CALIFORNIA SCHOOL LAW

CALIFORNIA SCHOOL LAW

Second Edition

FRANK KEMERER AND

PETER SANSOM

STANFORD LAW BOOKS
An imprint of Stanford University Press
Stanford, California

Stanford University Press
Stanford, California

Printed in the United States of America on acid-free, archival-quality paper

Library of Congress Cataloging-in-Publication Data

Kemerer, Frank R.
   California school law / Frank Kemerer and Peter Sansom.—2nd ed.
     p. cm.
   Includes bibliographical references and index.
   ISBN 978-0-8047-6037-9 (cloth : alk. paper)—ISBN 978-0-8047-6038-6 (pbk. : alk. paper)
   1. Educational law and legislation—California.   I. Sansom, Peter (Peter Andrew)   II. Title.

KFC648.K45 2009
344.794'07—dc22   2008054142

Typeset by Thompson Type in 10/13.5 Minion

CONTENTS

TABLES AND FIGURES

Tables

Figures

ABBREVIATIONS

AB	Assembly Bill
ADA	Americans with Disabilities Act of 1990; also average daily attendance
ADEA	Age Discrimination in Employment Act of 1967
API	Academic Performance Index
AUP	Acceptable Use Policy
AYP	Adequate Yearly Progress
CAHSEE	California High School Exit Examination
CAPA	California Alternate Performance Assessment
CBEST	California Basic Education Skills Test
CCTC	California Commission on Teacher Credentialing
CDE	California Department of Education
CELDT	California English Language Development Test
CFRA	California Family Rights Act
CFT	California Federation of Teachers
CIF	California Interscholastic Federation
CIPA	Children's Internet Protection Act
CPC	Commission on Professional Competence; the commission
CSEA	California School Employees Association
CST	California Standards Test
CTA	California Teachers Association
DFEH	Department of Fair Employment and Housing
DIS	designated instruction and services
EAA	Equal Access Act
EEOC	Equal Employment Opportunity Commission

EERA	Educational Employment Relations Act
EHCA	Education for All Handicapped Children Act of 1975
EIA	Economic Impact Aid
ELL	English-language learners
EMO	educational management organization
ERA	Equal Rights Amendment
ERAF	Educational Revenue Augmentation Fund
ESEA	Elementary and Secondary Education Act
ESY	extended school year
FAPE	free appropriate public education
FEHA	Fair Employment and Housing Act
FERPA	Family Educational Rights and Privacy Act of 1974
FMLA	Family and Medical Leave Act
GATE	gifted and talented education
HOUSSE	high, objective, uniform state standard of evaluation
IDEA	Individuals with Disabilities Education Act
IEE	independent educational evaluation
IEP	individualized education program
LEA	local education agency
LCI	licensed children's institution
LRE	least restrictive environment
NAEP	National Assessment of Educational Progress
NCIPA	Neighborhood Children's Internet Protection Act
NCLB	No Child Left Behind Act of 2001
NEA	National Education Association
NLRA	National Labor Relations Act
NPA	nonpublic agency
NPS	nonpublic school
OAH	Office of Administrative Hearings
OCR	Office of Civil Rights
OSEP	Office of Special Education Programs
OSERS	Office of Special Education and Rehabilitation Services
PAR	Peer Assistance and Review program
PERB	Public Employment Relations Board
PPRA	Protection of Pupil Rights Amendment
PRA	Public Records Act
PTA	Parent-Teacher Association
PTSA	Parent, Teacher, and Student Association
QEIA	Quality Education Investment Act

RSP	resource specialist program
RTI	response to intervention
SAIT	school assistance and intervention team
SARC	School Accountability Report Card
SAT	Scholastic Aptitude Test
SBE	State Board of Education
SEHO	Special Education Hearing Office
SLD	Specific Learning Disability
SPI	superintendent of public instruction
STAR	Standardized Testing and Reporting program
UCP	Uniform Compliant Procedure
USDOE	United States Department of Education

PREFACE

The law impacting the day-to-day operation of schools never stands still. Though this book is unique in having a free cumulative update posted on the book's website to keep readers current, in time the book itself needs to be brought up to date for ease of readership. Hence this new second edition. As with the first edition, the authors have endeavored to make sense of the seemingly incomprehensible maze of legislative laws, administrative rules, and judicial decisions that constitute "education law." This is particularly true for a large state like California, where education law emanates from a variety of sources and encompasses a host of topics.

Written in non-legalese language, this second edition of *California School Law* provides a comprehensive and current description of the law that affects the operation of the state's traditional public schools, charter schools, and private schools. It is intended for a wide audience including governing board members, school administrators, teachers, education professors and their students, policymakers, union leaders, school law attorneys, parents, and members of the general public. To serve such a broad constituency, we have simplified the writing and provided numerous illustrative figures and tables. While cases are referenced in the text, their citations are included in an index at the end of the book.

In the book's twelve chapters, readers will find a detailed, yet readable, account of the many ways in which the law structures the delivery of education services in California. We begin in Chapter One with an overview of the legal framework governing California schooling. The uninitiated may want to read this chapter first to gain an understanding of what education law is, the sources from which it emanates, and the components that make up the state's schooling system. We also review the rights of parents and the status of private schools in this chapter.

Subsequent chapters discuss the law in detail as it affects attendance and the instructional program, the financing of California traditional public and charter schools, the collective bargaining process, employment, teacher and student free speech, religion, the delivery of services to children with disabilities, student discipline, open meetings and records, privacy and student search and seizure, race and gender discrimination and harassment, and legal liability. Within each of these areas, myriad legal matters are examined. Readers who are interested in particular topics are advised to consult both the table of contents and the topical index.

In addition to a comprehensive discussion of how law affects the operation of California schooling, readers will find appendices providing a glossary of legal terms relating to education law, a discussion of how to find and read statutes and judicial decisions, and sources for additional information. The index of cases provides page references for those seeking to locate a particular judicial ruling.

Because the law is constantly changing, readers are encouraged to consult the book's website. Updating information found there is linked to the relevant chapter and page for easy reference. *California School Law* is designed to provide information regarding the subject matter covered and does not take the place of expert advice and assistance from a lawyer. It is published with the understanding that neither the authors nor the publishers are rendering legal services. If specific legal advice or assistance is required, the services of a competent professional should be sought.

While our co-author Jennifer Kemerer has opted to become a full-time mother since the publication of the first edition, we value her comments and suggestions for this second edition. We also are indebted to Richard C. Seder, a Sacramento-based school finance consultant, and Rebecca Heatherman, a graduate of the University of San Diego School of Law, for their assistance in the revisions of the school finance chapter. We are extremely grateful for the many laudatory comments that greeted the publication of the first edition, some of which are posted on the book's website. We hope that the California education community will find this second edition a useful means of unlocking the education law maze. The benefits of understanding the law and following its dictates are immeasurable. Not only is the potential for legal liability lessened, the school becomes a more ordered place. As a Harvard law professor wrote many years ago, an institution that prepares students for living in a democracy is more likely to accomplish its mission when it follows the law itself.

Frank Kemerer
Peter Sansom

CALIFORNIA SCHOOL LAW

1 LAW AND THE CALIFORNIA SCHOOLING SYSTEM

School law is a complex subject. The extensiveness of the California schooling system adds to its complexity. California elementary and secondary schools enroll over 6.8 million students. Traditional public schools enroll about 90 percent of them, with another 225,000 enrolled in charter schools. Some 570,000 students attend private schools enrolling 25 or more students. It is estimated that well over 100,000 students attend very small private schools or are homeschooled. The California public school system encompasses 1,052 school districts of various types. There are approximately 9,500 public schools, some 625 charter schools, and 3,500 private schools. About 40 percent of the total state budget is devoted to public schooling.

The law that governs this vast system emanates from several sources and has become extensive over time. Laws enacted by the California Legislature pertaining to precollegiate education alone constitute some 1,650 single-spaced, double-column pages of small print in the commonly used desktop edition of the California Education Code. Because the provisions of the Education Code have been enacted in piecemeal fashion over the years, they are difficult to find and often overlap. As early as 1922, a California court recognized the complexity of the Education Code: "At the outset it may be observed that any attempt to apply literally all the various provisions of the school law would lead to hopeless confusion" (*Horton v. Whipple,* p. 190).

Interplay among the various sources of school law adds to the complexity. To cite one example, California voters approved Proposition 187 in 1994 curtailing public social services and benefits for illegal aliens. Among other things, the proposition added Section 48215 to the California Education Code excluding illegal alien children from California public schooling. However, a year later, a federal district court ruled that the exclusion was unconstitutional. To the uninformed, it

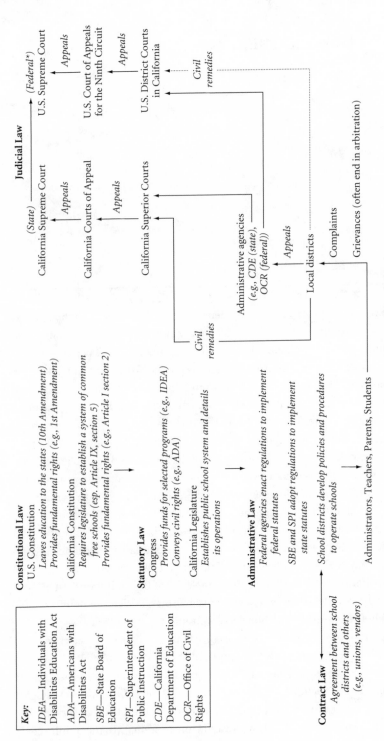

Figure 1.1 Relationship of Law to Establishment and Operation of California Public Schools

*Limited to rulings on federal issues.

[Some matters such as U.S. constitutional rights disputes can be taken directly from school districts to federal district court. Hence the dotted line.]

may seem strange that a single federal judge could thwart the wishes of a majority of the electorate and their representatives.

Our purpose in this introductory chapter is to identify the sources of California school law, the major players, and the structure of the system. We also will review the rights and responsibilities of parents, the role of private schools, and the efforts to expand schooling options through charter schools and voucher proposals. Once we have an understanding of the legal framework within which California public and private schools operate, we are in a good position to explore the influence of the law in their day-to-day operation in the remainder of the book.

WHAT COMPRISES SCHOOL LAW?

School law essentially is a combination of constitutional, statutory, administrative, contract, and judicial law. In this section, we identify each type of law and describe how they relate to one another. We have developed a flowchart to accompany the discussion (see Figure 1.1). Readers will find it useful to refer to the chart periodically.

Constitutional Law

Constitutional law is the highest form of law because it sets forth basic principles of governance. Constitutional law has two sources, federal and state. The federal constitution is an important source of school law for two reasons. First, it reserves to states the responsibility to establish and operate a schooling system. Article I, Section 8 of the U.S. Constitution lists the powers given to Congress; and Article I, Section 10 lists powers prohibited to the states. Since education is in neither list, it becomes a state responsibility under the Tenth Amendment to the U.S. Constitution, which provides that all powers not specifically delegated to Congress or prohibited to the states are left to the latter. The federal constitution is also an important source of individual rights. The Bill of Rights lists such fundamental rights as freedom of speech, the free exercise of religion, and the right to be free from unreasonable searches and seizures. It was a condition of state ratification of the Constitution in 1789 that the Bill of Rights was added to protect these fundamental rights from hostile action by Congress. The purpose of the Bill of Rights was well stated by Justice Robert Jackson in a 1943 ruling preventing the state from compelling all students to salute the flag. He wrote, "The very purpose of a Bill of Rights was to withdraw certain subjects from the vicissitudes of political controversy, to place them beyond the reach of majorities and officials and to establish them as legal principles to be applied by the courts" (*West Virginia State Board v. Barnette*, p. 638).

The due process clause of the Fourteenth Amendment extends nearly all of the original Bill of Rights protections to persons in the state setting, and many of them now apply to public school employees and students. The due process clause reads, "nor shall any State deprive any person of life, liberty, or property, without due process of law." Not only has the U.S. Supreme Court construed the word "liberty" in this clause to protect persons from state governmental intrusion on their constitutional rights, the Court also has ruled that these rights cannot be taken away without "due process of law." As we shall see in later chapters, both educator contract termination and the disciplinary removal of students from public school must be done in compliance with the due process clause.

The Fourteenth Amendment also provides that no state shall "deny to any person within its jurisdiction the equal protection of the laws." Beginning in 1954 with the famous *Brown v. Board of Education* desegregation case, the equal protection clause has figured prominently in efforts to integrate schools and, for a time, to assure equalized funding as well. When the U.S. Supreme Court backed away from becoming involved in equalization of school finance, state courts took over. Both of these matters are discussed in detail in subsequent chapters.

While public school districts and charter schools are included within the ambit of the Fourteenth Amendment, private schools are not. This is because the amendment is phrased in terms of "states." It requires some semblance of state action for the amendment to apply. Because private schools are not part of the state, they do not have to observe the constitutional rights of their constituents. The relationship between the private school and parents, teachers, and students is essentially contractual in nature, just as is true of a private corporation and its employees. At the same time, private schools are subject to other types of law that limit their autonomy. We will discuss how this is so later in the chapter.

When there is a conflict between state and federal law, federal law prevails as a general rule. This is the thrust of Article VI, Section 2 of the U.S. Constitution, which states:

> This Constitution, and the laws of the United States which shall be made in pursuance thereof; and all treaties made, or which shall be made, under the authority of the United States, shall be the supreme law of the land; and the judges in every state shall be bound thereby, any thing in the constitution or laws of any state to the contrary notwithstanding.

This provision is known as the federal supremacy clause. The complicated legal question of when a state law may survive a supremacy clause challenge is beyond the scope of our discussion. The supremacy clause figured prominently in the 1995 federal district court decision striking down the portion of Proposition 187 excluding illegal aliens from California public schools. The U.S. Supreme Court had ruled in 1982 that the exclusion of undocumented aliens from tuition-free public schooling violates the equal protection clause of the Fourteenth Amendment (*Plyler v. Doe*). Based on the federal supremacy clause, the federal judge in *LULAC v. Wilson* declared such exclusion by California's Proposition 187 unconstitutional. Later, most of the other provisions of the proposition were supplanted by federal law.

While the Tenth Amendment leaves education to the states, it does not specify that the state has to set up a schooling system. In fact, the amendment merely reads, "The powers not delegated to the United States by the Constitution, nor prohibited by it to the States, are reserved to the States respectively, or to the people." Picking up where the federal constitution leaves off, Article IX, Section 1 of the California Constitution indicates that since "a general diffusion of knowledge and intelligence being essential to the preservation of the rights and liberties of the people . . . ," the legislature is encouraged to promote it. Article IX, Section 5 specifies that "The Legislature shall provide for a system of common schools by which a free school shall be kept up and supported in each district. . . . " Article XVI, Section 8 specifies that "From all state revenues there shall first be set apart the moneys to be applied by the State for support of the public school system and public institutions of higher education." Taken together, these provisions not only require the California Legislature to provide for a public school system, they also make a student's entitlement to education a fundamental right. This determination was essential to the California Supreme Court's ruling in 1976 in *Serrano v. Priest* that expenditures across districts must be equalized, a matter addressed in some detail in Chapter 3.

The California Constitution also is an important source of individual rights. For example, California courts have held that the entitlement to free speech for students is greater under the California Constitution than under the First Amendment to the U.S. Constitution. Article I, Section 2, subdivision (a) of the California Constitution reads, "Every person may freely speak, write and publish his or her sentiments on all subjects, being responsible for the abuse of this right. A law may not restrain or abridge liberty of speech or press." In 1979 the California Supreme Court ruled that this provision protects the right of high school students to circulate a petition in a private shopping center (*PruneYard Shopping Center v. Robins*), a decision it affirmed as recently as 2007 when it struck down a shopping mall ban on all forms of speech urging customers to boycott a store (*Fashion Valley Mall v. National Labor Relations Board*). In the eyes of the court, the shopping center is the equivalent of a public forum where people exchange views. The U.S. Supreme Court earlier had ruled that the free speech clause of the First Amendment to the U.S. Constitution does not apply within the confines of a private shopping center (*Hudgens v. National Labor Relations Board*, 1976).

While federal law is supreme over state law when there is a conflict between them, the U.S. Supreme Court has recognized that state constitutions and laws can be *more* protective of civil liberties than the U.S. Constitution, but not less so. Just as the California Constitution is more protective of free speech than its federal counterpart is, so too is it more protective of privacy. For example, in cases involving teacher lifestyle choices, a portion of Article I of the California Constitution has surfaced, providing that among the inalienable rights enjoyed by Californians is the right of "obtaining safety, happiness, and privacy."

Statutory Law

A "statute" is a law made by a legislative body. Both the statutes enacted by Congress and those passed by the state legislature have significant influence over the operation of California schools. Congress has enacted numerous laws affecting education. A synopsis of some of the most important is provided in Table 1.1.

Since Congress does not have direct authority over education, most—but not all—of the statutes it has enacted are pursuant to its spending authority. The first provision of Article I, Section 8 of the U.S. Constitution provides that Congress has the authority to collect taxes and provide for "the general welfare of the United States." Congress uses this power to provide conditional monetary grants to states, trading federal dollars for state compliance with Congress's political agenda. For example, a school district could lose federal funding if it condoned the release of personally identifiable information about students or their families without complying with the provisions of the federal Family Educational Rights and Privacy Act. The state itself could lose millions of dollars by failing to comply with provisions of the No Child Left Behind Act, a federal statute enacted in 2001 that, as discussed in Chapter 2, has had great impact on teaching and learning.

Some federal statutes affect both public and private educational institutions regardless of whether they receive federal funding. These statutes are enacted pursuant to Congress's authority to enact laws affecting interstate commerce under another provision of Article I, Section 8. Recently, Congress has been less inclined to enact laws under the interstate commerce clause, in part because doing so limits the autonomy of states and in part because the U.S. Supreme Court has been more protective of the concept of federalism—the division of power between the central government and states. Nevertheless, as noted in Table 1.1, some very important federal statutes that are based on Congress's power under the interstate commerce clause remain and have significant influence over the operation of both

TABLE 1.1
Key Federal Statutes Affecting California Public Schools

42 U.S.C. § 1981	Accords all persons the right to make and enforce contracts free of racial discrimination and retaliation for filing complaints based on racial discrimination in both the public and private sectors. Based on Congress's power to enforce the terms of the Thirteenth Amendment to the U.S. Constitution outlawing slavery and its trappings, this law applies to discrimination occurring during the contract term as well. Thus, a private school student who is subjected to racial discrimination after enrolling would have a cause of action. Penalties include injunctive relief and money damages.
42 U.S.C. § 1983	Allows suits for injunctive relief and compensatory damages against persons acting under color of state law who deprive others of constitutional and federal statutory rights. The U.S. Supreme Court has interpreted the word "persons" in this statute to encompass state political subdivisions such as cities, towns, and school districts, as well as individuals. However, for reasons explained in Chapter 12, California school districts are not subject to suit under this statute.
Title VI of the 1964 Civil Rights Act	Prohibits intentional discrimination in the context of race, color, or national origin in federally assisted programs. Loss of federal funding, injunctive relief, and monetary damages are available. This law was instrumental in desegregating public schools in the South during the 1960s and 1970s.
Title VII of the 1964 Civil Rights Act	Prohibits direct discrimination and retaliation for filing complaints on the basis of race, color, religion, sex, and national origin in all aspects of public and private employment. In addition to equitable relief such as back pay and reinstatement, this law allows money damages for intentional discrimination. Title VII does not apply to organizations with fewer than fifteen employees for each working day in each of twenty or more calendar weeks in the current or preceeding year. It also does not apply to religious organizations with respect to the employment of individuals of a particular religion to perform work as, for example, in a Catholic school.
Age Discrimination in Employment Act of 1967 (ADEA)	Prohibits discrimination against individuals age forty and over in both public and private employment unless as a bona fide occupational qualification reasonably necessary to carry out job responsibilities (e.g., airline pilots). Thus, with few exceptions, there is no longer a permissible mandatory retirement age. Also prohibits retaliation for filing age-related complaints. Penalties are similar to those for Title VII.
Individuals with Disabilities Education Act (IDEA)	Requires public schools to identify children with certain specific disabilities and provide them a free, appropriate public education. IDEA affords parents extensive due process rights. Penalties include loss of federal funding, compensatory relief, and attorneys' fees. This law is

(continued)

TABLE 1.1 *(Continued)*

	procedurally complex and has spawned a vast network of federal and state regulations that school administrators must follow. We discuss it in detail in Chapter 8.
Section 504 of the Rehabilitation Act of 1973	Prevents discrimination against persons with disabilities in programs receiving federal financial assistance. Regulations issued by the Office for Civil Rights require a free appropriate public education and services for children who have a mental or physical handicap that substantially limits one or more major life activities. Penalties are the same as under Title VI of the 1964 Civil Rights Act.
Americans with Disabilities Act of 1990 (ADA)	Expands Section 504 by according persons with disabilities meaningful access to the programs and facilities of most businesses in the country. The ADA also prohibits discrimination against persons with disabilities in public and private employment and requires employers to make reasonable accommodation for disabled persons to enable them to perform their jobs. Penalties are similar to those for Title VII for public entities. The statute provides an exemption for religious organizations or entities controlled by religious organizations. Thus, a religious school would be exempt from the ADA.
Title IX of the 1972 Education Amendments	Prevents discrimination against persons on the basis of gender in educational programs receiving federal financial assistance. Also prohibits retaliation for filing sex discrimination complaints. Penalties against educational organizations can encompass both money damages and the loss of federal funding. Title IX has taken on renewed importance in recent years in the context of employee-on-student sexual harassment and student-on-student sexual harassment.
Family Educational Rights and Privacy Act of 1974 (FERPA)	Gives parents of children at educational institutions receiving federal financial assistance access to personally identifiable information contained in records, files, documents, and other materials containing information about their student and prevents disclosure of such information without parent permission. Exceptions include a legitimate educational interest (e.g., sending records to a substitute teacher). The statute also gives parents the right to request that directory information about them and their child (e.g., names, phone numbers, addresses, etc.) not be revealed through class rosters, athletic programs, and the like. A violation of FERPA can result in loss of federal funding.
No Child Left Behind Act of 2001 (NCLB)	Adds accountability measures to Title I of the long-standing Elementary and Secondary Education Act (ESEA), which provides federally funded programs for schools educating low-income students. NCLB requires states to meet teacher quality standards in all its public schools, to test students enrolled in them annually in grades 3–8 and once in grades 10–12, to publicly report achievement data by different categories of students, and to ensure that all students meet state proficiency standards by the year 2014. Parents in Title I schools that fail to make adequate yearly progress have the option to enroll their children in higher-performing schools or to receive supplemental educational services at school expense. NCLB also includes a number of other requirements that affect school operation, as discussed in subsequent chapters.

public and private schools. Included among them are Title VII of the 1964 Civil Rights Act, which, with few exceptions, prohibits discrimination on the basis of race, color, religion, sex, or national origin in both public and private employment, and the Americans with Disabilities Act, which does the same for persons with disabilities.

Another important federal statute included in the table is a civil rights law known as 42 United States Code Section 1983. Enacted after the Civil War, this law was designed to enforce the provisions of the Fourteenth Amendment by enabling persons to file lawsuits in federal court involving alleged violations of federal rights. This was Congress's effort to provide meaningful relief to victims of discrimination since state courts had not proven up to the task. Known generally as "Section 1983," the statute provides that

> Every person who, under color of any statute, ordinance, regulation, custom, or usage, of any State or Territory . . . subjects, or causes to be subjected, any citizen of the United States or other person within the jurisdiction thereof to the deprivation of any rights, privileges, or immunities secured by the Constitution and laws, shall be liable to the party injured in an action at law, suit in equity, or other proper proceeding for redress [in federal court]. . . .

Discussed at some length in Chapter 12, Section 1983 is the primary means by which claims involving deprivation of constitutional rights such as free speech and free exercise of religion by municipalities and public employees are taken directly to federal court. While school personnel in California public school can be sued individually under this statute, school districts in the state are not subject to suit because they are viewed to be part of the state, and the state itself is immune under the provisions of the Eleventh Amendment.

The California Legislature has enacted a vast number of statutes involving education in response to the California Constitution's educational mandate that it do so. And since the legislature is in session every year, new statutes are constantly being added and old statutes revised or repealed. State statutory law reaches deeply into the operations of public schools and, in some cases, private schools as well. For example, the legislature has decreed that every public and private school shall assure that every restroom is to be cleaned regularly, be fully operational, and stocked at all times with toilet paper, soap, and paper towels or functional hand driers (Educ. Code § 35292.5).

Most of the statutes affecting education are grouped together in the California Education Code. The code establishes the structure of the system and details its operation. Provisions of the Education Code will be a major focus in ensuing chapters and can be found in their entirety on the California Department of Education

(CDE) website at www.cde.ca.gov. Other important state laws also affect education. A case in point is the section of the California Government Code setting forth the Educational Employment Relations Act (EERA)—also known as the Rodda Act after its sponsor. EERA provisions spell out how collective bargaining is to be conducted in public schools. It will be explored in some detail in Chapter 4.

Administrative Law

When legislatures enact statutes, they cannot possibly write them specifically enough to give them operational value. This is where administrative law comes in. Administrative law is the body of law developed by administrative agencies under the authority of the legislature to carry out their statutory responsibilities. Congress has given federal agencies like the U.S. Department of Education the authority to develop administrative regulations implementing various federal statutes. For example, the department's Office for Civil Rights has developed regulations for determining how Title IX of the 1972 Education Amendments is to apply to curricular and extracurricular activities so as to assure gender equity. Likewise, extensive regulations have been developed by the department's Office of Special Education and Rehabilitation Services (OSERS) to implement the terms of the Individuals with Disabilities Education Act. Every school attorney and school administrator is familiar with federal "regs" that specify how the terms of federal statutes are to be implemented.

The California Legislature has given the California State Board of Education (SBE) broad authority to adopt whatever rules and regulations it deems necessary for the operation of elementary and secondary schools (Educ. Code § 33031), subject only to demonstrating their need to the Office of Administrative Law. As a practical matter, however, most of the SBE's rule making is in response to specific legislative directives. For example, Education Code Section 47605 (j)(2) requires the SBE to adopt criteria for the review and approval of charter school petitions presented to it. Like all state board rules, the set of regulations the board has developed for this purpose is included in Title 5 of the California Code of Regulations and can be found on the CDE website or directly on the California Code of Regulation's website at www.calregs.com. The state superintendent of public instruction (SPI) also has limited authority to adopt administrative regulations, which can be found as well in Title 5 of the California Code of Regulations. The administrative rules and regulations from the state board and SPI detail the operation of many facets of California schools, including such matters as special education, pupil accounting, student records, and the formation or reorganization of school districts.

While the complexity of modern government gives the legislature little alternative to enfranchise administrative agencies with broad authority, accusations sometimes arise that the legislature has delegated too much of its authority to administrative entities. However, as one California court of appeal has noted, "Reasonable grants of power to administrative agencies will not offend the nondelegation doctrine so long as adequate safeguards exist to protect against abuse of that power" (*Wilson v. State Board of Education*, 1999, p. 760). And as long as administrative agencies stay within the scope of the authority the legislature has given them, their regulations will be upheld. But if they stray too far afield, the regulations will be null and void. A good illustration of this fact involves a dispute over cash incentives involving teachers in a Sacramento elementary school and the State Department of Education. The school had well exceeded its one-year Academic Performance Index (API) minimum growth target to be eligible for cash awards under Education Code Section 44650, known as the Incentive Act. However, the SBE, which was given authority under the act to establish criteria for the awards, extended the qualification period to two years. The change resulted in the teachers being ineligible to receive their award. The teachers challenged the extension as contrary to the one-year period specified in the legislation. The California court of appeal agreed with the teachers, noting that the change was inconsistent with the statute and thus unenforceable (*Boyd v. Eastin*, 2002).

For school personnel, the best illustration of administrative law can be found in school board policies. Education Code Section 35010 requires school boards to develop and enforce rules for governing their district. The rules they adopt must not be in conflict with other law, including the rules prescribed by the SBE. In larger districts, board policies are accompanied by a set of district administrative procedures that detail the implementation of board policies at the school and program level. Taken together, board policies and administrative procedures are best known as "the law of the district." It is important for all school personnel to know and follow them because failure to do so can be grounds for contract termination, as well as for employee and district liability. And it is important for school district officials and attorneys to make sure that board policies and regulations are current and do not conflict with state or federal law.

When disputes arise over the application of statutes and their accompanying administrative regulations, administrative agencies often play a role in resolving them. In effect, they exercise quasi-judicial authority. At the federal level, for example, the Family Educational Rights and Privacy Act (FERPA) is enforced by the U.S. Department of Education through its Family Policy Compliance Office and its Office of Administrative Law Judges. Until the spring of 2002, it was possible for a student or the student's parents to file a lawsuit in federal court claiming a violation of FERPA and seeking money damages and attorneys' fees. But the U.S. Supreme Court cut off this manner of enforcing the privacy law by holding that the statute's enforcement mechanism is exclusively through the U.S. Department of Education (*Gonzaga University v. Doe*). The department's toughest sanction is the termination of federal funding. It cannot award money damages to victims. So, to some extent, the teeth of FERPA have been filed back.

As with federal law, California administrative law also governs the resolution of certain types of disputes. A process known as the Uniform Complaint Procedure (UCP) has been established within the CDE to channel and resolve complaints involving alleged violations by local agencies in administering federal or state law or regulations governing specific educational programs or committing unlawful discrimination against students. The UCP specifies the procedures and time lines for processing complaints within the school district and provides a right of appeal to the CDE. Its provisions can be found in Title 5 of the California Code of Regulations, Section 4600 and following sections. For example, if a parent claims that the football coach improperly cut his student from the team because of racial discrimination, the parent would follow the UCP complaint process. School districts now are required to use their uniform complaint process to help identify and resolve deficiencies relating to instructional materials, condition of facilities, teacher assignment, and instructional services provided for students who fail the state's high school exit exam (Educ. Code § 35186). This provision was added in 2004 as part of the settlement of the *Williams v. State of California* school finance lawsuit, described in Chapter 3 in the section "The Movement toward Adequacy." Complaints are first channeled to the principal or other appropriate school official, who then has up to thirty working days to resolve them and forty-five days to report back to the complainant. If not satisfied, the complainant can appeal to the governing board and, if the complaint involves dangerous conditions of school facilities, to the SPI. The statute requires notices in all classrooms stating that sufficient textbooks and teaching materials are to be provided; that facilities are to be clean, safe, and well maintained; and that complainants be informed of where complaint forms are available in case of a shortage. The notice also is to inform parents that there should be no teacher vacancies or misassignments. A misassignment means that the place of a teacher in the position for which the teacher does not have a credential. If such is not the case, the UCP provides a means of seeking redress.

Not all disputes involving federal or state law are resolved through the UCP. As explained in Chapter 8 in the section "Due Process Hearings," a different process must be followed for disputes over identification and placement of children with disabilities. Matters involving gender discrimination under Title IX go directly to the Office of Civil Rights in the U.S. Department of Education, while employment discrimination disputes are routed to the California Department of Fair Employment and Housing. The law is filled with such complexities, and it often requires a specialist to sort them out.

The reason that administrative bodies have a role in resolving disputes is to avoid flooding courts with matters that can best be resolved by knowledgeable experts who are close to the scene. Often complainants are required to "exhaust administrative remedies" before they seek judicial relief. Not all disputes involving federal and state law, however, are subject to the exhaustion requirement. Some matters can be taken directly to state court. For example, a parent may be able to go directly to state court to try to obtain an order overturning a principal's decision to exclude the parent's child from graduation ceremonies. And disputes involving the violation of federal constitutional rights generally can be taken directly to federal court without pursuing state or federal administrative remedies. For example, the parent's allegation that the elimination of his son from the team was racially motivated could be taken directly to federal court. The dotted line in Figure 1.1, going from local districts to the California federal court system, shows how matters involving federal claims can bypass the state administrative and judicial process altogether. The solid line linking school districts and California courts illustrates a similar bypass for civil remedies.

Contract Law

Most professional school employees are aware of the importance of contract law simply because they have an individual or collective contract that spells out the terms and conditions of employment. Contract law also is much involved in the daily operation of schools through purchasing, property acquisition, and lease arrangements. Campus-level administrators sometimes run into concerns about whether they have the authority to enter into contracts with vendors such as the purveyor of team uniforms. While the governing board can delegate its power to contract to the superintendent and to persons the superintendent designates, Education Code Section 17604 requires that all contracts binding the district must be approved by the governing board. If this is not done, then the contract is invalid. In the event that an official given the power of contract in accord with this section engages in unlawful behavior, the official is personally liable to the district for any money paid out.

In the private school sector, contract law is an important determinant of the relationship between the school and its parents, students, and teachers. This is so because constitutional rights do not exist within the private sector, relatively few provisions of federal and California law pertain to private schools, and the CDE has little influence over private school operation. To determine the relationship between the private school and its constituents, one must view the agreements between the school and its constituents, as well as the school's policies that are incorporated by reference in the contract. In some private schools, teachers do not have contracts of employment but rather serve at the pleasure of the governing board; and in others, students can be asked to leave at the school's discretion. Exactly what rights teachers and students have is determined by the policies of the school. If the policies are not to a person's liking, he or she is free to go elsewhere.

The collective bargaining agreement is another form of contract law. The Winton Act passed in 1965 allowed school employees to meet and confer with governing boards but did not involve the formalities or the sanctions inherent in formal collective bargaining. The Winton Act gave way in 1975 to the present Educational Employment Relations Act. The collective bargaining contracts negotiated between employee unions and school districts impose sets of rules governing the operation of schools that are ignored at one's peril. Included in most collective bargaining contracts is a grievance process that specifies how complaints arising under the administration of the contract are to be channeled and resolved. Because of their importance to the operation of California public schools, in Chapter 4 we focus specifically on unions and collective bargaining.

Judicial Law

The last source of school law that we will discuss involves the rulings handed down by courts. Much of school law, particularly student and teacher rights, is controlled by judicial law. Since there are two judicial systems—one federal and one state—we discuss each separately.

California has a four-tiered judicial system. At the bottom are the municipal courts that have limited jurisdiction over civil matters and over criminal matters such as misdemeanors, driving while intoxicated, and traffic offenses. Located in each of California's fifty-eight counties, the superior courts are the state's basic trial court. Because important matters involving schools begin here, we include them in Figure 1.1. Like the municipal courts, they are staffed by a single judge. The superior court system has an appellate division that hears cases appealed from the municipal courts. These courts are staffed by three judges. Decisions from the appellate division may be published in volumes known as court reporters, depending upon their importance in establishing a new rule of law, resolving conflict in the law, dealing with an important public interest, or making a significant contribution to the legal literature.

Decisions of the superior courts are appealable to the California courts of appeal, of which six are scattered around the state. These courts hear cases in panels of three judges. The role of the appellate courts is to determine whether the law was applied correctly in cases decided by superior court judges. The decisions of the courts of appeal may be reported in the official court reporters, depending upon their importance. The highest state court is the California Supreme Court. Composed of seven justices who sit as a panel, this appellate court is the court of last resort for matters of state law. The justices have the authority to choose most of the cases they hear, and their decisions are published in the official court reporters. Because of the precedents established by California courts of appeal and the California Supreme Court in many education matters, they are often cited in school board policies and in various publications on California school law. California judges are elected either directly or, for appellate judges, through a retention election following appointment by the governor.

In addition to these four courts of record, there are specialized courts for certain types of cases. For example, with exceptions for violent acts such as murder or rape, persons under the age of eighteen who violate state or federal laws or municipal ordinances other than those pertaining to curfew violations are within the jurisdiction of California's county juvenile courts. Persistent student truancy matters are directed to these courts.

Federal courts hear cases involving the federal constitution and federal statutes. They also have authority to hear disputes involving citizens from different states on matters of state law where the amount in controversy is over $75,000. This so-called diversity of citizenship jurisdiction rarely involves education matters. In addition, federal courts occasionally hear state claims when they are combined with federal claims. Article III of the U.S. Constitution specifies that there is to be one supreme court and such lower federal courts as Congress wishes to establish. In response, Congress has established the federal district courts and the federal courts of appeals, which together with the U.S. Supreme Court constitute a three-tiered federal judicial system. At the bottom are the U.S. district courts, of which four are located in California (see Figure 1.2). The federal district courts are trial courts, each staffed by a single judge. Decisions reached by one federal district court are not binding on another federal district court, though judges will consider each other's decisions carefully in the interest of uniformity of law. The same is true of state court judges. The only time a decision of one court becomes a binding precedent on another

Figure 1.2 California Federal District Courts

court is when the former is in the same circuit and higher in the judicial hierarchy. Decisions from the federal district courts in California are appealed to the U.S. Court of Appeals for the Ninth Circuit, whose jurisdiction extends over nine western states including Alaska and Hawaii. Usually hearing cases in panels of three, the Ninth Circuit decisions are binding on the federal district courts within the geographic jurisdiction of the Ninth Circuit.

The decisions of the Ninth Circuit Court of Appeals can be appealed to the U.S. Supreme Court in Washington, D.C. However, the chances of having the Supreme Court accept a case on appeal are very slim. From some 8,500 appeals, the high court in recent years has chosen fewer than one hundred to hear. Thus, the claim "I will take this matter all the way to the U.S. Supreme Court if I have to" is more wishful thinking than reality. When the Court does accept a case, all nine justices hear it together. The Court's decision will bind the entire country. As with other courts where more than one judge hears a case, the justices often will disagree, and there will be several concurring and dissenting opinions. A concurring opinion means that the justice writing it concurs with the majority's decision but for different reasons.

All federal judges are appointed by the president, with the advice and consent of the U.S. Senate. This explains why the confirmation process often is so heated, as presidents seek to appoint judges who share their political philosophy. However, there are never any guarantees that a federal judge may not change his or her judicial philosophy over time.

In sum, these are the five primary sources of California school law, and as noted in Figure 1.1, there is a pattern to their interaction. Constitutional law is preeminent over all other types of law. A statute that conflicts with either the state or federal constitution may be ruled unconstitutional and thus null and void. Both federal and California statutes and their related administrative law regulations play important roles in establishing the structure and governance of California schools. Contract law, often in the form of collective bargaining agreements, shapes the relationship between the school and its employees, and in the private sector, with parents and students as well. Contract law also governs the relationship between the school and various entities such as contractors and vendors. Unless subject to a contractually negotiated grievance process, disputes arising between the school and its constituents usually are first processed administratively at the school level or before an administrative agency prior to appeal to the judiciary. Some matters such as a request for an injunction against a school policy or practice can be taken directly to court without first exhausting administrative law remedies. Generally, matters involving state law are routed to state courts, and matters involving federal law are routed to federal courts. Cases start at the trial court level and can be appealed to higher courts, with the California Supreme Court (state law) and U.S. Supreme Court (federal law) having the last word.

While this is a simplistic explanation of a complex process, it will suffice for our purposes in explaining how law affects the establishment and operation of public schools in California.

THE CALIFORNIA SCHOOLING STRUCTURE

As noted at the beginning of the chapter, the California Constitution directs the legislature to establish public education. In essence, the legislature controls the public schooling system of the state. In a characterization that has been repeated many times, the California appellate courts have termed the authority of the legislature over education as "exclusive, plenary, absolute, entire, and comprehensive, subject only to constitutional constraints" (*California Teachers Association v. Huff*, 1992, p. 706).

At the same time, it would be naive in the extreme to underestimate the influence of others on educational legislation. The governor is a key player in setting the legislative agenda and in making trade-offs necessary to the success of the governor's proposals. The governor also can veto legislative enactments. Equally significant, the governor controls the education budget and can use the line-item veto power to reduce or eliminate the funding appropriated by the legislature for education programs. The governor relies extensively on an education secretary, who serves as a liaison between the governor's office and the legislature. The two-party system assures that conflict will occur in the legislative arena, stimulated by intensive lobbying from powerful interest groups. It is often said that the making of legislation is similar to the making of sausage: both are messy and distasteful. Still, reality dictates that if a person wants to change the California schooling system, he or she is best advised to lobby the legislature and gain the governor's support.

The California Constitution itself assures that politics is an integral part of educational policymaking by the way it structures the state's educational system. Article 9, Section 7 of the California Constitution requires the legislature to provide for the appointment or election of the State Board of Education (SBE). In response, the legislature has established a ten-member board appointed by the governor for four-year terms with the advice and consent of the senate (Educ. Code § 33000 and following sections). A student is similarly appointed to the board for a one-year term. Assisted by a small office staff and meeting at least six times per year, the SBE oversees the policies drafted and implemented by the California Department of Education (CDE) and is the liaison between the federal government and the state. The board elects its own officers and establishes its committees. As noted earlier, one of the most important functions of the SBE is to adopt administrative regulations detailing how state statutes are to be implemented at the school district level. Among the multifaceted responsibilities placed on the SBE by the legislature are the following: engaging in statewide study and planning for schooling; developing teacher evaluation guidelines; adopting instructional materials for K–8 grades; granting waivers of various Education Code provisions for both traditional public and charter schools; approving proposals for the unification of school districts; and approving and overseeing statewide curriculum content and performance standards, student assessment, and the public school accountability program.

Article IX, Section 2 of the California Constitution provides for the selection of a state superintendent of public instruction (SPI)—sometimes referred to in state statutes as the Director of Education—in a nonpartisan election, meaning that the candidates are not identified by political party on the ballot. The state superintendent takes office after the first day of January following the gubernatorial election and can serve no more than two terms. If there is a vacancy in the office, the constitution provides that the governor appoints the SPI. The legislature has designated the superintendent to be the secretary and executive officer of the SBE with responsibility for executing its policies (Educ. Code § 33100 and following sections). While the legislature cannot alter the constitutional status of the SPI, it can change the superintendent's powers and duties. The legislature has given the SPI numerous responsibilities, just a few of which include superintending the schools of the state; developing regulations pertaining to arrangements with the federal government; administering state funding and budgeting; working with the state board to develop and implement the state's curriculum standards, instructional materials adoption, school district reorganization, assessment, and school accountability programs; and compiling a directory of information on private schools.

The CDE and its various subunits administer the education laws under the oversight of the state board and at the direction of the SPI, who is the CDE's chief executive and administrative officer (Educ. Code § 33300 and following sections). The legislature has placed a wide range of duties on the CDE including such functions as disseminating information, developing budgeting guidelines and holding training workshops, gathering and reporting test results and other outcome data, coordinating the identification and development of effective programs and practices, supervising physical education and interscholastic athletics, and evaluating the effectiveness of programs for learning English. With regard to secondary school interscholastic athletics, the department works in collaboration with the California Interscholastic Federation (CIF), a voluntary organization composed of school and school-related personnel. The CDE is also charged with assisting the California Commission on Teacher Credentialing, an agency set up by the legislature for establishing professional standards, assessments, and examinations for entry and advancement in the education profession. More will be said about the commission and its responsibilities in Chapter 2. Though pared down significantly in recent years because of budget cuts, the CDE still has a staff of some 2,700 employees to carry out its responsibilities and those of the state SPI.

Given that the CDE is subject to the authority of both an elected state superintendent and an appointed board, it is not difficult to imagine that tensions would surface. Indeed, turf battles have spanned more than seventy years, reaching a high point in 1993 when the state board filed a lawsuit against the state superintendent for not carrying out its directives (*State Board of Education v. Honig*). Prior to the lawsuit, the California attorney general was called upon on several occasions to clarify who was to do what. In 1943, for example, the attorney general advised that the state board is similar to a board of directors and the state superintendent to its executive head. The former makes policy and the latter executes it through the department of education. The problem with this view is that, unlike the chief executive officer of a company, the state superintendent is not selected by the state board and may not feel any particular allegiance to it. Indeed, that was the situation in the 1993 lawsuit. In that case, the state board had directed the state superintendent to do certain things, and the superintendent refused, saying he had no obligation to do so.

The judges in *State Board of Education v. Honig* first rejected the state superintendent's argument that, because the SPI is a constitutionally recognized official, the legislature is without authority to define the superintendent's duties. The legislature can increase or diminish the powers of the SPI as it wishes. Likewise, the authority given by the legislature to the SBE in Education Code Section 33031 to adopt rules and regulations governing its own appointees and employees is sufficient to require the state superintendent to comply with the board's directives. Regarding the dispute at hand, the court ruled that the state board could direct the state superintendent to nominate a deputy SPI and three associate SPIs for board approval, in accordance with Article 9, Section 2.1 of the California Constitution. The state superintendent had refused to nominate them. The state board also can seek additional staff and direct the state superintendent to include them in the CDE budget. However, while the state board can review the performance of key personnel, it is without authority to exercise detailed budget oversight of the CDE. Such an activity would overstep the board's role as a policymaking entity and involve it in micromanagement. Finally, the court ruled that the state board could hire outside legal counsel to represent it in its lawsuit against the state superintendent and have the state superintendent pay the costs out of state department funds. Figure 1.3 depicts the state components of the public school system and their interrelationship.

The state educational governance structure is replicated in California's fifty-eight counties. In each, there is a county office of education, a county superintendent, and a county board of education. The county superintendent is elected in all but five counties. In three of these—San Diego, Santa Clara, and Sacramento—the

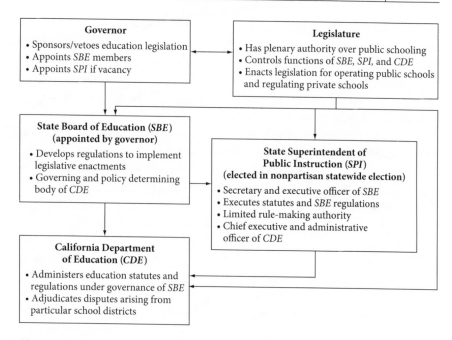

Figure 1.3 California State Structure for School Governance

county superintendent is appointed by the County Board of Education. In Los Angeles County, the county superintendent is appointed by the County Board of Supervisors, and in San Francisco County the San Francisco Unified School District superintendent is the county superintendent and operates under the auspices of the County Board of Supervisors. The county school board is composed of five to seven members elected from trustee areas within the county.

The Education Code includes extensive definitions of the responsibilities for county boards (Educ. Code § 1000 and following sections). The county board approves budgets submitted by the county superintendent, adopts rules for the administration of the office of the county superintendent, and implements legislative directives. The county school board also serves as an appeal board for the adjudication of student expulsion appeals, interdistrict attendance appeals, and charter schools whose applications are rejected by school districts. The county superintendent operates county schools where they exist (e.g., court and community schools) and otherwise serves as an intermediary between the local school districts within each county and the state (Educ. Code § 1200 and following sections). Among the superintendents' duties are operating programs for children with disabilities, parenting teens, and child care. In Kern County, the county superintendent even operates a county library and zoo. County superintendents provide a myriad of services to school districts within the county, including fiscal oversight, curriculum support and training, and media services. They also now have the responsibility of monitoring the sufficiency of textbooks and instructional material in low-performing schools that are not under review through state or federal intervention programs.

School district boards of trustees are responsible for governing school districts. They generally are composed of five members, elected to serve staggered four-year terms so that one-half are elected in each odd-numbered year (Educ. Code § 35000 and following sections). A unified school district may have a governing board of seven members who are elected either at large or by trustee areas as designated in the proposal for unification. For many years, the legislature has promoted unification of small districts in contiguous areas as a way of promoting efficiency and uniformity. In 1935 there were 3,500 school districts in the state. Today there are about a third as many, and of these, unified school districts comprise about 330. The rest are elementary (560), high school (87), county districts (58), and SBE charters (8), with a few additional schools operated by the California Youth Authority and by the state. These figures are subject to change because consolidation continues. The governing board of an elementary school district other than a union or joint union elementary district consists of three members elected at large. In districts with high schools, boards also must include at least one nonvoting student member if the students submit a petition requesting student representation. Education Code Section 35160 gives school boards broad authority to operate schools as they see fit—so long as their actions are not inconsistent with or preempted by law and are not in conflict with the purposes of school districts. This general grant of authority reflects an amendment to Article 9, Section 14 of the California Constitution added in 1972 and is often cited in school board policies, administrative regulations, and judicial decisions.

The law sets the maximum ratios of administrative employees to each 100 teachers as nine in elementary schools, eight in unified school districts, and seven in high school districts (Educ. Code § 41402). School superintendents constitute the chief executive officer of school districts (Educ. Code § 35035). Among the superintendent's duties set forth in Section 35035 are preparing and submitting budgets, assigning school district employees, and entering into contracts on behalf of the district. Other duties are specified elsewhere throughout the Education Code, usually in connection with programs or particular school district responsibilities. The qualifications for superintendents are set forth in Education Code Section 35028 and following sections. Superintendents must hold a valid administrator certificate unless the board has waived the requirement. However, the board may not employ a superintendent whose certificate has been revoked. The waiver option enables districts to employ as superintendents persons who are not educators. It is fairly common to see professionals from other fields like law, business, politics, and the military hired as superintendents in large districts. This reflects in part the desire for improved school management and in part disillusionment with the ability of traditionally credentialed administrators to bring about reform. Deputy, associate, and assistant superintendents must be certified as administrators, unless they function only in a clerical position. Superintendents and their deputies are limited to a maximum of four-year terms of employment, which can be renewed.

Public school principals, who basically serve at the pleasure of the school district, must hold an administrative credential and one or more teacher or services credentials (Educ. Code § 44860). However, a substitute principal with only a teacher's credential may be employed in an emergency situation for not more than five months in a school year, as long as the credential matches the grade level at the school to which the substitute principal is appointed (Educ. Code § 44861). While high school principals can act as principals of elementary schools in the same district, they require the approval of the county superintendent of schools to do so in another district. The powers and duties of principals are not detailed in the Education Code. Thus, what they do is determined largely by school boards and central office administrators. Included among the powers and duties listed in the Education Code are making annual reports to the school superintendent if directed to do so and suspending students from school. But rather than having too little to do, most principals soon realize upon taking office that there is not enough time in the day for them to complete the myriad and often unexpected tasks associated with running a complex educational facility. To help them, the legislature has established a grant program to provide administrator training in leadership activities (Educ. Code § 44681 and following sections) and an incentive training program targeted to principals in low-performing schools and administered by the SPI (Educ. Code § 48510 and following sections).

Principals also work with schoolsite councils and advisory committees. Adapted from the corporate decentralization model, these bodies are intended to promote a cohesive and cooperative campus culture. Education Code Section 52852 specifies that schools participating in school-based categorical funding programs must have a schoolsite council at each school. This body develops a school plan to better coordinate the categorical funds the school receives. Schoolsite councils also play a significant role in schools that opt to participate in the High Priority Schools Grant program that, as discussed in the next chapter, is targeted to low-performing schools.

Education Code Section 52176 requires each school with twenty or more limited English proficient students to have an advisory committee of parents and staff to assist the principal with planning and reviewing bilingual education, a requirement that continues even if funding for the program terminates (Educ. Code § 62002.5). For better coordination, the law permits the designation of a single schoolsite advisory council to carry out many of these functions (Educ. Code § 52870). Given the proliferation of special programs at many schools, a good deal of the principal's time can be taken up in committee work.

Continued low performance of the California public schooling system has prompted both the governor and the state superintendent of public instruction to commission comprehensive reform studies on how the system can be reconstituted. There is general agreement that the governance system should be less cumbersome with more discretion for administrators at the local level. However, changing a system so entrenched in law and practice will not be easy.

PARENT RIGHTS AND RESPONSIBILITIES

Despite the significant involvement of the state in schooling, education is a shared responsibility with parents. In fact, before there were public schools, parents either sent their children to private schools or educated them at home. With the advent of public schooling and compulsory attendance laws in the late nineteenth and early twentieth centuries, the role of parents in educating their children themselves declined. Parents were still responsible, of course, for child rearing and training during the first few years of life. But beyond that, education increasingly became a government responsibility. What rights do parents retain over the education of their children? With growing interest in school choice, this is an increasingly important question.

Choosing a Private School

The U.S. Supreme Court first confronted parent rights in the context of education in 1923. In *Meyer v. Nebraska*, a private school teacher challenged a state law that forbid the teaching of a foreign language in public or private school to any student who had not passed the eighth grade. The Court ruled that the state law intruded both on the teacher's right to teach and on the parent's right to control the child's upbringing. While the teacher's right to teach has never been well defined in the law, parent's rights are deemed fundamental. In the *Meyer* ruling, the Court observed that parents have the right "to control the education of their own." The justices found this right to exist in the word "liberty" of the U.S. Constitution's Fourteenth Amendment due process clause. Two years later, the Court revisited parent rights in the seminal *Pierce v. Society of Sisters* ruling. That case involved an Oregon statute requiring every child between the ages of eight and sixteen to attend a public school. Failure to do so was a misdemeanor offense. A Catholic school and a nondenominational military school challenged the law, arguing that if the law were strictly enforced, they would be forced to shut down. The U.S. Supreme Court unanimously declared the law to be an unconstitutional infringement on both the rights of parents and the rights of private schools.

With regard to parent rights, the Court noted that Oregon's compulsory public school attendance law "unreasonably interferes with the liberty of parents and guardians to direct the upbringing and education of children under their control." In a key passage, Justice James McReynolds, who wrote the opinion, observed that

> The fundamental theory of liberty upon which all governments in this Union repose excludes any general power of the state to standardize its children by forcing them to accept instruction from public school teachers only. The child is not the mere creature of the state; those who nurture him and direct his destiny have the right, coupled with the high duty, to recognize and prepare him for additional obligations. (p. 535)

Thus, parents have a constitutional right to enroll their children in private schools, and the state cannot require all children to attend public schools.

The Court reaffirmed its position on parent rights in a 2000 ruling. The case involved a Washington State statute giving state judges the authority to override a parent's objection to child visitation rights by grandparents. While a majority of justices reaffirmed the *Pierce* decision, four members of the Court went further to observe that the interest of parents in the care, custody, and control of their children "is perhaps the oldest of the fundamental liberty rights recognized by the Court" (*Troxel v. Granville*, p. 65).

It is clear from these decisions that parents have a right to select private schools for their children in lieu of public schooling. But beyond choice of a private school, the constitutional dimensions of parent educational rights appear quite limited. In a 2005 decision, the U.S. Court of Appeals for the Ninth Circuit rejected a parental claim that having elementary-age children respond to survey questions dealing with sex and sexual activity violated the parents' rights to control their children's upbringing. The survey was administered by a mental health counselor with the approval of the school. Parents were given an opt-out but several who did not exercise it became incensed when they discovered the nature of the questions, some of which related to sex (e.g., "Touching my private parts too much"). The appeals court observed that parent rights under *Meyer v. Nebraska* and *Pierce v. Society of Sisters* are limited to choosing the school their child attends. The court reviewed a number of previous federal court rulings upholding public school restrictions on parent rights in controlling the upbringing and education of their children (e.g., upholding mandatory health classes, uniform policies, a district's consensual condom distribution program, and a compulsory high school sex education assembly program). The judges observed that "Parents have a right to inform their children when and as they wish on the subject of sex; they have no constitutional right, however, to prevent a public school from providing students with whatever information it wishes to provide, sexual or otherwise, when and as the school determines that it is appropriate to do so" (*Fields v. Palmdale School District*, p. 1206). However, the court did not rule on application of state law to the claim. In California, parents have a statutory right to exempt their children from sex education and HIV/AIDS prevention education, as well as assessments pertaining to them (Educ. Code § 51938).

While the Old Order Amish were able to convince the U.S. Supreme Court that they should be able to withdraw their children from public school after eighth grade and educate them at home based on their separatist religious heritage, no other group successfully has done so (*Wisconsin v. Yoder*, 1972). Even in that case, the justices observed that the *Pierce* ruling provides "no support to the contention that parents may replace state educational requirements with their own idiosyncratic views of what knowledge a child needs to be a productive and happy member of society" (p. 239). Clearly, what made the difference in the *Yoder* decision was the central role of the Amish faith in family life and the education of the children within the Amish community. We examine in Chapter 7 the extent to which the free exercise of religion enhances parent rights to control the education of their children.

Homeschooling

Disillusionment with public schooling, coupled with the explosive growth of on-line learning, has resulted in the soaring popularity of homeschooling. However, federal courts have yet to extend the *Pierce v. Society of Sisters* ruling to encompass it. Thus, the right to homeschooling is a matter determined by state law. While California requires children between the ages of six and eighteen to attend school full time, there is an exemption for attendance at a full-time private school and for instruction by a tutor (Educ. Code §§ 48222 and 48224). The latter provides that children may be instructed for at least three hours a day for 175 days a year by a tutor in the subjects taught in the public schools. The instruction must be between 8 a.m. and 4 p.m. and in English. The statute provides that, unlike teachers in private schools, the tutor must hold a state credential for the grade taught. Until recently, parents who taught their children at home were considered tutors and consequently had to meet the credential requirement. In 2008 a California court of appeal ruled that the provision does not apply to homeschoolers. Though the legislature has never been explicit, the judges concluded after examining various statutes that homeschooling is a form of private schooling and not the equivalent of tutoring. In so ruling, the state court construed the liberty right of parents to control their children's upbringing to be sufficiently strong to require a compelling governmental purpose to restrict homeschooling. A finding by a dependency court that parents are not fit to instruct their children at home fulfills that requirement. The court concluded by observing that California has no laws overseeing homeschooling and that once a parent files an affidavit that they are teaching their children at home, the matter is at an end. The judges advised that in the interest of quality education, more clarity in this area of the law could be helpful (*Jonathan L. v. Superior Court*).

Parents who want to educate their children themselves have found a new venue in the form of charter schools that combine supervised homeschooling with various online and on-site programs. About a third of California's charter schools offer some degree of nonclassroom-based instruction, ranging from cyber schools with an online curriculum to schools that combine traditional classroom learning and independent study. Independent study programs also are available in many traditional public schools and can consist of nonclassroom-based instruction as well. State law imposes conditions on independent offerings in both settings, including a restriction on offering courses required for high school graduation in this manner (Educ. Code § 51745). In addition, traditional public schools often offer alternative programs that provide credentialed teachers to assist parents who homeschool their children.

Rights within Public Schools

Several sections of the Education Code give parents rights within public schools, recognizing that they are partners with public schools in the education of their children. Generally, the term "parent" means the natural parent or one who stands in a parental relationship with a child, such as a legal guardian or foster parent. One section of the Education Code details parent access to student records and the right to challenge information contained therein (Educ. Code § 49070 and following sections). Another gives parents the right to inspect instructional materials and assessments, teacher manuals, films, tapes, and computer software and to observe instruction and other school activities that involve the parent's child (Educ. Code

§ 49091.10 and following sections). Privacy rights involving both students and parents will be examined in detail in Chapter 10.

The Parental Involvement Act added by the legislature in 1998 conveys additional rights to parents, including the right to observe in their child's classrooms, to meet with their child's teachers and principal, to request a particular school for their child and to receive a response from the district, to refuse to give permission for psychological testing involving their child, to have a safe school environment, and to be eligible for membership on a school site committee (Educ. Code § 51100). The statute also reinforces other federal and state law provisions giving parents access to, and the right to challenge, their child's records. The statute requires school districts to develop a policy, in consultation with parents, outlining parental responsibilities and suggesting how parents and guardians can support the learning environment for their children. Suggestions may include checking student attendance, ensuring that homework is completed, monitoring television viewing, volunteering at school, and helping extend their children's learning activities at home.

The right of parents to have access to the school campus to visit with school personnel and to sit in on their children's classes is not unrestricted. Parents, guardians, and nonstudents over the age of sixteen who willfully interfere with classes or school activities are subject to criminal penalties (Educ. Code § 44810). A companion section provides that any parent, guardian, or other person who materially disrupts class work or extracurricular activities or who creates substantial disorder is guilty of a misdemeanor (Educ. Code § 44811). Penalties include fines and imprisonment. Parents also can be liable up to $10,000 for willful misconduct of their child resulting in injury or death to public or private school students, school personnel, or volunteers, as well as for damages caused by their child to property belonging to the school or school personnel (Educ. Code § 48904). This same section permits schools to withhold the grades, transcripts, and diploma of students who willfully damage school property or fail to return loaned property until the damages have been paid. If the minor and the parent or guardian are unable to pay the damages or return the property, the school must provide a voluntary work program to secure release of academic records and diploma.

Expanding Parent Choice

The school choice movement has not escaped the attention of California legislators. While parents have always had the right to choose private schools and public schools for their children through choice of residence, the options within traditional public schools have been limited. Starting in 1994 governing boards were required to adopt an intradistrict open enrollment policy (Educ. Code § 35160.5

(b)). Intradistrict open enrollment means that parents or guardians may select any school in the district for their children. The policy must include a random, unbiased selection criterion for chosen schools that are oversubscribed. Athletic and academic performance may not be considered, though the latter may be used for placement in gifted and talented programs. Specialized schools such as a mathematics academy can continue existing selection criteria. Districts are allowed to give special consideration to students who seek transfers even to overcrowded schools within the district because of unsafe and dangerous conditions to those students at their assigned school. Districts also may give priority to siblings of students already in attendance at a chosen school or whose parents or guardian work there. However, transferring students cannot displace students who currently reside in the chosen school's attendance zone.

One provision of this statute stands out. It provides that school districts retain the authority to maintain appropriate racial and ethnic balances among their schools, either at their discretion or pursuant to a court-ordered or voluntary desegregation plan. At the same time, Proposition 209 added in 1996 to the California Constitution prohibits discrimination against, or preferential treatment to, any individual or group on the basis of race, sex, color, ethnicity, or national origin in public employment, public education, or public contracting. In 2002 a California court of appeal ruled that the latter takes precedence over the former and struck down a racial balance policy at Westminster High School in the Huntington Beach Union High School District (*Crawford v. Huntington Beach Union School District*). A central concern with school choice dating back to the desegregation era of the 1960s is that it will result in racial and ethnic isolation. As discussed in some detail in Chapter 11, the concern is real, and the measures to prevent it are limited.

Congress gave parents increased choice opportunities within school districts when it enacted the No Child Left Behind (NCLB) Act in 2001. An amendment to the venerable Elementary and Secondary Education Act that provides federal funding for the education of low-income and minority students, NCLB permits parents whose children are in low-performing public schools receiving Title I funds to transfer to higher-performing traditional and charter schools in the district. More will be said about NCLB in Chapter 2 because of its extensive impact on the way public schools do business.

Parents also can seek to have their children attend other school districts pursuant to transfer agreements between two or more school districts. The agreements spell out the conditions for transferring and associated rights of appeal (Educ. Code § 46600 and following sections). The state also has an interdistrict school choice program whereby school districts may accept transfers from other districts (Educ. Code Section 48300 and following sections). If governing boards accept transfers, they must assure that no resident student is displaced and that transferring students are admitted through a random, unbiased process. Preference may be given to siblings of children presently enrolled. While no consideration may be given to academic or athletic performance, existing entrance requirements for specialized programs or schools may be applied. Either the district of residence or chosen district may refuse to permit a transfer if it would negatively impact a court-ordered or voluntary desegregation plan or the racial and ethnic balance of the district. The validity of this condition is questionable, for reasons discussed in Chapter 11 on racial segregation.

The district of residence may not block or discourage out-transfers. However, a district of residence with fewer than 50,000 students may limit the number of students transferring out to 3 percent of its enrollment. School districts may not charge a transfer processing fee, according to the state attorney general (Opinion No. 04-501, September 14, 2004). Districts are encouraged to hold informational meetings to inform parents of the options available, and parents are to be notified within ninety days after the chosen district has received the application if the transfer has been approved. The chosen district may not deny a transfer if the additional cost would exceed the amount of additional state aid received for the student, but it may refuse to accept a student transfer if a new program would be required to serve the student. It also may revoke the transfer if the student is recommended for expulsion. Once admitted, high school transfers may be automatically renewed, even if the district later cancels its transfer program. If parents so request, the chosen district may provide transportation assistance within the boundaries of the district in the same manner as for resident students.

Relatively few families take advantage of these interdistrict transfer programs because children do not wish to leave their neighborhoods and because of transportation burdens. It is also important to note that the California Interscholastic Federation requires a one-year moratorium on playing the same contact sport if a student transfers from a private or public school to another school without change of parent residence.

The adoption of magnet and thematic schools, together with transfer options and charter schools, has increased parent choice of schools significantly. The Policy Analysis for California Education research center at the University of California–Berkeley estimated in 1999 that one-fourth of all students in the state no longer attended neighborhood schools. The percentage is probably higher today.

CALIFORNIA CHARTER SCHOOLS

Charter schools have blossomed in the state since the Charter School Act was passed in 1992. A charter school essentially is a newly created public school that is relatively free of state regulation. Both its staff and students are there by choice. The purpose of charter schools is to give parents increased options for the education of their children and to generate new approaches to schooling. Because they are public schools, charter schools must recognize the constitutional rights of their students and teachers under the terms of the federal and state constitutions—just like traditional public schools. Thus, for example, teachers and students are entitled to constitutional rights of expression, the right to associate, and the right to due process. And like traditional public schools, charter schools must be neutral toward religion. They are subject to the federal statutes listed in Table 1.1 and must follow California statutes, such as the open meetings law, that are generally applicable to governmental entities. They also are bound by local building, health, and zoning laws. However, they are exempt from most state laws applying to traditional public schools.

A lengthy section of the Education Code known as the Charter Schools Act of 1992 spells out the details for the approval, operation, and accountability of charter schools (Educ. Code § 47600 and following sections). These provisions are augmented by SBE regulations. As an aid to understanding these requirements, the CDE maintains a charter school website that provides answers to commonly asked questions (www.cde.ca.gov/charter/). Charter schools either must be converted from traditional public schools or be newly created. Private schools cannot convert to charter school status. The law limited the number of charters to 250 in 1998–1999, with up to 100 charter schools authorized in each successive year. The petition to convert an existing public school to a charter school requires the signatures of at least 50 percent of the permanent teachers at the school. The petition to start a new charter school must be signed either by at least one-half of the parents or guardians of students expected to attend, or by at least one-half of the teachers interested in teaching in the school. The charter school can encompass any grade levels and operate as a single school or at multiple sites within the district.

There also are options for operating a charter school outside the district, as well as on a countywide and statewide basis. Such options are especially appealing to organizations seeking to operate large networks of charter schools. Charter schools that serve a large geographic region within the state often are the equivalent of a newly created school district. In federal statutory parlance, they are called "local education agencies" or LEAs. The same is true of start-up charter schools that operate independently of their authorizers. We will see the significance of the LEA classification in later chapters. A school district may even seek to convert all of its schools to charter schools if 50 percent of the teachers sign a petition to that effect. A district-wide charter requires approval of both the SBE and the SPI. However, since neither teachers nor students can be forced to work and study in charter schools, the district charter must include alternative arrangements for those opposed to the idea.

Starting a Charter School

Components of the petition to start a charter school are spelled out in detail in Education Code Section 47605. Among them are a description of the governance system; the educational program, its goals, and measurable outcomes; student outcome assessment; employee qualifications; admission requirements; facilities; start-up costs and three-year cash flow projection; the manner in which annual financial audits will be conducted; student suspension and expulsion procedures; a dispute resolution process; and procedures to be followed if the school closes. Also to be included are the rights of school district employees who leave employment in the district to work in the charter school and any rights of return, as well as the manner in which staff members will be covered by the State Teachers' Retirement System, the Public Employees' Retirement System, or social security. Petitioners must affirm that their school will be nonsectarian; shall not charge tuition; and shall not discriminate against students on the basis of ethnicity, national origin, gender, or disability. While schools can have admissions criteria that do not discriminate on these bases, no preference is to be given to any student in admissions, except that public schools converting to charter school status must give preference to students living within the previous attendance area. Petitioners also must affirm that the charter school will admit all comers but, if oversubscribed, will admit students by public random drawing. Preference is to be extended to students already attending the charter school and those residing within the school district. Other preferences, such as for siblings of enrolled students, must be approved by the chartering authority. If a full-time student is expelled or drops out, the charter school must inform the superintendent of the student's last district and provide a grade transcript and health information.

The petition also must specify "the means by which the school will achieve a racial and ethnic balance among its pupils that is reflective of the general population residing within the territorial jurisdiction of the school district to which the charter petition is submitted" (Educ. Code § 47605 (b)(5)(G)). Achieving this requirement is a major challenge to charter school operations in light of the state constitution's prohibition against affirmative action. It is important to note that the racial balance provision requires charter schools to reflect the racial balance of the *general population* within the school district, not the school district population. Since many persons do not have children or do not send them to public schools, the racial makeup of the community may be quite different from the racial makeup of the district's student body. Without efforts to assure integration, however, charter schools may become more racially isolated than traditional public schools. This matter is discussed in some depth in Chapter 11. District governing boards are to give preference to charter school petitions focused on low-achieving students. Another provision permits charter schools located in the attendance area of an elementary school with upwards of 50 percent of the student population eligible for free or reduced-price lunch to give preference in admissions to students enrolled in the school or living in the attendance area (Educ. Code § 47605.3). The law, however, does not specify that preference must be restricted to those who are actually receiving free or reduced-price lunches.

Once completed, the charter petition is presented to the district's governing board for a public hearing, followed by board action to approve or reject the petition. If the charter school is to serve students enrolled in schools operated by a county, such as schools for adjudicated youth, or to provide instructional services that are not provided by the county office of education—and that, in the county board's judgment, cannot be provided as effectively if the charter school were to operate in a single district—then the petition is presented to the county board of education. Petitions for charter schools to be operated statewide can be presented directly to the SBE. Petitions can be denied only if the chartering entity can establish in writing that they are incomplete, the educational program is unsound, the petitioners are unqualified, there are not enough signatures on the petition, or the petitioners have not agreed to comply with statutory conditions for operating a charter school. If the charter petition is rejected by the district governing board, the petitioners can revise and resubmit the proposal or appeal to the county board of education. If the county board rejects it, petitioners may submit the petition to the SBE. However, petitions for countywide charter schools rejected by county boards may not be appealed.

Operating a Charter School

Under current law, charters can be granted for up to five years. The schools may operate as, or be operated by, a nonprofit benefit corporation; if so, the school district granting the charter is entitled to one representative on the board of directors of the nonprofit public benefit corporation. This means that nonprofit educational management organizations like Aspire Public Schools can receive charters and must adhere to California laws applying to nonprofit corporations. Though California charter school recipients must be nonprofit, they can contract with for-profit education management companies like the Edison Schools to operate the school. In either case, the charter school remains a public school.

Charter schools are monitored by their authorizing entity, which must conduct annual site visits and perform specific oversight activities. County school boards also have authority to investigate charter schools operating within the county if there is a reason to do so, including auditing expenditures and internal controls of a charter school and reporting findings to the charter school and the school's authorizer. Charter schools must submit annual financial audits to the chartering entity, SBE, state controller, and county superintendent of schools unless encompassed in the authorizer's audit. Except for the charters it grants directly, the SBE has the option of delegating its supervisory responsibility by agreement to any local agency in the county, to the school district that originally denied the charter petition, or to any other third party. To underwrite its monitoring cost, the chartering entity can charge up to 1 percent of the revenue of the charter school—an amount defined as general-purpose and categorical block grant funding—unless the charter school obtains rent-free facilities from the entity, in which case the sponsor may charge up to 3 percent. In addition, some charter schools contract with their school district authorizer to provide services such as printing, payroll, and maintenance. In many instances, the school district works to help charter schools flourish, viewing them as partners rather than rivals. The legislature has charged the California Research Bureau with conducting an assessment of the current authorizer oversight system and recommending changes. The report is due early in 2009.

The authorizing entity may inspect the charter school at any time and may revoke the charter if it finds a material breach of a charter term, failure to meet the student achievement outcome specified in the charter, financial mismanagement, or a violation of the law. Before revocation, the authorizer must give the charter school a reasonable opportunity to correct the deficiencies unless student health and safety are at risk. Details of the process for revocation are spelled out in Education Code Section 47607. During the first decade of charter schools in California, twenty charters were revoked. To bolster credibility, some charter schools are seeking accreditation by the Western Association of Schools and Colleges, one of six regional accrediting bodies recognized by the U.S. Department of Education. While accreditation does not insulate a school from having its charter revoked, it does indicate that the school is conforming to generally accepted operating standards. A charter can be renewed by its grantor for five-year periods if the school continues to meet the conditions set forth for granting the initial charter and if the school meets specified academic proficiency standards. The standards are discussed in the school "Assessment and Accountability" section in Chapter 2. Renewals and revisions of charters are to include any new requirements enacted into law after the charter was originally granted or last renewed.

While generally exempt from state law applying to school districts, charter schools are not completely autonomous. In fact, they are now subject to some seventy provisions of the Education Code as the legislature has tightened accountability measures over the years. Charter schools must observe the minimum age for school attendance and must meet the same statewide student testing requirements as traditional public schools, including participating in the California High School Exit Exam (CAHSEE). Teachers of core subjects must hold a state credential. There are restrictions on independent study and nonclassroom-based instruction. These are intended to preclude excessive funding for schools that have no facilities or traditional classroom teaching (e.g., virtual schools that offer instruction via the Internet). Those who start charter schools must establish their qualifications for doing so, and charter schools must prepare financial and attendance statements and undergo auditing and periodic inspections. Charter schools must comply with the California Building Code as adopted and enforced by the local building enforcement agency unless the school already complies with the Field Act regarding building construction and repair or unless the facility is owned or controlled by the federal government or other entity not subject to the building code (Educ. Code §§ 47610-47610.5) Collective bargaining is permitted if teachers wish it. For this purpose, the charter must specify whether the charter school or the school district is the employer. If the teachers in a charter school choose to unionize, the union may bargain over teacher discipline and dismissal procedures since state employment law, much of which is not bargainable, does not apply to charter school teachers.

Some of these accountability measures are part of the original charter petitioning process, and others were added when the Charter School Act was amended in later years. In 2002 the legislature severely limited the ability of charters to operate satellite campuses outside the geographic boundaries of the chartering entity after financial abuses surfaced at the satellite schools. The burden of overseeing a wide network of campuses springing from a single charter proved too great for school district authorizers. The closing of a network of sixty charter schools operated by the California Charter Academy in 2004 demonstrated the point. Now, with limited exceptions, a charter school must operate within the geographic boundaries of the district granting the charter, though multiple sites are permissible if they are listed in the charter. Restrictions like these reflect a tendency found in a number of states for the legislature to impose more regulatory controls over time as charter schools become more numerous.

Creeping regulation from both the legislature and state education agencies remains a central concern of school-choice proponents. Every time stories surface about misuse of funds, of excess profits going to charter school management companies at taxpayer expense, and of efforts to teach unorthodox curricula, new accountability measures are added. The added cost of doing business results in fewer charter schools started by entrepreneurs and more by nonprofit organizations that can attract grant money and realize the efficiencies of operating a network of schools. Some charter school proponents fear that rising costs will drive entrepreneurs out of the charter field altogether, leaving vast networks of carbon-copy schools little different from traditional public schools. In response, charter support and advocacy entities have been established like the California Charter School Association and the Charter Schools Development Center to advance the cause for charter schools and ward off restrictive legislation.

Start-up and facility costs also are major concerns, but the federal Public Charter School Grant Program administered by CDE, together with the Charter School Facility Grant Program (Educ. Code § 47614.5) and the Charter School Revolving Loan Fund for newly created charter schools (Educ. Code § 41365), have ameliorated those costs to some extent. To assist with facility needs, Proposition 39, which passed in 2000, requires school districts to make facilities available to accommodate a charter school's in-district enrollment if the school enrolls eighty or more students (Educ. Code § 47614). The facilities must be comparable to other district schools including furnishings and equipment. They remain the property of the school district, which may charge the charter school the portion of cost for the facility that the district would otherwise have to pay. The district also must make reasonable efforts to provide the charter school with facilities near to where the charter school wishes to locate. Litigation between Ridgecrest Charter School and the Sierra Sands Unified School District focused on the meaning of these requirements. Ridgecrest sought a contiguous facility to accommodate its 223 elementary and middle school students. Desiring to minimize the dislocation of its students, the district offered Ridgecrest the use of 9.5 classrooms at five different school sites separated by sixty-five miles. Ridgecrest rejected the offer. The California court of appeal noted that a district must give the same degree of consideration to the needs of charter school students that it does to students in district-run schools, starting with the assumption that all charter school students will be assigned to a single site. Because the contiguous requirement had not been addressed, the school district had abused its discretion (*Ridgecrest Charter School v. Sierra Sands Unified School District*, 2005).

Sequoia Union High School District lost a court battle in 2003 over whether it, rather than the Redwood City Elementary School District, had to provide facilities under this provision for the Aurora Charter High School. The Redwood City district, which lies within Sequoia's borders, had granted the Aurora charter. Because Aurora served the minimum number of students who otherwise would be attending the Sequoia district, the appellate court ruled that the latter was responsible for providing facilities (*Sequoia Union High School District v. Aurora Charter High School*). The court noted that if a charter school served students in several districts, it could request facilities from all of them if it met the requisite minimum enrollment requirement in each. In 2004 a California court of appeal ruled that a charter school's facilities request must be based on a showing of enrollment projections supported by relevant documents. The court backed the Centinela Valley Union High School's refusal to grant a facilities request when the charter school would not provide names, date of birth, and other information about its students (*Environmental Charter High School v. Centinela Valley Union High School District*).

In a study commissioned by the California Legislative Analyst's Office, the RAND Corporation, a well-known independent nonprofit research organization, reported in 2003 that the state's charter schools performed about as well as traditional public schools on the state's academic performance index (API) rating system, even though charter schools receive less funding and have fewer credentialed teachers. Individual student reading and math test scores for students attending charter schools from 1998 through 2002 were somewhat lower than for traditional public school students. Most of the difference was attributable to charter schools with a nonclassroom-based instructional component. When these were removed from the comparison, charter and traditional public school students performed about the same, a finding echoed by more recent studies. The RAND researchers suggested that charter schools with a nonclassroom-based instructional component are more likely to serve students who are at risk of not attending school at all. A 2008 study conducted by EdSource, an independent California research entity in Mountain View, showed that charter schools operated by educational management organizations tend to do better than other charter schools. In all these comparisons, "selection bias" creates problems for making comparisons. That is, regardless of income levels, those families who select the schools their children attend are more likely to be motivated and more involved in the education of their children than are those who do not, and this translates into higher student performance. To assess the "value added" by the school requires that selection bias must be controlled—no easy task.

Constitutionality of Charter Schools

The Charter School Act survived a major court test in 1999 when a California court of appeal upheld its constitutionality. Noting that charter school legislation was designed to cut through the tangle of rules pervading the California public school system, the appellate court held that the legislature had not unconstitutionally delegated its constitutional duty set forth in Article IX, Section 5 of the California Constitution to provide for a system of free common schools. "From how charter schools come into being, to who attends and who can teach, to how they are governed and structured, to funding, accountability and evaluation—the legislature has plotted all aspects of their existence" (*Wilson v. State Board of Education*, p. 751). Charter schools, the court noted, are very much part of the California common school system. Their teachers have the same credentials as other public school teachers, the curriculum must meet state standards, and students are assessed in the same manner as other public school students.

Similarly, the court rejected the contention that charter schools are not school districts and thus violate Article IX, Section 14 giving the legislature the power to provide for the incorporation and organization of school districts of every kind and class. The court pointed out that the legislature had specifically classified charter schools as school districts in Education Code Section 47612 (c) for purposes of funding and compliance with the constitution. The court ruled that the charter legislation also conforms to Article IX, Section 6 that no part of the public school system shall be directly or indirectly transferred to any authority other than public authorities. Nor does the charter school program violate Article IX, Section 8 of the constitution that no public money may be spent for support of any sectarian or denominational school, or any school not under the exclusive control of public school officials. The destiny of charter schools, the court noted, is controlled by public entities. Charter schools must be operated on a nonsectarian basis and cannot be controlled by religious organizations. Therefore, there is no violation either of this article or of Article XVI, Section 5 prohibiting public entities from spending public money to help support or sustain schools controlled by religious organizations. The appellate court's decision gave a major boost to further development of charter schools in California. At the same time, charter schools are public schools and subject to a great deal of public law, as we note in subsequent chapters.

CALIFORNIA PRIVATE SCHOOLS

In addition to liberty rights, the Fourteenth Amendment to the U.S. Constitution prevents the state from taking away property rights without due process of law. In the 1925 *Pierce v. Society of Sisters* case, the operators of private schools complained that their property rights were being denied because Oregon was requiring all children to attend public schools. The U.S. Supreme Court agreed. It held that the Oregon statute was so arbitrary and unreasonable as to amount to a denial of due process.

While private schools have a right to exist by virtue of the *Pierce* decision, the justices recognized that the state has the right to regulate them, even in the absence of any public funding. In a key passage that many private school and voucher advocates often overlook, the Court noted that

> No question is raised concerning the power of the state reasonably to regulate all schools, to inspect, supervise and examine them, their teachers and pupils; to require that all children of proper age attend some school, that teachers shall be of good moral character and patriotic disposition, that certain studies plainly essential to good citizenship must be taught, and that nothing be taught which is manifestly inimical to the public welfare. (p. 534)

How much regulation is reasonable? When Hawaii imposed very restrictive regulations on its private foreign language schools in the 1920s in the interest of promoting Americanism, the U.S. Supreme Court declared them unenforceable (*Farrington v. Tokushige*, 1927). Among the requirements were paying an annual per-student fee for an operating permit; restrictions on when the schools could operate; teacher permits and pledges; and specifications on entrance requirements, subjects, courses, and textbooks.

Conversely, if a state legislature were to permit private schools to operate with no regulation, it could be argued that the legislature has unconstitutionally delegated its central responsibility for schooling to unaccountable private entities. While the unconstitutional delegation claim has lost its punch in federal courts, it remains viable in state court. Many commentators and private school organizations believe increased regulation of private schools is an inevitable by-product of publicly funded voucher programs.

In accord with *Pierce*, California provides an exemption from public schooling for children who attend private full-time day schools. Teaching in these schools must be in English, taught by capable teachers, and cover the several branches of study required in public schools (Educ. Code § 48222). Pupil attendance must be taken. Though California does not require private schools to be state accredited, they must file an affidavit annually with the state superintendent of public instruction (SPI) providing information on such matters as the school's operators, size of the teaching staff and enrollment, courses of study offered, names and qualifications of the teachers, and fingerprint and criminal record information (Educ. Code § 33190). The filing of the affidavit is not meant to confer any state approval, recognition, or endorsement of private schools, and it is not to be construed as a license or authorization. Most private schools are accredited through the Western Association of Schools and Colleges or by the associations to which they belong, such as the California Association of Independent Schools. An umbrella group of private schools, known as the California Association of Private School Organizations, maintains contact on behalf of its members with the California Department of Education (CDE) and state legislators.

Other provisions of the Education Code pertain to the operation of private schools. Among the more significant are those requiring private schools to comply with earthquake construction measures (Educ. Code § 17320 and following sections); earthquake emergency procedures (Educ. Code § 35295 and following sections); school safety measures such as fire drills, access gates, the wearing of eye-protective devices, having first-aid kits, avoiding toxic art supplies, and preventing hazing (Educ. Code § 32000 and following sections); school bus regulations (Educ. Code § 39830 and following sections); and employee sex offense notification requirements (Educ. Code § 44020). Private schools also must comply with local health and zoning requirements. It is readily apparent that homeschooling parents who seek to have their home declared a private school are unlikely to meet these requirements.

While the regulations may seem to be extensive at first glance, it is important to note what is not regulated: student admissions, teacher credentialing, textbooks, the instructional program, and reporting and finances. California private schools may participate in the state's student assessment system, but they are not required to do so. In essence, California private schools are relatively autonomous organizations. No doubt part of the reason for the general hands-off approach is that the majority of California private schools are religiously affiliated. For reasons discussed in the next section and in Chapter 7, the California Constitution erects a substantial barrier between church and state. In this regard, it is more stringent than the federal constitution.

As a matter of federal law, private schools do not have to observe the constitutional rights of their constituents, because these schools are not state entities. For this reason, they and their employees are exempt from lawsuits under 42 U.S.C. Section 1983 (see Table 1.1). While private schools can select students based on gender and religion, they cannot discriminate on the basis of race. The U.S. Supreme Court ruled as much in 1976 (*Runyon v. McCrary*). The Court cited 42 U.S.C. Section 1981, a federal statute enacted after the Civil War to implement the Thirteenth Amendment's ban on slavery and its trappings (see Table 1.1). That amendment and implementing statute apply to both public and private schools. The private schools in *Runyon* had argued that the statute would undercut the right of some parents to choose to have their children educated in racially segregated schools. But the justices pointed out that the state has the authority under *Pierce* to regulate the parents' choice of schooling for their children and that the schools could still teach whatever values they wanted; though presumably under the *Pierce* decision, the state could prevent the teaching of racial hatred. A few years later, the Court ruled that tax exemptions can be denied to private educational institutions that practice racial discrimination, even if those practices are religiously motivated (*Bob Jones University v. United States*, 1983).

Private schools are subject to several important federal statutes. Included among them are Title VII of the 1964 Civil Rights Act and the Americans with Disabilities Act (see Table 1.1), though there are exemptions for very small schools and for those controlled by religious organizations. Unless private schools receive federal funding—and most do not—they are not subject to the Individuals with Disabilities Education Act, Section 504 of the 1973 Rehabilitation Act, and Title IX of the 1972 Education Amendments. Interestingly, California law requires private secondary schools to observe the free speech rights of their students in the same manner that public schools do (Educ. Code § 48950). We will have more to say in subsequent chapters about this and other statutes affecting private schools.

VOUCHER PROGRAMS

When the U.S. Supreme Court ruled in *Pierce v. Society of Sisters* that parents have a constitutional right to choose private schools for the education of their children, it said nothing about any responsibility on the part of the state to finance the choice. Many parents view the *Pierce* decision as inequitable because only families of means can afford to exercise the right. Private schools are beyond the reach of most low-income families. Lacking the means to pay private school tuition or move to another district, these families have had little alternative in the past but to send their children to the assigned public school. In urban areas, this often meant a dilapidated school with inferior teachers and few high-achieving students to serve as positive role models. With the advent of magnet schools, intra- and inter-district transfer programs, and charter schools in California, more parents have been able to exercise control over where their children attend school. But their choices are all within the public sector. Private schools remain beyond the reach of most families, a reality especially resented by parents who seek a faith-based education for their children. Both federal and state constitutional laws require public schools to be secular. By contrast, over three-quarters of private schools in the nation are religiously affiliated.

Enter vouchers. At its purest and grandest, a publicly funded voucher system gives parents the means to send their children to the public and private schools of their choice. In addition to empowering parents, a voucher system represents a fundamental change in the financing of education because the money goes to parents, not schools. In effect, education becomes a market system whereby schools compete for students. Proponents believe that selection of schools should be an integral part of individual choice in a free society. Many low-income families view vouchers favorably because vouchers open the door to private schools. Middle- and upper-income families who send their children to private schools find vouchers attractive because they resent paying taxes for public schools they do not use. Many private school operators see vouchers as a means of shoring up their financial base and expanding enrollment. Opponents, on the other hand, believe a voucher system will undermine the common learning experience provided by the nation's public schools. They fear that many parents will not choose wisely, or at all, and that accompanying regulations will undermine the autonomy of private schools.

So far, experience with voucher programs has been limited. The first significant voucher program involved the Alum Rock school district on the east side of San Jose in the early 1960s. Launched by the Office of Economic Opportunity as an experiment in assisting low-income families, the program created a firestorm of opposition from many quarters and eventually was limited to giving parents a choice of thematic public schools in the Alum Rock district. Within a few years, the program disappeared. Growing concern about the quality of public schools in the 1980s generated renewed interest in vouchers and resulted in the development of private school voucher programs for low-income families in Milwaukee and Cleveland in the early 1990s. Florida enacted a private school voucher program in 1999 for parents with children in failing public schools and later expanded it to include the parents of children with disabilities. The portion pertaining to low performing schools was declared unconstitutional by the Florida Supreme Court in 2006. A voucher program was approved by Congress for the District of Columbia in 2004. Research findings on these programs remain mixed. While parent and student satisfaction levels generally are higher than in traditional public schools, student achievement remains about the same when all the variables, including the influence of the act of choosing, are controlled.

Vouchers attracted interest in California too, but proponents quickly realized that the state afforded an inhospitable constitutional climate. Article IX, Section 8 of the state constitution is very explicit: "No public money shall ever be appropriated for the support of any sectarian or denominational school, or any school not under the exclusive control of the officers of the public schools. . . . " Article XVI, Section 5 further provides that

> Neither the Legislature, nor any county, city and county, township, school district, or other municipal corporation, shall ever make an appropriation, or pay from any public fund whatever, or grant anything to or in aid of any religious sect, church, creed, or sectarian purpose, or help to support or sustain any school, college, university, hospital, or other institution controlled by any religious creed, church, or sectarian denomination whatever. . . .

Faced with these constitutional barriers, California voucher proponents nevertheless launched two initiatives to amend the state constitution to permit vouchers. Neither was successful. Proposition 174, known as the Parental Choice in Education initiative, was rejected by more than a two-to-one margin in 1993. Carrying the wordy title "The National Average School Funding Guarantee and Parental Right to Choose Quality Education Amendment," Proposition 38 failed by an even larger margin in 2000. Both demonstrated that when it comes to vouchers, the devil is in the details. Proposition 174 would have provided an educational scholarship of $2,600 for every resident school-age child in California. Scholarships could have been redeemed at any scholarship-redeeming school, which included public, private, and religious schools that met minimal requirements. The initiative strictly limited regulation of scholarship-redeeming schools. Proposition 38 would have given parents $4,000 to send their children to private schools. It too would have severely restricted the ability of the legislature and other governmental entities to regulate private schools. A flat voucher of the type proposed in these initiatives is too small to be of much benefit to low-income families. Unlike the voucher programs targeted to low-income families in Milwaukee, Cleveland, and the District of Columbia, both initiatives were open to criticism that they diverted taxpayer money to the wealthy. Fiscal concerns also were apparent since families already in private schools presumably would apply for the scholarships. Opponents saw the shift of money to private education as draining funds from public schools and shortchanging the education of children left behind. Restrictions on the state's ability to hold choice schools accountable raised fears about misuse of the money. Opponents capitalized on all of these design features to soundly defeat the voucher initiatives.

In the past several years, renewed interest has been shown in vouchers and other forms of indirect aid to private schools in the wake of U.S. Supreme Court decisions that clarified the law regarding their constitutionality to some extent. Because these decisions involve interpretation of both federal and state constitutional provisions involving government support for religion, we include them in our discussion of religious issues in Chapter 7.

SUMMARY

In this chapter, we have presented the basic sources of school law and discussed how they interrelate. School law is not a cohesive category of law. Rather, it is a multilayered mixture of constitutional, statutory, administrative, contract, and judicial law. Given the size and complexity of the California school system, it is easy to get lost in the details.

The federal constitution leaves the creation of an educational system to the states. California constitutional law places the major responsibility for the establishment and operation of the schooling system on the legislature. While the legislature has enacted a host of laws detailing the manner in which schools are to operate and has placed considerable oversight responsibility in state agencies, it has left the day-to-day operation of schools to county and district boards of education. Still, given that schooling is one of its most important functions and consumes 40 percent of the state budget, the legislature is never far away. In recent years, that has been evident in the enactment of comprehensive curriculum standards and assessment legislation. The legislature does not operate in a vacuum. It is significantly influenced by the governor, powerful interest groups, and the electorate. And it cannot act contrary to either federal law or to state constitutional law.

While the state and its political subdivisions have a major role in the education of children within its borders, so too do parents. The role of parents in the education of their children increasingly has been recognized by both the federal and California governments. An example of the former is Congress's enactment of the No Child Left Behind Act in 2001 that gives an opt-out to parents whose children attend low-performing schools. An example of the latter is the California Legislature's Parental Empowerment Act of 1998 that specifies parents' rights within the public schools. Increasingly, parents have been given a choice of public schools they wish their children to attend through intra- and interdistrict choice programs and the development of charter schools. Indeed, charter schools have become an integral part of the California schooling system. It is estimated that upward of half of all public school students are attending schools chosen by their parents, either through these programs or by choice of residence.

For many students, the California private schooling system has provided a viable alternative to public schools, especially for those seeking a faith-based education. While parents long have had a constitutional right to choose private schools, most lack the means to do so. The newest systemic reform is publicly funded vouchers that enfranchise parents with the right to select private schools. While California voters have decisively defeated two voucher initiatives, the design features of both played a large role in their demise. With polls showing that a sizeable portion of the California electorate remains interested in vouchers, new attempts to enact such a program will surface in the future.

With our overview of the legal framework for California schooling and of the major players involved in their operation completed, we now turn to an examination of how law affects school attendance, teacher preparation, and the instructional program.

2 ATTENDANCE, INSTRUCTION, AND ASSESSMENT

Before instruction can begin, students have to be in school. Accordingly, this chapter begins by examining California school attendance law and describing the consequences for those who violate it. Then the focus shifts to the instructional program. Increasingly, emphasis has been placed on specifying what students are to learn as they move from grade to grade, how their learning is to be assessed, and how schools are to be held accountable. Since teacher quality is an important influence on student learning, teacher preparation and credentialing also have received attention. An important stimulus to reform in these areas comes from Congress. When Congress reauthorized the Elementary and Secondary Education Act (ESEA) by passing the No Child Left Behind Act (NCLB) in 2001, it mandated high standards for teacher quality and for student achievement as a condition of receiving federal funding under the act. ESEA is the principal federal program affecting elementary and secondary education. Title I of the act provides funding for the education of disadvantaged children, and 60 percent of the California schooling population is enrolled in schools receiving Title I funds. Prior to the enactment of NCLB, California had made significant strides in developing curriculum content standards, student assessment, and school accountability. NCLB stimulated further reform.

A number of other legal issues arise in the context of curriculum and instruction. A prerequisite to effective learning is an orderly environment, and state law conveys some important tools for school administrators to use to assure it. While the authority of policymakers over what occurs in the classroom is extensive, it is not unlimited. The growing role of computers and the Internet in the instructional program poses a unique set of legal concerns. Copyright law imposes some important restrictions on the use of classroom instructional material. The education of English-language learners has undergone major change in California due to the passage of Proposition 227 in 1998. These and other concerns are addressed in this chapter.

A word to readers: What broadly can be termed "curriculum law" is in a state of flux, as reformers and policymakers seek to improve the performance of the public schooling system. For example, at this writing, changes are being made to NCLB and California's education reform programs. To keep up to date on legal developments in this area, readers should consult the book's update posted on its website at www .californiaschoollaw.org. Because many topics in this chapter are controlled by state law, we frequently cite the statutes for ease of reference, even though this may interfere a bit with the flow of the discussion. It is important to note as well that many of these statutes are very detailed and frequently amended. Thus, they should be consulted directly when the need arises. This can be easily done through the California Department of Education website at www.cde.ca.gov (click on "Laws and Regulations").

ATTENDANCE

The Compulsory Attendance Law

Compulsory education dates back to 1903 in California. Spurred by rapid economic growth during the late nineteenth and early twentieth centuries, states came to realize that education could not be left to the vagaries of parents and private tutors. For the state to have an educated and productive population, all children had to attend school. Current attendance law is set forth in Education Code Sections 48200 and 48204 and provides that, unless otherwise exempt, students between the ages of six and eighteen are to be admitted to public schools of the district on a full-time basis under the following conditions:

- Either the parent or legal guardian lives in the district.
- The student is placed in a licensed children's institution or foster home in the district.
- The student is admitted pursuant to an interdistrict transfer agreement under Education Code Section 46600.
- The student lives in the district and is emancipated from the control of parent or guardian. This means that the student is or has been married, is on active duty in the armed forces, or has been declared emancipated by a court.
- The student lives in the home of a caregiving adult in the district who is over the age of 18 and who has filed a caregiving affidavit to this effect as specified in Family Code Section 6550, unless the school district determines

to the contrary. The affidavit asks only for the name and address of the caregiver to authorize enrollment in school and to authorize school-related medical care. For any other medical care, additional items must be completed on the affidavit by a relative. If these items aren't completed, then additional medical care can be authorized only by the minor's parent or guardian. In any case, the affidavit is valid for one year only.

- The student resides in a state hospital located in the district.

In addition, until 2012, districts may admit a student if one or both of the parents or guardians are physically employed within the boundaries of the district (Educ. Code § 48204 (b)). If a district refuses to admit these students, it must not do so on the basis of race, ethnicity, sex, parental income, scholastic achievement, or any arbitrary consideration. The state attorney general has advised that overcrowding is a permissible reason to refuse admission, but not to deny continued attendance through the highest grade offered by the district as long as the parent continues to be employed within the district's boundaries (84 Ops. Atty. Gen. 198, 2001). In the same opinion, the attorney general advised that under Education Code Section 46601.5 relating to interdistrict transfers, once a student is admitted based on child-care needs, overcrowding does not justify denying them continued attendance through twelfth grade as long as the child-care needs remain.

Education Code Section 48204 (b) provides that either the sending or the receiving district may deny admission to a student whose parent or guardian works within the district's boundaries if the admission would negatively impact a court-ordered or voluntary desegregation plan. The receiving district also may deny admission if the cost of education would exceed the amount of state aid received for educating the student. The statute encourages districts that reject these transfers to communicate with parents and to record the reasons accurately in governing board minutes. The statute does not authorize out-of-district transfers beyond specified limits unless approved by the sending district. Once a student whose parent or guardian works within the boundaries of the district is admitted, the student does not have to reapply each year and may continue through the twelfth grade, subject to the conditions just described.

What if a child lives in a home that is only partly within a district's geographic boundaries, and the bulk of property taxes paid by the home's owners goes to a second district? Can the first district refuse to admit the student? A California court of appeal ruled in the negative in 2004, holding that Education Code Section 48200's requirement that students attend school in the district "in which the residence of either the parent or guardian is located" must be interpreted to include a residence that is only partly within a school district's boundaries. The fact that the bulk of property taxes may flow to another district is unfortunate—but a matter for the legislature, not the courts. Additionally, the fact that the county office of education construed the law otherwise was irrelevant because the judiciary has the final say (*Katz v. Los Gatos-Saratoga Joint Union High School District*).

Governing boards, with the approval of the county superintendent of schools, may admit students in adjoining states to its schools pursuant to an agreement with the district of residence or the parent or guardian reimbursing the chosen district for the cost of education (Educ. Code § 48050). The attendance of these students cannot be included in computing the average daily attendance for purposes of state funding. Students who live in Mexico and who regularly return there within a twenty-four-hour period may be admitted to district classes and schools with approval of the governing board if they are otherwise eligible to attend school (Educ. Code § 48051).

Foster children present a special challenge to California public and private schools. There are over 80,000 foster children in the state, most of whom experience multiple placements in foster homes and licensed children's institutions (LCI) that result in frequent transfers among schools. It has been estimated that a change in placement occurs about once every six months and that three-quarters of foster children are working below grade level, over 80 percent are held back by third grade, and nearly half drop out of high school.[1] Education Code Sections 48850-48859 stipulate that foster children are entitled to the same educational opportunities as other children and detail the notification requirements regarding educational options for children placed in LCIs. Agencies placing children in these institutions are required to notify the local county office of education, school district, and any charter schools participating as a member of a special education local plan area. Children placed in foster homes or LCI's are entitled to remain in their school of origin unless it is determined that a different placement would be appropriate.

Section 48853.5 requires every school district and county board of education to have an education liaison for foster children and details this person's responsibilities to ensure proper educational placement of foster children and assist with the transfer of their credits, records, and grades. If there is a change in a foster child's residential placement, the school district must permit the child to remain enrolled through the school year if it will best serve the needs of the child. That determination

---

[1] As quoted in 2008 Report to the Legislature and the Governor for the Foster Youth Services Program, California Department of Education, February 15, 2008, pp. 1–2.

is made jointly by the school district's foster care liaison, the person who holds education rights for the child, and the child. If it is determined that a foster child should be enrolled in a school other than the school of origin, the new school must admit the child immediately without regard to past due fees, fines, or textbooks at the previous school and without regard to the absence of records or inability to comply with a dress code. Other important Education Code provisions relating to foster children include Section 49069.3 (access of foster care agencies to student records), Section 49076 (access of case workers and probation officers to student records), Section 49069.5 (timely transfer of records for foster children and no academic penalties for school absences related to placement changes), Section 48645.5 (awarding credit for coursework completed satisfactorily at another public school, private nonsectarian school, or juvenile court school), and Section 42920 and following sections (establishment of a Foster Youth Services Program to provide services to foster youth for improving their education).

Several provisions of the Education Code exclude students from schooling. Section 48215 was enacted following approval of Proposition 187 in 1994 excluding illegal immigrants from various public services including public schooling. However, this provision conflicted with a 1982 U.S. Supreme Court ruling to the contrary and was declared null and void in 1995 (*LULAC v. Wilson*). Section 48216 gives governing boards the authority to deny admission to students who have not been immunized.

Children must be admitted to kindergarten at the beginning of the school year or anytime thereafter if the child will be five years old on or before December 2 of that year (Educ. Code § 48000). Children whose fifth birthday is after this date may be admitted on a case-by-case basis. They also may be admitted to the prekindergarten summer program for students who will be enrolling in kindergarten in September. To be admitted to the first grade, students must be six years old on or before December 2 (Educ. Code § 48010). If a child has completed a year of kindergarten in a private or public school, he or she must be admitted to first grade unless the parent or guardian believes the child should remain in kindergarten for another year. A child who is in kindergarten and judged ready for first grade may be admitted to that grade at the discretion of the administration and with the consent of the parent or guardian if the child is at least five years of age (Educ. Code § 48011). The attorney general has opined that a student who has completed a year of kindergarten in a private school is not automatically entitled to be admitted to first grade in a public school when the student does not meet the minimum age requirements. The decision is left to the school administration if the child is at least five years of age (66 Ops. Atty. Gen. 135, 1983).

Like most states, California equates quality learning with time spent in school. The minimum and maximum lengths of the school day for various grade levels are set forth in Education Code Section 46111 and following sections. While these provisions are quite detailed and contain numerous exceptions and conditions, the general thrust is to limit kindergarten to a minimum of 180 minutes and a maximum of 240 minutes per day exclusive of recesses (265 minutes per day in a multitrack year-round school). The minimum school day for the first through third grades is 230 minutes except in opportunity schools, classes, or programs. For grades four through eight, the minimum school day is 240 minutes, not counting the lunch period and recesses. For junior and senior high schools, the minimum school day is 240 minutes. The minimum is 180 minutes per day for eleventh and twelfth graders also taking courses on a part-time basis for academic credit at a junior college, the California State University, or the University of California. With some exceptions, seniors must take at least five courses each semester. As we will note later, California limits the amount of time students can spend learning on the Internet. Minutes of instruction per grade level for charter schools also are specified (Educ. Code § 47612.5 (a)(1)). These are, at a minimum, 36,000 minutes per year in kindergarten; 50,400 minutes in grades one through three; 54,000 minutes in grades four through eight; and 64,800 minutes in grades nine through twelve. These cannot be waived by either the State Board of Education or the Superintendent of Public Instruction.

Attendance Records

Parents and guardians enrolling a child in kindergarten or first grade must present evidence that the child has reached the minimum age (Educ. Code § 48002). When students transfer to a new school, administrators can request records from the former public or private school. Such records cannot be withheld from the requesting school because the student or parent has not paid fees. According to the attorney general, the withholding provision in Education Code Section 48904.3 applies to the student and the student's parents, not to a school to which a student is transferring (64 Ops. Atty. Gen. 867, 1981). This is so because another section of the code requires both public and private schools to forward student records to the new school upon request (Educ. Code § 49068). The county board of education may require the reporting of various types of attendance severance at both public and private schools. Such reporting is required for children with disabilities (Educ. Code § 48203). The California Administrative Code classifies student enrollment and academic achievement records as permanent records, which must be kept indefinitely. Other information such as the names of persons other than educators given access to a student's records, heath information, participation in special education programs, progress slips, and results of standardized tests administered within the preceding three years are disposable in accordance with California law (Admin. Code, title 5, §§ 432, 16023).

Exemptions from Attendance

Students who are exempt from having to attend public school include those who are attending a full-time private school and those who are being homeschooled by credentialed tutors or parents (Educ. Code §§ 48222, 48224). Students who hold a permit for working in the entertainment industry are permitted a maximum of five absences per school year of up to five consecutive days each (Educ. Code § 48225.5). They are to receive instruction from a qualified studio teacher. Students participating with a not-for-profit performing arts organization in a performance for a public school audience must be excused for up to five days per school year if the parent submits a written request. In either case, students must complete reasonably equivalent assignments and tests missed during the absence for full credit. Students who hold permits to work are exempt from the compulsory school law but must attend part-time classes. A student who is fifteen or older may take a leave of absence for up to one semester for supervised travel, study, training, or work not available in school if the district has a policy to this effect (Educ. Code § 48232). The child's parent or guardian must sign an agreement indicating the purpose and length of the leave, as well as the need for meeting periodically with a school official during the leave. The leave may be extended for an additional semester. The statute limits leaves of absence to no more than 1 percent of student enrollment in the district.

School districts, county boards of education, and charter schools may permit independent study for various reasons such as providing access to content not included in the curriculum and providing continuing education to students who are traveling (Educ. Code § 51745 and following sections). To include these students in average daily attendance for funding purposes, the district, county, or charter school must require the students to sign a detailed independent study agreement. It is not sufficient to have a general policy governing independent study (*Modesto City Schools v. Education Audits Appeal Panel*, 2004). The statute delineates the required components of the agreement in some detail (Educ. Code § 51747). Included among them are how completed work is to be submitted and evaluated, the resources to be made available to the student, and the duration of the agreement. State funding is not available for independent study if funds or anything of value is provided to these students that is not provided to students attending regular classes. Nor is funding available if funds or anything of value is provided for independent study, including home study, that a school district could not legally provide to a student in regular attendance or to the parent (Educ. Code § 51747.3). According to a 1995 attorney general opinion, the purpose of this provision is to prevent charter schools from offering "sign-up bonuses" to parents for home study so that the schools could obtain state funding. It does not prevent a charter school or other local education agency from spending funds for special education aids and materials that make independent study meaningful (78 Ops. Atty. Gen. 253, 1995).

Absences and Truancy

The law permits students to be excused from school for justifiable reasons such as illness, doctor's appointment, family emergency, and attendance at religious retreats (Educ. Code § 48205). The attorney general has advised that a school district cannot require prior written parental consent before releasing a student to obtain confidential medical services under this section. The district also cannot notify the parents when a student leaves school for this purpose. The attorney general noted that although parental permission is required under this statute for justifiable reasons, such as appearance in court, attendance at a funeral, and observance of a holiday, such is not the case for absences for medical, dental, optometrical, or chiropractic services (87 Ops. Atty. Gen. 168, 2004). Students who have excused absences must be allowed to complete missed assignments and tests for full credit, based on the classroom teacher's determination. Religious retreats are limited to four hours per semester. The latter limitation may invite dispute from devout parents, who may argue that it intrudes upon their free exercise of religion. Another provision of the code gives school districts the option of releasing students for up to four days per month to attend religious exercises or receive religious and moral instruction off campus. Such absences are not to be included in computing the average daily attendance.

Truancy provisions in the education code are elaborate (Educ. Code § 48260 and following provisions). A student is considered truant and must be reported to the attendance supervisor or school superintendent if he or she is absent from school without valid excuse for three full days in one school year or is tardy or absent for more than any thirty-minute period during the school day without a valid excuse on three occasions in one school year or a combination thereof. Parents and guardians of truant students are to be notified and reminded of their responsibility to see that the student attends the regular or alternative school program. Failure to do so can result in criminal penalties against the parent following an investigation and referral to a county-based school attendance review board, which, among other things, has authority to direct parents and students to participate in community services to address the truancy problem. Penalties include a fine of up to $100 upon first conviction,

$250 upon second conviction, and $500 upon third or subsequent convictions; or, in lieu of these fines, placement in a parent education and counseling program. Failure to pay the fine or attend the program will result in a contempt citation. The municipal court judge also may order that a parent immediately enroll the student in school with proof to the court. Failure to do so is punishable as civil contempt with a fine up to $1,000 but not imprisonment. Fines collected under these provisions are to be credited to the school district to support activities of the student attendance review board, as well as the parent education and counseling program.

Truant students also suffer penalties for nonattendance. A first-time truant may be asked to make up the missed classes and may receive a warning by any police officer. School attendance supervisors or designees, police officers, school administrators, and probation officers have the authority to take custody of a truant student during school hours. Custody is not considered punishment, but rather a step toward remediation by returning the student to school or to the student's parent or guardian. At the same time, police officers who have probable cause to suspect that a youth is truant have grounds to conduct a search of the student and the student's belongings (*In re Humberto O.*, 2000). The school may make a record of the truancy. The second truancy in the same school year may result in the student's assignment to an after-school or weekend program. A third offense results in classification of the student as a habitual truant. Habitual truants may be referred to the school attendance review board or a truancy mediation program. School attendance review boards may be established at the county and at the district level. They include a diversified membership reflective of the school community and are empowered to improve coordination among agencies dealing with student attendance and behavioral problems, as well as to develop alternative ways of dealing with truant students in the juvenile court system.

A fourth truancy in the same year places the student in the jurisdiction of the juvenile court, which may adjudge the student a ward of the court. If this occurs, the student will be required to do one or more of the following: perform court-approved community service, pay a fine, attend a court-approved truancy prevention program, or have driving privileges suspended or revoked. The court may also require the parent or guardian to bring the student to school. Districts are to submit data to the county superintendent of schools on the number and types of referrals to school attendance boards and juvenile courts.

There is no easy method of dealing with truant students. Students usually are truant because they do not like school or see no reason to attend. The legislature has enacted legislation encouraging school districts and county boards of education to adopt pupil attendance policies that incorporate active student, parent, and community involvement. At the same time, it discourages the use of suspensions for these students (Educ. Code § 48900 (v)). The legislature has directed the state superintendent of public instruction (SPI) to disseminate information on effective attendance strategies to school districts. Perhaps most useful is the development of alternative education programs and charter schools for at-risk students. Under Education Code Section 48432.5, for irregular attendance a high school student can be assigned to attend an alternative school, and many students find that environment more conducive to learning. Measures like these give truant-prone students greater opportunity to find an educational setting in which they can succeed.

CURRICULUM AND INSTRUCTION

Maintaining a Safe Learning Environment

Students learn best when classes are safe and orderly. Article I, Section 28 of the California Constitution provides that "All students and staff of public primary, elementary, junior high and senior high schools have the inalienable right to attend campuses which are safe, secure, and peaceful." The legislature has responded by passing several laws that give administrators at public, and in some cases private, schools the authority to maintain a safe learning environment. Here we discuss laws that restrict outsiders from interfering with campus activities. In Chapter 9 we address the discipline of students. It is important to note at the outset that while a traditional public or charter school is a public place and thus must observe the constitutional rights of individuals, it also serves a special purpose. Thus, unlike a public park or street corner, individual rights are more circumscribed in this setting. This is particularly true for outsiders. At the same time, the Civic Center Act allows governing boards to open school facilities for use by community organizations for literary, scientific, recreational, educational, and similar purposes (Educ. Code § 38130 and following sections). The act requires governing boards to permit nonprofit organizations such as the Girl Scouts, Boy Scouts, parent-teacher association, and the like to use its facilities when alternative locations are not available as long as doing so does not interfere with schooling. The school district may charge a fee for allowing outside organizations to use its facilities. While the district is liable for injuries arising from its negligence in maintaining the facilities, the outside group is liable for injuries arising from its negligence in using them.

Declaring that a disproportionate share of crimes committed on school grounds are committed by outsiders who have no lawful business there, the legislature added provisions to the California Penal Code in 1982 requiring outsiders to register with the principal or principal's designee during school hours (Penal

Code § 627 and following sections). They cannot simply walk onto campus to interact with staff members and students at will. School hours are defined to mean an hour before school begins and an hour after school ends. Registration is to include the visitor's name, address, and occupation; proof of age and identity; the purpose for being on campus; and any other information that may be relevant. Failure to register is a misdemeanor offense. The statute also provides that if it appears reasonable to a school official that an outsider may disrupt school activities, the official can direct the person to leave. Failure to comply also is a misdemeanor, as is reentry of a person onto school grounds within seven days of being asked to leave.

A California appellate court defined the scope of this important statute in a 2000 decision involving the Golden West Middle School in Fairfield (*In re Joseph F.*). The case involved a juvenile offender who challenged his conviction for violating this law and for committing battery on a police resource officer assigned to the school. The police officer testified that the assistant school principal asked him to detain the youth for questioning after the youth was unresponsive to the assistant principal's questions. In attempting to do so, the officer met with resistance and had to use force to subdue the youth. The youth was placed on probation and restricted from associating with gangs. He argued that he did not have to register because the school day had ended and that the officer had no reason to stop him for questioning. In a two-to-one decision, the court of appeal rejected his arguments. While the statute's registration requirement is restricted to school hours, the majority noted that nothing prevents a school official from inquiring why an outsider is on campus at any time. Contrary to the youth's assertion, it was not necessary for the officer to specify any particular law that was being broken. In a key passage, the court observed that

> unlike the rules applicable to public places in general, school officials, including police who assist in maintaining general order on school campuses, need not articulate a specific crime which appears to be violated in order to detain an outsider for the limited purpose of determining the fundamental factors justifying an outsider's presence on a school campus, such as who he is, why he is on campus, and whether he has registered. (p. 986)

The conviction of the youth for battery and resisting arrest was upheld.

The question of whether the school campus is a public forum that must accommodate outside groups intending to communicate with students surfaced in a 2003 California appellate court ruling (*Reeves v. Rocklin Unified School District*). The case involved an antiabortion organization that sought to register with the school principal for the purpose of handing out leaflets and engaging in communication with students at the Rocklin High School. When the request was denied, the group filed a lawsuit, arguing that its First Amendment rights had been violated. The court of appeal rejected the claim. It noted that the U.S. Supreme Court had declared in a 1983 ruling that in order to serve its dedicated purpose, some public property may not be open to communication by outsiders (*Perry Education Association v. Perry Local Educators' Association*). A high school campus is such a place. If the high school were considered a public forum, not only the antiabortion group but other organizations would have to be granted the same right since the government cannot discriminate on the basis of speech content in a public forum. The educational functioning of the high school and the safety of the students would be jeopardized as a result. The group pointed out a provision of Penal Code Section 627, which states that the law is not to impinge upon protected rights of expression. But because the high school is a closed forum to outsiders, this provision is inapplicable. In any case, the court noted that the group could still communicate with students by doing so at a public intersection near the school. It is important to note that this case involves the speech rights of outsiders, not students or teachers. The expression rights of students and teachers are discussed in Chapter 6.

A number of other Penal Code provisions can be relied upon by school officials and law enforcement to maintain a safe schooling environment. While it is beyond the scope of this chapter to discuss them, we have provided a list of the most relevant in Table 2.1.

Provisions of the Education Code also give school administrators authority to maintain order. Some of these statutes have their roots in the student activist period of the 1960s and early 1970s when civil rights and Vietnam antiwar demonstrations were common across the educational landscape. One statute provides that minors over the age of sixteen or adults who enter school grounds and willfully disrupt classes or interfere with administration of the school are guilty of a misdemeanor (Educ. Code § 44810). A companion statute provides that a parent, guardian, or other person whose conduct "in a place where a school employee is required to be" materially disrupts classwork or extracurricular activities is guilty of a misdemeanor (Educ. Code § 44811). An exemption is permitted for lawful union activity such as picketing and distribution of handbills. These statutes state that repeated offenses will result in increased penalties, including both a fine not exceeding $1,000 and imprisonment.

Education Code Section 32210 provides that anyone who willfully disrupts a public school or a public school meeting is guilty of a misdemeanor punishable by a fine of up to $500. Education Code Section 32211 directly relates to the classroom and mirrors many of the Penal Code provisions previously discussed. It provides that nonstudents who are requested to leave because the principal or designee is

TABLE 2.1

Selected California Penal Code Provisions for Maintaining Order at School

Section 186.22	Strengthened by the passage of Proposition 21 in 2000, this section of the Street Terrorism Enforcement and Prevention Act broadly defines a street gang to include any group of three or more persons having as one of its primary purposes the commission of specifically listed criminal acts, having a common name or identifying sign or symbol, and whose members individually or collectively engage in criminal activity. This section encompasses persons who actively participate in a gang activity even if they are not members. Other sections extend penalties to those in gangs who know that fellow gang members engage in criminal activities and to those who recruit gang members. Stringent penalties are delineated. Convicted offenders must register with the police.
Sections 407–408	A person who participates in a rout or unlawful assembly is guilty of a misdemeanor. Unlawful assembly means two or more persons gathering to do an unlawful act or gathering in a violent, boisterous, or tumultuous manner to do a lawful act.
Section 409	A person who fails to disperse during a riot, rout, or unlawful assembly, except law enforcement personnel and those assisting them, is guilty of a misdemeanor.
Sections 415–415.5	Penalizes unlawfully fighting in a public place (including a school), disturbing others by loud and unreasonable noise, and using offensive words which are likely to produce an immediate violent reaction.
Section 422.6	Penalizes hate crime that by force or threat of force injures, intimidates, interferes with, oppresses, or threatens a person in the enjoyment of any right because of the person's race or ethnicity, religion, national origin, disability, gender, or sexual orientation or perception thereof. Includes defacing, damaging, or destroying a person's personal property.
Section 626.2	Penalizes unauthorized entry upon public or private school grounds by a student or employee after written notification of suspension or dismissal for disrupting school operation.
Section 626.4	Anyone failing to leave the school premises after consent to remain there has been withdrawn because of concern about disruption of school operation is guilty of a misdemeanor.
Section 626.7	Permits chief administrative officer or designee of a public school or facility to request that an outsider who enters a nonpublic business area is to leave the campus if disruption appears likely. Failure of the person to leave, or returning without following the posted requirements, is a misdemeanor offense. An exception is a parent or guardian who needs to reenter the campus to retrieve a student for disciplinary reasons, medical attention, or family emergency.
Section 626.8	Applies to outsiders who enter public or private school premises without written permission of the school principal or designee and disrupt school activities. It is a misdemeanor offense if the person (1) remains after being asked to leave, (2) reenters within seven days of being asked to leave, or (3) has otherwise established a continued pattern of unauthorized entry.
Section 626.9	Prohibits possession or discharge of a firearm in an area in or on the grounds of a public or private school without written permission of the superintendent or designee. Among the exceptions are firearms carried by law enforcement and unloaded firearms capable of being concealed on a person and kept in a locked container or within the locked truck of a motor vehicle. Known as the Gun-Free School Zone Act.

concerned about disruption of classes or other school activities must do so promptly and not return for seven days. Included as nonstudents are parents, guardians, and off-duty school employees other than a union representative engaged in representational activities. Failure to comply will result in a misdemeanor charge. The person can file an appeal later with the school superintendent and, if the appeal is unsuccessful, with the school board. The attorney general has advised that under this section, school administrators may require members of the news media to register on campus and comply with whatever conditions the school has for interviewing students and observing events or teaching. If their presence would interfere with school activities, they may be requested to leave (79 Op. Atty. Gen. 58, 1996). This statute also requires that a notice setting forth school hours be posted at every entrance to the school and grounds. School hours are described as either the period one hour before classes begin and one hour after classes end, or the time period defined by the governing board.

NCLB supports the effort to create safe schools. It provides that under Title IV of the Elementary and Secondary Education Act, states must create a uniform management and reporting system to collect and publicize information on school safety and drug use among students. Funds are available to states under Title IV to support drug and violence-prevention programs. Parents whose children have been the victims of violent crime at school or who are enrolled in schools that the state determines are "persistently dangerous" are to be offered the opportunity to transfer to another public school in the district, including a charter school. As noted in Chapter 1, California law already has an intradistrict open enrollment program that permits a school district to give preference to students seeking to transfer for reasons of safety (Educ. Code § 35160.5).

Part of maintaining a safe school environment is to assure that students receive nutritional foods and beverages while at school. In recent years, the legislature has enacted laws requiring that full meals must be served during breakfast and lunch at elementary schools, that food served during breaks meet specific standards, and that consumption of nutritious fruits and vegetables be promoted outside the lunch period (Educ. Code § 49430 and following sections, § 49565). The California High School Coaching Education and Training Program, which is set forth in Education Code Section 35179.1 and following sections, provides information about the harmful effects of the use of steroids and performance-enhancing dietary supplements. Education Code Sections 49030-49034 specify which performance-enhancing substances are prohibited, restrict schools from accepting sponsorship from manufacturers of dietary supplements, and require that the California Interscholastic Federation's constitution and bylaws be amended to require participating athletes to sign a pledge not to use dietary supplements or anabolic steroids without a prescription. Parents also are to sign a notification form regarding these restrictions. Legislative concern about obesity has resulted in tightening up on the responsibility of the California Department of Education to assure through categorical program monitoring that each school is providing not less than 200 minutes of physical education each ten schooldays to students in grades one through six and not less than 400 minutes in the same time frame to students in grades seven through twelve, except for students who are exempted (Educ. Code § 33352). In addition, the Health and Safety Code now requires that both public and private school principals must notify school employees where an automatic external defibrillator (AED) is located in the school and ensure that staff members receive information on how to use it. The principal also is to designate the trained employees who shall be available during instruction and school-sponsored activities to respond to an emergency that may necessitate use of the AED.

Finally, public and private school teachers, teacher aides, and administrators, as well as classified staff at public schools, are among a long list of persons who have a mandatory obligation to report suspected child abuse or neglect under the terms of the Child Abuse and Neglect Reporting Act (Penal Code § 11164 and following sections). The report is to be made to law enforcement, a county welfare department, or a county probation department if authorized to receive it. The report is to be made as soon as the reporter knows or suspects abuse or neglect. An initial telephone call is to be followed up by sending, faxing, or electronically transmitting a written report within thirty-six hours. Failure to report can result in county jail confinement for six months, a fine of up to $1,000, or both. The law encourages employers to provide training in the duties of child abuse and neglect reporting. Employees who have a mandatory duty to report must be provided with a statement regarding this obligation and their confidentiality rights.

Curriculum Content Standards

Like legislatures in other states, the California Legislature has responded to criticism of public schools as unfocused and mediocre by specifying an elaborate set of academic content standards in each of the core curriculum areas of reading, writing, mathematics, history-social science, and science (Educ. Code § 60604 and following sections). The standards were developed by a broad-based, appointed commission and approved by the State Board of Education (SBE) and are intended to serve as a model for the development of school district standards (Educ. Code § 60618). Since the state student and school assessment program is tied into the standards, school districts have little alternative but to adopt them in some form. The idea behind the standards is to specify the content that students need to acquire as they progress through public schools. These standards reflect the judgment of educators and others about the knowledge students should possess and the skills they need in order to succeed as adults. Accompanying the content standards are performance standards established for measuring student academic achievement at various grade levels. The state assessment system is elaborate and provides feedback not only on student achievement but also on how well schools are doing.

The content standards are specific to grade levels. The English-Language Arts content standards provide an illustration. They specify the content students need to master by the end of each grade level or cluster of grades. The standards are separated into the four domains of reading, writing, written and oral English language conventions, and listening and speaking. These, in turn, are further broken down into specific categories with performance objectives set for each. Thus, for example, the reading domain for kindergartners includes three categories, one of which is literary response and analysis. Under this category are specific information and skills students are to acquire. Included are distinguishing fantasy from realistic text; identifying types of everyday print materials; and identifying characters, settings, and important events. While the four domains and subcategories remain the same for successive grade levels, the specific information and skills students are to acquire become increasingly complex. Thus, for eleventh and twelfth graders, the literary response and analysis category includes a long list of specific information and skills students are to master, such as analyzing the way in which authors through the centuries have used archetypes drawn from myth and tradition in literature, film, political speeches, and religious writings.

In addition to curriculum standards and detailed curriculum frameworks for teachers to use in developing standards-based lesson plans, the legislature has established requirements for the selection and disposal of instructional material (Educ. Code § 60000 and following sections). Among other things, the legislature with certain exceptions requires the SBE to adopt for each elementary grade level and subject-matter area at least five separate basic instructional materials that are aligned with the curriculum content standards; requires school governing boards to involve teachers and community members in the adoption of instructional materials; requires instructional materials to portray cultural and racial diversity; specifies that instructional materials are to address certain topics in certain ways (e.g., the necessity for environmental protection and the harmful effects of tobacco, alcohol, narcotics, and dangerous drugs); and requires religious neutrality. Instructional materials are to be free of charge to public school students. Private schools may order at cost instructional materials adopted by the SBE.

Critics argue that the detailed nature of the content standards in combination with state-approved curriculum materials diminishes the autonomy of the school district and the classroom teacher, as well as dampens classroom spontaneity. The English-Language Arts content standards alone encompass eighty-four single-spaced pages. While charter schools are relatively free to develop their own instructional program, they cannot as a practical matter stray very far from the state standards, because their students must participate in the state assessments. To make sure the students do well, charter schools need to address the content standards in their curricula. There also is concern that the backgrounds and characteristics of some students (e.g., students with disabilities, those with a poor grasp of the English language, or those from impoverished backgrounds) stand in the way of their mastering the standards, and they do poorly on state assessments as a result. This places special responsibility on educators to make sure these students have an equal educational opportunity to learn. As we will see, under both the No Child Left Behind Act and state law, there are serious consequences for schools and educators who fail to do so.

Curriculum Censorship

The U.S. Supreme Court has been reluctant to intrude on state and school governing board authority in developing curricula and selecting classroom instructional materials. Its general orientation to the issue was well expressed in a 1968 decision: "By and large, public education in our Nation is committed to the control of state and local authorities" (*Epperson v. Arkansas*, p. 104). However, the authority of state and local school officials to control the classroom curriculum is not unlimited. In a seminal 1969 decision, the Court observed that "state-operated schools may not be enclaves of totalitarianism" (*Tinker v. Des Moines Independent Community School District*, p. 511). The problem is one of balance. As one California appellate court has observed, "there exists an inherent tension between two essential functions of a school board, exposing young minds to the clash of ideas in the free marketplace and the need to provide our youth with a solid foundation of basic, moral values" (*McCarthy v. Fletcher*, 1989, p. 719).

The difficulty is determining when the exercise of curricular authority crosses the line of constitutionality. In the *McCarthy* case, the school board in the Wasco Union High School District school board removed two books, *Grendel* by John Gardner and *One Hundred Years of Solitude* by Gabriel Garcia Marquez, for use as supplemental reading in a senior English class. School administrators believed the books contained too much profanity, vulgarity, and sordid imagery to be appropriate and were antireligious. The school board approved a book list with the two books deleted. A teacher, student, parent, and taxpayer argued that the board's action constituted unconstitutional censorship. The appellate judges noted that school officials must have legitimate educational reasons for their curricular decisions. They cannot substitute "rigid and exclusive indoctrination" for the right to make educational choices. The case was sent back to the trial court to determine the motives of the school board members in approving the altered reading list.

A particularly sensitive Arizona case came before the U.S. Court of Appeals for the Ninth Circuit in 1998 (*Monteiro v. Tempe Union High School District*). The geographic jurisdiction of the Ninth Circuit encompasses Arizona and a number of other western states in addition to California. African American parents objected to having their children read *The Adventures of Huckleberry Finn* by Mark Twain and *A Rose for Emily*, a short story by William Faulkner, in a ninth-grade English class. These parents found the required readings racially offensive and asked the school board to delete them. They alleged that following the assigned reading, their children were subjected to racial harassment. The Ninth Circuit ruled that a student's First Amendment rights are infringed when approved instructional material subsequently is removed due to the threat of lawsuits. Furthermore, removal of books that some parents find objectionable would establish a dangerous precedent. The court noted that whites might seek removal of books by Toni Morrison, Maya Angelou, and other black authors; Jews might file lawsuits over the writings of William Shakespeare; and females might seek damages for assignments of works by Tennessee Williams. The court pointed out the value of reading materials with which one disagrees.

At the same time, the judges were sensitive to the parents' allegations about a racially hostile environment. They held that under Title VI of the 1964 Civil Rights Act, school authorities have a responsibility to take action to stop racial harassment as soon as they learn it is occurring. Title VI prohibits discrimination on the basis of race in any federally assisted program. Failure to do so can result in liability, a matter discussed in more detail in Chapter 11. One judge in the case wrote a short concurring opinion, in which he noted that a school board's requiring students to read books with overt messages of racial hatred may well violate Title VI.

In a related matter, a California appellate court ruled in 1994 that school districts can contract with a commercial entity (in this case, Channel One) to provide a current events video program for classroom viewing, provided there is an opt-out for students who object to viewing the program because of its advertisements. The court could find no justifiable educational purpose to require students, who are compelled to attend school and thus are a captive audience, to view advertisements (*Dawson v. East Side Union High School*). Under prevailing constitutional law, commercial speech is not entitled to the same degree of constitutional protection as noncommercial speech. Additionally, as noted earlier in the chapter, outsiders do not have unfettered access to come onto a public school campus for expressive purposes.

Classroom Instruction

Class size reduction. In recent years, attention has been directed to reducing class size as a way to improve student learning. Teachers and teacher organizations love the idea. So do parents. If classes are smaller, teachers can give more attention to each student. California embraced the idea in 1996 by enacting a voluntary program that encourages school districts and charter schools to reduce class size in kindergarten through grade three from thirty to twenty students (Educ. Code § 52120 and following sections). Districts that do so are entitled to additional funding. Emphasis is placed on reading and mathematics instruction, with priority given to reducing class sizes in grades one and two. The program requires that student achievement must be maintained. A portion of the funding is available for facility-related costs. Similar programs exist to reduce class size for ninth-grade English and one other ninth-grade program required for graduation, and for grades ten through twelve (Educ. Code § 52080 and following sections). At the same time, the legislature imposes funding penalties on districts and charter schools that exceed designated maximum class sizes (Educ. Code §§ 41376 and 41378).

But reducing class size has not been accomplished without problems. Policymakers and administrators have been concerned about finding enough highly qualified teachers, enough space to accommodate additional classes, and enough money to implement the reform. Research findings on class size reduction have been mixed. Evaluations have found only marginal improvement in student achievement, though student discipline problems have declined and more students are receiving individual attention. There is some indication that class sizes must be reduced considerably for positive outcomes to occur. Smaller class sizes are least likely in districts serving high concentrations of low-income minority students, because of limited resources, and teacher qualifications have declined in these schools as more experienced teachers transfer to other schools. Recent budgetary problems at both the state and school level have prompted some pullback from class size reduction efforts. Other strategies to improve classroom instruction have focused on tailoring programs to special categories of students and improving teacher quality.

Educating targeted groups. Several student groups have been identified as needing special instructional attention. Clearly, children with disabilities are the most prominent. In Chapter 8 we describe how their instructional needs are met. Other groups with tailored programs include English-language learners, gifted and talented students, and those who are educationally disadvantaged.

In June 1998 California voters approved Proposition 227, largely replacing bilingual education with English immersion. Legislation incorporating the terms of Prop. 227 begins by noting that "all children in California public schools shall be taught English by being taught in English" (Educ. Code § 305). Under the provisions of this and accompanying statutes, English-language learners (ELL) are taught primarily in English-language classrooms, beginning with a one-year transition period. During the transition period, the student is taught in a sheltered English immersion classroom where nearly all classroom instruction is in English, but the curriculum and instruction are designed for students who are not proficient in the language. Waivers from the sheltered English immersion requirement are permitted for students who already are fluent in English.

Schools must offer bilingual instruction if they have twenty or more students with waivers from sheltered English immersion because the students are not succeeding. Bilingual learners are taught in their native language while they learn English. In the past, there has been concern that students in bilingual education classes tend to remain there. If fewer than twenty receive waivers, the students must be allowed to transfer to a school where such instruction is offered. The parents of ELL children with special needs who are not succeeding in an English-language classroom also are entitled to a waiver from the statute's requirements, provided that school officials approve. With parent consent, a student aged ten or older may be educated in bilingual classes where available, if the principal and instructional staff believe such a course of study would be better suited to the student's rapid acquisition of English. However, parents in this instance have a right to refuse to agree to a waiver. The statute also provides funding for adult English language instruction for parents and other community members so they can help tutor ELL children.

The fact that all ELL students are not automatically placed in English-only classrooms avoids running afoul of a 1974 U.S. Supreme Court ruling involving the San Francisco Unified School District (*Lau v. Nichols*). In that case, the Court ruled that regulations accompanying Title VI of the 1964 Civil Rights Act required school districts to eliminate language barriers that deny students an equal opportunity to learn. Because English is the primary language of instruction and a graduation requirement, the school board was required to take affirmative steps to rectify language deficiencies. Simply placing Chinese students who spoke no English in all-English classes would not suffice.

The passage of Prop. 227 was quickly followed by a similar lawsuit challenging the law as discriminatory toward non-English-speaking students. The Ninth Circuit rejected the claim, holding that the proposition was not enacted for a racially discriminatory purpose but rather to improve education for English-language learners (*Valerie v. Davis*, 2002).

To put some teeth in the new English-immersion law, the drafters included a section giving parents the right to sue for its enforcement and, if successful, to be awarded attorneys' fees and damages (Educ. Code § 320). School board members, schoolteachers, and administrators themselves can be liable if they "willfully and repeatedly" refuse to implement the statute. Another provision requires that all California students whose primary language is not English must undergo an assessment to determine their level of proficiency (Educ. Code § 313).

The California English Language Development Test (CELDT) has been developed for this purpose. First given in 2001, this test tracks the progress of these students toward full proficiency in English, a determination also encompassing teacher evaluation, parental views, and basic skills testing. CELDT coincides with a requirement under the federal No Child Left Behind Act (NCLB) that all children, including ELL students who have had at least one year of English instruction, be tested in English proficiency. Parents cannot opt out of the CELDT, because English-language assessment is both a federal and state requirement. To avoid penalties, NCLB requires that schools must show annual increases in the number and percentage of ELL students who become proficient in English and those who make progress toward proficiency. Parents are informed of their children's scores on CELDT; and results at the school, district, county, and state level are available on the CELDT website (http://celdt.cde.ca.gov/). Additionally, school site and district advisory committees afford parents an opportunity to have a role in their children's education (Educ. Code § 62002.5).

Among the other targeted groups are gifted and talented students. The provisions for gifted and talented education (GATE) encompass both high-achieving and underachieving elementary and secondary students. Emphasis is placed on ensuring participation of students from different cultural, as well as economic, backgrounds (Educ. Code § 52200 and following sections). The term "gifted and talented" encompasses a range of intellectual and artistic abilities and achievement as defined by governing boards in accord with standards set by the SBE. The subset of "highly gifted pupil" is defined in the statute to mean a student with an IQ of 150 or more or demonstrated extraordinary aptitude and achievement in academic subjects. The subset is limited to 1 percent of the student population. GATE programs include special classes or groupings during the regular school day, as well as supplemental learning experiences such as accelerated learning, independent study, and college courses. The SPI apportions funds for the education of

GATE students. Before districts can offer a GATE program, they must submit an application to the SBE. If approved, the program continues for up to three years or, in the case of exemplary programs, five years.

A continuing concern about the education of high-achieving students is that separating them from other students denies the latter the positive role models GATE students provide. The positive (or negative) influence of the student peer group is an important influence on learning. Schools try to address this concern by including, as much as possible in the regular curriculum, enrichment activities for these high-achieving students. The same concern is expressed regarding advanced placement and honors courses, which siphon off higher-performing students.

Tracking has been the focus of litigation in the past when it has had a disproportionate impact on disadvantaged students and students of color. In the case of special education students, for example, multiple criteria generally are utilized to determine whether a student needs special education rather than relying on a single means of assessment such as an IQ score. An important lawsuit against the sole use of IQ tests for this purpose is *Larry P. v. Riles*, a 1984 decision of the U.S. Court of Appeals for the Ninth Circuit. Reliance on multiple measures is less likely to screen out students based on their racial, cultural, or socioeconomic backgrounds. With the stringent standards for prevailing in disproportionate impact cases, tracking is now less successfully challenged. Under Title VI of the 1964 Civil Rights Act and its implementing regulations, for example, plaintiffs must show that disproportionate assignment of students of color to lower academic tracks resulted from intentional discrimination—no easy task.

Teacher preparation and evaluation. While the content standards somewhat diminish teacher autonomy and local control, they do not end it. School districts, principals, and teachers still must design instructional strategies to bring about mastery of the subject matter. Research has consistently shown that teacher quality and experience play a role in student achievement. This is especially true in high-poverty schools. Unfortunately, these schools have trouble attracting and retaining high-quality teachers. Both federal and California law are seeking to address the problem.

When Congress enacted the No Child Left Behind Act in 2001, it was as much concerned about the quality of teaching as it was about student performance. Accordingly, the law requires that all public schoolteachers, including those in charter schools, must be highly qualified to teach the core academic subjects of English, reading or language arts, math, science, foreign languages, civics and government, economics, arts, history, and geography. This requirement does not apply to private schoolteachers. The stakes for failing to meet the terms of NCLB are high, given the amount of federal aid involved. California receives some $1 billion a year in federal Title I funding.

Under the accompanying federal regulations, elementary teachers are deemed highly qualified if they are fully state certified, or have passed a state teacher licensing exam and hold a license to teach in the state; have a bachelor's degree; and demonstrate subject-matter knowledge in reading/language arts, writing, mathematics, and other areas of the elementary curriculum. If new to the profession, the teacher must have passed a rigorous state test. If not new to the profession, the teacher must either pass such a test or demonstrate competency through an alternative approach that recognizes relevant teaching experience combined with other measures of proficiency. This alternative approach is defined by the state based on criteria for a high, objective, uniform state standard of evaluation (HOUSSE). Middle and secondary schoolteachers must be similarly state certified and hold at least a bachelor's degree. If new to the profession, the teacher must have a college degree in the subject being taught or its equivalent, have advanced credentialing, or pass a rigorous state test in the subject area that he or she teaches. If not new to the profession, the teacher can establish competency in this manner or through HOUSSE.

For both elementary and middle/secondary schoolteachers, a temporary, emergency, or provisional certificate will not be acceptable toward a highly qualified designation. This has proven a problem in California because continued enrollment growth, along with class size reduction, has resulted in a shortage of teachers in many districts. At the time NCLB was enacted, it was estimated that one in five teachers in a quarter of the state's public schools did not meet NCLB standards. The problem was especially acute in schools serving low-income families. To meet the demands, California has focused on teacher recruitment and developed alternative routes to teacher credentialing. Whether these will result in sufficient numbers of highly qualified teachers to meet both the demand and NCLB standards remains to be seen.

NCLB also requires that paraprofessionals or teachers' aides who provide instructional support must work under the direction of a highly qualified teacher. In addition they must have at least an associate's degree or two years of college, or meet quality standards through a formal academic assessment. There is an exception for those who are serving as translators for limited-English-proficient students or involved solely in parental support services.

The Individuals with Disabilities Education Act requires special education teachers to hold at least a bachelor's degree and have full state certification as a special education teacher or have passed the state special education licensing exam. Special education teachers who teach core academic subjects exclusively to children who are assessed against NCLB's alternate achievement standards will be deemed highly qualified if they meet the applicable NCLB standards for their counterparts teaching regular education students. If these special education teachers teach above the elementary level, they will meet the highly qualified standard if the state determines they have the subject-matter knowledge appropriate to teach the level of instruction effectively.

Special education teachers teaching two or more core academic subjects exclusively to students with disabilities will be deemed highly qualified if they meet the same standards that their regular education counterparts must meet. In the case of a teacher not new to the profession, competence may be demonstrated through HOUSSE covering multiple subjects. A new special education teacher who teaches multiple subjects and who is highly qualified in mathematics, language arts, or science may demonstrate competence in other core academic areas in the same manner as any elementary or secondary teacher through HOUSSE. Such demonstration of competence must be met not later than two years after the date of employment.

For more information about NCLB, consult its website at www.ed.gov/nclb. At the state level, a particularly useful source is the NCLB Teacher Requirements Resource Guide, to be found on the California Department of Education's website at www.cde.ca.gov/nclb.

California has sought to address teacher quality by developing a comprehensive system of credentialing over the years and fine-tuning it to meet NCLB requirements. It is beyond the scope of this book to address the details of the system, which are set forth in Education Code Section 44200 and following sections and in the regulations developed by the California Commission on Teacher Credentialing (CCTC). Basically, the credentialing system requires that teacher candidates complete a bachelor's or higher degree in a field other than professional education at a regionally accredited college or university, take the California Basic Education Skills Test (CBEST) unless exempted, and complete both a teacher preparation program and performance assessment approved by CCTC. Elementary teachers also must pass the Reading Instruction Competency Assessment. The preparation program must be linked to state curriculum content and student performance standards, and its teacher assessment component linked to the research-based competencies set forth in the California Standards for the Teaching Profession. These encompass six areas: engaging and supporting all students in learning, creating and maintaining effective environments for student learning, understanding and organizing subject matter for student learning, planning instruction and designing learning expectations for all students, assessing student learning, and developing as a professional educator.

Other requirements for obtaining a credential include studying alternative ways of developing English-language skills, completion of a subject-matter program aligned with the state content and performance standards, demonstrating knowledge of the U.S. Constitution, and showing competency in the use of computers (Educ. Code § 44259 and following sections). General education teaching credentials in California are of two types: multiple subject and single subject. A multiple-subject teaching credential is necessary for teaching in the elementary school self-contained classroom. A single-subject credential is required to teach the subject in middle schools and high schools. Candidates for both must demonstrate competency in their subject area either by taking a subject-matter test or by completing an approved program at a college or university. For elementary teacher candidates, the test covers the multiple subjects taught at this level, such as language studies, mathematics, and science. As noted, NCLB places considerable emphasis on subject-matter competency.

Teacher candidates who meet basic credentialing requirements and are recommended for a credential by their teacher preparation institution are given a preliminary certificate valid for up to five years. During this time, they complete additional requirements including a school-based induction program in order to receive a professional clear credential. The induction program is linked to ongoing assessment of the teacher's effectiveness. The professional clear credential is valid for life so long as the holder functions effectively on the job and submits a renewal application and fee every five years.

There is a similar program for credentialing administrators in traditional public schools. Administrators in charter and private schools are not required to hold a state credential. Like teacher credentialing, the requirements for an administrator credential are ever changing. At this writing, the public school administrative services credential encompasses a five-year preliminary credential followed by a professional clear credential. The preliminary credential requires a valid teaching or services credential, three years of full-time teaching experience, completion of a professional administrator preparation program or a one-year internship in administrative services, and current employment as a public or private school administrator. The professional clear credential requires two years of successful administrative experience and completion of additional academic, field-based training, or a national administrator assessment. The clear credential is issued for five years and is renewable.

As noted earlier, all teacher and administrative credential candidates are required to take the CBEST, which assesses basic reading, writing, and mathematics skills, unless exempted. Among those exempt are candidates receiving scores on the Graduate Record Exam, Scholastic Aptitude Test, or the ACT Plus Writing test at a level determined by the Superintendent of Public Instruction. Also exempt are persons who have a teaching credential from another state and have passed a basic skills test in that state. Because nonwhite candidates have received disproportionately failing scores on CBEST, several organizations challenged its validity under Title VI and Title VII of the 1964 Civil Rights Act. As noted earlier, Title VI prohibits discrimination on the basis of race in federally assisted programs. Title VII prohibits discrimination on the basis of race, color, religion, sex, and national origin in both public and private employment. In a divided decision, the judges of the U.S. Court of Appeals for the Ninth Circuit ruled in 2000 that the test is a valid measure of minimum competency for both teaching and nonteaching positions and that the passing rates were appropriately established (*Association of Mexican-American Educators v. State of California*).

The legislature has directed the superintendent of public instruction (SPI) and the CCTC to develop a system of teacher support and assessment to help beginning teachers become effective and weed out those who are not (Educ. Code § 44279.1). California for some time has required school districts to have a uniform system of evaluation and assessment of performance for all certificated employees. Districts are required to evaluate performance as reasonably related to student achievement on grade-level assessments and, if applicable, the state-adopted content standards; instructional techniques and strategies; adherence to curricular objectives; and the establishment of a suitable learning environment (Educ. Code § 44662). Details are discussed in Chapter 5, on employment. As part of the California Education Information System, the legislature has directed the California Department of Education in association with the Commission on Teacher Credentialing to oversee the development of an individualized tracking system for teachers to be called the California Longitudinal Teacher Integrated Data Education System (CALTIDES). Teacher data tracking provides a central repository of information for enhancing understanding of the teacher workforce and the effectiveness of teacher preparation programs. However, CALTIDES data may not be used "for purposes of pay, promotion, sanction, or personnel evaluation of an individual teacher or groups of teachers or any other employment decisions related to individual teachers" (Educ. Code § 10601.5 (c)). For more on CALTIDES, see Education Code Section 10600 and following sections.

Copyright Law

Article I, section 8 of the U.S. Constitution provides Congress with the authority to "promote the progress of science and useful arts, by securing for limited times to authors and inventors the exclusive right to their respective writings and discoveries."

While copyright law is designed to protect authors' rights over their works, these protections are not unlimited. Thus, the Copyright Act enacted by Congress in 1976 specifies that copyright protection does not encompass "any idea, procedure, process, system, method of operation, concept, principle, or discovery regardless of the form in which it is described, explained, illustrated, or embodied" in a published work (17 U.S.C. § 102 (b)). The most important limitations to author rights are embodied in the doctrine of "fair use" and are codified in section 107 of the Copyright Act. The principle of fair use attempts to balance the author's and the public's interests in the dissemination of information, and is rooted in consideration of four factors: the purpose and character of the use, including whether it is for nonprofit educational purposes; the nature of the copyrighted work; the amount and substantiality of the portion used in relation to the whole work; and the effect of the use on the potential market for or value of the work.

These factors accord educators in nonprofit educational environments some latitude in reproducing works for classroom use, but do not explicate the extent to which school personnel fairly may use copyrighted works. Because the law left the scope of fair use in the educational setting somewhat ambiguous, a committee of educators, authors, and publishers has established a set of guidelines for use of copyrighted materials in nonprofit schools (see Table 2.2).

With respect to print items, these guidelines permit teachers to make and retain a single copy of a chapter from a book; an article from a periodical or newspaper; an entire short story, essay, or poem; or a chart, graph, diagram, drawing, cartoon, or picture for personal use or for class preparation. Teachers may also make multiple copies of these items for classroom use so long as the copies are for one class, are made at the instance and inspiration of the teacher, and there is not sufficient time to request permission to use the materials. A more complete listing of the specific guidelines related to the use of copied print materials is included in Table 2.2.

Teachers may not use the copied class materials in repeated school terms. If teachers wish to use the copied items again, their best approach is to request permission from the publisher. A publisher's permission trumps the standard copyright limitations, and many publishers are quite accommodating. Others may charge a fee, and in some cases, teachers may find it is less expensive simply to purchase the printed work.

Many school personnel assume that materials posted on the Internet are freely available for reproduction and use. This assumption may be rooted in the absence of a copyright notice on many materials available via the Internet. The federal Copyright Act of 1976 specifically includes the Internet, and nearly everything on the Internet is or can be copyrighted. Thus, the safest approach is to assume that,

TABLE 2.2
Copyright Law Guidelines

Type of copyrighted material	School personnel may	School personnel may not
Books, newspapers, magazines (specific items)	Make multiple copies for classroom use of the following: • 250 words or less from poems printed on two pages or less • 2,500 words or less of an article, short story, or essay • 1,000 words or 10%, whichever is less, of a play, novel, or letter (Note: No matter how short the work, educators may copy up to 500 words without risking copyright infringement.) • Two pages or 10%, whichever is less, of illustrated books such as picture or comic books	Copy consumables such as workbooks and standardized tests Copy items for use term to term Copy more than one poem, article, or essay by the same author, nor more than two excerpts from a collection
Music	Make emergency copies for performance with the understanding that the emergency copy soon will be replaced with a purchased copy Make multiple copies for nonperformance classroom use of less than a performance unit so long as the copy does not exceed 10% of the entire work Simplify or edit printed music so long as the changes do not alter the fundamental character of the work Make single copies for exercises or exams	Make copies in order to substitute for the purchase of a complete work Copy consumables Copy for performance (unless an emergency) Add or alter lyrics
Multimedia (Microsoft PowerPoint)	Play multimedia presentations that support direct instruction that include • 10% or 3 minutes, whichever is less, of a video, film, or television recording • 10% or 1,000 words, whichever is less, of a novel, play, story, or long poem • Poems of 250 words or less in their entirety • Up to 10% but not more than 30 seconds of a musical work • No more than five illustrations from a single artist or photographer • Up to 10% or 2,500 fields or cells, whichever is less, of a copyrighted numerical data set	Use the same multimedia presentation for more than two years
Software	Make backup copies of purchased software	Make copies (other than backup) unless pursuant to lease or purchase Network software unless it is licensed for networking (be aware of license limitations)

unless specifically indicated otherwise, any material or design on the Internet is copyrighted. Teachers should be aware that a copyright notice is not required in order for materials to enjoy protection. In addition, teachers may not copy Web pages, portions of Web pages, or Web graphics; and they may not copy, reprint, or distribute unpublished e-mail. Because Web page links are recognized as facts and are not protected by copyright, their use is not restricted.

Copyright violations may also occur in the use of microcomputer software. The Copyright Act of 1976 includes computer software in its protections and defines a computer program as "a set of statements or instructions to be used directly or indirectly in a computer in order to bring about a certain result" (17 U.S.C. § 101). The disk containing the software and its accompanying manual are protected by copyright laws. Educators may make backup copies of purchased software but may not make additional copies unless pursuant to a lease or purchase agreement. Software must be licensed for networking in order to be included on a school or district computer network.

The increasing use of programs such as Microsoft PowerPoint and Hypermedia in school settings raises concerns when presentations incorporate materials from copyrighted sources. The copyright guidelines for multimedia presentations are quite detailed and are included in Table 2.2.

Video and audio recordings that directly relate to instruction may be used in the classroom even if these recordings are labeled "for home use only." These recordings may not be used for the purpose of entertainment or reward (e.g., during noninstructional periods or as a reward for performance on a difficult test). Off-air recording of television programs is permitted so long as the recording is used within ten days of taping and is destroyed within forty-five days. Teachers may not routinely copy a program for use in the classroom or copy in anticipation of need. In addition, teachers may not alter or combine off-air recorded copies or make backup copies of their recordings. Cable-only channels such as HBO, The History Channel, and The Disney Channel have developed their own off-air recording policies. Educators will need to comply with these policies when taping from cable-only networks.

Teachers in traditional face-to-face teaching environments enjoy broader fair-use exemptions than do teachers who present their lessons via distance-learning arrangements. This is an emerging and rapidly changing area of copyright law and is likely to have the greatest impact on educators working in online or independent study charter or private schools. Currently, teachers who work in distance-learning or Web-based teaching environments are limited to the use of nondramatic works such as novels, short stories, or symphonies. Dramatic works, including videos, films, plays, operas, and musicals, may not be used in distance-learning teaching arrangements.

Because lawsuits charging copyright infringement against schools have increased in recent years, administrators are well advised to develop clear policies regarding the use of copyrighted work and to monitor their compliance. In addition, administrators may wish to take the extra step of marking equipment capable of copying with reminders of copyright limits and liabilities.

The Internet

From the educational perspective, the Internet is a vast electronic library that increasingly is being used to secure information and enrich learning. The legislature has established the California Technology Assistance Project to provide a regional network of technical assistance to school districts and schools (Educ. Code § 51871). The purpose of the project is to help schools use technology in a variety of ways, including improving teaching and learning and developing high-speed telecommunications networks. The California Department of Education (CDE) administers the program. The state superintendent of instruction is required to ensure that each school district has access to technical assistance and an approved online technology plan builder. The legislature enacted the Educational Technology Grant Program in 2002 to provide funds to school districts, county offices of education, and charter schools for developing and implementing technology to improve student achievement (Educ. Code § 52295.10 and following sections). Priority is given to schools with high percentages of low-income students, small and rural schools, and low-performing schools under the No Child Left Behind Act. The grants may be used only to serve students in grades four through eight.

As a vast communication and information-conveying system, the Internet has become the focus of litigation. In response to this and prodded by the federal government, school districts have developed Internet user agreements generally called Acceptable Use Policies (AUPs). These policies spell out the conditions for the use of the Internet and other technology by school personnel and students. They typically specify the purposes for which school technology and equipment can be used, set forth applicable rules, inform users about the extent of privacy, and spell out such matters as copyright and privacy requirements. As a condition of employment, teachers must adhere to the AUP terms. Since students are not employees, they and their parents generally sign the policy, indicating that they have read, understand, and agree to abide by it. Failure to do so can result in disciplinary action.

E-mail warrants separate mention. For schools, e-mail is an electronic form of the school mailbox system. And just like the mailbox system, the school can control and monitor the contents of its e-mail system. In the Perry decision discussed earlier, the U.S. Supreme Court ruled that school mailboxes are not automatically open forums for any type of communication among school personnel, their unions, and other persons. Since the mailbox system is a channel of communication owned and operated by the school, it can control how it is used. Thus, for example, the school could limit the mailbox system to business only. Or it could open the system for certain types of communication but not other types. This is called a "limited open forum." Once open to a particular category of communication, the school cannot discriminate within that category. As an example, if the school permits its mailbox system to be used for school business and community announcements, it cannot prohibit certain types of community announcements.

Frequently, school districts will specify that the district reserves the right to monitor e-mail usage as well as any and all files on computers or servers connected to the district's network, and that no employee or student should have any expectation of privacy as to his or her usage. When students and parents sign a responsibility contract incorporating this provision, they agree to the condition. The same is true of employees who must abide by the district's AUP. Obtaining consent in this way dissolves any reasonable expectation of privacy, and thus the school can monitor e-mail or Internet use without violating the Electronic Communications Privacy Act, a federal law criminalizing the interception of e-mail communications unless at least one party to the communication gives consent to the interception.

Controlling access to inappropriate material. Obscenity is not entitled to any constitutional protection under the First Amendment. This was the teaching of the U.S. Supreme Court in *Miller v. California* in 1973. In that case, the majority set forth a three-part test for determining when material is obscene: whether the average person, applying contemporary community standards, would find that the work, taken as a whole, appeals to the prurient interest; whether the work depicts or describes, in a patently offensive way, sexual conduct specifically defined by the applicable law; and whether the work, taken as a whole, lacks serious literary, artistic, political, or scientific value. Pornography that is determined to be obscene under these standards is not constitutionally protected under either the federal or California Constitution. The California Penal Code has provisions providing criminal penalties for distributing/possessing obscene materials.

In 1990 the Supreme Court ruled that, while adults have a right to possess and view in their own homes pornography that is not legally obscene, a state can criminalize the possession and viewing of pornography involving children (*Osborne v. Ohio*). This is so because, unlike adult pornography, child pornography is always obscene (*New York v. Ferber*, 1992). Adult possession of obscene materials, including child pornography, is not protected by the speech or privacy provisions of the California Constitution either (*People v. Luera*, 2001). The California Penal Code has provisions imposing criminal penalties for distributing/possessing obscene materials.

The federal Children's Internet Protection Act (CIPA), which took effect in April 2001, requires public libraries as well as schools using federal E-rate or Elementary and Secondary Education Act funds for Internet use or connections to have filtering devices in place to block out visual depictions deemed harmful to children. Failure to do so can result in loss of federal money. Inappropriate material includes visual depictions that appeal to a prurient interest in nudity, sex, or excretion; that depict actual or simulated sexual acts or lewd exhibition of genitalia; and that lack serious artistic, literary, political, or scientific value to minors. CIPA provisions apply to students seventeen years of age and younger. For adult library patrons who wish access to pornography that is not obscene, CIPA permits libraries to disable the filters. In 2003 the U.S. Supreme Court upheld the statute (*American Library Association v. United States*).

While CIPA provisions pertain to pictures, images or graphic image files, or other visual depiction, they do not apply to Internet text. However, along with CIPA, Congress added a measure called the Neighborhood Children's Internet Protection Act (NCIPA) to require libraries and school districts to develop an Internet safety policy as a condition for receiving federal assistance. The policy must address access by minors to inappropriate matter on the Internet and the Web; the security and safety of minors when using electronic mail, chat rooms, and other forms of electronic communication; hacking or other illegal activities; unauthorized disclosure, use, and dissemination of personal identification information regarding minors; and measures designed to restrict minors' access to material deemed harmful to them. What is deemed "harmful" is to be determined by the school or library.

While the application of CIPA to school computers gives the governing board considerable control over what material can be accessed on the Internet through school computers, the control is not unlimited. As a vast electronic library, the use of the Internet in public schools is likely to fall within the parameters of the U.S. Supreme Court's 1982 decision that school boards may not remove books from the school library merely because they disagree with their contents (*Board of Education of Island Trees v. Pico*). In that case, three members of the Court held that students have a "right to receive ideas" as a necessary correlate to the right to express them. Two other justices did not endorse such a right but nevertheless agreed that the First Amendment limits the board's discretion in removing library books (but the Court said nothing about refusing to purchase library books). In response to this decision, school districts usually employ some type of deliberative process for handling complaints about library books so that there are legitimate pedagogical purposes for their removal. These might include inappropriateness for the age level of the students, obsolescence, and redundancy. How much authority California districts have to remove books from the school library remains uncertain. While Education Code Section 18111 gives governing boards the authority to exclude books, publications, or papers of a sectarian, partisan, or denominational character, doing so may well constitute unconstitutional viewpoint censorship and discrimination against religion. One California appellate court has ruled that school governing boards have no authority at all to remove books from a school library under state law (*Wexner v. Anderson Union High School District*, 1989). Further, removal would conflict with the expansive recognition given student rights of expression in Education Code Section 48907. However, in denying review of the decision, the California Supreme Court ordered that the opinion not be published, which means that it has no value as a precedent.

In the context of Internet access in the public school, when does filtering or blocking go beyond the school district's legitimate right to control the content of the curriculum to constitute impermissible or inappropriate censorship? Suppose a filtering system eliminates access to any message that has the word "intercourse." Such restrictive screening could be considered an intrusion on protected free speech because it prevents access to various forms of commercial and intellectual discourse. Likewise, a school district that prevents Internet access on the district's high school library computers to material with the words "gay," "lesbian," and "homosexual" because the governing board opposes a gay lifestyle could run afoul of the thrust of the *Pico* decision. Since there are likely to be print materials in the library containing such terms, the inconsistency inherent in such a policy is readily apparent. Matters like these are of less concern in the classroom because the U.S. Supreme Court has recognized that school board control in this setting is extensive (*Hazelwood School District v. Kuhlmeier*, 1988). As noted later in this chapter and in Chapter 6, both teacher and student rights in this setting are quite limited.

The best safeguard to losing in court is to employ a blocking or filtering system that is narrowly tailored to achieve its goal of eliminating access to inappropriate material without at the same time eliminating material that is entirely appropriate for library and classroom use. This is easier said than done, because no screening system is foolproof. Some districts acknowledge up front that their screening system is imperfect and warn parents in their AUPs that students might encounter inappropriate material when using the school's computers. The assumption is that parents will accept some responsibility for educating their children about inappropriate Internet use. Lessening district concern about liability is the federal Telecommunications Act of 1996, which provides that interactive computer service providers are not considered content providers but rather information conduits.

Privacy and the Internet. As discussed in greater detail in Chapter 10, the federal Family Educational Rights and Privacy Act (FERPA) prevents disclosure of personally identifiable information about students and their families contained in school records without prior parent permission (the student's permission if the student is over eighteen years of age). Education Code Section 49061 and following sections track this law. Educational records are those that are directly related to the student and are maintained by the school. The term is defined more broadly than just information in the student's cumulative folder. As defined in FERPA, educational records include "records, files, documents, and other materials which contain information directly related to the student" maintained by the school or its personnel (20 U.S.C. § 1232 g). FERPA also requires that parents be notified of the posting of directory information by the school (names, addresses, etc.) and be given an opportunity to opt out prior to posting.

Privacy becomes an issue when personally identifiable information (e.g., a student's academic record or photograph) or school directory information (e.g., names and statistics about the district's football players) is included on the school's website. This is particularly a cause for concern when students create their own websites at school for uploading to the Web. In these instances, parents should be informed and given the opportunity to decline to have personally identifiable information posted. If students and faculty members grant their permission, their original works may be published on school websites.

Disciplining students for Internet misuse. As discussed in some depth in Chapter 6, students have the right under both the federal and California constitutions to exercise free speech rights. In the famous *Tinker v. Des Moines Independent Community School District* case, the U.S. Supreme Court held that students cannot be disciplined for exercising their right of free speech on campus in the absence of material disruption or substantial invasion of the rights of others. Education Code Section 48907 gives all students a broad right to exercise freedom of speech and press. Education Code Section 48950 provides that high school students have the same rights of free speech on campus that they retain off campus. However, subsection (d) of this section states that "nothing in this section prohibits the imposition of discipline for harassment, threats, or intimidation, unless constitutionally protected."

School district control over student expression on the Internet is greatest when students are using school computers, given their agreement to abide by the district's AUP. But this control is considerably less when students use their own computers at home to communicate about school matters. For example, a Missouri school district was without authority to discipline a student who created a website on his home computer and vulgarly criticized his teachers, the school principal, and the school's home page. While the student's home page had a link to the school's home page, there was no corresponding link that permitted someone at school to access what the student had written. A classmate accessed the student's home page at school during a computer class and showed it to a teacher. Before long, students, teachers, and the school administration became aware of the student's home page. The student was suspended from school. The court overturned the suspension, noting that "Disliking or being upset by the content of a student's speech is not an acceptable justification for limiting student speech under *Tinker*" *(Beussink v. Woodland R-IV School District,* 1998, p. 1180).

However, a student's free speech rights can be lost if the student goes too far in criticizing the school and its constituents on his home computer. A good illustration is an eighth grade student in upstate New York who used AOL Instant Messaging (IM) software on his parents' home computer to create a small icon of a pistol firing a bullet at a person's head. Above the head were dots representing splattered blood and below it were the words "Kill [name of the student's English teacher]." The student sent IM messages displaying the icon to some fifteen members of his IM "buddy list." The icon came to the attention of one classmate who gave a copy to the English teacher. The school board imposed a semester-long suspension of the student. The case ended up in federal court after the student and his parents contested the suspension as violating the student's rights of free speech. Both the trial and federal appellate courts rejected the contention. As the appellate court judges noted, "there can be no doubt that the icon, once made known to the teacher and other school officials, would foreseeably create a risk of substantial disruption within the school environment" (*Wisniewski v. Board of Education of Weedsport Central School District,* 2007, p. 40). Bullying, including by electronic means, against a school employee or student is now a suspendable or expellable offense in California. What has become known as "cyberbullying" involves communication through an electronic device such as a telephone, wireless telephone, computer, or pager (Educ. Code § 32261). To prevail against free speech claims, school officials must document carefully the harm created by student use of these devices.

Online courses and cyberschools. Distance learning has been around for a while, chiefly in the form of two-way interactive videoconferencing. Distance learning enables persons at remote sites to be linked together. This is a great advantage to classes in rural schools that lack the means to offer specialized classes. It also enables students in different settings to explore a common topic together. There are also some disadvantages, chiefly cost. The cost of having site-based instructors and technicians can be great. The equipment used by educational institutions often is inferior, resulting in sound lags, video failures, and the like.

Internet classrooms are the modern derivative of distance learning. They are even less place-bound than distance learning classes are. Web-based classes can be taught interactively or can be made available to students when it is convenient for them to learn. Online courses enrich the education for students attending schools with limited educational offerings (e.g., no AP classes or qualified teachers for hard-to-staff subjects). Web-based classes have an advantage over distance telecommunication because they are cheaper. All that is necessary is Internet access. Web-based curricula are easily updated and eliminate hard-copy texts.

The Internet classroom appears to be the classroom of the future. The virtual school opens up new opportunities for homebound students and for home-schooling parents who lack the time or qualifications to provide a quality education for their children. An increasing number of charter schools in California offer some or all of their programs online. For some time, the California legislature has recognized and encouraged the development of distance learning through a variety of mediums including television, video and teleconferences, and computer-based instruction. A key piece of legislation is Education Code Section 51865 enacted in 1991 that sets a number of goals for distance learning. These include providing equal access to educational opportunities, enabling interaction with students from other cultures and geographic locations, enhancing diversity, and fostering efficiency and accountability. The statute spells out ways in which a coordinated distance learning system should be developed. The movement toward more "on-line" instruction is apparent in many schools, particularly charter schools. As described in the next chapter, charter schools classified as "nonclassroom-based" are entitled to state funding, though the funding may be less than for their classroom-based counterparts.

ASSESSMENT AND ACCOUNTABILITY

Along with the specification of curriculum content standards has come unprecedented emphasis on performance for students, their teachers, and their schools. The roots of so-called high-stakes testing go back to 1983, when the U.S. Department of Education issued a report on the relatively poor performance of American public school students. Entitled *A Nation At Risk,* the report called for renewed emphasis on academic rigor and assessment. Over the intervening years, many reforms have been instituted, yet student performance is little improved. In recent years, for example, about 30 percent of the nation's fourth and eighth graders performed at or above the proficient level on the National Assessment of Educational Progress (NAEP) reading test. For California, the percentage is lower. In fact, California ranks near the bottom of all fifty states in student performance on NAEP tests in reading and math. Part of the reason for the low performance is the nature of the California public schooling population: 70 percent are nonwhite, half are low-income, and one-quarter are English-language learners. Administered by the U.S. Department of Education, NAEP is the nation's only representative and continuing assessment of what students know and can do in various subject-matter areas. It is known as "the nation's report card," though its findings have been viewed with some skepticism because states have different participation rates. Along with tightened state curricular requirements has come more frequent and rigorous state assessment to determine how well students, their teachers, and their schools are doing.

The Influence of the No Child Left Behind Act

Concerned that the federal government's expenditures under Title I to improve the education of disadvantaged students have increased dramatically over the years with relatively little improvement in student achievement, Congress now requires under the No Child Left Behind that states must annually assess every public school student's progress in reading and math in grades three through eight, and once during grades ten through twelve. Tests in science are now required not less than one time in grades three through five, grades six through nine, and grades ten through twelve. The tests must be aligned with the state's curriculum standards, and each school must make adequate yearly progress as determined by the state on the state's assessments toward having all students achieve 100 percent proficiency by 2013–2014. Achievement data must be broken down by race, ethnicity, gender, English-language proficiency, migrant status, disability status, and low-income status, so that low-performing schools can be identified. In addition, states are required to participate every two years in the NAEP math and reading assessments for fourth- and eighth-grade students. This requirement is designed to compare results in one state with another state, as well as to demonstrate the degree of rigor of a state's assessment program. Penalties are required under NCLB for persistently low-performing schools on the state's assessment tests, though the penalties apply only to schools receiving Title I money. The force behind NCLB is the loss of some or all federal funding for education. In 2008, Congress began debating changes necessary for reauthorizing the law. Check this book's website for updates.

Student Assessment

Coinciding with the development of curriculum content standards in the late 1990s, California enacted a comprehensive student assessment system both for students and for schools. Its major components are detailed in Table 2.3. For students, the basic grade-level assessments in core curriculum areas are done pursuant to the state's Standardized Testing and Reporting (STAR) system, which is found in Education Code Section 60640 and following sections. STAR consists of multiple measures of student performance. Its core component is the California Standards Test that assesses student progress in grades two through eleven in achieving the state's curriculum content standards. Various levels of performance are designated, with "proficient" being the state's desired performance level for all students. A second part of the STAR system is a basic skills test that assesses how California students compare with students nationwide. The third component is a test administered to Spanish-speaking English learners. When the STAR program was reauthorized in 2004, CDE was directed to develop tests in the primary language of dominant groups of English-language learners and align them with the state academic content standards. It is important to note that not all California students are assessed through the STAR system. While STAR applies to traditional public and charter schools, it does not apply either to private schools or home schools. Furthermore, parents and guardians can opt to have their children excused from taking state assessments (Educ. Code § 60615). However, CDE rules prohibit a district and its employees from soliciting or encouraging parents to do so (Admin. Code title 5, § 852). At the same time, both NCLB and CDE rules require that 95 percent of every student subgroup must participate in state assessments.

School administrators and teachers are prohibited from engaging in test preparation activities for the state assessment program and its individual tests. (Educ. Code § 60611). The statute does permit educators to utilize instructional materials provided by CDE for statewide assessment preparation if embedded in the instructional program. And a provision of the California Code of Regulations permits the use of practice tests provided by the test publisher to familiarize students with testing format and tabulating (Admin. Code title 5, § 854). In accord with federal disability law, accommodations must be made for children with disabilities. Where appropriate, alternate assessments are permitted for these students. California has developed a test known as the California Alternate Performance Assessment (CAPA) to meet NCLB and state law requirements for them. Under NCLB regulations as they existed in 2008, children with the most significant cognitive disabilities were subject to the

TABLE 2.3
California Public School Accountability System

Curriculum content ⟶	Student assessment ⟶	School accountability
Ed. Code §§ 60605 and following sections • Model for districts • Specific to grade levels and subject areas Ed. Code § 60811 • English proficiency	Ed. Code §§ 60640 and following sections, 60810, 60850 • STAR program (esp. CST for grade-level assessments) • Alternative assessment for some special ed students through CAPA • Rigor of CST measured against NAEP • NCLB (requires 100% proficiency or higher on state assessments by 2014) • CELDT (test of English proficiency for English-language learners) • CAHSEE	Ed. Code §§ 52051, 33126 and following sections • AYP (schools required by NCLB to make AYP toward 100% proficiency by 2014) • API (state-determined growth rate on STAR and CAHSEE for each public school toward 100% proficiency by 2014) • SARC (state's annual report card for each public school containing accountability data)

API	Academic Performance Index (Calif. Statute)
AYP	Adequate Yearly Progress (part of NCLB)
CAHSEE	California High School Exit Examination (Calif. Statute)
CAPA	California Alternate Performance Assessment (part of STAR)
CELDT	California English Language Development Test (Calif. Statute)
CST	California Standards Test (part of STAR)
NAEP	National Assessment of Educational Progress (U.S. Dept. of Educ. criterion-referenced testing program in reading and math)
NCLB	No Child Left Behind Act (federal statute)
SARC	School Accountability Report Card
STAR	Standardized Testing and Reporting

same curriculum content standards as other students were, but their levels of performance could be based on alternative academic achievement standards.

School districts and charter schools are considered agents of the California Department of Education (CDE) for test administration and are shielded from liability when acting in accordance with State Board of Education (SBE) and state superintendent instructions. Tests are confidential but may be viewed by governing boards in closed session pursuant to SBE rules and by individual governing board members who agree in writing to keep the tests confidential. The tests cannot inquire into personal or family beliefs or practices. Nor may they contain questions designed to evaluate personal behavioral characteristics such as honesty and self-esteem.

STAR results on individual students are reported directly to their parents. Schools also receive individual test results, which can be used by teachers to identify student weaknesses and to alter instruction accordingly. Districts have the option of using STAR results in student promotion and retention decisions in lieu of grades (Educ. Code § 48070.5 (b)). Individual test results are private and cannot be released to anyone other than the student's parent, guardian, teacher, counselor, or administrator without written consent of the parent or guardian, or of the student if eighteen or emancipated. County and district superintendents can receive STAR results for each teacher's class, thus enabling them to link teaching behavior to student performance. The testing agency also reports STAR results to the SBE for each school, district, county, and the state as a whole. The state board, in turn, is required by law to post the information on the Internet (http://star.cde .ca.gov/). This process likely will become more precise when the state has the ability to track over time the performance of individual students on state assessments. Such a system is now underdevelopment and is known as the California Longitudinal Pupil Achievement Data System (CALPADS). For more on CALPADS, see Education Code Section 60900. Federal regulations implementing the Family Educational Rights and Privacy Act (FERPA) are being amended to accommodate individual student data tracking systems like CALPADS, though privacy issues will remain a central concern under both federal and state law.

To make test outcomes more meaningful, NCLB and state law require that STAR results be disaggregated by student subgroup. Thus, the scores are reported by race/ethnicity, language fluency, program participation, special education, and parent education, together totaling more than forty separate subgroupings. This enables educators and policymakers to discern which categories of students are not performing up to expectations. The thrust of disaggregation is to hold schools accountable for the education they deliver. California has indicated to the U.S. Department of Education that it expects to have all students at or above the proficient level on the state's English language arts and mathematics standards tests by the 2013-2014 academic year. In the spring 2007 testing, half or less of California fourth and eighth graders scored at this level in these subjects. For some subgroups, the percentage was much less.

In addition to STAR, the state legislature has mandated that students must take an exit exam to graduate from high school (Educ. Code § 60850 and following sections). School districts and charter schools functioning as local education agencies may require additional assessments for high school graduation. Known as the California High School Exit Exam (CAHSEE), the test assesses how well high school students have mastered English language arts and mathematics as specified in the state's curriculum content standards. Students must pass both sections of CAHSEE to receive a diploma. The law requires assistance for those who have trouble doing so, including more focused coursework and supplemental instruction. To avoid legal problems, the statute requires that students receive annual notice of the exam after completing ninth grade, that the exam be constructed so that it is not racially discriminatory, and that the test measure mastery of subject matter found in classroom textbooks and taught by teachers. All of this is important in light of the fact that CAHSEE is a criterion-referenced test, meaning that student performance is assessed against a set of performance expectations related to the instructional program, not to the performance of other students on the test.

To assist students with disabilities, accommodations are to be permitted during CAHSEE administrations. The Education Code specifies that at the request of a parent, the school principal is to ask the governing board to grant a waiver from successfully passing the test in whole or part for a child with a disability if the individualized education program (IEP) calls for accommodations or modifications in taking the test, the child has attained the knowledge and skills needed to pass the test, and the child has achieved the equivalent of a passing score on the exit exam while using a modification that fundamentally alters what the high school exit examination measures (Educ. Code § 60851 (c)). Litigation over this provision spurred the legislature to grant an exemption from CAHSEE for children with disabilities in the classes of 2006 and 2007 who met certain conditions. While English-language learners cannot secure a diploma without passing CAHSEE, the district may defer the requirement for up to two years until the student has completed six months of instruction in the English language (Educ. Code § 60852).

School Accountability

Not only students and teachers are assessed; so too are all schools and districts, as well as charter schools (see Table 2.3). NCLB requires all schools to make adequate yearly progress (AYP) toward 100 percent proficiency or higher for all students in 2014. In calculating AYP progress for each school, NCLB requires that the test scores of children with disabilities be included with those of other students. Under current U.S. Department of Education regulations, no more than 1 percent of the number of students who score at or above the proficient level in the grades assessed on state tests may be composed of cognitively impaired students taking an alternate achievement assessment (e.g., CAPA) unless an exception has been granted by the U.S. Department of Education. In addition, the Department of Education allows modified grade-level content standards and assessments for AYP purposes for students with disabilities up to 2 percent of the testing population. The additional 2 percent is not limited to those with severe cognitive disabilities.

Under NCLB, schools and local education agencies receiving Title I funding that do not make AYP for two consecutive years are designated for program improvement. About two-thirds of California public schools are Title I schools. School officials then have two years to turn the school around. In the meantime, parents must be given the opportunity to transfer their children to higher-performing schools within the district, with priority given to the lowest-achieving students from low-income families. Subject to a funding cap, transportation costs are paid by the district. In California, schools are required to take steps to eliminate racial segregation regardless of cause, and a few districts remain under desegregation court orders. Thus, the transfer option may not be unfettered in some districts.

If the Title I school does not make AYP for three years, parents continue to have the option to transfer their children. In addition, students from low-income families become eligible for no-cost supplemental services such as tutoring or remedial classes chosen by their parents from a list of nonprofit or for-profit state-approved providers. These could include public schools, charter schools, educational service agencies, and private faith-based organizations. Continued low performance by the school triggers more aggressive remedial efforts such as replacing staff or implementing a new curriculum. If this doesn't work, NCLB requires the school to be completely restructured. In addition to replacing most of the staff, NCLB suggests converting the school to a charter school or allowing a private educational management organization (EMO) to operate the school. In the case of the latter, the EMO must have a demonstrated record of effectiveness. Critics view these provisions as a step in the direction of privatizing schooling. Throughout this process, federal law requires that parents in low-performing schools be encouraged to participate in school improvement efforts. The law details measures that state education departments, school districts, individual schools, and private schools served by Title I funds are to take to assure meaningful parent involvement. Through one means or another, California has indicated to the U.S. Department of Education that it expects to have all Title I schools in the state making adequate yearly progress by the 2013–2014 school year. In 2007, slightly over 60 percent were doing so.

In 2004 the legislature instituted a comprehensive assistance program for any local educational agency (LEA) that CDE has identified as in danger of being designated as a program improvement institution under NCLB (Educ. Code § 52055.57). The term "local educational agency" encompasses school districts, county offices of education, and those charter schools that receive their funding directly from the state. Under its early warning provision, the statute requires a voluntary self-assessment if the LEA is in danger of being a program improvement entity within the next two years. Once identified as in need of program improvement, the LEA is required to conduct a self-assessment and contract with the county office of education or other external entity for assistance. Subject to availability of funds, grants may be awarded to LEAs for up to two years to implement the recommendations they receive. If corrective action is required under NCLB, the LEA is subject to sanctions imposed by the SPI with approval of the SBE. These include replacement of personnel, removal of schools from the LEA's jurisdiction, appointment of a receiver to operate the LEA, restructuring the entity, authorizing students to transfer to higher-performing schools, instituting a new curriculum, contracting with a district assistance and intervention team, and restructuring or abolishment. If program improvement does not occur, the LEA must appear before the SBE within three years to review its progress and may be subject to additional sanctions. In 2008, Governor Schwarzenegger and State Superintendent Jack O'Connell announced plans to improve ninety-seven school districts that had persistently failed to meet NCLB goals. Interestingly, the quirkiness of the NCLB's classification system resulted in several high-performing school districts being included on the list. Among them was the Berkeley Unified School District, where too few students in particular subgroups at several of the district's schools had participated in STAR.

In 1999 the California legislature enacted the Public School Performance Accountability Program, encompassing a state assessment program for conventional public and charter schools, an intervention program for low-performing schools, and a reward system for high-performing schools (Educ. Code § 52051 and following sections). An alternative accountability system is required for schools under the jurisdiction of a county board or superintendent, community day schools, alternative schools, and private nonsectarian schools serving children with disabilities under contract with public school districts. The first component requires the SPI, with SBE approval, to develop a system for assessing school performance. Known as the Academic Performance Index (API), it focuses on student academic achievement and is a determinant of a school's adequate yearly progress under NCLB. The SBE periodically sets the performance target on a scale for all schools. Each school must establish a minimum 5 percent annual API growth rate over its previous API score toward the statewide performance target. If the school already is performing at the target level, it must continue to do so. One concern is that it may take many years for schools with low initial API scores to reach the API performance target of 800.

The API is calculated primarily from student achievement scores on the California Standards Tests that are part of STAR and on passing rates on CAHSEE. It also includes attendance and graduation rates. The scores are reported for each school and district, and for subgroups in the school that constitute at least fifty students and at least 15 percent of the school's total enrollment or, if less than 15 percent, constitute at least 100 students. Subgroups encompass ethnic subgroups, socioeconomically disadvantaged students, English-language learners, gender, and students with disabilities. The ethnic subgroup encompasses African American, American Indian or Alaska Native, Asian, Filipino, Hispanic or Latino, Pacific Islander, and White. The legislature prohibits graduation rates from dropout recovery high schools to be included in the API and has specified that secondary school four-year graduation rates are to be calculated based on the number of graduates who entered ninth grade three years before, plus the number transferring into the graduating class less those transferring out during the same time period. Fifth- and sixth-year graduation rates also are to be calculated in accord with a formula set forth in the statute. The SPI is to make graduation and dropout rates available to the public for socioeconomically disadvantaged students and for subgroups scoring below average on statewide standards tests for each school, school district, and the state as a whole (Educ. Code § 52052). Section 52052.1 of the Education Code requires that beginning July 2011, each school's API calculation include test scores and other accountability data for students assigned to alternative education programs so that these programs are accountable to the public. API information also is to include dropout rates for students enrolled in grades eight and nine. The requirements of Section 52052.1 become operative only if per pupil allocations are in place for implementation of the California Longitudinal Pupil Achievement Data System (CALPADS), a system that, as noted earlier, is intended to provide performance data on the progress of each student through the education system.

Schools are ranked in deciles on API by school type when compared to schools with similar characteristics. A score of ten is the highest decile, while a one is the lowest. There is also a "similar schools" ranking that compares schools serving students of similar socioeconomic backgrounds, thus fostering an "apples-to-apples" comparison system.

Schools that achieve their API growth rates are eligible for performance rewards under the High Achieving/Improving Schools Program (Educ. Code § 52056 and following sections). Those that do not have been subject to interventions spelled out in the Immediate Intervention/Underperforming Schools Program (Educ. Code § 52053 and following sections). In recent years, the Immediate Intervention program has given way to targeting low-performing schools under the High Priority Schools Grant Program (Educ. Code § 52055.600 and following sections). It is similar to the Immediate Intervention/Underperforming Schools Program but targets supplemental funding to schools in the bottom 10 percent of the API rankings—the decile I schools. While voluntary, if a school opts not to participate, the statute requires the school district to hold a public hearing explaining the reasons and rationale for not accepting the invitation and how it intends to address the needs of the school and its students. In order to receive funding, a school must present an action plan to the SPI that is based on scientifically justified practices and grounded on an initial needs assessment. The statute details the components of the action plan, the professional development requirements for both teachers and principals, and the submission of annual reports to the California Department of Education. Schools are given three years to make significant growth on the API. If little or no improvement occurs, the SPI with approval of the SBE assumes control of the school and appoints a school assistance and intervention team (SAIT) with targeted responsibilities. The SPI can take various actions including reorganizing or closing the school or allowing parents to apply to the SBE for establishing a charter school at the site. Low-performing schools also will find assistance in a third program, mentioned in the next chapter, stemming from the settlement of a major school finance lawsuit against the state over conditions in these schools. That program is known as the Quality Education Investment Act. How much improvement these programs will have is questionable. The complexities of turning around underperforming schools on a broad scale, especially schools serving disadvantaged students, are immense.

Charter schools also are held accountable under the API system. For a charter to be renewed, the school must satisfy one of the five standards delineated in Education Code Section 47607 (b). These include meeting the school's API growth target in the prior year, in two of the past three years, or in the aggregate over the past three years; achieving an API rank of four or above in the prior year, or in two of the past three years, either at the state level or in comparison with a demographically comparable school; submitting data to the charter grantor showing that the school's academic performance is equal to the performance of public schools its students would have attended and to other schools in the district where the school is located, considering the student population served by the charter school; or qualifying for an alternative accountability system developed by the SPI under Education Code Section 52053 (h). Each is a rigorous standard and may prove particularly challenging to charter schools serving at-risk student populations. In fact, these schools may well be labeled as low performing during their first few years of operation.

In addition to academic assessment data, the API report also includes general subgroup and demographic data such as number of students in each subgroup, class size, average parent education level, percentage of teachers with full or emergency credentials, number of students excused from testing by parent written consent, and so on. API data for each school and district are readily available on the CDE website. All of this information, of course, is relevant to complying with the terms of NCLB.

API results also are part of the School Accountability Report Card (SARC) required each year by NCLB and mandated by state law (Educ. Code § 33126 and following sections). The report card originated with Proposition 38 in 1988. In return for a stable source of school funding, public schools are required to prepare and disseminate information about themselves to the public. The intent is to enable parents to make informed decisions about the schools their children attend. The information typically includes a school profile that sets forth mission and goals, demographic information, student achievement by grade level under STAR, teacher and staff information, conditions of facilities, and the like. Responding to continuing concern over inequities among schools, the legislature has added new provisions to SARC. These include the percentage of students who lack sufficient standards-assigned textbooks or instructional materials in each subject area, estimated expenditures per student and types of services, average salaries paid to certificated personnel at the school-site, and percentage of secondary school graduates who pass course requirements for entrance to the University of California and California State University systems. Since the posting of this information will highlight differences among schools within the same district, it could generate concern over disparities in resources among schools, particularly those populated by students from low-income families. The full list of components for SARC is described in the Section 33126. The report cards are available to parents in hard copy and via the Internet. They also can be obtained through the CDE website at www.cde.ca .gov/ta/ac/sa/.

SUMMARY

This chapter began with a detailed examination of California school attendance law. But there is more to quality education than getting students to attend school. First, the learning environment must be safe, and there are numerous provisions in California law to make it so. Equally important, the curriculum must be challenging, teachers must be of high quality, and instruction must be effective. Even before Congress enacted No Child Left Behind (NCLB) in 2001, California had embarked on an ambitious route toward school improvement. As we have noted, the curriculum content standards, the accompanying student assessment system, and the Academic Performance Index are testimony to this fact.

NCLB is particularly important because it places great pressure on states to make sure that all students become proficient in mastering state standards by the 2013-2014 school year. This is a tall order. The danger is that the resources will not be available to improve the performance of disadvantaged students. Litigation in the past has focused on this form of inequality and is doing so again, as described in Chapter 3. California has taken steps to avoid liability by specifically targeting many of its reforms to disadvantaged students and others needing special instructional attention. In particular, the state's class size reduction program and enhanced teacher preparation measures are designed with these students in mind.

How well federal and state-mandated reform of traditional public schools will succeed remains to be seen. This much is sure: If traditional public schools falter, it is likely that policymakers will look to alternative delivery systems in the form of expanded school choice, privatization, and Web-based instruction. As we have seen, the Internet already has become an important new form of educational delivery.

3 EQUITY, ADEQUACY, AND SCHOOL FINANCE

Throughout the 1960s and early 1970s California's spending on public education was among the highest in the nation, with average per-pupil expenditures that were 10 percent higher than schools in other states. Throughout the 1980s, California's school spending declined to the national average. By the mid-1990s, it fell well below the national average, with per-pupil expenditures that were as much as 17 percent below those of the rest of the nation, according to the National Center for Education Statistics. Although California's school spending has begun to recover somewhat, it still spends considerably less per student than most other states.

What has caused this dramatic change in fortune for California's schoolchildren? As this chapter indicates, the answer is multifaceted. Throughout the 1970s California courts wrestled with the issue of equitable school funding in the landmark *Serrano v. Priest* school equity case. The *Serrano* rulings prompted the legislature to overhaul the distribution of California's school resources. A significant setback to such efforts occurred in 1978 when California voters limited their property tax burdens by approving Proposition 13. This resulted in a centralized system of school finance that slowed the growth of per-pupil expenditures at the very time the California school system was both expanding and undergoing significant demographic changes. A combination of inadequate resources and glaring funding inequities among school districts, and even schools within districts, spawned new litigation and stimulated reform efforts.

Understanding the problems of the state's school finance system is made more difficult by its sheer complexity. As one state appellate court noted in 1992, California's system of funding schools is "Byzantine in its intricacy and complexity" (*California Teachers Association v. Hayes*, p. 707). Such complexity merits more than a chapter's discussion, and in fact a book-length treatment of the subject may well prove insufficient to fully address the many forces that have shaped California's approach to funding public education, how the system works in day-to-day school budgeting, and its effect on schoolchildren. Instead, this chapter examines the role of money in schooling and seeks to explain how California's school finance litigation has shaped the ways in which both this state's and the nation's schools are funded. We describe the litigation and how it changed the way schools are funded. We also look at competing approaches to funding public education that frame the legal arguments. In addition, we examine how both traditional public and charter schools currently are funded in California.[1]

DOES MONEY MATTER?

The relationship between school spending and student achievement has been the source of heated debate since 1966, when the federally commissioned Equality of Educational Opportunity study—commonly known as the Coleman Report, after its principal investigator Professor James S. Coleman—asserted that schools have little influence on student performance that can be separated from family background. Since then researchers have worked to identify educational production functions that measure the effect of a wide variety of student, parent, community, and school influences on students' academic achievement. School spending is a key ingredient in such analyses as well as one of the most hotly disputed. Clearly, money is important—it buys school buildings and textbooks, and it pays the salaries of trained teachers, counselors, and administrators—but how much money is necessary in order to educate students effectively? The research is divided on this point, because school spending does not demonstrate a clear or consistent relationship with student achievement. Many high-spending districts have disappointing student outcomes, while many low-spending districts are able to produce high levels of student achievement.

Funds spent on uniform policy changes designed to improve achievement frequently prove ineffective. Research indicates that policies such as increasing teacher salaries, installing classroom computers, or reducing class size have not consistently improved student achievement. Class size reduction is an interesting case in point. While it makes intuitive sense that teachers are better able to affect the learning of smaller student groups, the research on smaller classes and achievement increases

---

[1] Texas educational researcher Catherine Maloney is added as coauthor of this chapter.

is disappointing. California presents an interesting example. In 1997 the California legislature approved funding to reduce the size of K–3 classrooms to twenty students. Evaluation of the program during its early stages by a consortium of research institutions found that math scores increased slightly, and reading scores were unchanged, despite an expenditure approaching $2 billion a year.

While class size reduction has had a weak effect on California's student achievement, it has proven to be a strong force in the state's labor market for teachers. Reductions in the number of students per teacher create an increased demand for teachers as more teachers are needed to teach the same number of students. In California this increase in demand was not met with a corresponding increase in the supply of credentialed teachers willing to teach. Many teachers working with hard-to-serve student populations in predominately low-income and nonwhite schools moved when class size reduction created new teaching positions in what they viewed as more desirable districts. Administrators in many predominately low-income and nonwhite schools were unable to find credentialed teachers to fill vacancies and were forced to hire uncertified teachers with little or no classroom experience. Policymakers likely were unaware of the burden class size reduction would create for these schools and students most in need of improved outcomes, but it is certain that the policy's effects have raised questions as to whether the money could have been spent more effectively and efficiently.

The lack of convincing research on the relationship of funding to student achievement was one of the reasons the U.S. Supreme Court refused to rule that interdistrict funding disparities are unconstitutional (*San Antonio Independent School District v. Rodriguez*, 1973). Writing for the five-to-four majority in that decision, Justice Lewis F. Powell observed:

> On even the most basic questions in this area the scholars and educational experts are divided. Indeed, one of the major sources of controversy concerns the extent to which there is demonstrable correlation between educational expenditures and the quality of education—an assumed correlation underlying virtually every legal conclusion drawn by the District Court in this case. (pp. 42–43)

But common sense suggests that funding does indeed matter. Justice Thurgood Marshall, dissenting in *Rodriguez*, noted ironically that if financial variations do not affect educational quality, "it is difficult to understand why a number of our country's wealthiest school districts, which have no legal obligation to argue in support of the constitutionality of the Texas legislation [which reduced interdistrict funding disparities but did not eliminate them], have nevertheless zealously pursued its cause before this Court" (p. 85).

The central policy concern is not that money doesn't matter, for clearly schools with modern and well-equipped facilities, a strong and comprehensive curriculum, and high-quality teachers are preferable to schools with poor facilities, a sparse curriculum, and unqualified teachers. Instead, the central policy issue is how best to distribute school resources in order to maximize the opportunity for all students to learn. For a time, the preferred means to achieve this goal centered on ending the often glaring per-pupil spending disparities among school districts. More recently, attention has shifted to see that every child is provided the necessary resources to reach a certain level of proficiency on state-mandated achievement tests. These are very different goals, and, as we will see, California policymakers have wrestled with both.

THE QUEST FOR EQUITY

Foundation Funding

The local property tax has long been the primary source of funding for local governments in the United States. In most states, the property tax is levied by local governments, and each taxing jurisdiction sets its own tax rate through the budgetary decision-making processes or voter initiative or both. The generally decentralized and local character of property taxes provides the opportunity for local communities to have a strong voice in how the tax is levied and how much support is provided to public schools. In many states, property taxes satisfy the principles of horizontal and vertical equity because landowners in similarly situated residences can expect to pay about the same in taxes, and homeowners residing in more expensive homes can usually expect to pay more. As discussed later in this chapter, Proposition 13 has largely eroded horizontal equity in California's property tax structure by restricting the reassessment of a property's market value until it is sold or changes ownership.

One advantage of using property taxes to fund public schools is that they are a generally stable source of revenue. Unlike the sales and income tax, which are highly sensitive to economic trends, property values—and subsequently property taxes—are less affected by short-term economic fluctuations and remain relatively constant through economic downturns. Thus, funding public education through property taxes ensures a stable funding base for schools during difficult economic times.

Property taxes are ad valorem taxes. This means they are calculated as a percentage of property value. Different types of property may be taxed at different rates depending on how the properties are used. Residential, business, and agricultural properties generally are taxed differently. To determine the amount of tax, the assessed value of a property is multiplied by the locally determined levy rate. For example, a home owner living in a home with assessed value of $150,000 in a community that levies a property tax of $1.50 per $100 of assessed value would pay property taxes in the amount of $2,250.

Historically a wealthy state, California was well able to fund its public schools by relying on the local property tax, augmented by a system of state-funded flat grants for all students. This was true until the 1940s, when the state experienced rapid population growth. The emergence of communities with sizable amounts of industrial and residential property meant that they were able to raise far larger amounts of revenue through the local property tax, at relatively low tax rates, than more sparsely settled regions of the state could raise with higher tax rates. This resulted in growing disparities across the state in the amount of revenue communities could raise for local public services, including schooling. Pressed with the need to develop a more efficient method of funding its rapidly expanding system of public education, California adopted the foundation plan approach to school finance in 1947.

Foundation programs have been a popular method of funding public education. Organized around the principle that students throughout a state should receive some minimum level of educational services, foundation plans strive to offset local district wealth and equalize the distribution of educational resources by ensuring that each student has access to a basic education, paid for by a threshold level of education spending. Each school district is responsible for a share of this funding through its property tax effort at some predetermined uniform tax rate, and for districts with revenues that fall short, the state makes up the difference. Because state resources are distributed in inverse proportion to a local district's ability to raise revenue, poorer districts with low assessed property values receive more state support while wealthier districts receive less.

In the years prior to the *Serrano* decisions, California operated two foundation programs: one for equalization aid and a second for supplemental aid. Although state equalization contributions diminished as a district's per-pupil wealth increased, the California Constitution had provided each district with a basic aid floor of $120 per student regardless of wealth since 1952 (Article IX, § 6). The basic aid provision, a holdover from the state's early flat grant program, ensured that even the wealthiest districts received some state aid. For supplemental aid, however, the foundation level was set just above the median assessed property value per pupil, and most supplemental aid went only to low-wealth districts.

Foundation plans equalize spending up to the established minimum foundation level, but beyond the minimum, local districts generally enjoy latitude in generating additional school funding. In principle, this ensures that local communities with differing preferences for schooling are able to obtain their desired level of educational services through local tax effort. In practice, however, differences in the fiscal capacity of local districts frequently translate into wide variances in the amount of revenue available for schools. Noting that the differences in the amount of resources available to wealthy and poor school districts implied differences in the quality of education provided, school finance reform efforts began to address concerns about the equity of school finance systems that relied primarily on local property tax bases for school funding. The concern over inequity in the distribution of school resources was well aligned with the changing legal interpretations of the equal protection clause in the Fourteenth Amendment to the U.S. Constitution and, later, state constitutions as well.

By the 1960s it was apparent that the equal protection clause had taken on new meaning in the eyes of the U.S. Supreme Court. Worded simply, the clause specifies that no state shall "deny to any person within its jurisdiction the equal protection of the laws." In 1954 the U.S. Supreme Court relied on the clause to find segregated schools unconstitutional in the landmark case *Brown v. Board of Education*. The Court held that "Separate educational facilities are inherently unequal" and that the inequity created by segregated schools deprived black children of the equal protection of the laws. Although the Court stopped short of defining education as a fundamental right under the Constitution, its language straightforwardly addressed the importance of education to American society:

> Today, education is perhaps the most important function of state and local governments. Compulsory school attendance laws and the great expenditures for education both demonstrate our recognition of the importance of education to our democratic society. It is required in the performance of our most basic public responsibilities, even service in the armed forces. It is the foundation of good citizenship. (p. 493)

The importance that the high court gave to education in *Brown* and the aggressive stance it took in the 1960s to compensate the victims of racial segregation by requiring school integration caught the attention of school finance reformers. If the equal protection clause could be used to halt unequal treatment based on race in schooling, could it not also be used to halt unequal treatment based on wealth? This thinking led to litigation in both state and federal courts on the application of the equal protection clause to interdistrict disparities in school finance.

Litigation

State court: **Serrano v. Priest I** *(1971).* On behalf of a class of public school students in all but the richest school district in California, John Serrano filed a lawsuit in state court against state treasurer Ivy Priest and others who administered the California school finance system, contending that it denied them the equal protection of the laws under both the federal and California constitutions. It would become a seminal ruling in school finance. The question for the California Supreme Court was whether the trial court judge was correct in dismissing the case. The justices began by noting that over 90 percent of public school funding in the state was derived from local district property taxes and aid from the state foundation program known as the State School Fund. Of these funds, the local property tax was by far the major source, contributing over half of all educational revenue. The amount of money that a local district could raise was dependent upon the assessed valuation of real property within its borders and upon its tax rate. Tax bases varied on a ratio of 1 to 10,000 across California school districts. While the state had placed a cap on the property tax rate, nearly all districts had voted to override the statutory limit. The central problem was that even with a high tax rate, school districts with low assessed valuations could not match the spending levels of property-rich school districts.

The court noted that the state's foundation program did little to ameliorate funding differences. While the equalization component of the foundation program varied inversely with the property wealth of the district, substantial disparities remained. In the Los Angeles County school district of Baldwin Park, the school district of plaintiff John Serrano, per-pupil spending for the 1968–1969 school year was $577. For the same school year, the nearby Beverly Hills school district spent $1,231 per pupil. The source of this variance in spending was not the willingness of Beverly Hills residents to tax themselves at a higher rate. Instead, the difference emerged because Beverly Hills had much greater property wealth than did Baldwin Park. For the 1968–1969 school year, Beverly Hills had $50,885 in per-pupil assessed property value, and residents paid school taxes of $2.38 per $100 of assessed property value. In marked contrast, Baldwin Park had per-pupil assessed property value of $3,706. Its residents paid $5.48 per $100 of assessed valuation, yet were able to spend less than half as much on their children's education. Differences like these existed across the state.

In overturning the trial judge's ruling by a six-to-one margin, the California high court chiefly relied upon the Fourteenth Amendment equal protection clause. The majority did note in a footnote that the court previously had construed several provisions of the California Constitution to be the substantial equivalent of the equal protection clause. These included Article I, Section 11 (now Article IV, § 16), which provided that "all laws of a general nature shall have a uniform operation," and Article I, Section 21 (now Article I, § 7 (b)), which provided no citizen or class of citizens shall be granted privileges or immunities "which, upon the same terms, shall not be granted to all citizens." The court's footnoted observation would become central to its second *Serrano* ruling in 1976.

The justices began by noting that while the U.S. Supreme Court had not directly ruled that wealth, like race, to be a "suspect" classification under the equal protection clause, it appeared to be poised to do so. This is important because a suspect classification requires the state to establish a compelling justification for the unequal treatment, a very high criterion. The California Supreme Court rejected the claim of state defendants that wealth could not be a suspect classification like race, because wealth related to school districts, not individuals. The court was equally unimpressed by the state's assertion that levels of educational expenditure do not affect the quality of education. Nor was it necessary for the plaintiffs to prove that the state had intentionally discriminated against residents in property-poor districts. The court pointed out that it had held eight years before that racial segregation in schools was unconstitutional regardless of cause (*Jackson v. Pasadena City School District*, 1963) and that it should be the same with wealth discrimination.

The justices also accepted Serrano's argument that education is a fundamental constitutional right even though not mentioned in the U.S. Constitution. The court pointed to the U.S. Supreme Court's observation in *Brown v. Board of Education* that "education is perhaps the most important function of state and local governments" and noted its own observation in the *Jackson* decision that education must be made available to all on an equal basis. While citing U.S. Supreme Court decisions to support this assertion, the justices also referenced the California Constitution in discussing why education is so fundamental that its funding must be equalized.

Having concluded that wealth is a suspect classification and education a fundamental right, the justices rejected the state's argument that deference to local control satisfied the compelling interest criterion. Under the present system, the court noted, "such fiscal freewill is a cruel illusion for the poor districts" because though they express their willingness to tax themselves high for quality education, they are precluded from matching the spending levels of the rich districts (p. 611). The justices also rejected the contention of the state defendants that if spending for education had to be equalized, then so would spending for other social services—an argument commonly termed "the parade of imaginary horribles." Education, they wrote, is unique among public services.

The case was sent back to the trial court for further proceedings, meaning that the trial judge was now in a position to order the state to develop a system of school financing that would satisfy a compelling interest test. Meanwhile, another case on the same issue would soon reach the U.S. Supreme Court. The question among school finance reformers was whether the California Supreme Court had accurately prophesied how the justices on the nation's highest court would rule. It had not.

Federal court: San Antonio Independent School District v. Rodriguez *(1973).* As noted, the California Supreme Court based its *Serrano I* decision primarily on the Fourteenth Amendment equal protection clause. An important case from Texas reached the U.S. Supreme Court in the early 1970s, giving the Court the opportunity to rule definitively on the subject. In the late 1940s, Texas established the Minimum Foundation School Program (MFSP) to help ameliorate glaring inequities among school districts in per-pupil expenditures. The program involved both local and state contributions to a special fund to help pay for teacher salaries, operating expenses, and transportation costs in property-poor school districts. Eighty percent of the funding came from the state, with the remaining amount coming from local school districts on an ability-to-pay basis. Each district was required to levy a property tax to support its contribution, and any excess could be retained to support local schools.

MFSP helped reduce the inequities but did not eliminate them. For example, in 1967–1968, Edgewood Independent School District, serving a predominately Mexican American population in the inner city of San Antonio, retained $26 per pupil in local funding above its MFSP contribution at a property tax rate of $1.05 per $100 of assessed evaluation. MFSP added $222 per pupil, with an additional $108 coming from federal funds. Altogether, Edgewood had $356 per pupil to spend. By contrast, Alamo Heights Independent School District, which is located in an affluent area of San Antonio, retained $333 per pupil for its schools beyond its MFSP contribution at a property tax rate of 85 cents per $100 of assessed evaluation. MFSP added $225 per pupil. An additional $36 from federal funds gave the district a total of $594 per pupil, nearly twice that of the per-pupil expenditure in Edgewood. Differences like these existed elsewhere in Texas and in states across the nation.

As in *Serrano*, the property-poor districts argued that education is a constitutionally protected fundamental right and that a system of public finance that discriminated against poor districts violated the equal protection clause of the Fourteenth Amendment to the U.S. Constitution. They also argued that poverty, like race, is a "suspect" classification under the Fourteenth Amendment requiring the state to establish a compelling state reason to justify inequality in school finance. If poverty were to be declared a suspect classification, Texas agreed it could not justify its finance program. For its part, the state sought to argue that education is not a fundamental right protected by the U.S. Constitution and that poverty is not a suspect classification. This being the case, all the state had to do to prevail under the equal protection clause was to show that its program served a rational purpose.

The state was confident that the fact that MFSP did ameliorate the differences, though imperfectly, would satisfy this lower criterion.

By a narrow five-to-four margin, the Court agreed with the state (*San Antonio Independent School District v. Rodriguez*, 1973). The majority noted that education is not specifically listed as a constitutional right in the U.S. Constitution and chose not to infer it from explicit constitutional protections like freedom of speech. With regard to the suspect classification argument, the majority noted that, unlike racial minorities, the "poor" are not easily definable. Indeed, the Court noted that there was no evidence that the poorest families were necessarily clustered in the poorest school districts. Thus, all the state had to do to survive the equal protection challenge was to establish that its plan was rational. And while imperfect, the MFSP did reduce the disparities significantly.

The decision came as a great blow to those who had hoped that the Court would do for the poor what it had done for racial minorities. And, for school finance reformers in California, the decision came as a serious setback because the California Supreme Court had based its ruling primarily on the Fourteenth Amendment equal protection clause. The U.S. Supreme Court majority did offer some hope, however, because it conceded that inequities in school finance were apparent. Wrote Justice Powell: "We hardly need add that this Court's action today is not to be viewed as placing its judicial imprimatur on the status quo. The need is apparent for reform in tax systems which may well have relied too long and too heavily on the local property tax." He added, "And certainly innovative thinking as to public education, its methods, and its funding is necessary to assure both a higher level of quality and greater uniformity of treatment" (p. 58). However, any reform in school finance would have to come from state legislators and state judges. With the door to the federal courthouse closed, attention shifted back to these entities in California.

State court: **Serrano v. Priest II** *(1976).* Meanwhile, the California Legislature had swung into action after the California Supreme Court's *Serrano I* decision. It passed Senate Bill 90 and Assembly Bill 1276 in 1972. These bills attempted to comply with the *Serrano* decision by increasing both the foundation level of state aid and the computational tax rate used to assess the districts' share of funding. All districts continued to receive basic aid of $125 per average daily attendance (ADA)—$120 of which was constitutionally mandated. What had changed was a substantial increase in the foundation level. For elementary students, the foundation level rose from $355 to $765, and for high school students, from $488 to $950. This is the minimum amount that the state guaranteed to all districts from state or local funds. Increases in the maximum computational tax rate meant that local districts' share of the foundation plan funding also increased. The rate rose from $1 to $2.23 per $100 of assessed valuation at the elementary level and from 80 cents to $1.64 at the high school level. If districts were unable to reach the foundation levels at these rates, then the state made up the difference. Of course, many districts could do so at much lower tax rates. The bills provided some property tax relief by increasing the home owner exemption for residential property and the property tax exemption for business inventories.

The most lasting and significant effect of this legislation was the introduction of the revenue limit system. A district's initial or base revenue limit in 1973–1974 was its total per-pupil funding from both property tax revenues and noncategorical state aid for the 1972–1973 school year. A district could not levy taxes at a higher rate that would increase its 1972–1973 base revenues beyond a permitted yearly inflation rate unless the voters decided otherwise. Wide variances in districts' assessed property values resulted in large differences among districts' initial 1973–1974 base revenue limits, with the wealthiest districts generating three to four times as much in per-pupil funding as the poorest districts, often at very low tax rates. To equalize these differences over time, districts having a tax rate that produced revenues in excess of foundation levels would receive inflation adjustments from the state, which decreased in magnitude as those revenues rose above foundation levels. Districts having base revenues that when added to the full inflation allowance did not reach the foundation level were permitted growth rates of up to 16 percent of the preceding year's revenue limit. The goal of this approach, known as the "squeeze formula," was that per-pupil spending of high- and low-wealth districts would converge over time—the spending of low-wealth districts would be leveled up and the spending of high-wealth districts would be leveled down.

While the central intent of the legislation was equalized per-pupil spending, it allowed districts to increase their revenue limit spending by increasing the local tax rate if a majority of voters approved an override. The idea was that because education is a local enterprise, the residents of a particular district ought to have the discretion to decide how much they wish to spend on their school systems. Many districts adversely affected by the constraints of the revenue limit and squeeze systems were able to pass such initiatives and thus weaken the effect of the law. Viewing the revised finance system as still inequitable, the plaintiffs once again filed suit. Citing *Serrano I*, the trial court struck down the revised finance system, and the plaintiffs appealed the decision to the California Supreme Court.

By a four-to-three vote, the California Supreme Court ruled that despite the legislative reforms, the unconstitutional features that existed in *Serrano I* remained. The basic aid allotment required by the California Constitution had an anti-equalizing effect because all districts, rich or poor, received the same amount on a per-pupil basis. Property-rich districts could reach their foundation levels with a tax rate below the computational level. The new revenue limit system perpetuated inequities that already existed in the 1972–1973 school year by making that the base year. As a result, the system would require up to twenty years to achieve convergence between property-rich and property-poor districts. Even if convergence were to occur, there would still be inequity because the property-rich districts could achieve the foundation level at less than the computational property tax rate. And the entire revenue limit system was compromised by permitting property tax rate overrides so that districts could secure additional property tax revenues.

As to the nature of the constitutional wrong, the majority noted that they had based their *Serrano I* decision on both the federal and state constitutions. They also noted that the state constitution now contained its own equal protection clause with the passage of Proposition 7 in 1974 adding Article I, Section 7. That section read, "A person may not be deprived of life, liberty, or property without due process of law or denied equal protection of the laws." Holding that education is a fundamental right and interdistrict funding disparities a form of wealth discrimination under the California Constitution, the majority of the justices ruled against the state once again.

As to how the system could be rectified, the majority identified several options that the legislature had the authority to pursue. Among them were full state funding through a statewide property tax, consolidation of school districts into geographic areas with equalized property valuations, shifting of commercial and industrial property taxation from local to state control, instituting a school voucher system, and school district power equalizing. As articulated by three school finance experts,[2] district power equalizing reduces the effect of local property taxes on school finance by having the state assume a much greater role in assuring some basic level of funding. In addition, district power equalizing permits unequal spending in a way that works to end the correlation between spending and district wealth. Given finite state resources and the large role of local property taxes in school funding, this usually means that excess revenues raised at a state-mandated minimum tax rate in wealthy districts are siphoned off by the state and distributed to poor districts. Aside from a shift in the control of school finance away from lo-

---

[2] John Coons, William Clune, and Steve Sugarman, *Private Wealth and Public Education* (Cambridge, MA: Harvard University Press, 1970). Both Coons and Sugarman were law professors at the University of California, Berkeley. Their book is a seminal work in school finance reform that has significantly influenced the thinking of both judges and state policymakers across the nation. The writings of these authors were cited frequently in *Serrano I* and in much of the commentary on school finance reform.

cal districts to the state, district power equalizing generates resentment among residents in property-wealthy districts who see their tax dollars diverted away from their schools. But for a time, what was dubbed "the Robin Hood system" intrigued state policymakers around the country. Whatever system the state used, the justices affirmed the trial court's decision that the California school finance system was unconstitutional and had to be remedied within six years.

Following the *Serrano II* ruling, the matter of school finance reform was back in the hands of the California legislators. They responded by enacting Assembly Bill 65 (AB 65) in 1977. AB 65 increased revenue limits and embraced district power-equalizing in the form of the Guaranteed Yield Program, which was designed to increase the financial capacity of property-poor districts. Under this program, a district was guaranteed a certain amount of money at a specified tax rate. If the district fell short of producing the money guaranteed at the tax rate, the state made up the difference. Because property-rich districts produced excess funds at the same tax rate, their funds were subject to recapture by the state for redistribution to the property-poor districts. In addition, AB 65 continued the inflation squeeze system whereby the higher a district's base revenue limit, the lower its inflation adjustment. Thus, the thrust of AB 65 was to raise the spending levels in low-wealth districts while capping spending in the very high wealth districts.

AB 65 was short lived. On June 6, 1978, California voters approved Proposition 13, which was spearheaded by antitax activist Howard Jarvis in a revolt against high property taxes. A year later, voters approved Proposition 4, known as the Gann Limit after its sponsor, Paul Gann. Proposition 4 amended the state constitution to limit spending growth among state and local governments, including school districts, to the rates of inflation and population growth.

Proposition 13

Because in most states the property tax is a largely decentralized form of taxation, local tax jurisdictions must employ assessors to determine the fair market value of properties even if those properties will not change hands. This results in what many taxpayers refer to as "paper wealth." When property values increase, the property owner is subject to higher taxes even though he has not experienced a parallel increase in well-being. The taxpayer still lives in the same home, but when assessment establishes a higher value for the home, he is subject to higher property taxes even when the tax rate remains unchanged. During the early 1970s, housing values began to increase rapidly in many communities, resulting in increased property taxes. When soaring assessments in combination with increased social services were not met with lowered tax rates, homeowners became restless. In

1972, a proposition known as the Watson Initiative that would have reduced property taxes and effectively converted them into a state property tax was defeated at the polls. But by the end of the decade, homeowners reversed directions and supported Proposition 13.

Proposition 13 limited property taxes to 1 percent of assessed value (Calif. Const. Article XIIIA, § 1). It also required a two-thirds vote of the legislature to increase state taxes and prohibited imposition of a statewide property tax. It prohibited increasing property taxes and required a two-thirds majority vote in order for cities, counties, and special districts to impose any special taxes. And it eliminated voter overrides on state-set local property tax rates, a significant blow to property-rich school districts. As a practical matter, Proposition 13 established a system that taxed everyone at the same low rate and centralized authority over school funding at the state rather than the local level. It resulted in a substantial benefit to home and business owners who saw their property tax bills drop by more than 50 percent because of the combination of rolled-back assessments and the reduction in tax rates. This reduction in property tax revenues required that California use other funding sources, such as the sales and income taxes, to fund its public schools and other social services. Many critics argue that this shift in revenue sources, coupled with the centralization of school funding at the state level, has resulted in a system of school finance that is more sensitive to California's economic fluctuations and less responsive to the needs of individual school districts.

Under Proposition 13, assessed value was established at the 1975–1976 assessed value of the property, and inflationary increases of this value were limited to no more than 2 percent a year. Property is reassessed at market value only when it is sold. Home owners may challenge assessments and frequently seek reductions when property values drop. Because the assessed and market values may differ substantially, many property owners pay real property taxes that are less than 1 percent of assessed value. In addition, Prop. 13's requirement that reassessment occurs only when the property is sold or changes hands results in large differences in the taxes paid for similarly situated properties.

Billionaire investor Warren Buffet, who acted as a financial advisor to Arnold Schwarzenegger during the 2003 recall election, irritated some Californians when he suggested the law should be revised to permit increases in property taxes. Buffet pointed to his Emerald Bay home as an example of the disparities caused by the law. While he purchased his home for less than $100,000 in 1971, its 2002 market value was estimated at about $4.5 million. Because of Proposition 13's restrictions on reassessment, Buffet paid property taxes of $2,265 on an assessed property value of $217,350 in 2002. If he had paid taxes on the home's 2002 market value, his taxes would have increased to about $47,000 (*Los Angeles Times*, August 19, 2003). Under this framework, a taxpayer's property tax burden depends on when he bought his home, and new home owners pay considerably more than tenured residents for the same schools, fire and police protection, trash collection, and other public services.

Ironically dubbed the "welcome stranger" law because a newcomer to the community will contribute much more in taxes for local government than settled neighbors, Proposition 13's constitutionality was challenged in 1990 by Stephanie Nordlinger, who found that the tax bill for the Baldwin Hills home she purchased in 1988 was more than five times that of her neighbors living in similar homes. Nordlinger argued that the burden imposed on new home owners deterred people from moving to California and violated the constitutional right to travel. She further argued that the law was a violation of the equal protection clause of the Fourteenth Amendment because it treated taxpayers differently without legitimate justification. Although California state courts rejected these arguments, the case made its way to the U.S. Supreme Court in 1992. In an eight-to-one decision, the Court also rejected Nordlinger's claims. There was no infringement on her right to travel because she already resided in California prior to purchasing her home. On the equal protection clause claim, the Court noted that a state needed only a "plausible policy reason" for imposing differing property taxes contingent upon purchase dates. The justices held that Proposition 13 met this standard. California has a legitimate interest in preserving local neighborhoods by discouraging the rapid turnover of homes and businesses. Furthermore, the state can distinguish between a new owner and one who has vested rights in retaining his property (*Nordlinger v. Hahn*).

Following the enactment of Proposition 13, the California Legislature returned to the drawing boards on school finance. After a one-year state block grant stopgap measure, it enacted Assembly Bill 8 (AB 8) in 1979. Under this measure, high-wealth districts received very low inflation increases each year to their revenue limits, and low-wealth districts received high inflation increases, a continuation of the convergence or "squeeze" approach of the previous foundation program. AB 8 restricted the revenue limit concept to general operating funds, excluding categorical funding for such purposes of educating children with special needs, providing transportation, and deferred maintenance, which vary from district to district. Because the legislature no longer could recapture excess property taxes from high-wealth districts and had no immediate source of state revenue to raise funding levels in low-wealth districts, per-pupil funding levels expanded much less rapidly.

But the *Serrano* litigation had not ended. Plaintiffs returned to court following the implementation of AB 8 to argue that it too was inequitable. The trial court disagreed, and the decision was upheld by the Court of Appeal for the Second District, whose judges were so impressed by the superior court judge's carefully reasoned opinion that they incorporated it as their own (*Serrano v. Priest*, 1986, known as *Serrano III*). A good deal of controversy surrounded the standard for determining equity. The superior court judge looked back to what the trial judge had decided in 1974 following the California Supreme Court's decision in *Serrano I*. In that decision, the trial judge had determined that other than categorical funding, wealth-related disparities between districts had to be reduced to insignificant differences, meaning considerably less than $100 per pupil, within six years. While the California Supreme Court had affirmed that decision in *Serrano II* in 1976, it had not specifically discussed the extent of permissible interdistrict disparities.

Referring to the earlier judge's ruling, the superior court judge, whose decision was embraced by the California Court of Appeal for the Second District in *Serrano III*, concluded that the term "insignificant differences" as applied to base revenue funding across districts did not mean that the $100 figure had to be mechanically applied. Rather, it was to serve as a guide, and the revised system imposed by AB 8 and subsequent legislation achieved the desired equity. The judge also pointed out that the plaintiffs first had to establish that their fundamental right to education under the state constitution has been substantially impaired before the court will scrutinize the constitutionality of funding legislation. This threshold requirement is necessary to avoid having judges second-guess every legislative funding enactment that may treat persons and districts differently. For example, it may be that it is more costly to educate a secondary student than an elementary student. Such a funding difference would not by itself warrant judicial review.

Serrano v. Priest had come to an end. While equity appeared to have been achieved, it came at the expense of local control of school funding. In addition, the shift to state-centered funding resulted in a system of school finance that was less responsive to the needs of individual districts and that failed to keep pace with the need for additional school funding. As a result of *Serrano*, the passage of Propositions 13 and 4, and a rapidly growing schooling population, California's per-pupil spending grew more slowly relative to other states, and by the 1990s, the state's average per-pupil expenditures were well below the national average. Some attribute the slowdown to the reticence of California's political leaders to introduce new taxes. While this explanation may have some merit, it is undermined by state public spending patterns over the past decade. While school funding has lagged, other public services have not, leading some to conclude that the lack of resources for public education is the result of deliberate decision making on the part of policymakers and voters. These critics point to demographic changes as the source of California's school funding problems, asserting that white voters are reluctant to invest in schooling for the state's increasingly nonwhite and low-income school population. In 2007–2008, 70 percent of California public school students were students of color, half came from low income families, and one-quarter were English language learners. Others contend that legislators no longer believe increasing school funding will lead to improved student outcomes. Whatever the reason, the shape of equity in the wake of *Serrano* was not what reformers had expected, and the failure of California school funding to keep pace with other states fostered a growing perception that California's public schools were rapidly becoming equally mediocre.

THE CURRENT CALIFORNIA SCHOOL FINANCE SYSTEM

California's system of public education is supported by a variety of state, local, and federal sources. The major components are listed in Table 3.1 and described in this section. State funds generally make up about 60 percent of California's school revenues and are derived largely from the state sales and income taxes. Local sources, such as property taxes, which the state allocates to school districts, and developer fees, comprise the next largest share of school revenues (about a quarter in 2005–2006), and the remaining revenues come from federal funding for categorical aid programs, receipts from the state lottery, and other miscellaneous sources.

The amount of funding derived from each source varies from year to year depending on the decisions and compromises made by the legislature and governor in developing the state's budget. This process begins in January when the governor releases a proposed budget and generally concludes sometime in July or August when the finalized budget is formally adopted. While the California Legislature has substantial influence over how California's schools are financed, its authority is not exclusive. California's system of K–14 education has been guaranteed a minimum level of funding by the state's voters. Proposition 98, approved in November of 1988, amended the state constitution to establish a funding floor for the state's public schools and community colleges (Article XVI, § 8). It also focused on educational outcomes by requiring the establishment of the School Accountability Report Card (SARC) discussed in Chapter 2. The funding floor was initially set at 40 percent of California's general-fund tax revenues, but during the recession of the early 1990s, this minimum was reduced to about 34 percent. As a means to keep funding for public education largely intact, the legislature and then Governor Pete Wilson enacted the Educational Revenue Augmentation Fund (ERAF) in 1992. ERAF made up for the lost general-fund revenues by shifting some of the property tax revenues of counties and cities to public schools.

TABLE 3.1

Major Components of California's School Finance System

Revenue Limit Funding
- Set percentage of state general fund tax revenues for public schools and community colleges (Prop. 98)
- State and local property tax funds (latter controlled by Prop. 13)

Categorical Aid
- State sources
- Federal sources

Other Sources
- State lottery revenue
- Parcel taxes
- Private contributions
- Interest income
- Leases and rentals

Facilities Funding
- State and local bonding process
- Developer fees
- Mello-Roos Community Facilities District Act (1982)
- Leroy Greene School Facilities Act (1998)

Proposition 98 provides that state revenues for school districts and community colleges in high-revenue years are to be the larger of the first two formulas in Table 3.2. Formula three is applicable in low-revenue years.

The first formula is used when economic times are good and general-fund revenues high and where the portion of the budget for schools is 39 percent. This formula has been operational since 1988–1989. The second formula is available only in fiscal years when the growth in per capita income is less or equal to the percentage of growth in per capita general-fund revenues plus one-half percent. This formula is used most often because it is not as heavily dependent on economic factors as are the other two. The third formula is used when general-fund revenues do not grow as rapidly as per capita income. And, as noted in the table, the proposition gives the legislature the further option of suspending the proposition's base funding provisions for one year by passing urgency legislation. This happened for the first time in 2004. Shortly after Proposition 98 was passed, several groups including the California Teachers Association tried to argue that the proposition had shifted authority away from the state and had given school districts the exclusive right to decide how funding allocated to them is to be spent. The argument was rejected (*California Teachers Association v. Hayes*, 1992). The California Court of Appeal ruled that the proposition did not alter the legislature's plenary authority over school funding.

TABLE 3.2

Tests for Determining a Minimum Base Funding for Schools under Proposition 98

High-Revenue Years

Formula One   The same share of state general fund taxes received in the base year of 1986–1987, adjusted for shift of property taxes to schools under ERAF.

Formula Two   The same amount of state and property tax funding received in the previous year with adjustments for increases in enrollment and inflation.

Low-Revenue Years

Formula Three   Same criteria as Formula Two but inflation defined as the growth of taxes per capita plus one-half percent. Any reduction compared to the previous year must be no worse than cuts in state spending per capita for other budgeted services.

State has the option of suspending Proposition 98's base funding provisions for one year by passing urgency legislation requiring two-thirds approval of both houses and signature of the governor pursuant to Article IV, Section 8 of the California Constitution.

General-purpose funds make up about two-thirds of California's school revenues. The legislature provides these funds to school districts on an unrestricted basis. Consisting of a combination of local contributions through the applied property tax and the state's contribution toward the district's predefined revenue limit, general purpose funds are primarily devoted to classroom needs such as teacher salaries, instructional materials, textbooks, and school maintenance. The remaining one-third of school revenues comes from state and federal categorical funds, which are earmarked for specific educational purposes such as programs for low-income students, students with limited English proficiency, and children with special educational needs. Differences in the amount of categorical aid that districts receive are one reason for the continuing inequities in per-pupil funding across districts.

Revenue Limit Funding

Districts continue to receive the bulk of their general-purpose funds through revenue limit foundation funding (Educ. Code § 42238 and following sections; see Table 3.1). A district's revenue limit is calculated through a complex formula that adjusts a base revenue limit amount according to a variety of factors, including increases for inflation or cost-of-living adjustments (COLAs) and decreases for deficits, as well as adjustments for summer school programs and policies that extend the school day and year.

The amount of funding a district receives under the revenue limit system is calculated by multiplying the per-pupil amount of its revenue limit by its average daily attendance, or ADA. Additional funding is provided for "necessary small schools" located in geographically isolated areas with low levels of attendance. To protect against revenue losses caused by declining enrollments, districts are permitted to use either the current or the previous year's ADA when calculating their revenue limit funding. Initially, districts were permitted to include students with excused absences in their ADA calculations. However, in 1998–1999, revenue limit ADA was restricted to only those students who were actually present in school.

The legislature combines state funds with local property tax revenues to meet the revenue limit requirements. Because districts are generally prohibited from receiving money in excess of their revenue limit, the exact mix of state and local funds is of little concern. Each year, however, between 60 and 80 districts have property tax revenues that either meet or exceed their revenue limits. These districts are not subject to a state recapture plan and were designated as "basic aid" districts until the 2003–2004 school year because they kept their property tax receipts and received the basic aid guaranteed by the California Constitution—a flat grant of $120 per pupil. In 2003, however, legislators agreed to eliminate state basic aid to these districts, reasoning that all districts receive the constitutionally guaranteed minimum in the form of categorical aid. The districts are still permitted to retain their excess property tax revenues and are now designated as "excess tax" districts.

By largely eliminating the connection between local wealth and school spending, the revenue limit system moved California's public schools to a position of equality relative to general-purpose funding. Differing revenue limit growth rates forced a convergence to a median level for all districts. In the late 1970s, some high-wealth districts had revenue limit funds that were more than 30 percent above the revenue limit median, and some low-wealth districts had per-pupil revenue limit spending that was less than 85 percent of the median. By the 1990s, however, the upper band on spending had been reduced to about 7 percent, and the lower band had been increased to about 99 percent of median revenue limit funding.

Categorical Aid

About a third of California's school funds are committed to categorical aid (see Table 3.1). Funding for categorical programs is drawn from both federal and state sources and is generally accompanied by regulations ensuring that the money is used for the educational purpose or special student population for which it is designated. In California, the largest share of categorical funding is dispensed for special education. Although special education receives more than $2.7 billion in federal and state categorical aid each year, the funding does not cover the full cost of special education services; districts must contribute some of their general-purpose funds to make up the difference—a practice known as encroachment. As its name indicates, this practice results in less expenditure in other areas and generates resentment from those who see funding for regular students siphoned off to make up the shortfall in special education. This is a continuing source of controversy and generates assertions that the federal government has, in effect, imposed an unfunded federal mandate on the states.

The needs of low-income and English-language learners are another important focus of categorical aid in California. Economic Impact Aid (EIA) is the primary state program supporting low-income and limited-English-speaking students. EIA funding is determined on a per-pupil basis, and districts receive funding based on the number of low-income and English-language learners they serve. Federal funding for these students is split into two programs: Title I provides funding for low-income students, and Title III funds programs for students with limited proficiency in English.

In addition, California's public schools receive varying amounts of funding for some fifty other categorical aid programs (this number may vary depending on how "programs" are defined). These include federally funded programs for preschool students, child development and nutrition, and vocational programs as well as state-funded programs for school improvement, desegregation, and a variety of compensatory educational programs. Like special education, programs for class size reduction, early childhood development, and adult education receive both state and federal funding. The number of programs and the amount of funding per program varies from year to year, reflecting legislative preferences.

The antitax Proposition 4 corollary to Proposition 13, approved by voters in 1979, added Article XIII B to the California Constitution. Section 6 of this article requires the state to reimburse local governments whenever the legislature or state agency mandates a new program or higher level of service. The term "program" in this provision has been construed to encompass public education (*Long Beach Unified School District v. State of California*, 1990). Thus, the proliferation of categorical programs has resulted in increased funding, particularly for schools serving large numbers of children with special needs.

From 1992 to 2000, California grouped about thirty of its state-funded categorical programs into one line item in the state budget. Termed "mega-item" funding, the grouping was intended to protect special programs from governor-initiated funding cuts. Districts were granted some flexibility with mega-item allocations and were allowed to redirect small amounts of money between programs blocked for mega-item funds. The mega-item fund was eliminated in 1999–2000, though some discretion in the use of categorical funding remained.

In 2004, the legislature consolidated over twenty categorical programs accounting for some 18 percent of annual categorical funding into six block grants. These include pupil retention, school safety, teacher credentialing, professional development, targeted instructional improvement, and school and library improvement (Educ. Code § 41500 and following sections). School officials welcomed the provision, which gave them the discretion to transfer up to 15 percent of four of the block grants (pupil retention and teacher credentialing are excluded) to cover costs in other block grants or categorical programs not to exceed 20 percent of the total amount allocated for those programs (Educ. Code § 45000 (a)). Before this can be done, the district or county board of education must discuss the matter at a public meeting.

Other Sources of School Revenue

There are several other sources of school revenue, as outlined in Table 3.1. In 1984 California voters approved a constitutional amendment enabling the creation of a state lottery, with 34 percent of revenues tagged for public education. Although the lottery provides less than 2 percent of K–12 funding, the money is valuable to districts because it may be spent at the district's discretion on any school expense except school construction or the purchase of property.

Despite the centralization of California's system of school finance, districts still retain some local avenues for school funding. Districts are able to generate local revenues through leases and rentals of school property and earned interest on general-fund balances. In addition, with two-thirds voter approval districts are permitted to levy parcel taxes on parcels of real estate in order to raise revenue for specific school purposes. The tax may be variable, or it may be a flat per-parcel rate, but it may not be levied ad valorem. That is, the tax is levied on the parcel itself and not on the value of the parcel. During the 1999–2000 school year, parcel taxes generated about $63 million in additional school funding. The voter approval requirement makes the parcel tax a somewhat cumbersome funding mechanism for many California districts, and parcel tax revenues are enjoyed only by districts in which voters are willing to approve the tax.

The slowing pace of increases in California's per-pupil spending have caused many local districts to rely on voluntary private contributions in order to support school programs. In the wake of Proposition 13, an increasing number of California districts have established nonprofit educational foundations for the purpose of raising private revenues for local school districts. More than five hundred of these foundations currently operate in California. At the school level, however, the primary source of private revenues continues to be parent groups, such as the Parent-Teacher Association (PTA) and booster clubs. In most school districts, private donations contribute less than $100 per pupil, though there can be wide disparities among schools in the same district.

Facilities Funding

Rapidly increasing enrollments coupled with aging school buildings have placed considerable pressure on California's public school districts to build new school facilities and renovate existing ones. In 2001, the California Legislative Analyst's Office estimated that one-third of California's school-aged children attended school in an overcrowded or outdated facility.

California's system for funding new schools and school renovations is independent of its basic school finance system and relies heavily on the state and local bonding process. Prior to the passage of Proposition 13 in 1978, local school districts held the primary responsibility for financing school facilities through general obligation bonds. Districts that experienced rapidly increasing enrollments and had reached the limits of their bonding capacity were eligible for state school construction aid. With the passage of Proposition 13, property taxes were restricted to 1 percent of assessed valuation, and local districts were no longer able to use general obligation bonds supported by a local ad valorem tax as a funding source for school construction.

At the state level, voters have passed bonding measures in recent years that have generated billions of dollars for school land acquisition and facility construction / repair. Proposition 47 raised $11.4 billion in 2002, and Proposition 55 generated $10 billion in 2004. As discussed later in the chapter, the settlement of a class action lawsuit brought by poor districts generated additional funds.

From 1978 to 1986, the state held the central role in school facilities funding. In 1986 California voters passed Proposition 46, which restored local district authority to issue general obligation bonds with two-thirds voter approval. Bond issues for school renovations and repair required a simple majority of voter approval. From 1987 to 1999, revenue raised through local general obligation bonds paid more than 30 percent of California's school building and renovation costs. Despite the passage of Proposition 46, the state still retained considerable control over school construction because state school construction bonds could be passed by a simple majority vote instead of the two-thirds vote required by local districts. In November of 2000, however, California voters approved Proposition 39, which reduced the voter approval threshold needed to pass local school facility bonds from two-thirds to 55 percent. The reduction in required voter approval makes it substantially easier for school districts to generate funds for school construction.

In addition to Proposition 46, 1986 also saw the approval of Assembly Bill 2926, which permitted local districts to levy developer fees on new commercial, industrial, and residential construction projects. Districts are permitted to impose the fees when they can demonstrate that the new construction will create a need for additional school facilities (Educ. Code § 17620 and following sections). The law initially permitted fees of up to $1.50 per square foot for residential construction projects and up to 25 cents per square foot for commercial and industrial projects (Govt. Code § 65995). Provisions permitting increases for inflation as determined by the State Allocation Board raised the fees to $2.05 per square foot for residential and 33 cents for commercial and industrial construction in 2000. Developer fees provide substantial revenue in rapidly growing communities but are not important sources of revenue in stagnant communities.

School districts may also raise capital revenues through the creation of Mello-Roos districts with two-thirds voter approval. Introduced in 1982, the Mello-Roos Community Facilities District Act enables local districts to create special financing districts in order to raise money for community construction needs such as schools, libraries, and roads (Govt. Code § 53311 and following sections). The Leroy Greene School Facilities Act of 1998 is another measure designed to assist schools with facilities funding. Under the terms of the Leroy Greene program, eligible school districts may apply to the State Allocation Board for school construction funds (Educ. Code § 17070 and following sections). The program requires schools to meet state-developed criteria for inadequate school facilities according to a point system. The application process is competitive and complex, and schools that qualify must match state funding with local revenues.

Voter approval in November 2006 of Proposition 1D channeled $7.3 billion of the $10 billion measure for K–12 facility modernization, new construction, relief grants for overcrowded schools, career technical education facilities, charter school facilities, environmentally friendly projects, and joint-use projects such as gyms and libraries. In each case, local contributions are necessary for release of funds. It is estimated that some 1,800 schools (20 percent of all schools) are eligible for overcrowding grants.

Although California's spending on school facilities has increased steadily since the mid-1980s, it still lags the rest of the nation by about 20 percent. In addition, differences in local communities' ability to pass general obligation bonds as well as differences in the amount of state aid received have resulted in wide disparities in the amount of facilities funding available to California school districts.

FUNDING CHARTER SCHOOLS

The Block Grant System

Prior to 1999, California's charter schools were funded by the revenue limit system used by traditional school districts. Thereafter, the system of charter school funding was restructured to develop a simpler method of providing charters with operational funds equivalent to those received by traditional school districts serving similar student populations. Charters authorized after June 1, 1999, were automatically funded under the new system. Charter schools authorized before that time were permitted the option of converting to the new model or using a district apportionment system through the 2001–2002 school year. District-wide charters were permitted to convert to the new system or to retain the revenue limit funding model.

The revised system of charter school funding is composed of two block grants (Educ. Code § 47633 and following sections). The first, a general-purpose entitlement, replaces revenue limit funding. The charter school general-purpose entitlement is computed annually by the Superintendent of Public Instruction (SPI) and funded through a combination of state aid and local funds; it is distributed to charter schools on the basis of average daily attendance across a set of four grade ranges: K–3, 4–6, 7–8, and 9–12. Charter schools receive per-pupil funding equivalent to the statewide average revenue limit funding of traditional public school districts serving similar student populations. Like the revenue limit funds received by a traditional district, a charter school's general-purpose entitlement is unrestricted and may be used for any school purpose. Charters are restricted, however, from receiving necessary small-school revenue limit funding available to traditional schools (Educ. Code § 47633).

The second, a categorical aid block grant, replaces some of the categorical aid available to traditional schools. In place of applying separately for certain categorical aid programs, charter schools receive a categorical aid block grant that includes funding for general categorical programs and for educationally disadvantaged students. For 2007–2008, the SPI set a base funding level of $500 per ADA that is to be adjusted each year thereafter for inflation. Charter schools enjoy more flexibility than do traditional schools in the use of state categorical aid funds and are not bound by programmatic restrictions. Like the general entitlement funds, a charter school may use its state categorical aid revenues for any school purpose (Educ. Code § 47634.1 (f)).

The categorical aid block grant includes some but not all state-funded categorical programs. Among the programs included are the Agricultural Vocational Education

Incentive Program, the Beginning Teacher Support and Assessment System, college preparation programs, gifted and talented programs, the Class Reduction Act, and California's Peer Assistance and Review program. Charter schools may not apply for separate funding for any program included in the block grant. They also may not apply for categorical programs administered by a county office of education. They must apply separately in order to receive funding for state categorical aid programs omitted from the grant as well as for federal categorical aid programs. Charters are not granted the same flexibility with the funds they receive from categorical programs outside of the block grant. Charters that apply for federal categorical aid programs such as Title I funding for disadvantaged students or for state programs such as California's Principal Training program are bound by the program's regulations and may use the funds only for their specified purposes.

A charter school may elect to receive funds either directly or through the local authorizing agency that granted its charter or was designated as the oversight agency by the state board of education (Educ. Code § 47651). Charters that choose the direct funding option have their funds deposited in the school's appropriate account in the county treasury. The same is true for charters that have been granted by the State Board of Education (SBE) but for which the board has not delegated oversight responsibilities. For charters that are funded through their local authorizing agent, the funds are deposited in the account of the authorizing local education agency and then dispensed to the charter. The method of allocating funds affects neither the amount of funds provided to charters nor the oversight responsibilities of the local authorizing agent. Charter school authorizers are permitted to charge an administrative fee of up to 1 percent of a charter school's revenues for oversight responsibilities or up to 3 percent of revenues if they provide the school with substantially rent-free facilities (Educ. Code § 47613).

The method by which a charter school chooses to have its funds allocated may affect its ability to apply for state and federal categorical aid. Those schools that have their funds allocated directly may apply for categorical aid individually, just like a school district. If the funding flows through the local education agency that granted the charter or has been designated by the SBE as the oversight entity, then the charter school may receive considerable administrative support in the application process and in managing the program from that agency. RAND's 2003 analysis of charter schools, which compared the amount of categorical aid received by charter schools and traditional district schools, found that as a group, charter schools received considerably less categorical aid but that these differences were largely attributable to start-up charters that preferred the direct method of fund allocation. Conversion charters, which generally choose to be funded locally through their authorizing district, had categorical aid participation rates that were similar to and in some cases greater than those of traditional public schools. RAND's survey of school administrators indicated that many charter school administrators did not know they were eligible for some categorical programs and had given up applying for others, such as Title I, due to the complexity of the program's application process and regulatory requirements. Locally funded charter schools that were able to be included in their authorizing district's application for categorical programs outside of the block grant had much higher participation rates in these categorical programs.

In addition to state and federal funding sources, many charter schools rely on private donations to offset start-up costs, provide instructional materials, and substitute for categorical aid programs for which the charter was ineligible or failed to apply. The RAND study also found that charters receive substantially more in private funding than traditional schools. On average, charters received $433 per pupil in private funding compared with $83 for similarly situated conventional public schools. Start-up charters were the primary recipients of private funds, receiving $576 per pupil compared with $56 per pupil in conversion charters. It is unclear whether this funding was the result of one-time gifts to cover the start-up costs of the new schools or whether the contributions were spread over a period of years to supplement operating and capital costs.

The Special Case of Nonclassroom-Based Charters

The Education Code defines a charter school's program as "classroom-based instruction" when the following four criteria are met: (1) the charter school's students are engaged in educational activities and are supervised by a teacher who holds a valid teaching certificate, (2) at least 80 percent of instructional time is offered at the school site, (3) the charter school site is used principally for classroom instruction, and (4) the charter school requires its students to be in attendance at the school site for at least 80 percent of the minimum instructional time required by law for the appropriate grade level (Educ. Code § 47612.5 (e)(1)). During the 2007–2008 school year, about 20 percent of California's charter schools did not meet these criteria and were classified as "nonclassroom-based instructional programs" and tended to serve a different population than traditional charters. These charters offered programs for independent study, home study, and work study as well as distance and computer-based instructional programs.

Many assume that the costs of operating a nonclassroom-based charter are less than for a classroom-based school. Others believe that these schools are not providing a quality education and point to the RAND study showing that students in these schools do not perform as well as those in the more traditional classroom setting. As we noted in Chapter 1, it may be that the students in these schools are more difficult to educate and that is why their performance lags behind. In any case, the California Legislature has instituted a reduced funding schedule for nonclassroom-based charter schools. Nonclassroom-based charters may receive an amount not more than 70 percent of the per-ADA funding provided to classroom-based programs (Educ. Code § 47634.2). The State Board of Education may determine that less or more funding is appropriate based on the amount the charter school spends on certificated employee salaries and benefits, school site expenses, teacher-student ratio, and other factors the board considers appropriate to school funding. One caveat is that a non-classroom-based charter school may not receive state funding for instruction of students who do not reside in the county where the school is chartered or in an adjacent county (89 Ops. Atty. Gen. 166, 2006). This is because the State Board of Education requires nonclassroom-based instruction in any school to comply with independent study requirements. State funding is available only for independent study programs when the students are residents of the county in which the school is located or an adjacent county (Educ. Code § 51747.3 (b)).

Facilities

Obtaining adequate school facilities has been a central obstacle for many charter schools and for start-up charters in particular. While conversion charters often occupy the same facilities they used as traditional public schools, start-up charters must contend with locating appropriate facilities, as well as rental costs and expenses for maintenance and utilities. Responding to the difficulties inherent in starting a new school, California recently implemented legislative changes designed to assist charters with capital expenses.

As part of Proposition 39, voters in 2000 approved a measure requiring traditional school districts to provide charter schools serving eighty or more in-district students with facilities sufficient to serve those students (Educ. Code § 47614). The facilities must be "reasonably equivalent" to those of other schools operating within the district. These facilities must be "contiguous, furnished and equipped" and remain the property of the host school district. Districts are required to provide facilities even if unused facilities are not available and must make reasonable efforts to accommodate the charter school with facilities in the area of its desired location. Charter school facilities must be provided even if districts will incur costs in providing them. However, some charter operators have complained that districts are providing poor-quality facilities that are not reasonably equivalent to other district schools. Districts are permitted to charge charter schools a pro rata share of school facilities costs, which the school district pays for with unrestricted general-fund revenues. Because districts use nongeneral funds for most capital expenditures, general-fund expenses are likely to include only costs for maintenance and upkeep. Districts are not required to use their unrestricted general-fund revenues for charter school capital expenses and instead may use state or local bonds to fund the facilities.

Proposition 47, approved by voters in November 2002, provided up to $100 million for the construction of new charter schools and presented the first opportunity for charter schools to apply directly for state facilities bond funds. These funds were rapidly depleted when more than twenty charters applied for funding in the spring of 2003. In March 2004, however, voters approved Proposition 55, which included provisions granting charter schools with an additional $300 million in state bond funds for facilities.

In 2003–2004 California implemented Senate Bill 740 and established the Charter School Facility Grant Program, which is designed to assist charter schools with the costs of renting and leasing facilities (Educ. Code § 47614.5). Eligible charters may receive up to $750 per pupil as reimbursement for up to 75 percent of the annual cost of leasing or renting a school facility. The California Department of Education was charged with informing charter schools about the program and determining eligibility requirements. Charter schools are eligible for the program (1) if they are located in the attendance zone of a public elementary school in which at least 70 percent of students are eligible for free or reduced-price meals, and the charter gives preference in admissions to students who either attend the public elementary school or reside in its attendance area; or (2) if they enroll 70 percent or more students eligible for free or reduced-price meals. The availability of funds depends on the state's budget for each fiscal year and funds are not appropriated until the subsequent year's fiscal budget has been approved.

Discussions of how California's charter schools spend their revenues are limited by the absence of reliable data sources and inconsistencies in charter school reporting. Because California collects data on school expenditures at the district level, school-level analysis of the expenditure patterns of charter and traditional district schools has been difficult.

THE MOVEMENT TOWARD ADEQUACY

The fiscal complexities and political difficulties inherent in equalizing school resources across districts, coupled with an increased emphasis on state-mandated educational standards, led to a subtle but significant shift in school finance reform efforts in the 1990s across the nation. This shift was marked by a movement away from concern over equitable school funding to discussion of adequate funding and school quality. Instead of pressing equal protection clause arguments to shape more equitable distributions of school resources, school finance reform advocates now focused on the education clauses of state constitutions, arguing that the clauses obligate states to provide a minimum level of education for all students. These efforts appealed more readily to American understandings of fairness and opportunity and were better aligned with the growing curriculum standards movement than were the arguments for increased equity. An important stimulus to the adequacy argument was the enactment of the federal No Child Left Behind Act in 2001. That act, which is discussed in Chapter 2, requires that all students must achieve proficiency levels or higher on state-mandated assessments by 2014.

The focus on adequacy of school resources has placed school quality at the center of the debate over how best to distribute school revenues. Although a school's quality is not necessarily a function of its revenues, some students require more resources than others do in order to attain minimum levels of achievement. Urban schools serving large populations of low-income students of color, in particular, are challenged to provide an adequate education for their students, many of whom arrive at schoolhouse doors with significant educational deficiencies resulting from low-income backgrounds or limited-English-proficient households. These students have greater educational needs and frequently require more resources in order to bring their achievement in line with state-required minimum standards.

While the education clause in California's constitution is relatively vague with respect to standards of achievement—Article IX, Section 1 holds that "a general diffusion of knowledge and intelligence" is essential to California's citizenry—California's State Board of Education adopted some of the most rigorous academic content standards in the nation in 1997. California began assessing each school's performance based on these standards in 1999. The results of the assessments comprise a school's Academic Performance Index (API) and may be used to compare California's schools to each other and to schools throughout the country. Academic content standards, student assessment, and school accountability are all discussed in Chapter 2.

California's expectations for its schools are notably higher than those of other states, but it provides substantially fewer resources to help schools achieve these goals. According to the Public Policy Institute of California, between 1969 and 1998 California's per-pupil funding fell about 15 percent relative to the average spending in other states. As noted at the start of this chapter, nationwide comparisons of per-pupil expenditures rank California among the states with the lowest expenditures on education. In addition, California's schools have larger class sizes, fewer instructional materials, and older facilities than schools in most other states.

Although there is little evidence that school expenditures are directly related to student achievement, some question whether California's record of poor student achievement over the past decade is a result of the shift to state-based school finance policymaking and the slowing of increases in per-pupil expenditures. Before equalization got under way, California's students performed about the same as students in the rest of the nation on nationally administered tests of student achievement. In 1992, the U.S. Department of Education revised the National Assessment of Educational Progress (NAEP) testing program to include state-level as well as national information about academic achievement. Throughout the 1990s, California's NAEP scores lagged behind those of the rest of the nation. For example, in 2007, California's eighth graders earned reading scores that were below those of forty-four of the fifty-two states and jurisdictions that participated in the tests. The percentage rated proficient or higher stood at 21 percent, the same as in 1997. The math scores for these students were slightly higher with some improvement over prior years.

While California's poor record of academic achievement may be linked in some way to school finance, it is likely that the state's changing demographics also have influenced testing outcomes. California's immigrant population grew throughout the 1980s and 1990s, and students from low-income families and from households with limited English proficiency on average earn lower scores on standardized measures of academic achievement. On comparisons of 1992 NAEP test takers, California's students were more likely to come from minority and recent immigrant households and to have parents who were less educated than those of students in the rest of the nation. It is likely that these characteristics of California's test takers have contributed to the state's relatively poor academic performance.

Irrespective of student outcomes, many critics of California's reduced expenditures for public schooling fault Proposition 13's restrictions on property tax revenues and point to the increased susceptibility to economic conditions of state-based systems, such as California's, that rely heavily on sales and income taxes. These critics argue that the economic downturn of the early 1990s was particularly hard on California and that the current recession coupled with increasing per capita enrollments are at the center of California's school finance difficulties.

Other critics take a different tack. Some fault the strength of California's teachers unions, arguing that while California ranks among the lowest in per-pupil expenditures, its teachers are among the highest paid in the nation. During the 2007 school year, California's teachers ranked first in the National Education Association's statewide comparison of teacher salaries. Critics of these high salaries contend that expenditures on teachers absorb a disproportionate share of California's school resources, leaving little money for instructional materials, counselors, and other services. In response, teacher organizations maintain that the cost of living is higher in California than in other states.

Still others point to the influence of Proposition 98's minimum funding for education. These critics argue that since Prop. 98 was implemented in 1988, funding for California's schools has declined relative to other states while its spending on other government services has remained high. They suggest that the California Legislature has focused somewhat narrowly on meeting previous school-funding requirements without giving much thought to actual costs of educating California's current public school population. This focus on meeting districts' past funding levels has effectively transformed Prop. 98 from a funding floor to a funding ceiling. While 40 percent of California's general revenue is devoted to education, the national average is 48 percent.

Adding strength to the argument are statistics showing that the current California funding system remains inequitable despite over thirty years of pursuing equity. A class action lawsuit that was filed in May 2000 against the state by civil rights organizations clearly demonstrates the point by focusing on the deplorable facilities, absence of textbooks and materials, and inadequately prepared teachers in schools serving students who are disproportionately nonwhite and poor. These conditions are not just apparent across districts. They show up among schools within particular districts too. The plaintiffs' trial brief in *Williams v. State of California* detailed substandard conditions in forty-six schools across the state, attended by the named plaintiffs. Relying on its numerous expert witnesses, the brief also included statistical information documenting disparities. For example, it presented a table showing that at schools with upward of 90 percent students of color, a quarter of the teaching staff was noncredentialed. This compared with about 4 percent for schools with less than 10 percent students of color. The same inverse relationship was evident in schools serving children from poor families.

The lawsuit argued that these conditions not only violate the California Constitution, they also constitute racial discrimination under Title VI of the 1964 Civil Rights Act and violate Education Code Section 51004. The latter states that it is the policy of California to provide every student, without regard to race, creed, color, national origin, sex, or economic status, an educational opportunity sufficient to enable the student to secure a job.

Plaintiffs' expert witnesses maintained that test-based accountability is a cheap, but not necessarily effective, way of addressing school quality. A marketplace approach placing responsibility to improve on schools whose students do not do well on state tests and relying on parents to search out better schooling for their children is misguided, they asserted, because it penalizes schools for lack of adequate resources. Rather than focus solely on outputs, these experts maintained that the state must assure that the quality of facilities, textbooks, and teachers is sufficient to enable students in all schools to reach levels of proficiency. This means a funding system that recognizes that some schools will need disproportionately greater state-guaranteed funding than others, based on student needs. Under an adequacy system, districts that already meet the adequacy standard would be free to spend more, assuming they have the discretion to do so and that voters agree.

The problem with adequacy, however, is that it is hard to define. If set too low, then adequacy begins to look like the discredited minimum foundation programs that triggered the first round of school finance litigation. One rather crude measure is to assume that adequacy is the national average spent on education. A 2004 study considered how many students in each state are funded at or above this figure, finding that more than 75 percent of California's students attended schools with fewer resources than the national average ("Count Me In," *Education Week*, January 8, 2004). The difficulty of identifying the standards necessary to determine educational adequacy was the central thrust of the reply brief filed by the state defendants in the *Williams* litigation. The state argued that the plaintiffs had not specified what the minimal standards for teachers, textbooks, and facilities are under the California Constitution and how the state has fallen short.

Commentators generally agree that once school facilities are made safe and accommodating, simply spending more money in low-performing schools by itself is no guarantee of improved student outcomes.[3] As noted at the start of this chapter, the key concern is *how* the money is spent. It also is important to make sure that the money finds its way through the district and school bureaucracy to reach targeted students. But first, the factors that directly improve student achievement must be identified and then the extent of their influence determined. Funding would be directed to those factors that are most positively correlated with student outcomes. This asks a lot of social science research, and concurrence among experts is likely to

---

[3]For a detailed exploration of the issues involved in the debate over equity versus adequacy, see Rob Reich (2007), *"Equality and Adequacy in the State's Provision of Education: Mapping the Conceptual Landscape."* This paper is one of over twenty completed for a comprehensive study of school finance and governance issues in California. All can be found on the website of the Institute for Research on Education Law and Practice at Stanford University. Go to www.stanford.edu/group/irepp and click on the "Getting Down to Facts" link.

be elusive. Consider teacher quality. Is it measured by the possession of a state teaching credential or a subject-matter degree? From a state university or a virtual university? By years of experience, the accumulation of continuing education credits, glowing evaluations from administrators, or high student scores on state assessments? Is research methodology sufficiently sophisticated to separate one from the other and to control for other factors that positively influence student learning? If high-quality teaching is an art, then can it be taught to the less gifted? However defined, would the investment in teacher preparation be better spent in some other way, such as Web-based classes or vouchers for parents?

Additionally, some factors that are positively correlated with student performance may only be minimally affected by how schools are funded. For example, spending more money on the education of low-income students in racially isolated schools does not address the positive impact on learning and socialization of student bodies that are integrated by both race and class. Nor does it influence parenting skills.

Research on teaching and learning is inexact, and politics plays a major role in the determination of standards and assessment. Given that education is a fundamental right under the California Constitution and measured against constitutional provisions requiring a general diffusion of knowledge and equal protection of the laws, how a school finance system built on the concept of educational adequacy will fare in court is open to question. Late in the summer of 2004, the parties in the *Williams* litigation agreed to settle the case rather than engage in a long and expensive court battle. The settlement affected more than 1 million students across the state in schools that rank in the bottom 30 percent on state tests. Most of the money is to be spent on instructional materials and facilities improvement.

Despite the new money resulting from the *Williams* settlement, the California Teachers Association and other educator organizations criticized the governor's failure to restore $2 billion taken from Proposition 98 when it was suspended by the legislature to deal with a budget shortfall in 2005 on the promise that the funding would be restored. These organizations joined the State Superintendent of Public Instruction (SPI) in a lawsuit to force the governor to pay back the money plus the increase in school funding that would have accrued to public education if Prop 98 had remained in effect—a total of over $3 billion. The lawsuit was dropped when the governor agreed to restore the money by adding $2 billion to Prop 98 base funding for 2006 and an additional $3 billion in "settle-up" funds through 2013. The funding is committed to low-performing schools ranking in the bottom 1 and 2 of the state's Academic Performance Index (API) categories and is administered in accord with the Quality Education Investment Act (QEIA) (Educ. Code § 52055.700 and following sections). Under QEIA, school districts and charter authorizers with low-performing schools may apply for supplemental funding that is to be used in the implementation of their Single Plan for Student Achievement, a requirement necessary to receive funding from a number of categorical programs. Districts and charter school authorizers must monitor each school's compliance with the terms of the act and insure that principals are to have exemplary qualifications and experience. The California Department of Education is required to prepare periodic progress reports on QEIA to the governor and legislature, with a final report due at the start of 2014.

In recent years, the state's top political leaders have acknowledged the need for fundamental school finance reform. In 2005, Governor Schwarzenegger established the Governor's Advisory Committee on Education Excellence. Together with legislative leaders, the Advisory Committee requested a comprehensive study of school finance and governance. The study, entitled "Getting Down to Facts," was released in the spring of 2007. Composed of twenty-two reports by an array of researchers from thirty-two institutions across the country and orchestrated by the Institute for Research on Educational Policy and Practice at Stanford University, "Getting Down to Facts" provided a critical look into the school finance and governance systems of California's public education system. However, the return of hard times in 2008 drew attention away from systemic reform. While few support the current Byzantine system of California school finance, developing a consensus as to when and how it should be reformulated has been and will continue to be no easy task.

SUMMARY

The lack of a strong positive correlation between money and student outcomes is one reason the U.S. Supreme Court has refused to mandate reform. The California Supreme Court has expressed no such inhibitions. In 1971, the California high court struck a blow for school finance reform by ruling in *Serrano v. Priest* that the great disparities in per-pupil funding in districts across the state caused by excessive reliance on the local property tax were unconstitutional. Simply put, property-rich districts could spend more at lower tax rates than could property-poor districts, and this amounted to a violation of the equal protection clause of the Fourteenth Amendment. That decision was undermined by the U.S. Supreme Court's contrary decision in its 1973 *San Antonio Independent School District v. Rodriguez* decision. But the California Supreme Court ruled the same way in a 1976 installment of the *Serrano* case, this time based on provisions in the California Constitution.

Thereafter, state policymakers sought to revise the system to curtail funding disparities so that per-pupil expenditure among students varied only insignificantly across school districts. The idea was to institute what was then known as district power-equalizing: Excess revenues from the property taxes in rich districts would be siphoned off to raise spending levels in poor districts at a state-determined tax rate. This noble venture, however, was sidetracked by passage of several propositions, the most famous being Proposition 13 that limited the yield obtainable from local property taxes.

The *Serrano* decisions in combination with Proposition 13 resulted in a significant shift of school financing control to the state. And faced with limited resources, the state responded with various measures to secure equity in per-pupil spending. Pursuant to Proposition 98, enacted in 1988, public schools generally are guaranteed a basic percentage of the state's general tax revenues. School districts receive the bulk of their general-purpose funds through revenue limit funding consisting of a combination of state funds and local property tax revenues. They also receive categorical aid, which by its nature is not distributed equally across districts. While restrictions on the issuing of local school facility bonds have eased in recent years, voters in many districts are reluctant to pass them. The lack of sufficient funding to maintain school buildings has resulted in rapidly deteriorating facilities in many districts, especially those serving low-income students of color. California's per-pupil expenditures on public education have declined in relation to other states and now rank well below the national average.

Charter schools have budget problems as well, especially start-up charters that need facilities to operate and nonclassroom-based charters that receive less state funding than their classroom-based counterparts. Facilities costs have eased somewhat, since the state now requires traditional school districts to provide charter schools with facilities if they serve a certain number of in-district students. The charter school funding process also has been simplified by the adoption of a block grant system. How the block grants reach the schools has some impact on the schools' ability to secure state and federal categorical aid. Charter schools have been able to tap into private funding more readily than traditional public schools have.

A class action lawsuit filed in 2002 threatened to bring state courts once again into the school finance fray. This time, the argument was that the state has shirked its responsibility of providing sufficient resources for all students to receive an adequate education. Rather than seeking equalization, reformers sought to tie funding to the needs of students. From this perspective the state should guarantee disproportionately greater funds for schools serving students who are difficult to educate, so that the students can succeed on state-mandated proficiency tests. In 2004 the parties reached a settlement that channels many millions of dollars to secure textbooks and other instructional material for these students, as well as upgrade the facilities they attend. But the greater questions remain: What are the standards of educational adequacy, and how should limited resources be spent in the best way to achieve them?

4 | UNIONS AND COLLECTIVE BARGAINING

Unionization has become a way of life in American public education. In 1959 Wisconsin was the only state with a public sector collective bargaining law. Today, most states either have such statutes or permit bargaining without them. Only a few prohibit collective bargaining outright. Eighty-five percent of teachers in American public schools are represented by unions. Like other states, California began with so-called meet and confer legislation that required management to confer with unions but did not permit the negotiation of a binding contract. California's meet and confer legislation gave way in 1975 to the Educational Employment Relations Act (EERA), also known as the Rhodda Act. With the legal framework in place, unionization progressed rapidly.

Today, nearly all of California's 1,056 school districts are unionized. Of these, the California Teachers Association (CTA), an affiliate of the National Education Association, represents teachers, counselors, and other professional employees in the majority of districts; its major competitor, the California Federation of Teachers (CFT), an AFL-CIO affiliate, represents professional employees in some 140 districts. Classified workers also are unionized in most districts. The California School Employees Association (CSEA) is the largest classified school employees union in the country, representing more than 220,000 public employees in California. CSEA is affiliated with the AFL-CIO. However, unions have not made as much headway in representing employees in charter schools, other than in those where the district continues to be the employer. About a third of the state's charter schools have unions. Unions are not a presence in California private schools. Further, key members of educational management in public schools are not eligible for unionization under EERA.

EERA, like other public sector collective bargaining laws, is modeled on the National Labor Relations Act (NLRA). NLRA provides full bargaining rights to employees in the private sector, including lay faculty members at several large Catholic school systems in the East. Briefly stated, full bargaining rights consist of:

- The right of employees to organize collectively if they so choose
- The right of employees to be represented by a single agent
- Bilateral (management-labor) determination of wages, hours, and other terms and conditions of employment
- The right to a binding contract between the employer and the union
- The right to strike or to negotiate binding arbitration of both grievance disputes (those arising under the contract) and interests disputes (those arising from the negotiation of a new contract)

By virtue of EERA, teacher unions in California have become major players in public education. They sponsor legislation, influence school board elections and state politics, negotiate collective agreements, and represent employees on the job. The collective bargaining contract they negotiate is a source of law that rivals school board policy in governing day-to-day school administration.

We begin by sketching the three stages of collective bargaining to get a sense of how the process works. Then we examine in detail how EERA shapes collective bargaining in California and what the implications are for both union members and school administrators. We conclude by exploring the challenges that school restructuring and reform pose for traditional teacher union bargaining.

THE THREE STAGES OF COLLECTIVE BARGAINING

Once a collective bargaining law conveys bargaining rights to employees, the collective bargaining process generally follows three stages. Table 4.1 depicts the three stages.

Unionization Stage

During the unionization stage, unions compete to gain representational rights of employees within the bargaining unit. The bargaining unit is determined by an overseeing public employment relations board, commonly known as PERB, based on a community of interest among employees (e.g., all teachers and professional employees, other than administrators, within a school district). Depending upon how much support a union has among employees in the bargaining unit, the employer

TABLE 4.1
Stages of Collective Bargaining

	Unionization stage	Contract negotiation stage	Contract administration stage

Character	1. Drive to organize unions
	
	2. Competition among unions
	
	3. Elections for certification and decertification
		1. Bilateral (employer/employee)
		
		2. Adversary ("we-they" mentality)
		   a. Least common denominator
		   b. Use of sanctions
			1. Parties meet and confer
			
			2. Grievance processing
			
			3. Adjudication by arbitrators

Results	1. One union selected as exclusive agent
	
	2. Contract negotiation begins
		1. Transcribed agreements with language specificity
		
		2. Differentiation of role relationships
		
		3. Contract expansion over time
			1. Rationalization of organizational processes
			   a. Define role relationships
			   b. Legitimize exercise of authority
			   c. Channel and resolve conflict
			
			2. Highlight contract inadequacies, pointing way for new rounds of negotiation

either may recognize the union as the exclusive bargaining agent or ask PERB to schedule an election. Evidence is usually required that at least 30 percent of the bargaining unit supports a union before an election can be scheduled. This is termed a "showing of interest." Once a union is chosen by a majority of employees in the bargaining unit, that union becomes the exclusive bargaining agent for all employees in the unit, even those who voted for a different union or no union.

This concept of "exclusivity" is central to collective bargaining. It gives the union great power at the bargaining table as the single spokesperson for all employees in the bargaining unit. Conversely, the individual employee loses the right to negotiate individually with the employer. With few exceptions, all relations with the employer must go through the union unless the union decides otherwise. In this sense, collective bargaining is about group rights, not individual rights, though the provisions of the contract serve to protect individual rights. It is the union that negotiates the collective bargaining contract, and it is the union that sees that it is enforced. Exclusivity also eliminates free riders—those who do not support the union but still receive the benefits the union negotiates. In return for exclusivity, the union has a legally enforceable fiduciary responsibility to represent all employees fairly, whether or not they are union members.

The unionization stage is very political as unions compete among themselves to represent employees within the bargaining unit and as the employer seeks to avoid having any union chosen by a majority of the employees. Once the majority of employees choose a union to represent them, the conflict shifts to the bargaining table.

Contract Negotiation Stage

Because there is only one union representing all employees in the bargaining unit at the bargaining table and only one employer, negotiations are bilateral. Whether blue collar or professional, union members are clear about one thing: Their interests at the bargaining table are divergent from those of their employer, at least during the first few rounds of negotiation before a collective bargaining relationship has been formed. The union takes on the character of a well-prepared interest group whose chief goal is to gain enough influence to increase economic and organizational benefits for its members. The bargaining sessions are likely to be adversarial in tone as each side alternately threatens, persuades, and modifies its position. In effect, the negotiation stage is best characterized as a power struggle between the employer and the union, conducted within the confines of a legal framework. As an interest group, the union employs the familiar tactic of asking for more than it expects to get. Management, on the other hand, is just as insistent on getting as much productivity from its employees as it can at the least cost. Thus, the parties often begin from the least common denominator and work toward an agreement. This is particularly true when the bargaining relationship is new and relationships between management and labor have yet to be formed. If bargaining is particularly adversarial, either or both sides may engage in verbal abuse, threaten to file an unfair labor charge against the other, or even employ sanctions. Depending upon what is possible under a collective bargaining statute, unions may threaten to go out on strike, while management may threaten to lock out or discharge union members. Both sides quickly learn the meaning of quid pro quo—never make a concession without exacting a price.

Generally, collective bargaining statutes specify what the parties can bargain about. Mandatory subjects of bargaining refer to those matters that the parties must bargain about if one side wishes to do so. Typically, economic matters such as wages and hours of employment fall into this category. Permissive subjects of bargaining are those that the parties can negotiate if both parties agree to do so. For public education, these might include involvement of teachers in the selection of administrators or in curriculum development. Prohibited subjects of bargaining are those that cannot be bargained even if both parties want to do so. Procedures for the termination of teachers that are set forth in a state statute might fall into this latter category. When there is disagreement about whether a particular subject is bargainable, PERB and perhaps the judiciary will be called on to sort it out.

Eventually, the parties will reach agreement and sign a collective bargaining contract. The contract will have certain characteristics. First, most terms will be very explicit. Specificity of contract language assures that little ambiguity exists that could trigger interpretation disputes later on. The role of the union will be spelled out as it relates to involvement in school district operation. The same is true for delineating the role of management.

As time goes on, there is a tendency for collective bargaining contracts to expand. This is so for several reasons. First, despite efforts to be as explicit as possible, areas of ambiguity are certain to remain, in part because the parties chose to compromise on some issues in order to reach agreement. During the next go-round, the parties will seek to clarify the ambiguity. Second, the bargainers will anticipate as many conflict situations as possible and include contingency mechanisms for their resolution. Third, new legislation may provide topics for negotiation (e.g., benefits resulting from the enactment of the federal Family Medical Leave Act). The union can never rest on its laurels. To justify its existence and the cost of union dues, it must continue to win benefits for its members.

In addition to economic benefits, the union is equally concerned about working conditions and will strive to negotiate matters that fall within the permissive area of bargaining. This is particularly true of unions representing professional employees. The union might say, for example, that development and implementation of a new middle school curriculum, while a permissive subject of bargaining, will affect the preparation time of teachers, a mandatory subject of bargaining. To avoid having to build more preparation time into the contract, school board negotiators may decide to give teachers greater say in curriculum development. In these ways, the scope of bargaining expands, and contracts can become quite lengthy as a result. The days of the "shirt pocket contract," which members could readily carry around and refer to when needed, are over in most districts.

Contract Administration Stage

In contrast to the political character of the unionization and contract negotiation stages, the contract administration stage is more impersonal and bureaucratic. Similar to a government constitution, the agreement regulates the diverse activities of individuals with conflicting interests within the same organizational setting. It rationalizes organizational functioning through a set of mutually acceptable work rules that define the respective roles of the employer, the employees, and the union. It legitimizes the exercise of management authority. It fosters communication between the union and management through periodic deliberative sessions regarding administration of the contract. And equally important, the grievance provisions, including arbitration by a neutral party, are a channel through which disputes may be resolved. If conflict is a basic characteristic of life in an organization like a school, which depends upon many people to carry out its functions, then the collective bargaining agreement affords a means of controlling it. Inevitably, of course, contract inadequacies will surface during the years the contract is in force. These, coupled with changing conditions, will become the focus of the next round of negotiations.

The presence of collective bargaining is no assurance that employees will not be too weak to check absolute, arbitrary administrative power. Or conversely, there is no guarantee that management can preserve enough authority to direct the organization and prevent worker demands from becoming an impregnable wall against needed innovative change. At best, collective bargaining represents a workable balance between management prerogative and membership rights that is not externally imposed but decided by the parties themselves.

Having sketched out the collective bargaining process, we turn now to examine how collective bargaining in California operates under the terms of EERA and what the implications are for both administrators and teachers.

COLLECTIVE BARGAINING UNDER THE EDUCATIONAL EMPLOYMENT RELATIONS ACT (EERA)

Before the enactment of EERA in 1975, unions had been around for many years in California. In fact, CTA and CFT date back to 1863 and 1919, respectively. CSEA was started in 1927. However, the absence of a collective bargaining law kept them from having much leverage with school districts. Until 1961, school districts could unilaterally determine working conditions. That year, the California Legislature became one of the first states to move toward public sector collective bargaining by enacting the Brown Act, which gave public employees the right to join or not join employee organizations and recognized the right of these organizations to meet with employers to discuss working conditions. However, the school board retained the prerogative to make the final decisions, and there was no process for adjudicating disputes over the application of the Brown Act. In 1965, the Winton Act was passed for public school employees, thus splitting them away from California public employees in general. The latter were accorded collective bargaining rights with enactment of the Meyers-Milias-Brown Act in 1968.

The Winton Act continued the meet and confer provisions of the Brown Act for school employees, but added measures establishing dispute resolutions mechanisms such as fact-finding and mediation. While the Winton Act gave teacher unions more influence, it did not accord them full bargaining rights. That came with the enactment of EERA ten years later. Because unions already were on the scene, unionization moved quickly after EERA was passed.

EERA does not impose collective bargaining on school districts. It leaves the decision to form and join a union to employees and the process of negotiating a contract to the union and the school district. But it does provide the legal framework within which collective bargaining occurs. This lengthy and detailed statute can be found in California Government Code Sections 3540–3549. Its purpose is to promote

> the improvement of personnel management and employer-employee relations within the public school system of the State of California by providing a uniform basis for recognizing the right of public school employees to join organizations of their own choosing, to be represented by the organizations in their professional and employment relationships with public school employees, to select one employee organization as the exclusive representative of the employees in an appropriate unit, and to afford certificated employees a voice in the formulation of educational policy. (Govt. Code § 3540)

The statute sets forth a number of unfair, or prohibited, labor practices for both public school employers and employee organizations. It is unlawful for both employers and unions to penalize employees for exercising their rights under EERA, to refuse to meet and negotiate in good faith, and to refuse to participate in efforts to resolve differences when negotiations break down. EERA also requires good-faith negotiations over mandatory subjects of bargaining before employers can impose a change unilaterally. In addition, employers are prohibited from denying unions their rights under EERA and from seeking to dominate or interfere with unions by such actions as contributing financial support or preferring one union to another.

Government Code Section 3540 specifies that EERA is not to supersede the provisions of the California Education Code and the rules and regulations of public school employers relating to tenure or a merit or civil service system. Thus, the California Supreme Court has ruled that a teacher union cannot negotiate due process rights for the nonextension of probationary teacher contracts. Other than timely notice, the Education Code provides no due process rights to probationary teachers in the context of a contract nonextension. As the court observed in a 1996 decision:

> the Legislature has determined that the due process protection enjoyed by permanent certified employees should not apply to probationary employees, and that the state's interest in discharging unsuitable teachers in the first two years of employment outweighs any due process rights sought by these teachers. (*Board of Education of the Round Valley Unified School District v. Round Valley Teachers Association*, p. 125)

However, EERA does permit a union to negotiate the layoff of probationary employees, as well as employee discipline (Govt. Code § 3543.2).

The Role of the Public Employment Relations Board (PERB)

EERA is administered by an independent state agency known as the Public Employment Relations Board (PERB), comprised of five members appointed by the governor with the advice and consent of the senate. The governor also appoints the chairperson. PERB selects an executive director, who in turn appoints a staff and general legal counsel. PERB's principal functions are to decide appropriate bargaining units; conduct representation elections and certify the results; determine what is within the scope of negotiations and of meeting and conferring; investigate unfair labor practice claims; establish lists of mediators, arbitrators, and fact finders; and undertake other actions necessary to implement EERA. To this end, it has developed a set of administrative regulations that can be found in Title 8 of the California Code of Regulations beginning with Section 31001. The regulations are included as well on the PERB website, www.perb.ca.gov.

As a quasi-judicial administrative entity, PERB has established a body of labor law through the hundreds of decisions it and its administrative law judges have handed down over the years. A summary can be found on the PERB website. PERB enforces its orders and decisions by court action, where its judgments are accorded substantial deference by judges. In 1988 the California Supreme Court observed that "the PERB's interpretation will generally be followed unless it is clearly erroneous" (*Banning Teachers Association v. Public Employment Relations Board*, p. 674).

Covered Employees and Schools

EERA governs public school employers and public school employees. It defines "public school employee" as any person employed by any public school employer except persons elected by popular vote (e.g., school board members), persons appointed by the governor, management employees, and confidential employees. Management employees are those who have significant responsibilities for formulating and administering district policies. These employees are designated by the public school employer subject to review by PERB. Confidential employees are those who have access or possession of information relating to employer-employee relations.

Management and confidential employees are permitted to represent themselves individually in employment matters with the school district or through an organization of similar employees. However, the organization cannot meet and negotiate with the governing board. The statute specifically prohibits the organization from negotiating any benefit or compensation for these employees. As we noted in Chapter 1, school principals as members of management essentially serve at the discretion of the school district. Supervisory employees, meaning those given the authority to exercise independent judgment to hire, transfer, suspend, lay off, recall, promote, discharge, assign, reward, or discipline other employees, are permitted to engage in bargaining, providing the bargaining unit includes all supervisory employees employed by the district and does not include employees they supervise.

"Public school employer" is defined by the act as the governing board of a school district, a school district itself, a county board of education, a county superintendent of schools, or a charter school that has declared itself and not the district that granted the charter to be the public employer (Govt. Code § 3540.1 (k)).

Deciding on the Appropriate Bargaining Unit and Choosing a Representative

EERA permits one organization to represent all employees within the bargaining unit on matters specified in the statute. If there is a conflict over what the bargaining unit should be, PERB makes the determination based on "the community interest between and among the employees and their established practices" (Govt. Code § 3545 (a)). A negotiating unit that includes classroom teachers is not considered an appropriate unit unless it includes all classroom teachers employed by the school district. A negotiating unit of supervisory employees is not deemed appropriate unless it includes all supervisory employees employed by the district. However, supervisory employees cannot be included in the same unit with persons that they supervise, nor can classified and certificated employees be included in the same unit, because their interests are different.

If an employee organization can satisfy a public school employer that it represents the majority of all employees in an appropriate bargaining unit, the employer must recognize the organization as the exclusive bargaining agent unless the employer doubts the appropriateness of the unit. The employee organization is required to post its request for recognition on employee bulletin boards in all of the district's facilities, as well as to submit proof of its majority support claim to PERB for verification. EERA grants employee organizations the right of access to employees at reasonable times and the right to use institutional bulletin boards, mailboxes, and other means of communication subject to reasonable regulation. Verification of union support is established through review of dues deduction authorizations, notarized membership lists, or signed petitions. The employer does not have to recognize the union as the exclusive representative if another employee organization contests the bargaining unit or submits—within fifteen days of the first organization's posting—a competing claim that is supported by at least 30 percent of the members of the unit. In the latter scenario, PERB schedules an election. No election can be held if a collective bargaining agreement already is in existence unless the request for recognition by another union is filed in accord with time lines set forth in EERA. No election can be scheduled if the employer has recognized another employee organization as the exclusive bargaining agent within the past year.

If by January 1 of any school year, no employee organization has established majority support in the bargaining unit, a majority of employees may submit a petition to the public school employer asking for an election to be conducted by PERB. An employee need not be a member of an employee organization to sign the petition. Any employee organization that establishes support from at least 30 percent of the members of the bargaining unit may appear on the ballot.

As the overseeing agency, PERB has the authority to investigate and resolve matters submitted to it by petition involving the appropriateness of a proposed bargaining unit and recognition or withdrawal of recognition of a bargaining agent. If PERB finds that a question of representation exists, it will order an election by secret ballot and certify the results. Time lines and procedures are specified in the statute. Ballots must include "no representation" as one of the options. Each voter is entitled to choose only one option. If no choice on the ballot receives a majority, then a runoff election is conducted between the two highest contenders. Once an employee organization is selected as the exclusive representative, it has a duty to "fairly represent each and every employee in the appropriate unit" (Govt. Code § 3544.9).

Scope of Bargaining

While the Winton Act permitted education unions to meet and confer over a wide range of items, it did not require management to negotiate and reach agreement over any of them. EERA increases the power of unions by specifying that certain matters are mandatory subjects of bargaining and according representatives of certificated employees the right to consult on certain matters. All other matters are left to the discretion of the public school employer. Within certain limits, the parties are free to expand the scope of consultation and negotiation should they desire. An item that is not a mandatory subject of bargaining can trigger a duty to bargain if it impacts a matter that is within the scope of bargaining. Table 4.2 provides an overview of the categories discussed in this section.

TABLE 4.2

Key Mandatory, Consultative, and Nonnegotiable Topics under EERA

Mandatory bargaining	Mandatory consulting	Management prerogative
Wages Hours Terms and Conditions of Employment • Health and welfare benefits • Leave, transfer, and reassignment policies • Safety conditions • Class size • Evaluation procedures • Organizational security agreements • Grievance procedures • Layoff of probationary certificated employees • Alternative compensation or benefits if adversely affected by pension limitations Causes and procedures for disciplinary action other than dismissal of certificated employees* Procedures and layoff of certificated employees for lack of funds* Payment of additional compensation based on criteria other than years of training and experience* Salary schedule based on criteria other than years of training and experience* Other topics (per PERB decision) if: • Logically and reasonably related to wages, hours, and an enumerated term and condition of employment • Conflict likely to occur if not negotiated • Will not significantly undercut management prerogative	Representatives of certificated employees have the right to consult on the following: • Definition of educational objectives • Determination of course and curriculum content • Selection of textbooks Note: The parties may agree to consult on other matters.	All matters not specifically enumerated are reserved to the public school employer and may not be a subject of meeting and negotiating unless the employer and union agree otherwise and the matter is not preempted by the Education Code. EERA does not limit the right of the public school employer to consult with any employees or employee organization on any matter outside the scope of representation.

*If no agreement, provisions of Education Code control.

Note: Matters that are not themselves mandatory topics may trigger a duty to bargain if they impact an item that is within the scope of bargaining.

As indicated in the table, mandatory topics of bargaining encompass matters relating to wages, hours, and other terms and conditions of employment. Government Code Section 3543.2 delineates specific topics that fall within terms and conditions of employment, including health and welfare benefits; leave, transfer, and reassignment policies; safety conditions; class size; evaluation procedures; organizational security arrangements (to be discussed later in this chapter); grievance processing procedures; layoff of probationary certificated employees; and alternative compensation or benefits for employees adversely affected by pension limitations.

In an important decision, the California Supreme Court has ruled that subjects for mandatory bargaining may range beyond those specifically listed in EERA but may not supersede provisions of the Education Code. The case involved unfair labor charges filed with PERB against two school districts for their refusal to bargain in good faith on selected topics. The San Mateo City School District refused to bargain over instructional duty and preparation time, and the effects of unilaterally making changes in the length of the instructional day. The Healdsburg Union School District refused to negotiate a list of items presented to it by the California School Employees Association. When the unions filed unfair labor practice charges against the districts, the matter came before PERB. The school districts argued that because the matters were not specifically listed in the statute as topics of negotiation, they did not have to be bargained. PERB disagreed with the school districts' position, ruling that a subject is negotiable even if not specifically enumerated in the statute. PERB developed the following three-part test to determine which topics are mandatory topics of bargaining.

1. The subject is logically and reasonably related to hours, wages, or an enumerated term and condition of employment;

2. The subject is of such concern to both management and employees that conflict is likely to occur and the mediatory influence of collective negotiations is the appropriate means of resolving the conflict;

3. The employer's obligation to negotiate would not significantly abridge its freedom to exercise those managerial prerogatives (including matters of fundamental policy) essential to the achievement of the district's mission.

Using an earlier version of this test, PERB had ruled that all contested items in the San Mateo case and some items in the Healdsburg case were negotiable. The California Supreme Court endorsed use of the test, noting that the legislature had not exclusively listed all negotiable items in the statute. Rather, by using terms such as "matters relating to," it left such a determination to PERB's expertise. The high court did note that while explicit provisions of the Education Code such as layoff of classified employees may not be bargained, they may be added to a collective bargaining agreement. Doing so, wrote the court, "would not supercede the relevant part of the Education Code, but would strengthen it" (*San Mateo City School District v. Public Employment Relations Board*, 1983, p. 811).

Upon request of either party, EERA also includes within the scope of bargaining causes and procedures for disciplinary action other than dismissal for certificated employees, including suspension of pay for up to fifteen days, procedures for the layoff of certificated employees for lack of funds, payment of additional compensation based on criteria other than years of training and experience, and a salary schedule based on criteria other than uniform allowance for years of training and experience. If no mutual agreement is reached, then the provisions of the Education Code control. These are, respectively, Sections 44944 (disciplinary action), 44955 (layoff), and 45028 (uniform salary schedule).

The provision dealing with additional compensation based on criteria other than years of experience puts a union in the difficult position of negotiating provisions that may benefit some bargaining unit members but not others. The matter was an issue in a 2002 California court of appeal ruling involving a one-time retroactive payment of 3 percent of base salary to teachers who returned to work or who had retired at the end of the previous year, but not to eight teachers who had resigned or left. Though the payments complied with the terms of a mediated settlement package reached with the teachers union, the agreement was negotiated with difficulty and involved the work of a mediator. The union subsequently sued the school district, contending that the payment was not additional compensation but rather a uniform salary payment under Education Code Section 45028 that should have been given to all teachers. The section provides that, except for those holding administrator or supervisor credentials, each person employed in a certificated position is to be classified on a salary schedule based on uniform allowance for years of training and years of experience unless the union and employer agree otherwise.

The questions for the court in this case were whether the one-time payment to all teachers except those who resigned or left after the school year could be characterized as a salary payment or as additional compensation. If additional compensation, was it based on criteria other than years of training and experience? The court answered yes to both. As a one-time payment, the 3 percent emolument was additional compensation. And the criterion upon which it was based was whether or not the teachers returned to work for the 1998–1999 school year or had retired at the end of the previous year. The teachers in question had resigned or left, so they did not meet the criterion. Thus, the one-time payment provision in the contract was justified as an incentive payment and did not violate the uniform pay provisions of Education Code Section 45028 (*California Teachers Association v. Governing Board of the Hilmar Unified School District*).

Such was not the case with an effort by the Stockton Unified School District and its teacher union to catch up with the salary levels of neighboring school districts by accelerating teacher pay though compression of steps on the salary schedule. While this benefited teachers on the lower levels of the schedule, it worked the reverse on teachers who were on the eliminated steps. These teachers were shifted to lower steps and thus had to work longer to attain higher salaries. They filed suit, arguing that the compressed salary schedule violated the uniformity requirement. Both the trial court and the appellate court agreed, noting the absence of new criteria such as teaching in an economically depressed area or teaching special needs students to justify the differential treatment. The compressed salary schedule could remain in place, but the district was required to adjust the affected teacher salaries so that the uniformity requirement was met (*Adair v. Stockton Unified School District*, 2008).

As noted earlier, the Winton Act's meet and confer approach was carried over to EERA in the form of mandatory topics for consultation between the union and the public school employer. Consultation means that the parties can talk about the topics but are not required to bargain over them unless both parties agree to do so. Government Code Section 3543.2 (a) specifies that the exclusive representative of certificated employees "has the right to consult on the definition of educational objectives, the determination of the content of courses and curriculum, and the selection of textbooks to the extent such matters are within the discretion of the public school employer under law." Several of these matters, such as curriculum content, are significantly influenced by the Education Code and implementing regulations, thus leaving less discretion to the employer. While the substance of these matters is not bargainable, PERB has ruled that the procedures by which consultation takes place are subject to negotiation.

Beyond bargainable and consultative topics are those reserved to the public school employer. Government Code Section 3543.2 (b) states that "All matters not specifically enumerated are reserved to the public school employer and may not be a subject of meeting and negotiating." At the same time, in a 1983 decision, PERB noted that in enacting EERA, the legislature did not intend to deny employees without an exclusive representative the opportunity to speak to their employers individually or through a nonexclusive representative about matters affecting employment, a right that they had under the predecessor Winton Act. Thus, in this situation, the employer has an obligation to provide reasonable notice and a time to meet and discuss fringe benefits and other matters of fundamental concern to the employment relationship before making a final decision (*Service Employees Industrial Union v. Los Angeles Unified School District*). Even when there is an exclusive representative, the statute provides that "nothing herein may be construed to limit the right of the public school employer to consult with any employees or employee organization on any matter outside the scope of representation" (Govt. Code § 3543.2 (a)). School districts and individual schools have any number of advisory committees and channels of communication for receiving information and commentary about matters other than those governed by EERA.

Nothing precludes the union and employer from extending the scope of bargaining and consultation should they wish to do so. However, PERB has ruled that when a school district agrees to bargain over a permissive topic of bargaining, the topic then does not become a mandatory topic. In other words, a district can withdraw the topic from bargaining during negotiations or, if already in a contract, can refuse to bargain over it in future negotiations (*Poway Federation of Teachers v. Poway Unified School District*, 1988). A case in point is a dispute over implementing a no-smoking policy in the Eureka City School District in accordance with Education Code Section 48901. That section requires school districts to forbid students from smoking and using nicotine products at school, at school-sponsored activities, or while under the supervision of school employees. The dispute centered on whether the district could impose the policy on teachers as well as students. PERB decided that the smoking policy was a permissive topic of bargaining, meaning that the parties could bargain over it if they wished. Once agreement is reached concerning a permissive subject, then it becomes part of the agreement. In this case, the contract contained a provision permitting smoking by teachers in designated areas. The new no-smoking policy for teachers would go into effect at expiration of the agreement. The union contended that the matter had become a mandatory topic of bargaining during the next round of negotiations because it was already in the contract. But PERB followed the *Poway* decision and rejected the contention. Either the district or the employee organization can indicate prior to the expiration of the agreement that it does not intend to bargain over a nonmandatory topic. Thus, there was no violation of EERA when the district chose to adopt the tobacco-free policy at the expiration of the agreement as a matter of management prerogative (*Eureka Teachers Association v. Eureka City School District*, 1992).

As noted earlier, charter schools now fall within the ambit of EERA. As amended in 1999, Education Code Section 47611.5 specifies that the school's charter must indicate whether it is to be the exclusive public school employer for purposes of collective bargaining if the school's employees opt to unionize. If the charter school is not so designated, then the school district where the charter school is located becomes the employer for this purpose. At the same time, the section provides that the approval or denial of a charter petition by a charter authorizer is not controlled by collective bargaining agreements, nor is it subject to review or regulation by PERB. To date, unions have made limited headway in organizing charter school employees, though in some districts the conversion of a traditional public school to a charter school has continued employee union representation.

Following the 1999 amendment to the charter school law, conflict arose in a few districts over the employer designation issue. For example, controversy arose in the Ravenswood City School District over termination of several teacher contracts by the Edison Brentwood Academy, a charter school operating in the district. The teacher's union brought an unfair labor practice charge against the Ravenswood district, contending that the teachers were terminated for engaging in union activities and citing language in the collective bargaining contract that the district was the employer. The district claimed that the charter school was the employer and should face the charges. In compliance with the statute, Edison Brentwood Academy's principal had sent out a letter confirming that it, and not the district, was the employer. The teacher union argued that this declaration did not change the fact that the district had authority over personnel matters at the school. The PERB administrative law judge observed that while the collective bargaining agreement between the teacher union and the Ravenswood district did have provisions setting terms and conditions for the employment of charter schoolteachers, the charter stipulated that these provisions did not apply if they were in conflict with the design and operation of the school. Thus, the charter school had the unilateral discretion to make personnel decisions about its teachers. This being so, the charter school was the employer and was the proper entity to face the unfair labor charge (*Ravenswood Teachers Association v. Ravenswood City School District,* 2001).

Complicating the matter in the Ravenswood case was the fact that the charter school was operated by Edison Schools. While the management agreement between the charter school and Edison recognized that the company and the Ravenswood School District would be involved in teacher selection and evaluation, that teachers remained public employees, and that the district would provide due process protections in the event of contract teacher termination, the administrative law judge ruled that the charter between the district and the charter school took precedence. Conflict of this type is not unusual when multiple agreements are involved—here, a collective bargaining contract between the union and the school district with some provisions applying to the charter school, a charter document between the district and the charter school, and a management agreement between the charter school and the private educational management organization.

The 1999 amendment to the charter school law states that if the charter or the charter school does not specify that the school will comply with statutes and regulations governing tenure or a merit or civil service system, then the discipline and dismissal of teachers at that charter school become mandatory topics of bargaining. This depends on who is the employer, the terms of the charter, and whether the teachers at the school have opted to unionize. At the same time, the statute directs PERB to take into account the Charter Schools Act when deciding cases coming before it involving these institutions, suggesting that the innovative character of charter schools should be safeguarded whenever possible.

Contract Negotiation

EERA specifies that negotiations are to begin well in advance of adoption of the final budget for the ensuing school year. This allows time for an agreement to be reached should negotiations become prolonged or even break down. Negotiations involving public schools significantly implicate the public. Thus, EERA requires that all initial proposals of the parties are to be presented at a public meeting and become public records. Negotiating cannot begin until the public has had a reasonable time to become familiar with the proposals and express its views at a governing board meeting. Though negotiation sessions are not open to the public, new subjects arising in the course of negotiation must be made public within twenty-four hours, and the public must be informed of any votes cast upon the subject by the governing board within the same time period. Prior to approval of the written agreement, the provisions and implementation costs are to be presented at a public meeting.

The assumption is that if the negotiating stance of the governing board and costs associated with its position are not supported by the public, board members will feel the pressure and conform to public wishes. However, as a powerful interest group, the union sometimes can have significant influence on school board elections, especially when voter turnout is small. If school board members realize that union members constitute a good portion of their backers, they may be particularly attentive to union interests. And while school board members are always concerned about public opinion, unions are adept at influencing it. As portrayed in Figure 4.1, the union's presence thus can be felt on *both* sides of the bargaining table. This is less true of charter schools whose governing board is the employer, because the members of charter school governing boards are not elected but gain their status through the granting of the charter. However, if the school district re-

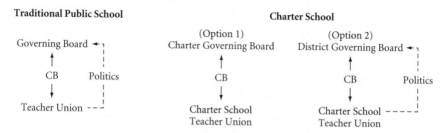

Figure 4.1 Teacher Contract Negotiation in California Public Schools

mains the employer of charter school employees and charter school employees agree to unionize, the union can exert any political influence it has on the governing board. Figure 4.1 illustrates these lines of union influence.

In many districts with a long history of amicable relations between the union and the governing board, collective bargaining is not extremely adversarial, and agreement is quickly reached. In other situations, however, strained relations in combination with limited resources lead to conflict at the bargaining table over key issues such as salary and benefits. During the negotiation process, the parties may reach impasse, meaning that they have been unable to reach agreement on a contested item of bargaining. EERA defines "impasse" to mean that the "differences in positions are so substantial or prolonged that future meetings would be futile." If PERB agrees that impasse is evident, several things can happen, as outlined in Figure 4.2. Note that a district's locking out or discharging teachers is not among them. Nor can a union resort to a strike except in rare circumstances, as described later in the chapter. The reason is that public schooling is a constitutional right under the California Constitution and its continuation takes precedence over the interests of the governing board and the union.

First, PERB can appoint a mediator to help the parties reach agreement. The parties also can develop their own mediation process. But impasse can apply only to mandatory bargaining items. This is so because there is no obligation to negotiate a consultative or permissive topic. Some years ago PERB declared that the South Bay Union School District had committed an unfair labor practice by declaring impasse over negotiating a provision restricting the union's right to file grievances in its own name. The contract eventually was signed without the provision. The district insisted that the matter was a mandatory topic of bargaining because it related to negotiating a grievance system. The union argued that because it has a statutory right to file grievances, the district could not force it to bargain over the matter to the point of impasse. The district sought to overturn the PERB ruling against

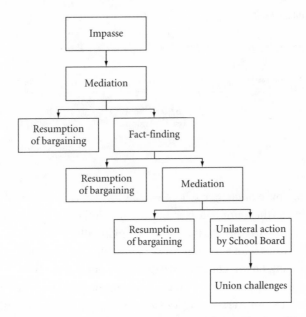

Figure 4.2 Resolving Impasse over Negotiating Mandatory Topics of Bargaining under EERA

it without success. Noting its obligation to defer to the judgment of PERB, the California court of appeal cited several PERB decisions holding that a union has a statutory right to file a grievance in its own name. Thus, the district's declaration of an impasse over this nonmandatory bargaining topic constituted bad-faith bargaining (*South Bay Union School District v. Public Employment Relations Board,* 1991). EERA was amended in 2000 to permit employees to file grievances in their own name without the involvement of the union as long as the resolution is reached prior to arbitration and is not inconsistent with the terms of the collective bargaining agreement. However, the public school employer may not agree to a resolution of the grievance until the union has received a copy and has had a chance to file a response (Govt. Code § 3543 (b)).

Government Code Section 3548 provides that a mediator can meet with the parties or their representatives either jointly or separately and take whatever steps the mediator thinks advisable to help the parties over the impasse. Like negotiation sessions, meetings held by the mediator with either or both parties are not open to the public. If the mediator is not successful within fifteen days after appointment, then either party may request that their differences be submitted to a three-person fact-finding panel. Each party selects a person to serve on the panel, with the chairperson selected either by PERB or by mutual agreement of the parties. Unless the parties agree, the chairperson cannot be the same person who served as mediator. Within the time frames specified in the statute, the fact-finding panel meets with the parties, holds hearings, and conducts investigations. These activities take place in private. The panel has the power to compel persons to attend, give testimony, and produce evidence. Following a set of criteria spelled out in the statute, the panel sets forth its findings and settlement recommendations. These are advisory only and are submitted to the parties before being released to the public. The mediator previously appointed can resume mediation based on the findings of fact and recommendations for settlement. Throughout this period, the parties have an obligation to continue to seek resolution of their differences, and when impasse is broken, to resume bargaining in good faith.

Section 3549 of the act permits the school district to take unilateral action to implement the last offer the union has rejected. When can this occur? A California court of appeal ruled in 1983 that a school district can impose unilateral changes in employment conditions within the scope of bargaining only after the impasse procedures as just described have been completed. The court agreed with PERB that allowing the employer to do so prior to this time would generate conflict, undercut effective employee representation, and diminish the bilateral duty to negotiate (*Moreno Valley Unified School District v. Public Employment Relations Board*). Even after fact-finding, however, if one party makes concessions, the duty to bargain resumes. Thus, the employer cannot simply impose the last best offer rejected by the union without returning to the bargaining table. Further, when a unilateral change is implemented, it must be reasonably consistent with the last offer (*Public Employment Relations Board v. Modesto City Schools District*, 1982).

Of course, even after post-impasse actions have been exhausted and the employer unilaterally implements changes in the terms and conditions of employment, the matter is not likely to end. Union challenges are likely on a variety of fronts, including going out on strike. The Educational Employment Relations Act (EERA) does not expressly approve a post-impasse right to strike. But neither does it prohibit that right. In 1979 the California Supreme Court discussed the matter in conjunction with a strike occurring in the San Diego Unified School District. Both parties filed unfair labor charges against each other. The school district obtained a judicial restraining order halting the strike. The parties then agreed to resume negotiations. A few days later, the trial judge filed contempt charges against the union and its president for violating the restraining order. Both were subsequently found guilty. The union and its president were fined and the latter sentenced to jail for a short time. They appealed, arguing that while Section 3549 does state that a provision of the Labor Code permitting strikes is inapplicable to public school employees, EERA does not itself prohibit strikes. The California high court did not rule directly on the question, because it found the district had sought the injunction without pursuing the steps EERA provides when the parties fail to reach agreement, including letting PERB seek the restraining order. While the court noted that the impasse procedures discussed earlier "almost certainly were included in EERA for the purpose of heading off strikes," it did not preclude strikes after the impasse procedures have been exhausted (*San Diego Teachers Association v. Superior Court*, p. 898). The court annulled the contempt order and penalties against the union and its president.

Taking its cue from the California Supreme Court's *San Diego* decision and a 1985 decision by the same court refusing to apply an automatic ban against strikes that do not impose an imminent danger to public health and safety (*County Sanitation District No. 2 v. Los Angeles County Employees Association, Local 600*), PERB subsequently developed a two-part test to determine whether a post-impasse strike constitutes an unfair labor practice. For such a strike to be an unfair labor practice, it must cause a total breakdown of basic education and be used to leverage gains at the bargaining table by holding education hostage (*Compton Unified School District v. Compton Education Association*, 1987). In *Compton*, teacher work stoppages coincided with failure to reach agreement on a contract and continued intermittently, lasting a total of sixteen days. The district was not able to replace most of the striking teachers. Over the four-month period when periodical work stoppages occurred, attendance was down 40 percent, reaching 70 percent when the strikes were occurring. Considerable disruption occurred in the administration building, interrupting a school board closed meeting and resulting in police action. The district asserted that strikers encouraged students to join the picket lines around the district's schools or sent them home when they arrived for school. Several fires of suspicious origin occurred in the district's schools. Viewing education as a fundamental right, the majority members of PERB found that a considerable number of the district's students received little or no meaningful education during this period. Based upon the facts and its lengthy analysis of the importance of education, PERB ruled that the strike constituted an unfair labor practice and sought a court order against it.

By contrast, PERB ruled the other way in an unfair labor practice claim filed by the Vallejo Unified School District against its teacher union over a two-day walkout occurring after impasse procedures had concluded (*Vallejo City Unified School District v. Vallejo Education Association*, 1993). Though only 100 teachers out of a normal day attendance of approximately 800 arrived for work, the district was able to replace all of them with substitutes. While student attendance was down by half during the strike, there was no evidence that attendance suffered beyond the week of the strike. Nor was there evidence that the strike caused a breakdown in negotiations, because neither side sought to continue negotiations during the time when the strike occurred.

It is important to note that PERB has not supported a union's right to strike either before or during impasse to achieve economic goals, because such a strike undermines the mandatory procedures set forth in EERA to end the impasse. For example, the Irvine Teachers Association resorted to several tactics to advance its cause in contract negotiations with the Irvine Unified School District in the mid-1980s. Included among the tactics was a work-to-rule job action and a one-day strike. The work-to-rule job action meant that the teachers refused to perform any discretionary duties beyond those specified in their contracts. The strike occurred on the first day of the beginning of the spring semester. Three-quarters of the 750 members of the bargaining unit participated in the work stoppage. It was conducted peacefully, with striking teachers spending most of the day engaged in informational picketing at their respective school sites. The PERB administrative law judge ruled that the work-to-rule job action was a lawful bargaining tactic, but the strike was not. The strike was unlawful because it was motivated not by an unfair labor practice engaged in by the school district, but solely by the teacher union's desire to advance its economic demands at the bargaining table. In effect the strike amounted to a refusal to negotiate contrary to the mandatory procedures set forth in EERA (*Irvine Unified School District v. Irvine Teachers Association, CTA/NEA*, 1987).

A few years later, PERB ruled that the post-impasse intermittent strike is impermissible under EERA. The decision involved a series of short work stoppages by teachers in the Fremont Unified School District in 1990 following an unsuccessful effort to reach agreement. Each of the strikes coincided with an impasse in negotiations and lasted no more than two days. The district filed an unfair labor practice charge against the union. PERB noted that the intermittent strike is an unfair pressure tactic because it enables employees to retain the benefits of working and striking at the same time. It also precludes the district from hiring long-term substitutes. Because it disrupts the delivery of education services and violates the duty to bargain in good faith, a post-impasse intermittent strike is both unprotected and unlawful (*Fremont Unified School District v. Fremont Unified District Teachers Association*).

Contract Administration

Once a contract has been signed and is in force for up to three years, its provisions must be followed in day-to-day school and district management. Usually, a joint contract administration committee is established to assist the parties in handling matters that arise in applying contract provisions such as access to district premises; use of association leave for association business; negotiating the master calendar; reviewing monthly class size reports; and developing a collaborative approach to achieving alignment of standards, curriculum, staff development, and student assessment.

Occasionally, disputes arise that cannot be resolved informally. To resolve these peacefully requires resort to the grievance and arbitration clause.

The grievance and arbitration system. A grievance system is a standard provision of a collective bargaining contract. It consists of a number of steps by which an individual employee can, with or without union support, seek a remedy for a violation of the contract. The first step normally involves bringing the matter to the attention of the employee's immediate supervisor. If no satisfactory adjustment is forthcoming, the employee and/or union may appeal to a higher level and so on through the grievance steps. If no agreement can be reached, the matter usually is referred to arbitration. EERA provides that a public school employer and exclusive representative may include in the agreement final and binding arbitration for disputes involving the interpretation, application, or violation of the agreement (Govt. Code § 3548.5). Even if the agreement does not include such an arbitration clause, both parties mutually may agree to submit a dispute to final arbitration in compliance with rules established by PERB. Compliance with an agreement to arbitrate is enforceable by court order. Once an arbitrator has made an award, the award is final and binding upon the parties. Subject to certain exceptions, it too is enforceable by court order. An arbitrator's award may be challenged in court only on limited grounds (Code of Civil Procedure § 1281 and following sections).

More than any others, the grievance and arbitration features of the collective bargaining contract give it its constitutive character. In the words of Justice William O. Douglas writing for the U.S. Supreme Court over forty years ago:

> the grievance machinery under a collective agreement is at the very heart of the system of industrial self-government. Arbitration is the means of solving the unforeseeable by molding a system of private law for all the problems which may arise and to provide for their solution in a way which will generally accord with the variant needs and desires of the parties. (*United Steelworkers of America v. Warrior and Gulf Navigation Company*, 1960, p. 581)

The role of the arbitrator. The arbitrator's role is particularly significant to the ongoing relationship between the employer and the union. Often, under pressure to reach agreement, negotiators will leave certain clauses relatively ambiguous simply to avoid further conflict. Naturally, the parties will interpret these clauses differently, each to its own advantage. Sooner or later the conflicting views will coalesce around a specific grievance. The resolution of the question will be up to the arbitrator, who legally has been given the power by the parties to render a decision. In some cases, all provisions in the contract are subject to the arbitration clause; and in others, the arbitrator has the authority to determine whether a grievance is arbitrable. Justice Douglas observed in another 1960 Supreme Court ruling that, "so far as the arbitrator's decision concerns construction of the contract, the courts have no business overruling him because their interpretation of the contract is different from his" (*United Steelworkers of America v. Enterprise Wheel and Car Corporation*, 1960, p. 599). Consequently, judges are reluctant to interfere with the arbitrator's broad powers to decide both procedural and substantive issues arising under a contract. Thus, the arbitrator plays an important adjudicatory role in the continuing relationship between the parties and, in the process, provides a way of settling disputes without expensive and time-consuming litigation.

But despite the authority of the arbitrator and the reluctance of judges to interfere, there are limits to what an arbitrator can do. In 1996 the California Supreme Court was faced with a school district's refusal to arbitrate a dispute with its teacher union over the nonextension of a probationary teacher's contract. The union had succeeded in getting a clause into the collective bargaining agreement extending due process rights to probationary teachers in such situations. The school district notified a teacher of contract nonextension without complying with the clause. A provision of the Education Code provides that probationary teachers have no due process rights other than notice of contract nonextension by March 15 during the second consecutive year of their probationary contract (Educ. Code § 44929.21). In effect, they may be nonreelected without a showing of cause, without a statement of reasons, and without a hearing or right to appeal. A California lower court ordered the district to submit the dispute over the contract nonextension to binding arbitration in compliance with the collective bargaining contract. The arbitrator later found the district had violated the agreement and ordered it to comply with the due process procedures it had agreed to. The school district challenged the decision.

While the California high court recognized that arbitrator awards are accorded great judicial deference, exceptional circumstances may justify judicial involvement. Here, the arbitrator's decision conflicted with a provision of the Education Code governing nonextension of probationary teacher contracts and hence violated a provision of EERA that it "shall not supersede other provisions of the Education Code" (Govt. Code § 3540). Further, EERA specifies that matters not specifically enumerated as bargaining topics are not negotiable and left to the discretion of the employer. As we noted earlier in the chapter, while the layoff of probationary teachers is listed as a negotiable item, the nonextension of their contracts is not. Thus the arbitrator exceeded his authority in attempting to enforce a provision in a contract that required due process procedures for contract nonextensions (*Board of Education of Round Valley Unified School District v. Round Valley Teachers Association*, 1996).

A somewhat similar decision a few years earlier by a California court of appeal involved the remedial powers of an arbitrator. In this case, the arbitrator ordered the school district to reinstate a probationary teacher whose contract had not been extended. The teacher maintained that her performance had not been evaluated in compliance with evaluation procedures set forth in the contract. The arbitrator agreed and gave her another year as a probationary employee so that the evaluations could be administered. The district challenged the decision, maintaining that the arbitrator's action to reinstate the teacher was preempted by the Education Code that gives districts exclusive authority to nonextend contracts. The appellate court agreed. While employee evaluation is within the scope of bargaining, the remedy of reinstatement is beyond the remedial powers of the arbitrator. Were it otherwise, the statutory authority of the school board to make this decision would be undermined. The court did uphold the arbitrator's order that the district cease and desist from violating the evaluation provision of the collective bargaining contract (*Bellflower Education Association v. Bellflower Unified School District*, 1991).

Decisions like these, however, are the exception, not the rule. The chances of overturning an arbitration award are slim. A case in point involves the Bonita Unified School District's effort to overturn an arbitrator's decision against bypassing progressive discipline to terminate a classified employee. The employee received notice of termination and suspension without pay for a number of reasons including incompetence, dishonesty, insubordination, and immoral conduct. The collective bargaining agreement with the California School Employees Association (CSEA) required that the district could not terminate a classified employee without first going through "progressive discipline"—verbal warnings, written warnings, and a letter of reprimand. However, if the offense was sufficiently serious, the district could bypass these steps. The agreement provided that in accord with Education Code Section 45113 (e), this determination could be submitted to final and binding arbitration. The district and CSEA agreed to do so. If the arbitrator did find the alleged offenses sufficiently serious, the arbitrator would become the district's hearing officer for a termination hearing, with the board having the right to accept, reject, or modify the hearing officer's findings and recommendations. The matter never got this far, because the arbitrator found lack of evidence to support many of the charges against the employee, thus leading to a conclusion that the offenses were not sufficiently serious to warrant bypassing progressive discipline. The district vacated that decision, citing a provision of Section 1286.2 of the California Code of Civil Procedure that permits overturning arbitration awards when the arbitrator exceeds his powers. The union and the employee filed suit. Both the California trial court and court of appeal ruled against the district. The appellate court noted that school boards, like courts, have very limited statutory grounds to overturn arbitration awards. Here the arbitrator was well within his authority to determine what constitutes "serious" for purposes of bypassing progressive discipline (*California School Employees Association v. Bonita Unified School District*, 2008).

Unfair labor disputes. Occasionally during the duration of the contract, an unfair labor dispute will arise that will require involvement of PERB and even the courts. A good example is a dispute over the use of the school district's internal mail system that arose recently in the San Leandro Unified School District. The San Leandro Teachers Association (SLTA) filed a lawsuit against the San Leandro governing board because the board refused to permit it to circulate a newsletter that included a section discussing support for SLTA-endorsed governing board candidates. A second newsletter pertaining mostly to employment issues included a sentence urging bargaining unit members to volunteer to phone or walk in support of the candidates. PERB dismissed the unfair labor charge based on Education Code Section 7054 that prohibits use of school funds, services, supplies, or equipment for political endorsements. The union then took the matter to court. The trial court decided in favor of the union. However, a California court of appeal overturned that decision, citing Education Code Section 7054. The school's mail system, the judges observed, can be viewed as both a service and as equipment. The union argued that Section 3543.1 (b) of the Educational Employment Relations Act gives it the right to contact employees through institutional bulletin boards, mailboxes, and other means of communication. The court agreed, but noted that the provision conditions the right upon "reasonable regulation." Here, denying use of the school district's mail system for political activity, as contrasted with employment matters, serves a valid public purpose and is reasonable. The union also argued that the restriction violates its freedom of speech under the federal and California constitutions, but the court rejected the argument, noting that the San Leandro internal mail system was not being operated as a public forum. Further, the union had other ways to communicate its political messages to its members, including leaving material in the faculty lounge and mailing newsletters to teacher home addresses. In 2007 the California Supreme Court agreed to hear the matter, thus vacating the appellate court's decision (*San Leandro Teachers Association v. Governing Board of San Leandro Unified School District*).

Organizational Security Arrangements

Organizational security arrangements are critically important to unions because they provide the union with the money needed to be effective. EERA requires that once a union is recognized as the exclusive representative of employees in the bargaining unit, each employee who chooses not to be a dues-paying union member must pay a fair share service fee—also known as an agency or agency-shop fee—that is not to exceed the dues paid by union members (Govt. Code § 3546). Government Code Section 3546.3 permits those having religious objections to either joining a union or paying a service fee to opt out of doing so. However, to prevent making this an incentive for bargaining unit members to avoid paying anything at all, the law provides that the money must be routed to a nonreligious charitable organization. Several years ago a teacher in the Chino Valley School District filed a lawsuit against her union, contending that having to pay an amount equivalent to full union dues to a charitable organization while agency fee payers paid a lesser amount to the union constituted discrimination against religion and a denial of equal protection of the laws. The federal district court rejected the contention, noting that religious objectors are not in the same category as agency fee payers. Religious objectors get the full benefits of union representation without having to pay anything and at the same time get to advance the cause of their charities (*Madsen v. Associated Chino Teachers* (2004).

Like exclusivity, service fees are designed to eliminate free riders. Since the union has a legal obligation to represent both members and nonmembers equitably, it is only fair that nonmembers contribute their share of the union's costs. Upon request by the union, the public school employer is required to deduct the fee from the employee's salary and turn the amount over to the union, even without employee authorization (Educ. Code § 45061). The fee may include, but is not limited to, the cost of negotiation, contract administration, and similar activities germane to the collective bargaining process. It also may include costs of union lobbying targeted to fostering collective bargaining negotiations and contract administration or to securing benefits for union members outside the collective bargaining process. In 1989 the California Supreme Court excluded most such costs in the absence of specific statutory authority (*Cumero v. Public Employment Relations Board*). In 2000 the legislature provided that authority. Since the service fee is a large portion of what a regular union member pays, it is not uncommon for fee-payers to decide to join the union so that they have a voice in union affairs. Once a union member, the person is obligated to maintain membership in good standing for the duration of the agreement. However, the member can terminate membership within a period of thirty days following expiration of the agreement.

The organizational security arrangement can be rescinded by majority vote of members in the bargaining unit if the voting request is supported by a petition signed by at least 30 percent of the membership (Govt. Code § 3546 (d)). The vote may be conducted only once during the term of the collective bargaining contract. The school district's governing board must be careful not to influence the rescission process lest an unfair labor charge be filed against it and the election blocked. This could occur, for example, if the school administration speaks out against the agency fee and refuses to enforce it. Such a situation occurred in a dispute between the representative of classified employees and the governing board in the Mount Pleasant Valley Elementary School District some years ago (*Charles H. Allen, et al., Petitioners-Appellants, and California School Employees Association and Pleasant Valley Elementary School District, Respondents,* 1984). If the vote is successful, then the union may petition for the reinstatement of the organizational security arrangement by requesting another election to be held not earlier than one year after the rescission pursuant to a petition signed by at least 30 percent of the bargaining unit members, or the union may negotiate the matter.

Over the years, the fair share service fee has been the source of controversy. Much of the controversy has centered on what the money is used for—especially lobbying activities that the nonunion payee objects to. In its *Cumero* decision, the California Supreme Court faced this question in a case involving a teacher who objected to having to support any union expenses beyond those incurred in the negotiation and administration of the contract. While the scope of what can be supported by the agency fee has expanded by the later amendment to the statute, the decision is instructive on several counts. First, the court rejected the teacher's argument that having to support any lobbying to which he objected would violate his First Amendment rights. The court cited a 1977 U.S. Supreme Court decision, *Abood v. Detroit Board of Education,* in support of a distinction between lobbying to support collective bargaining activities and lobbying for ideological causes unrelated to collective bargaining. Only the latter violates the nonunion payee's First Amendment rights.

Second, the court agreed with the teacher that union organizational activities in other school districts to build union strength is too attenuated from the costs of negotiating contracts to be within the scope of an organizational security arrangement. But the court rejected the teacher's contention that the agency fee could be used by the local affiliate only to support its work and not to support its state and national affiliates. The court noted that the word "employee organization" as defined in EERA includes not only the bargaining agent but also "any person such an organization authorizes to act on its behalf." Because the local teacher union utilized the services of the California Teachers Association (CTA) and its national affiliate, the National Education Association, in representing its members, payment of a portion of the agency fee to them was permissible.

A related matter concerns a nonunion member's access to information on how the agency fee is spent. Agency feepayers have a right to receive a rebate or fee reduction of the portion of the fee that is not used for its intended purposes. EERA requires that the public employer must provide the bargaining agent with the home address of each unit member, regardless of when the member begins employment, so that the union can comply with notification requirements set forth in a 1986 U.S. Supreme Court decision. In that decision, the high court ruled that the union has an obligation to provide nonmembers with an explanation of the basis of the fee, a reasonably prompt opportunity to challenge the amount of the fee before an impartial decision maker, and the establishment of an escrow account for the disputed amount pending the outcome of the challenge (*Chicago Teachers Association, Local No. 1 v. Hudson*, 1986). This has become known as the *Hudson* notice. If the union does not issue a Hudson notice, it can be liable to nonconsensual feepayers. While school district employers have the responsibility to assure procedures that protect nonunion member rights, they are not required to assure that feepayers receive a *Hudson* notice before agency fees are deducted (*Foster v. Mahdesian*, 2001). They could be liable, however, if they take adverse action against a feepayer because the feepayer challenges the union's handling of the matter.

Does the union have to provide nonmembers with a formal audit? The U.S. Court of Appeals for the Ninth Circuit ruled in the negative in 2003. The case concerned nonunion teachers in eight California school districts who sued their unions and CTA, asserting that to comply with the *Hudson* decision, the unions had to submit audited financial statements so that the nonmembers could be sure that their agency fees were being spent for authorized purposes. At the time, CTA did require a local union to secure a financial statement by an outside certified public accountant if the estimated annual revenue from membership dues and agency fees totaled $100,000 or more. If the amount were less than $100,000, the financial disclosure could be reviewed by a certified public accountant or audited by CTA staff auditors. If it were less than $50,000, the local union only had to provide feepayers access to its check register and canceled checks, along with a form required by the IRS and another by PERB. The Ninth Circuit found fault only with the policy involving the smallest local unions. No outside reviewers verified the accuracy of the financial records, and only partial information was made available. The court noted that the unions do not provide feepayers access to such financial records as bills or inventories. The judges left it to the union and its state affiliate to devise a better system (*Harik v. California Teachers Association*).

Finally, the U.S. Supreme Court weighed in the matter of agency-shop fees in 2007. The case involved a State of Washington law requiring unions representing public employees to seek permission from nonmembers before spending agency fees for political purposes. In effect, the Washington statute imposed on the union the obligation to secure permission before spending the money rather than requiring nonmembers to inform the union not to do so or seek a rebate after the money has been spent. The union argued that imposing the consent requirement intruded on the union's First Amendment rights. The Court unanimously rejected the argument (*Davenport v. Washington Education Association*). While California does not have such a requirement, the matter has surfaced in the past.

FUTURE CHALLENGES

Both the National Education Association and the American Federation of Teachers are professional associations as well as unions. However, it seems fair to say that they have not been as successful as other trade unions in securing the professional interests of their members. For many trade unions representing professional employees, the collective agreement is intended not only to secure economic benefits, but to prevent erosion of the employees' traditional influence over their work. Contemporary examples are the American Federation of Musicians, an AFL-CIO affiliate that includes most symphony orchestras in its membership; the Air Line Pilots Association, also an AFL-CIO affiliate that represents some 66,000 airline pilots in the United States and Canada; and Actors Equity, another AFL-CIO affiliate that represents some 45,000 theatrical performers. Teachers, on the other hand, have never had substantial influence over their working conditions.

Teacher unions have become more aggressive in advancing the professional interests of their members through collective bargaining. For example, they have sought a voice for teachers in the development of the school curriculum. This reflects in part the nature of unions to continue to serve their members' interests and in part the growing concern about the quality of public schoolteachers as well as schools. Teacher union advocates point out that having public policymakers, bureaucrats, and school administrators make decisions about curriculum standards and student assessment leaves out of the loop the valuable input of teachers who face students every day. Opponents contend that such assertions mask a union power drive that would stifle innovation. For the moment, EERA gives California teacher unions the right to consult on, but not negotiate, educational objectives, course and curriculum content, and textbook selection. Union polling shows that many newer members are very interested in education reform issues. This is one of the reasons why the California Teachers Association (CTA), for example, has become involved in the implementation of the Quality Education Investment Act as described in the previous chapter.

The area most troubling to teacher unions is expansion of school choice through charter schools and particularly vouchers for private school attendance. Charter schools pose a dilemma for unions because, in many cases, teachers are among those who develop the charter petition and undertake the design of the school and its program. They both teach and oversee the operations of the school. Many teachers consider themselves part of the administration of the school and are not predisposed to unionize. Even if they desired to do so, would it be contrary to EERA because, in effect, teachers would be sitting on both sides of the bargaining table? According to a 2003 PERB decision, however, the fact that some members of the charter school bargaining unit may rotate into and out of management and supervisory roles cannot deny all members of the bargaining unit their rights under EERA to organize (*Robert L. Mueller Charter School*). PERB ruled that exclusion of eight certificated members of the charter school's thirteen-member leadership team from the bargaining unit would result in a unit consisting of just classroom teachers. Whether or not the eight should be excluded, however, was an issue left to future determination should the charter school challenge the ballot process.

While California law does permit charter schoolteachers to unionize, few have done so in schools that begin without a faculty union. The rapid growth of nonunionized charter schools threatens to erode the traditional union power base. They also raise the free rider question in that unrepresented charter school employees benefit from union lobbying on behalf of public schools generally, particularly regarding funding. Partly for this reason, California teacher unions have been reluctant supporters of charter schools and have pressured the legislature to impose more regulations on them. They were behind the move in 1998 to limit the number of charter schools, to require that charter schoolteachers be credentialed, and to require that half of all permanent teachers in a public school approve the school's conversion to charter school status. At the same time, unions advise their members to think carefully about moving to charter schools, where they may not have the job protections that unionization affords, and strive to extend provisions in the existing contract to them. For example, the collective bargaining contract negotiated by the San Diego Education Association with the San Diego district has a section pertaining to charter schools, one provision of which states that the district must urge charter school petitioners who desire to waive all or portions of the collective bargaining agreement to discuss their concerns with the teacher union prior to submitting the charter for board approval. The section also stipulates conditions for bargaining unit members who seek to transfer to or from a charter school, as well as declaring them eligible for the same health and welfare benefits as teachers in traditional schools as long as the charter school purchases group health coverage through the school district and abides by the group eligibility requirements.

Adding to the complexity is the question of the status of teachers in a charter school operated by a private educational management organization (EMO). Suppose, for example, that a charter school recipient contracts with an EMO to provide instructional services. The EMO then hires the teachers to staff the school. Are these teachers the employees of the public charter school or of the private EMO? If the latter, a union seeking to represent them would have to do so under the terms of the National Labor Relations Act (NLRA), the law applicable to the private sector. This is so because EERA applies only to public employees. NLRA presents a whole new set of legal concerns for public sector unions, not the least of which is that unless the school substantially affects interstate commerce, it is not likely to be subject to NLRA at all.

So far there is little law on the question, though the matter has surfaced in California. In 2003 a regional director of PERB ruled that the employees of a charter school remain public employees for purposes of EERA, even though the operators of the school contended otherwise. A private nonprofit public benefit organization known as Options for Youth (OFY) sought and received a charter from the Victor Valley Union High School District in 1993 to operate learning centers for at-risk students. Employees of the school were hired by the board of directors, and the learning centers operated in leased commercial space. A majority of the school's twenty full-time teachers opted for representation by a teacher association, which sought to gain collective bargaining rights under EERA. OFY opposed the move, claiming that the teachers were private, not public, employees and could organize only under NLRA.

The PERB regional director began by noting that NLRA excludes from the definition of "employer" a state or a political subdivision of a state. So the key question was whether the charter school, despite being operated by a private nonprofit benefit corporation, remained a political subdivision of the state. The PERB director observed that the U.S. Supreme Court had developed a test for making this determination in a 1971 decision (*National Labor Relations Board v. Natural Gas Utility District of Hawkins County, Tennessee*). Named after the case, the *Hawkins* test requires either that the entity is created directly by the state or is administered by officials who are responsible to public officials or the general electorate.

To apply the test, the PERB director examined provisions of the Education Code creating charter schools and also *Wilson v. State Board of Education*, a 1999 California court of appeal decision upholding the constitutionality of the charter school act. Both the statutes and the decision are discussed in some detail in Chapter 1. Based on his analysis, the regional director found that charter schools, even those operated by nonprofit benefit corporations, are clearly part of the public school system and carry out educational functions under the auspices of the legislature and the public school district granting the charter. Indeed, the OFY charter petition recognized this fact. Thus, there was no question that OFY Charter School was a political subdivision of the state. Nor was there any question that the charter school officials were fully accountable to the chartering entity, the State Board of Education, and the superintendent of public instruction. Thus, the teachers at the OFY charter school could organize under EERA (*Options for Youth—Victor Valley, Inc. v. Victor Valley Options for Youth Teachers Association*). Interestingly, the PERB regional director chose not to follow a contrary decision by a NLRB administrative law judge regarding an Arizona charter school (*C. I. Wilson Academy and William E. Safriet*, 2002). After PERB accepted the regional director's decision as its own, Options for Youth sought to take the matter to court. However, to do so, the charter school had to obtain PERB's consent, and PERB did not grant it. The matter remains disputatious, and future legal developments are likely to occur, particularly if for-profit EMOs insist upon a right to make their own personnel decisions independent of the entity granting the charter and the charter recipient.

Even more threatening to teacher unions are publicly funded vouchers and tuition tax credit programs that open up the private educational sector to many parents. Both the National Education Association and the American Federation of Teachers are philosophically opposed to vouchers and tuition tax credits, which they see as threatening the ideal of universal public education. But they also fear that expansion of private school choice will undermine union power. Few private schools are unionized, because most are too small to come within the terms of NLRA and because the U.S. Supreme Court has ruled that NLRA does not apply to private school religious faculty members (*National Labor Relations Board v. Catholic Bishops of Chicago*, 1979). Recall that most private schools in California are religiously affiliated. The ruling does not preclude unions from seeking to unionize lay faculty at such schools. Even if some unionization is possible in the private school sector, teacher unions would have to shoulder the costs of organizing teachers and negotiating and administering contracts in both the public and private sectors. Further, union influence on private school management likely would be lessened because private school boards, like charter school boards, are not popularly elected. Finally, expansion of private school choice inevitably siphons off both students and teachers from public schools, thus reducing the traditional union power base. This, of course, is precisely what many voucher advocates hope will occur. For all these reasons, unions oppose voucher and tuition tax credit programs.

In some quarters, calls are being made for changing the role of unions and the nature of the collective bargaining process in education to make both more compatible with the systemic changes occurring throughout public education. For example, it has been suggested that greater accommodation to nuances at the campus level would be realized by having the union negotiate a master contract with the school district regarding basic salary levels and benefits, and then a series of separate agreements at the campus level governing school operation.[1] Another is that unions should be able to operate schools as an independent contractor. In a few states, unions have toyed with the idea of operating charter schools, though this places the union on both sides of the negotiating table. In the San Diego Unified School District, the San Diego Teachers Association did operate a charter school for a time, but the experiment was not successful in part because the union was reluctant to have a strong administrative presence in the school and in part because the district did not give the school a lot of support. However, several union efforts to start charter schools now are under way elsewhere in the state. Operating charter schools and partnering with administrators in education reform initiatives require significant changes in how unions view themselves and perhaps in the legal framework governing unionization and collective bargaining. However, if public schooling continues to undergo structural changes, teacher unions will have no choice but to adapt.

SUMMARY

Until the 1960s, California school district operation was essentially controlled by elected officials and school administrators. While teacher unions had been around for many years, their role was limited. They had little clout to influence how education decisions were made, including those affecting working conditions. The

---

[1] See, for example, Charles Kerchner et al., *United Mind Workers: Unions and Teaching in the Knowledge Society* (San Francisco: Jossey-Bass, 1997); Paul Hill, et al., *Reinventing Public Education: How Contracting Can Transform America's Schools* (Chicago: University of Chicago Press, 1997).

enactment of the Brown Act in 1961 and the Winton Act in 1965 gave unions the right to meet and confer with public employers. While this was a significant step forward, it did not deprive the public employer of the right to have the final say. That changed for public schools with the enactment of the Educational Employment Relations Act (EERA) in 1975. Modeled on the venerable National Labor Relations Act that had governed labor relations in the private sector since 1935, EERA enfranchises public school employees with the right to form and join unions; the right to select an exclusive bargaining agent; the right of the agent to negotiate a binding contract with the school district governing wages, hours, and other terms and conditions of employment; and the right to negotiate dispute settlement procedures.

Because unions had been on the scene so long in California and had lobbied so hard for the right to bargain collectively, unionization proceeded rapidly. It was not long before the professional and classified staffs of most districts in the state were unionized. Over the past thirty years, a vast body of law has developed around the process of determining bargaining units, certifying and decertifying unions, negotiating contracts, and settling disputes. Most of this law emanates from the regulations and rulings of the Public Employee Relations Board (PERB), the state agency charged with implementing and overseeing EERA. Given the technical nature of its work and the expertise it has developed over the years, PERB decisions are accorded significant deference by judges.

Aside from charter and private schools, the collective bargaining process has become ingrained in the operation of California schooling. To a large extent, the relations between educational employees and their employers are governed by the collective bargaining agreement. Through unions, employees have gained economic benefits and a greater say in educational decision making. Employers have benefited by having a body of law that regularizes day-to-day school operation. Both employers and employees benefit from having a mutually agreed upon process for channeling and resolving disputes.

Collective bargaining is not without its problems. It is time-consuming and expensive. Critics accuse unions of having too much influence at the bargaining table because, as powerful interest groups, they shape legislation and influence school board elections. Unions are said to be more concerned with serving their own interests than with reforming public education. Unions counter that they are the ones that have done the most to improve working conditions for teachers and other school employees who have been mistreated and underpaid in the past. They argue that until teachers and their representatives have a significant voice in the development of educational policy, efforts to improve schools will fall short.

Systemic reforms now being touted for schooling will pose major challenges for unions and traditional collective bargaining. Teacher assessment, the growth of charter schools, the privatization of public schooling, and growing utilization of Web-based instruction all carry significant implications for how unions function in the future.

5 | EMPLOYMENT

California's public school system relies on over 600,000 employees to perform the myriad tasks necessary to keep school doors open and students learning. The rights of these employees are a combination of state and federal statutes, regulations, and constitutional principles. Our focus in this chapter is the Education Code's specific provisions regarding the employment, classification, discipline, dismissal, release, and layoff of public school employees.

The Education Code's patchwork of statutes regarding public school employees is complicated and, at times, quite confusing. Even judges have found the Education Code employment statutes to be less than a model of clarity. In a California court of appeal decision regarding the Education Code's dismissal statute for teachers, the first sentence in the opinion reads, "in this case, we confront the formidable task of making sense out of the California Education Code" (*Woodland Joint Unified School District v. Commission on Professional Competence*, p. 229).

In this chapter we start with a discussion of the different types of public school employees, focusing on the two main categories: certificated and classified. This sets the stage for reviewing due process of law and its application to employee discipline and dismissal. The procedures applicable to the discipline or dismissal of an employee are a function of the employee's category (i.e., certificated or classified).

Attention is then given to the process for nonreelecting or releasing certificated and classified employees prior to their attainment of permanent status. After obtaining permanent status, certificated and classified employees retain their jobs until dismissal, layoff, resignation, or death. We detail the permissible circumstances for layoff after a brief word on the employment rights of administrators and a comment on the rights of public school employees regarding their personnel files. The final pages of the chapter concern the leave rights of public school employees and applicable antidiscrimination laws.

Unless otherwise noted, our discussion concerns the employees of a governing board in a school district with 250 or more average daily attendance (ADA). ADA measures student attendance for receipt of state funding. School districts with less than 250 ADA are subject to a number of different statutes governing the employment, discipline, and release of employees.

CLASSIFICATIONS AND CATEGORIES
OF PUBLIC SCHOOL EMPLOYEES

There are two basic classifications of public school employees: certificated and classified. A certificated employee is an individual who is required to hold a credential issued by the California Commission on Teacher Credentialing (CCTC). CCTC oversees the issuance, denial, suspension, and revocation of credentials. A teacher is the most common type of certificated employee. Counselors, school site administrators, and other administrators who are required to hold a credential are also certificated employees. Classified employees are all other employees of the school district not specifically exempted by the Education Code from classified service. Classified employees include those who keep a school running through janitorial services, grounds maintenance, cafeteria operation, and the provision of administrative support. Classified employees also include supervisory management employees who oversee other classified employees (e.g., assistant superintendent of business, director of food services).

The distinction between certificated and classified employees is important for reasons beyond the employees' job duties. Certificated and classified employees have different employment, discipline, dismissal, and layoff rights. Important distinctions among employment rights also occur within the different types of certificated and classified employees. For example, a certificated employee in the employee's first year of employment as a teacher may be released solely with written notice. The employee completes the current school year and does not return. This is known as nonreelection. Alternatively, if the same employee works more than two years with the district as a probationary teacher, the employee is entitled to a formal hearing, if the employee so desires, prior to dismissal. Nonreelection is not an option.

Administrators also are critical to the daily operations of public schools. However, the generic term "administrator" does not constitute a third category of public school employee. While the employment terms and conditions of an administrator differ greatly from a certificated or classified employee, the administrator may nonetheless be a certificated or classified employee who is simply working in an administrative position. The administrator still retains any rights he or she accrued as a certificated or classified employee. For example, reassignment of an administrator may require the school district to place the ex-administrator in a classroom teaching position if the individual requests it and meets certain criteria (generally certification and two or more years of consecutive service).

The vast majority of public school employees work for the governing board of a school district. Education Code Section 35160 and following sections set forth the general powers and duties of school district governing boards. The Education Code requires governing boards to employ certificated (Section 44831) and classified (Section 45103) employees. In addition to these two basic types of employees, governing boards also employ individuals in senior management positions (e.g., superintendent, assistant superintendent of personnel) and special consultants or experts. The latter include attorneys for legal services, architects, accountants, and any other service providers whose services are not otherwise in conflict with or preempted by law. This last catchall category of special consultants or experts is permissible under Education Code Section 35160.

Public school employees may also work for a county superintendent. A county board of education does not have hiring authority. The county superintendent, however, may permit its employees to assist the county board of education (Educ. Code § 1290 and following sections). A county superintendent may enter into a contract of employment with a certificated employee for a period not to exceed the end of the school year in which the county superintendent's term expires. No contract of employment between a county superintendent and a certificated employee may exceed four years and six months. Certificated employees under contract with the county superintendent have the same rights with respect to leaves of absence, sick leave, and bereavement leave as do certificated employees working for a governing board (Educ. Code § 1294). Education Code Sections 44922 (part-time employment) and 44949 and 44955 (layoffs) also apply to certificated employees working for the county superintendent.

Public school employees also work for charter schools. As noted in Chapter 1, charter schools are newly created public schools (although some have already been in existence for years) that are relatively free from state regulation. Charter schools are not subject to any of the Education Code provisions applying to the employees of governing boards. These include the extensive classification systems, discipline and dismissal procedures, and leave rights we address in this chapter. However, charter schools are nonetheless employers subject to a wide range of state and federal antidiscrimination laws. For example, charter schools are subject to the federal Americans with Disabilities Act and the state Fair Employment and Housing Act.

PROPERTY RIGHTS IN EMPLOYMENT

In 1972 the U.S. Supreme Court ruled that public schoolteachers have a protected property right in employment under the terms of the Fourteenth Amendment to the U.S. Constitution if the state gives them a "legitimate claim of entitlement" to it (*Board of Regents v. Roth*). The Fourteenth Amendment provides in part that no state (or political subdivision of the state, like a public school district) shall deprive a person of "life, liberty, or property, without due process of law." Thus, the dimensions of property rights in public employment are to be found in state law, local policies, collective bargaining agreements, and contractual provisions. Once a governmental entity has created a property right protected by the Fourteenth Amendment, it may not take that right away without providing the employee due process of law.

Employees who do not have property rights and are not protected by civil service rules or union contract are said to be employed "at will." This means that they serve at the pleasure of the employer. For example, Education Code Section 44953 states that substitute teachers may be dismissed at any time at the pleasure of the governing board. Because there is no expectation of continued employment in an at-will arrangement, the employee is not entitled to notice and a hearing before dismissal. Conversely, the employee need not give the employer any notice before quitting. The employment arrangement continues at the discretion of both parties. But as we shall see, there are some limitations on employer discretion to end an at-will arrangement.

The Education Code defines property rights for public school employees in California. Property rights vary, however, between certificated and classified employees, and among different classifications of certificated and classified employees. The interrelationship between property rights and employee classification underscores the importance of properly determining a public employee's classification prior to initiating disciplinary action or dismissal.

CERTIFICATED EMPLOYEES

Credentials

A public school employee in a certificated position must hold an appropriate credential from CCTC. CCTC can issue two types of credentials: a teaching credential and a service credential. We will comment briefly on the most common types of teaching and service credentials (see Chapter 2 for a more detailed discussion of teacher credentialing). The Education Code and Title Five of the California Code of Regulations contain extensive statutes and regulations regarding credentials (Educ. Code § 44250 and following sections; Admin. Code, title 5, § 80000 and following sections).

The holder of a Multiple Subject Teaching Credential may teach grades kindergarten through twelve, preschool, and adults in a self-contained classroom (the setting commonly associated with elementary schools). The holder of a Single Subject Teaching Credential may teach the same range of students in a departmentalized, rather than self-contained, classroom. Middle, junior high, and high schools commonly contain departmentalized classrooms. As the name implies, a Single Subject Teaching Credential is issued for a specific subject (e.g., Art, English, Mathematics).

The most common types of service credentials include Administrative Services, Pupil Personnel Services, Health Services, and Clinical or Rehabilitative Services. An individual holding an Administrative Services Credential may work in the position of superintendent, assistant superintendent, principal, or vice principal. The Pupil Personnel Services Credential will specifically authorize the holder to serve in the position of school counseling, school social work, school child welfare and attendance services, or school psychology. School nurses hold the Health Services Credential. The Clinical or Rehabilitative Services Credential will authorize its holder to perform a specific clinical or rehabilitative service (e.g., speech and hearing).

CCTC may also issue emergency permits for an individual who has not completed all of the requirements for a credential (Educ. Code § 44300 and following sections). Emergency Multiple and Single Subject Permits are available for assignments of greater than thirty days. A school district seeking to employ an individual with an emergency credential must justify the need for the emergency credential to CCTC (Educ. Code § 44300). An individual with a bachelor's degree who passes the California Basic Educational Skills Test (CBEST) is eligible to receive an emergency Substitute Permit to perform day-to-day substitute teaching for no more than thirty days in any one assignment during the school year. Holding an emergency credential can have important implications for determining the classification of a certificated employee. We address this aspect of an emergency credential later in the chapter.

The employment of teachers with emergency credentials may not be an option under No Child Left Behind (NCLB). As we discussed in Chapter 2, NCLB is a federal law that imposes major reforms on testing, accountability, and the qualifications of teachers throughout the nation. NCLB presently requires all teachers who are teaching core academic subjects to meet NCLB's definition of "highly qualified." An emergency credential does not satisfy this definition. Readers desiring more information on NCLB can consult the California Department of Education website at www.cde.ca.gov.

CCTC issues a permit rather than a certificate to preschool teachers. An individual employed in a position requiring a child development permit for the instruction and supervision of children is "deemed to be employed in a position requiring certification qualifications" (Educ. Code § 8366). As an individual working in a position requiring certification qualifications, a preschool teacher receives many of the rights afforded to other certificated employees. Education Code Sections 8360–8370 govern preschool teachers.

A credential cannot be issued to an individual who has been convicted of any of the following offenses: a sex offense as defined in Education Code Section 44010, a narcotics offense as defined in Education Code Section 44011, or a crime listed in Education Code Section 44424. These Education Code sections cross-reference various portions of the Penal Code. An individual who has been judicially determined to be a mentally disordered sex offender is also ineligible for a credential.

Classifications

In addition to a wide range of credentials, there are different statutorily recognized classifications of certificated employees. The property rights a certificated employee has are a function of the employee's classification. Property rights, in turn, drive the level of due process necessary for discipline and dismissal. Therefore, before a school district can determine how—or even if—it can discipline or dismiss a certificated employee, there must be a preliminary determination as to the employee's appropriate classification. Determining an employee's classification can sometimes be difficult because there are circumstances in which an employee is hired in one classification and through subsequent events attains an entirely different classification. The Education Code recognizes four different categories of certificated employees: substitute, temporary, probationary, and permanent. Of the four classifications, substitute affords an employee the least job protection. This is where we start our discussion. Throughout this section, we will refer to certificated employees as teachers because they constitute the largest category of such employees.

Substitute. A substitute teacher generally provides day-to-day service in place of a regular school district employee who is absent. Through the nature of their work, substitute teachers are "at-will" employees and do not have an expectation of continued employment. In other words, there is no property right in continued employment with the school district. A governing board may dismiss a substitute teacher "any time at the pleasure of the board" (Educ. Code § 44953). A school district may employ a substitute teacher for an entire school year if no qualified regular employee of the district is available (Educ. Code § 44917). Absent a written notice of release by the end of the school year, the teacher must be reemployed for the next school year in any vacant position. A substitute teacher working in a certificated position at least 75 percent of the school year will be deemed to have served a complete school year as a probationary teacher if the employee is employed as a probationary teacher for the next school year (Educ. Code § 44918 (a)). A substitute teacher serving in an on-call status to replace absent regular teachers of the district on a day-to-day basis cannot attain probationary status (Educ. Code § 44918 (d)).

Temporary. Temporary employees are those persons working in positions requiring certification qualifications, other than substitute employees, who work for a school district on a temporary basis (Educ. Code § 44919). For example, a high school Spanish teacher may enter into a contract with a governing board to teach for a semester to replace a permanent teacher who is on leave. "At the time of initial employment," a school district must give a temporary certificated employee a written statement "clearly indicating the temporary nature of the employment" and the duration of the employment (Educ. Code § 44916). If a written statement does not indicate the temporary nature of the employment, the teacher is deemed a probationary employee. The presence or absence of the foregoing written notice is critical because an individual working in a probationary certificated capacity is accruing time toward permanent status.

In the 2003 California Supreme Court decision of *Kavanaugh v. West Sonoma County Union High School District*, the court interpreted the phrase "at the time of initial employment" in Section 44916 to settle a dispute over a teacher's classification. Alta Kavanaugh applied for a position as an English teacher with the West Sonoma County Union High School District (West Sonoma County UHSD) for the 1999–2000 school year. Alta interviewed for and received the job. According to Alta, however, it was never made clear to her whether the position was temporary or probationary. A few weeks after Alta's first day of employment, West Sonoma County UHSD's Board of Trustees ratified Alta's hiring as a teacher. Alta received a letter confirming her employment "as a temporary teacher" a few days after the West Sonoma County UHSD Board of Trustees meeting.

Near the end of the school year, West Sonoma County UHSD was experiencing financial difficulties. Alta and some other temporary employees were not reemployed. Alta challenged this decision in court, making a two-part argument. First, she argued that she was a probationary employee by default because she did not receive written notice of her temporary status "at the time of initial employment" as required by Section 44916. Second, she argued that because she was a probationary employee and did not receive notice of nonreelection, she was entitled to reemployment for the following school year. Failure to timely nonreelect a probationary employee automatically results in rehiring of the employee for the next school year. Alta prevailed on both arguments. Because Alta did not receive written notice of her temporary classification "on or before her first day of paid service" the court concluded that she "must be considered a probationary employee as a matter of law" (p. 823).

A temporary teacher may also attain probationary status with retroactive probationary credit for time served as a temporary employee if: (1) the temporary teacher performs the duties normally associated with a teacher for at least 75 percent of the school year and (2) the teacher is employed as a probationary teacher for the following school year. In this scenario, the teacher (who is now a probationary teacher) receives retroactive credit for the prior year of service as though the employee were serving as a probationary employee (Educ. Code § 44918 (a)). This means the probationary teacher has one year of probationary service credit toward attaining permanent status.

Education Code Sections 44909, 44917, and 44919–44921 detail the remaining types of temporary employees a school district may employ. Depending on the nature of the temporary employee's position, the employee will have different reemployment rights, and in some instances, the prospect of attaining permanent status after only three or four months. For example, Education Code Section 44919 describes the following two types of temporary employees who attain probationary status after working beyond the three- or four-month period for which the employees were hired:

- Three Months: Individuals employed "to serve from day-to-day during the first three months of any school term to teach temporary classes not to exist after the first three months of any school team or individuals employed to perform any other duties which do not last longer than the first three school months of any school term."

- Four Months: Individuals employed to "teach in special day and evening classes for adults or in schools or migratory population for not more than four school months of any school term."

Deviation from the specific criteria in the relevant code section can result in the "temporary" employee acquiring probationary credit. For example, a school district seeking to utilize Section 44920 to classify employees as temporary must ensure that the temporary employee is, as the section requires, replacing a certificated employee on leave or experiencing long-term absence. Deviation from this key requirement of Section 44920 will prohibit classification of the employee as temporary and afford that employee probationary credit (*Bakersfield Elementary Teachers Association v. Bakersfield City School District,* 2006).

Temporary employees who serve more than 75 percent of the school year in a position requiring certification and are hired as probationary employees for the next school year receive retroactive probationary credit for their service. This retroactive credit is not available to temporary employees serving in the previously noted three- or four-month positions. This distinction is critical because it requires the employee to work longer as a probationary employee before attaining permanent status (i.e., for an extra three or four months).

Education Code Section 44954 permits the release of a temporary employee at the "pleasure of the board" prior to the employee's completion of at least 75 percent of a school year. If a temporary employee serves more than 75 percent of a school year, the employee may be released with a written notice of the "district's decision not to reelect the employee for the succeeding school year."

School districts may employ certificated employees in categorically funded programs (Educ. Code § 44909). Certificated employees in these positions are essentially temporary employees. In certain circumstances, however, they can obtain permanent status with a school district. The Class Size Reduction Program, in which school districts reduce class size to receive funding from the state, is one example of a categorically funded program. Receipt of categorical funding, however, is contingent on the recipient school district adhering to the terms and conditions upon which the funding is made available. If the funding is no longer available or the school district is no longer eligible for the funding, how is a school district to classify the certificated employees who were hired to work in the program?

The 2002 California court of appeal decision of *Zalac v. Governing Board of the Ferndale Unified School District* addressed this question. Mary Jo Zalac was hired by the Ferndale Unified School District (Ferndale USD) to serve in the program. After Mary Jo's second year of employment, Ferndale USD was unable to meet certain statutory criteria for the program, and the program funding ceased. Ferndale USD decided nonetheless to retain Mary Jo and offered her a contract as a temporary teacher in essentially the same position. Mary Jo received two notices from Ferndale USD in March of her third year. The first notice said she would not be reemployed as a temporary teacher, due to the loss of program funding. The second notice said she was going to be laid off under Education Code Section 44955. The layoff notice (which is not required for a temporary employee) was a likely hedged bet on behalf of Ferndale USD that Mary Jo may not actually be a temporary certificated employee. We address the layoff of certificated employees later in this chapter.

Mary Jo initiated a court action challenging her dismissal. She argued that the district had improperly classified her as a temporary employee, thus rendering her termination void. Prior to determining if Mary Jo was a temporary employee, the court addressed whether the program was a categorically funded program under Section 44909. The court determined it was. The court then focused on the following language in Section 44909 to determine if Mary Jo was a temporary employee of the District:

> Service pursuant to this section shall not be included in computing the service required as a prerequisite to attainment of, or eligibility to, classification as a permanent employee unless (1) such person has served pursuant to this section for at least 75 percent of the number of days the regular schools of the district by which he is employed are maintained and (2) such person is subsequently employed as a probationary employee in a position requiring certification qualifications.

The court interpreted the foregoing language to mean that Mary Jo should be granted a year toward permanent status for each year she served in the program. Focusing on the district's decision to rehire Mary Jo, the court determined that she was rehired in her third year as a probationary employee, thereby retroactively granting her two years of service credit as a probationary teacher and affording her permanent status upon commencement of her third year of employment. Note the distinction between this result and the statutory analysis for a temporary teacher who serves 75 percent or more of the school year in a position requiring certification and is rehired as a probationary teacher. The latter receives only one year of credit as a probationary employee and must survive the entire subsequent year without a notice of nonreelection.

Mary Jo's victory on this point was a hollow one, however, for the court upheld her layoff as an independent basis to sever her employment from the district. Under *Zalac,* school districts must immediately decide whether or not to terminate certificated employees hired under a categorical funding program when the program no longer exists. Rehiring the employees for a subsequent year after the applicable categorical funding program expires may result in their attaining probationary or permanent status.

Probationary. Prior to attaining permanent classification, a teacher must either serve as a probationary employee or receive retroactive credit for service as a probationary employee. A school district has an opportunity to evaluate an employee's performance during the employee's probationary period. This permits the district to make an informed decision as to whether the employee should attain permanent status. Governing boards of school districts must classify as probationary employees "those persons employed in positions requiring certification qualifications for the school year, who have not been classified as permanent employees or as substitute employees" (Educ. Code § 44915). A key feature of probationary status is nonreelection, which we discuss in more detail later in the chapter. Nonreelection permits a school district to notify a probationary teacher in writing that the teacher's service with the district will not continue into the next school year. The employment relationship ends at the close of the school year in which the notice is given, without any further action on the school district's behalf. Upon receipt of the written notice, the probationary teacher has no recourse. Nonreelection is not available for permanent teachers. This is why Marilyn and Lori, each a teacher in separate cases we review later in this chapter, initiated legal actions to have a court grant them permanent status. While probationary status does not provide the job security of permanent status, it is still important because it is a precursor to permanent status.

Under certain circumstances, interns employed by school districts in certificated positions may attain probationary status. The Education Code recognizes three types of intern programs: pre-internship teaching internships, school district internships, and university internships. While the Education Code is silent on the employment status of pre-interns, it is unlikely that they are serving in a probationary position. Education Code Sections 44325 to 44328 govern school district internships. Education Code Section 44885.5 details the two circumstances in which a district intern is a probationary employee. First, an individual hired as a district intern is a probationary employee. Second, an individual who is not hired as a district intern may nonetheless become a probationary employee when the individual completes service in the intern program and is reelected in the next succeeding school year to a position requiring certification.

Can a school district alter the probationary status of a district intern through a contract identifying the intern as a temporary employee? The 2001 California court of appeal decision of *Welch v. Oakland Unified School District* answered this question in the negative. Melanie Welch was offered a teaching position by the Oakland Unified School District (Oakland USD) in September of 1998. Melanie was a participant in the Partnership Program at California State University. On Melanie's behalf, Oakland USD applied for an internship Multiple Subject Teaching Credential with CCTC. Approximately one month later, the district gave Melanie a contract of employment identifying her as a temporary teacher. The contract specified that either party could terminate the contract with fifteen days' notice.

Melanie's employment with Oakland USD did not go smoothly. According to Melanie, the principal at her school introduced himself by explaining that the culture at the school was Christian and that Melanie would "not fit in if Jesus talking bothered [her]" (p. 376). Melanie alleged that she was later attacked by a student and threatened by a parent. After bringing her concerns to the principal, Melanie alleged that he would "have [twenty] kids say [she] hit and kicked them" (Id). In November of 1998, Melanie was placed on administrative leave for allegations regarding erratic behavior and hitting and kicking students. By February of 1999, Oakland USD sent Melanie a letter releasing her from her temporary employment contract. A temporary certificated employee generally may be released midyear unless a contract of employment provides otherwise.

Melanie filed a legal action arguing that she was improperly released. She argued that because she was an intern in a district internship program she was a probationary, not temporary, employee. The district rested its argument on a narrow interpretation of Education Code Section 44885.5, which states in relevant part:

> Any school district shall classify as a probationary employee of the district any person who is employed as a district intern pursuant to Section 44830.3 and any person who has completed service in the district as a district intern . . . and is re-elected for the next succeeding school year to a position requiring certification qualifications.

Oakland USD argued that a district intern is not a probationary employee until the intern is hired, completes a year of service, and is reelected for the next school year. The court disagreed, observing that the phrase "any person" in the statute preceded a second, separate manner in which a district intern could attain probationary status. Because Melanie was employed as a district intern, she was a probationary employee. This entitled her to thirty days' notice and the right to a hearing for a midyear dismissal. The contract identifying her as a temporary employee was invalid. *Welch,* among other things, demonstrates the inability of a school district to contract around a certificated employee's appropriate classification under the Education Code.

A university internship is established by a school district in cooperation with an approved college or university. Education Code Section 44450 and following sections govern university internships. The intern serves under an internship credential issued by CCTC and cannot obtain permanent status while serving under the internship credential. A university intern obtains permanent status by completing the internship program, serving a complete school year, and being reelected for the next succeeding school year (Educ. Code § 44466). After completion of the university internship but prior to attaining permanent status, the intern is a probationary employee. The Education Code is silent on the classification (i.e., probationary or temporary) of a university intern prior to completion of the intern's internship.

Permanent. Except for those in very small districts, a full-time teacher must serve two consecutive school years as a probationary employee before becoming a permanent employee (Educ. Code § 44929.21 (b)). In school districts with less than 250 average daily attendance (ADA), a full-time certificated teacher must serve three consecutive years as a probationary employee before becoming a permanent employee (Educ. Code § 44929.23 (a)). There are numerous other distinctions in the classifications of certificated employees for school districts with less than 250 ADA that we do not address. A probationary teacher who has served for at least 75 percent of a school year is deemed to have served a complete school year (Educ. Code § 44908).

A certificated employee serving in a "teaching position" for a county superintendent with 250 ADA or more must do so for two consecutive years before attaining permanent status (Educ. Code § 1296 (b)). The county superintendent or county board of education designates those positions that qualify as teaching positions (Educ. Code § 1296 (c)). These "teaching positions" may not necessarily be the same types of positions occupied by the probationary teachers of governing boards. Permanent status is generally not available for a certificated employee employed by a county superintendent with less than 250 ADA.

As noted earlier, one exception to these general rules regarding permanent status exists when a temporary employee serves for more than 75 percent of the school year and is subsequently hired into a probationary position. For this event, the school district must retroactively count the employee's year of service as a temporary employee as though it were a year of service as a probationary employee. Permanent status, or "permanency" or "tenure" as it is sometimes referred to, is established only with the current employer. A school district's governing board may, but does not have to, extend permanent status to a newly hired teacher who established permanent status elsewhere in the state (Educ. Code § 44929.28).

May a school district grant permanent status to a teacher prior to the teacher's completion of two consecutive school years of service as a probationary employee? The 1988 California court of appeal decision of *Fleice v. Chualar Elementary School District* addressed this question for Marilyn Fleice. Marilyn taught for one year as a probationary teacher before she was given a contract by the Chualar Elementary School District (Chualar ESD) to work the next school year as a permanent employee. Marilyn executed the contract. At the start of the next school year, a new superintendent took office. The superintendent decided that Marilyn was not entitled to be a permanent teacher, notwithstanding the contract, because Marilyn did not complete two years of consecutive service as a probationary teacher. The superintendent corrected the mistake by sending Marilyn a letter explaining that tenure was erroneously granted and that Marilyn was now a probationary certificated employee. Marilyn was not rehired for the next year.

Marilyn filed a legal action seeking to compel Chualar ESD to rehire her as a permanent certificated employee. Marilyn argued that the Education Code did not prohibit the district from granting permanent status to an employee prior to completion of the employee's two-year probationary period. The court did not agree. Viewing the two-year probationary period as a mandatory prerequisite to attaining permanent status, the court concluded that the governing board did not have the power to grant Marilyn early permanent status. Thus, the contract rehiring Marilyn as a permanent certificated employee was not legally enforceable, and Marilyn was properly reclassified as a probationary teacher subject to release through nonreelection.

Save for certain narrow exceptions, time spent serving under a "provisional credential" does not count toward attaining classification as a permanent teacher (Educ. Code § 44911). Is a provisional credential the same as an emergency credential? This was the question Lori Summerfield posed to a California court of appeal in 2002 (*Summerfield v. Windsor Unified School District*). Lori served as a certificated employee for the Windsor Unified School District (Windsor USD) under a series of emergency credentials from September of 1996 to March 1998. In March of 1998, the district informed Lori that she had successfully completed her probationary period and would be rehired as a permanent employee for the next school year. A month later, however, the governing board advised Lori that it believed her service under an emergency teaching credential did not count toward permanent employee status. Like Marilyn, Lori was reclassified as a probationary teacher, worked another school year, and was thereafter released through nonreelection.

Lori filed a legal action requesting the court to order Windsor USD to grant her permanent classification. Lori argued that the phrase "provisional certificates" in Section 44911 did not include emergency credentials. The court did not adopt Lori's argument, ruling that the phrase "provisional certificate" in Section 44911 means the same thing as an emergency credential. Because Lori did not satisfy any of the exceptions in Section 44911, the time she served under her emergency credentials did not count toward attainment of permanent status. Although the district told Lori that she attained permanent status, the court dismissed this by citing *Fleice* for the proposition that "it is well settled that the two-year probationary period for teachers is mandatory and may not be shortened by the advice or actions of a school district" (p. 240).

Once a probationary teacher completes the requisite number of consecutive school years of service, the teacher automatically attains permanent status at the commencement of the next school year (*Vittal v. Long Beach Unified School District*, 1970). No action by the school district's governing board is required. Once elevated to permanent status, a teacher has a vested property right in employment within the scope of the teaching credential when tenure was conferred (*Adelt v. Richmond School District*, 1967). Permanent teachers can be dismissed only for grounds specified in the Education Code and are afforded full due process rights, as discussed later in the chapter. A teacher attaining permanent status is entitled to continued employment with the school district until retirement, resignation, death, dismissal, or layoff. Probationary teachers like Marilyn and Lori do not have these same rights and may be nonreelected prior to March 15 during their second year of probationary status. In effect, the property right ends at this time, and due process other than timely written notice of nonreelection is not required. It is primarily for this reason that a school district carefully considers whether a certificated employee should ascend from probationary to permanent status.

Evaluation and Reassignment

The evaluation of teachers plays an important role in year-to-year retention, which may lead to permanent status, and in documenting employee performance for purposes of discipline or dismissal. Education Code Section 44660 and following sections, commonly known as the "Stull Act," set forth the guidelines a school district is to consider in developing and implementing an evaluation system of its teachers. While the Education Code delegates a fair amount of discretion to school districts in this process, all evaluation systems must have certain key features. The criteria used to evaluate teachers must be negotiated with the exclusive representative of the teacher union.

Teacher evaluation is to be done on a uniform basis. For "compelling reasons," however, a governing board may use different evaluation criteria for teachers of certain schools within the district (Educ. Code § 44660). The statute does not provide further detail regarding these reasons. However, one potential example is attempting to impose a different evaluation system on teachers in a school receiving substandard test scores either by state or federal (No Child Left Behind) standards. The governing board must consider the advice of teachers within the district in developing an evaluation system. A school district may, by mutual agreement with the teacher union, include objective standards from the National Board for Professional Teaching Standards or from the California Standards for the Teaching Profession.

Education Code Section 44662 sets forth the minimum criteria by which a governing board must evaluate and assess teacher performance. These criteria include the instructional techniques and strategies used by the teacher, the teacher's adherence to curricular objectives, and whether the teacher established and maintained a suitable learning environment. The performance of the teacher's students toward the standards of expected student achievement established by the governing board is another component of the evaluation. Student achievement may also focus on state-adopted academic content standards. If a school district participates in the Peer Assistance and Review (PAR) program for teachers, the teacher's participation in PAR must also be made part of the teacher's evaluation. PAR provides mentor-type assistance to permanent teachers whose evaluation results in a rating of "unsatisfactory performance." School districts are not technically required to participate in PAR; however, those that do receive state money. Those that do not are ineligible for funding for other programs such as the Administrator Training and Evaluation Program. Education Code Section 44500 and following sections detail PAR's requirements. PAR is also a mandatory subject of bargaining.

An evaluation must be reduced to writing and given to the teacher not later than thirty days prior to the end of the school year in which the evaluation occurred (Educ. Code § 44663). Prior to the last day of the school year, the evaluator and the teacher meet to discuss the evaluation. The teacher may issue a written response, which becomes a permanent attachment to the employee's personnel file. Special time lines regarding the evaluation of certificated noninstructional employees such as an administrator are detailed in Education Code Section 44663 (b). A teacher not performing his or her duties in a satisfactory manner is given an evaluation of unsatisfactory performance. The superintendent, or superintendent's designee, must meet with any teacher receiving an unsatisfactory performance, give the employee specific recommendations regarding areas that require improvement, and endeavor to assist the teacher to improve.

Education Code Section 44664 sets forth the frequency with which teachers must be evaluated. A probationary teacher is evaluated at least once every school year. A permanent teacher is evaluated at least once every other year. A permanent teacher receiving an unsatisfactory performance is evaluated annually until the employee receives a positive evaluation or is no longer employed by the district. A permanent teacher with ten years of service in a school district may be evaluated at least once every five years if the teacher satisfies the definition of "highly qualified" under the No Child Left Behind Act, the teacher met or exceeded standards in the teacher's previous evaluation, and both the teacher and the evaluator agree to an evaluation at least once every five years. A school district may exclude substitute teachers from evaluations. The evaluation process does not apply to teachers who are employed on an hourly basis in adult education classes.

Subject to the approval of the governing board, it is the superintendent's duty to assign all certificated employees of the district to the position in which they will serve (Educ. Code § 35035(c)). As a general rule, the superintendent has the power to transfer a certificated employee from one school to another when the superintendent concludes that the transfer is in the best interests of the district. A teacher does not have a vested property right in the location of the teaching assignment (*Bolin v. San Bernardino City Unified School District*, 1984). A collective bargaining agreement, however, can dictate a process for determining how employees are transferred (e.g., on the basis of seniority). Additionally, a superintendent may not transfer a teacher to a school with a 1-3 API ranking over the objection of the principal (Educ. Code § 35036.) For a discussion of API ranking, see Chapter Two.

Discipline of Probationary and Permanent Employees

Discipline consists of action against an employee short of dismissal. Save for egregious acts, the discipline of public school employees generally follows a format known as progressive discipline. An oral warning may precede a conference, which can escalate to a written warning. A stronger tone can be taken with a letter of reprimand. An unfavorable evaluation may command even more attention from the offending employee. Suspension, which is the last resort before dismissal, is technically available in many instances, yet often not worth the time and expense of the hearing an employee may request to challenge it. The Education Code contains specific provisions concerning suspension and derogatory statements or comments entered into an employee's personnel file. Our focus here is suspension. Later in the chapter we discuss the placement of a derogatory statement or comment in the personnel file. A governing board may negotiate the causes and procedures for disciplinary action, other than dismissal, including a suspension of pay for up to fifteen days with the exclusive representative of the employee's union (Govt. Code § 3543.2(b)). In this instance, a collective bargaining agreement details and governs the suspension process for both permanent and probationary teachers.

Absent a collective bargaining agreement, a school district is left with the relatively inflexible and cumbersome suspension provisions of the Education Code. A governing board may "suspend without pay for a specific period of time on grounds of unprofessional conduct" a permanent teacher (Educ. Code § 44932 (b)). A governing board may also suspend a permanent teacher for "grounds of unprofessional conduct consisting of acts or omissions other than those specific in Section 44932," but the charge must specify the instances of behavior deemed to be unprofessional conduct. Suspension of a probationary teacher is permissible for cause under Education Code Section 44932 or unsatisfactory performance under Education Code Section 44948.3.

Immediate suspension of a permanent teacher is permissible based on written charges of immoral conduct, conviction of a felony or of any crime involving moral turpitude, incompetency due to mental disability, or willful refusal to perform regular assignments without reasonable cause (Educ. Code § 44939). A charge permitting immediate suspension will result in the employee's suspension unless the employee requests a hearing within thirty days after receipt of the written charge(s). For a charge permitting immediate suspension, the employee may be suspended without pay unless the employee provides a bond or some other security to the governing board. This typically occurs when a teacher is placed on suspension pending dismissal. The purpose of the bond or security is to permit the governing board to recover salary paid to the employee during the suspension if the employee is dismissed. If the employee ultimately prevails, the governing board must reimburse the employee the costs of the bond or other security.

Education Code Section 44942 contains a detailed process for the suspension and dismissal of a permanent certificated employee if the employee is "suffering from mental illness of such a degree as to render him or her incompetent to perform his or her duties." The expense and complexity of the process, which includes a panel of psychologists or psychiatrists to examine the employee, makes it a largely impracticable option for school districts. Dismissal or suspension for evident unfitness for service under Education Code Section 44932, however, may be a more practical solution.

A "Skelly" conference is a prerequisite to the suspension of a certificated employee without pay. The conference is an informal meeting between administration and the employee and takes its name from the 1975 California Supreme Court decision of *Skelly v. State Personnel Board*. The essence of *Skelly* is that a government employee is to receive written notice and an opportunity to respond prior to the deprivation of a property right. Loss of pay during a suspension constitutes the loss of a property right. A *Skelly* conference, in which the employee is apprised of the basis for the suspension and is given an opportunity to respond, thus satisfies due process of law prior to the suspension.

Nonreelection and Dismissal of Probationary Teachers

If a probationary teacher of a school district with 250 or more ADA does not receive a written notice of nonreelection by March 15 of the employee's second consecutive year of employment, the teacher is automatically reelected for the following school year and obtains permanent classification. A special nonreemployment, rather than nonreelection, process applies to probationary teachers in school districts with less than 250 ADA.

A governing board meeting must occur in which the board adopts a resolution to nonreelect probationary teachers. The meeting can be held in closed session (i.e., no members of the public or press or notice to the teacher) (*Fischer v. Los Angeles Unified School District*, 1999). Under the Ralph M. Brown Act, the board must properly notice the closed session in which this decision is made. After the closed session, the board's decision must be reported out to the public. A notice of nonreelection, including a copy of the board's resolution, must be given by personal notice or an equivalent means to the teacher. Service of the notice by certified mail is not sufficient (*Hoschler v. Sacramento City Unified School District*, 2007). No hearing to challenge the nonreelection is available. A probationary teacher can, however, challenge the nonreelection if the employee can prove the nonreelection was for an unlawful reason such as race or sex discrimination or retaliation for union activity.

May a school district give written notice of nonreelection to a probationary teacher after March 15 during the employee's first year of employment? The 1987 California court of appeal decision of *Grimsley v. Board of Trustees* addressed this question. Sherilyn Grimsley was a first-year probationary teacher working for the district when she received a notice of nonreelection on April 23, 1984. The notice said that her employment with the district would terminate on June 30, 1984. In the ensuing legal action, Sherilyn argued that her nonreelection was invalid because it was issued after March 15. The court disagreed and held that nonreelection is permissible any time prior to March 15 of the probationary teacher's second consecutive year of employment. In a footnote, however, the court did note that a notice of nonreelection issued on June 29 for release on June 30 may well be unreasonable given the teacher's reliance on continued employment until that time.

Given the ease with which the governing board of a school district can nonreelect probationary teachers, it is quite rare for a midyear dismissal action to be undertaken against them. Education Code Section 44948.3 governs the dismissal of probationary teachers in a school district with 250 or greater ADA. These employees may be dismissed during the school year for unsatisfactory performance determined under the Stull Act (Educ. Code §§ 44660–44664). Dismissal may also be for cause, as delineated in the next section.

A probationary teacher must receive at least thirty days prior written notice of dismissal. If the teacher is in the second year of employment, the written notice must be received no later than March 15. The notice must include a statement of the reasons for the dismissal and notice of the opportunity for a hearing. This is necessary because the teacher has a property right during the term of the contract (i.e., to complete the full term of the school year), a right that cannot be taken away without providing due process of law. Notice of dismissal for unsatisfactory performance must include a copy of the teacher's evaluation. The teacher thereafter has up to fifteen days to submit a written request for a hearing to the governing board. Failure to request a hearing within fifteen days after receipt of the dismissal notice results in a waiver of the right to a hearing. Although the Education Code provides a statute covering the dismissal of a permanent teacher, it does not contain a statute setting forth the requirements for the dismissal hearing of a probationary teacher. Hearing procedures, which the governing board develops, must comport with due process of law (e.g., notice, right to representation, right to testify, and right to call and question witnesses). A governing board may conduct the hearing or delegate the matter to an administrative law judge. If an administrative law judge conducts the hearing, a recommendation is given to the governing board. The governing board reviews the recommendation and makes its own decision regarding dismissal. Once again, the employee can appeal the decision on the grounds that the dismissal was unlawfully motivated.

Dismissal of Permanent Teachers

Dismissal of a permanent or probationary teacher may occur under one of the specific causes set forth in Education Code Section 44932. These causes are

- "Immoral or unprofessional conduct"
- "Dishonesty"
- "Unsatisfactory performance"
- "Evident unfitness for service"
- "Physical or mental condition unfitting him or her to instruct or associate with children"
- "Persistent violation of or refusal to obey school laws of the state or reasonable regulations prescribed for the government of the public schools by the State Board of Education or by the governing board of the school district employing him or her"
- "Conviction of a felony or of any crime involving moral turpitude"
- "Violation of Section 51530 or conduct specified in Section 1028 of the Government Code"
- "Alcoholism or other drug abuse which makes the employee unfit to instruct or associate with children"

A permanent teacher may also be dismissed on grounds of unprofessional conduct other than those specified in Section 44932, but any such charge(s) must specify instances of behavior deemed to constitute unprofessional conduct (Educ. Code § 44933). Next we present an overview of four of the most common grounds for dismissal: immoral or unprofessional conduct, unsatisfactory performance, evident unfitness for service, and persistent violation of or refusal to obey school laws or reasonable regulations.

Immoral or unprofessional conduct. In the case of immoral or unprofessional conduct, it must be established that the conduct undermined the teacher's effectiveness. This was the thrust of the seminal ruling of *Morrison v. State Board of Education,* a decision of the California Supreme Court in 1969. That case involved a teacher who had resigned when confronted with evidence of a private, consensual homosexual relationship. Though the relationship had not been known among students or teachers, the state revoked the teacher's credential. The court ruled in favor of the teacher, noting the absence of evidence that the relationship had negatively affected the teacher's performance. The court delineated seven criteria to be used in assessing whether or not immoral or unprofessional conduct has such an effect. Known as the Morrison factors, these factors are

- "The likelihood that the conduct may have adversely affected students or fellow teachers"
- "The degree of such adversity anticipated"
- "The proximity or remoteness in time of the conduct"
- "The type of teaching certificate held by the party involved"
- "The extenuating or aggravating circumstances, if any, surrounding the conduct"
- "The likelihood of recurrence of the questioned conduct"
- "The extent to which disciplinary action may inflict an adverse impact or chilling effect upon the constitutional rights of the teacher involved or other teachers"

The inquiry is whether the teacher is fit to teach, considering these factors in the aggregate.

The sexual harassment of female students by a teacher can constitute immoral conduct under the Morrison factors (*Governing Board of ABC Unified School District v. Haar,* 1994). Kenneth Haar was a certificated music teacher in a middle school. The school district initiated dismissal proceedings against Kenneth on the grounds that he engaged in immoral conduct by sexually harassing his female students. Allegations against Kenneth included touching a female student on the thigh; hugging a female student tightly until the student pushed Kenneth away;

and, while dressed up as Santa Claus, indicating to female students that an extra raffle ticket for a drawing was available in return for a kiss. Kenneth's dismissal was upheld by a California court of appeal because substantial evidence demonstrated that Kenneth's conduct rendered him unfit to teach. The Morrison factors have also been applied to the causes of dishonesty and evident unfitness for service.

Seeking to dismiss a teacher on the basis of unprofessional, but not immoral, conduct requires the school district to give the employee written notice specifying the nature of the conduct and the "behavior with such particularity as to furnish the employee an opportunity to correct his or her faults and overcome the grounds for the charge" (Educ. Code § 44938 (a)). The written notice must also include the most recent evaluation. After issuance of the foregoing written notice, the school district must wait at least forty-five calendar days before filing a charge of unprofessional conduct to initiate the dismissal process. Teachers are therefore given an opportunity to learn of the nature of their unprofessional conduct and change their conduct prior to the initiation of formal dismissal proceedings. Failure to provide this written notice is fatal to a school district's efforts to suspend or dismiss a teacher for unprofessional conduct (*Crowl v. Commission on Professional Competence*, 1990).

Unsatisfactory performance. A 1995 amendment to Education Code Section 44932 substituted the phrase "unsatisfactory performance" for "incompetency." As in dismissal for unprofessional conduct, a teacher receives prior written notice of unsatisfactory performance. The school district cannot initiate formal dismissal proceedings until ninety calendar days after the employee is given written notice of the unsatisfactory performance (Educ. Code § 44938 (b)(1)). The written notice is in the same form and detail as described in the preceding section regarding unprofessional conduct (albeit with a description of the specific instances of behavior that constitutes unsatisfactory performance). Unprofessional conduct and unsatisfactory performance are the only grounds for dismissal requiring prior written notice to the teacher and a grace period for the teacher to alter conduct prior to initiation of a dismissal proceeding.

Evident unfitness for service. The 1992 California court of appeal decision of *Woodland Joint Union School District v. Commission on Professional Competence* addressed when a certificated employee's conduct rises to the level of evident unfitness for service within the meaning of Education Code Section 44932 (a)(5). In *Woodland,* the district sought to terminate a permanent English teacher. The district's charges for dismissal were based on an allegation of evident unfitness for service and persistent refusal to obey school laws of the state or reasonable regulations. Writing sarcastic and belittling notes about students, insulting students in class, behaving rudely and contemptuously toward parents, displaying insubordination and disrespect toward administrators, and bullying and threatening other teachers were among the allegations supporting the charges of dismissal. A Commission on Professional Competence (CPC) convened to hear the charges and found the allegations either not supported by the evidence or insufficient to justify dismissal. We discuss the role of a CPC when we explain the dismissal process later in this chapter.

The district challenged the commission's findings in a superior court action and requested a finding that the teacher's conduct showed him temperamentally unfit to teach, so that his continued employment would pose a substantial danger to faculty, administrators, students, and parents. The superior court agreed, and the teacher appealed. The first question for the court of appeal was whether the charge of "evident unfitness for service" is synonymous with the charge of "unprofessional conduct." The teacher argued that because these charges were synonymous, the district erred in not providing him with the forty-five-day written notice that must precede a charge of unprofessional conduct. Recall that failure to provide this notice for dismissal on the basis of unprofessional conduct effectively terminates the dismissal proceeding, thereby resulting in the teacher's reinstatement. The court first observed that the purpose of the notice requirement for unprofessional conduct is to allow the teacher to correct his or her conduct. After noting that no such requirement applies to dismissal for evident unfitness for service, the court held that "unlike 'unprofessional conduct,' 'evident unfitness for service' connotes a fixed character trait, presumably not remediable merely on receipt of notice that one's conduct fails to meet the expectations of the employing school district" (p. 235). Otherwise, the Education Code would also provide a teacher with prior written notice of conduct constituting evident unfitness for service to enable the teacher to alter his or her conduct. This teacher, at least in the opinion of the court, was not an individual who could change his conduct.

In upholding the teacher's dismissal, the court also clarified the role of the Morrison factors in a dismissal for evident unfitness for service. The teacher had argued that the court must apply the Morrison factors individually to each allegation. The court rejected the teacher's argument and upheld an application of the Morrison factors to the evidence in the aggregate. In the words of the court, "when a camel's back is broken we need not weigh each straw in its load to see which one could have done the deed" (p. 244). If application of the Morrison factors indicates unfitness for service in the aggregate, the only remaining question is whether the offensive conduct is the result of a defect in temperament, thus demonstrating evident unfitness for service.

Persistent violation of or refusal to obey school laws. School laws and regulations are taken from numerous sources. Among these are statutes, regulations, and board policies. Title Five of the California Code of Regulations contains the Rules of Conduct for Professional Educators. While these rules may not themselves be reasons for dismissal, they can be cited as additional evidence that the certificated employee is persistently violating or refusing to obey school laws. Some governing boards add to these provisions through their own code of ethics. The code prohibits the following conduct:

- Failure to use professional candor and honesty required in letters and memoranda of employment recommendation.
- Withdrawal from professional employment without good cause.
- Unauthorized private gain or advantage from use of confidential information relating to students or fellow professionals.
- Performance of duties when substantially mentally impaired for any reason, including alcohol or substance abuse. This rule also includes the assignment of such a person to perform duties.
- Harassment or retaliation against those who report actual or suspected wrongdoing.
- Failure to perform duties for a person because of discriminatory motives.

A teacher's failure to adhere to a goal in an evaluation may also constitute persistent violation of or refusal to obey school laws or reasonable regulations. Such was the case with a teacher in the 1985 California court of appeal decision of *San Dieguito Union High School District v. Commission on Professional Competence.* The teacher's evaluation set forth a goal of "providing thorough lesson plans when absent, and calling early for a substitute when needed" (p. 353). The teacher did not meet her goal. One substitute testified that for twelve of the seventeen times she substituted in the teacher's classroom, she could not locate lesson plans. Absenteeism (in the form of an evident unfitness for service charge) was another ground on which the court upheld the teacher's dismissal.

The Dismissal Hearing Process

The dismissal hearing process starts with the filing of written charges with the governing board. Importantly, suspension or dismissal of a teacher may not generally be based on charges or evidence of any nature relating to matters occurring more than four years prior to the filing of charges (Educ. Code § 44944 (a)). The California Supreme Court recently held that a school district may seek to introduce evidence of wrongdoing from more than four years prior to the filing of charges where it can be shown that the employee induced the school district to avoid bringing charges within

Step One: Written charges filed with governing board (Educ. Code §§ 44934, 44938)

- Person signs and verifies, or governing board formulates, written charges of grounds for dismissal or suspension without pay as specified in Education Code §§ 44932 or 44933. Teachers may be suspended only for unprofessional conduct. Teacher unions may negotiate the terms and conditions for suspensions up to 15 days (Govt. Code § 3543.2 (b)).
- If charges of unprofessional conduct, teacher must be given written notice that he or she has at least 45 days to improve before any action on charges will be taken.
- If unsatisfactory performance, teacher must be given written notice that he or she has at least 90 days to improve before action on charges taken. The notice must include the teacher evaluation. Governing board may act during the time period composed of the last one-fourth of the school days it has scheduled for computing apportionments in any fiscal year if, prior to the time period, the teacher has received written notice of unsatisfactory performance, including the teacher evaluation.
- For both unprofessional conduct and unsatisfactory performance, notice must be sufficiently specific to enable the teacher to correct the faults and overcome grounds for charges.

Step Two: Governing board gives notice of intent to dismiss or suspend (Educ. Code §§ 44934, 44936, 44937)

- Governing board decides by majority vote whether to dismiss or suspend without pay at the end of 30 days from the date of service of the notice. The notice cannot be served on the teacher between May 15 and September 15.
- Charges of unprofessional conduct or unsatisfactory performance must be sufficiently specific so that the teacher can prepare a defense. The statutes and rules the teacher is alleged to have violated must be stated, as well as the facts relevant to the charges.
- If no hearing is requested, teacher is dismissed or suspended without pay at expiration of the 30-day period.

Step Three: Hearing (Educ. Code §§ 44943, 44944, 44945)

- If teacher requests a hearing, the governing board has the option either of rescinding its intention to dismiss or suspend, or of scheduling a hearing.
- The hearing must be held within 60 days from the date of the request.
- The process now takes on the formality of preparation for a civil trial, with a formal accusation required from the board and, within 30 days thereafter, the exercise of discovery rights by both parties. Oral depositions may occur after this time frame.
- The hearing is conducted by the Commission on Professional Competence (CPC) composed of a member selected by the teacher, a member selected by the governing board, and an administrative law judge. The law judge serves as chairperson.
- The CPC determines by majority vote whether or not the teacher should be dismissed in a dismissal case, or whether or not the teacher should be suspended (and the period of suspension) in a suspension case.

Step Four: Appeal

- On petition by either party, the decision of the CPC may be reviewed by a court.
- The court exercises independent judgment on the evidence.

Figure 5.1 Steps to Dismiss for Cause—Permanent Teacher

the four-year time period (*Atwater Elementary School District v. California Department of General Services*, 2007).

As previously noted, charges of unprofessional conduct or unsatisfactory performance provide a grace period for the teacher to improve. Upon receipt of the charge(s), the teacher has thirty days to request a hearing. Failure to request a hearing results in dismissal. If a hearing is requested, a rather formalized process initiates, including pre-hearing discovery, and the CPC conducts the dismissal hearing. The CPC is an ad hoc panel of three: One panel member is chosen by the teacher, one is chosen by the governing board, and the third is an administrative law judge. A majority vote of the CPC is required for dismissal. On petition by either party, judicial review of the CPC's decision may occur. Figure 5.1 outlines key steps in the dismissal process and cites the relevant sections of the Education Code.

Layoff

In difficult financial times, school districts may lay off certificated employees for cost savings. A detailed explanation of the layoff process is beyond the scope of this book. We will, however, address the main contours of the process which applies if the matter is not covered by the collective bargaining agreement. The Education Code sets forth three circumstances in which layoffs of certificated employees are permissible: average daily attendance (ADA) layoffs, particular kinds of services (PKS) layoffs, and budget act/revenue limit layoffs. We address the first two types of layoffs.

Elimination of certificated positions is permissible through ADA layoffs if the ADA for the current year is lower than that in either of the previous two school years. Education Code Section 44955 details the process for determining if ADA layoffs are permissible. A mathematical formula is used to produce a percentage corresponding to the decline in ADA.

PKS layoffs permit a reduction in certificated employees, "whenever a particular kind of service is to be reduced or discontinued not later than the beginning of the following school year" and in the opinion of the governing board it becomes necessary to decrease the number of certificated employees in the district (Educ. Code § 44955 (b)). Unlike ADA layoffs, PKS layoffs are not tied to a mathematical formula. PKS layoffs permit the governing board to eliminate certain positions in the district (e.g., school psychologist, nurses) without demonstrating a decline in ADA.

Regardless of the basis for the layoff, the same notice, procedure, and hearing rights extend to all certificated employees to whom the layoffs apply. Additionally, the layoff rights set forth in Education Code sections 44979 and 44959 apply to teachers who hold provisional credentials (e.g., an emergency teaching permit)

(*California Teachers Association v. Vallejo City Unified School District*, 2007). Written notice of layoffs, including the reasons for them, must be given to employees no later than May 15 of the school year in which the layoffs are being conducted. The layoff of a permanent teacher generally cannot occur while any probationary teacher, or any other teacher with less seniority, is retained to render a service the permanent teacher is certificated and competent to render. If necessary, the governing board must reassign a certificated employee with such seniority to another position instead of terminating the employee through a layoff. In the event of a tie between two certificated employees hired on the same date, the governing board must determine the order of termination based solely on the needs of the district and its students. These criteria are known as tie-breaking criteria. If the reassignment requires a permanent teacher to instruct in an area for which the employee does not have a teaching credential or that is not in the teacher's major area of post-secondary study, the governing board must require the employee to pass a subject-matter competency test in the relevant area.

A governing board has some discretion to deviate from the seniority-driven ordering of certificated employees in layoffs. This is known as skipping and is permissible in the following two instances (Educ. Code § 44955 (d)):

- "The district demonstrates a specific need for personnel to teach a specific course or course of study, or to provide services authorized by a services credential with a specialization in either pupil personnel services or health for a school nurse, and that the certificated employee has special training and experience necessary to teach that course or course of study or to provide those services, which others with more seniority do not possess."
- "For purposes of maintaining or achieving compliance with constitutional requirements related to equal protection of the laws."

The layoff process requires a school district accurately to apply all of the statutory rules regarding employee classification. For example, misclassification of a certificated employee as a temporary employee when the employee attained permanent status can result in a chaotic domino effect on the district's seniority list developed for the layoffs.

Employees receiving notices regarding layoffs may request a hearing. An administrative law judge conducts the layoff hearing and prepares a proposed decision containing findings of fact regarding the layoff and a recommendation as to its disposition. The findings of fact address whether the layoffs are permissible. After considering the findings of fact and recommendation, the governing board makes the final decision. A permanent teacher who is laid off is placed on a thirty-nine-month reemployment list. The teacher is given preferential consideration for rehiring based on the order in which the employee was laid off. The process for a laid-off probationary teacher is similar, but reemployment preference is limited to a twenty-four-month period. Under a showing of specific need, however, a governing board may deviate from the general preference to rehire based on seniority. Education Code Sections 44956 and 44957 address reemployment rights for laid-off permanent and probationary certificated employees.

CLASSIFIED EMPLOYEES

Classified employees comprise the other primary classification of public school employees. While classified employees do not hold a credential, they enjoy rights that are similar to certificated employees in the areas of permanent status, discipline and dismissal, and layoff.

Categories

We previously discussed the four main categories of certificated employees (substitute, temporary, probationary, and permanent). Classified employees also serve in different categories. The employment, discipline, termination, and layoff rights of a classified employee are a function of the employee's classification. Technically, there are only two categories of classified employees: permanent and probationary. An individual may serve in a classified position, however, as a short-term or substitute employee. Short-term and substitute employees are not part of the classified service. Rounding out the classified service are individuals serving in senior management.

Slightly complicating our discussion is the existence of merit system school districts. In a merit system school district, the classified employees are subject to different rules and have different rights as compared their counterparts in a nonmerit school district. We note the major differences later in the chapter.

A classified employee attains permanent status after completion of a prescribed period of probation not to exceed one year (Educ. Code § 45113). Prior to attaining permanent status, a classified employee is considered probationary unless the employee is serving in a short-term or substitute capacity. A short-term employee is "any person who is employed to perform a service for the district, upon the completion of which, the service required or similar services will not be extended or needed on a continuing basis" (Educ. Code § 45103 (d)(2)). An individual hired solely to repaint the bleachers on a high school football field without additional assignments is an example of a short-term classified employee. A short-term employee is not part of the classified service of the school district. Prior to hiring someone in this capacity, the governing board must identify the specific duties the employee will perform and the ending date of the employee's service. An individual contract between the short-term employee and the governing board sets forth the terms and conditions of employment. Although the ending date of the short-term classified employee's service may be shortened or extended by the governing board, the ending date cannot exceed 75 percent of the school year. Seventy-five percent of the school year is defined in this section of the Education Code as "195 working days, including holidays, sick leave, vacation and other leaves of absence, irrespective of the number of hours worked per day."

A substitute employee is defined as "any person employed to replace any classified employee who is temporarily absent from duty" (Educ. Code § 45103 (d)(1)). An individual hired for one week to stand in for a janitor on sick leave due to illness is an example of a substitute employee. A substitute employee is not part of the classified service of the school district. One or more substitute employees also may serve for a period not to exceed sixty calendar days to fill a vacancy for which the school district is currently seeking to hire a permanent classified employee. A collective bargaining agreement, however, may provide for a different period of time.

A governing board may adopt a resolution designating certain positions as senior management of the classified service (Educ. Code § 45100.5). An individual serving in this capacity cannot obtain permanent status. The employment terms are a function of the employee's individual contract with the governing board.

In addition to short-term and substitute employees, the following non-certificated positions are not part of the classified service of a school district: part-time playground positions, apprentices, professional experts employed on a temporary basis for a specific project regardless of the length of employment, full-time students employed part-time, and part-time students employed part-time in any college work-study program or work experience program (Educ. Code § 45103). These employees serve on an at-will or contract basis for the governing board.

Evaluation and Discipline

We previously discussed the Education Code's guidelines for use in the evaluation of certificated employees. No similar provisions apply to the evaluation of classified employees. A governing board, however, must "prescribe written rules and regulations, governing the personnel management of the classified service" (Educ. Code § 45113 (a)). These rules and regulations may include criteria for evaluation. The procedures for the evaluation are negotiable with the classified employees' union.

Rules and regulations prescribed by the governing board dictate the causes for which suspension of a classified employee may be imposed. Such rules and regulations generally set forth a wide range of inappropriate behavior warranting suspension and/or dismissal. A collective bargaining agreement may also address the suspension of a classified employee.

As a general rule, misconduct occurring beyond two previous years or during the employee's probationary period cannot form the basis for discipline (Educ. Code § 45113 (d)). However, misconduct may form the basis for discipline charges if the misconduct was concealed or not disclosed by the employee when it could be reasonably assumed that the employee should have disclosed the facts to the school district.

A governing board must also adopt procedures governing the suspension of classified employees, including informing the employee of the specific charges being brought and the employee's right to request a hearing. Notice of the specific charges must be in "ordinary and concise language of the specific acts and omissions upon which the disciplinary action is based" (Educ. Code § 45116). The notice must also contain a statement of the cause for the disciplinary action. If violation of a regulation or rule is involved, the rule or regulation also must be in the notice. Citing the rule or regulation without further detail as to the specific charges and cause for the disciplinary action is insufficient for imposing discipline. A Skelly conference is required prior to placing an employee on an unpaid suspension. As we previously discussed, a Skelly conference is an informal meeting during which the charges against the employee are explained and the employee may issue a response. If the employee requests a hearing, the hearing will occur under the procedures adopted by the governing board, or in some instances, pursuant to the terms of a collective bargaining agreement. The hearing results in a proposed decision the governing board may accept, reject, or modify.

Dismissal and Layoff

Dismissal of a permanent classified employee may occur only for cause pursuant to rule or regulation prescribed by the governing board. The same notice and hearing rights discussed for suspension of a classified employee also apply to the dismissal of a permanent classified employee. This includes the necessity of specific charges, right to a hearing, and a Skelly conference if suspension without pay is ordered. Education Code Section 45113 (d)'s general prohibition against basing discipline on conduct occurring more than two years prior or before the employee attainted permanent status also applies to dismissal. Service of the charges by mail may not be sufficient to provide notice consistent with due process of law if the employee does not work the entire school year because the employee could be gone for an extended period of time and not receive the notice (*California School Employees Association v. Livingston Union School District*, 2007). Absent an unlawful motivating factor (e.g., retaliation against free speech), a probationary classified employee may be dismissed without notice or any other due process.

The layoff of classified employees is permissible for "lack of work or lack of funds" (Educ. Code § 45308). A layoff of classified employees is initiated by resolution of the governing board. Classified employees are generally to receive written notice of a layoff thirty days in advance. The governing board has discretion to determine the positions or classifications subject to the layoff. As with the layoff of certificated employees, the order of the layoff is a function of seniority or, as the phrase is used in Education Code Section 45308, "length of service." Length of service consists of all hours in paid status, whether during the school year, a holiday, recess, or during any period that a school is in session or closed, but does not include overtime pay. Under a collective bargaining agreement, length of service may be defined as the date of hire. A collective bargaining agreement may also include bumping rights for more senior classified employees. Exercise of a bumping right permits a classified employee who would otherwise be laid off to bump a more junior employee. In some instances, the employee subject to the bump may be in a position that was not even within those positions or classifications originally subject to the layoff. As an alternative to being laid off, a school district may permit a classified employee to accept a voluntary demotion or transfer or reduction of hours. Special rules contained in Education Code Section 45117 govern the layoff of classified employees due to the expiration of a specially funded program.

Laid-off classified employees are placed on a reemployment list for thirty-nine months. Reemployment occurs in the reverse order of the layoff. Classified employees accepting a voluntary demotion or reduction in hours have these same rights plus twenty-four additional months of eligibility on a reemployment list. Education Code Section 45298 governs the reemployment rights of classified employees in the context of a layoff or voluntary demotion or reduction in hours.

Merit System School Districts

In a merit system school district, a three-member personnel commission and a personnel director are responsible for the administration, regulation, discipline, and dismissal of classified employees. Education Code Section 45220 and following sections detail the various ways in which a school district may adopt the merit system. These include through vote of the classified employees, vote of the governing board of the school district and the county board of education, and vote of the electorate of the school district. A personnel commission composed of three members governs a merit system. The governing board of the school district appoints one member of the commission, and the classified employees of the school district appoint another. These two members of the commission choose the third member. The commission thereafter appoints a personnel director who is responsible for carrying out the administration of the classified employees of the district.

The commission is responsible for classifying all of the classified employees in the district. The governing board retains the power to prescribe the duties of the various positions. The commission also prescribes rules governing a wide array of items pertaining to the classified employees of the district. These include rules regarding applications, examinations, eligibility, appointments, promotions, demotions, vacations, discipline, leaves of absence, performance evaluations, and compensation within classifications. If a collective bargaining agreement exists, these rules must be consistent with the agreement (Educ. Code § 45261(b)). Although the commission makes recommendations to the governing board regarding salary schedules for the classified service, the governing board may approve, amend, or reject these recommendations (Educ. Code § 45268). The commission also oversees the discipline of classified employees. Aside from promulgating the rules governing the discipline of classified employees, the commission also hears appeals regarding the suspension, demotion, or dismissal of classified employees.

ADMINISTRATORS

An administrator does not have a property interest in the administrator's position. This means the administrator does not have the right to a due process hearing prior to dismissal, release, or reassignment to a non-administrative position. However, an administrator may acquire permanent status to a previously held certificated or classified position. The Education Code contains special notice provisions applicable to the release of administrators, including certain high-level administrators such as superintendents and assistant superintendents.

A school district's internal policies and procedures for reassignment of administrators may provide a due process right that would not otherwise exist and which can be enforced in state court (*Berstein v. Lopez*, 2003). While the administrators in *Berstein* were unsuccessful in federal court, they prevailed in state court after the judge determined that the district violated due process of law by reassigning administrators to less well-paid teaching positions without following the district's own procedures for reassignment of administrators.

An administrator serves in an administrative position at the pleasure of the governing board. Education Code Section 44951 provides that these employees may be released (through written notice by March 15) for the following year. Absent written notice, the employee will continue in the position through the following school year and be once again subject to the prospect of release prior to March 15. Section 44951 does not apply to administrators who have a written contract specifying an ending date beyond the current school year. Section 44951 also does not apply to an administrator in a position funded for less than a school year or serving in an acting position. Section 44951's March 15 notice requirement also applies to the reassignment of an administrator to another administrative position.

An administrative employee may have permanent status in a previously held certificated or classified position. Thus, even if the employee is released from an administrative position, the employee may return to the position in which permanent status was obtained. Dismissal from that position must adhere to the applicable certificated or classified dismissal procedures. Prior to reassignment to a teaching position, the administrator has a right to request the governing board to state the reasons for the reassignment in writing (Educ. Code § 44896). If the reason for the reassignment is incompetency, the employee is also entitled to an evaluation under the Stull Act.

Education Code Section 35031 governs the release or reassignment of superintendents, associate or assistant superintendents, or senior management employees who serve for a period of four years. A written notice of nonreemployment for these administrative employees must be provided forty-five days prior to the expiration of the employee's contract term. Failure to timely provide this notice results in reelection of the employee for a subsequent term of equal length.

THE PERSONNEL FILE

The Education and Labor Codes govern the rights of public school employees regarding their personnel files. These rights are important because the personnel file often serves as the largest source of information and/or evidence for employee evaluation, discipline, and dismissal. Labor Code Section 1198.5 permits an employee to inspect personnel records regarding either the employee's performance or any grievance concerning the employee. Additionally, Education Code Section 44031 gives an employee the right to receive notice and comment on any derogatory statement before the comment is entered into the employee's personnel file. The employee also can attach the employee's own response to the derogatory statement. An employee without a credential has the right to access the employee's numerical score on a written examination used to screen or qualify for a position. Education Code Section 44031 and Labor Code Section 1198.5 give an employee the right to inspect certain records in the employee's personnel file. An employee is entitled to copies of only those documents that the employee signs (Labor Code § 432). The employee's union, however, may have a right to examine the entire personnel file if the file is necessary and relevant to representation of the employee in a grievance.

A school district's failure to observe these rules can frustrate or invalidate efforts to impose discipline or dismissal. In the 1979 California Supreme Court decision of *Miller v. Chico Unified School District*, Hal Miller was reassigned from administrator to teacher. The reassignment was based, in part, on numerous confidential memoranda that were never shown to Hal prior to the reassignment. Rather than reinstate Hal to his prior position, however, the court sent the case back to trial to determine if the absence of these documents from Hal's personnel file was prejudicial.

PUBLIC SCHOOL EMPLOYEE LEAVE RIGHTS

A collection of state and federal statutes governs the leave rights of public school employees. These statutes consist of select provisions of the Education and Labor Codes, a state law entitled the California Family Rights Act (CFRA), and a federal law entitled the Family and Medical Leave Act (FMLA). The CFRA and FMLA are almost identical. To the extent either law affords an employee a greater benefit, the employee receives the greater benefit. Although we do not address the CFRA or FMLA in this book, a reference to useful websites regarding them can be found in Appendix C.

Certificated and classified employees receive personal necessity leave. Personal necessity leave permits an employee to use sick leave pursuant to rules and regulations of the governing board or in certain statutorily defined circumstances (e.g., death or serious illness of a family member, an accident involving the employee's person or property). Unless a collective bargaining agreement specifies otherwise, certificated and classified employees are generally limited to seven days per school year of personal necessity leave. Education Code Section 44981 governs personal necessity leave for certificated employees. Education Code Section 45207 governs personal necessity leave for classified employees.

Education Code Section 44043.5 permits the establishment of a catastrophic leave program. Under this program, district employees may donate accrued sick and vacation leave to another employee for use when the employee or a member of the employee's family experiences a catastrophic illness or injury. A "catastrophic illness" or "injury" is an illness or injury expected to incapacitate the employee (Educ. Code § 44043.5 (a)(1)). An illness or injury expected to incapacitate a member of the employee's family, which requires the employee to care for the family member for an extended period of time, is also a catastrophic illness or injury. An employee must exhaust all sick leave and other paid leave before accessing a catastrophic leave program. If a school district desires to establish a catastrophic leave program, the program's terms and conditions must be negotiated with the exclusive representative of the employees' union.

After exhausting all paid leave, certificated and classified employees become eligible for differential pay. For a period not to exceed five months, certificated and classified employees on an extended leave receive their salary minus the salary paid to their substitute replacement. Education Code Section 44977 governs differential pay for certificated employees. Education Code Section 45191 governs differential pay for classified employees. Among the differences in differential pay between certificated and classified employees are determining when the period of five months starts to run, and how salary is calculated if no substitute employee is hired.

Certificated and classified employees exhausting all paid leave, including differential pay, who remain unable to return to work are placed on a reemployment list. While on the reemployment list, the employee can return to a position for which the employee is qualified. Education Code Section 44978.1 governs the reemployment list for teachers. A probationary teacher may remain on a reemployment list for twenty-four months, and a permanent teacher may remain on the list for thirty-nine months. Education Code Section 45192 governs the reemployment list for classified employees.

FEDERAL AND STATE ANTIDISCRIMINATION LAWS

A number of state and federal antidiscrimination laws applicable to the private sector also apply to public school employers and their employees. Taken in the aggregate, these civil rights laws protect applicants, employees, and even ex-employees from discriminatory employment practices on the basis of race, color, national origin, religion, sex, age, disability, and, among other protected classifications, sexual orientation. In certain areas, state law affords a public school employee greater protections than federal law. In this section we highlight the major differences between federal and state law.

Title VII

Title VII of the Civil Rights Act of 1964, commonly known as Title VII, is a federal antidiscrimination law governing private and public employers (42 U.S.C. § 2000e and following sections). The Equal Employment Opportunity Commission

(EEOC) is the federal agency charged with promulgating regulations interpreting Title VII. EEOC also investigates allegations that an employer violated Title VII. Title VII applies to state and local government entities, which include the entire range of public school employers. Title VII prohibits employment practices or discrimination based on race, color, religion, sex, or national origin. These protections extend to job applicants, current employees, and even former employees in some instances.

Race or color discrimination includes discrimination based on associating with persons of another race. Title VII's prohibition against discrimination based on religion requires an employer to accommodate the religious beliefs or observations of employees. This matter is discussed in Chapter 7. Sex discrimination includes discrimination on the basis of pregnancy and extends to sex discrimination in which the offender and victim are the same sex. Title VII does not extend to discrimination on the basis of sexual orientation. Sexual harassment is a form of sex discrimination that violates Title VII and includes a variety of circumstances such as unwelcome sexual advances, requests for sexual favors, or other verbal or physical conduct of a sexual nature that explicitly or implicitly affects an individual's employment, interferes with work performance, or otherwise creates an intimidating, hostile, or offensive work environment. The victim does not necessarily have to be the person harassed but may be anyone affected by the offensive conduct. Unlawful sexual harassment may occur despite the absence of economic damage or loss of employment to the victim. EEOC's regulations define national origin discrimination as "including, but not limited to, the denial of equal employment opportunities because of an individual's, or his or her ancestor's, place of origin; or because an individual has the physical, cultural, or linguistic characteristics of a national origin group" (29 C.F.R. § 1606.1).

Title VII case law contains a number of different discrimination theories. These include a straightforward allegation of discrimination against an individual (known as disparate treatment claim), an allegation that a facially neutral policy is having a discriminatory effect on a protected class and the policy is not justified by a business necessity (known as a disparate impact or adverse impact claim), and an allegation of a regular policy or procedure of discrimination on a class-wide basis (known as a pattern and practice or systematic disparate treatment claim). The theory of discrimination is important because it dictates the manner in which the plaintiff employee and defendant employer must put forth their respective cases to the court. For example, if a school principal alleges that he was terminated based on race, he must prove the following to maintain a Title VII disparate treatment lawsuit: (1) he was a member of a protected class; (2) he was qualified for his position;

(3) he was discharged; and (4) he was replaced by a person outside of the protected class. If the principal can demonstrate each of these factors by a preponderance of the evidence (i.e., more than 50 percent of the evidence), there is an inference of discrimination the employer school district must rebut by demonstrating that there was a legitimate, nondiscriminatory reason for the adverse employment action. If the school district can make this showing, the burden then shifts back to the principal to demonstrate that the school district's reason was not the true reason for his termination, but a pretext for discrimination.

Title VII requires an individual to first file a charge with EEOC or Department of Fair Employment and Housing (DFEH), a state agency, before bringing a legal action in court. Accessing a necessary intermediate administrative process prior to bringing suit in a court is referred to as exhaustion of an administrative remedy. The charge must be filed with EEOC within 180 days after the employee knew or should have known of the allegedly discriminatory act. If a complaint is first sent to a state agency (e.g., pursuant to a parallel state employment antidiscrimination law), the complainant has 300 instead of 180 days to file the complaint with EEOC. Once EEOC completes its investigation, the charging party receives a right-to-sue letter. In some instances EEOC, or DFEH if the complaint is made at the state level, may bring a legal action on behalf of the complainant. If a lawsuit is to be filed by the employee, the employee must do so within ninety days after the issuance of the right-to-sue letter. Failure to first bring a charge alleging a violation of Title VII with EEOC or timely initiating a legal action after receipt of the right-to-sue letter may foreclose the aggrieved party from suing the employer in court.

A successful plaintiff in a Title VII lawsuit may be entitled to a range of remedies, including back pay, front pay, reinstatement, and compensatory damages. Under the Civil Rights Act of 1991, punitive damages are available under Title VII for intentional discrimination by a private, but not government, employer. A prevailing plaintiff is also entitled to recover attorneys' fees and costs. Title VII, like other civil rights statutes, contains a fee-shifting provision to encourage attorneys to represent individuals alleging employment discrimination. This operates as an exception to the general rule in America that each party bears their own costs in a lawsuit.

Americans with Disabilities Act and Section 504

The Americans with Disabilities Act of 1999 (ADA) and Section 504 of the Rehabilitation Act of 1973 (Section 504) are federal laws prohibiting discrimination on the basis of disability. ADA applies to public and private employers, while Section 504 applies only to recipients of federal funding. As public employers in receipt of federal funding, all public school employers are subject to ADA and Section 504.

ADA and Section 504's antidiscrimination provisions also extend to certain students meeting the statutes' definition of disability. This aspect of ADA and Section 504 is addressed in Chapter 8. Our focus in this chapter is the application of these statutes to employment. ADA and Section 504 provide essentially identical obligations to public school employers and rights to public school employees. Unless otherwise indicated, our reference to ADA also applies to Section 504. Effective January 1, 2009, the ADA Amendments Act of 2008 significantly changes the ADA and Section 504. Updates regarding the ADA Amendments Act of 2008 will be available at this book's website at www.californiaschoollaw.org.

ADA's protections extend to a "qualified individual with a disability." ADA defines a disability as (1) a physical or mental impairment that substantially limits one or more major life activities; (2) a record of such an impairment; or (3) being regarded as having such an impairment. An individual who meets one of the foregoing criteria satisfies ADA's definition of disability. The first definition of disability contains multiple components. A physical or mental disability is broadly defined to include any physiological, mental, or psychological disorder. Major life activities are functions such as caring for oneself, performing manual tasks, walking, seeing, hearing, speaking, breathing, learning, and working. The phrase "a record of such impairment" means that the person has a history of, or has been misclassified as having a mental or physical impairment that substantially limits one or more major life activities. The phrase "being regarded as having such an impairment" refers to an individual who is treated as though the individual has a physical or mental impairment that substantially limits a major life activity and the individual does not. The ADA Amendments Act of 2008 requires interpretation of the definition of "disability" in favor of broad coverage.

In determining whether an individual satisfies ADA's definition of disability, is the individual to be considered with or without corrective devices (e.g., glasses for an individual with poor eyesight)? The 1999 U.S. Supreme Court decision of *Sutton v. United Airlines* addressed this question for Karen Sutton and her twin sister Kimberly. Karen and Kimberly both have severe myopia, resulting in poor uncorrected vision. In 1992, the twins applied for employment with United Airlines as commercial airline pilots. They were invited to an interview and flight simulator tests. At their interview, however, the twins were informed that a mistake had been made because their uncorrected vision did not meet United Airline's minimum requirements. The interviews were terminated, and neither twin was offered a position.

The twins sued United Airlines under ADA, alleging discrimination on the basis of disability. United Airlines raised a single defense: the twins are not disabled within the meaning of ADA, and thus not entitled to the law's protections, because neither is substantially limited in a major life activity while wearing glasses. The U.S. Supreme Court agreed with United Airlines in holding that "the use or nonuse of a corrective device does not determine if an individual is disabled; that determination depends on whether the limitations an individual with an impairment actually faces are in fact substantially limiting" (p. 488). The ADA Amendments Act of 2008 largely overruled *Sutton* and, except for ordinary eyeglasses or contact lenses, prohibits consideration of ameliorative measures to determine if an impairment substantially limits a major life activity.

Satisfying ADA's definition of disability is not the end of the inquiry to determine if ADA's protections apply to an employee. The individual must be a qualified individual with a disability. This aspect of ADA is unique to the employment context and does not apply to ADA or Section 504 issues for students. ADA defines a qualified individual with a disability as "an individual with a disability who, with or without reasonable accommodation, can perform the essential functions of the employment position that such individual holds or desires" (29 C.F.R. § 1630.2(m)). Determining if an individual satisfies this definition is a fact-intensive inquiry.

The ADA requires an employer to make reasonable accommodations for qualified individuals with a disability. Reasonable accommodations include making existing facilities readily accessible, restructuring jobs, and acquiring or modifying equipment (29 C.F.R. § 1630.2 (o)). For example, permitting a blind employee to bring a guide dog to work is a reasonable accommodation. Employers do not have to provide an accommodation that will impose an undue hardship on the employer. An undue hardship is an action requiring significant difficulty or expense (29 C.F.R. § 1630.2 (p)). Interpretive guidance accompanying the ADA's regulations cites an example of a waiter with a disabling visual impairment requesting the employer nightclub to provide bright lights as a reasonable accommodation. The guidance concludes that this request will impose an undue hardship if the bright lights will destroy the ambiance of the nightclub or make it difficult for patrons to view the stage show. An employer is required to engage in an interactive process with an employee to determine if a reasonable accommodation is necessary, and if so, the nature of the accommodation.

The EEOC enforces ADA with the same powers, remedies, and procedures applicable to Title VII. An individual seeking to initiate a legal action against an employer under ADA must first file a timely complaint with EEOC, wait for a right-to-sue letter, and thereafter bring suit within ninety days of receipt of the letter. The time period for filing a complaint under Title VII also applies to ADA.

An individual may demonstrate disability discrimination under ADA with the same discrimination theories applicable to Title VII. For example, a plaintiff alleging wrongful termination in violation of ADA must prove the following: He or she meets ADA's definition of disability; he or she is able to perform the essential functions of the job, with or without reasonable accommodation; and he or she was terminated because of disability. A prevailing employee in an ADA action may generally seek and receive the same relief available under Title VII (e.g., back pay, front pay, reinstatement, compensatory damages). Punitive damages, however, are not available under ADA.

Fair Employment and Housing Act

The Fair Employment and Housing Act (FEHA) is a California law governing employment discrimination (Govt. Code § 12900 and following sections). FEHA applies to private and public employers. FEHA defines public employers as the State of California, cities, counties, local agencies, special districts, and any other political or civil subdivision of the state. Governing boards, county superintendents of schools, and charter school operators are subject to FEHA. FEHA, however, does not apply to nonprofit religious organizations or to corporations exempt from state and federal taxes. FEHA's protections extend to both employees and job applicants. An applicant does not include a person who voluntarily, and without coercion, withdraws his or her application before being interviewed, tested, or hired.

FEHA's antidiscrimination provisions are broader than those in Title VII or ADA. FEHA prohibits discrimination on the basis of race, religion, color, national origin, ancestry, physical or mental disability, medical condition, sex, age, pregnancy, or sexual orientation. Title VII does not extend to physical or mental disability, medical condition, age, or sexual orientation. FEHA also differs from federal law (ADA) on the definition of disability. Recall that ADA requires a mental or physical impairment to substantially limit one or more major life activities. FEHA, however, merely requires a physical or mental impairment to limit a major life activity. Unlike the holding in *Sutton*, FEHA explicitly provides that the determination of whether a mental or physical impairment "limits" a major life activity is to be undertaken without regard to mitigating measures such as medications, assistive devices, or reasonable accommodations. FEHA therefore affords public school employees a number of rights not available under federal law.

FEHA also prohibits two types of sexual harassment applicable to the workplace. The first is quid pro quo sexual harassment in which a person in a position of authority conditions tangible benefits (e.g., a favorable job review, increase in salary, promotion, etc.) on sexual favors. The second is a hostile workplace environment. Unlike quid pro quo sexual harassment, a hostile workplace environment does not require the loss of a tangible job benefit, nor the harasser to be in a position of authority as to the victim. A hostile work environment exists where the employee can demonstrate (1) that he or she was subjected to sexual advances, requests for sexual favors, or other verbal or physical conduct of a sexual nature; (2) that this conduct was unwelcome; and (3) that the conduct was sufficiently severe or pervasive to alter the conditions of the victim's employment and create an abusive working environment (*Ellison v. Brady*, 1991).

FEHA contains an exhaustion of administrative remedies requirement like that in Title VII. Before bringing a legal action based on FEHA, an individual must file a verified complaint with the Department of Fair Employment and Housing (DFEH), wait for DFEH to investigate, and receive a right-to-sue letter.

SUMMARY

A public school employee's due process rights are a function of the employee's classification. Depending on the employee's classification, due process may range from a phone call informing a substitute teacher that the substitute's services are no longer necessary to a time-consuming and expensive dismissal proceeding for a permanent teacher. Within the two primary classifications of certificated and classified employees, there is a stepladder series of subclassifications defining the employee's property right and attendant amount of process due prior to deprivation of that right. The four classifications of certificated employees are substitute, temporary, probationary, and permanent. Substitute employees enjoy the least job protections while permanent employees have the most. Substitute teachers serve at the pleasure of the governing board, and the release of temporary teachers is permissible with written notice. The nonreelection process requires written notice to a second-year probationary teacher prior to March 15 of the teacher's year of employment. Otherwise the teacher is reemployed for the subsequent school year and attains permanent status.

Classified employees are either probationary or permanent, although an individual may serve in a classified position in a substitute or short-term capacity. Like their certificated counterparts, permanent classified employees enjoy the most job protections, including the right to a formal hearing prior to dismissal.

The dismissal of permanent teachers may occur only for cause, as defined in the Education Code. The grounds of unprofessional conduct and unsatisfactory performance require advance written notice and an opportunity for the teacher to improve prior to initiation of dismissal proceedings. Dismissal and suspension of probationary teachers is quite rare because the nonreelection process for these individuals is so simple.

The Education Code sets forth a number of unique leave and reemployment rights for certificated and classified employees. Federal and state leave laws complement these rights. Federal and state antidiscrimination laws also govern the rights of public school employees and the obligations of their employers. These laws prohibit discrimination on the basis of race, national origin, color, sex, religion, age, and, among other protected classifications, disability. To the extent a state law affords an employee a greater benefit than federal law does, the employee receives the benefit of the state law.

6 | RIGHTS OF EXPRESSION

For most of the history of public schooling, neither teachers nor students had constitutionally protected free speech rights at school. By the late 1960s, major judicial rulings had extended rights of expression to both. The decisions coincided with the expansion of civil rights in the wake of the 1954 *Brown v. Board of Education of Topeka, Kansas,* school desegregation decision. Student activism of the 1960s added further stimulus. More recently, both federal and state courts have retreated somewhat from the early decisions, but the core constitutional principles remain.

In this chapter we discuss the extent to which both educators and students have rights of expression within traditional public and charter schools and what the implications are for school administrators in making personnel and student discipline decisions. Because the right to freedom of the press and the right to association are closely associated with free speech, our discussion will encompass them as well. As we noted in the first chapter, constitutional rights generally do not exist in the private sector. Thus, what expression rights educators and students have in this setting depends upon the policies of these institutions.

EDUCATOR EXPRESSION RIGHTS

Speaking Out on Matters of Public Concern

In 1968 the U.S. Supreme Court was confronted with a case involving an Illinois teacher who was dismissed after he wrote a letter critical of the school board's handling of a bond election. The letter was published in a local newspaper. The school board contended that Marvin Pickering owed his employer a certain amount of allegiance and that the letter writing was detrimental to the efficient administration of the schools. Pickering, on the other hand, maintained that he had a First Amendment right as a citizen to comment on school board matters and doing so should not compromise his position as a teacher. The First Amendment to the U.S. Constitution provides in part that Congress shall make no law "abridging the freedom of speech, or of the press; or the right of the people peaceably to assemble, and to petition the Government for a redress of grievances." As we noted in the first chapter, the Fourteenth Amendment extends these provisions to states and their political subdivisions. The Illinois Supreme Court decided in favor of the school board. However, had the case arisen in California, the outcome may have been different because by the 1960s the California Supreme Court had become particularly sensitive to the claims that public employees were being dismissed for exercising their rights as citizens. The *Pickering* case was appealed directly to the U.S. Supreme Court.

In a unanimous decision, the U.S. Supreme Court overruled the Illinois Supreme Court and decided in favor of Marvin Pickering (*Pickering v. Board of Education*, 1968). But the Court recognized from the start that both the school board and the teacher had credible arguments. The Court's task, wrote Justice Thurgood Marshall, was to "arrive at a balance between the interests of the teacher, as a citizen, in commenting upon matters of public concern and the interest of the State, as an employer, in promoting the efficiency of the public services it performs through its employees" (p. 568). In this case, the justices found insufficient evidence to justify Pickering's dismissal. The Court observed that the bond election clearly was a matter of public concern and that teachers are the community members most likely to have informed and definite opinions on how funds allotted to schools should be spent. While it was true that the teacher's letter contained some false statements, the Court observed that the school board could easily have corrected them by writing its own letter to the newspaper. There was no evidence that Pickering's statements had undermined his effectiveness as a teacher or disrupted the school. Likewise, there was no evidence that he had made false statements knowingly or recklessly.

Pickering is a seminal decision both for public schoolteachers and for governing boards. For teachers, it clearly establishes the right to speak out on matters of public concern and not fear loss of employment. In fact, the California Supreme Court has ruled that any form of retaliation for the exercise of First Amendment rights is out of bounds. In the words of that court:

> Any sanction imposed for the exercise of protected First Amendment conduct must be viewed as having a chilling effect on speech and on the right of teachers to

engage in those activities which are protected by the First Amendment. Lesser penalties than dismissal can effectively silence teachers and compel them to forego exercise of the rights guaranteed them by our Constitution. (*Adcock v. San Diego Unified School District*, 1973)

For governing boards and administrators, *Pickering* establishes the necessity to assemble sufficient documentation to show that the exercise of free speech has been abused. This can be done by showing that the teacher's effectiveness has been significantly compromised, that school operation has been disrupted, or that false statements have been made knowingly or recklessly. Assertions that a teacher's speech "might" or "could" prove disruptive in some way rarely will suffice. This is so because most judges give special weight to robust free speech in a democratic society.

Suppose Marvin Pickering had voiced his comments at school during school hours. To what extent can a teacher exercise free speech on school grounds? A year after the *Pickering* ruling, the California Supreme Court was faced with a challenge to a directive from the Los Angeles City Board of Education that teachers cease circulating a petition on campus during noninstructional time. The petition related to public school financing. The school district conceded that teachers do have a right under the *Pickering* decision to speak among themselves during duty-free periods about such issues. But the district contended that petitioning would be disruptive and hence not constitutionally protected. The California high court disagreed. In a bit of judicial rhetoric characteristic of this period, the justices observed that the governing board could not seriously argue that its teachers should be "unthinking 'yes men'" who never share ideas or fear to do so. The court unanimously ruled that the ban on the petition violated the teachers' free speech rights (*Los Angeles Teachers Association v. Los Angeles City Board of Education*, 1969). At the same time, however, the court did note that the school district could issue a regulation protecting teachers in faculty rooms and lunchrooms from unwelcome interruptions. Called "time, place, and manner" rules, such restrictions are permissible because they do not constitute an outright ban on speech content but rather determine the conditions under which speech rights can be exercised.

A somewhat similar situation arose a number of years later in the San Diego Unified School District. The California Teachers Association filed a lawsuit against the district's ban on the wearing of political buttons anytime during school hours. The school district relied on a provision of the California Education Code that permits, but does not require, school districts to regulate officer and employee political activity during working hours on school grounds and to restrict political activities in general (Educ. Code §§ 7050–7058). The law does permit the use of public resources to provide information to the electorate in a fair and impartial manner on bond issues or ballot measures. The union argued that the San Diego school district restriction intruded on protected free speech. It cited both the First Amendment and Article I, Section 2 of the California Constitution, which provides that "every person may freely speak, write and publish his or her sentiments on all subjects, being responsible for the abuse of this right. A law may not restrain or abridge liberty of speech or press."

The California appellate court ruled that neither the First Amendment nor Article I, Section 2 of the California Constitution limits the power of school authorities to dissociate themselves from political controversy by prohibiting employees from engaging in political advocacy in the classroom (*California Teachers Association v. Governing Board of San Diego Unified School District*, 1996). Wrote the judges, "Most self-evident is the conclusion that when public schoolteachers and administrators are teaching students, they act with the imprimatur of the school district which employs them and ultimately with the imprimatur of the state which compels students to attend their classes" (p. 479). Thus the district's ban on partisan political activity in that setting did not violate the teachers' rights of free speech. However, outside the classroom, the ban could not be enforced because it conflicted with the precedents set by the U.S. and California supreme courts in *Pickering* and *Los Angeles Teachers Association*, respectively, supporting the right of teachers to express their political opinions to each other.

In 1979 the U.S. Supreme Court unanimously ruled that a teacher who expresses views on matters of public concern privately—for example, in the principal's office—also is protected by the First Amendment (*Givhan v. Western Line Consolidated School District*). The case involved a junior high school English teacher whose contract was terminated after she complained about school policies and practices she found racially discriminatory. The Court did recognize that the supervisor-employee relationship may be of greater concern when private expression is involved. If the exercise of free speech impairs institutional efficiency, it may not be entitled to constitutional protection.

Mt. Healthy Test

Let's assume that Bob Instructor is a marginally effective teacher on a probationary contract. Bob is concerned that his contract may not be extended at the end of the year, and he realizes that he is not entitled to notice and a hearing to challenge such an action. He is thinking about filing a grievance or lawsuit should this occur, but wonders what he might allege. A colleague tells him about the *Pickering* decision. Bob has a great idea. He simply will write a letter to the editor of the local newspaper in which he criticizes a school policy on a matter of public concern.

Then, should his contract not be extended, he can allege that he was the victim of retaliation for the exercise of free speech, just as Marvin Pickering had contended. A brilliant strategy and one often used until the U.S. Supreme Court's 1977 decision in *Mt. Healthy City School District Board of Education v. Doyle.*

In *Mt. Healthy*, Ohio teacher Fred Doyle's two-year term contract was not renewed following his phone-in discussion to a radio talk show about the school's faculty dress code policy. While he was not entitled to either notice or a hearing under Ohio law, he requested a statement of reasons for the action. He received a letter from the superintendent explaining that the radio station incident was a factor in the decision. Doyle promptly sued, claiming retaliation for the exercise of free speech. Both the federal trial and appellate courts supported his claim based on *Pickering*. But the U.S. Supreme Court did not. The high court noted that the radio station incident was not the only incident involving Doyle. The record revealed that Doyle had argued with another teacher, culminating in Doyle's being slapped by the other teacher. Both were suspended for a short time. In other incidents, he had argued with cafeteria workers about the amount of spaghetti he had been served, referred to students as "sons of bitches," and made an obscene gesture to two female students when they failed to follow his directive.

Given this record, the Court observed that while a borderline teacher should not be denied tenure because of the exercise of constitutional rights, "that same candidate ought not to be able, by engaging in such conduct, to prevent his employer from assessing his performance record and reaching a decision not to rehire on the basis of that record, simply because the protected conduct makes the employer more certain of the correctness of the decision" (p. 286). The California Supreme Court had expressed much the same sentiment several years earlier, noting that while it would not permit school officials to mask an unconstitutional dismissal behind a statement of valid causes, it also would not allow an ineffective teacher to avoid dismissal by engaging in political activities (*Bekiaris v. Board of Education of City of Modesto*, 1972). The U.S. Supreme Court sent the *Mt. Healthy* case back to the trial court for a determination of whether the governing board would have reached the same decision had it not considered Doyle's comments on the radio. Applying the so-called *Mt. Healthy* test, both the trial and appellate courts later decided in favor of the governing board.

The significance of *Mt. Healthy* cannot be underestimated. The Ninth Circuit has articulated a three-part test for applying the *Mt. Healthy* principles. First, the school employee must show that the speech is constitutionally protected, a relatively easy task if it relates to a matter of public concern. Second, the employee must show that the exercise of free speech played a substantial role in a negative employment decision. This is not an easy burden when there is little evidence and especially when an employee is not entitled to either notice or a hearing, as in the case of the nonextension of a probationary contract. In 2001 the Ninth Circuit upheld a lower-court ruling against three members of the deputy superintendent's cabinet who contested their reassignments as retaliation for free speech. In this case, the employees were unable to overcome a two-year time lap between their speech charging the deputy superintendent with mismanaging federal funds and their reassignments. Nor were they able to establish convincingly that the central office administrator knew of the speech by one of the employees or was opposed to what the other two had said (*Keyser v. Sacramento City Unified School District*). However, in the *Mt. Healthy* case, Doyle had little trouble meeting this burden because the superintendent had sent him a letter telling him that the radio talk show incident played an important role in the contract nonrenewal, even though Doyle was not entitled to written notice of the reasons for the action. The lesson for school administrators, of course, is to avoid citing legally impermissible reasons.

Third, even when free speech does play a substantial role in a negative employment decision, the governing board still can prevail if it can show the existence of job-related deficiencies unrelated to the exercise of the protected right. To do this, the governing board must have been provided documented evidence from school administrators. Without it, the governing board cannot meet the terms of the *Mt. Healthy* test.

An excellent illustration of the *Mt. Healthy* test at work is a 2004 Ninth Circuit decision involving Pamella Settlegoode, an adaptive physical education teacher employed on a probationary contract in the Portland, Oregon, public schools. Her contract was not extended after she wrote lengthy letters to school officials expressing concern about the way disabled students were treated in the school system. At one point, she drew an analogy to discrimination experienced by black students in the South. Before Settlegoode wrote the letters, her performance evaluations were generally positive. But afterward they were more negative, particularly with regard to alleged deficiencies in writing individualized education programs (IEPs) for disabled students. Officials noted in their reply memos that the teacher's communiqués were highly critical of special education services, administrators, and other staff. After Settlegoode's contract was nonextended, she filed a lawsuit seeking damages for violation of her First Amendment rights. The jury found for the teacher on all claims, awarding her $902,000 in economic and compensatory damages. In addition, $50,000 in punitive damages was assessed against her supervisor and one other administrator. The entire award was set aside by the trial judge, but the Ninth Circuit overruled that decision and reinstated the damage awards. The appeals court noted the teacher also was entitled to have her attorney fees paid by the Portland school system.

What is important about the case is the sensitivity that the Ninth Circuit expressed toward the right of school employees to express negative views about school programs that concern the public and the necessity for school administrators to document effectively the justification for negative employment decisions. In this case, Settlegoode's supervisor had based the nonextension recommendation on the teacher's inability to write effective IEPs. However, the court noted that IEP writing is not done by an individual teacher but rather by the IEP team. Further, there was no independent confirmation of the teacher's deficiencies from anyone other than her immediate supervisor, nor was there any evidence that the IEP drafts the teacher had written had been discarded or even substantially revised. In short, the *Mt. Healthy* and *Keyser* requirement of establishing other reasons unrelated to the exercise of the protected right to justify a negative employment decision had not been met. Additionally, the appeals court refused to dismiss punitive damages against the individual administrators, noting that it would have been "patently unreasonable" for them not to conclude that Settlegoode's speech was constitutionally protected (*Settlegoode v. Portland Public Schools*). This decision makes it abundantly clear that administrators should solidly anchor negative employment decisions in job-related deficiencies, and those deficiencies should not suddenly materialize after an employee exercises protected rights.

In 2006 the U.S. Supreme Court tightened up on public employee free speech rights by ruling five-to-four that employee speech on matters of public concern made pursuant to official duties is not constitutionally protected (*Garcetti v. Ceballos*). The case involved an assistant attorney general who alleged that he suffered retaliation by his supervisor after he wrote an internal memo in his official capacity recommending dismissal of a case because of prosecutorial misconduct. He claimed that the memorandum involved a matter of public concern and thus was constitutionally protected. The majority ruled that even if the subject of the memorandum was a matter of public concern, it was written in the assistant attorney general's official capacity as an employee. At the same time, the Court recognized that public employees who make such statements outside their official duties may be entitled to constitutional protection. However, such might not be the case if the employee is in a policymaking position such as a school principal or superintendent. The Ninth Circuit noted in a 1998 decision that "we are most doubtful that the Constitution ever protects the right of a public employee in a policymaking position to criticize her employer's policies or programs simply because she does not share her employer's legislative or administrative vision" (*Moran v. State of Washington*, p. 850).

The case involved a deputy insurance commissioner who was dismissed based on philosophical differences with the insurance commissioner. The deputy commissioner argued unsuccessfully that the dismissal violated her free speech rights.

The U.S. Supreme Court in *Ceballos* added two other caveats to its ruling. First, the justices rejected the contention that employers may curtail employee free speech rights on the job by creating excessively broad job descriptions. Second, they observed that speech related to scholarship or teaching may be treated differently. However, the majority seemed to be talking about academic freedom at the public college and university level, not in public schools where academic freedom exists only minimally, if at all. Despite this ruling, it is important to note that public employee free speech rights are broadly protected under the California Constitution. Furthermore, when a California public employee speaks out about possible wrongdoing, the Whistleblower Protection Act comes into play as described later in this chapter. Given the legal implications, it is always wise to consult the school attorney before penalizing employees for what they say on the job.

Complaints about Working Conditions

In the *Pickering* and *Mt. Healthy* decisions, the U.S. Supreme Court focused on speech relating to matters of public concern. Are employees likewise protected when they complain about their own working conditions? Sheila Myers was employed as an assistant district attorney in New Orleans serving at the pleasure of the district attorney, meaning that she had no contract and hence no expectation of continuing employment. She became disgruntled over a decision to transfer her to prosecute cases in another section of the criminal court. Believing that others also were unhappy about such matters, she constructed a questionnaire and circulated it to fifteen co-workers. The questions centered on office morale, levels of trust in various supervisors, the transfer policy, and the need for a grievance committee. When Harry Connick Sr., the district attorney (and father of the well-known singer by the same name), learned of her action, he considered it insubordinate and terminated her employment. Myers filed suit, contending that she was being penalized for exercising free speech. Both the trial and appellate courts ruled in favor of Myers based on the *Pickering* decision. The U.S. Supreme Court agreed to hear the case.

Once again as in *Pickering*, the Court was faced with balancing the interests involved. But this time in a closely divided opinion, it struck the balance in favor of the employer, distinguishing between speech on matters of public concern and on matters of internal office concern (*Connick v. Myers*, 1983). While the former is entitled to constitutional protection, the latter is not. On balance, the Court found the questionnaire focused on internal matters. It also observed that Myers circulated the questionnaire both at lunch and at other times during working hours, thus undermining the efficiency of the workplace.

In 1997 a California court of appeal handed down a decision that is instructive on how state courts apply the *Pickering, Givhan,* and *Connick* precedents to speech by school employees (*Kirchmann v. Lake Elsinore Unified School District*). The case involved a secretary in the school district's facilities department. The secretary was directed by her supervisor to draft a memo to the superintendent recommending a particular architectural firm be chosen as project manager for future construction projects. Concerned that a consultant to the firm had been involved in its selection, the secretary faxed a notice from her home to the unsuccessful bidders about the appearance of a conflict of interest and suggesting they attend the board meeting to question the matter. After learning of the fax, the secretary's superiors sought her suspension for thirty days, a recommendation accepted by the governing board following an administrative hearing. The secretary challenged her suspension as retaliation for the exercise of free speech.

The appellate court first considered whether the secretary's fax addressed a matter of public concern under the *Pickering* decision or a matter relating to her working conditions under *Connick.* The judges noted that courts in California have been protective of public employee speech critical of governmental operations and that California Government Code Section 81000 and following sections prohibit conflicts of interest by governmental employees and consultants. This being the case, the secretary's fax addressed a matter of public concern. It did not matter that her fax was not aired in public, because *Givhan* protects privately expressed speech on public issues. Nor did it matter that the secretary may have sent the fax because she sought revenge against her supervisor for a threatened layoff. If the speech addresses a matter of public concern, the motive behind its utterance is irrelevant.

Noting that free speech on matters of public concern can lose its protection under the *Pickering* rationale if abused, the judges next examined whether this was the case. They did not find the fax to be knowingly or recklessly false. The secretary's action did not undermine her relationship with her supervisor or the consultant, because no unusual level of loyalty to either was demanded. If the superior-subordinate relationship had been that critical, the judges observed, the district would have sought to reassign the secretary to another position or terminate her employment rather than give her a short-term suspension. Nor was there evidence of any significant disruption of the project manager selection process. Finally, the fact that the secretary was only suspended and not terminated does not diminish her right to protected free speech. As the court noted, "if the speech is protected, any sanction, whatever its severity, is prohibited" (p. 281).

Expression through School Channels

When employees communicate through school-maintained channels of communication, their free speech rights are subject to much greater control than when speaking face-to-face. This is because the school can control its own channels of communication. The key ruling to this effect is a 1983 U.S. Supreme Court decision involving a challenge to a collective bargaining agreement between an Indiana school district and its recognized teachers union granting the union exclusive access to an interschool mail system (*Perry Education Association v. Perry Local Educators' Association*). Another union argued that the restriction violated the First Amendment. The Court decided in a narrow five-to-four ruling that the school mail system is not automatically a public forum available to teachers, their associations, and others to disseminate information. A public forum is a place for virtually unrestricted communication. Street corners and parks are prime examples of public forums. To enforce a content-based exclusion in this setting, the government must have a compelling reason that is very precise in its application (judges term this as being "narrowly tailored" to serve the state's interest). For example, a municipality might be able to curtail an inflammatory racist speech on a public street corner if the harangue threatens imminent lawless action. The municipality would argue that it had a compelling interest in preventing a riot and that its action was very precise (or "narrowly tailored") because it applied to only a single speaker.

At the opposite end of the spectrum from the open forum is the closed forum. A closed forum is governmental property that is traditionally not a place for public communication. A prison is a good example. The Court in Perry viewed the public school mail system to be inherently a closed forum under school district control unless the school has opted to convert it into a "limited open forum." A limited open forum accommodates certain types of communication but not other types. For example, a school district could choose to open up its mail or e-mail system to certain types of communication—say, announcements by community organizations—but not to commercial advertising. Once the communication system is open to certain categories of information, however, the school cannot discriminate within categories. Thus, if community organizations like the garden club have access to make announcements of their meetings through the school communication system, the school would have difficulty denying access to Planned Parenthood or a gay-lesbian community organization for a similar purpose. In the *Perry* case, the rival union argued that once the school permitted the recognized teachers union to use the school mail system, it had to permit rival unions to do so too. But the majority noted that there was a difference between the recognized union and its rivals. When the teacher union was selected as the exclusive bargaining agent, it became the official representative of all teachers in the school system on matters relating to the collective bargaining contract. Its status had become quite different from those of rival labor organizations. Permitting the recognized bargaining agent to use the interschool mail system to communicate with teachers about labor-management relations did not create a limited open forum for competing labor organizations. The majority noted that these entities still could communicate with teachers through school bulletin boards, meetings on school property after hours, and outside of school.

The *Perry* ruling was cited in a 1996 case involving the open session of a school board meeting in the Moreno Valley Unified School District. Like many districts, the school board's policy specified that no oral or written presentations in open session could include charges or complaints about district employees, whether or not such employees were identified. A parent and president of a statewide Mexican activist organization identified a middle school principal and the district superintendent during remarks she made about parent complaints during an open session. She was ejected from the meeting and later filed suit, contending the restriction was a violation of free speech. The federal judge agreed (*Baca v. Moreno Valley Unified School District*). Under the California open meeting law, known as the Brown Act, school board meetings are open to the public, and the public has a right to address the school board on matters related to school affairs (Govt. Code § 54954.3). The open session thus constitutes a limited open forum. While the governing board can confine the discussion to school business under *Perry*, the judge noted that it cannot restrict speech within that category unless it can establish a compelling interest for doing so and can show that its action was narrowly tailored to serve that interest.

In *Baca*, the court found no compelling interest to prevent criticism of the named school officials. Wrote the judge: "It is difficult to imagine a more content-based prohibition on speech than this policy, which allows expression of two points of view (laudatory and neutral) while prohibiting a different point of view (negatively critical) on a particular subject matter (District employees' conduct or performance)" (p. 730). It did not matter that employees cannot bring defamatory actions against their attackers under California law, because comments at open sessions of board meetings are absolutely privileged (Civil Code § 47 (b)(3)). The constitutionally protected right of members of the public to speak freely to elected officials at board meetings takes precedence. Even though they are employees, teachers have the same right to address the school board and cannot be penalized for doing so. A provision of the Education Code gives all school employees this right (Educ. Code § 44040). The U.S. Supreme Court likewise has ruled that a teacher has a constitutional right to speak out during the open session of a school board meeting. The case arose when a member of a Wisconsin teacher union was permitted to speak at a school board meeting on a matter involving the union; the union later filed an unfair labor practice claim against the district, claiming that only the union could speak to the board about employment matters (*City of Madison v. Wisconsin Employment Relations Commission*, 1976).

The lesson of *Perry* and *Baca* is that whether or not a school-maintained channel of communication is open to free speech to any extent depends upon state law and governing board policy. If a limited open forum has been created, then school authorities cannot discriminate within the categories of speech that are allowed.

Educator Association Rights

The right of association is anchored both in constitutional and statutory law. The U.S. Supreme Court long has supported the right of teachers to join groups and causes without fear of losing their jobs. A key ruling is *Shelton v. Tucker*, handed down in 1960. In that case, the Court ruled that this right had been violated by an Arkansas statute requiring teachers as a condition of continued employment to file annually an affidavit listing every organization they belonged to or regularly supported during the previous five years. Wrote Justice Potter Stewart for the Court, "It is not disputed that to compel a teacher to disclose his every associational tie is to impair that teacher's right of free association, a right closely allied to freedom of speech and a right which, like free speech, lies at the foundation of a free society" (pp. 485–486). Stewart added, "The vigilant protection of constitutional freedoms is nowhere more vital than in the community of American schools" (p. 487). There are less intrusive means, noted the Court, for the state to inquire into the fitness and competency of its teachers.

To some degree the right of association overlaps with the right of privacy. Teachers have a right to their own lifestyle outside of school. The California Supreme Court ruled as much in a 1969 decision (*Morrison v. State Board of Education*). *Morrison* involved a teacher in the Lowell Joint School District. The teacher had a virtually unblemished record, but his lifetime teaching credential was revoked because he had engaged in private homosexual acts with a consenting adult outside of school some years before. As discussed in more detail in Chapter 10, the court ruled that a public schoolteacher cannot be dismissed for lifestyle behavior unless evidence is presented showing unfitness to teach.

Neither free speech nor the right to associate is absolute. In a free speech case with overtones of associational rights, the Ninth Circuit decided against a teacher who aggressively advanced his religious beliefs to students in and out of class. The teacher complained that the school principal directed him not to discuss religion or to attempt to convert students to Christianity while meeting with students on campus, including lunch and before and after school. For reasons discussed in Chapter 7, the appeals court found that the restriction was justified in light of the school's interest in avoiding advancing religion (*Peloza v. Capistrano Unified School District*, 1995).

The right of association in the context of labor organizations is a well-established statutory right in California. One of the purposes of the Educational Employee Relations Act is "to promote the improvement of personnel management and employer-employee relations within the public school systems in the State of California by providing a uniform basis for recognizing the right of public school employees to join organizations of their own choice" (Govt. Code § 3540). The entire matter of unions and collective bargaining is discussed in Chapter 4.

Whistleblowing

The term "whistleblowing" refers to reporting illegal activity in the workplace to appropriate authorities. Like most states, California has enacted a statute that protects public employees who "blow the whistle" on improper governmental activities. Known as the California Whistleblower Protection Act, it is found in California Government Code Section 8547 and following sections. Its provisions are applied to schools by a 2000 statute bearing the ungainly title of the Reporting by School Employees of Improper Governmental Activities Act (Educ. Code § 44110 and following sections). In essence, the latter provides that a school employee who reports a suspected violation of law in good faith is protected from retaliation. The statute encompasses both illegal orders and improper governmental activities. An "illegal order" means a directive that is contrary to federal, state, local law, rule, or regulation or a directive to work outside the scope of employment in conditions that would unreasonably threaten the health of the employee or the public. Improper governmental activity encompasses a work activity by a school district or employee that violates a state or federal law or regulation including, but not limited to, corruption, malfeasance, bribery, theft of government property, fraudulent claims, fraud, coercion, conversion, malicious prosecution, misuse of government property, or willful omission to perform a duty. Also falling into this category are activities that are economically wasteful or involve gross misconduct, incompetency, or inefficiency. Reports of alleged wrongdoing are to be directed to an official agent such as a school administrator, member of the governing board, county superintendent of schools, or superintendent of public instruction.

School employees who believe they have suffered actual or threatened reprisal for exercising their whistleblower rights can file a written complaint with their supervisor, school administrator, or governing board and also may file a claim with local law enforcement. Those who intentionally interfere with the right of an employee to report alleged wrongdoing in good faith are subject to criminal penalties. The latter encompasses a fine of not more than $10,000 and a jail term of not more than one year. Civil damages, including punitive damages and attorneys' fees, also can be imposed if the injured party has notified local law enforcement when filing the complaint with the district. Intentional interference with an employee's whistleblowing rights can result in disciplinary action by the school district, including termination of employment. Finally, the statute provides that it does not diminish any rights that employees have under a collective bargaining agreement or any other state or federal law. There also is a whistleblower provision in the state's Labor Code that can be applied in the education context (Section 1102.5). A California court of appeal ruled in 2005 that the reassignment of a junior high school principal to a magnet school after she complained to a state assembly member about the transfer of surplus school funds violated this section. The court agreed with the principal that her transfer to the magnet school, while an easier administrative position, would deny her the opportunity to become adept at turning around low-performing schools, something she strongly desired (*Patton v. Grant Joint Union High School District*).

As with the *Mt. Healthy* decision discussed earlier, nothing precludes a school district from taking an adverse action against a school employee who exercises whistleblower rights if there are other reasons unrelated to the whistleblowing to justify the action. Thus, marginally effective employees cannot use the whistleblower act to shield themselves from an adverse personnel action.

STUDENT EXPRESSION RIGHTS

Traditionally, school officials have stood in loco parentis with regard to students, meaning they have the same right to control students in school that parents have to control them at home. Accordingly, the old maxim "children are to be seen and not heard" pretty much applied to the status of student free speech. But in 1969, this all changed. In one of its most important education law decisions, the U.S. Supreme Court advised that "It can hardly be argued that either students or teachers shed their constitutional rights to freedom of speech or expression at the schoolhouse gate." That decision begins our discussion of student expression and associational rights.

Face-to-Face Communication

Christopher Eckhardt, John Tinker, and Mary Beth Tinker, secondary students in the Des Moines School District, were involved with their parents in the peace movement during the Vietnam War. To publicize their objections to the war and their support for a truce, the students opted to wear black armbands to school in December 1965. Learning that this might be the case, school officials announced a policy that anyone who came to school with an armband would be asked to remove it, and if he failed to do so, would be suspended from school. Undeterred, the trio wore their armbands to school. All were suspended and did not return until after the planned period for wearing armbands had ended. In addition to these students, eleven-year-old Hope Tinker and eight-year-old Paul Tinker also wore armbands to their elementary school. Because the suspension rule applied only to the secondary students, the elementary school students were not suspended. Instead, their teachers took advantage of the opportunity to engage the elementary students in a discussion about dissent in a democratic society.

A year after the *Pickering* decision and in one of the last decisions of the progressive Court headed by Chief Justice Earl Warren, former governor of California, the justices voted seven-to-two to uphold the right of students to wear their symbolic armbands in school as a form of free speech (*Tinker v. Des Moines Independent Community School District*, 1969). The Court did not confine student expression to any particular part of the campus. A student's speech rights "do not embrace merely the classroom hours," wrote Justice Abe Fortas for the majority. Fortas added: "When he is in the cafeteria, or on the playing field, or on the campus during the authorized hours, he may express his opinions, even on controversial subjects like the conflict in Vietnam" (pp. 512–513). At the same time, the Court recognized that the public school is not the equivalent of the public park. The environment must be conducive for teaching and learning. Accordingly, a student loses the right of free speech if the student materially disrupts the school or substantially interferes with the rights of others. The majority cited with approval a 1966 ruling by the U.S. Court of Appeals for the Fifth Circuit in which that court had upheld a school prohibition against the wearing of "freedom buttons" after students at an all-black high school in Mississippi engaged in boisterous distribution of the buttons by trying to pin them on others, throwing buttons through windows, and refusing to attend class (*Blackwell v. Issaquena County Board of Education*). Conversely, in the Tinker case, the school had no convincing evidence that any disruption had taken place. A highlight of the oral argument before the high court occurred when Justice Thurgood Marshall asked the attorney for the school district about the extent of the armband wearing:

Q. How many were wearing armbands?

A. There were five suspended for wearing armbands.

Q. Any wearing armbands that were not suspended?

A. Yes, sir, I think there were two.

Q. That makes seven . . . Seven out of 18,000? And the school board was advised that seven students wearing armbands were disrupting 18,000? Am I correct?

A. I think, if the Court please, that doesn't give us the entire background that builds up to what was existing in the Des Moines Schools at the time the armbands were worn.

In addition to the material disruption/substantial invasion of the rights of others condition on the exercise of student free speech, the Court's decision pertained only to the three named secondary school students. The majority never mentioned the two elementary students. Consequently, there are few decisions supporting free speech rights at the elementary level. In one of the few, the U.S. Court of Appeals for the Seventh Circuit observed that "grammar schools are more about learning, including learning to sit still and be polite, than about robust debate" (*Muller v. Jefferson Lighthouse School*, 1996, p. 1538). The case involved a Wisconsin fourth grader who sought permission to hand out invitations to a religious meeting during school hours. Expressing some ambivalence about what the law is in this area, the court nevertheless allowed the student to hand out the invitations but regarded the elementary school as a nonpublic forum subject to reasonable regulation by school officials.

The majority in *Tinker* clearly opted for a view of the secondary school as a marketplace of ideas. Writing for the Court, Justice Fortas phrased it this way:

> In our system, state-operated schools may not be enclaves of totalitarianism. School officials do not possess absolute authority over their students. . . . In our system, students may not be regarded as closed-circuit recipients of only that which the state chooses to communicate. They may not be confined to the expression of those sentiments that are officially approved. (p. 511)

Expressing quite a different view, Justice Hugo Black in dissent observed that "one may, I hope, be permitted to harbor the thought that taxpayers send children to school on the premise that at their age they need to learn, not teach" (p. 522). For Black, the school is a place for the inculcation of the values, skills, and knowledge that the community wishes students to learn. These two perspectives on the purpose of school—to serve as a marketplace of ideas or to inculcate community values and beliefs—underlies much of the tension in the case law in this area and continues to dominate dialogue among educators as well.

The *Tinker* decision robustly protects inter-student communication. California law goes even farther. Education Code Section 48907 gives all students in California public schools a broad right of free speech and free press, including access to bulletin boards, distribution of printed material including petitions, and the wearing of buttons and insignia. Citing both the First Amendment and Article 1, Section 2 of the California Constitution, Education Code Section 48950 gives California public and private secondary school students, except those in private schools controlled by religious organizations, the same rights of expression on school grounds that they enjoy off campus. This section also gives them the right to seek a court order against enforcement of a school rule that violates this provision. School officials may impose reasonable time, place, and manner regulations. No protection is given to harassment, threats, or intimidations that are not constitutionally protected. The question, of course, is when does speech fall into this category so as not to be entitled to constitutional protection? Much speech is intended to be disputatious. Both Section 48907 and Section 48950 prohibit negative employment actions against school employees who support student expression rights.

In addition to being disputatious, student speech sometimes can be offensive as well. A case in point is a high-profile case triggered by Poway high school student Chase Harper's decision to wear a T-shirt with an anti-gay message to school during a "Day of Silence" organized by the Gay-Straight Alliance and permitted by the school. Believing the observance endorsed homosexuality, Harper donned a T-shirt bearing the words "I will not accept what God has condemned" on the front and "Homosexuality is Shameful 'Romans 1:27' " on the back. He wore another T-shirt with a similar message the next day. Considering the T-shirts too aggressive and the words inflammatory, the principal had Chase remain in the office for the remainder of the day. Through his parents, Harper filed suit against the school district, seeking among other things a preliminary injunction against the high school's refusal to let him wear the T-shirts. The federal district court judge denied the preliminary injunction, maintaining that the student was unlikely to be successful at the forthcoming trial in asserting a First Amendment right to wear the T-shirt because of potential disruption. In a controversial two-to-one decision, the U.S. Court of Appeals for the Ninth Circuit agreed with the judge's decision but then went on to articulate a new basis for denying student free speech on campus (*Harper v. Poway Unified School District*, 2007). The majority held that student speech loses its protection under the First Amendment if it constitutes derogatory and injurious remarks directed at student's minority status such as race, religion, and sexual orientation. The dissenting judge found this rationale unworkable, as did many commentators after the decision was announced. The later hearing before all the judges assigned to the Ninth Circuit did not change the ruling. The case was then appealed to the U.S. Supreme Court, which declared the request for a preliminary injunction moot, because Harper had graduated. This had the effect of canceling out the Ninth Circuit opinion. However, the litigation resumed at the trial court level when Chase's sister became involved. Early in 2008 the trial court judge ruled in favor of the school district, observing that school officials can restrict student speech that expresses damaging statements about sexual orientation and that school officials can require students to state views in a positive manner. How this ruling will fare on appeal in light of the protection of the armband wearing in *Tinker* that clearly offended students in the Des Moines school district remains to be seen.

In 1996 the Ninth Circuit provided clarification on when students can be disciplined for making threats. The case involved a tenth grade student in the Poway Unified School District who had spent several hours trying to get her schedule changed. When she met with her counselor for what she thought was the last time, the counselor told the student that the classes she wanted were overloaded. Though there was some apparent confusion as to what transpired next, the appellate court wrote that the student responded, "I'm so angry, I could just shoot someone." The counselor maintained that the student said, "If you don't give me this schedule change, I'm going to shoot you!" The student apologized for her inappropriate behavior, but the counselor was sufficiently concerned that she later notified school administrators. The student was given a three-day suspension, which she and her parents challenged as a violation of her right to free speech under the First Amendment and Education Code Section 48950.

The lower court decided in favor of the student. However, the Ninth Circuit reversed, opting to believe the counselor. The judges agreed that threats of physical violence, whether made on or off campus, are not protected by the First Amendment; and two of the three agreed that threats are not protected by Section 48950 of the Education Code either (*Lovell v. Poway Unified School District*, p. 372). The judges noted that in light of violence prevalent in many schools, school officials are justified in taking student threats against faculty and students seriously. A few years later, the Ninth Circuit noted that "Although schools are being asked to do more to prevent violence, the Constitution sets limits as to how far they can go. Just as the Constitution does not allow the police to imprison all suspicious characters, schools cannot expel students just because they are 'loners,' wear black and play video games. Schools must achieve a balance between protecting the safety and well-being of their students and respecting those same students' constitutional rights" (*Lavine v. Blain School District*, 2001, p. 987). In this case, however, the appeals court did uphold the temporary expulsion of a troubled student who had written a threatening poem that he showed to his English teacher. The action, the appeals court concluded, did not violate the student's right to expression but rather was based on concern for the safety of other students. But the appeals court did disallow any mention of the incident in the student's records.

California has a hate-crime statute outlawing force or threat of force that intimidates, oppresses, or threatens a person's exercise of protected rights because of the person's race, color, religion, ancestry, national origin, disability, gender, or sexual orientation or perception of having one or more of these characteristics (Penal Code § 422.6). A subsection prohibits defacing, damaging, or destroying property of any person on these grounds. At the same time, the statute specifies that no person is to be penalized for speech alone; it must be shown that the speech threatened violence against a specific person or group and that the speaker had the apparent ability to carry out the threat. A few years ago, a student sought to overturn his delinquency conviction under this statute for using a permanent black marking pen to write "Nigger" on the classroom door of his school's only African American teacher at the school and "Kill the Niggers" on a concrete post outside the music building where African American students congregated. The student first argued that the school door and the concrete post were not the property of the targeted persons but of the school. The California court of appeal chose to construe the statute broadly so that ownership is not required. Wrote the judges, "As long as the property is regularly and openly used, possessed, or occupied by the victim so that it is readily identifiable with him or her, it falls within the statutory scope" (*In re Michael M.*, 2001, p. 16). The student next argued that the mere scrawling of the words on the door and concrete post did not constitute a credible threat of violence but was instead protected free speech. The appellate court noted that the California Supreme Court had ruled earlier that the statute is targeted at conduct that results from hate speech, not hate speech itself (*In re M.S.*, 1995). Here, the words had a violent connotation. The teacher testified that she was shocked, felt belittled, and was fearful of entering her classroom. The court noted that the words "Kill the Niggers" could reasonably be interpreted as a direct, violent threat. Thus, the speech had lost its protection and could be grounds for the conviction.

While some conduct such as the wearing of armbands or peaceful picketing is a form of expression, conduct that is only tangentially related to expression may not be. In a situation that had a sad ending, several middle school students in the Ontario-Montclair Unified School District left school without permission to walk by themselves to another school to participate in a protest against immigration policies. Later, the students walked home. The assistant principal confronted the students two days later, advising them that their absences were unexcused and that they would be precluded from participating in an end-of-the-year school celebration as a result. One of the students went home and shot himself. He later died. In his suicide note, he mentioned, among other things, the confrontation with the assistant principal. Later, a lawsuit was filed against the principal and the district seeking damages for violation of First Amendment rights and, in the case of the deceased student, his death. While *Tinker* gives public school students the right to express views at school on an issue like immigration after passing through the schoolhouse gate, the judge noted, it "does not give a child license to *exit* the schoolhouse gate with neither permission nor supervision of school personnel, parents, or guardians" (emphasis in the original). The First Amendment claim was rejected. With regard to the contention that the assistant principal's confrontation caused the one student to commit suicide, the federal judge noted that the student's act was unforeseeable and extraordinary, and that the principal had not intended to cause such an act. The case was dismissed (*Corales v. Bennett*, 2007).

In 1986 the U.S. Supreme Court once again visited student free speech. But this time a much more conservative Court headed by Chief Justice Warren Burger drew back from its rigorous protection of student free speech in *Tinker*. The case involved a Washington State high school student, Matthew Fraser, who sought to tailor his speech to his audience to get their attention. Fraser, a member of the school debate team, had won the top speaker award at two statewide debate championships. The audience was a voluntary assembly of high school students brought together to hear nominating speeches for student body officers. Fraser's speech contained abundant sexual metaphor (e.g., "I know a man who is firm—he's firm in his pants, he's firm in his shirt, his character is firm—but most . . . of all, his belief in you, the students of Bethel, is firm"). The speech was every bit as successful as Fraser had intended. Indeed, Fraser was later elected by write-in vote to give the high school graduation speech. But not all were pleased. The school administration suspended Fraser, who thereafter filed suit contending that his First Amendment rights had been violated. Both the federal trial court and the Ninth Circuit decided in his favor under the *Tinker* ruling because there was little evidence of any significant material disruption or interference with the rights of others. But the majority on the Supreme Court ruled that student speech that is lewd, profane, or indecent is not entitled to any constitutional protection at all (*Bethel School District v. Fraser*). Viewing the school as a vehicle for inculcating community values, Chief Justice Burger pointed out that one of its most important functions was to teach students to speak in civilly acceptable ways.

In 2007 the high court by a five-to-four margin rejected a Juneau, Alaska, student's claim that his holding up a sign with the words "Bong Hits 4 Jesus" during released time to view an Olympic parade passing in from of the high school is protected by the First Amendment. Five justices agreed with the school principal that the sign evidenced support for drug use and held that such speech is not constitutionally protected. But the decision was very narrow. Chief Justice John Roberts, who wrote for the majority on the First Amendment issue, refused to endorse the school's position that any student speech viewed as plainly offensive enjoys no constitutional protection. "After all," he wrote, "much political and religious speech might be perceived as offensive to some. The concern here is not that [the student's] speech was offense, but that it was reasonably viewed as promoting illegal drug use" (p. 2629). Two justices who agreed that the speech in this case was not protected drew the line at extending the ruling to other forms of student expression. "I join the opinion of the Court," Justice Samuel Alito wrote, "on the understanding that the opinion does not hold that the special characteristics of the public schools necessarily justify any other speech restrictions." Justice Anthony Kennedy agreed with him. It is important to note that both the California Constitution and Education Code are more supportive of student expression rights than are the rulings of the U.S. Supreme Court. Whether a California court would rule similarly on the "Bong Hits" sign is questionable (*Morse v. Frederick*).

In recent years, students increasingly communicate at school through wireless electronic devices such as cell phones, iPhones, and BlackBerrys. Misuse includes students receiving calls during classes, text messaging during examinations, and taking and transmitting photos that invade student privacy. In accordance with Education Code Section 48901.5, school officials can regulate the use of such electronic signaling devices at school, school-sponsored activities, and at other times when students are under the supervision of school employees. The law also provides that no student shall be prohibited from possessing or using such a device if a licensed physician and surgeon determines it is essential to the health of the student and used for that purpose. The extent to which free speech issues are implicated in student use of electronic devices has yet to be determined.

Expression through School Channels

Two years after the *Bethel* decision, the U.S. Supreme Court was faced with a challenge to school administrator censorship of a school-sponsored student newspaper (*Hazelwood School District v. Kuhlmeier*, 1988). The matter arose when the school principal in a Missouri school district decided that two articles in *Spectrum*, the high school newspaper, should not be published. One dealt with the impact of divorce on students and the other on the experiences of three pregnant, unwed high school students. The editor of the paper, Cathy Kuhlmeier, filed suit, contending that the deletion of the articles violated the First Amendment freedom of the press. The Supreme Court began by reaffirming the *Tinker* ruling that students have First Amendment rights at school. But in quoting from that ruling, the majority in the six-to-three ruling did not cite Justice Fortas's comments about student rights in the classroom. Rather, the Court was careful to limit its affirmance of *Tinker* to inter-student communication occurring elsewhere on campus. Here, by contrast, the student communication was flowing through a channel of communication operated by the school—the student newspaper.

While evidence was conflicting, the majority concluded that the school had not converted the newspaper into an open forum for student expression. Had it done so, the censorship would have been harder to justify. As a closed forum, the newspaper remained under the control of school authorities. Writing for the majority, Justice Byron White observed that educators can control the contents of school-sponsored publications, theatrical productions, and other expressive activities that are part of the school curriculum and supervised by school personnel "to assure that participants learn whatever lessons the activity is designed to teach, that readers or listeners are not exposed to material that may be inappropriate for their level of maturity, and that the views of the individual speakers are not erroneously attributed to the school" (p. 271). The only justification for the control is that it addresses legitimate pedagogical concerns. Applying that rationale to the censorship of *Spectrum*, the Court deferred to the judgment of the principal, noting that he had legitimate concerns that the articles were not well written and did not sufficiently shield the identity of students.

As we have noted, California law is more supportive of student free speech rights than the First Amendment is. In according students the right to exercise freedom of speech and of the press, Education Code Section 48907 specifically includes the right of expression in official school publications "whether or not such publications or other means of expression are supported financially by the school or by use of school facilities." In other words, by statute, school-sponsored publications are limited public forums open for student free expression. The statute provides that student editors of school publications are responsible for assigning and editing the news, editorial, and features content of their publications. While school officials can preview what is being written in school-sponsored publications, they can exercise content control only on narrow grounds. These encompass expression that is obscene, libelous, or slanderous; that so incites students as to create a clear and present danger of the commission of unlawful acts on school premises or the violation of lawful school regulations; or that threatens substantial disruption of school operations. The fact that school officials might disagree with the viewpoints being expressed is not grounds for censorship. School officials have the burden of showing justification "without undue delay" prior to any limitation of student expression under these conditions.

The application of this statute to school-sponsored newspapers was the focus of an important 1988 California appellate court ruling (*Leeb v. Delong*). The case arose after the school principal of Rancho Alamitos High School in the Garden Grove Unified School District prohibited distribution of the April Fools' Day edition of the student newspaper, a decision upheld by the superintendent. The principal particularly was concerned about an article entitled "Nude Photos: Girls of Rancho" in which it was stated that a future issue of *Playboy Magazine* would carry nude photos of Rancho Alamitos students. The article was accompanied by a photo showing five fully clothed female students standing in line, purportedly with applications in hand. The principal believed the article and photo would damage both the girls' reputations and the reputation of the school. The father of one of the girls threatened legal action if the article were published. The principal also felt that the April Fools' Day disclaimer in the paper was too inconspicuous to be noticed and that, because time was short, he had no choice but to ban distribution of the entire issue following his review.

The student editor filed suit, arguing that the limited prior review authorized by Section 48907 is contrary to Article I, Section 2 of the California Constitution. The trial court ruled in favor of the school district, and the student editor appealed. While the appellate court affirmed the lower-court ruling because the passage of time had rendered printing of the newspaper moot and because the student did not challenge the lower court's finding that the article was defamatory, the judges discussed the limits of school board censorship. The court recognized that, while *Hazelwood* does not apply in California and while public publishers do not have the same extensive authority over their publications as do private publishers, the school does not lose all authority to regulate student expression in school-sponsored newspapers. The court noted that Education Code Section 48907 gives school officials the right to preview for limited purposes what students want to include in school-sponsored publications.

The court refused to accept the student's argument that any form of prior review is unconstitutional. The limited use of prior review authorized by Section 48907 serves a valid purpose, the judges observed, in that the school would be vulnerable to defamation suits if it could not preview what students write. This in turn could cause the school to discontinue school-sponsored publications. Accordingly, Education Code Section 48907 does not violate the state constitution by permitting school officials to censor expression from official school publications that they believe reasonably will contain actionable defamation, meaning that the targeted expression contains a false statement likely to harm the reputation of another or hold that person up to shame, ridicule, or humiliation.

However, the threat of a lawsuit is not enough to justify suppression, the judge wrote. There must be a factual determination of potential liability. If public officials are targets of the article, the court advised that actual malice would have to be established. Actual malice means that students deliberately intended to commit an injury by including statements they know to be false or with reckless disregard as to their truth or falsity. School officials may not censor "as a matter of taste or pedagogy." The judges also rejected the principal's contention that prepublication censorship could be justified by concerns over tarnishing the school or district reputation, adding that "The mere reputations of government entities may never be defended by censorship in a society governed by the governed" (p. 503). While the court did affirm the lower court decision against the student, it required the district to implement a set of procedural guidelines providing for a speedy opportunity to be heard and a swift procedure for administrative review in exercising prior review as mandated by Section 48907.

Editorials written by students in school-sponsored school newspapers often address controversial issues that can upset the school community. However, school officials need to be aware that controversy alone is insufficient to justify censorship. A case in point involves an editorial written by Andrew Smith, a Novato High School student, in the high school newspaper, *The Buzz*, in which he spoke out critically against illegal immigration. Among other things, he stated, "[I]f they can't legally work, they have to make money illegal way [sic]. This might include drug dealing, robbery, or even welfare" and "Criminals usually flee here in order to escape their punishment." He ended his editorial by writing "I feel like there has to be some major reforms in immigration policy. I just hope it happens before our country rots from within." The acting principal of the school reviewed and approved *The Buzz* before it was distributed. The editorial upset students and their parents, resulting in an assembly to discuss the matter. At the meeting, the principal apologized for misinterpreting board policy in allowing publication of the editorial but warned that the school would not tolerate any retaliation against Andrew. Without reading the editorial, the superintendent ordered all undistributed copies of *The Buzz* be retrieved and, together with the principal, sent a letter home with all students in which they stated that the editorial shouldn't have been printed. They maintained that student rights of expression under board policy are limited to maintain an orderly school environment and protect the rights, health, and safety of all members of the school community. The student filed suit, alleging that these comments violated his right to free expression, pointing to Education Code Section 48907. The trial court rejected the claim, but a California court of appeal reversed.

The appellate court noted that under Section 48907 student expression is protected unless it incites students to engage in unlawful acts or disrupt school operation. While the article was disrespectful and unsophisticated, it did not incite students to engage in such actions and thus was protected speech. While the court applauded school officials for holding the assembly and found no fault with distancing the school from Andrew's comments, their statement that the editorial shouldn't have been printed violated Section 44907. The court also disapproved of the superintendent's intent to retract undistributed copies of *The Buzz*. The judges advised that "when faced with offensive student speech, school districts must proceed cautiously with due regard to the valuable rights at stake, rather than reacting impulsively because of protest about the speech" (*Smith v. Novato Unified School District*, 2007, p. 527). The U.S. Supreme Court later refused to hear the case.

While the grounds for content censorship are very narrow under California law, nothing precludes school officials from assigning a low grade to a student whose article is poorly researched or sloppily written. Further, the inclusion of a disclaimer would advise readers that the contents of a school-sponsored publication do not bear the school's imprimatur.

Unofficial publications in the form of printed materials that students want to distribute on school grounds cannot be previewed. The prior review procedure of Education Code Section 48907 that was the focus of the court's attention in the Leeb case applies only to official school publications. In the case of unofficial publications, school officials can only impose reasonable time, place, and manner regulations and discipline students for violating them. Because the school in this instance is merely a place of distribution, it has no legal responsibility for content of the materials. The *Leeb* court noted that "the power to regulate time, place, and manner expression cannot be converted into a right to control content" (p. 501).

In sum, by virtue of Education Code Section 48907, California public school students are entitled to greater free expression rights in school-sponsored publications than is true in most other states. School control over content is limited, and the procedures for exercising it are spelled out. At the same time, because the statute concerns only students, the school district's control over the access of nonstudents to school publications and the content of what they wish to convey is greater, as long as the publications remain closed forums to outsiders. Even in this instance, however, the school cannot engage in viewpoint discrimination by permitting expression on only one side of an issue. For example, while a school could not censor from the school-sponsored newspaper a well-written story about birth control penned by one of its high school students, it might very well exclude an advertisement by a birth control clinic in the advertising section of the paper if that section were operated as a closed forum and no ads were permitted on the subject of procreation and birth control. The issue remains tricky, however; and for this reason, school publication policies and practices should be carefully reviewed with the school attorney.

Student Dress, Grooming, and Uniforms

In 1971 the U.S. Court of Appeals for the Ninth Circuit rejected the claim advanced by a high school student and a community college student that they have a First Amendment right to have long hair (*King v. Saddleback Junior College District*). However, in making the contention, neither student explained what the expression was. The appellate court discussed possible sources of such a right other than the First Amendment but noted a lack of consensus among judges generally as to what it might be. "No doubt their confusion is fostered by the tenuous nature of the right asserted," the judges mused (p. 938). Finding no interference with a significant constitutional right, the court ruled against the students.

The same year, a California court of appeal addressed the issue. The case involved a fourteen-year-old student who was suspended from school for three days because he refused to cut his hair in conformity with the school's rule regarding hair length for males. Like their federal counterparts in the *King* case, the state appellate judges were wary of anchoring a student's right to personal grooming in the First Amendment. Nor did they feel comfortable equating it to a right of marital privacy. However, they did find a right to personal grooming in the word "liberty" of the Fourteenth Amendment. But the judges in this case were reluctant to give personal grooming much weight, opting to defer to the judgment of school officials. "At most," wrote the judges, "hair style is an indefinite and vague expression of personality, individuality or of an idiosyncrasy much like the color or style of clothes or deportment" (*Montalvo v. Madera Unified School District Board of Education*, pp. 600–601). All that is necessary to justify controlling the length and style of hair is a legitimate concern on the part of the school administration relating to the educational process. The judges found such in interest in maintaining discipline and protecting the health and safety of students. The court pointed to testimony that long hair might subject a male student to danger in a shop class or to razzing from other students, testimony that clearly dates the case. The trial court's decision in favor of the school district was upheld.

Education Code Section 35183 recognizes that "gang-related apparel" is hazardous to the health and safety of the school environment and gives governing boards the authority to ban it through a dress code policy. At the same time, the statute acknowledges the difficulty of identifying constantly changing gang attire and gang affiliation, and suggests the adoption of a school uniform as an alternative. No particular style of uniform is described. The statute leaves this detail to the school principal, staff, and parents. Adoption of a dress code banning gang attire or instituting a school uniform, according to Section 35183, does not violate the students' free speech rights under Education Code Section 48950.

In 2008, the Ninth Circuit confronted the constitutionality of mandatory student uniforms. The case arose when several Nevada students contended that the uniforms established by their schools in conformity with a school district policy violated their rights of expression and free exercise of religion. The court ruled against the students by a two-to-one vote in *Jacobs v. Clark County School District*. The policy, the majority observed, had nothing to do with prohibiting a particular form of "pure speech" like the restriction in *Tinker* against armbands protesting the Vietnam War. Rather the policy prohibited all forms of "expressive conduct" via dress and thus warranted a less searching level of judicial scrutiny than used for viewpoint-based speech restrictions like the one in *Tinker*. The majority was a little troubled by the fact that the school district did permit uniforms to display school logos on clothing but concluded this was less for purposes of expressing a viewpoint than for an identifying mark. The court also noted that students still had the right to engage in interstudent communication during the school day, publish articles in school newspapers, join student clubs, and dress as they like outside of school. So could students in the Nevada district wear armbands on their school uniform protesting the uniform policy? While the majority didn't address the matter, it appears from the ruling that any form of communication on a school uniform other than the school logo would be impermissible. The dissenting judge argued that the majority's rationale was inconsistent with *Tinker* and contrary to its own 1992 *Chandler v. McMinnville School District* ruling permitting students to wear pro-teacher buttons on their clothing.

While lawsuits always are possible over dress code restrictions, especially those attempting to define and prohibit gang-related attire, a uniform policy in California schools is less likely to result in litigation. This is so because Section 35183 provides that "the governing board shall provide a method whereby parents may choose not to have their children comply with an adopted school uniform policy." Presumably, those who are likely to bring lawsuits would avail themselves of the opt-out opportunity. The statute also provides that if a uniform policy is adopted, it may not be implemented without less than six months' notice to parents and without the availability of resources to assist economically disadvantaged families.

Right of Association

In 1981, the U.S. Supreme Court handed down an important First Amendment decision pertaining to student associational rights on a public college campus. This decision led directly to an important federal statute extending associational rights to public secondary school students. In *Widmar v. Vincent* (1981), the question arose whether the University of Missouri, which had made its facilities available to registered student groups, could refuse to accommodate a student religious group that wished to meet for worship and religious discussion. Writing for the Court in this eight-to-one decision, Justice Lewis F. Powell observed that by accommodating student groups, the university had created a limited public forum and, having done so, could not discriminate among them on the basis of speech content. While the university contended that the separation of church and state provision in the First Amendment known as the establishment clause (the focus of our attention in Chapter 7), as well as a similar provision in the Missouri Constitution, required that it not permit religious groups to practice their religion at a public university, the Court disagreed. Wrote Justice Powell: "Having created a forum generally open to student groups, the university seeks to enforce a content-based exclusion of religious speech. Its exclusionary policy violates the fundamental principle that a state regulation of speech should be content-neutral" (p. 277).

Congress extended the ruling in *Widmar v. Vincent* to public secondary school student groups when it enacted the Equal Access Act (EAA) in 1984. Originally intended to apply only to student religious groups, the statute makes it unlawful for any secondary school receiving federal funding to "deny equal access or a fair opportunity to, or discriminate against, any students who wish to conduct a meeting within that limited open forum on the basis of religious, political, philosophical, or other content of the speech at such meetings" (20 U.S.C. § 4071 (a)). Under EAA, a limited open forum exists when the school allows one or more noncurriculum-related student groups to meet on campus during noninstructional time. The U.S. Supreme Court defined the term "noncurriculum-related" when it upheld the EAA in *Board of Education of Westside Community Schools v. Mergens* in 1990, a decision discussed in more detail in Chapter 7. A group is directly related to the curriculum if the subject matter of the group is taught, if the subject matter of the group concerns the curriculum as a whole, if participation in the group results in academic credit, or if participation is related to a specific course. If the secondary school accommodates one or more groups that do not fall into any of these categories, then it has created a limited open forum under the act and must accommodate all similar groups that wish to meet.

In the *Mergens* case, the school argued that it had a closed forum because it permitted only curriculum-related groups to meet. But using the Court's definition, the justices concluded that the scuba diving and chess clubs, as well as a service group that worked with special education classes, were not curriculum related. Thus, the school had a limited open forum and Bridget Mergens's religious club had a right to meet on campus during noninstructional time. The same would be true for any other student-initiated group that desired to meet.

Some noncurricular student groups can be quite controversial. Such was the case with the Gay-Straight Alliance (GSA) that sought to meet under EAA at the El Modena High School in the Orange Unified School District. Anthony Colin and a friend decided to form the club after Matthew Shepherd, a Wyoming youth, died following a brutal assault motivated at least in part by his homosexuality. The purpose of the club was to raise public awareness and promote tolerance by providing a safe forum for discussion of issues related to sexual orientation and homophobia. Colin found a faculty member to sponsor the group and submitted a club constitution in compliance with school policy. While the school had a limited open forum, school officials had their doubts and forwarded the application to the school board. While the application was pending before the board, the group was not allowed to participate in a one-day informational fair about student groups. Nevertheless, over fifty students signed a petition in support of the club. Administrators tried to get the students to change the club's name and to steer its mission away from sexual orientation. The school board denied the club's application because it allegedly infringed on the school's teaching of sex education. The students sought an injunction under EAA to overturn the board's decision.

In a carefully reasoned opinion, the federal district court granted the injunction (*Colin ex rel. Colin v. Orange Unified School District*, 2000). The judge rejected the school's novel argument that because the GSA was curriculum related, the school could refuse to recognize it. The club's mission was not concerned with the physiology of sex education. Even if it were, it would be inconsistent for the governing board to exclude the club and at the same time teach sex education. Moreover, the court observed that the board did not have authority to foreclose access to the campus because a group's speech content may relate to the curriculum in some way: "The only meetings that schools subject to the Act can prohibit are those that would 'materially and substantially interfere with the ordinary conduct of educational activities with the school'" (p. 1146). There was no evidence that a community gay-lesbian support group controlled the GSA contrary to the terms of EAA. Efforts by the administration to change the name and mission of the club violated the group's speech and associational rights. Furthermore, the court noted that the board's delay and discrimination against the students ran counter to legislation prohibiting discrimination based on sexual orientation in public schools (Educ. Code § 200).

In sum, the right of older students to associate has become clearly established. While the public secondary school may find the content of expression objectionable, even contrary to the mission of the school, it has little authority to intervene once a limited public forum has been created. To this extent, the school is a marketplace of ideas. However, the authority of the state and the school over what transpires in the classroom is quite a different matter.

EXPRESSION RIGHTS IN THE CLASSROOM

Teacher Academic Freedom

Academic freedom remains at best a nebulous concept. The U.S. Supreme Court did recognize the right in a seminal 1923 decision (*Meyer v. Nebraska*). The case involved Robert Meyer, a German American teacher in the Evangelical Lutheran Church of Zion Corners, who was arrested for violating a Nebraska statute preventing instruction in non-English languages to students below the eighth grade. The law had been enacted during the backwash of resentment against the foreign-born following World War I. Meyer had been reading the German version of the Bible story "Jacob's Ladder" to a ten-year-old student during a period in his private school reserved for religious classes. Meyer refused to switch to an English text after being warned by both the county attorney and school superintendent. He refused to pay a fine of twenty-five dollars—a month's salary—even though members of the church offered to pay it for him. Meyer appealed through the state court system, where he lost, and then to the U.S. Supreme Court. With little elaboration, the justices unanimously declared the law unconstitutional as a violation of Meyer's "right to teach" and of a parent's right to control the upbringing of the parent's children.

However, despite such an auspicious beginning, academic freedom has never become a definitive right, though it has been mentioned in later U.S. Supreme Court rulings. In *Epperson v. Arkansas* in 1968, Justice Abe Fortas observed for the Court that "it is much too late to argue that the State may impose upon the teachers in its schools any conditions it chooses" (p. 107). *Epperson* involved a challenge by a teacher to an Arkansas statute prohibiting the teaching of evolution in the state's public schools. Noting that the ban was motivated by a preference for the biblical view of the origin of man, the Court declared the statute an unconstitutional advancement of religion. In his concurring opinion in that case, Justice Potter Stewart recognized that while a state could decide that only one foreign language should be taught in its schools, he doubted that a state could punish a teacher for asserting in the classroom that other languages exist. Justice Lewis F. Powell noted in a 1979 ruling upholding New York State's right to deny public school teaching certificates to aliens that "in shaping the students' experience to achieve educational goals, teachers by necessity have wide discretion over the way the course material is communicated to students" (*Ambach v. Norwick*, p. 78).

Despite these views, judicial support for a public schoolteacher's right to academic freedom is sparse. Most of the few supportive cases date back to the early 1970s during the student rights movement. One of the most supportive was handed down by the U.S. Court of Appeals for the First Circuit in 1969 (*Keefe v. Geanakos*). The First Circuit has jurisdiction for several New England states. In that case, the appeals court recognized that academic freedom encompasses a teacher's explaining to his senior English class the nature and origin of the term "motherfucker" as contained in an assigned article from *Atlantic Monthly*. The judges noted that the discussion was educational in nature and that the same term appeared in books in the school library. If students had to be protected from exposure to such a word, the court observed, "we would fear for their future" (p. 361). Later, however, this same court drew back some from its strong support for academic freedom, noting in another case that it did not intend in the *Keefe* ruling to "do away with what, to use an old-fashioned term, are considered the proprieties, or to give carte blanche in the name of academic freedom to conduct which can reasonably be deemed both offensive and unnecessary to the accomplishment of educational objectives" (*Mailloux v. Kiley*, 1971, p. 566).

A somewhat similar case came before the California Supreme Court during this period; the case involved a probationary teacher whose contract was not extended because he read to his tenth-grade English class a theme containing objectionable language (*Lindros v. Governing Board of Torrance Unified School District*, 1973). The teacher, who also was a Catholic priest on leave from his church, asked his class to write a short paper on a personal emotional experience. To illustrate what he had in mind, he read a story he had written entitled "The Funeral." The story concerned one of the teacher's former students at a predominately black high school in Watts who had died of a heroin overdose. In his poignant and moving story, the teacher had used the term "white mother-fuckin Pig." Teachers had considerable authority to select supplementary instructional material at the high school, and the teacher had not consulted school administrators before reading the story. Books with similar terms were available in the school library. Though no students or parents complained, the teacher's contract was not extended because of the incident.

The California Supreme Court ruled in favor of the teacher. The court distinguished between the use of profane words in a classroom and their inclusion in teaching material. The judges noted that such words have long been used to convey emotion in works of literature. "In sum, we could not impose upon teachers of writing, as a matter of law, that they must tell and teach their students that in depicting the jargon of the ghetto, the slum, or the barrack room, characters must speak in the pedantry of Edwardian English" (p. 536). It is important to note that the court did not rule that the teacher had an academic freedom right to read the story with the offensive terms. Rather, the court based its decision on the lack of good cause for the board not to extend his contract. Today this case would not arise in the same way, because the contracts of probationary teachers can be nonextended at the discretion of the governing board.

Exactly what the status of teacher academic freedom is in California is unclear. The matter arose in the Ninth Circuit in conjunction with the passage of Proposition 227 requiring that English-language learners be taught in English. Among other things, it requires that teaching be "overwhelmingly" in English in English-language classrooms and that "nearly all" classroom instruction be given in English in sheltered English-immersion classes. The California Teachers Association filed suit, claiming that these terms are vague and have a chilling effect on teacher classroom free speech. The Ninth Circuit decided against the association. Wrote the two judges in the majority, "Here, in the context of curriculum presentation, it is the state's pedagogical interests that take clear precedence over the teacher's First Amendment interests" (*California Teachers Association v. State Board of Education*, 2001, p. 1154). But the appeals court did not delineate what First Amendment rights a public schoolteacher has in the classroom.

While there are decisions in other circuits that have recognized a teacher's entitlement to some degree of academic freedom, the U.S. Supreme Court's 1988 decision in the *Hazelwood* case discussed earlier dampened further development, even though it involved students, not teachers. There the Court recognized the authority of the school to control the school curriculum. In 2005 a California federal district court cited *Hazelwood* in ruling against an elementary school teacher's claim that his classroom free speech rights were violated. An avowed orthodox Christian, the teacher, Stephen Williams, alleged among other things that his principal in the Cupertino Union School District had expressed concern over incorporation of religion in his teaching. On one occasion, Williams did not submit a lesson plan to the principal for preapproval. The lesson plan handout contained the history of the National Day of Prayer on one side and President Bush's proclamation of a Day of Prayer on the other. A parent complained. After this incident, Williams maintained that his principal directed him to stop distributing religious materials to students and to provide her with advance copies of handout materials so that she could make sure the materials would not upset parents and would not violate the separation of religion and public education. She specifically did not approve the distribution of an "Easter activity" sheet to his class. The federal district court judge observed that under *Hazelwood* the school can exercise content control over the classroom for legitimate pedagogical purposes. Here, the judge ruled that the classroom in an elementary school is a nonpublic forum and that the school principal had a legitimate pedagogical reason for her directives—avoiding advancing religion. Further, the restrictions were not issued until after a series of conferences between Williams and the principal over the religious nature of his materials. Thus, there was no violation of the teacher's free speech rights. And because no constitutionally protected activity was restricted, Williams was not denied any due process rights through what he alleged were unconstitutionally vague policies and practices. While these claims were dismissed, the judge did not dismiss Williams' claim that he was denied equal protection of the laws under the Fourteenth Amendment because other teachers were allowed to include religious expression in their supplemental handouts without principal permission while he as a Christian was not. This matter could proceed to trial (*Williams v. Vidmar*).

The lack of supportive case law has led the California Attorney General to advise that a classroom teacher may not decline to present an abstinence-based sex education program, based on the inclusion of an academic freedom clause in the district's collective bargaining contract. First, the attorney general noted that a collective bargaining contract cannot convey authority on teachers to determine course content and curriculum on sex education, because both are specified by state law and hence nonnegotiable. With regard to academic freedom, the attorney general gave it short shrift: "We find no judicial precedent for the notion that a secondary schoolteacher has a constitutional right to academic freedom" (77 Ops. Atty. Gen. 204, 1994, p. 208).

In a matter tangential to academic freedom, a Los Angeles Unified School District high school teacher attached postings to a bulletin board across the hall from his classroom that took a general anti-gay/lesbian approach. His action was in response to a bulletin board the school established in recognition of Gay and Lesbian Awareness Month. Faculty and staff were permitted to post materials on the board, subject to the oversight of the school principal. Because the teacher's postings were contrary to the message the school wished to convey, the principal directed the teacher to remove his postings. The teacher, Robert Downs, filed a lawsuit against the district, contending that the school had created a free speech forum and that he should be allowed to present an alternative view. The school countered that its bulletin boards are not free speech forums but rather are reserved for messages that the school wants to communicate. The case is interesting because it pits a teacher's speech claims against the speech claims of the school.

Here, the U.S. Court of Appeals for the Ninth Circuit concluded that the school district's speech claims should prevail because it was speaking as the educator. The bulletin boards were its channels of communication. The school had not opened this channel of communication to general discussion and had not opted to let Downs speak as its representative. Thus, the school could insist that its teachers convey the school's chosen curricular message. Downs could advance his own views on homosexuality on his own time, but not "when he is speaking as the government, unless the government allows him to be its voice" (*Downs v. Los Angeles Unified School District*, 2000, p. 1016). The court did not specifically address the extent to which Downs could advance his views in face-to-face discussions with students and other teachers on campus. Given the case law, he should do so with caution.

While there is no academic freedom right to determine a student's grade, California teachers have been given significant authority to do so under state law. Education Code § 49066 provides that a teacher's grade can be changed only if based on clerical or mechanical mistake, fraud, bad faith, or incompetency, and then only in consultation with the teacher. In a 2001 ruling, a California appellate court determined that conduct grades are included within the statutory term "grade" and can be changed only for the reasons listed in the statute (*Las Virgenes Educators Association v. Las Virgenes Unified School District*). The case involved a teacher whose conduct grades were changed after the teacher failed to alert parents as required by district policy. The court noted previous decisions that NM (meaning "no mark") and W (meaning "withdrawal") fall within the term "grade." Since failure to notify a parent is not among the reasons listed to change a teacher's grade, the principal was without authority to do so. While the principal could not change the grade, the principal could hold the teacher responsible for failing to follow district policy. When parents request changes in student records including grades, the teacher who awarded the grade must be present (Educ. Code § 49070). If the parent is unsuccessful, the parent can file an objection that becomes part of the student's record.

While the right of a teacher to teach is not well established in case law and is significantly confined by state curriculum content standards, teachers must have some discretion to address the needs of their students. Teachers and administrators are well advised to check school governing board policy, teacher handbooks, and the collective bargaining agreement to determine the extent to which teachers can introduce supplementary materials into their classrooms, lead students in discussing controversial subjects, and invite outside speakers. When in doubt, always consult the supervisor to avoid trouble later on.

Student Classroom Expression

The U.S. Supreme Court was quite clear in holding in its 1969 *Tinker* decision that student rights of expression encompass the classroom. But in later decisions, the Court drew back from this position. As noted earlier, in its 1986 *Bethel School District v. Fraser decision*, the Court embraced the concept that the purpose of public schools is to inculcate community values and beliefs, not to permit unfettered student free speech. And two years later in *Hazelwood School District v. Kuhlmeier*, the Court indicated that school officials have the authority to determine what manner of speech is inappropriate in the classroom and other venues controlled by the school. While provisions of the California Education Code strongly support student speech rights on campus, as described earlier, they do not expressly include the classroom (Educ. Code §§ 48907, 48950). Further, they do not deny school personnel the right to impose reasonable time, place, and manner regulations on the exercise of student speech. Thus, student expression could be confined to a classroom discussion period and not permitted during a lecture or demonstration. Additionally, any student speech that creates material disruption or substantially interferes with the rights of other students is not constitutionally protected. For example, a student who desires to speak out about the recall election process in California during a physics class would not be entitled to do so, because the speech would clearly disrupt the teaching of physics.

A 1995 California appellate court ruling sheds light on the extent of student classroom expression rights (*Lopez v. Tulare Joint Union High School District*). The case involved students in Valley High School (a continuation school in the district) who had produced a video in their fine-arts class addressing problems of teenage parenting. The video was to be shown to students and parents and entered in an off-campus film competition. Entitled *Melancholianne* after the name of the baby, the film depicted a day in the life of teenage parents in a seedy, unkempt motel room. The father had just been released from prison after serving time for raping another girl. The dialogue included considerable profanity (e.g., "shit," "ass," "pimp," "fuck"), which the students maintained added realism because it was the language they heard every day. The arts instructor agreed. But the principal found the language highly offensive and educationally unsuitable. Relying on an administrative regulation dealing with school publications, he directed that it be removed from the script. Among other things, the regulation specified that school publications must reflect professional standards of English grammar and journalistic writing style, and must not include profanity, defined as language which would not be used in area newspapers. The school board backed the administration; and the students, with assistance from the American Civil Liberties Union, filed a lawsuit contending that the censorship violated their expression rights.

Two of the three appellate court judges accepted the premise that the video was an official school publication, a position that the students and their attorneys apparently did not contest. Thus, the provisions of Education Code Section 48907 applied. As noted earlier, this statute gives public school students broad rights of free speech and press, subject to limited school oversight. The court noted that the statute requires school governing boards to have a written publication code and to review official school publications to make sure that professional standards of English and journalism are followed. Here, the court held that school officials were acting in accordance with Section 48907 when they refused to permit profanity to be included in the video. Further, the judges pointed out that this section of the Education Code does not violate the California Constitution. As an official school publication, the video was a limited public forum subject to the control of the school to achieve a specific purpose. Here the purpose was to teach students not to use profane and vulgar language. Nor did the suppression of the speech violate Education Code Section 48950, which gives secondary school students the same free speech rights at school that they have off campus. This is so because that section expressly indicates that it does not limit or modify the provisions of Section 48907.

The third judge reached the same conclusion, but by a different route. He concluded that *Melancholianne* was not an official school publication. Thus, all the discussion about journalistic standards and prior review of school publications under Section 48907 did not apply. Instead, he viewed the case as one pertaining to student expression within the classroom. Rather than viewing the classroom as an open forum for the exchange of ideas, as had the justices in *Tinker*, this judge viewed the classroom as a closed forum subject to school control. Hence, school officials could prevent students from using profanity in the film because doing so served a legitimate pedagogical purpose.

Given the different perspectives expressed in the *Lopez* case, the degree to which student classroom expression is protected remains unclear. Classroom expression that may involve threats against others is subject to particularly careful scrutiny in light of the recent history of school violence.

SUMMARY

Because public school employees owe some degree of allegiance to their employer, their free speech rights at school are limited. They can speak out on matters of public concern and be free from retaliation so long as they do not abuse the right.

However, they have no constitutional entitlement to complain about working conditions. The manner and extent to which they can do so are determined by school policy and union contracts. The school's interest in controlling the curriculum generally takes precedence over a teacher's claim to academic freedom in the classroom unless governing board policy or the union contract provide otherwise. Some districts explicitly accord teachers the right to choose supplemental teaching materials, to engage students in discussing controversial topics, and to invite speakers to their classes. Others, however, retain tight control over classroom teaching, in part to assure that the state's curriculum content standards are implemented and student achievement targets are met. Thus, it is important for educators to determine what the policy and practices are in their districts and follow them. When uncertain, the best strategy is to ask the supervisor.

As a corollary to the right to speak, school employees have a constitutional right to associate with others. This encompasses the right to join and participate in organizational affairs and to engage in lifestyle activities. Like freedom of speech, however, the right to associate is not absolute. If such activity disrupts the learning environment or undermines the employee's effectiveness, the employee's job may be in jeopardy. Under state law, school employees have a right to participate in labor activities and engage in collective bargaining.

Because students are not employees, they do not owe the same allegiance to their schools as do employees. Therefore, their expression rights are more extensive. As we have noted, the U.S. Supreme Court clearly opted for the view of the school as a marketplace of ideas in recognizing the free speech rights of public school students in the landmark *Tinker v. Des Moines Independent Community School District* decision. At the same time, however, because the school is a place for learning, speech that creates material disruption or invades the rights of others is not constitutionally protected. California law is even more protective of free speech for public school students, giving them broad access to school channels of communication such as bulletin boards and school newspapers. The law even goes so far as to say that both public and nonreligious private secondary school students' expression rights are as extensive in school as outside of school. However, federal and state judicial decisions provide little constitutional protection for student speech that is profane, indecent, or threatening to the safety of others. And, as we have seen, judicial deference to school board authority over classroom instruction has undercut student expression rights in this setting.

The school can impose reasonable time, place, and manner rules that channel when and how student speech can be exercised. While the school has a right to preview what students wish to express in school-sponsored channels of communication such as the school newspaper, its authority under California law to engage in content censorship is quite limited. The school does have a broader right to regulate student dress and grooming, but even here expression rights may surface. Indeed, the wearing of symbolic armbands was what triggered the U.S. Supreme Court's *Tinker* ruling.

The student right of association is safeguarded by the federal Equal Access Act, which gives noncurriculum-related student groups broad access to secondary schools that receive federal financial assistance. The rights of elementary students to free speech and association are much less well defined. This is understandable, given their age and maturity level.

7 | THE SCHOOL AND RELIGION

Education and religion have long been intertwined. Before there were public schools, religious private schools provided most formal education in America. Enacted in 1787, two years before the ratification of the U.S. Constitution, the Northwest Ordinance set aside lands for public education, noting that "Religion, morality, and knowledge being necessary to good government and the happiness of mankind, schools and the means of education shall forever be encouraged." Even after the public common school system began to take shape in the nineteenth century, religion was an integral part of schooling. Much of the early public school curriculum was focused on religion. The famous McGuffey's Reader, introduced in 1836 and used by millions of students until the mid-twentieth century, drew heavily on Protestant religion. In fact, the Protestant character of public schools drove many Catholics to start their own parochial school systems in the late nineteenth century.

Over the years, America has become more religiously diverse. Today, some 140 million Americans are affiliated with 149 different religious groups. Increasing religious heterogeneity within public schools generated conflict and litigation after World War II that has continued unabated to the present. Gradually, a body of law has developed governing many manifestations of religion in public education. It is this body of law that we discuss in this chapter, beginning with a review of applicable constitutional law.

FEDERAL AND CALIFORNIA CONSTITUTIONAL LAW

No Government Establishment of Religion

The writers of the Constitution knew from their experiences that government involvement in religion inevitably generates conflict. If government were to prefer one religion to another, the question arises, "Whose religion?" If religion in general were favored over nonreligion, then nonbelievers and those holding secularized belief systems would be penalized. Seeking to avoid such problems, the founders included a provision in the First Amendment of the U.S. Constitution preventing Congress from making laws "respecting an establishment of religion." By virtue of the Fourteenth Amendment, the provision applies to states and political subdivisions of states like school districts and charter schools. Exactly what the establishment clause means in practice, however, has long been the subject of debate.

To some, the establishment clause merely prohibits government from setting up a state church similar to the Anglican Church in England. To others, the word "an" before establishment of religion indicates that the clause was intended to prevent government involvement with any one or all religious denominations. The latter approach has been characterized as maintaining a "wall of separation between church and state." The wall metaphor originated in a letter President Thomas Jefferson sent to the Danbury Baptist Association in 1802. The U.S. Supreme Court first used the phrase in its 1878 decision holding that, while Mormons have a right to believe in polygamy, Congress can ban its practice (*Reynolds v. United States*). The Court again referred to the wall metaphor in its first prominent ruling involving religion and education (*Everson v. Board of Education*, 1947). What is interesting about the latter decision is that after citing Thomas Jefferson to exclaim how stringent the establishment clause is, the five-justice majority found no bar to the use of public funds to underwrite bus transportation for students attending parochial schools. Writing for the majority, Justice Hugo Black observed that the purpose of the New Jersey legislation was to get students safely to and from school, regardless of what type of school they attended. The four dissenters viewed the aid program as tax support for religion because it furthers the mission of these schools to provide religious training and teaching.

Continued uncertainty as to how to apply the establishment clause is evident in later decisions. In 1948, one year after the *Everson* decision, the Court ruled against a released-time program whereby religious instruction was given to public school students on school premises during the school day (*McCollum v. Board of Education*). Four years later, the Court upheld a released-time program that allowed public school students to leave school during the school day to receive religious instruction off school grounds (*Zorach v. Clauson*, 1952). Justice Black, who had written for the Court in the *Everson* and *McCollum* decisions, found this degree of accommodation unconstitutional and dissented.

As time went on, the Supreme Court developed criteria for deciding when a law violates the establishment clause. While the Court has not used them consistently and has modified them in cases involving government assistance to religious institutions, lower federal courts continue to rely upon some or all of them in resolving conflict over religion in public schools. The criteria of constitutionality are:

1. A secular, as contrasted with a sectarian or religious, governmental purpose
2. A primary effect that neither advances nor inhibits religion
3. No excessive entanglement of government with religion
4. No government endorsement of religion
5. No coercive effect on objectors to participate in government-directed religious activities

The California Constitution also has provisions restricting government involvement with religion. Article I, Section 4 provides in part that "The Legislature shall make no law respecting an establishment of religion." Article XVI, Section 5 states, "Neither the Legislature, nor any county, city and county, township, school district, or other municipal corporation, shall ever make an appropriation, or pay from any public fund whatever, or grant anything to or in aid of any sectarian sect, church, creed, or sectarian purpose, or help to support or sustain any school, college, university, hospital, other institution controlled by any religious creed. . . . " This section has particular relevance for both direct and indirect forms of aid to religious private schools, a matter discussed in the last section of the chapter.

Protection for Free Exercise of Religion

While both federal and state constitutions have limits on governmental involvement with religion, they also recognize the fundamental right of individuals to exercise their religious beliefs freely. Religious freedom is a central tenet of our society. Many of the colonists who left Europe for the new country did so to escape religious persecution. To prevent repression in America, the founders provided in the First Amendment that Congress is not to make laws prohibiting the free exercise of religion. The Fourteenth Amendment added after the Civil War extends the same prohibition to states and their political subdivisions.

The system the founders designed guarantees that all religions can flourish. This includes secularized belief systems because the word "religion" in the free exercise clause has been interpreted more broadly than in the establishment clause. Judicial decisions involving the establishment clause generally have confined the term "religion" to theistic belief systems, that is, to those that relate to a supreme being. For this reason, the argument that schools are promoting a "religion of secularism" by not teaching theistic religion has not been generally accepted. As defined in the dictionary, *secular* means "not sacred or ecclesiastical." At the same time, however, schools cannot ignore theistic religion to the point that they become religion-free zones. As the U.S. Supreme Court noted in its well-known 1963 decision against state-mandated prayer in public school, "We agree of course that the State may not establish a 'religion of secularism' in the sense of affirmatively opposing or showing hostility to religion, thus 'preferring those who believe in no religion over those who believe'" (*School District of Abington Township v. Schempp*, 1963, p. 225). Confinement of the term "religion" to theistic beliefs for purposes of the establishment clause does not preclude complaints from parents and students that public schools are promoting nonmainstream belief systems like Wicca or Satanism through the curriculum. We will have occasion to examine some of these cases later in this chapter.

While secularism is not a religion under the establishment clause, the U.S. Supreme Court has recognized that it does fall within the definition of religion in the free exercise clause. The 1961 ruling to this effect involved a state requirement that public officers must declare a belief in God to hold public office. Such a requirement, the Court unanimously ruled, violates the individual's right to freedom of conscience, noting that the free exercise clause encompasses nontheistic beliefs "such as Buddhism, Taoism, Ethical Culture, and Secular Humanism and others" (*Torcaso v. Watkins*, p. 495, fn. 11). Were it otherwise, the argument could be made that religion is being favored over nonreligion, a violation of the establishment clause. The Court recognized this by ruling in 1965 that a conscientious objector who expressed skepticism about the existence of God but who did acknowledge a belief in and devotion to goodness and virtue for their own sakes was entitled to an exemption from the military draft. Writing for the majority, Justice Tom Clark concluded that "the beliefs which prompted his objection occupy the same place in his life as the belief in a traditional deity holds in the lives of his friends, the Quakers" (*United States v. Seeger*, p. 187). Toward the end of the Vietnam War, the Court extended this rationale to a conscientious objector who maintained that the taking of a life is morally wrong (*Welsh v. United States*, 1970).

The validity of a belief system is beyond the purview of public officials. As the Supreme Court ruled long ago:

> Freedom of thought, which includes freedom of religious belief, is basic in a society of free men. It embraces the right to maintain theories of life and of death and of the hereafter which are rank heresy to followers of orthodox faiths. Heresy trials are foreign to our Constitution. Men may believe what they cannot prove. They may not be put to the proof of their religious doctrines or beliefs. (*United States v. Ballard*, 1944, p. 886)

As long as a belief system is sincere, government officials may ask no more.

While rare in education, assertion of an expanded definition of religion has surfaced in criminal law. A somewhat humorous example involves a Wyoming defendant, charged with possession and trafficking of marijuana, who claimed that prosecuting him would violate his religious rights as the Founder and Reverend in the Church of Marijuana. The U.S. Court of Appeals for the Tenth Circuit rejected his claim (*United States v. Meyers*, 1996). While the defendant has a right to believe in such a religion, the judges observed, he cannot escape being penalized for violating a law against the use or trafficking in illegal drugs that is applied to everyone, regardless of religious beliefs. The appeals court drew on the rationale of a 1990 U.S. Supreme Court ruling that a religious claim cannot provide an exemption from a valid law prohibiting conduct that the state is free to regulate (*Employment Division, Department of Human Resources v. Smith*). Presumably, this rationale would work with a student who makes the same claim when faced with disciplinary action for drug possession.

The California Constitution has a provision protecting free exercise of religion as well. Article I, Section 4 states in part that "Free exercise and enjoyment of religion without discrimination or preference are guaranteed." Since most litigation over free exercise of religion has occurred in federal courts, the California provision has not been relied upon as often.

MANIFESTATIONS OF RELIGION ON CAMPUS

Judicial rulings reveal the many ways that religion manifests itself on the public school campus. In some instances the manifestations violate the constitutional principles previously discussed, and in other instances they do not. We differentiate the permissible from the impermissible in this section.

The Pledge of Allegiance

In 2004, the U.S. Supreme Court sidestepped ruling on whether a school district policy requiring teachers to lead students in reciting the Pledge of Allegiance constitutes a violation of either the First Amendment establishment clause or the free exercise clause, even though the words "one nation under God" are part of the pledge (*Elk Grove Unified School District v. Newdow*). The high-profile case began when the father of an elementary school student objected to the practice. Education Code Section 52720 permits use of the pledge to satisfy the requirement of daily patriotic exercises in public schools. An attorney and avowed atheist, Michael Newdow did not contend that his daughter was compelled to salute the flag. This could not be required by virtue of a 1943 Supreme Court ruling, *West Virginia State Board v. Barnette*. In that case, the Court ruled that the First Amendment prevents a public school from compelling anyone to salute the flag. Writing for the majority in that case, Justice Robert Jackson observed that "We think the action of the local authorities in compelling the flag salute and pledge transcends constitutional limitations on their power and invades the sphere of intellect and spirit which it is the purpose of the First Amendment to our Constitution to reserve from all official control" (p. 642). Nor did Newdow contend that his daughter was required to stand rather than remain quietly seated during the pledge. Years ago, the U.S. Court of Appeals for the Second Circuit in a case from New York set forth the generally accepted precedent that being compelled to stand is an unconstitutional violation of the student's right to be free from having to profess a belief because standing is part of the pledge (*Goetz v. Ansell*, 1973).

Rather, Newdow contended that having his daughter watch and listen to the teacher proclaim the existence of a God, and that the country is a nation under God, constituted a violation of the establishment clause. Congress added the "under God" phrasing in 1954. The Ninth Circuit ruled in favor of the father in a highly controversial two-to-one decision that originally applied to recitation of the pledge in any setting but was later modified to apply only to public school students. Amidst a public outcry and flurry of legal maneuvering, the full panel of judges assigned to the Ninth Circuit refused to overturn the decision, and the matter headed to the Supreme Court. The justices found that Newdow lacked "standing"; that is, he could not sue on his daughter's behalf because he was not the parent who had authority under the divorce settlement to make decisions when both parents disagreed. Rather, the mother had that right, and she was not opposed to the pledge. Because Newdow lacked standing, he could not file the suit in the first place. The effect of the ruling was to moot the Ninth Circuit decision. Thus, the wording of the pledge remains unchanged.

Newdow was not deterred. He sought out other parents, also atheists, to join him in a new suit against the U.S. Congress, four California public school districts, and others. The school districts sought dismissal of the case. In a September 2005 ruling, the federal district court judge rejected Newdow's assertion that, as the child's father, he had the requisite standing to file the lawsuit. But such was not the case with the other parents, who had custody of their children. The judge then noted that the Ninth Circuit's ruling striking down the pledge remains good law. This being the case, the judge was without authority to second-guess the appellate court. However, the judge refused to rule against reciting the pledge as presently worded at school board and other government meetings. The decision in *Newdow v. Congress of the United States* is on appeal to the Ninth Circuit and has not gone into effect.

Several judicial decisions involving the pledge from other jurisdictions are instructive. In one, the U.S. Court of Appeals for the Third Circuit ruled that a Pennsylvania law requiring the school to inform parents of students who opt not to participate in the recitation of the pledge or national anthem violates the students' First Amendment rights because it amounts to viewpoint discrimination. That is, the state weighs in on the matter only when the student refuses to participate. The appeals court also ruled that the law could not be applied to private schools, because to do so would violate the schools' expressive rights (*Circle Schools v. Pappert*, 2004). The U.S. Court of Appeals for the Eleventh Circuit ruled that a principal in Alabama violated a student's rights of expression when he paddled the boy for standing and silently raising his fist during the daily flag salute. Further, the boy's teacher breached the establishment clause by soliciting prayer requests from her students and leading the class in a moment of silent prayer. Neither the teacher nor the principal was immune from the lawsuit. Nor was the school board itself. The matter was returned to the lower court for trial (*Holloman v. Harland*, 2004).

School Prayer

In the early 1960s, the U.S. Supreme Court handed down two decisions involving prayer in public schools that have generated controversy to this day. In 1962, the Court ruled that this prayer composed by the New York State Board of Regents for reading in the public schools violated the establishment clause: "Almighty God, we acknowledge our dependence upon Thee, and we beg Thy blessings upon us, our parents, our teachers, and our Country." That the prayer was nondenominational and that its recitation could be voluntary made no difference. Concluded the majority:

we think that the constitutional prohibition against laws respecting an establishment of religion must at least mean that in this country it is no part of the business of government to compose official prayers for any group of American people to recite as a part of a religious program carried on by government. (*Engle v. Vitale*, p. 425)

A year later, the Court struck down a Pennsylvania statute mandating the daily reading of ten verses from the Bible, without comment, at the beginning of the school day. The readings were done by either student volunteers or homeroom teachers. While recognizing the important role of religion in American life, as it had done the year before in the *Engle* case, the Court found the practice a violation of the establishment clause (*School District of Abington Township v. Schempp*, 1963).

Some commentators argued that these decisions in essence removed religion from the public schools. They cited Justice Potter Stewart's dissent in *Schempp* in support of the contention. Stewart noted that compulsory education so structures a child's life that "if religious exercises are held to be an impermissible activity in schools, religion is placed at an artificial and state-created disadvantage" (p. 313). He argued that permission should be granted for those who want to exercise their religious beliefs at school. If such accommodation is not granted, then "a refusal to permit religious exercises thus is seen, not as the realization of a state neutrality, but rather as the establishment of a religion of secularism, or at the least, as government support of the beliefs of those who think that religious exercises should be conducted only in private" (Id.). As we have noted, clearly public schools cannot become religion-free zones because, as Stewart noted, this would place the state in a position of hostility to religion. The question thus becomes, how can prayer be accommodated in the public schools without either overly promoting it or being hostile to it? Following these two U.S. Supreme Court rulings, lower courts have struggled to find a workable rationale. The dividing line that has emerged separates school-sponsored or endorsed prayer from private prayer and religious exercise. The former is impermissible. The latter is not.

School-sponsored or endorsed public prayer. Clearly, school-sponsored public prayer at the beginning of the school day is unconstitutional. What about a period of silent meditation? In 1985 the U.S. Supreme Court was faced with an Alabama statute that required a moment for "silent meditation or prayer" at the start of the school day. The majority was concerned about the legislature's amending an earlier statute to include the words "or prayer." Based on legislative testimony, the majority viewed the addition as a subtle way to get around the Court's prayer decisions, rejecting Chief Justice Warren Burger's assertion in dissent that the addition was merely an effort to let schoolchildren know that prayer was an option.

Without a secular legislative purpose, the statute was unconstitutional. But writing for the six-justice majority, Justice John Paul Stevens observed that "The legislative intent to return prayer to the public schools is, of course, quite different from merely protecting every student's right to engage in voluntary prayer during an appropriate moment of silence during the school day" (p. 59). In other words, setting aside a time for silent meditation would, by itself, not violate the Constitution. The U.S. Court of Appeals for the Eleventh Circuit so ruled with regard to Georgia's Moment of Quiet Reflection in Schools Act in 1997 (*Bown v. Gwinnett County School District*). California does not have a similar statute.

Sometimes it is difficult to know what is school sponsored and what is not. In 1981 the U.S. Court of Appeals for the Ninth Circuit ruled that an Arizona school principal's allowing the student council to open voluntary school assemblies with prayer constitutes impermissible government endorsement of religion (*Collins v. Chandler Unified School District*). The student council selected a student from the student body, and the student was free to choose the prayer and manner in which it was delivered. The appeals court observed that school endorsement of the practice conveys a subtle message to impressionable students. Furthermore, nonconsenting students were forced either to listen to the prayer or to forgo attending an important school function.

Seeking to avoid a problem with sponsorship under the establishment clause, a Texas school district attempted to convert a brief time during pregame ceremonies of home football games into a free speech forum for an "invocation and/or message" to solemnize the event, to promote good sportsmanship and student safety, and to establish the appropriate environment for competition. According to the policy, the high school student council was to conduct an election to determine whether to have a message or invocation and, if so, to elect a student from a list of volunteers to deliver it. The school board viewed turning the matter over to the student council as a "circuit breaker" between the school and religious endorsement. The policy further provided that any message or invocation had to be nonsectarian and nonproselytizing. The U.S. Supreme Court struck down the policy in 2000 as lacking a secular purpose (*Santa Fe Independent School District v. Doe*).

The six-justice majority first rejected the district's contention that the comments delivered during this period constituted private student speech and thus were beyond the thrust of the establishment clause, which applies only to government. Rather, the justices considered the invocation and/or message to be public speech because it was authorized by government to take place on school property at a school-sponsored event. The district had not created a true free speech forum for private speech, because only one student could speak during the entire semester and then could give an invocation or message only for the limited purpose of solemnizing the event. The Court viewed the words "invocation" and "solemnize" as evidence of the school's support for religion. Indeed, the school district had a long history of incorporating religion into its program. The justices also were troubled by the student council majority vote process, viewing it as a means of stifling minority views and assuring that only one viewpoint was expressed. After this decision, it appears dubious whether a school district could create a free speech forum prior to a special-purpose school event like an athletic contest. Even doing so before the opening of school would require some artful drafting by the school attorney.

Invocations before the convening of the school board came under challenge a few years ago in the Palo Verde Unified School District. Noting that the U.S. Supreme Court had upheld prayers before the convening of legislative bodies in *Marsh v. Chambers* (1983), the school board contended that its practice was similarly constitutional. In an unpublished decision, the Ninth Circuit disagreed (an unpublished decision has no value as judicial precedent, but it does convey some idea of judicial thinking). Unlike the prayers upheld by the Supreme Court, the court noted, the Palo Verde prayer was sectarian because it included the words "In the Name of Jesus," thus advancing one faith. Further, there was no rotation system allowing a different individual to give a different invocation. Rather, the record showed that the same individual always gave the prayer with the same reference. The school board argued that restricting invocations would inhibit free exercise of religion. But the appeals court rejected the contention, noting that members of the board are always free to pray privately as they choose. Thus, because the prayer was part of the board's official agenda and gave favored status to one faith, it violated the establishment clause. The judges sidestepped addressing whether a nondenominational invocation or rotational prayer would be unconstitutional (*Bacus v. Palo Verde Unified School District*, 2002).

Private prayer and religious exercise. It is quite clear that both students and teachers have a right on their own to engage in nondisruptive private prayer during the school day. As described in Chapter 6, neither students nor teachers shed their constitutional rights at the public schoolhouse gate under the U.S. Supreme Court's 1969 *Tinker v. Des Moines Independent Community School District* decision. As the U.S. Court of Appeals for the Eleventh Circuit put it in a decision dealing with an Alabama student prayer statute, "so long as prayer is genuinely student-initiated, and not the product of any school policy which actively or surreptitiously encourages it, the speech is private and protected" (*Chandler v. Siegelman*, 2000, p. 1317). This right extends to groups of students as well. For example, as long as it is not disruptive, nothing precludes students from holding a prayer rally around the school flagpole or engaging in group prayer at a lunch table in the school cafeteria. Similarly, students can distribute religious literature on the school campus because handing out literature is a form of free speech. At the same time, the school has the right to limit the time, place, and manner of such distribution to prevent disruption of normal school activities. School officials could, for example, require student distributors to identify themselves and restrict distribution to a table outside the school cafeteria during certain times of the school day.

The U.S. Department of Education issued guidelines in 2003 providing that students have a right to engage in private prayer in schools receiving federal financial assistance. The guidelines give as examples reading Bibles or other religious literature, saying grace before meals, and praying or studying religious materials with other students when not engaged in school activities or instruction. According to the guidelines, teachers too can meet with each other before school and during lunch for prayer or Bible study, provided they are not acting in their official capacities. However, the Seventh Circuit has ruled that a school district can prevent teachers from holding organized prayer meetings on campus before the school day begins, so long as this time is restricted to school business (*May v. Evansville–Vanderburgh School Corporation*, 1986). The case involved an Indiana elementary school that refused to permit Evangelical Christian teachers from using the campus before the school day began for praying, singing, and reading the Bible. The appeals court commented that the school is not inherently a public forum, and that to be able to hold the prayer meetings, the teachers had to establish that the school had opened its campus to other than school business during this time. This they could not do. While it is possible to reconcile the guidelines and the court ruling—informal communication is permitted while organized meetings on closed campuses are not—it is important to note that when there is a conflict between judicial law and administrative guidelines, the former takes precedence.

While teachers generally have a right to discuss religious matters on the public school campus, there are some limits. Recall that teachers as public officials must remain neutral when addressing religion with students. Several federal courts have recognized that while students can hold prayer rallies, teachers are not to join them. As the U.S. Court of Appeals for the Fifth Circuit recognized in a case involving a Dallas area school district, if school personnel "join hands in a prayer circle or otherwise manifest approval and solidarity with student religious exercises, they cross the line between respect for religion and endorsement of religion" (*Doe v. Duncanville Independent School District*, 1995, p. 406). However, the court noted that employees need not leave the room when students pray on their own or otherwise treat student religious beliefs with disrespect. In 1994 the Ninth Circuit upheld a school district's directive that a teacher refrain from attempting to convert students to Christianity or initiating conversation about the teacher's religious beliefs with students at any time during the school day, given the teacher's penchant for proselytizing. The appeals court commented that "the school district's interest in avoiding an Establishment Clause violation trumps [the teacher's] right to free speech" (*Peloza v. Capistrano Unified School District*, 1994, p. 522). Two years later the same court ruled that a complete ban on religious advocacy anywhere in the workplace imposed by a department in the California Department of Education was not justified, because the employees performed no educational functions (*Tucker v. State of California Department of Education*, 1996).

Public school employees cannot be penalized for their religious beliefs. A case in point is a 1997 Ninth Circuit ruling in favor of an Idaho elementary school principal who challenged his reassignment to a teaching position because he opted to educate his children at home for religious reasons. While the school district was concerned that the homeschooling decision would engender a loss of confidence in the principal by teachers and parents, that concern and supporting evidence were not sufficiently compelling to override the exercise of the principal's religious beliefs and his liberty right to determine the education of his children (*Peterson v. Minidoka County School District No. 331*). It would have been different, the court noted, if the principal's action was not motivated by a religious belief but by lack of confidence in the district's educational program, or if there were other job-related reasons unrelated to the principal's rights to justify the reassignment.

Religion in the Classroom

As we will see from our review of the case law in this section, teaching about religion in a public school classroom is entirely appropriate; but promoting it is not. This distinction is evident in a 1980 U.S. Supreme Court ruling that displaying a religious symbol like the Ten Commandments in the classroom is impermissible (*Stone v. Graham*). It did not matter that private contributions underwrote the cost of implementing the statute, nor that the statute required a notation on the display to the effect that "The secular application of the Ten Commandments is clearly seen in its adoption as the fundamental legal code of Western Civilization and the Common Law of the United States." In an unsigned opinion, five justices wrote that the statute lacked a secular purpose because the Ten Commandments is undeniably a sacred text in the Jewish and Christian faiths and because several of the commandments address religious duties of believers (e.g., worshiping the Lord God alone, avoiding idolatry, not using the Lord's name in vain, and observing the

Sabbath Day). However, the Court recognized that the Ten Commandments can be included as a topic of study within the school curriculum. In 2005, the U.S. Supreme Court distinguished displaying the Ten Commandments in public school classrooms from displaying them on other government property, noting that *Stone* "stands as an example of the fact that we have 'been particularly vigilant in monitoring compliance with the Establishment Clause in elementary and secondary schools'" (*Van Orden v. Perry*, p. 691).

Teachers need to be sensitive to the wearing of religious attire in the classroom. School districts must reasonably accommodate the wearing of religious attire under Title VII of the 1964 Civil Rights Act, but not to the point of imposing an undue hardship. In addition, employees have rights of free speech and the free exercise of religion. At the same time, however, the school must assure that it and its employees remain neutral with regard to religion. This is especially true in elementary grades, where students are highly impressionable. It thus becomes a matter of balancing the interests of the school in avoiding the advancement of religion and the rights of employees to exercise their religious beliefs. While the wearing of a small religious symbol such as a cross or a Star of David would be appropriate, the wearing of an extremely large cross or a Star of David that lit up periodically would not be.

Teaching about religion. Despite the claims of many critics, the U.S. Supreme Court did not remove religion from the public schools when it struck down school-sponsored prayer in the 1960s. In fact, the Court was careful to protect it. In the *Schempp* ruling, Justice Tom Clark, who wrote the opinion, noted that "it might well be said that one's education is not complete without a study of comparative religion or the history of religion and its relationship to the advancement of civilization. It certainly may be said that the Bible is worthy of study for its literary and historic qualities" (p. 225). He added, "Nothing we have said here indicates that such study of the Bible or of religion, when presented objectively as part of a secular program of education, may not be effected consistently with the First Amendment."

Section 51511 of the California Education Code similarly recognizes that religion can be incorporated in the curriculum. It states:

> Nothing in this Code shall be construed to prevent, or exclude from the public schools, references to religion or references to or the use of religious literature, art, or music or other things having a religious significance when such references or uses do not constitute instruction in religious principles or aid to any religious sect, church, creed, or sectarian purpose and when such references or uses are incidental to or illustrative of matters properly included in the course of study.

In essence, both the U.S. Supreme Court and the California Legislature permit the school to teach *about* religion but not teach religion. Teaching religion is the province of the home, the church, and the private religious school. Despite the simplicity of this guideline, however, schools have run into legal challenges over incorporation of religion in the curriculum.

Comparative religion classes have generated litigation because much of the time they are not neutral toward religion. A good illustration of what is acceptable and what is not comes from a federal district court decision in Mississippi. For some fifty years, a Bible committee composed of members of local Protestant churches had sponsored Bible classes in the Pontotoc County School District. The course was taught once every four days in the elementary classrooms and as an elective in the high school grades. The committee hired the teachers to teach the classes. The district supervised them and provided classroom space and materials. The course was entitled simply "Bible" until the Mississippi State Department of Education refused to approve it. Thereafter, the committee developed a new course called "A Biblical History of the Middle East," which was subsequently approved by the department. But it did not fare as well with the federal judge, who found that despite the new name, the course was being taught from a fundamentalist Christian perspective just as it had been in the past (*Herdahl v. Pontotoc County School District*, 1996).

Employing each of the five guidelines for deciding establishment clause cases outlined at the beginning of this chapter, the judge found the religion course unconstitutional. Despite the name change, the course was designed by the committee to inculcate students into a particular religious belief system. Therefore, it lacked a secular purpose and had the primary effect of advancing religion. The inclusion of the course in the school's regular program also constituted excessive entanglement of the school with religion. Furthermore, the district's involvement amounted to official endorsement of religion over nonreligion and fundamentalist Christianity over other belief systems. Finally, the teaching of the course to children in the elementary grades placed undue coercion on young children to participate in the classes. For all these reasons, the religion course was unconstitutional.

In a closing footnote, the judge outlined several conditions that would make the course constitutionally acceptable as part of the school's curriculum: It must be taught objectively as part of a secular program of education; the Bible must not be used as the only source of historical fact or as if the Bible were actual literal history; students must be assigned readings from nonbiblical sources of ancient Middle East history; the course must not teach religious doctrine or a sectarian interpretation of the Bible; and the district is not to accept instructors for the course based in whole or part on a religious test or profession of faith.

Charter schools have not escaped litigation over allegations of impermissible advancement of religion. Parents in Michigan filed suit in federal court against the Vanguard Charter School Academy in Grand Rapids and its operator, National Heritage Academies, contending among other things that the elementary school permitted parents to pray on school grounds, permitted distribution of religious materials in student folders, and taught morality from a religious perspective. They were unsuccessful on all counts (*Daugherty v. Vanguard Charter School Academy*, 2000). With regard to permitting parents to pray on campus, the school had set aside a room for parents to meet during and after school hours. The fact that a "Moms' Prayer Group" had access to the room did not violate the establishment clause, the judge noted, because other parent groups also were allowed to meet there. Further, the room was off-limits to students, and meetings were held behind closed doors. The inclusion of religious materials from community groups in student folders did not impermissibly advance religion, because announcements from other community groups also were included. The school's Moral Focus Curriculum, the judge noted, did not mention religion. The use of words and concepts that happen to coincide with tenets of religion did not render the curriculum unconstitutional.

Though dismissing all the claims in *Daugherty*, the judge noted that federal courts are more sensitive to allegations of establishment clause violations at the elementary level because of the age and impressionable nature of the students. For example, the court observed that allowing parents to read Bible stories to students during classroom time was "questionable." What helped the school avoid liability in this case was the school's development of a set of First Amendment guidelines intended to prevent unconstitutional conduct by teachers and excessive entanglement with religion.

The matter of teaching creation-science came before the U.S. Supreme Court in 1987 (*Edwards v. Aguillard*). The case involved a statute enacted by Louisiana bearing the ungainly title "The Balanced Treatment for Creation-Science and Evolution-Science in Public School Instruction Act." The thrust of the statute was to require that whenever evolution was taught in the public school curriculum, the science associated with creation had to be taught. Proponents labeled it a way of promoting academic freedom by teaching all the information relating to the origins of man. Opponents viewed it as a confining measure restricting academic freedom by permitting only two views to be taught. They considered it an effort to infuse a fundamentalist Christian perspective into the teaching of science. By a seven-to-two vote, the Court agreed with opponents. The justices ruled that Louisiana's creation-science act lacked a secular purpose. The majority noted that "teaching a variety of scientific theories about the origins of humankind to school children might be validly done with the clear secular intent of enhancing the effectiveness of science instruction" (p. 594). But rather than add to the science curriculum, the creation-science act served to discredit evolution by advancing a particular religious view.

A few years later, creation-science came before the Ninth Circuit when a biology teacher in the Capistrano Unified School District alleged that by being required to teach only evolution in his science classes, he was being forced to proselytize "evolutionism" to his students under the guise of its being a valid scientific theory. The teacher contended that the school district was establishing a religion by teaching only evolution. The appellate judges affirmed the lower court's rejection of the claim, noting that neither the U.S. Supreme Court nor any court within the Ninth Circuit has ever held that "evolutionism" or secular humanism are "religions" within the meaning of the establishment clause. The judges pointed out that evolution is a biological concept holding that higher life-forms evolve from lower ones and is not religious (*Peloza v. Capistrano Unified School District*, 1995).

The year before the *Peloza* decision, the Ninth Circuit rejected a claim that the school was advancing the Wicca belief system by permitting its teachers to use *Impressions*, a series of fifty-nine books containing some 10,000 literary selections and classroom activities (*Brown v. Woodland Joint Unified School District*, 1994). Of particular concern to the parents were selections they contended promoted witchcraft and that asked students to discuss witches or create poetic chants. This, they contended, amounted to advancement of the Wicca religion. Assuming, but not ruling, that Wicca is a religion, the appeals court rejected the claim. Merely reading and discussing witches does not have the effect of advancing religion. "If an establishment clause violation were to arise every time a student believes a school practice has advanced or disapproved of religion," the judges wrote, "school curricula would be reduced to the lowest common denominator, permitting each student to become a 'curriculum review committee' unto himself or herself" (p. 1379). The court expressed more concern about having students act out rituals, but noted that the activities in this case were drawn from a secular source and used for a secular purpose. The appeals court also rejected the parents' claims under the California Constitution. It noted that since no California decision indicates that the state's establishment clause in Article I, Section 4 is stricter than its federal counterpart, California courts would uphold use of the challenged selections from *Impressions*.

In a case that largely escaped notice in California because it never was officially reported yet reached the U.S. Supreme Court, the matter of acting out religious rituals once again was challenged. This time, the dispute arose over the Byron Unified School District's unit on Islam in the seventh grade world history class. During the three-week unit, students simulated Islamic history and culture. Students could choose to wear Arabic costumes, simulate a pilgrimage to Mecca, and engage in make-believe fasting during the holy month of Ramadan. The parents of one student objected, contending the school was teaching religion. Noting the option of an opt-out, the federal district court rejected their contention. The Ninth Circuit upheld the lower court decision in a short unpublished memorandum opinion, noting that the Islam program activities were not overt religious exercises. The U.S. Supreme Court refused to hear the case (*Eklund v. Byron Unified School District* 2005).

A coalition of seventeen national religious and educational organizations has developed six guidelines that remain very helpful in deciding what public schools can and cannot do in incorporating religion into the instructional program. The guidelines for teaching about religion are set forth in the following list.

- The school's approach to religion must be academic, not devotional.
- The school may strive for student awareness of religion but should not press for student acceptance of any one religion.
- The school may sponsor study about religion but may not sponsor the practice of religion.
- The school may expose students to a diversity of religious views but may not impose any particular view.
- The school may educate about all religions but may not promote or denigrate any religion.
- The school may inform the student about various beliefs but should not seek to confine him or her to any particular belief.

Student religious papers and presentations. As noted in Chapter 6, school officials have considerable authority to control the content of the curriculum and what transpires in the classroom. Occasionally, disputes arise over the desire of students to write papers and give presentations on religious topics. The general pattern of federal judicial decisions to date is to defer to the judgment of educators. One early ruling involves a second grader in a Michigan public school who wanted to show to her classmates a videotape of herself singing a proselytizing religious song during a church service. The teacher had started a "VIP of the Week" program to afford each child an opportunity to gain confidence and experience in verbal communication by telling the class about the child's interests and what the child considers important. The child later testified that she wanted to show the videotape so that she might be able "to help people be saved."

After viewing the videotape, the teacher told the child that the videotape could not be shown. The teacher concluded that showing the video would not satisfy the purpose of the VIP program by giving the student an opportunity to talk before the class. The teacher also was concerned that if other students brought videos, she would have to spend considerable time viewing them to see if they were suitable. She also feared that the religious message of the video would convey a message of school endorsement. The parents filed a lawsuit, contending the denial violated their child's First Amendment rights of expression and free exercise of religion. The trial court decided that the teacher's concerns were valid and ruled against the parents. The U.S. Court of Appeals for the Sixth Circuit concurred. Relying on the *Hazelwood School District v. Kuhlmeier* decision (discussed in Chapter 6), the Sixth Circuit noted that the school can exercise content control over the classroom as long as the classroom is not an open forum and a legitimate pedagogical purpose justifies the control. Here, the teacher had opened the classroom for the limited purpose of giving students the learning experience of orally presenting information to their classmates. The videotape would not serve this purpose. And it would place additional burdens on the teacher (*DeNooyer v. Merinelli*, 1993).

Two years later, the same circuit ruled similarly in a case involving a ninth grader who planned to write a paper on the life of Jesus to satisfy a research paper assignment. Initially, the student indicated she was going to write her paper on drama, but then changed the topic without the teacher's approval. When the student handed in an outline of the paper, the teacher was concerned that the student's strong Christian beliefs could lead to misunderstandings over the grade the teacher might give the paper and doubted the student would have to do much research on the topic. The teacher disapproved the topic and gave the student a failing grade when the student chose not to write a paper. The trial court dismissed the lawsuit, and the Sixth Circuit affirmed the judgment. The appellate court noted that teachers should have wide latitude in giving assignments and awarding grades. Here the teacher had legitimate reasons for her action. "So long as the teacher limits speech or grades speech in the classroom in the name of learning and not as a pretext for punishing the student for her race, gender, economic class, religion, or political persuasion," the judges noted, "the federal courts should not interfere" (*Settle v. Dickson County School Board*, 1995, p. 155). In 2008, the Sixth Circuit returned to the issue again in the context of a fifth grader in Saginaw, Michigan, who intended to sell candy canes with an attached religious card promoting Jesus during a mock marketplace exercise called Classroom City. Noting that younger students would be permitted to purchase products in Classroom City and concerned that they and their parents would receive an unsolicited religious message, the school disallowed the religious card. The student was permitted to sell candy canes without the card in Classroom City and with the card in the school parking lot. The Sixth Circuit once again upheld the actions of school officials as serving a legitimate pedagogical purpose, given that the school retained control over Classroom City as a classroom activity including approving the products to be sold (*Curry v. Hensiner*).

That the matter of religious topics in student works is controversial is evident in an evenly divided opinion by the U.S. Court of Appeals for the Third Circuit. The case involved a New Jersey kindergartner whose poster on Jesus was removed from a hallway display, then reinstated but in a less conspicuous location. Later when the same student was in first grade, his teacher told him that he could not read his Bible story to the class but instead could share it with her. The teacher's practice was to preview what students intended to read to the class to determine if the work would be appropriate in length and degree of complexity. In this case, the teacher considered the story inappropriate because of its religious content.

The trial court concluded that the poster moving was justified by the school's desire to avoid the appearance of advancing religion. The teacher's action was justified by her concern that the children might assume the teacher endorsed the message if she let the student read the story. Eventually, the full panel of judges assigned to the Third Circuit heard the case. They avoided ruling on the poster moving on procedural grounds and divided equally on the Bible story reading. This had the effect of mooting the trial court's decision on the poster issue but affirming it regarding the Bible story reading (*C. H. ex rel. Z. H. v. Oliva*, 2000).

The thrust of these decisions is to give teachers considerable control over making decisions about student expression in the classroom. If religious topics will not serve the lesson plan, then teachers have the authority to disallow them. Guidelines issued by the U.S. Department of Education in 2003 under the No Child Left Behind Act seem to be less deferential to educators than the federal courts. The guidelines state that

> students may express their beliefs about religion in homework, artwork, and other written and oral assignments free from discrimination based on the religious content of their submissions. Such home and classroom work should be judged by ordinary academic standards of substance and relevance and against other legitimate pedagogical concerns identified by the school.

Thus, "if a teacher's assignment involves writing a poem, the work of a student who submits a poem in the form of a prayer (for example, a psalm) should be judged on the basis of academic standards (such as literary quality) and neither penalized nor rewarded on account of its religious content." In California, the dearth of case law suggests that the guidelines should be followed unless the school attorney advises otherwise. While federal guidelines do not have the legal weight of statutes or judicial decisions, noncompliance could result in sanctions including the loss of federal funding.

Holiday Observances and Religious Music

The leading case on holiday programs in public schools is a 1980 decision from the U.S. Court of Appeals for the Eighth Circuit, whose geographic jurisdiction encompasses several Midwestern states. The case involved a school district policy advising teachers on how to address holidays that have both a religious and secular basis such as Christmas, Easter, Passover, and Hanukkah. The policy permitted teachers to recognize the religious nature of the holidays through references to art, music, literature, and religious symbols. The policy had been developed by a representative committee of various faiths in the community. In a two-to-one decision, the appeals court found the new policy had a secular purpose, did not advance religion, and did not excessively entangle the school and its teachers in religion. The dissenting judge found the holiday program too closely tied to the Christian and Jewish faiths. His commentary has more relevance today now that nontraditional belief systems are increasingly represented in school districts. He advised that "the observance of the holidays of religions less familiar to most American public school children than either the Christian or Jewish holidays would seem more likely to increase student knowledge and promote religious tolerance" (*Florey v. Sioux Falls School District*, p. 1324). While there are practical limits, the more encompassing a school district or charter school's holiday observance program is of faiths represented in the community, the more likely it will withstand constitutional challenge by those who resent the noninclusion of holidays associated with their belief system.

Occasionally, lawsuits will be filed against state statutes declaring school holidays on days that happen to coincide with a religious observance. The few courts that have considered the question generally have accepted school district arguments that not holding school on these days is justified by the economic savings when few children are likely to attend school.

Several federal courts have ruled that religious music may be included in the school music program. The most well-known case arose in the Tenth Circuit. The case involved a Jewish choir member who contended that the choir director at her Salt Lake City high school had long promoted his Mormon beliefs by including religious songs in the choir repertoire and scheduled performances at churches. She objected to the choir's singing "May the Lord Bless You and Keep You" and "Friends" at the high school graduation ceremony. The student's lawsuits generated considerable controversy in her community, much of it aimed at her. The appeals court decided against her in a two-to-one decision. The majority noted that a public school choral program is intended to introduce students to a wide range of music, including religious songs. Performing in churches can be based on secular reasons such as better acoustics, adequate seating, and an appropriate setting for serious music. In this case, the majority noted that the student had not alleged that the program lacked a secular purpose and had not produced sufficient evidence to show a primary effect of advancing religion (*Bauchman v. West High School*, 1997).

Graduation Prayer and Religious Speeches

In a seminal 1991 decision, the California Supreme Court ruled that school-sponsored invocations and benedictions at a high school graduation ceremony violate the state constitution (*Sands v. Morongo Unified School District*). The high court construed one of the three state constitutional provisions it considered, Article XVI, Section 5, as prohibiting "*any* official involvement that promotes religion" (italics in original). In short, the California Constitution asserts a very strong separation of church and state.

The next year, the U.S. Supreme Court came to the same conclusion in a case involving a middle school student who contested her principal's asking a rabbi to give a nondenominational invocation and benediction at her graduation ceremony (*Lee v. Weisman*, 1992). The majority in this five-to-four ruling viewed the principal's involvement in inviting the rabbi to give the prayer and then advising him to deliver a nondenominational prayer as impermissible government endorsement of religion. It made no difference that the prayer was nondenominational. Writing for the majority, Justice Anthony Kennedy noted, "The suggestion that government may establish an official or civic religion as a means of avoiding the establishment of a religion with more specific creeds strikes us as a contradiction that cannot be accepted" (p. 590). The majority also ruled that the prayer placed psychological coercion on nonbelievers. The fact that the student did not have to attend the graduation ceremony did not erase the coercion, because few students would choose to miss such an important event in their educational career. In his dissent, Justice Antonin Scalia decried the lack of sensitivity the majority exhibited toward the wishes of the majority of parents, students, and others attending graduation. But Justice Anthony Kennedy countered that "While in some societies the wishes of the majority might prevail, the Establishment Clause of the First Amendment is addressed to this contingency and rejects the balance urged upon us" (p. 596).

Can school officials turn the matter of invocation and benediction over to students and let them decide whether to have a prayer and, if so, to select someone to give it? In 2000, the Ninth Circuit dismissed a lawsuit filed against the Oroville Union School District after the district refused to permit the co-valedictorian to give a religious presentation and another student to give a sectarian invocation. The pair subsequently delivered their proselytizing presentations in defiance of the directive. The Ninth Circuit ruled that the refusal to permit both the proselytizing invocation and valedictory speech was necessary to avoid breaching the establishment clause. The appeals court observed that the graduation ceremony is held on district property, financed with district funds, and only selected students are allowed to speak. The principal retains supervisory control and has final authority to approve speech topics. The school district requires students to sign a contract obligating them to act and dress in a certain manner. And the school broadcasts the speech over a public address system. Given the control the school has over the graduation ceremony, allowing the student to give a proselytizing valedictory speech would constitute government endorsement of religion and have a coercive effect on nonbelievers. The two students were free to pray and proselytize outside of school (*Cole v. Oroville Union High School District*).

In another case with nearly identical facts, the lawyer for the student graduation speaker whose speech contained proselytizing remarks suggested that the district could provide a disclaimer stating that the views of the student speakers do not represent those of the school district. But the school officials rejected the suggestion and excised offending portions of the speech. The student was permitted to distribute the unedited version of the speech outside the graduation ceremony. The student later filed suit against the school district and its officials, alleging violation of his First Amendment rights. As in the *Cole* decision, the Ninth Circuit affirmed the lower court's decision in favor of the district. With regard to the disclaimer suggestion, the appeals court judges noted that a disclaimer would not address the coercive effect of such a speech on nonbelievers: "Although a disclaimer arguably distances school officials from 'sponsoring' speech, it does not change the fact that proselytizing amounts to a religious practice that the school district may not coerce other students to participate in, even while looking the other way" (*Lassonde v. Pleasanton Unified School District*, 2003, pp. 984–985).

U.S. Department of Education guidelines provide that

> Where students or other private graduation speakers are selected on the basis of genuinely neutral, evenhanded criteria and retain control over the content of their expression . . . that expression is not attributable to the school and therefore may not be restricted because of its religious (or anti-religious) content.

The guidelines go on to assert that school officials may use disclaimers to clarify that such speech reflects the views of the speakers, not the school. In light of the Ninth Circuit rulings, the key phrase in the guidelines appears to be "retain control over the content of their expression." These rulings indicate that because the graduation ceremony is a closed forum controlled by the school, the speakers do not retain such control. Because the matter is contentious, the school attorney should be involved in developing the school's graduation speaker policy.

Access of Religious Groups to Campus

Student religious groups and the Equal Access Act. Constitutional law precludes a public school from recognizing a student religious group as a school-sponsored organization. This is clear from a 1977 California appellate court ruling. The court ruled that permitting a voluntary student Bible club to meet on the campus during the school day as a recognized student club with a faculty sponsor would have the primary effect of advancing religion and would create excessive entanglement between the school and religion (*Johnson v. Huntington Beach Union High School District*).

As we discussed in Chapter 6, Congress enacted the Equal Access Act (EAA) in 1984 making it unlawful for any public secondary school that receives federal funding and has a limited open forum to deny any noncurricular-related group access to the campus during noninstructional time to engage in various forms of speech. In 1997 the Ninth Circuit ruled that noninstructional time includes an activities period during the day when classes do not meet. In that case, the appeals court ruled that a student religious club could meet at this time because other clubs were allowed to do so. Accommodating the club in this way does not constitute impermissible advancement of religion (*Ceniceros v. Board of Trustees of the San Diego Unified School District*). In a later ruling, the Ninth Circuit permitted a student religious group to meet during "student/staff time" when individual student tutoring takes place. While agreeing that EAA does not require this degree of accommodation, two judges on the three-judge panel held that because the school district had permitted officially recognized Associated Student Body clubs to meet during this period, it could not engage in viewpoint discrimination under the First Amendment by preventing the student religious club and similar student-sponsored clubs from doing so (*Prince v. Jacoby*, 2002). The dissenting judge argued that permitting a student group to conduct religious activities during instructional time violates the establishment clause. The *Prince* ruling is discussed in more detail later in this section.

In 1990, the U.S. Supreme Court upheld EAA against a charge that it violates the establishment clause as applied to student religious groups that seek access under its terms to a public secondary school (*Board of Education of Westside Community Schools v. Mergens*). The Court ruled that EAA does not violate the establishment clause, because it does not extend just to student religious groups but to all groups regardless of the content of their speech. Further, the speech that is being protected by EAA is private, not government, speech. Writing for the majority, Justice Sandra Day O'Connor added, "We think that secondary school students are mature enough and are likely to understand that a school does not endorse or support student speech that it merely permits on a nondiscriminatory basis" (p. 250).

EAA requires that noncurriculum groups must be student initiated. School personnel are prohibited from sponsoring their meetings and may be present at religious meetings only in a nonparticipatory capacity. The Act prohibits the district and its personnel from influencing the form or content of prayer or other religious activity or from requiring any person to participate in prayer or other religious activity. The school retains authority to maintain order and discipline and to assure that student attendance is voluntary. School personnel may be asked to serve in a custodial role at meetings unless the content of the speech at such meetings conflicts with their beliefs. Nonschool persons may not direct, conduct, control, or even regularly attend activities of student groups. The school may restrict the times outsiders may attend meetings or deny access altogether.

Noncurricular student groups have access to the school media, including the public address system, school paper, and bulletin boards, to announce their meetings if the school grants similar groups access. The Ninth Circuit's *Prince* decision mentioned earlier addressed the extent to which this must be permitted for religious groups. The case involved the "World Changers," a student religious group addressing issues of concern to students from the Gospel of Jesus Christ. The Spanaway Lake High School in Washington State had a policy distinguishing Associated Student Body (ASB) clubs from those meeting under the terms of EAA. Unlike ASB clubs, EAA clubs at the school did not have access to ASB funding; did not appear in the yearbook; could not meet during student/staff time; could not publicize events as extensively at school; and did not have the same access to school supplies, use of audiovisual equipment, and school vehicles for field trips. The World Changers challenged this as a form of discrimination under both EAA and the First Amendment.

In a lengthy decision, the Ninth Circuit first discussed whether the school had violated EAA. The court noted that the Spanaway Lake High School student council, not the school, controls the budgeting process for student groups and generates funds from sale of ASB cards and from fund-raising events. Likewise, ASB-generated funds are used to produce the yearbook. Denying student religious groups access to ASB funding and making them pay for appearing in the school yearbook is a violation of EAA. The court held that denial of the same access to the public address system and bulletin boards as ASB clubs also violates EAA. However, as discussed earlier, the court ruled that the student religious club does not have a right under EAA to meet during student/staff time, because instruction occurs then. Nor do non-ASB groups have a right under EAA to school supplies, audiovisual equipment, or vehicles.

While such benefits are not available under EAA, two members of the three-judge panel then went further to decide that they nevertheless must be provided because it would be a form of First Amendment viewpoint discrimination to deny them. In the words of the majority:

> Spanaway Lake High School has created a limited public forum in which student groups are free to meet during student/staff time, as well as to use school vehicles for field trips, to have priority for use of the AV equipment, and to use school supplies such as markers, posterboard, and paper. (p. 1091)

Therefore, without a compelling reason, the high school could not deny World Changers (and any other non-ASB group) the right to meet during student/staff time and have access to these benefits without violating the First Amendment. The majority rejected the school's claim that accommodating World Changers in this way would put the school in the position of advancing the religious mission of the club and thus violate the establishment clause. Treating World Changers in the same way as any other student club ensures neutrality, the majority noted. The fact that school supplies and school vehicles involve public funds rather than ASB student funds did not alter the outcome. Any concern the school might have about conveying the perception of endorsing the World Changers' religious mission could be dispelled "by making it clear to students that a club's private speech is not the speech of the school" (p. 1094). The dissenting judge agreed with the school district that allowing World Changers to meet during student/staff time and giving or lending them supplies, AV equipment, and transportation on school vehicles advances the religious mission of the group and thus violates the establishment clause.

The *Prince* decision applies to California and other states within the geographic jurisdiction of the Ninth Circuit. The decision seems to have blurred the distinction in *Mergens* between noncurricular and curricular student clubs by permitting both to meet during student/staff time and to benefit from nonschool funds controlled by the student council. It may be that a more direct form of public funding would breach the federal or state constitution. Given the complexity and sensitivity of this issue, it is a matter requiring involvement of the school district's attorney.

In another case originating in Washington State, the Ninth Circuit sided with the school district when the district backed its Associated Student Body (ASB) Council's refusal to grant a charter to a student religious club called Truth. Without the charter, the club could not be a recognized student club at the school. The club divided its membership into three categories: attendees, non-voting members, and voting members. Becoming an attendee or non-voting member was contingent upon a student's complying in good faith with Christian character, Christian speech, Christian behavior, and Christian conduct as described in the Bible. To be a voting member or an officer, a student had to sign a "statement of faith" requiring an affirmation that the student believes "the Bible to be the inspired, the only infallible, authoritative Word of God." The member also had to pledge that he or she believes "that salvation is an underserved gift from God" and that only by "acceptance of Jesus Christ as my personal Savior, through His death on the cross for my sins, is my faith made real." ASB and the school district require equal educational treatment without regard to race, creed, and other statuses. "Creed" encompasses religious beliefs. The Ninth Circuit agreed with the school district and lower court that Truth's membership requirements violated the school district's non-discrimination policies and were not protected by the First Amendment. The court also found such action consistent with the terms of the Equal Access Act, because the district's action in denying access to Truth was not based on the club's religious speech but rather on its discriminatory membership criteria. The court noted that two other Bible clubs at the school receiving ASB recognition did not have membership requirements at odds with the district's non-discrimination policies. However, the case was sent back to the trial court for a determination if Truth could prove its contention that other clubs were granted exemptions from the nondiscrimination policy while it was not because of its religious character and speech (*Truth v. Kent School District,* 2008).

Community use policies. The U.S. Supreme Court ruled unanimously in 1993 that the First Amendment prevents a school district from denying a religious group access to its facilities if it permits other organizations to use them under the terms of a community use policy (*Lamb's Chapel v. Center Moriches Union Free School District*). In effect, the district has created a limited open forum. As described in Chapter 6, a limited open forum accommodates certain categories of expression but not others. With regard to those categories of expression that are permitted, there can be no discrimination based on the viewpoints being expressed.

Subject to conditions set forth in the statute and the rules and regulations of the governing board, California's Civic Center Act provides that school districts may allow community groups to use their buildings and grounds for recreational, educational, political, economic, artistic, or moral activities including the conduct of religious services by churches that have no suitable meeting place (Educ. Code § 38130 and following sections). School districts are required to authorize the use of their facilities or grounds to nonprofit organizations, clubs, and associations such as the Girl Scouts and Boy Scouts when an alternative location is not available (Educ. Code § 38134). In effect, public school districts in this state are limited open forums under the terms of the Civic Center Act.

The basic principles involved in administering a limited open forum surfaced in a 1999 Ninth Circuit decision. The case centered on whether the Downey Unified School District's refusal to post a local businessman's sign containing the text of the Ten Commandments on a fence surrounding the high school's baseball field was a violation of the First Amendment. The district permitted commercial advertisements for fund-raising purposes but excluded ads it deemed inappropriate for the secondary school. Accordingly, advertisements promoting alcohol and taverns were refused, as was a Planned Parenthood advertisement. Additionally, the district asserted that permitting the posting of a sign with the Ten Commandments would violate the establishment clause and might cause disruption.

In upholding the lower court's ruling in favor of the district, the Ninth Circuit ruled that the district had not designated the fence as a public forum for any form of expressive activity. Rather, it had created a limited open forum that excluded certain categories of speech. Accordingly, the district had to cite only a reasonable basis for excluding the Ten Commandments sign. It had done so by citing its desire to avoid disruption and the possibility of litigation that would undercut the purpose of posting ads in the first place. The district's action did not constitute viewpoint discrimination, because it limited posting to commercial advertisements, and the contested sign was not commercial. Nor did the district's decision to stop posting advertisements altogether in response to the litigation constitute viewpoint discrimination (*DiLoreto v. Downey Unified School District Board of Education*, 1999). A few months earlier, a California court of appeal had ruled similarly in the case with regard to the state constitution. That court held that posting the advertisement would have violated Article I, Section 4 preventing establishment of religion and that the refusal to do so did not violate either the free exercise of religion provision in that section or the free speech provision of Article I, Section 2 (*DiLoreto v. Board of Education*, 1999).

The wording of community use policies is critical for determining what kinds of communication and activity are allowed on public school grounds and what are not. A few years ago the Milford Central School in Milford, New York, refused to allow the Good News Club, a private Christian organization for children ages six to twelve, to hold after-school meetings in the school cafeteria. The Good News Club is sponsored by Child Evangelism Fellowship, which operates in over 140 countries and has some 4,600 clubs meeting on public school property in this country. The Milford School District had a community use policy that allowed community residents access to school campuses for, among other things, "instruction in any branch of education, learning, or the arts" and for "social, civic and recreational meetings and entertainment events, and other uses pertaining to the welfare of the community." However, the policy prohibited use by any individual or organization for religious purposes. Under the policy, the district permitted the Boy Scouts, Girl Scouts, and 4-H Club to meet. The school district refused to grant similar access to the Good News Club, maintaining that the club essentially was engaging in religious instruction and Bible study. According to documents filed in the case, the adult Good News Club instructor begins each meeting by having a student read a Bible verse and receive a treat for doing so. After attendance is taken, the Club sings songs and then engages in games focused on Bible verses. The adult leader reads a Bible story and explains its application to the students' lives. The meeting ends with a prayer and with the distribution of treats and Bible verses for memorization.

The U.S. Supreme Court decided in a six-to-three decision that the exclusion of the Good News Club constituted impermissible viewpoint discrimination under the First Amendment (*Good News Club v. Milford Central School*, 2001). The majority noted that the district had established a limited open forum by permitting outside groups to meet on school facilities for educational and recreational purposes. The Court found no establishment clause justification for the district's permitting secular organizations to address character and moral development but denying access to organizations addressing the same concerns from a religious perspective. The meetings were to be held after school, not sponsored by the school, and not limited just to Good News Club members. The majority rejected the school's concern about conveying a message of religious endorsement to impressionable children. The relevant audience was parents, not children, because parents had to give permission for their children to participate. Further, the meetings were not held in an elementary school classroom but in a combined high school resource room and middle school special education room. Because the meetings were held after school, no students or teachers were present. The Good News Club instructor was not a teacher, and the students were from six to twelve years old. Excluding the club, the Court observed, could be perceived as a message of hostility toward religion.

The Ninth Circuit later applied the *Good News Club* precedent to an Oregon school district that similarly excluded the Good News Club from holding meetings after school at an elementary school serving children from kindergarten through grade three. Pursuant to a state law similar to California's Civic Center Act, the district had adopted a policy encouraging the use of school buildings at no cost for educational and recreational purposes. A number of groups met at the elementary school after school hours, including the Birth-to-Three program, Cub Scouts, and the Upper Willamette Youth sports program. With one modification, the Ninth Circuit affirmed the lower court's decision in favor of the Child Evangelism Fellowship of Oregon, which had applied as a sponsor of the Good News Club. The appeals court observed that requiring teachers to hand out permission slips puts them in the position of advancing the religious mission of the club. This would be a violation of the establishment clause. However, teachers could hand out the club's brochures just as they did for other organizations (*Culbertson v. Oakridge School District No. 76*, 2001).

In 2003 the Ninth Circuit revisited the matter of community use policies. The decision in *Hills v. Scottsdale Unified School District No. 48* well illustrates the complexity of designing and administering such policies. In this case, the district had a policy and practice of allowing nonprofit outside groups to distribute or display brochures and other promotional literature to students. But material of a commercial, political, or religious nature was not allowed. Hills, the organizer of a nonprofit summer camp, sought to advertise his camp by distributing a flyer at the district's elementary schools. In the flyer, he described the courses to be offered, including two addressing religious subjects. Both courses emphasized coming to know Jesus Christ and the importance of Bible reading. The school district halted the distribution and then permitted it with the addition of a disclaimer. Later, it changed its mind and again disallowed distribution until Hills changed the brochure to, among other things, remove descriptions of the Bible classes. Hills filed suit, contending that the district's actions violated his rights to freedom of speech and religious exercise.

The Ninth Circuit found the application of the district's community use policy flawed. Based on testimony of school officials, the judges concluded that the district had created a limited open forum for community announcements that were intended to notify students and their parents of extracurricular activities or issues of general interest to all students. Having done so, a refusal to permit Hills to circulate his camp brochure constituted viewpoint discrimination. The judges noted that the district had conceded that summer camps are permissible subjects and so too the Bible if taught as history or literature. Thus, the district could not refuse outright to permit Hills to distribute the brochure.

However, the judges noted that the district could exercise some control over the contents of what Hills intended to communicate. For example, the court noted that the district could restrict some of the phrasing that exhorted the reader to involve children in religious observance. At one point, the original brochure stated that if children do not come to the knowledge of Jesus Christ and learn the importance of Bible reading by age twelve, chances are slim that they ever will. In the words of the court, "the District cannot refuse to distribute literature advertising a program with underlying religious content when it distributes quite similar literature for secular summer camps, but it can refuse to distribute literature that itself contains proselytizing language." The court added, "The difference is subtle, but important" (p. 1053). A concern that the court did not address is whether there may be a violation of the establishment clause when school officials begin reviewing the contents of religious materials and deciding what is and what is not permissible. Recall that the school principal ran into difficulty in doing this with regard to the rabbi's invocation and benediction in *Lee v. Weisman*, discussed earlier in the chapter.

Given the Civic Center Act, school districts in California appear not to have the option of declaring their facilities and grounds to be closed to outside nonprofit groups. But governing boards do have the authority to develop rules and regulations governing their use. Therefore, it is important to involve the school attorney in drafting a community use policy and advising school officials on how to enforce it so that violations of free speech and free exercise of religion do not occur. In deciding the *Hills* case, the Ninth Circuit recognized the complexity of the matter but agreed with the observation of the Seventh Circuit that "The school's proper response is to educate the audience rather than squelch the speaker.... Schools may explain that they do not endorse speech by permitting it" (*Hedges v. Wauconda Community Unit School District No. 118*, 1993, pp. 1299–1300).

Religiously Based Exemptions

The California Education Code has several provisions dealing with religiously based exemptions. Public school students are exempt from school attendance for, among other things, observance of a religious holiday or ceremony or attendance at religious retreats (Educ. Code § 48205). Attendance at the latter is limited to four hours per semester. Governing boards have the discretion to give students excused absences for receiving moral or religious instruction off school grounds with the consent of their parents for up to four days a month (Educ Code § 46014). As noted earlier, the U.S. Supreme Court upheld such released-time programs in 1952 (*Zorach v. Clauson*). A California court of appeal ruled similarly with respect to the state constitution in 1947 (*Gordon v. Board of Education of the City of Los Angeles*). Teachers have the right to opt out of school district evaluations and surveys that ask about religious beliefs (Educ. Code § 49091.24). Teachers also may opt out of teaching weekend classes if doing so would conflict with their religious beliefs or practices (Educ. Code § 44824).

The extent to which parents can rely on religion to seek exemptions for their children from public school programs and activities has generated recent litigation. In 1985 the Ninth Circuit faced the question whether a school district's refusal to remove a novel entitled *The Learning Tree*, by Gordon Parks, from the sophomore English literature curriculum violated the free exercise rights of an objecting parent. The book looks at the world through the eyes of a black teenage boy from a working-class family. The appeals court noted no significant intrusion on the student's religion, because she had been given an exemption from reading the book. Additionally, she could leave the class when the book was discussed, though she chose not to do so. The judges pointed out that if everything objectionable to someone had to be eliminated from the public school curriculum, nothing would be left. The parents also argued that including the book violated the establishment clause because it advanced secular humanism. The court rejected the contention, noting that *The Learning Tree* was religiously neutral (*Grove v. Mead School District No. 354*). The key to the outcome in this case was the fact that the student had been given an exemption.

More recent cases have questioned the extent to which parents can demand religiously based exemptions from required schooling practices. In Chapter 1, we discussed how the Old Order Amish were successful in convincing the U.S. Supreme Court that their religious beliefs and practice justified exempting their children from school attendance beyond the eighth grade, an exemption that has not been accorded to other belief systems (*Wisconsin v. Yoder*, 1972). More recently, the U.S. Supreme Court has ruled that the free exercise of religion, which was the basis of the *Yoder* decision, cannot provide an exemption from a neutral and generally applied law (*Employment Division, Department of Human Resources v. Smith*, 1990). The case involved denial of unemployment benefits to an Oregon worker who was terminated for using peyote, an illegal hallucinogen, in a Native American religious ceremony. The state argued that every terminated worker who used an illegal drug was denied unemployment benefits, regardless of the reason for such use, and that religion should not provide an exemption to the state's interest in eradicating illegal drug use. The Court agreed. But what about the *Yoder* decision, which provided an exemption from the compulsory school law for the Old Order Amish, based on their religion? The Court avoided overruling *Yoder* by pointing out that *two* rights were involved in that case—the parent's right to control their child's upbringing *and* the religious beliefs of the Old Order Amish—thus constituting a "hybrid" claim.

The hybrid claim has received a mixed reception from lower federal courts. For example, in 1995 the U.S. Court of Appeals for the First Circuit, whose jurisdiction encompasses several New England states, ruled against parents who asserted that requiring their children to attend a sexually explicit AIDS awareness program violated both parental rights and the free exercise of religion. The court noted that the one-time attendance at the program did not threaten the parents' way of life in the same manner as did the compulsory school law for the Amish children in *Yoder* and that parents do not have the right to dictate the public school curriculum (*Brown v. Hot, Sexy and Safer Productions*, p. 534). In California, parents have a right to exempt their children from HIV/AIDS prevention and sex education programs (Educ. Code § 51938).

The Tenth Circuit observed in 1998 that merely invoking the parental rights doctrine in combination with a free exercise claim will not suffice. "Whatever the *Smith* hybrid-rights theory may ultimately mean," the judges wrote, "we believe that it at least requires a colorable showing of infringement of recognized and specific constitutional rights, rather than the mere invocation of a general right such as the right to control the education of one's child" (p. 700). The case involved the Oklahoma parents of a homeschooled student who argued that the school district's refusal to permit the child to attend part-time violated their rights (*Swanson v. Guthrie Independent School District*). The appeals court rejected the contention.

Citing this ruling, the Ninth Circuit decided against Nevada parents who cited parental rights in combination with the Individuals with Disabilities Education Act (IDEA) in support of a reimbursement claim for speech therapy services for their homeschooled disabled child (*Hooks v. Clark County School District*, 2000). The Ninth Circuit noted that IDEA leaves to the states the question of whether home education constitutes a private institution for purposes of receiving IDEA services and that parents do not have the right to pick and choose the services they wish from a school district.

But there are a few decisions where the hybrid claim has been successful. As we noted in Chapter 6, students in California public schools have strong protection under both federal and state law for exercising rights of free speech. The wearing of a religious symbol, like the wearing of the black armband as a political symbol in the well-known *Tinker v. Des Moines Independent Community School District* U.S. Supreme Court ruling, is a form of protected speech. While there are few cases involving the wearing of religious symbols by public school students, two from Texas are particularly instructive. In the first, the federal district court judge ruled that a hair-length regulation intruded on Native Americans' sincerely held religious belief to have long hair. It made no difference that the practice was not a fundamental tenet of Native American religious orthodoxy. Sincerity, not centrality, sufficed. Nor was the judge persuaded that religion ought not to be entitled to an exemption to neutral rules that are generally applied to all, as the U.S. Supreme Court had held in its 1980 *Employment Division, Department of Human Resources v. Smith* decision. A literal interpretation of that decision, Judge William Wayne Justice wrote,

> would represent the erosion, if not the absolute obliteration, of one of the most basic principles our Founders, recently freed from the oppression of European government, sought to establish through the Bill of Rights—the free exercise of religion as a fundamental right of the new American democracy. (p. 1332)

In any case, the judge found the case fell into the Supreme Court's hybrid context because the hair-length rule as applied to the Native American students would violate their rights of religious freedom and free speech, as well as interfere with their parent's right to control their children's upbringing (*Alabama and Coushatta Tribes of Texas v. Big Sandy Independent School District*, 1993).

The second ruling involved an antigang-related school rule that was applied to students wearing rosary beads. The federal judge found that the wearing of the rosary beads was a sincere form of religious expression. Citing the free exercise clause and the free speech clause, the judge held that the case fell into the hybrid category and thus required very careful review of the school district's action. Because the rule was poorly worded, it constituted an unconstitutional intrusion upon the students' sincere expression of their religious beliefs (*Chalifoux v. New Caney Independent School District*, 1997).

In sum, there is no assurance that religion can provide the basis for an exemption to activities that public schools require of all students, even when coupled with parental rights. Parents who strongly oppose the experiences of their children within public schools on religious grounds have a constitutional right to enroll their children in religious private schools. The problem for most families, however, is the high cost of private education. To make private schooling more accessible to parents, policymakers have endeavored over the years to find ways to provide financial support to private education. The final section of this chapter addresses the legality of these efforts.

AID TO RELIGIOUS PRIVATE SCHOOLS

In many states with sizable numbers of private schools and legislatures populated by their graduates, efforts have long been taken to channel public funding to private schools. As discussed at the beginning of the chapter, the U.S. Supreme Court's first major case involving religion and education dealt with a New Jersey statute underwriting the cost of bus transportation to private schools (*Everson v. Board of Education*, 1947). Rather than seeing this program as advancing the religious mission of the private school, the majority of justices viewed it as a pupil benefit program. The state was doing nothing more than assuring that all students got to and from school safely. A California court of appeal took the same position a year earlier in upholding a similar state law against a charge that it violated the state constitution (*Bowker v. Baker*, 1946). Currently, Education Code Section 39808 permits the governing board of a school district to provide transportation to students attending private schools upon the same terms, in the same manner, and over the same routes as public school students. However, the statute does not permit providing transportation reimbursement money to parents or guardians of students attending private schools. In addition, Education Code Section 37253 permits districts to offer supplemental instruction in core academic areas at various times, including the summer. The attorney general has advised that private school students can be permitted to attend during the summer because the primary beneficiaries are the students and parents, not the private schools (70 Op. Atty. Gen. 282, 1987).

Direct Aid Programs

Beyond police and fire protection and student transportation, private schools in California receive few direct financial benefits from the state. The U.S. Supreme Court upheld a New York law authorizing public school authorities to lend secular textbooks free of charge to private school students (*Board of Education v. Allen*, 1968). But a similar effort failed in this state before the California Supreme Court in 1981 (*California Teachers Association v. Riles*). Wrote the judges in a unanimous decision, "it is not the meaning of the First Amendment which is critical to our determination, but section 8 article IX and section 5 of article XVI of the California Constitution" (p. 311). Those provisions require that public funds must be spent for public schools and specifically prohibit appropriations that help support or sustain schools controlled by religious organizations. Unlike police and fire protection, the court found that the provision of textbooks would advance the educational mission of the religious private school and thus be clearly unconstitutional.

Direct aid cases have come before the U.S. Supreme Court, and the Court has responded over the years with a plethora of rulings that often seem contradictory. While the history of this litigation is beyond the scope of our discussion, two rulings well portray the current stance of the Court regarding direct assistance to religious and nonreligious private schools. In 1997 the Court upheld the use of public schoolteachers to deliver remedial instruction to educationally at-risk children on the premises of private schools under Title I of the Elementary and Secondary Education Act, overturning an earlier ruling to the contrary. The majority noted that the aid was not being used to advance the religious mission of the private schools (*Agostini v. Felton*). A number of California private schools have students who receive Title I services in this manner. In deciding this case, the justices modified the guidelines for deciding direct aid cases. First, there must be a secular purpose. Then it must be determined if the aid has the effect of advancing religion. To determine the latter, three criteria must be addressed: whether the aid results in government indoctrination, whether it defines recipients by reference to religion, and whether it creates excessive entanglement between government and religion.

The Court used these criteria three years later to uphold the lending of educational materials such as computer hardware and software, library materials, and reference and curriculum materials to private schools under the Education Consolidation and Improvement Act of 1981 (*Mitchell v. Helms*, 2000). Chapter 2 of that law permits the federal government to channel funds to state educational agencies, and through them, to local education agencies. The local educational agency uses the funds to purchase the materials and then loans them to both public and private schools. The program was deemed secular because it provides money for both public and private education. In providing the key fifth vote to the majority, Justice Sandra Day O'Connor observed that the program only loans the materials to the private schools and requires that the materials must be secular, neutral, and nonideological. Thus, Chapter 2 money never reaches the coffers of religious schools. The other four justices in the majority, however, went further to maintain that even if the materials were used for sectarian purposes, that would not violate the establishment clause. In the words of Justice Clarence Thomas, who wrote for these four justices, "So long as the governmental aid is not itself 'unsuitable for use in the public schools because of religious content,' and eligibility for aid is determined in a constitutionally permissible manner, any use of that aid to indoctrinate cannot be attributed to the government and is thus not of constitutional concern" (p. 820). In effect, this approach would eliminate the distinction between direct aid and indirect aid and permit unrestricted expenditure of public money in private religious schools. However, only four justices took this position.

Indirect Aid Programs through Vouchers and Tax Credits

Indirect aid does not raise the same constitutional concerns as direct aid, because funding arrives at religious and other private schools via the decisions of others. In 2002, the U.S. Supreme Court relied on this rationale to breathe new life into the voucher movement by upholding the Pilot Project Scholarship Program for children in the failing Cleveland public school system against a challenge that it constituted impermissible aid to religious private schools in violation of the establishment clause of the federal constitution (*Zelman v. Simmons-Harris*). While parents had a choice of out-of-district public schools, none chose to participate. Ninety-six percent of the scholarship recipients enrolled in religious private schools. The majority in the five-to-four decision found the fact that parents had a range of choices encompassing traditional public schools, magnet schools, and charter schools and that funding flowed through parents to the private schools diminished concern about advancing religion. Writing for the majority, Chief Justice Rehnquist cited earlier rulings in observing that

> where a government aid program is neutral with respect to religion, and provides assistance directly to a broad class of citizens who, in turn, direct government aid to religious schools wholly as a result of their own genuine and independent private choice, the program is not readily subject to challenge under the Establishment Clause. (p. 652)

Thereafter, voucher measures were introduced in a number of state legislatures. However, about one-third of the states including California have strict antiestablishment of religion provisions in their state constitutions. The possible continued viability of these provisions came before the Supreme Court in 2004 in a case involving a Washington State student who was denied a state scholarship that he intended to use to help defray expenses at a Bible college in preparing for the ministry (*Locke v. Davey*). But the Court sidestepped the issue by ruling narrowly. The justices upheld the denial of the scholarship based on a state constitutional provision restricting payments of public money for religious worship, exercise, or instruction, or the support of any religious establishment. The Court did not rule on another provision in the Washington State Constitution that requires public schooling to be free from sectarian control or influence. It is provisions like these in many state constitutions, including California's, that bar publicly funded vouchers to help parents send their children to religious private schools.

The future for vouchers in California is uncertain. Clearly, the state constitution continues to be a bar against channeling taxpayer money directly to schools not controlled by public officials. Aside from an initiative that would amend the state constitution or a judicial ruling that would alter its meaning, efforts to open up private schools to California parents who cannot afford them depend upon legislative interest and creativity. As noted in Chapter 1, Californians decidedly voted down voucher initiatives on two occasions.

In other states, legislatures have looked at individual income tax credits as a way of enfranchising parents with the right to choose private schools. It is argued that income tax credits are more likely to be considered private, not government, money and thus less vulnerable to state constitutional attack than are state-funded vouchers. Because they are not government funds, tax credits are less likely to be accompanied by restrictive regulatory measures imposed on private schools. In enacting its program in 1997, the Arizona Legislature established a school tuition organization that distributes the money to parents. Thus, there are two layers of insulating private action between the government and religious schools: the school tuition organization and the parents. The Arizona Supreme Court upheld the program by a narrow margin in 1999 (*Kotterman v. Killian*). Later, a lawsuit against the program was filed in federal court. After the U.S. Supreme Court permitted the lawsuit to go forward, the federal district court ruled that it did not violate the establishment clause of the First Amendment (*Winn v. Hibbs*, 2005).

A general tax credit has a distinct advantage over the individual tax credit. Any taxpayer, not just parents, can obtain a tax credit for making contributions to a tuition scholarship fund. As a result, the amount of accumulated money is likely to be much greater. This is especially true in states like Florida and Pennsylvania, which give tax credits to corporations as well. In 2006 the Arizona Legislature expanded its individual tax credit program to encompass a general tax credit program whereby businesses can donate up to $10 million for private school tuition grants. In 2007 a state superior court judge dismissed a lawsuit against that law. Whether there will be any interest in a similar program in California and how it might fare in the state courts remain to be seen.

As the battles over state initiatives demonstrate, any program that expands school choice to encompass private schools will encounter stiff resistance.

SUMMARY

Conflict over the role of religion in public schooling is unlikely to abate any time soon. With advocates on all sides of the issue ready to challenge any school action they consider unwarranted, it is incumbent on school personnel to know the law and stay abreast of legal developments. While this chapter has covered many facets of religion and schooling, several key points emerge from our discussion.

First, while public schools cannot promote prayer, nothing precludes students from engaging in nondisruptive private religious discussion and prayer. The same is true of employees, though teachers and others in direct contact with students need to be especially circumspect in not conveying the impression of religious endorsement.

Second, schools can teach about religion but cannot teach religion. The incorporation of religious materials, artifacts, and music in the instructional program and during holiday observances is appropriate as part of a secular program of instruction. Whether students can write papers and give presentations on religious topics depends upon the purpose of the assignment. If such topics would serve the goals of the lesson plan, then students cannot be denied the opportunity to do so lest the school and its officials portray hostility toward religion. However, in accord with recent Ninth Circuit rulings, student speeches on religious topics at graduation ceremonies, along with an invocation and benediction, breach the separation of church and state in both the federal and California constitutions.

Aside from several statutory exemptions, parents generally do not have a right to exempt their children from curricular activities to which they object on religious grounds when those activities are required of all students as part of a secular program of instruction.

While public schools cannot sponsor student religious organizations, such organizations have a right under the federal Equal Access Act as noncurricular groups to meet on campus during noninstructional time at public secondary schools and may have a similar right at public elementary schools under the terms of the district and school's community use policy. Religious organizations may be allowed access to a school's campus and facilities under the terms of the California Civic Center Act and in compliance with a school district's community use policy.

California school districts have the discretion to provide transportation to children attending private schools and to include them in a supplementary summer school program, but private schools receive few other benefits from the state. However, federal assistance to religious private schools that is routed through state, county, and local educational agencies for the education of certain categories of students does not violate the establishment clause of the First Amendment. Giving parents publicly funded vouchers for tuition expenses at religious private schools in combination with other choice programs is permissible under the federal Constitution but not under the California Constitution. How the California Legislature and judiciary will respond to efforts to privatize schooling, and how private schools that pride themselves on their autonomy will respond, await the future. Much like incorporating religion in public schools, the channeling of public funding to religious private schools remains a contentious and litigious subject.

8 | STUDENTS WITH DISABILITIES

Federal special education law brought wide-sweeping changes to public education, a matter historically left to the states. In this chapter, we explore the events and context spurring federal special education law into existence. We then turn our attention to the entire process of special education under federal and state law. The contours and requirements of a free appropriate public education (FAPE) are explained. We discuss how students are located, referred for initial evaluation, and determined eligible for special education under the Individuals with Disabilities Education Act (IDEA). The role, composition, and requirements of individualized education program (IEP) teams are detailed, and precede an explanation of the contents of an IEP. A comment on behavior-related plans and services, mental health services, transition plans and services, and private school students follows. An overview of the impact of the Americans with Disabilities Act (ADA) and Section 504 of the Rehabilitation Act of 1973 (Section 504) concludes the chapter. This chapter is not the final word on these topics, but an introduction to their general contours and requirements. Readers desiring greater specificity should reference the resources noted in the appendix and consider consultation with a competent legal professional.

Special education law is an amalgamation of hundreds of pages of statutes, regulations, judicial and administrative decisions, and administrative guidance. To breathe life into these pages of black-and-white law, we have created Amy. She is our imagined student through whom we will explain IDEA while retaining a connection to the law's primary focus and beneficiary: children with disabilities.

Amy is a cute and engaging fifth grader attending an elementary school in California. Rhonda, Amy's mother, has become increasingly concerned about Amy's ability to complete class work at the same level as that of her classroom peers. Recently, Rhonda had a conference with Amy's teacher to discuss the level of Amy's schoolwork and classroom performance. A main concern addressed in the conference was Amy's reading. The teacher believes that Amy is reading at a noticeably lower level than her peers are. At the end of the conference, Amy's teacher mentions that a referral for an evaluation may be appropriate to determine if Amy is eligible for special education. Before making such a referral, however, Amy's teacher explains that she wants to see if some modifications to Amy's general education program will help. Amy's teacher offers extra time for tests and additional tutoring as some options. These modifications will be provided through a Student Study Team that will monitor Amy's performance.

Rhonda is shocked. Rhonda always thought special education was for students with severe physical or mental disabilities. According to the teacher, the special education referral would be made only to ensure that "all the bases are covered." Further, the referral will be made only if the modifications to Amy's current program are not successful. Rhonda goes home with a lot on her mind. While eager to determine the source of Amy's difficulties, Rhonda has mixed feelings about the possibility of a special education referral for her daughter.

SPECIAL EDUCATION LAW

A Brief History

Federal and state laws afford special education students numerous protections and entitlements that are not available to general education students. Among these are a guarantee for a particular type and level of education, numerous procedural safeguards, and recourse to an administrative hearing process to challenge almost any aspect of the educational program offered by the school district. To those first encountering these laws, a simple question may arise: why does special education law exist?

To gain an understanding of why special education law exists, we must look back over thirty years and examine the landmark decisions of *Pennsylvania Association for Retarded Children (PARC) v. Commonwealth of Pennsylvania* (1972) and *Mills v. Board of Education of the District of Columbia* (1972). We must also listen to Leonard Kalish, a father speaking on his daughter's behalf in *PARC*, describing special education in Pennsylvania at the time:

> I would just like to call to the Court's attention to what the realities of that situation are, and I think I can speak with some authority because for the last nine years, my fifteen-year-old daughter has been denied access to public education

without due process, but consistently denied, and as a result of which we have had her in private schools for the last nine years. Now in those nine years . . . we have spent approximately forty thousand dollars on her private schooling.

There is no pride or status symbol involved in having a child in a private school such as the private schools to which my daughter and others in the same situation would go. In other words, it isn't out of any feeling of status that I am undertaking this heavy financial burden. It is simply because there is no public facility.

Now the moment a public facility is indicated, even just on the drawing board or on brochures, or papers of any kind which will look reasonably appropriate, I will assure Your Honors that ninety-five per cent or more of all parents will rush to get their children in there because every one of the parents is laboring under a backbreaking financial burden. We're not talking about wealthy people here. We are talking about ordinary people.

Mr. Kalish's daughter—like the other minor plaintiffs in *PARC*—did not have access to a public education, because she was mentally retarded. Under Pennsylvania law at the time, the state board of education was not obligated to educate any child whom a public school psychologist certified as uneducable or untrainable. After such a certification, the state's burden to care for the child shifted to the Department of Welfare, which had no obligation to provide any educational services. These children had no place in a Pennsylvania public school.

The plaintiffs in *PARC* argued that this and other similar Pennsylvania laws violated the due process and equal protection clauses of the United States Constitution. The plaintiffs argued that due process was denied because their children were excluded from a public education without any notice or a hearing to challenge the exclusion. The equal protection argument was aimed at the state's current practice of providing a public education to nondisabled children while denying that education to mentally retarded children. *PARC* ended in a judicial consent decree repealing the exclusionary laws and practices at issue. A consent decree is a judicial order requiring the parties to abide by its terms. The historical significance of *PARC* extends beyond its then immediate impact on Pennsylvania law. Some of the key terms and conditions in the *PARC* consent decree influenced Congress in its deliberation and drafting of the nation's first federal special education law a few years later.

Mills also dealt with the exclusion of children with disabilities from public education. Peter Mills was in the fourth grade when he was identified by the principal as a "behavior problem." Without a full hearing or review, Peter was approved for exclusion from public education without any other publicly funded educational alternatives. Unlike *PARC*, laws already existed in the District of Columbia providing for the education of children with disabilities and due process protections prior to their removal from school. The board of education, as it admitted in court, simply failed to follow these laws. In response to the plaintiffs' due process and equal protection arguments, the defendants made a single argument: we do not have the money to provide special education. The court made short work of this defense, noting that limited financial resources must be spread equitably among all students.

The court ordered the board of education to provide "each child of school age a free and suitable publicly supported education regardless of the degree of the child's mental, physical, or emotional disability or impairment." The order forbid the practice of exclusion from public school without a hearing and set the board of education to the task of notifying thousands of parents that their children, regardless of their disability, were entitled to a public education. To this end, newspaper and radio advertisements ran for weeks after the decision.

PARC and *Mills* brought reforms to the school districts within Pennsylvania and the District of Columbia. Nationwide, however, there was no uniformity among state laws in how children with disabilities were, if at all, educated. All of this changed in 1975 with passage of the Education for All Handicapped Children Act (P.L. 94–142) (EHCA). Congressional findings preceding EHCA noted the widespread nature of the circumstances litigated in *PARC* and *Mills*. The House Report accompanying EHCA's enactment set out the grim statistics. In 1974, over 1.75 million children with disabilities did not receive any educational services. Of those attending school, approximately 2.5 million were not receiving appropriate services and were "left to fend for themselves in classrooms designed for education of their nonhandicapped peers." Millions of children with disabilities "were either totally excluded from schools or [were] sitting idly in regular classrooms awaiting the time when they were old enough to 'drop out.'"

To address these inequities, EHCA made federal money available to states in return for a promise to abide by EHCA's requirements. Many of EHCA's core requirements came from *PARC* and *Mills*. School districts were charged with locating and evaluating students for receipt of special education services. EHCA guaranteed eligible students a free appropriate public education (FAPE), comprised of special education and related services. The requirement of individualized education program (IEP) team meetings for making decisions regarding a child's special education program was codified into the law. The IEP team was required to detail the student's educational program in a written document entitled an IEP. Parental involvement in their child's special education program was mandated. Special education students were to be placed with their nondisabled peers to the maximum extent appropriate. EHCA contained a procedural framework to ensure parent participation and timely compliance with the law's requirements. Parents also were given an administrative hearing process for bringing grievances regarding their child's educational program.

Congress enacted EHCA to remedy the inequalities in public education facing disabled children and their families. In signing EHCA in 1975, however, President Gerald Ford acknowledged some of the concerns that had been raised regarding the expense and administrative burden of this new law:

> Unfortunately, this bill promises more than the federal government can deliver, and its good intentions could be thwarted by the many unwise provisions it contains. Everyone can agree with the objective in the bill—educating all handicapped children in our nation. The key question is whether the bill will really accomplish that objective.
>
> Even the strongest supporters of this measure know as well as I that they are falsely raising the expectations of the groups affected by claiming authorization levels which are excessive and unrealistic.
>
> Despite my strong support for the full educational opportunities for our handicapped children, the funding levels in this bill will simply not be possible if the federal expenditures are to be brought under control and a balanced budget achieved over the next few years.
>
> There are other features of the bill which I believe to be objectionable and which should be changed. It contains a vast array of detailed, complex and costly administrative requirements which would unnecessarily assert federal control over traditional state and local government functions. It establishes complex requirements under which tax dollars would be used to support administrative paperwork, and not educational programs. Unfortunately, these requirements will remain in effect even though Congress appropriates far less than the amounts placed [in the law].

President Ford's concerns remain as pressing today as they did nearly three decades ago. Despite authorizing federal funding up to 40 percent, Congress has never appropriated more than 20 percent. The funding shortfall is absorbed by states and local school districts. Some special educators and school administrators feel as though the majority of their time is not spent educating, but performing the myriad administrative tasks necessary to ensure compliance with IDEA's procedural requirements. Disagreements between parents and school districts are increasingly subject to timely and expensive litigation, both at the administrative and federal court levels.

These criticisms are shaping the modern debate over IDEA, which Congress reauthorized in 2004 with the passage of the Individuals with Disabilities Education Improvement Act of 2004 (IDEA 2004). In 2006, the United States Department of

Education's Office of Special Education and Rehabilitative services published new regulations for IDEA 2004. Our discussion incorporates IDEA 2004's most significant amendments.

Sources of Special Education Law

Reflecting on the structure of school law as described in Chapter 1, we can divide the sources of special education law into three categories: statutory, administrative, and judicial law. At the federal level, IDEA is the vehicle through which Congress seeks to "open the doors of public education to handicapped children." IDEA sets forth the rights of eligible students, their parents, and the obligations of covered public entities for every aspect of special education law. The United States Department of Education (USDOE) publishes comprehensive regulations interpreting IDEA. The complete text of IDEA and its implementing regulations can be found in Title 20 United States Code, Section 1400 and following sections, and in the Code of Federal Regulations, Chapter 34, Part 300. The Office of Special Education Programs (OSEP) provides administrative guidance on how to interpret IDEA. OSEP's opinion may be relied on as persuasive, but not binding, legal authority by courts.

At the state level, California Education Code Section 56000 and following sections contain parallel provisions to IDEA. Title Five of the California Code of Regulations contains specific regulations enacted by the State Board of Education (SBE) detailing the implementation of various provisions of the Education Code. The Office of Administrative Hearings (OAH) conducts administrative hearings applying these state and federal laws to disputes between parents and school districts. Unlike judicial decisions, OAH decisions do not create legal precedent binding other OAH administrative law judges. OAH decisions are considered nonbinding, persuasive authority by OAH administrative law judges in future hearings. OAH decisions can be appealed to state and federal district courts in California.

IDEA applies to each state that receives federal funding under the statute. IDEA's coverage thereafter extends to all political subdivisions of the state that are involved in the education of children with disabilities. These include the state educational agency, local educational agencies, other state agencies and schools such as the Department of Mental Health and Welfare, state schools for children with disabilities, and state and local juvenile and adult correctional facilities. School districts are understandably the primary public entity subject to IDEA's requirements.

Charter schools that are deemed a local educational agency (LEA) are also responsible for complying with IDEA. Education Code Sections 47640 and 47641 define when a charter school is a LEA for purposes of IDEA responsibility. The key inquiry is whether the charter school elected to be a LEA in its petition for establishment or renewal of its charter (Educ. Code § 47641 (a)). As a LEA, a charter school is essentially an independent entity for purposes of complying with IDEA and attendant Education Code sections. A charter school that is not a LEA is deemed a "school of the district" of the LEA that granted the charter (Educ. Code § 47641 (b)). In this latter situation, the school district granting the charter remains responsible for ensuring the charter school's IDEA compliance (e.g., funding educational programs and being subject to a due process hearing when a dispute arises). The SBE also can grant a charter to a charter school but delegate oversight of the charter school to a school district. In this situation, the school district must ensure the charter school's adherence to IDEA.

IDEA's procedural and substantive rights extend to a child with a disability and the child's parent. The California Education Code uses the phrase "individual with exceptional needs" in lieu of "child with a disability." Unless otherwise noted, the words "school district" or "school districts" are used in this chapter for purposes of referring to any public agency within California covered by IDEA. Students who qualify for special education under IDEA are referred to as IDEA-eligible, special education students, or children with disabilities.

The Language of Special Education

Special education has its own language populated with acronyms. Students do not receive a free appropriate public education, but a FAPE. Instead of individualized education program team meetings, IEP team meetings are held. The following is a brief explanation of the most common acronyms and terms encountered. Further detail and context regarding each term are provided throughout the chapter.

- Individuals with Disabilities Education Act (IDEA): The federal law governing all aspects of special education and requiring school districts to provide eligible students with a free appropriate public education or FAPE. IDEA's precursor was EHCA.

- Free appropriate public education (FAPE): Special education and related services that are provided at public expense, meet the standards of the state educational agency, and are in conformity with the student's individualized education program or IEP.

- Special education: Specifically designed instruction, at no cost to the parents, that meets the unique needs of a student with a disability.

- Related services: Related services encompass a wide variety of supportive services that are necessary for a student to benefit from the student's educational program. These services may include transportation, occupational therapy, speech and language therapy, and counseling.

- Designated Instruction and Services (DIS): California's phrase for related services.

- Child with a Disability: A student who meets one or more of thirteen defined categories in IDEA (e.g., Specific Learning Disability, Mental Retardation) and by reason of the student's disability needs special education and related services.

- Parent: A parent includes a guardian, person acting in the place of a parent if the individual is legally responsible for the child's welfare, a surrogate parent, or a foster parent.

- Individualized Education Program (IEP): The master document that charts a student's educational program. An IEP contains a description of a student's educational needs, goals for the year, progress on goals from the previous year if applicable, and, among other items, the nature and type of special education and related services for the student.

- IEP Team: The group of individuals responsible for developing, reviewing, or revising an IEP for a child with a disability. IEP teams have both mandatory and discretionary team members.

- Independent Educational Evaluation (IEE): Parents disagreeing with a school district's evaluation of their child may request an independent evaluation at public expense. If certain criteria are met, a school district must pay for the IEE unless it can demonstrate at a due process hearing that its evaluation was appropriate.

- Extended School Year (ESY): ESY is a continuation of a student's special education and related services beyond the normal school year to prevent regression.

- Due Process Hearing: An administrative hearing that can be requested by either a parent or school district. A common issue is whether a FAPE was offered or provided.

- Stay Put: When a parent files for a due process hearing, a student generally remains in the student's last agreed-upon and implemented educational placement. The student's stay-put placement maintains the educational status quo pending completion of the due process hearing.

FREE APPROPRIATE PUBLIC EDUCATION (FAPE)

Special education students have an entitlement to a FAPE under IDEA. FAPE has a procedural and substantive aspect. The procedural component of FAPE refers to the numerous procedural requirements that a school district must follow in developing, providing, and revising the substantive component. Procedural elements of FAPE include, among other things, notice requirements, time lines, the composition of the IEP team, and the contents of the IEP. The substantive component of FAPE is the student's educational program, which consists of special education and designated instruction and services (DIS).

Procedural Component

Congress placed emphasis on both the procedural and substantive aspects of FAPE. If school districts follow the procedural requirements of the law, Congress reasoned, the substantive requirement of making FAPE available would be met. There are a seemingly infinite number of ways in which school districts can commit a procedural violation. Among these potential procedural violations are missing a time line, failing to provide adequate written notice, not having a mandatory IEP team meeting member at an IEP team meeting, or not drafting the IEP document in conformity with the IDEA. However, a procedural violation does not always equate to a denial of a FAPE.

The United States Court of Appeals for the Ninth Circuit held that only procedural violations that result in a "loss of educational opportunity" or "seriously infringe the parents' opportunity to participate in the IEP formulation process" are a denial of FAPE (*W. G. v. Board of Trustees of Target Range School District No. 23*, 1992). There must be some demonstrable harm to the student's education or the parents' opportunity to participate in the IEP process for a procedural violation to rise to the level of a denial of a FAPE. In other words: no harm, no foul.

IDEA 2004 permits an OAH administrative law judge to determine that a procedural violation is a denial of a FAPE only if the violation:

- "Impeded the child's right to a [FAPE]";
- "Significantly impeded the parents' opportunity to participate in the decision making process regarding the provision of a [FAPE] to the parents' child"; or
- "Caused a deprivation of educational benefits" (20 U.S.C. § 1415 (f)(3)(E)(ii)).

The latter two standards appear consistent with the analysis in *Target Range School District*. An understanding of what it means to impede a child's right to a FAPE, however, will evolve over time through OAH and court decisions interpreting this aspect of IDEA 2004.

Substantive Component

FAPE is statutorily defined as special education and DIS that are provided at public expense under public supervision and direction, without charge; meet the standards of the state educational agency; include preschool, elementary school, or secondary school education; and are provided in conformity with an appropriate IEP. IDEA is silent on the level of education FAPE requires. Should a special education student be entitled to a basic level of services, or to the best possible program that focuses on maximizing the student's potential? In 1982, the U.S. Supreme Court took up this question in special education's most famous case: *Board of Education of Hendrick Hudson School District v. Rowley*.

Amy Rowley, no relation to our hypothetical Amy, was a deaf student attending elementary school. In the first grade, Amy Rowley's IEP provided her with an FM hearing aid, one hour of instruction per day from a tutor for the deaf, and instruction from a speech therapist for three hours per week. In lieu of some of these services, Amy's parents asked the school administrators to provide a qualified sign language interpreter for all of Amy's academic classes. The school district initially provided the requested interpreter. After two weeks the interpreter concluded that Amy did not need her assistance. The school district then discontinued the interpreter, and Amy's parents initiated their long journey through the legal system.

After completing an administrative hearing, administrative appeal, federal district court trial, and federal appellate court trial, Amy and her parents appeared before the U.S. Supreme Court. Amy's parents urged the high court to find, as the federal district and appellate court had, that FAPE requires school districts to "maximize the potential of each handicapped child commensurate with the opportunity provided nonhandicapped children." Carefully examining the legislative history of EHCA, the Court disagreed in a five-to-three split.

The majority concluded that EHCA confers a "basic floor of opportunity" onto eligible students and not the potential maximizing services Amy and her parents sought. Because Amy performed better than the average child in her class and was easily passing from grade to grade, the majority held that she did not require a sign-language interpreter to receive a FAPE. The importance of *Rowley* cannot be overstated; it is the legal standard that school districts throughout the nation must meet to provide FAPE or make FAPE available. The latter (making FAPE available) refers to those students who are never enrolled by their parents in the school district's offered program.

Based on *Rowley*, OAH requires that a school district's special education program satisfy four elements to constitute a FAPE. OAH requires the school district's program to:

1. Be designed to meet the student's unique educational needs;
2. Be reasonably calculated to provide the student with some educational benefit;
3. Be provided in conformity with the student's IEP; and
4. Be in the least restrictive environment or LRE.

Appropriate administration and interpretation of assessments play a key role in the first element. If, for example, a student is not assessed in all areas of suspected disability (as IDEA requires), the IEP team may not be aware of one or more of the student's unique needs. The same result can occur if a student is appropriately assessed, but the IEP team does not develop any goals to address one of the student's unique needs resulting from the student's disability. A special education program that cannot meet this first element does not constitute a FAPE and will in all likelihood be determined inappropriate to some degree by CSEHO.

Once a student's unique needs have been identified, the question becomes whether the special education student's program is reasonably calculated to provide some educational benefit. As noted in *Rowley*, FAPE does not require the absolute best or "potential maximizing" education for the student. A number of judicial decisions have further defined FAPE. As the Ninth Circuit ruled in 1987, the correct inquiry is not whether the student may obtain more benefit from the placement preferred by the parents, but whether the school district's placement is reasonably calculated to provide the student with some educational benefit (*Gregory K. v. Longview School District*). The phrase "some educational benefit," however, has substance. De minimis or trivial educational benefit will not satisfy the *Rowley* standard (*Walczak v. Florida Union Free School District*, 1998). The limitations imposed by the student's disability are taken into consideration when determining if some educational benefit has been conferred (*Mrs. B. v. Milford Board of Education*, 1997). A 1999 Ninth Circuit decision refers to an IEP as a "snapshot," in which a review of its appropriateness focuses on what "was, and was not, objectively reasonable . . . at the time the IEP was drafted" (*Adams v. Oregon*, p. 1149). Under *Adams*, hindsight is irrelevant in determining the appropriateness of an educational placement.

The third element pertains to implementation of a student's IEP. A failure to implement a student's IEP, however, is not necessarily a denial of a FAPE. Rather, only a material failure to implement the IEP constitutes a denial of a FAPE. The services a school provides must fall significantly short of the services required by a student's IEP to constitute a material failure (*Van Duyn v. Baker School District*, 2007). One factor that is considered in determining whether a material failure to implement occurred is the progress, or lack thereof, of the student.

The fourth element of FAPE, LRE, warrants separate discussion.

FAPE and the Least Restrictive Environment (LRE)

LRE is both part of FAPE and its own distinct concept. A student cannot receive FAPE unless the student is in the LRE. IDEA's LRE requirement has two related aspects. First, school districts must ensure "that to the maximum extent appropriate, children with disabilities . . . are educated with children who are not disabled" (20 U.S.C. § 1412 (a)(5)(A)). Second, the "removal of children with disabilities from the regular education environment occurs only when the nature or severity of the disability of a child is such that education in regular classes with the use of supplementary aides and services cannot be achieved satisfactorily" (Id.).

Given the wholesale exclusion in *Mills* and *PARC*, it is not surprising that Congress sought to include special education students with their general education peers. As the second aspect of LRE indicates, however, there are circumstances in which a special education student cannot receive a satisfactory education in the regular education environment and a more restrictive setting is appropriate. In the context of LRE, restrictiveness is primarily a function of the degree to which the special education student is educated with nondisabled peers. For example, spending the entire school day in a special day class that contains no nondisabled students is more restrictive than attending a special day class for two periods of the school day and spending the remainder of the school day in the general education setting. The definitive ruling addressing LRE for California came from the Ninth Circuit in 1994 (*Sacramento City Unified School District v. Holland*).

In this case, Rachel Holland's parents, citing the IDEA's LRE requirement, wanted their daughter to be placed in a general education classroom for the entire school day. Taking note of Rachel's moderate mental retardation and her forty-four IQ, the school district denied her parents' request. From the school district's perspective, Rachel was too severely handicapped to benefit from a full-time placement in a general education classroom. Over the next four years the school district and Rachel's parents argued their respective positions to a CSEHO hearing officer, federal district court, and the Ninth Circuit Court of Appeals. The school district lost at every level.

For *Holland,* the federal district court was charged with interpreting IDEA's directive to educate disabled children "to the maximum extent appropriate" with their nondisabled peers. The federal district court created a four-factor balancing test to determine if a full-time placement in a general education classroom would be appropriate for Rachel. The four factors are the educational benefits of placement full-time in a regular class, the nonacademic benefits of such a placement, the effect Rachel had on the teacher and other children in the regular class, and the costs of mainstreaming Rachel. The Ninth Circuit affirmed the four-factor test.

In applying *Holland,* OAH routinely rejects school district arguments that a student will receive a better education in a special day class as opposed to a general education classroom. The appropriate inquiry, as OAH states, is whether or not the student can receive a satisfactory education in a general education classroom with the use of supplementary aides and services. Supplementary aides and services cover a wide range of items, such as classroom accommodations and modifications, behavior plans, or the provision of a full-time, one-to-one aide. IDEA requires school districts to appropriately use these aides and supports to enable a special education student to be educated with the student's nondisabled peers to the maximum extent appropriate. However, the LRE mandate is not so strong as to overcome the student's entitlement to an appropriate education or FAPE. If a student cannot receive a satisfactory education in a general education classroom (e.g., does not address the student's unique needs and provide some educational benefit), even with supplementary aides and services, the student can be placed in a more restrictive setting without violating the IDEA's LRE mandate. Remember, IDEA requires the education of children with disabilities with nondisabled peers only to the "maximum extent *appropriate*" (emphasis added).

Having commented on the procedural and substantive aspects of FAPE, we again turn our attention to the hypothetical case of Amy and the special education process under IDEA.

CHILD FIND, REFERRAL, ASSESSMENT, AND ELIGIBILITY

School districts must affirmatively seek out students who may be IDEA-eligible, undertake comprehensive assessments, notice and convene initial IEP team meetings to determine if the students qualify for special education, and make FAPE available for those students who are children with disabilities under IDEA. Parental notice

and consent are integral components of this process. Notwithstanding the important role of parents in the education of their children, a school district's obligations
under IDEA remain the same regardless of how involved, apathetic, or even hostile
parents may be regarding their child's special needs.

Child Find and Referral for Initial Assessment

Amy is on the cusp of the "child find" process and a potential referral for a special
education assessment. A student study team (SST) comprised of Rhonda, Amy's
teacher, and the local school site principal meet to determine what modifications
to Amy's general education program may improve her classroom performance. No
law requires SSTs. They are a function of local school district policies. The goal of
the SST is to address academic difficulties through the use of general education
modifications and accommodations. Through an interactive process, parents and
educators can address educational issues (whether academic or behavioral) before
considering more intensive interventions that may be available under IDEA or
Section 504. SSTs may also consider and issue referrals to determine eligibility under IDEA or Section 504.

Over the next few months Amy receives extra time on tests and is tutored in reading by a general education teacher. After two months, the SST convenes to discuss
Amy's performance. The SST agrees that the extra test time and tutoring are not improving Amy's class work or test scores. Amy's teacher decides to refer Amy for an assessment to determine if Amy qualifies as a child with a disability under IDEA.

Under IDEA's child-find provision, school districts are under an affirmative obligation to identify, locate, and assess all children residing within the district's geographical boundaries who may need special education and related services. This
obligation extends to children such as Amy who are suspected of having a disability and may require special education and DIS. A school district's child-find obligations are not relieved if a parent does not request a special education evaluation
for the parent's child. The duty to identify, locate, and assess also extends to children who are not attending a public school. For example, if Amy had never set foot
on a public school campus, her school district would still have an obligation to
identify, locate, and assess her for special education and related services.

Like the court's order in *Mills*, school districts are under an obligation to get the
word out about the availability of special education. Neither IDEA nor the Education Code details what public schools in California must do to fulfill their child-
find obligation. For students already attending public schools, a teacher referral
system coupled with notices to parents about the availability of special education
is typical. To reach private school students, some school districts use newspaper

advertisements. Some school districts go an extra step and mail notices regarding the availability of special education directly to private schools within the school district's geographical area.

IDEA 2004 provides that school districts are required to conduct child find for children *attending* private schools located within the geographical boundaries of the district. If assessment of a child is warranted, the new regulations provide that the school district where the child is attending school must undertake the assessment, determine if the child is eligible for services, and, if the parents do not desire services for the child, develop an individual services plan (ISP) for the child (34 C.F.R. § 300.131(a)). See page 319 of this chapter for a brief discussion of ISPs.

Why did the school district convene an SST to provide extra time on tests and reading tutoring prior to the referral by Amy's teacher for a special education assessment? Because a referral for special education may be made only "after the resources of the regular education program have been considered, and where appropriate, utilized" (Educ. Code § 56303). There are, of course, instances in which a child is referred for a special education assessment with no modification of the child's general education program. For example, upon entering preschool, a child who has been diagnosed with autism will undoubtedly be referred directly to a special education assessment with no attempts to modify the child's general education program. Consideration should also be given to Section 3021(a) of California Code of Regulations, Title 5, which states that all referrals "shall initiate the assessment process" and has been interpreted by at least one OAH administrative law judge to require a school district to automatically move forward with assessment of a student when requested to do so by a parent.

Amy's teacher placed the referral in writing because all referrals for special education assessment must be documented. If Amy's mother, Rhonda, had made a verbal request for an assessment, the school district would be required to assist Rhonda with placing her request in writing. Amy's referral contains a brief reason for the referral, documents the resources of the regular education program that were considered or modified, and describes the results of intervention.

Amy's referral goes to Bob Smith, a program specialist in the district. Mr. Smith takes note of the lack of improvement in Amy's reading and test taking despite the extra time and tutoring. Mr. Smith believes the district is obligated to assess Amy for special education because he has reason to believe that Amy may qualify for special education. Amy has passed an invisible legal threshold; the school district is now required to determine if she is eligible for special education under IDEA.

School districts are not required to assess a child simply because a referral for assessment is made. In rare instances, Mr. Smith has denied a request for a special education assessment when he has no conceivable reason to suspect that the student in question has a qualifying disability. When a request for a special education assessment is denied, Mr. Smith sends the parent a letter informing the parent of the basis for the decision not to assess. Because Mr. Smith has only to "suspect" that a student may qualify for receipt of services under IDEA in order to be required to assess, there are very few instances when an assessment referral is denied. Sometimes Mr. Smith issues an assessment plan even in doubtful cases, just to make sure the school district does not miss anything.

Mr. Smith's decision to assess Amy for special education eligibility triggers the first of many procedural rights Amy will have under IDEA. Education Code Section 56321 details the procedural requirements concerning assessment. Mr. Smith must provide Rhonda with a proposed assessment plan within fifteen days of receiving Amy's referral. The proposed assessment plan must be accompanied by a document explaining the procedural safeguards available to Rhonda under IDEA. The procedural safeguards are Rhonda's rights as a parent. IDEA's implementing regulations detail the necessary components of the procedural safeguards notice. A school district need only provide a parent with a notice of procedural safeguards one time per year and in the case of assessment, the first occurrence of a state complaint or due process hearing, or upon the request of the parent (Educ. Code § 56301(d)(2). Both an obligation to inform parents of their rights and a deadline requiring completion of a task within a set time are recurrent themes throughout IDEA. The former provides parents with the knowledge to understand their rights; the latter with the assurance that educational issues are addressed in a timely manner.

Initial Assessment

Rhonda receives the proposed assessment plan and the accompanying procedural safeguards notice from Mr. Smith. The plan is a single page and contains a description of the areas in which the school district desires to assess Amy. A few of the assessment tools that may be given to Amy are named. A cover letter from Mr. Smith explains that the school district cannot assess Amy under the plan without Rhonda's written consent.

Amy has been identified as a potential candidate for services under IDEA through the child-find process. However, the school district can take no further action unless Rhonda provides her written consent to the proposed assessment plan. Before deciding to sign the plan, Rhonda makes a telephone call to Mr. Smith to ask a few questions. After some polite conversation, Rhonda asks why the school district wants to assess her daughter. Because the district suspects that Amy may qualify for special education services under IDEA, Mr. Smith explains to Rhonda, the district is required by the law to assess Amy for special education eligibility.

Rhonda asks if Amy will automatically become a special education student if the plan is signed. Mr. Smith explains that the assessments in the plan are merely to determine if Amy qualifies for special education services and that the district cannot legally provide Amy any special education services without further consent from Rhonda. After a pause in the conversation, Rhonda asks, "What if I don't want to sign the plan?"

Mr. Smith responds that Rhonda does not have to sign the plan and can exercise her parental discretion to refuse consent. "But," continues Mr. Smith, "if you do not sign the plan, the school district may request a hearing to seek an order to assess Amy over your consent." Somewhat taken aback, Rhonda asks why the school would undermine her authority as a parent. Mr. Smith's response is simply, "Because we have to." Mr. Smith breaks a moment of awkward silence in the conversation by telling Rhonda that he understands her being nervous and uncertain about this process. He tells Rhonda that the school district is simply trying to determine if Amy needs extra help in school. A bit more at ease, Rhonda decides to sign the assessment plan.

Education Code Section 56320 and following sections detail the requirements of an assessment plan, assessments, related assessment reports, and the follow-up IEP team meeting. An assessment plan must be in terms easily understood by the general public, must be in the parent's primary language or mode of communication (unless to do so is not feasible), must explain the types of assessments to be conducted, and must state that no IEP will result from the assessment without the parent's consent. A school district does not have to identify every specific assessment tool that may be used in the assessment. Most assessment plans, like Amy's, contain a short list of potential assessment tools. As noted, an explanation of the parent's procedural rights and safeguards must accompany the assessment plan.

Assessment must occur in all areas "related to the suspected disability." In Amy's situation, there is suspicion that she may have a learning disability in reading. Her assessment plan is therefore primarily focused on areas relating to reading. The school personnel undertaking the assessment must be qualified to administer their respective portions of the plan; use assessments that are not racially, culturally, or sexually discriminatory; and administer the assessments in Amy's primary language. In addition to these statutory requirements, school districts in California are prohibited from using intelligence tests with black students, regardless of parental consent (*Larry P. v. Riles*, 1984). In *Larry P.*, the court found that the use of intelligence tests with black students was inaccurate due to a cultural bias in the tests and led to racially discriminatory over-inclusion of black students in classrooms for educable mentally retarded students. IDEA permits the use of nonstandardized assessment tools. School districts therefore are not obligated to use intelligence tests with nonblack students (*Ford v. Long Beach Unified School District*, 2002).

Only a credentialed school psychologist can administer tests of intellectual or emotional functioning. No single procedure can be used as the sole criterion for determining either eligibility or Amy's educational program if she is found eligible for special education. The individuals assessing Amy must prepare written reports noting, among other items, whether she may need special education and related services; the relevant behavior noted during any observations; the relationship between the observed behavior and Amy's academic and social functioning; and where appropriate, a determination concerning the effects of environmental, cultural, or economic disadvantage. To the extent protocols are completed with information specific to Amy, these documents are pupil records and Rhonda may request, and the school district must provide, copies notwithstanding any concerns on the district's behalf regarding potential copyright infringement regarding the publisher of the test(s) to which the protocol(s) relate (*Newport-Mesa Unified School District v. State of California Department of Education*, 2005).

An IEP team meeting to discuss Amy's eligibility under IDEA must be held within sixty days after the school district's receipt of Rhonda's written consent to the assessment plan. School breaks in excess of five days are not calculated as part of the sixty-day period. Rhonda can also agree in writing to a longer period of time. Copies of all written reports and documentation of the determination regarding eligibility must be given to Rhonda when Amy's IEP team meeting is held. If Rhonda disagrees with a school district's assessment, she can request an independent educational evaluation (IEE) at public expense. If Amy is determined eligible for services, the school district can, if it desires, wait an additional period not to exceed 30 calendar days to develop and offer an educational program to Amy (Ed. Code §§ 56043(f)(2) and 56344(a)). Many school districts elect to combine the determination of eligibility and, where appropriate, development and offer of an educational program, into a single IEP team meeting to be held no later than sixty calendar days after receipt of consent for assessment.

The process for an initial assessment contains many of the procedural requirements that reoccur throughout IDEA: notice of a proposed action, attendant notice to a parent regarding his or her rights, parental consent, minimum criteria for the action undertaken by the school district, and the imposition of specific time lines.

Eligibility

After signing the assessment plan, Rhonda meets with a school psychologist and nurse. The nurse asks Rhonda questions about Amy's medical history and health. The psychologist gives Rhonda a questionnaire to complete regarding Amy's behavior at home. The psychologist also gives Amy a number of tests. After both the nurse and psychologist conclude their interviewing and testing, Mr. Smith calls Rhonda. Mr. Smith explains to Rhonda that an IEP team meeting will be held to determine if Amy qualifies for special education. A few days later, Rhonda receives a written notice for an IEP team meeting. The notice contains the time, location, and date of the meeting. The notice also lists the other individuals who will be attending and states the purpose of the meeting. Rhonda sends the notice back to the school district, indicating that she will attend.

An IEP team meeting must be held to determine if Amy is eligible for special education under IDEA. If Amy is found eligible, the IEP meeting will be referred to as her initial IEP. Amy, like all children, will be found eligible for special education under the Individuals with Disabilities Education Act (IDEA) if she is evaluated as having one or more of the thirteen defined disability categories in IDEA *and* her disability "requires instruction, services, or both, which cannot be provided with modification of the regular school program." Consideration of both elements is critical. For example, a student with attention deficit hyperactivity disorder (ADHD) can, if other criteria are met, be evaluated as having an "Other Health Impairment," which is one of IDEA's defined disability categories. However, our hypothetical ADHD student may be able to access the curriculum successfully in a general education classroom with preferential seating, extra time for testing, and a homework contract to ensure timely completion of assignments. If these modifications to the general education classroom are sufficient, our student with ADHD does not qualify for special education under IDEA despite being evaluated as having one of the defined disability categories.

The age criterion for special education is generally three to eighteen years of age. However, a student may qualify for special education in certain circumstances from birth to three and from nineteen to twenty-one years of age. School districts' IDEA obligations do not apply to children under three years of age. These children, to the extent they are identified, are served under Part C of IDEA by a regional center. At age three, the children transition to Part B of IDEA and are served by their local school district. Education Code Section 56426.9 details school districts' obligations for transitioning children with disabilities into a public education program at age three. A student's eligibility for special education ends upon receipt of a high school diploma or after the end of the current fiscal year in which the student reaches age twenty-two. A student may also cease to be eligible if the student does not continue to meet one of IDEA's defined disability categories or to need special education.

IDEA contains thirteen categories by which a student may qualify as a child with a disability. California's terminology for a category is noted in parenthesis when different from IDEA. The thirteen categories are (1) Autism (Autistic-Like Behaviors); (2) Deaf-blindness (Hearing and Visual Impairments); (3) Deafness (Hearing Impairment); (4) Emotional Disturbance (Serious Emotional Disturbance); (5) Hearing Impairment; (6) Mental Retardation; (7) Multiple Disabilities; (8) Orthopedic Impairment (Severe Orthopedic Impairment); (9) Other Health Impairment; (10) Specific Learning Disability; (11) Speech or Language Impairment (Language or Speech Disorder); (12) Traumatic Brain Injury; and (13) Visual Impairment. Specific requirements for each category are detailed in Code of Federal Regulations, Title 34, Section 300.8 and Section 3030 of California Code of Regulations, Title 5.

At Amy's IEP team meeting, the school psychologist gives a copy of her written report based on Amy's evaluations to all IEP team members. The school psychologist describes the testing and interviewing that were completed in order to write the report. Both academic and cognitive testing were done. According to the report, Amy's intellectual ability is average for her age. Amy's reading and writing abilities, however, are significantly below her intellectual ability. Amy has a severe discrepancy between her ability and achievement in the areas of reading and writing. Amy also has an auditory processing disorder, determined through other evaluations undertaken by the school psychologist.

Based on the school psychologist's report, the IEP team discusses whether Amy meets the definition of a child with a disability under IDEA. The only category under which Amy might qualify is Specific Learning Disability (SLD). The IEP team reviews the criteria that Amy must satisfy under Education Code Section 56337 in order to meet the SLD eligibility category.

> A severe discrepancy exists between intellectual ability and achievement in one or more of the following academic areas: oral expression, listening comprehension, written expression, basic reading skills, reading comprehension, mathematics calculation, or mathematics reasoning.
>
> The discrepancy is due to a disorder in one or more of the basic psychological processes and is not the result of environmental, cultural, or economic disadvantages.
>
> The discrepancy cannot be corrected through other regular or categorical services offered within the regular instructional program.

The school psychologist elaborates on the intellectual and academic testing that was undertaken and explains how the discrepancy between Amy's intelligence and her reading and writing does constitute a severe discrepancy under the law. The school psychologist continues by noting how the presence of an auditory processing disorder satisfies the second element of the definition. The IEP team considers this information with the unsuccessful nature of the extra time for testing and reading tutoring to conclude that Amy does qualify under the SLD eligibility category. The previous modifications to Amy's general education program also convince the IEP team that Amy does need special education because of her disability. The IEP team has found Amy eligible for special education. The next step is for the IEP team to draft Amy's initial IEP.

In regards to the eligibility category of SLD, IDEA 2004 provides that an IEP team "shall not be required to take into consideration whether a child has a severe discrepancy between achievement and intellectual ability in oral expression, listening ability, written expression, basic reading skill, reading comprehension, mathematical calculation, or mathematical reasoning" (20 U.S.C. § 1414 (b)(6)(A)). A school district therefore may, but does not have to, use the "severe discrepancy" model to determine if a student has a SLD. Response to intervention, or "RTI," is an alternative means to determine if a student satisfies the criteria for a specific learning disability and, in broad terms, focuses on how the student performs in comparison to peers after receipt of scientific, research-based intervention. Specific guidance on the use of RTI in California, and in determining eligibility under the category of SLD, will be developed by the CDE.

Independent Educational Evaluation (IEE) and Reevaluation

An IEE is a second opinion. A parent has the right to obtain an IEE, at public expense, if the parent disagrees with a school district assessment (Educ. Code § 56329 (b)). A parent is only entitled to one IEE in each area assessed by the school district. The individual performing the IEE must be a qualified specialist under the Title 5 regulations. If Rhonda disagreed with the school psychologist's evaluation of Amy, Rhonda can request the school district to fund an IEE for Amy. The school district can either pay for the IEE or request a due process hearing before OAH to determine if the school psychologist's evaluation was appropriate. If OAH determines that the school psychologist's evaluation is appropriate, the school district does not have to pay for the IEE. Regardless of whether a parent or school district pays for an IEE, the IEE must always be considered by an IEP team.

Special education students must be reevaluated at least once every three years. Conversely, a student cannot be assessed more than one time per year unless the parent and school district agree. A three-year reevaluation is referred to as a triennial. A reevaluation must conform to all of the requirements noted for Amy's initial evaluation. A special education student's needs may change before his or her triennial is due. In these instances, reevaluation can occur if conditions warrant reevaluation. The individuals comprising a student's IEP team can meet or communicate informally to determine if conditions warrant reevaluation. An IEP team meeting is not required to determine if reevaluation is warranted nor to develop an assessment plan.

THE IEP PROCESS

No single document is more critical to the education of a special education student than the student's individualized education program (IEP). An IEP operates as a road map to a special education student's educational program; all individuals working with the student must consult it. Before exploring the specific components of an IEP, however, we will comment on the process by which IEPs are created: IEP team meetings. Education Code Section 56340 and following sections contain the requirements for both IEP team meetings and IEPs.

IEP Team Meetings

Before Amy can receive any services under IDEA, she must have an IEP to which Rhonda consents. Amy's initial IEP must be developed through a properly noticed and convened IEP team meeting. For as long as Amy remains eligible for special education under IDEA, all key decisions regarding her educational program will occur through an IEP developed or revised in an IEP team meeting. A parent and school district may agree in writing to amend a student's IEP after the student's annual IEP team meeting is held without convening a meeting.

IEP team meetings must be held at least once annually to review a special education student's educational program, when the student demonstrates a lack of anticipated progress, when the parent requests an IEP team meeting, and for purposes of discussing school district assessments. A student who has already been found eligible for special education under IDEA must have an IEP in effect at the beginning of each school year.

An IEP team meeting includes both mandatory and discretionary team members. Mandatory IEP team members are required by law to attend an IEP team meeting. Discretionary IEP team members are not required to attend, but may be invited by either the student's parent or the school district.

The California Education Code requires that an IEP team meeting *must* include the following individuals:

- Not less than one general education teacher if the student is, or may be, participating in the general education environment. The general education teacher does not have to be the student's teacher.

- No less than one special education teacher, or if appropriate, a special education provider of the student.

- An administrative representative from the school district.

- If applicable, an individual who undertook an assessment of the student on the school district's behalf. Otherwise, an individual who is knowledgeable about the assessment procedures used, familiar with the assessment results, and qualified to interpret the instructional implications of the assessment results must attend.

- At least one parent of the student, unless the school district is unable to convince the parent to attend.

- If applicable, a representative of the student's group home.

- Whenever appropriate, the student.

Amy's IEP team included her general education teacher, a special education teacher, the local school site principal, the school psychologist, the school nurse, and Rhonda. A parent and school district may consent to a mandatory IEP team member not attending the meeting. The parent must agree to the nonattendance in writing, and if the absent team member's area of curriculum is going to be modified or discussed, that team member must submit written input into the development of the IEP to the parent and IEP team prior to the meeting.

Either the parent or school district may invite individuals who have knowledge or special expertise about the student to attend the IEP team meeting. These individuals are the discretionary IEP team members. The determination of whether an invitee has such knowledge or special expertise is made by the party inviting the individual to be a member of the IEP team. Discretionary IEP team members typically include educational advocates, attorneys, and independent experts or assessors. May discretionary IEP team members include a reporter from a local newspaper or television station? As absurd as the question may sound, the California Attorney General wrote a thorough opinion in response to this question (85 Ops. Atty. Gen. 406, August 26, 2002). The answer is no. These individuals, the attorney general reasoned, do not have the requisite knowledge or special expertise required for an individual to be a discretionary member of an IEP team. For now, the possibility of an IEP team meeting on the evening news appears foreclosed.

A parent must be notified of an IEP team meeting early enough to ensure an opportunity to attend. Most school districts opt for the unofficial "ten-day rule" and give notice of IEP team meetings ten days in advance. If all parties are in agreement, however, an IEP team meeting can be held on as little notice as possible. Typically, as in Amy's situation, a written notice is sent to the student's parent or guardian. The notice must specify the purpose, time, and location of the meeting and the attendees. The law does not require written notice. A telephone call conveying the same information is sufficient. To avoid confusion and to document compliance, school districts often use written notice. Because an IEP team must be held at a mutually agreed-upon time and place, a school district generally defers to a parent's schedule. A school district, however, cannot force a parent to attend an IEP team meeting. When the relationship between a parent and a school district becomes litigious, the parent may abuse the requirement that an IEP team meeting be at a mutually agreeable date and time by continually requesting a new date for the IEP team meeting. In these difficult circumstances, school officials must carefully balance the parent's right to participate in an IEP team meeting with the student's right to have the student's educational program continue regardless of any disagreement between the student's parent and the school district.

If the parent refuses to attend an IEP team meeting (as opposed to merely requesting another meeting date or time), the school district must document its efforts to encourage attendance and then convene the meeting. Both the parent and school district have the right to make an audio recording of an IEP team meeting if notice of the intent to record is given at least twenty-four hours prior to the IEP team meeting. If, however, the school district initiates the notice of intent to record and the parent or guardian refuses to attend or objects to recording, the school district cannot record. Depending on the relationship between the parent and the school district, audiotape recordings of IEP team meetings may be standard practice.

IEP Contents

IDEA 2004 and attendant California Education Code sections set forth the minimum requirements of an IEP. The particular format of the document is left to each school district. While there may be hundreds of different formats for IEPs throughout California, all IEPs must, at a minimum, contain the following:

- Present levels of educational performance. Present levels of performance include, among other items, academic skills (reading, math, writing), social skills, and physical abilities.

- Measurable annual goals. Under Education Code Section 56345 (a)(2), annual goals must include short-term objectives related to meeting the student's needs that result from the student's disability to enable the student to be involved in and progress in the general education curriculum, and to meeting each of the student's other educational needs that result from the student's disability. IDEA 2004 eliminates the requirement in federal law for short-term objectives to support goals unless the student is taking alternate assessments aligned to alternate achievement standards.

- Special education instruction and services and program modifications. The instruction and services, and a statement of program modifications or supports for school personnel, must be provided for the student to advance appropriately toward attaining the annual goals, to be involved and progress in the general curriculum, to participate in extracurricular and other nonacademic activities, and to be educated and participate with other students with disabilities and nondisabled students.

- An explanation of the extent, if any, to which the student will not participate with nondisabled students in general education.

- Any modifications necessary for the student to participate in state or district-wide assessments. If the IEP team determines that the student will not participate in such assessments, the IEP team must note why assessment is not appropriate and how the student will be assessed.

- The projected date for the beginning of special education instruction and/or services, including the anticipated frequency, location, and duration of those services.

- Appropriate objective criteria, evaluation procedures, and schedules for determining, on at least an annual basis, whether the annual goals are being achieved.

- One year before the student reaches age eighteen, a statement that the student has been informed of his or her rights that will transfer to the student upon the student's turning eighteen.

- A statement of how the student's progress toward annual goals will be measured.

- A statement of how the student's parents will be informed of the student's progress.

Depending on the student's needs, additional IEP requirements contained in Education Code Section 56345 may apply.

In Amy's case, her present levels of performance will contain the results of the school psychologist's written report and perhaps some input from the general education teacher who made the special education referral. Amy's goals are drafted by the IEP team to focus on her educational needs that result from her learning disability: reading and writing. Goals are written for implementation over a one-year period, which also coincides with the requirement that Amy's IEP be reviewed at least annually. Goals are accompanied by short-term objectives that lead up to the goal. The following reading comprehension goal is written for Amy:

Goal—Amy will demonstrate an understanding of fourth-grade-level written text by orally answering who, what, where, and when questions independently with 80 percent accuracy.

Short-Term Objective One—Amy will demonstrate understanding of fourth-grade-level written text by orally answering who, what, where, and when questions independently with 60 percent accuracy.

Short-Term Objective Two—Amy will demonstrate understanding of fourth-grade-level written text by orally answering who, what, where, and when questions independently with 70 percent accuracy.

As IDEA requires, the foregoing goal was written to meet one of Amy's needs (reading comprehension in this instance) to enable her to be involved in and progress in the general curriculum. Amy's reading comprehension was determined to be at the third-grade level during her initial evaluation. The goal is therefore to increase her reading comprehension to the fourth-grade level over the next year. Because the IEP team meeting for Amy is being held in December, the goal is written to be met by December of the following year; short-term objectives one and two are to be met in March and June, respectively. The IEP team also drafts goals focusing on Amy's other reading and writing needs.

Amy's goals are all academic in nature. Other special education students may require goals addressing areas of need that do not appear to be traditionally academic. However, these goals address needs that are impacting the student's education. For example, a special education student may have goals addressing social skills, behavior, attention, school attendance, and any number of other educational needs resulting from the student's disability. The provision of designated instruction and services (DIS) is also accompanied by goals specific to the need being addressed by the DIS (e.g., an articulation goal for the provision of speech and language therapy).

The number and type of goals in an IEP are dependent on the unique needs of the student in question. Accurately identifying all the needs of a special education student through the assessment process is therefore an important, if not necessary, step to drafting appropriate goals. If Amy's school psychologist did not assess Amy's writing abilities, the IEP team may have not recognized Amy's needs in the area of writing. Absent recognition of Amy's difficulty with writing, the IEP team may have failed to draft any writing goals for Amy. In this manner, an inappropriate or incomplete assessment may lead to a detrimental domino effect on Amy's special education program.

Special Education and DIS

After completing the bulk of Amy's IEP, the IEP team discusses what type of special education and DIS to make available to Amy. Because the impact of Amy's disability is only in the areas of reading and writing, the IEP team decides that specialized instruction in reading and writing will appropriately address Amy's needs. The IEP team offers a resource specialist program (RSP) in which Amy will be one of only six other students in the classroom. The RSP teacher is a special education teacher who will use individualized instructional techniques to assist Amy with her reading and writing. RSP will be available to Amy for the first two periods of her school day.

After the IEP team discusses the RSP placement, Rhonda holds up a brochure from ABC Reading Company. Rhonda asks the IEP team if the school district can provide the service described in ABC's brochure. The brochure details the research-based, multimodal instructional techniques that "specially trained ABC staff use to obtain excellent results in improving reading with learning disabled children." Rhonda explains that she learned about ABC on the Internet and believes ABC's program could really help Amy catch up with her peers.

Mr. Smith explains to Rhonda that the RSP placement and ABC program both address the same educational need for Amy: reading. The only difference is in the methodology each program uses. Other school district IEP team members echo Mr. Smith's comments. If the programs are both designed to improve Amy's reading, Rhonda replies, then why not give Amy ABC? Mr. Smith politely informs Rhonda that school districts have the discretion to choose the methodology that will be used with a special education student as long as that approach is appropriate, or provides FAPE, for the student. The U.S. Supreme Court has been clear that "once the requirements of [IDEA] have been met, questions of methodology are for resolution by the States" (*Board of Education v. Rowley*, p. 207). As long as Mr. Smith and the IEP team are correct that Amy can receive a FAPE with the RSP placement, the school district is free to exercise its discretion in offering the RSP placement over a different program preferred by Rhonda. A similar rule applies to the personnel that school districts can choose to implement a special education student's program. If the chosen individual is qualified and can appropriately implement the service in question, school districts are free to exercise their discretion regarding who is chosen to work with the student (*Gellerman v. Calaveras Unified School District*, 2000). In *Gellerman*, a parent unsuccessfully argued that only the aide that worked with her autistic son at home could meet his classroom needs.

Special education is specially designed instruction without cost to parents that meets the unique needs of the student. Special education also includes DIS when the DIS is necessary for the student to benefit educationally from the student's instructional program. DIS includes both specialized instruction and services. The list of DIS in the Education Code is not exhaustive, and it includes audiological services, orientation and mobility services, instruction in the home or hospital, physical and occupational therapy, vision services, specialized driver training instruction, counseling and guidance, psychological services, parent counseling and training, specially designed vocational education and career development, and recreation services. A common related DIS is transportation, which may be necessary depending on the student's needs and/or the distance the student must travel to school.

A wide variety of DIS may be necessary for special education students, depending on their needs. However, IDEA makes it clear that medical services are available for diagnostic and evaluation purposes only. The U.S. Supreme Court provided a definitive ruling in 1984 on the obligation of school districts to provide medical services in *Irving Independent School District v. Tatro*. In *Tatro*, the parents of an eight-year-old child with spina bifida requested that the school district empty their daughter's bladder every three to four hours through a process called clean intermittent catheterization (CIC). The process takes a few minutes and can be taught to a layperson in an hour. The school district argued that CIC was a medical service and therefore not a related service under IDEA. The high court disagreed, holding that the medical exclusion to related services applies only to those services that must be performed by a physician or a hospital. In 1999, the Supreme Court reiterated this clear exception in *Cedar Rapids Community School District v. Garrett F.*, where the school district was ordered to provide a student paralyzed from the neck down with, among other things, a full-time nurse, suction of a tracheotomy tube, assistance with eating and drinking, and placement in a reclining position for five minutes each hour.

Despite the compelling nature of the disputes in *Tatro* and *Garrett F.*, cases such as these are quite rare. Rather, parents and school administrators more typically find themselves debating the necessity of an additional thirty minutes of speech and language therapy a week, provision of relatively controversial services such as vision or sound therapy, or in Amy's case the necessity of ABC instead of the district's RSP classroom.

Extended School Year (ESY)

ESY services are available beyond the regular school year to prevent certain special education students from regressing beyond a point where they cannot obtain the level of self-sufficiency and independence (i.e., educational progress) they would otherwise be expected to obtain. ESY services are commonly, but not always, made available during the summer and can be part of a school district's obligation to provide FAPE. For example, some children with autism receive services that extend through part of the school district's winter break. California's regulations describe the type of student that requires ESY services:

> Such individuals shall have handicaps which are likely to continue indefinitely or for a prolonged period, and interruption of the pupil's educational programming may cause regression, when coupled with limited recoupment capacity, rendering it impossible or unlikely that the pupil will attain the level of self-sufficiency and independence that would otherwise be expected in view of his or her handicapping condition. (Admin. Code, Title 5, § 3043)

The IEP team determines that an interruption in Amy's schooling over summer break is not likely to cause regression, and ESY is not made available to Amy.

Behavior-Related Assessments and Plans

School districts must consider strategies, including positive behavioral interventions and supports, in circumstances in which a student's behavior impedes his or her learning or that of others (Educ. Code § 56341.1 (b)(1)). IEP teams can develop behavior plans or, where appropriate, develop goals or offer accommodations and modifications, for special education students to address a wide range of behaviors that are impeding learning. A plan seeking to address a serious behavior problem that significantly interferes with the implementation of the goals and objectives of a student's IEP is a behavioral intervention plan (BIP). Serious behavior problems include maladaptive, recurring behaviors such as self-injury or property destruction. All other plans are referred to as behavior plans or behavior support plans. Plans in this latter category address behavior that is impeding the learning of the student or others, but that does not rise to the level of serious behavior requiring a BIP. For example, a behavior plan can be written requiring a student to complete a homework contract every week and attend class on a regular basis. Alternatively, a BIP may be developed for a student who engages in self-injurious or violent behavior.

A BIP can be developed only after completion of a functional analysis assessment (FAA). An IEP team is required to consider undertaking an FAA where the behavior approaches specified in the IEP are determined to be not effective. An FAA requires a detailed, systematic series of observations that results in a comprehensive report regarding the behavior(s) at issue. To undertake an FAA, an individual must have, or be under the supervision of, someone with documented training in behavior analysis with an emphasis on positive behavioral analysis.

When the FAA is completed, the special education student's IEP team must meet to determine if a BIP is necessary to address the behaviors at issue. One goal of a BIP is to replace maladaptive behaviors with alternative acceptable behaviors. The detailed requirements for an FAA and BIP are found in California Code of Regulations, Title 5, Section 3052.

A behavior plan, not to be confused with a BIP, is the result of a functional behavioral assessment (FBA). The term "FBA" comes from IDEA, not the Education Code. IDEA, however, does not define the term. Comments to IDEA indicate that an FBA is a process that searches for an explanation of the purpose behind a problem behavior. An FBA may be an assessment requiring parental consent or a review of existing data by the IEP team. An FBA can consist of record review and consultation among school district employees, or it can take the form of a more in-depth evaluation requiring parental consent. Neither IDEA nor the Education Code mandates an FBA before developing a behavior plan. Rather, sound educational practice makes it advisable for some level of record review or evaluation before developing a behavior plan. The FBA can also play an important role in the discipline of a special education student, as discussed more fully in Chapter 9.

Mental Health Services

In some instances, the needs of a special education student may require mental health services or placement in a residential facility. Mental health services and residential placement are the responsibility of the local branch of the State Department of Mental Health (referred to as county mental health or CMH). The responsibilities of the CMH in relation to special education students are detailed at Government Code Section 7570 and following sections.

Before CMH becomes involved in the education of a special education student, however, a referral for assessment by CMH must be made by the student's IEP team. A referral to CMH to evaluate the necessity of mental health services is sometimes termed an AB 2726 referral, in reference to the 1996 legislation detailing the referral process. Government Code Section 7576 details the prerequisites for an AB 2726 referral. Parent consent is required. If certain criteria are met, an order from OAH can be obtained to permit an AB 2726 referral without parental consent. If CMH accepts the referral, an assessment is undertaken, a report written, and an IEP team meeting held within fifty days after the parent consents to the referral. If an IEP team recommends residential placement for a special education student, the IEP team must be expanded to include a member of CMH. Government Code Section 7572.5 details the requirements for a residential placement.

Placement

A continuum of program options must be available to meet the needs of a special education student. These program options must include, but are not necessarily limited to, all or any combination of the following: a general education program; resource specialist program (RSP); DIS; special classes and centers; nonpublic, nonsectarian schools; state special schools; itinerant instruction; instruction using telecommunication; and instruction in the home, in hospitals, and in other institutions (Educ. Code § 56361). Recall the LRE discussion and take note of how the continuum of program options goes from the least (general education program) to the most restrictive environment (home or hospital setting). Referring to the continuum of program options, we can see that Amy's IEP team made a placement available that is a combination of a general education program and RSP.

In the context of special education, a nonpublic school (NPS) is a private school that has been certified by the California Department of Education (CDE) to contract directly with school districts. A private school that is not certified by the CDE is simply a private school. There are NPSs outside of California. In some instances, a student may be able to receive a FAPE only in an NPS outside of California, thereby obligating the school district to fund the placement. A school district may also have a shortage of a particular DIS provider. The school district can contract with a nonpublic agency (NPA) to provide the DIS to special education students. An NPA is a private company that is certified by the CDE to provide services to special education students. Absent a waiver from the CDE, school districts cannot prospectively contract with a school or agency that is not certified as an NPS or NPA (Educ. Code § 56366 (d)). OAH administrative law judges are also prohibited from ordering prospective placement or services with a school or agency that is not certified (Educ. Code § 56505.2 (a)).

Under IDEA, an IEP team meeting is supposed to be a collaborative effort whereby all team members work together to determine the appropriate placement for a student. The IEP team is to consider the continuum of placement options and reach agreement on the placement that is appropriate (or makes FAPE available) for the student.

At the end of the IEP team meeting, regardless of whether the parents and the school district IEP team members agree or disagree, the school district must present the parents with a formal written offer of placement. In 1994, the Ninth Circuit held that one purpose of a written offer of placement is to permit the parents to seriously consider the school district's offer (*Union School District v. Smith*). At a minimum, a formal written offer of placement should note the school site, classroom(s), and DIS (including type, frequency, and location) being made available to the student. A failure to make a formal written offer of placement is a procedural violation that may constitute a denial of a FAPE.

Parents also have the right to observe and have an expert of their choosing observe the placement made available by the school district. If a parent seeks an IEE, the parent's independent assessor is entitled to observe the parent's child in the school district's offered placement to the extent the district's assessors did so or to the extent such observation is permissible under the district's assessment procedures (Educ. § 56329(b)). Section 56329(b) has been interpreted to permit observation of a school district's placement by a parent's selected expert regardless of whether an IEE was being sought (*Benjamin G. v. Special Education Hearing Office*, 2005).

TRANSITION PLANS, THE AGE OF MAJORITY, AND EXITING SPECIAL EDUCATION

IDEA does not focus solely on a special education student's educational program during the time the student attends school. There is also an emphasis on preparing the student for independent living and life after special education services under IDEA cease. To this end, transition plans are created for students. Education Code Section 56345.1 details the requirements of transition plans.

At sixteen years of age, or younger if determined appropriate by the IEP team, a student's IEP must contain a plan detailing the transition services the student is to receive. The specific legal requirements of a transition plan are vague. The statute refers to a "coordinated set of activities" designed to promote movement from school to postschool activities. The transition plan must be based on the student's preferences and include instruction, related services, community experiences, and—when appropriate—acquisition of daily living skills and a functional vocational evaluation. IDEA 2004 requires an IEP for a student who is sixteen years of age or older to contain "appropriate measurable postsecondary goals based on age appropriate transition assessments related to training, education, employment, and where appropriate, independent living skills" as well as the "transition services (including courses of study) needed to assist the child in reaching those goals" (20 U.S.C. § 1414 (d)(1)(A)(i)(VIII)).

Once a student is eighteen years of age, the student (save for imposition of a conservatorship) holds his or her own educational rights. On or before the student's eighteenth birthday, the school district is required to provide both the student and the student's parents with a copy of the procedural safeguards. Despite the age at which educational rights transfer to a student, the age of majority in and of itself has no impact on eligibility for special education services. To examine how students are exited from special education, let us return to Amy.

Years later, Amy appears to be doing well in school. Her test scores, reading, and writing have all improved. Amy's RSP teacher does not believe that Amy continues to need special education. Amy's most recent IEP reduced her time in RSP to one period a day for language arts. At the RSP teacher's suggestion, the school district prepares an assessment plan for Amy. Mr. Smith explains to Rhonda that the plan is to determine if Amy continues to qualify for special education services. Rhonda signs the plan, and a month later, an IEP team meeting is held to discuss the results of the evaluations.

The same school psychologist who previously found Amy eligible for special education reports that Amy's standardized scores in reading and writing have noticeably improved. The school psychologist shares with the team that while Amy is still not performing at the same level as her peers, there is no longer the severe discrepancy upon which Amy's eligibility was originally based. The school psychologist explains that while Amy still has an auditory processing deficit, she has been able to implement successfully the learning techniques she has been taught. The severe discrepancy that at one time existed between her cognitive ability and achievement in the areas of reading and writing no longer exists.

Rhonda asks if this means that Amy no longer qualifies for special education. The other members of the IEP team express their opinion that Amy would not qualify, because she no longer meets the eligibility category of Specific Learning Disability or any other category. Rhonda is happy to see Amy exit special education, but she is concerned that Amy may still need some assistance with her education because of her auditory processing disorder. At this point, Mr.Smith speaks up and explains to Rhonda that Amy may qualify for accommodations and modifications under a different law entitled Section 504, a matter discussed later in the chapter.

There are three circumstances in which a special education student is no longer eligible for services under IDEA. First, like Amy, a special education student may no longer meet one of the thirteen eligibility categories or need special education and DIS. While many of the eligibility categories are based on permanent disabilities, other categories do present an opportunity for students to improve in the relevant area so that they do not continue to qualify for special education. A school district must undertake an evaluation of a special education student before determining that the student is no longer eligible for special education under IDEA.

For students who cannot or will not cease to qualify for their respective eligibility category under IDEA, the termination of special education eligibility turns on either age or the receipt of a high school diploma. A special education student receiving a high school diploma is no longer eligible for services under IDEA. However, a student receiving a certificate of completion remains eligible for services under IDEA. Special education students may continue to receive services until they are twenty-two. A school district does not have to evaluate a special education student before terminating services if the student receives a high school diploma or "ages out" of eligibility.

PRIVATE SCHOOL STUDENTS AND IDEA

We have already seen that a school district's child-find obligations extend to students in private schools. But do students in private schools have an entitlement to a FAPE? The answer, like so much in special education law, depends. There are two general categories of private school students: (1) students placed by a school district in a private school certified by CDE (known as an NPS); and (2) students placed by their parents in an NPS or private school (not certified by CDE). The second category can be further divided into (a) students placed by their parents in an NPS or private school when the parents dispute the school district's offer of FAPE; and (b) students placed by their parents in an NPS or private school when the parents do not dispute the school district's offer of FAPE. The Education Code prohibits school districts, but not parents, from placing students in a private school that is not certified as an NPS.

Let us examine the first category of students, those special education students who have been placed by a school district in an NPS for the student to receive a FAPE. These students clearly have an ongoing entitlement to FAPE. The students have been placed at the NPS to receive it. Placement in an NPS by a school district is permissible only if the school district itself does not have an appropriate public education program for the student (Educ. Code § 56365 (b)).

But what about students who are in an NPS or private school due to a unilateral decision by their parents? These are the students in the second group, which contains two subgroups. Returning to Amy, let us imagine that Rhonda believed the initial IEP proposed by the school district was not appropriate (i.e., did not make a FAPE available for Amy). In response, Rhonda removes Amy from the school district and enrolls her at an NPS or private school. Per our classification, Amy is a group 2(a) student. The disagreement between Rhonda and the school district does not terminate Amy's entitlement to a FAPE. If the school district believes that its proposed educational program provides a FAPE to Amy, then the district must make the program available to her. Rhonda, however, may choose not to partake of it. If Rhonda requests a due process hearing and the school district cannot demonstrate that it made a FAPE available to Amy, Rhonda may be able to obtain reimbursement for all or part of the costs of the NPS or private school. We address the remedies available in a due process hearing later in the chapter.

The last category of students pertains to those special education students placed by their parents at an NPS or private school when the school district's offer of FAPE is not in dispute. In this scenario, Rhonda would not disagree with the appropriateness of the school district's initial IEP for Amy, but would place Amy in an NPS or private school as a matter of parental preference. A private school student in this latter category does not have an individual entitlement to special education and related services, and thus no recourse to a due process hearing. This group of students is rare because the parents must pay the NPS or private school expenses. To avoid potentially falling into this subgroup of privately placed students, some parents maintain their child in a private school or NPS and summarily disagree with any IEP offered by the school district to leave open the possibility of reimbursement through a OAH due process hearing. A private school student can request an individual services plan (ISP) to receive services in an amount proportionate to the student's share of federal funding. This generally amounts to some consultation, but not direct services.

DUE PROCESS HEARINGS

A key concern in *Park* and *Mills* was the lack of recourse available to children who were prohibited from attending a public school. These children were deprived of due process of law because there was no mechanism available to challenge their exclusion. The Education for All Handicapped Children Act (EHCA) and its modernday namesake, IDEA, have changed all of this dramatically. Virtually every aspect of a special education student's program can be challenged in a due process hearing before an impartial hearing officer.

IDEA contains its own administrative hearing process in which both parents and school districts can request a hearing regarding identification, evaluation, placement, or the provision of FAPE. In California, OAH oversees due process hearings. Due process hearings are governed by a combination of state and federal laws and regulations (34 C.F.R. § 300.507 and following sections; Educ. Code § 56500 and following sections; and Admin. Code, Title 5, § 3080 and following sections).

Due process hearings are informal in comparison to proceedings in a court. A request for a due process hearing, in the form of a letter, needs only to note the name of the student, the address of residence, a description of the nature of the problem (including facts relating to the problem), and a proposed resolution of the problem to the extent known. A request for a due process hearing must be made within three years from the date the party initiating the request knew, or had reason to know of, the facts underlying the basis for the request.

IDEA 2004 provides that a party may not have a due process hearing until a notice meeting the above-noted requirements is filed. IDEA 2004 further provides that the hearing request will be deemed sufficient unless the party receiving the request notifies the other party and the hearing office within fifteen days that the request is not sufficient. IDEA 2004 thereafter requires the hearing officer to make a determination regarding whether or not the hearing request contains the requisite information. The importance of a hearing request is heightened under IDEA 2004 because a party is not permitted to raise issues at the due process hearing that were not raised in the hearing request without the agreement of the other party.

After a school district receives a due process hearing request, IDEA 2004 requires the district to send a written notice to the parent within ten days. The written notice must contain:

- "An explanation of why the agency proposed or refused to take the action requested in the complaint";
- "A description of other options that the IEP team considered and the reasons why those options were rejected";
- "A description of each evaluation procedure, assessment, record, or report the agency used as the basis for the proposed or refused action"; and
- "A description of the factors that are relevant to the agency's proposal or refusal." (20 U.S.C. § 1415 (c)(2)(B)(i))

IDEA 2004 also requires a parent to respond in writing to a hearing request filed by a school district. The parent must specifically address the issues raised in the school district's hearing request.

Before going to hearing, the parties are encouraged to resolve their dispute through mediation. State mediators are made available and have a very high degree of success in assisting the parties in resolution through settlement. IDEA 2004 contains a new provision designed to encourage resolution through settlement, entitled "resolution session." Under this provision, a school district is required to respond to a due process hearing request within fifteen days by convening a meeting with the parents and relevant members of the IEP team. The school district cannot have an attorney present unless an attorney accompanies the parent. If a settlement agreement is executed during the resolution session, either party has three business days to void the agreement. The school district and parent can agree in writing to waive the resolution session.

Stay Put during Hearing

From the date a due process hearing is requested to the time a written decision is issued, a student must generally remain in the student's last agreed-upon and implemented educational placement, unless the school district and the parent agree otherwise. This placement is referred to as "stay put." Stay put is maintenance of the status quo for the student's educational placement. Returning to Amy, let us imagine that four months after her initial IEP, another IEP team meeting is held. At that meeting, the IEP team reduces Amy's time in RSP to one period. If Rhonda disagrees and requests a due process hearing, the school district must maintain Amy's RSP for two periods (the last agreed-upon and implemented placement) until a decision issues from the due process hearing.

The contents of an IEP or settlement agreement may have unintended consequences for a student's stay-put placement. For example, an IEP naming a specific individual as a service provider may convince an OAH administrative law judge to obligate the school district, which otherwise has discretion in choosing personnel, to continue the provision of services by the named individual. Likewise, a settlement agreement's provision of a service or placement on a temporary basis may become a student's stay-put placement for the duration of a due process hearing.

Due Process Rights

Ten days before the hearing, the parties are required to inform each other of the issues and their proposed resolutions. Clarification of the issues can be sought through a prehearing telephone conference, in which the parties and/or their attorneys talk with an OAH administrative law judge. Returning to our last example with Amy, Rhonda could request a hearing on the reduction of RSP and frame the following proposed issue and resolution: Does Amy require two periods of RSP a day to receive a FAPE? Yes. The school district, of course, would answer the issue with a no.

Unlike a civil trial, a due process hearing has no discovery phase during which each party can depose (question under oath) witnesses and request documents. The entire administrative record is usually composed of the student's educational records and perhaps some independent assessments. All of the documentary evidence a party intends to rely on must be given to the opposing party at least five business days before the hearing commences. A list of witnesses, including their general areas of testimony, must also be exchanged at least five business days prior to the hearing. Rhonda would therefore prepare and exchange an evidence binder with all relevant documents as well as provide notice of all potential witnesses.

Parties to a due process hearing may be accompanied by an attorney if notice is given ten days prior to the hearing. Once the hearing convenes, the party requesting the hearing usually puts on its case first. The party seeking relief in a due process hearing bears the burden of persuasion (i.e., the burden of proving their claim(s) by a preponderance of the evidence) (*Schaffer v. Weast*, 2005). Therefore, if Rhonda requests a hearing on the proposed decrease in RSP time, she must prove that Amy requires two periods of RSP to receive a FAPE.

Despite the informal nature of due process hearings, emotions can run high. Rhonda could literally place Mr. Smith under oath and question his professional competency. Alternatively, Rhonda may be asked difficult questions regarding the nature and extent of Amy's disability and her willingness to realistically acknowledge it. Regardless of the outcome of the hearing, hard feelings may last for years on both sides. The hearing may damage the relationship between Rhonda and the school district even though both parties are bound together by Amy's education for an additional six to ten years. Beyond the emotional toll of a hearing there is the financial cost. Rhonda and/or the school district may employ legal counsel at a cost of tens of thousands of dollars. If Rhonda unilaterally places Amy in an expensive NPS or private school, the educational costs at issue can also be in the tens of thousands of dollars. The prospect of further litigation in federal court only compounds these costs.

Due Process Remedies

The most common remedies sought in a due process hearing are reimbursement for educational expenses already incurred, reimbursement for an independent educational evaluation or IEE, compensatory education, and/or a specific placement or DIS to be ordered prospectively.

Compensatory education. IDEA grants a court the power to grant such relief as the court determines is appropriate. OAH administrative law judges have broad powers to remedy a finding that a school district did not provide a FAPE by ordering compensatory education. The purpose behind such an order is to replace the lost educational opportunity that accompanies the denial of a FAPE.

A simple example of compensatory education is a single DIS like speech and language therapy. Returning to Amy, let us imagine that Rhonda believes the school district erred in not assessing her receptive communication skills (e.g., failure to assess in all areas of suspected disability). If an administrative law judge agrees with Rhonda and finds that Amy should have received speech and language therapy, Amy will most likely receive compensatory education. The compensatory education will probably be in the form of speech and language therapy for an amount of time to be determined by the judge. In calculating the amount of compensatory education, the judge does not have to undertake a one-to-one calculation. The judge can exercise discretion to award an amount that is, within the words of the Ninth Circuit, reasonably "designed to ensure that the student is appropriately educated within the meaning of IDEA" (*Parents of Student W. v. Puyallup School District*, 1994).

Reimbursement for educational expenses. A parent seeking to obtain reimbursement for educational expenses must satisfy two criteria. First, during the time period in which the educational expenses were incurred, the school district did not provide or make available a FAPE. Second, the educational services obtained by the parents must be designed to meet the student's unique needs and provide the student with educational benefit. Does this mean that a parent must meet the FAPE standard to which school districts are held? No. A 1986 Fifth Circuit ruling held that parents are not required to provide a placement that conforms to all of IDEA's requirements in order for their child to obtain reimbursement (*Alamo Heights Independent School District v. State Board of Education*, 1986). The U.S. Supreme Court also has ruled that it is immaterial if the student was at a private school not certified by the state (*Florence County School District Four v. Carter*, 1993). The impact of these cases is that if a school district does not provide or make a FAPE available, a parent stands a good chance of obtaining reimbursement for educational services that would not constitute a FAPE if provided by a school district.

While expert witnesses may be critical to a parent, or school district, obtaining a favorable decision from OAH, expert fees are not recoverable as a cost by a prevailing parent in a due process hearing (*Arlington Central Unified School District Board of Education v. Murphy*, 2006).

Attorneys' Fees

Parents who prevail in a due process hearing may recover their attorneys' fees. IDEA contains a fee-shifting provision to encourage attorneys to represent the class of individuals protected by the law: children with disabilities. School districts usually cannot recover attorneys' fees. Attorneys' fees in due process hearings are serious business. Depending on the length and complexity of the due process hearing, a prevailing parent may be entitled from $25,000 to in excess of $100,000. The attorneys' fees that may result from a hearing can significantly exceed the cost of the educational services at issue. For better or worse, IDEA's attorneys' fees provision has had a profound impact on the number of due process hearings, the decisions parties to a hearing make for or against settlement, and the financial costs school districts must consider in ensuring compliance with IDEA.

In 1994, the Ninth Circuit held that a "prevailing party for the purpose of awarding attorney fees [under IDEA] is a party which succeeds on any significant issue in litigation which achieves some of the benefit the parties sought in bringing suit" (*Parents of Student W. v. Puyallup School District*). A parent does not need to prevail on all issues to be considered a prevailing party. A parent, however, must obtain more than merely technical or de minimis (minimal) relief to be a prevailing party entitled to attorneys' fees. For example, imagine that Rhonda places Amy in an NPS and seeks reimbursement for all educational expenses (approximately $20,000) a year later. If all of Rhonda's claims are denied save for reimbursement on a $200 independent educational evaluation (IEE), the school district has a good argument that Rhonda merely obtained de minimis relief.

It is not unusual for OAH to issue a decision in which the student prevails on some, but not all, of the issues. If the student was represented by an attorney, the degree of the student's success is used as the criteria to determine the amount of attorneys' fees and costs that are properly recoverable (*Aguirre v. Los Angeles Unified School District*, 2006). For example, if Rhonda seeks 100 hours of compensatory education and is awarded fifty, the school district has a fair argument that her entitlement to attorneys' fees and costs should be 50 percent, which was her degree of success.

There are additional grounds for reducing or denying an award of attorneys' fees. A school district can issue a written offer of settlement at any time more than ten days before the due process hearing begins. If the offer is not accepted within ten days and the relief finally obtained by the parents is not more favorable than the offer, the parents cannot obtain attorneys' fees and related costs subsequent to the school district's issuance of the offer. Parents can avoid the limiting effect of a written offer of settlement if they are substantially justified in rejecting it. Attorneys' fees are not available for attendance at an IEP team meeting unless the meeting is ordered by OAH or a court. Attorneys' fees can be reduced or denied if the parent acts unreasonably during the proceeding, the hourly rate for attorneys' fees being sought is unreasonable, and/or the time spent on legal services was excessive.

IDEA 2004 permits an award of reasonable attorneys' fees to a prevailing school district "against the attorney of a parent, or against the parent, if the parent's complaint or subsequent cause of action was presented for any improper purpose, such as to harass, to cause unnecessary delay, or to needlessly increase the cost of litigation" (20 U.S.C. § 1415 (i)(3)(B)(i)(III)).

SECTION 504 AND AMERICANS WITH DISABILITIES ACT (ADA)

A complete discussion of Section 504 of the Rehabilitation Act of 1973 (Section 504) and the Americans with Disabilities Act (ADA) is beyond the scope of this chapter. Indeed, entire books have been written about Section 504 and ADA. Our intention is merely to provide a general overview of each law as it pertains to California public schools. Effective January 1, 2009, the ADA Amendments Act of 2008 brings about significant changes to ADA and Section 504. Key changes are noted below. Updates regarding the ADA Amendments Act of 2008 will be available at this book's website at www.californiaschoollaw.org.

Section 504

Section 504 is an antidiscrimination law that applies to all recipients of federal funding, such as California public schools. Covered entities are prohibited from discriminating against an individual on the basis of disability. A school district may also be required to provide educational services to students who qualify as individuals with a disability under Section 504. The ADA Amendments Act directly impacts interpretation and application of Section 504.

An individual with a disability, or handicapped person as the phrase is used in Section 504, is "any person who (i) has a physical or mental impairment which substantially limits one or more major life activities, (ii) has a record of such an impairment, or (iii) is regarded as having such an impairment" (34 C.F.R. § 104.3 (j)(1)). Only students in the first category have a right to educational services. The latter two categories are aimed at preventing discrimination on the basis of disability. Section 504's coverage is not limited to students. Section 504's impact on employment in public schools is discussed in Chapter 5.

The first category for eligibility has three requirements. A student must have (1) a physical or mental impairment (2) that substantially limits (3) one or more major life activities. A student must be assessed by a school district before being found eligible under Section 504. A school district does not have to assess all students for whom a referral for assessment is made, and may inform a parent of its decision to refuse assessment. Section 504's implementing regulations contain an illustrative, but not exhaustive, list of qualifying physical and mental disorders. These disorders include "any physiological disorder or condition" or "any mental or psychological disorder." The variety of qualifying physical or mental impairments is seemingly infinite. Eligibility under Section 504 also requires that the physical or mental impairment *substantially* limits one or more major life activities. Major life activities are defined as "functions such as caring for one's self, performing manual tasks, walking, seeing, hearing, speaking, breathing, learning, and working" (34 C.F.R. § 104.3 (j)(2)(ii)). This list also is not exhaustive and the ADA Amendments Act of 2008 provides that major life activities include "the operation of a major bodily function, including but not limited to, the function of the immune system, normal cell growth, digestive, bowel, bladder, neurological, brain, respiratory, circulatory, endocrine, and reproductive functions" (42 U.S.C. § 12102(2)(B)).

Section 504 does not define the phrase "substantially limits." In the context of the major life activity of learning, the phrase has been interpreted by the Office for Civil Rights (OCR), which enforces Section 504, to require an important and material limitation (*Pinellas County School District*, 1993). Like the criteria for eligibility under IDEA, the presence of a disability is not sufficient in and of itself to confer coverage to a student under Section 504. A student diagnosed with attention deficit disorder who nonetheless made academic progress was not substantially limited in the major life activity of learning (*Worth County Schools*, 1997). When determining if a student meets Section 504's eligibility criteria, a school district should compare the student's performance to that of the average student in the general population (*Bervcovitch v. Baldwin School*, 1998). The ADA Amendments Act of 2008, however, notes that the definition of disability (i.e., whether an individual is eligible for the protections of the ADA and Section 504) "shall be construed in favor of broad coverage . . . to the maximum extent permitted by the Act" (42 U.S.C. § 12102(4)). The ADA Amendments Act of 2008 may therefore expand eligibility beyond the contours established by prior case law and guidance from OCR. Future court cases and guidance from OCR will provide clarification on the full impact of the ADA Amendments Act of 2008.

What role do mitigating measures (e.g., medication, glasses) play in determining if a student is eligible under Section 504? The ADA Amendments Act of 2008 reverses existing case law from the U.S. Supreme Court by providing that the determination of whether an impairment substantially limits a major life activity is to be made without reference to the effects of mitigating measures (42 U.S.C. § 12102(4)(E)(i)). Ordinary eyeglasses or contact lenses are an exception and "shall be considered in determining whether an impairment substantially limits a major life activity" (42 U.S.C. § 12102(4)(E)(ii)).

We know that IDEA-eligible students are entitled to FAPE. But what services are available to a student who is not eligible for services under IDEA but is covered by Section 504? According to Section 504's implementing regulations, school districts must also provide a FAPE to qualifying students under Section 504. But is this the same FAPE that IDEA requires? Perhaps, but probably not.

Section 504 defines the provision of an appropriate education as either regular or special education and related aides and services that are designed to meet individual educational needs of handicapped persons as adequately as the needs of nonhandicapped persons. It is difficult to conceive of any student who requires special education under Section 504 yet is not eligible for special education services under IDEA. In other words, if Section 504 requires a school district to provide special education to a Section 504 student, that student should actually be an IDEA-eligible student receiving special education services under IDEA. However, if there is a Section 504–eligible student who requires special education, yet does not satisfy one of IDEA's thirteen eligibility categories, then the student would have an entitlement to special education services under Section 504. One, but not the only, way to satisfy Section 504's definition of an appropriate education is to develop an IEP for a student in conformance with IDEA. School districts can also develop a Section 504 Plan. A Section 504 Plan is a written document noting the educational services, accommodations, and modifications a student receives under Section 504.

Section 504 does not have a due process hearing system like IDEA. However, school districts are required to develop an internal hearing process to address complaints. An allegation of noncompliance regarding Section 504 can also be filed with OCR. OCR will investigate the allegation and issue a written letter of findings. Corrective action may be ordered by OCR. A lawsuit may be filed in federal court under a Section 504 claim. The Ninth Circuit recently held that the FAPE requirement under Section 504 is separate and distinct from the FAPE requirement under IDEA (*Mark H. v. Lemahieu*, 2008). The decision may invite increased litigation under Section 504 because while money damages have been foreclosed under IDEA, money damages can, under certain circumstances, be recovered under Section 504. If a Section 504 claim can be "redressed to some degree by the IDEA's administrative procedures and remedies," the due process hearing system overseen by OAH must be utilized before bringing a legal action in federal court (*Robb v. Bethel School District #403*, 2002). If a plaintiff prevails in litigation on a Section 504 claim, attorneys' fees may be available.

After Amy is exited from special education, a Section 504 team meeting is held to determine if Amy qualifies as an individual with a disability under Section 504. The Section 504 team reviews the recent assessment reports that were used to exit Amy from special education. The school psychologist explains how Amy's auditory processing deficit is a mental impairment. There is some disagreement as to whether the auditory processing deficit substantially limits a major life activity. However, after further discussion it is agreed that Amy meets the definition of an individual with a disability under Section 504. A Section 504 Plan is thereafter written for Amy. The Section 504 Plan contains accommodations and modifications that Amy is to receive in the general education classroom (e.g., preferential seating, extra time on tests, etc.).

Americans with Disabilities Act (ADA)

Application of the ADA to an entity, public or private, is not contingent on the receipt of federal funding. The most relevant portion of the ADA for our discussion is Title II, which prohibits public entities from discriminating on the basis of disability.

Title I, which prohibits discrimination on the basis of disability in employment, is reviewed in Chapter 5.

Title II applies to school districts in California. The ADA uses the same three-part test contained in Section 504 (e.g., physical or mental impairment that substantially limits one or more major life activities, a record of such impairment, or regarded as having such an impairment) to define the word "disability." Title II's protections extend to a "*qualified* individual with a disability," which means:

> [A]n individual with a disability who, with or without reasonable modifications to rules, policies, or practices, the removal of architectural, communication, or transportation barriers, or the provision of auxiliary aids and services meets the essential eligibility requirements for the receipt of services or the participation in programs or activities provided by a public entity. (42 U.S.C. § 12131(2))

Take note of the definition's reference to reasonable "modifications." Reasonable "accommodations" are reserved for Title I of the ADA in the employment context. Also note the series of items following the phrase "with or without." These are the areas in which Title II may require a school district to undertake a specific action to ensure access to a program or activity for a student who meets the definition of a qualified individual with a disability. A school district, however, is not required to modify a rule, policy, or procedure if making the modification would fundamentally alter the nature of the service, program, or activity. Detailed regulations governing school districts' obligations concerning architectural barriers, transportation, communication, and the provision of auxiliary aids and services are in Title 28 Code of Federal Regulations Section 36.301 and following sections.

OCR enforces Title II of the ADA. Like Section 504, an allegation regarding a school district's noncompliance with the ADA will trigger an OCR investigation that will result in a letter of findings. A lawsuit also may be filed in federal court alleging a violation of the ADA. If the ADA claim can also be addressed by a due process hearing, the IDEA's due process hearing system must be accessed before bringing a claim in federal court (*Robb v. Bethel School District #403*, 2002). Attorneys' fees are available under the ADA to a prevailing plaintiff.

SUMMARY

The Individuals with Disabilities Education Act (IDEA) is a comprehensive statutory scheme governing the education of children with disabilities. A school district must identify, locate, and assess all children residing within the district's geographical boundaries who may need special education and related services. To receive services under IDEA, a child must meet one of IDEA's disability categories and, by reason thereof, need special education and related services. If a child satisfies both of these criteria, the child is entitled to a free appropriate public education (FAPE).

FAPE has a procedural and substantive component. Not all procedural violations, however, constitute a denial of a FAPE. The substantive component of FAPE requires a school district's educational program to be designed to meet the student's unique educational needs, be reasonably calculated to provide the student with some educational benefit, be provided in conformity with the student's individualized education program (IEP), and be in the least restrictive environment (LRE). FAPE's substantive component does not require a potential maximizing program. In this regard, school districts need only provide an educational program that is reasonably calculated to offer some educational benefit.

A special education student's educational program is created by an IEP team during an IEP team meeting. An IEP team includes both mandatory (e.g., parent, general and special education teachers, administrator) and discretionary (e.g., attorney, advocate, or independent assessor) team members. An IEP team meeting must be held at least annually. IEP team meetings also must be held if requested by a parent, if there is a lack of anticipated progress, or if school district assessments need to be reviewed.

A special education student's IEP functions as a road map to the student's educational program. An IEP must include present levels of educational performance; measurable annual goals; special education instruction and services and program modifications; an explanation of the extent, if any, the student will not participate with nondisabled peers in general education; any modifications necessary for the student to participate in state- or district-wide assessments; the projected date for the beginning of special education services, including the anticipated frequency, location, and duration of those services; appropriate objective criteria, evaluation procedures, and schedules for determining, at least on an annual basis, whether goals are being achieved; a statement of how a student's progress toward goals will be measured; and a statement of how a student's parents will be informed of the student's progress.

Special education is specifically designed instruction without cost to the parents that meets the unique needs of the student. Special education also includes designated instruction and services (DIS) when necessary for the student to benefit from the student's instructional program. A wide variety of DIS are available. However, medical services are available only for diagnostic and evaluation purposes. School districts do not have to provide DIS if the service must be performed by a physician or hospital. Some special education students receive extended school year (ESY) services over the summer to prevent regression.

An IEP must also address a student's behavior when the behavior impedes the learning of the student or others. A behavior intervention plan (BIP) can address serious behavior problems that significantly interfere with implementation of the goals and objectives in the student's IEP. A BIP is the product of a functional analysis assessment (FAA), which is a detailed, systematic series of observations resulting in a comprehensive report regarding the behavior at issue. A functional behavioral analysis can be undertaken to address behaviors that do not rise to the level of seriousness triggering an FAA and consideration of a BIP.

A continuum of placement options must be available to meet a special education student's needs. All placement decisions must consider the IDEA's LRE mandate, which requires that to the maximum extent appropriate, children with disabilities are educated with children who are nondisabled; and the removal of children with disabilities from the regular education environment occurs only when the nature and severity of the disability is such that the education in regular classes with the use of supplementary aides and services cannot be achieved satisfactorily. The IDEA's LRE presumption does not supersede FAPE. Depending on a student's needs, placement in a more restrictive environment may be necessary in order for the student to receive a FAPE.

The due process hearing system is available to address special education disagreements between parents and school districts. The Office of Administrative Hearings (OAH) oversees due process hearings. Virtually every aspect of a student's educational program can be challenged in a due process hearing. A prevailing parent may be entitled to attorneys' fees.

Section 504 and the Americans with Disabilities Act (ADA) prohibit discrimination on the basis of disability and provide eligible students with affirmative rights. A student who is determined not to be eligible for services under IDEA may meet the eligibility criteria under Section 504 and the ADA. A student who is an individual with a disability under Section 504 (or a qualified individual with a disability under ADA) may be entitled to special services and accommodations. In the context of Section 504, these services and accommodations can be implemented through a Section 504 plan.

9 | STUDENT DISCIPLINE

The escalation of violence in society coupled with recent fatal shootings on public school campuses has prompted greater attention to assuring that schools are safe. Article I, Section 28 of the California Constitution specifies that all public school students and staff have the "inalienable right to attend campuses which are safe, secure, and peaceful." In Chapter 2, we discussed laws that restrict outsiders from disrupting school activities. In this chapter, we focus on student discipline. We begin our discussion with the importance of effective and legally defensible student discipline rules. Then we explore the acts for which a student may and must be disciplined. We address informal types of discipline, suspension, and expulsion. The constitutional and statutory requirements for imposing discipline are included in the discussion. We then examine in some detail the expulsion process, its components, and the power to expel, which is vested in the governing board. An explanation of the expulsion appeal process follows. Relevant case law and opinions of the California Attorney General are interspersed throughout.

We have also included a discussion of the Individuals with Disabilities Education Act's (IDEA) unique requirements for the discipline of students who qualify, or are suspected to qualify, for special education. We recommend reading Chapter 8 before reading this chapter in the context of students with disabilities.

THE IMPORTANCE OF STUDENT DISCIPLINE RULES

Student rules do more than merely inform students as to what conduct is impermissible. When written and implemented effectively, student rules provide order. In the wake of a 1982 U.S. Supreme Court decision, courts generally defer to the judgment of school officials on the development, interpretation, and application of student rules. The case involved a student who challenged the school board's reliance on a rule against drug use to expel him for drinking. The lower courts agreed that the rule was flawed and overturned the youth's expulsion. But the Supreme Court reversed the judgment, noting that "the District Court and the Court of Appeals plainly erred in replacing the Board's construction of [the rule] with their own notions under the facts of the case" (*Board of Education of Rogers, Arkansas v. McCluskey*, p. 971). Since alcohol can be classified as a drug, the school board was within its discretion to apply the rule as it had. As we have noted in earlier chapters, however, judges do not hesitate to become involved when student rules intrude on constitutionally protected behavior. Perhaps the best example is the seminal 1969 U.S. Supreme Court ruling in *Tinker v. Des Moines Independent Community School District*, discussed in Chapter 6. In that case, the school instituted a rule against the wearing of symbolic black armbands and then used it to suspend several students who did so. The Supreme Court held that the suspensions were unconstitutional because they deprived the students of their freedom of speech under the First Amendment.

The fact that judges normally do not second-guess educators on the development and use of student discipline rules does not mean that rule development should be taken casually. The better the rules are constructed, the more likely the students will follow them. A few simple illustrations will demonstrate the point. Consider a rule that states "disruptive offenses include gum chewing." Is the intent of the rule to prohibit only gum chewing that is disruptive, or all gum chewing? If the school intends to ban gum chewing, the rule should state that gum chewing is not permitted in school. Otherwise, the rule is ambiguous, and students will not know exactly what its intent is. Similarly, a rule providing that "students may be placed in an alternative education setting for insubordination to school personnel" invites uncertainty because "insubordination" is not likely to be well understood by a majority of students. A more precise and less authoritarian way of stating the rule is to say "students may be placed in an alternative education setting for failing to follow the directives of school personnel." Here are several key guidelines for improving the quality of student discipline rules:

- Conduct periodic audits of the student code of conduct.
- Delete rules that deal with trivial matters and are not worth the cost of enforcement. Use oral directives instead.
- Make sure that rules are understandable to students. For example, elementary school rules will be worded differently than will secondary school rules.
- Transpose the wording of criminal statutes in terms students can understand.

- Make sure rules are worded carefully so they do not intrude on constitutionally protected behavior (e.g., rules pertaining to campus rallies or the distribution of student literature).

- Exercise special care in developing and applying rules of off-campus student behavior (e.g., use of the Internet). Link off-campus discipline to the legitimate interests of the school.

- Make sure that students know what the rules are.

- Enforce the rules consistently and fairly.

All public schools in California publish a student code of conduct. Education Code Section 35291 requires school districts to prescribe rules for student discipline. At least every four years, public schools may review the rules and adopt new ones if necessary (Educ. Code § 35291.5). In developing rules under Section 35291.5, schools are to involve parents; teachers; administrators; school security personnel; and, for junior and senior high schools, students. Governing boards may prescribe procedures for giving continuing students written notice of the rules at the beginning of each school year and to transfer students when they enroll. And every school employee has the responsibility to see that the rules and discipline procedures are enforced.

Rules also serve a necessary constitutional purpose. The presence of clearly defined rules is a prerequisite to due process. The Fourteenth Amendment to the U.S. Constitution provides that no state (the public school is a political subdivision of the state) shall deprive any person of life, liberty, or property without due process of law. Article I, Section 7 (a) of the California Constitution contains a similar provision. Due process requires that students first be on notice of what behavior will subject them to sanctions. Fundamental fairness requires no less.

The school campus is a microcosm of society. A school campus without order is like a society on the verge of rebellion and anarchy. Rules, however, have limits. School violence and disharmony among students can still occur despite the most meticulously written and equitably enforced rules. And when this occurs, discipline must be administered. California has developed a comprehensive set of student discipline requirements, and it is to them we now turn.

CALIFORNIA'S LEGAL FRAMEWORK
FOR STUDENT DISCIPLINE

Student discipline is governed by Education Code Section 48900 and following sections. In some instances, consideration must also be given to local school district policy, the state and federal constitutions, and IDEA. Chapters 6 (Rights of

Expression) and 10 (Public Access, Privacy, and Student Search and Seizure) detail the relevant constitutional issues. Judicial decisions and California Attorney General opinions interpreting these statutes and constitutional provisions complete the legal framework for student discipline.

Who Can Discipline

Classroom teachers, principals or superintendents, and the school district's governing board all have the power to discipline a student under the Education Code. Teachers can suspend students from class for specified misbehavior or impose other related forms of discipline (Educ. Code § 48910). The principal or superintendent can suspend students and recommend expulsion (Educ. Code § 48900). While the school district's governing board can also suspend a student, only the governing board can order an expulsion (Educ. Code §§ 48912, 48915).

A principal's designee may also discipline students. A principal may designate, in writing, one or more administrators at the school site as the principal's designee to assist with disciplinary procedures. If there is no administrator in addition to the principal, a certificated employee can be the principal's designee. An additional backup employee may also be identified for imposing discipline if neither the principal nor a principal's designee is available. The names of all individuals identified as a principal's designee must be on file in the principal's office. Education Code Section 48911 (h) details the requirements for classifying an individual as a principal's designee. Section 48911 also applies to the disciplinary actions of a site principal at a nonpublic school (NPS) in which a special education student is enrolled (Educ. Code § 48911.5). An NPS is a private school that has been certified by the California Department of Education to provide an educational program to special education students.

Education Code Section 48910 (a) permits a teacher to suspend a student from class for the day of the offense and the following day. The teacher must immediately report the suspension to the local school site principal and send the student to the principal or principal's designee. A parent-teacher conference must be scheduled as soon as possible following the suspension. Instead of issuing a suspension, a teacher may send the student to the principal's office. During the classroom suspension, the student may not be placed in another class scheduled at the same time, but may continue to attend other classes during the day.

Due Process of Law

Before exploring the specific grounds for suspension and expulsion, it is necessary to comment on due process of law. As noted, the Fourteenth Amendment to the United States Constitution prohibits a public school from depriving any person of property without due process of law. Is attending a public school a property right under the Fourteenth Amendment, and if so, what process is due prior to deprivation of that right (e.g., discipline resulting in removal from school)? In 1975, the U.S. Supreme Court took up this question in the context of short-term suspensions in the case of *Goss v. Lopez*.

In 1971, Dwight Lopez was a student attending Central High School in Columbus, Ohio. During February and March 1971, there was widespread student unrest at Central High School and other schools within the Columbus Ohio Public School System (CPSS). Dwight was suspended for ten days in connection with a disturbance in a lunchroom resulting in damage to school property. Dwight maintained he was an innocent bystander, noting that at least seventy-five other students were suspended on the same day. Dwight was not given an opportunity to respond to the charges resulting in his suspension.

Dwight and eight other students suspended in a similar manner brought a legal action against the CPSS alleging that a suspension without a hearing was unconstitutional under the Fourteenth Amendment. The Court agreed. The Court held that through the compulsory schooling law, public education is a state-created property right under the Fourteenth Amendment, invoking the necessity of due process of law prior to deprivation. Focusing on the length of the suspension (ten days), the Court held that due process of law requires that a student be given oral or written notice of the charges, and if the student denies the charges, an opportunity to present his or her side of the story. Significantly, the Court did not require school districts to provide full adversarial hearings for suspensions of up to ten days. However, the Court did note that longer suspensions (e.g., more than ten days) and permanent removal from school through an expulsion may require more formal procedures.

When students are asked to repeat a course or are retained in the same grade for the next year, are they entitled to procedural due process as in *Goss v. Lopez*? The purpose of procedural due process essentially is to elicit truth. When academic decisions are made, truth normally is not in question. Test score performance, grades, and consultations with the student and the student's parents reveal the reason for these actions. In a 1978 decision involving a challenge from a student to her dismissal from medical school because of poor clinical skills and lack of personal hygiene, the Court observed:

> Like the decision of an individual professor as to the proper grade for a student in his course, the determination whether to dismiss a student for academic reasons requires an expert evaluation of cumulative information and is not readily adapted to the procedural tools of judicial or administrative decisionmaking. (p. 90)

Thus, the justices refused to require a *Goss v. Lopez*–type hearing for academic disputes (*Board of Curators of the University of Missouri v. Horowitz*).

Some years later the Court ruled similarly in a case involving the dismissal of a student from a six-year program leading to a medical degree (*Regents of the University of Michigan v. Ewing*, 1985). This time, the student contended that the university's decision not to allow him to retake a qualifying test midway through the program when others had been given the opportunity to do so was so unfair as to deprive him of a property right in his continuing education. He did not argue a procedural due process violation, because he had been allowed to pursue internal appeal procedures. Instead, he argued that the decision denied him substantive due process. Substantive due process relates to the rationale of the decision itself. In order to make out a successful substantive due process claim, a person has to establish that the decision was lacking in basic fairness. Judges rarely overturn decisions on this basis because doing so invites them to second-guess other decision makers. As the Supreme Court noted in the *Ewing* case, judges may not override an academic decision "unless it is such a substantial departure from accepted academic norms as to demonstrate that the person or committee responsible did not actually exercise professional judgment" (p. 225). In this case, university decision makers had adequate grounds to deny the student an opportunity to retake the test, though the justices did note that had the university done so, it may have avoided the lawsuit.

Whether procedural or substantive, there must be a deprivation of a liberty or property interest for due process to be required under the federal constitution. Does a student have such an interest in extracurricular and athletic activities? In the first California appellate decision to consider the matter, the answer insofar as the federal constitution is concerned was no. But the court was less certain in the context of the California Constitution (*Ryan v. California Interscholastic Federation—San Diego Section*). In this 2001 ruling, the court was faced with a case involving a student from Australia who was determined by the California Interscholastic Federation (CIF) not to be eligible for interscholastic football, because he had already completed eight semesters of schooling beyond initial enrollment in the ninth grade. Established in 1914, CIF was recognized by the legislature in 1981 as a voluntary, nonprofit organization responsible for administering interscholastic athletics in California secondary schools under a set of eligibility rules and complaint procedures (Educ. Code § 33353 and following sections; see also § 35179 and following sections). CIF also determined that the student was not eligible under the Federation's transfer rule, because his family had not changed their Australian residence. The student challenged the decision as a violation of his due process rights under both the federal and California constitutions.

Citing a long line of federal court decisions, the California court of appeal held that participation in interscholastic sports, like being a class officer or acting in a school play, is a privilege, not a right, under the Fourteenth Amendment. Thus, a *Goss v. Lopez*–type hearing is not required when a student is denied an opportunity to participate. The student also argued that his constitutionally protected Fourteenth Amendment liberty right to a good reputation was damaged by CIF's ruling that the district's head football coach had violated the federation's undue influence rule in working with the student. But the court was not supportive, noting that the U.S. Supreme Court has ruled that reputation becomes a protected liberty only when the person's reputation is stigmatized by public officials in the context of loss of a significant state-conferred benefit, such as employment or welfare. Here the student's athletic ineligibility did not rise to this level. Further, the court questioned how the student's reputation had been damaged over a matter involving the coach.

With regard to the California Constitution, the court recognized that the state supreme court had ruled in 1979 that neither a liberty nor a property right has to be involved for a person to invoke the due process clause of Article 1, Section 7 (a) (*People v. Ramirez*). However, the amount of process due depends upon the nature of the statutorily conferred benefit or interest that is at stake. If the benefit is minor, then informal due process will suffice prior to deprivation. But if the benefit is significant, then more formal due process becomes necessary. In this case, the appellate court could not identify what statutorily conferred benefit was at stake. While students have a constitutionally protected right not to be charged for participating in extracurricular activities and on athletic teams as part of a free public education, there is no statutory entitlement to participate. The judges noted that even if some procedural due process were necessary in this case, CIF's eligibility rules and internal appeal process satisfied it.

The requirements of due process under the federal constitution as identified in *Goss v. Lopez* and particularly under the more supportive California Constitution account for the due process procedures set forth in Section 48900 and following sections of the California Education Code for student discipline. To those we now turn.

TYPES OF DISCIPLINE

School discipline can be divided into three categories: discipline short of suspension, suspension, and expulsion. All three categories are vital for the maintenance of order and control in a public school. It is the latter two categories, however, that invoke the Education Code and both the informal and formal procedures noted in *Goss*. Corporal punishment is not among the disciplinary options available as it is explicitly prohibited by Education Code Section 49001.

Discipline Short of Suspension

Education Code Section 48925 (d) defines which types of discipline are not considered suspension. These types of discipline include reassignment to another education program or class at the same school, where the student will receive continuing instruction for the duration of the school day as other students in the same grade level; referral to a certificated employee designated by the principal to advise students (e.g., counselor); and removal from class, but without reassignment to another class or program, for the remainder of the class period without sending the student to the principal or the principal's designee. Removal of a student from a particular class cannot occur more than once every five school days. These low-level types of discipline are the stock-in-trade of teachers and administrators who must reign in disruptive and inappropriate student behavior on a daily basis. They are a function of school district policy and do not invoke the statutory requirements of the Education Code. For special education students, implementation of behavior management techniques in an individualized education program (IEP) or reassignment of a student's classroom per an IEP does not constitute a suspension. Chapter 8 addresses behavior plans and IEPs.

Suspension

The Education Code's grounds for suspension are a catalogue of foolish, inappropriate, and dangerous student conduct. Column A of Table 9.1 lists the acts for which suspension may or must be imposed. These are all of the acts contained in Education Code Sections 48900, 48900.2, 48900.3, 48900.4, and 48900.7. We have included the statutory citations for offenses in cell A3 of Table 9.1 because they are specifically referenced elsewhere in the discipline statutes. Readers need to keep in mind, however, that these sections of the Education Code are frequently amended. Thus, it is advisable to consult a current copy of the Education Code in conjunction with studying this table.

A1 details the particular circumstances under which an act in Section 48900 requires immediate suspension. All of the particular circumstances in this section are derived from an act or acts in Section 48900. For example, brandishing a knife is a combination of Section 48900 (a)(1) (attempting to cause or threatening physical injury to another person) and Section 48900 (b) (possession of a knife). Section 48915 (a) also sets forth particular circumstances based on an act or combination of acts in Section 48900 (e.g., assault or battery upon any school employee).

The general rule is that a suspension must be imposed only when other means of correction fail to bring about proper conduct (Educ. Code § 48900.5). A suspension for a first-time offense is typically not an option. However, certain acts permit, and may require, suspension regardless of whether other means of correction may bring about proper conduct. Suspension for a first offense is permissible for a student who:

- Is determined to have committed an act violating Section 48900 (a)–(e) as set forth in cell A3 of Table 9.1, or
- Through his or her presence causes a danger to persons or property or threatens to disrupt the instructional process (cells B2 and B3).

Additionally, immediate suspension must occur for a student determined to have committed an act listed in cell A1. Either the principal or superintendent must determine if the student did the act for which suspension may, or must, be imposed.

Implementation of a suspension requires the informal notice and meeting requirements discussed in *Goss*. At the time of a student's suspension, a school employee must make a reasonable effort to contact the student's parent in person or by telephone. A report of the suspension, including the cause for the suspension, must be sent to the school district's governing board or superintendent consistent with district policy. Certain acts require the principal or principal's designee to inform the appropriate law enforcement agency prior to suspension (Educ. Code § 48902). Law enforcement reporting is required for acts that may violate Penal Code Sections 245 (assault with a deadly weapon or force likely to produce great bodily injury), 626.9 or 626.10 (possession of weapons on campus), and Education Code Section 48900 (c) and (d) (controlled substances, alcohol, intoxicants, and look-alike substances). A principal or principal's designee who willfully fails to make a report to a law enforcement agency required by Section 48902 commits an infraction subject to a fine not to exceed $500. A principal or principal's designee reporting to law enforcement a potential violation of Penal Code Section 245 or Education Code Section 48900 (c) and (d) may not be held civilly or criminally liable unless a knowingly false report is made or the report is made with a reckless disregard for the truth.

Consistent with *Goss*, the Education Code generally requires a suspension to be preceded with an informal conference between school administration, the student, and whenever practicable the school employee who referred the student for discipline. A parent must respond without delay to a request to meet with school administrators regarding their child's behavior. At the conference, the student is informed of the evidence against him or her and is given an opportunity to present the student's side of the story. However, if an "emergency situation" exists, a student may be suspended without an informal conference. An emergency situation means a situation determined to constitute a clear and present danger to the life, safety, or

Table 9.1
Disciplinary Acts and Consequences

Column A	Column B	Column C	Column D
Student Act (Acts are specified in Educ. Code Sections 48900–48900.4, 48900.7, and 48915)	School Administration Response to Act	Finding to Recommend Expulsion to Governing Board	Final Action if Governing Board Adopts Recommendation from Expulsion Hearing
A1 Possessing, selling, or otherwise furnishing a firearm. Possession must be verified by a school district employee. Brandishing a knife at another person. Unlawfully selling a controlled substance listed in the Health and Safety Code. Committing or attempting to commit a sexual assault as defined in subdivision (n) of Section 48900 or committing a sexual battery as defined in subdivision (n) of Section 48900. Possession of an explosive.	**B1** Immediate suspension and mandatory recommendation for expulsion.	**C1** Student committed the act.	**D1** The governing board must order expulsion of the student. The governing board *may* suspend enforcement of the expulsion order.
A2 Causing serious physical injury to another person, except in self-defense. Possession of any knife or other dangerous object of no reasonable use to the pupil. Unlawful possession of any controlled substance listed in the Health and Safety Code, except for the first offense for the possession of not more than one avoirdupois ounce of marijuana, other than concentrated cannabis.	**B2** The student *may* be suspended for a first-time offense if (1) The student is determined to have committed an act violating Section 48900 (a)–(e); or (2) through his or her presence the student causes a danger to persons or property or threatens to disrupt the instructional process.	**C2** Student committed the act. Other means of correction are not feasible or have repeatedly failed to bring about proper conduct, and/or due to the nature of the act, the student's presence creates a continuing danger to the physical safety of the student or others.	**D2** The governing board *may* order expulsion. If the governing board orders expulsion, the governing board *may* suspend enforcement of the expulsion order.

Robbery or extortion.

Assault or battery, as defined in Penal Code Sections 240 and 242, upon any school employee.

Otherwise, suspension can be imposed only when other means of correction fail to bring about proper conduct.

The student must be recommended for expulsion unless inappropriate due to the particular circumstances.

A3

Caused, attempted to cause, or threatened to cause physical injury to another person (Educ. Code § 48900 (a)(1)).

Willfully used force or violence upon the person of another, except in self-defense (Educ. Code § 48900 (a)(2)).

Possessed, sold, or otherwise furnished any firearm, knife, explosive, or other dangerous object, unless, in the case of possession of any object of this type, the pupil had obtained written permission to possess the item from a certificated school employee, which is concurred in by the principal or the designee of the principal (Educ. Code § 48900 (b)). *Except for possession or sale of a firearm or possession of an explosive (see A1) or possession of a knife or other dangerous object of no reasonable use to the student (see A2).*

B3

The student *may* be suspended for a first-time offense if (1) The student is determined to have committed an act violating Section 48900 (a)–(e); or (2) through his or her presence the student causes a danger to persons or property or threatens to disrupt the instructional process.

Otherwise, suspension can only be imposed when other means of correction fail to bring about proper conduct.

The student may be recommended for expulsion.

C3

Student committed the act.

Other means of correction are not feasible or have repeatedly failed to bring about proper conduct, and/or due to the nature of the act, the student's presence creates a continuing danger to the physical safety of the student or others.

D3

The governing board *may* order expulsion.

If the governing board orders expulsion, the governing board *may* suspend enforcement of the expulsion order.

(Note: Education Code Section 48915 does not specifically reference Education Code Sections 48900 (d)–(q) and (s) or 48900.7 No court has addressed the possible implications of this omission. However, some school districts have taken a conservative approach by still requiring the findings noted in cell C3 before ordering expulsion.)

(continued)

Table 9.1
(Continued)

A3 (Continued)

Unlawfully possessed, used, sold, or otherwise furnished, or been under the influence of, any controlled substance listed in the Health and Safety Code, an alcoholic beverage, or an intoxicant of any kind (Educ. Code § 48900 (c)). *Except for unlawful sale (see A1) or possession (see A2) of a controlled substance.*

Unlawfully offered, arranged, or negotiated to sell any controlled substance listed in the Health and Safety Code, an alcoholic beverage, or an intoxicant of any kind; and either sold, delivered, or otherwise furnished to any person another liquid, substance, or material and represented the liquid, substance, or material as a controlled substance, alcoholic beverage, or intoxicant (Educ. Code § 48900 (d)). *Except for unlawful sale (see A1) or possession (see A2) of a controlled substance.*

Committed or attempted to commit robbery or extortion (Educ. Code § 48900 (e)). *Except for committing robbery or extortion (see A2).*

Caused or attempted to cause damage to school property or private property (Educ. Code § 48900 (f)).

Stole or attempted to steal school property or private property (Educ. Code § 48900 (g)).

Possessed or used tobacco, or any products containing tobacco or nicotine products, including, but not limited to, cigarettes, cigars, miniature cigars, clove cigarettes, smokeless tobacco, snuff, chew packets, and betel. However, this section does not prohibit use or possession by a student of his or her own prescription products (Educ. Code § 48900 (h)).

Committed an obscene act or engaged in habitual profanity or vulgarity (Educ. Code § 48900 (i)).

Unlawfully possessed or unlawfully offered, arranged, or negotiated to sell any drug paraphernalia, as defined in Section 11014.5 of the Health and Safety Code (Educ. Code § 48900 (j)).

Disrupted school activities or otherwise willfully defied the valid authority of supervisors, teachers, administrators, school officials, or other school personnel engaged in the performance of their duties (Educ. Code § 48900 (k)).

Knowingly received stolen school property or private property (Educ. Code § 48900 (l)).

Possessed an imitation firearm. "Imitation firearm" means a replica of a firearm that is so substantially similar in physical properties to an existing firearm as to lead a reasonable person to conclude that the replica is a firearm (Educ. Code § 48900 (m)).

Harassed, threatened, or intimidated a pupil who is a complaining witness or a witness in a school disciplinary proceeding for the purpose of either preventing that pupil from being a witness, retaliating against that pupil for being a witness, or both (Educ. Code § 48900 (o)).

Unlawfully offered, arranged to sell, negotiated to sell, or sold the prescription drug Soma (Educ. Code § 48900 (p)).

Engaged in, or attempted to engage in, hazing as defined in Education Code Section 48900 (q).

Engaged in bullying, including cyberbullying, against a pupil or school personnel, as defined in Education Code Section 32261 (Educ. Code § 48900 (r)).

Aiding or abetting, as defined in Penal Code Section 31, the infliction or attempted infliction of physical injury to another person may result in suspension of the offending student. However, a student who has been adjudged by a juvenile court to have committed, as an aider and abettor, a crime of physical violence in which the victim suffered great bodily injury or serious bodily injury will be subject to discipline under Education Code Section 48900 (a) (Educ. Code § 48900 (t)).

Committed sexual harassment (inapplicable to students enrolled in kindergarten and grades 1 to 3, inclusive) (Educ. Code § 48900.2).

Caused, attempted to cause, threatened to cause, or participated in an act of hate violence as defined in Education Code Section 233 (e) (Educ. Code § 48900.3).

Intentionally engaged in harassment, threats, or intimidation, directed against school district personnel or students, that is sufficiently severe or pervasive to have the actual and reasonably expected effect of materially disrupting classwork, creating substantial disorder, and invading the rights of either school personnel or students by creating an intimidating or hostile educational environment (Educ. Code § 48900.4).

Made terroristic threats against school officials, school property, or both (Educ. Code § 48900.7).

health of other students or school personnel (Educ. Code § 48911 (c)). A student subject to a suspension in an emergency situation must receive an informal conference within two school days of the suspension unless the student waives his or her right to the conference or is unable to attend.

May a student suspected of sexual harassment learn the names of his accusers during the informal pre-suspension meeting? No. In the 2003 decision of *Granowitz v. Redlands Unified School District,* Evan Granowitz was given a five-day suspension for sexual harassment. During the pre-suspension conference, Evan and his father, an attorney, requested the names of the students who had accused Evan. The principal did not disclose the names of these individuals, due to the nature of the accusations. Evan served his suspension and graduated. A few months later Evan, with his father as his attorney, sued the school district and the principal alleging a denial of due process of law. The principal was sued in his individual capacity and found liable by the superior court in excess of $100,000 under a federal statute known as 42 U.S.C. § 1983 that is discussed in Chapter 12.

The school district appealed and prevailed on all issues. The principal, in the appellate court's view, gave Evan all the process he was due under *Goss.* Citing the confidentiality provision in Education Code Section 48918 (f) for expulsion hearings, which permits witnesses to remain anonymous to avoid psychological harm, the court also upheld the principal's decision not to identify these individuals. After disposing of Evan's entire case on appeal, the court finished its opinion with the following parting comment:

> As a final note, we join the Seventh Circuit in deploring the exploitation of the legal system to pursue a case of this ilk. A minor suspension of trivial effect, accomplished with proper constitutional safeguards, has resulted in a costly expenditure of judicial, public, and private resources.
>
> We also adopt the sentiments of Judge Kozinski expressed in a case where he called the complaint of a disciplined student "a triumph of petulance over common sense. A teenager who gets into trouble . . . might, for lack of better judgment, feel that [he] is the one who has been wronged. But [he] can't turn his wishful thinking into a lawsuit without support from [his] parents and the services of a lawyer-adult who do not have youth and inexperience as excuses. Before bringing a suit, [a student's] parents might profitably have pondered their own culpability. . . . [A parent-lawyer] might have thought about whether it was right to impose the cost, risk and pain of a civil lawsuit on a civil servant who acted responsibly under difficult circumstances. . . . [The student] and the adults who abetted [him] might all have taken a lesson in common sense from the students . . . suffered the same 'harm'—but did not make a federal case out of it" (pp. 417–418).

Evan did not appeal.

A single suspension cannot exceed five consecutive school days (Educ. Code § 48911). As a general rule, a student cannot be suspended for more than twenty school days in one school year (Educ. Code § 48903 (a)). The two exceptions to the limit of twenty school days pertain to a student who transfers to another school or has his or her suspension extended. The school may extend the suspension of a student committing an act resulting in a recommendation for expulsion while the expulsion is being processed (Educ. Code § 48911 (g)). An extension of a suspension can occur only if it has been determined, following a meeting in which the student and the student's parents are invited to participate, that the student's presence at school or at an alternative school placement would cause a danger to persons or property or a threat of disrupting the educational process. This meeting can be held with the informal conference that generally precedes a suspension. A thirty-school-day limit on suspensions applies to a student who enrolls in or is transferred to another regular school, an opportunity school or class, or a continuation education school or class (Educ. Code § 48903 (a)). A school district may, but does not have to, count suspensions a student received in another school district toward the foregoing limitations on the length of suspensions.

While there is no appeal of a suspension, a school district's governing board may meet to consider suspension of a student prior to issuance of the suspension. The governing board's meeting can be in closed session if holding a public hearing would result in the disclosure of private student information (as defined in Education Code Section 49073 and following sections). Prior to holding a meeting for this purpose, the governing board must inform the student and the student's parents in writing, or the student if he or she is eighteen years of age, of the intent of the governing board to hold a closed session. Within forty-eight hours of this notice, a student may make a written request for a public meeting. If disclosure of private student information will occur in a public meeting, however, a closed meeting may be held.

Traditional suspensions are not the only options available as discipline for acts that do not warrant expulsion. Instead of suspension from school, a student may be required to perform community service on school grounds during nonschool hours (Educ. Code § 48900.6). With written parental consent, a student may be required to perform community service off school grounds. Community service includes, but is not limited to, work in the areas of outdoor beautification; community or campus betterment; and teacher, peer, or youth assistance. Community service is not an option if the student is suspended pending expulsion.

Another option is to order a supervised classroom for the entire period. Instead of suspension from school, a student may be ordered to a supervised suspension classroom for the entire period of the suspension (Educ. Code § 48911.1). A supervised suspension classroom is not available if expulsion proceedings have been initiated or the student poses an imminent danger or threat to the campus, students, or staff. During imposition of a supervised suspension classroom, the student remains separated from other students at the school site. A parent must be notified in person or by telephone when the parent's child is assigned to a supervised suspension classroom. Written parental notice is required when a student is assigned to a supervised suspension classroom for longer than one class period.

Interestingly, a teacher may also require a student's parent to attend school with a student suspended from a class (Educ. Code § 48900.1). Such unusual punishment is reserved for violations of Education Code Sections 48900 (i) (obscene act, habitual profanity, or vulgarity) or (k) (disrupting school activities or otherwise willfully defying authority). The parent attends the class from which the student was suspended. School districts may adopt a policy to require parent attendance. The policy must require the parent to meet with a school administrator after the classroom visit.

Expulsion

The same acts that qualify a student for suspension can also result in a recommendation for expulsion. There are three classes of offenses for which a recommendation for expulsion is permissible. The acts in cell A1 of Table 9.1 require a recommendation for expulsion. The acts in cell A2 require a recommendation for expulsion unless such a recommendation is inappropriate under the circumstances. A school administrator may recommend expulsion for a student determined to have committed an act in cell A3. As Table 9.1 indicates, a recommendation for expulsion from a school administrator is the first step in the expulsion process. The other three steps are detailed in the following subsections.

Mandatory recommendation for expulsion. A student committing an act described in cell A1 of Table 9.1 must be immediately suspended and recommended for expulsion. The acts committed under these particular circumstances are known as the "Big Five."

Possession of a firearm requires an employee of the school district to verify the student's possession of the firearm. Student possession of a firearm on school grounds is permissible if prior written permission is obtained from a certificated employee (e.g., a teacher), and the permission is concurred in by the principal or principal's designee (Educ. Code § 48915 (c)(1)). Most likely due to the unfortunate and tragic school shootings of recent years, the authors are not aware of any contemporary instances in which a school district has allowed a student to possess a firearm on a school campus under this provision of the Education Code. Further, possession of a firearm on a school campus would also have to comply with the Gun-Free School Zone Act (Penal Code § 626.9). Under this criminal law, a school district superintendent, his or her designee, or equivalent school authority must give written permission for a student to possess a firearm in a school zone.

Does a student impermissibly have possession of a firearm if he or she finds the weapon on campus and is merely delivering it to school officials for disposal? No. A 1997 California Attorney General opines that "possession" requires a student to knowingly and voluntarily have direct control over a firearm and does not include brief possession solely for the purpose of delivery to school officials (80 Ops. Atty. Gen. 91).

The Education Code defines a knife as "any dirk, dagger, or other weapon with a fixed, sharpened blade fitted primarily for stabbing, a weapon with a blade fitted primarily for stabbing, a weapon with a blade longer than three and one-half inches, a folding knife with a blade that locks into place, or a razor with an un-guarded blade" (Educ. Code § 48915 (g)). The term "explosive" has the same meaning as the phrase "destructive device" as described in Section 921 of the Title 18 of the United States Code (Educ. Code § 48915 (h)). The United States Code provides a broad definition of the phrase "destructive device," which includes, among other items, a bomb, grenade, any similar device, and a weapon capable of expelling a projectile (save for a shotgun). Although a shotgun is not considered a "destructive device," it is still prohibited as a firearm.

These are not the only instances in which a school administrator has to cross-reference another statute to determine if a student has committed an act warrant-ing expulsion. For example, drug offenses reference the Health and Safety Code and sexual assault and battery references the Penal Code. The entire California Code is available on the Internet at www.leginfo.ca.gov or in a law library. In the following list, we comment on the Health and Safety and Penal Code sections rel-evant to acts that mandate a recommendation for expulsion.

- A recommendation for expulsion is mandated for a student who is deter-mined to have unlawfully sold a controlled substance listed in Chapter 2 (commencing with Section 11053) in the Health and Safety Code (Educ. Code § 48915 (c)(3)). Health and Safety Code Section 11053 and the perti-nent following sections contain an exhaustive list of controlled substances ranging from the commonly known (opium, cocaine, marijuana) to the obscure (Levoalphacetylmethadol).

- A recommendation for expulsion is mandated for a student who is deter-mined to have committed or attempted to commit a sexual assault as defined in Sections 261, 266c, 286, 288, 288a, or 289 of the Penal Code or committing a sexual battery as defined in Section 243.4 of the Penal Code (Educ. Code § 48915 (c)(4)). These provisions of the Penal Code supply detailed definitions of a wide range of deplorable acts, from touching a person against their will for purposes of sexual gratification to rape.

May a school district enforce a "zero tolerance" policy mandating an immediate suspension and recommendation for expulsion for a student who committed an act other than those described in cell A1 of Table 9.1? This was the issue a California court of appeal addressed in a 2004 decision (*T. H. v. San Diego Unified School District,* 2004). T. H. was a twelve-year-old student who engaged in three fighting incidents during the school year. Under the district's zero tolerance policy, a school principal or designee was required to suspend and recommend for expulsion all students who "'are involved in three or more incidents of fighting that inflicts injury or trespassing within one year'" (p. 538). After his third fighting incident, T. H. was immediately suspended and recommended for expulsion.

After reviewing the evidence, the expulsion panel determined that T. H. violated the regulation. The panel also noted that T. H. had been suspended on five previous occasions for acts ranging from sexual harassment to inflicting physical injury. The panel determined that expulsion was appropriate because other means of correction were not feasible and T. H.'s continued presence at school caused a physical danger to T. H. and others. As we discuss later in the chapter, these additional findings must be made for a student committing acts in cells A2 and A3 of Table 9.1 if the expulsion hearing is to result in a recommendation of expulsion to the governing board. T. H. brought a legal action challenging the zero tolerance policy.

In relevant part, T. H. argued that the policy violated the Education Code by removing a principal's statutory discretion to not recommend expulsion. Recall that only those acts in Education Code Section 48915 (c) (as detailed in cell A1 of Table 9.1) entirely remove a principal's discretion in recommending expulsion. The offense described in the district's regulation is not among the acts in Education Code Section 48915 (c). T. H. argued that, except for those acts described in Education Code Section 48915 (c), a principal must always be able to exercise discretion in determining whether or not to recommend expulsion. The appellate court did not agree with T. H. The court held that the Education Code's imposition of a mandatory recommendation for expulsion to certain acts did not preclude a school district from applying a mandatory recommendation for expulsion to other acts (e.g., three or more instances of fighting that inflict injury in the case of T. H.).

Mandatory recommendation for expulsion unless inappropriate. A determination that a student has committed an act described in cell A2 of Table 9.1 mandates a recommendation for expulsion unless it would be inappropriate due to the circumstances. Assault or battery, as defined in Sections 204 and 242 of the Penal Code, upon any school employee is one of the particular circumstances warranting expulsion (unless inappropriate due to the circumstances) in cell A2. Penal Code Section 240 defines an assault as an unlawful attempt, coupled with a present ability, to commit a violent injury on the person of another. Penal Code Section 242 defines a battery as any willful and unlawful use of force or violence upon the person of another.

Another particular circumstance in cell A2 is possession, not sale, of a controlled substance (Educ. Code § 48915 (a)(3)). The previously noted definition of a controlled substance (which was discussed in the context of selling a controlled substance) also applies to the possession of a controlled substance.

While the acts in cell A2 are still quite serious, the California Legislature has given school administrators some discretion in recommending expulsion. The initial recommendation for expulsion, however, is a distinct and separate step from the findings necessary for the expulsion hearing to result in a recommendation for expulsion to the governing board. Cell C2 of the table notes the additional findings necessary to expel a student for committing an act in cell A2. We discuss these additional findings next.

Discretionary expulsion. A student determined to have committed one of the remaining acts in Education Code Section 48900 may be recommended for expulsion. A student cannot be expelled for committing one of the acts described in cells A2 and A3 of Table 9.1 unless there is a further determination of either of the following as delineated in cells C2 and C3:

- Other means of correction are not feasible, or have repeatedly failed to bring about proper conduct; or
- Due to the nature of the act, the presence of the pupil causes a continuing danger to the physical safety of the student or others (Educ. Code § 48915 (b) and (e)).

The Education Code does not require either of the preceding determinations prior to a principal or superintendent making a recommendation for expulsion. However, the expulsion hearing cannot result in a recommendation for expulsion to the governing board without such a determination. If a school administrator does not consider this issue prior to making a recommendation for expulsion, the school district may terminate the expulsion proceedings prior to the hearing. For example, a student with a clean disciplinary record who violates Education Code Section 48900 (l) (receiving stolen property) will most likely be suspended and not recommended for expulsion. This is because the absence of prior discipline is evidence that other means of correction may be feasible, and there have not been any prior attempts to bring about proper conduct. Additionally, receiving stolen property is not an act that typically causes physical danger to the student or others. An entirely different result may occur in our hypothetical if the act of receiving stolen property is replaced with a violation of Education Code Section 48900.7 (terroristic threats against school officials).

Certain subdivisions of Section 48900 cross-reference the Health and Safety and Penal Codes. Education Code Sections 48900 (c) and (d) reference the same Health and Safety Code definition of a controlled substance that we addressed on page 347. Education Code Section 48900 (n) references the same Penal Code definition of sexual assault and battery that we also discussed on page 347. Expulsion may also be recommended for a student who is determined to have unlawfully possessed or unlawfully offered, arranged, or negotiated to sell any drug paraphernalia, as defined in Section 11014.5 of the Health and Safety Code (Educ. Code § 48900 (j)). Section 11014.5 defines the term "drug paraphernalia" broadly as:

[A]ll equipment, products and materials of any kind which are designed for use or marketed for use, in planting, propagating, cultivating, growing, harvesting, manufacturing, compounding, converting, producing, processing, preparing, testing, analyzing, packaging, repackaging, storing, containing, concealing, injecting, ingesting, inhaling, or otherwise introducing into the human body a controlled substance in violation of this division.

Drug paraphernalia includes devices designed for preparing, testing, and measuring controlled substances (e.g., kits, testing equipment, and scales).

Education Code Section 48900.2 permits discretionary expulsion for sexual harassment, which is defined in Education Code Section 212.5 as:

[U]nwelcome sexual advances, requests for sexual favors, and other verbal, visual, or physical conduct of a sexual nature, made by someone from or in the work or educational setting, under any of the following conditions:
  (a) Submission to the conduct is explicitly or implicitly made a term or a condition of an individual's employment, academic status, or progress.
  (b) Submission to, or rejection of, the conduct by the individual is used as the basis of employment or academic decisions affecting the individual.
  (c) The conduct has the purpose or effect of having a negative impact upon the individual's work or academic performance, or of creating an intimidating, hostile, or offensive work or educational environment.

(d) Submission to, or rejection of, the conduct by the individual is used as the basis for any decision affecting the individual regarding benefits and services, honors, programs, or activities available at or through the educational institution.

Swift school district action against student-on-student sexual harassment does more than maintain the decency of the educational setting and the dignity of students. It can also be an important defense to a civil rights lawsuit against a school district and its employees, based on an alleged failure to adequately address student-on-student sexual harassment. Chapter 11 explores the issue of school district and school district employee liability for student-on-student sexual harassment.

Discipline for an Act Not on School Grounds

A student may be suspended and/or expelled for an act that does not occur on school grounds. A student may be disciplined for an act relating to a school activity or attendance that occurs while on school grounds; while going to or coming from school; during lunch period, whether on or off campus; and during, or while going to or coming from, a school-sponsored event (Educ. Code § 48900 (r)). These circumstances in which discipline is permissible for an act not on school grounds are illustrative rather than exhaustive.

Can a student be disciplined for an act occurring on a campus the student is not attending? Yes. A 1991 California court of appeal decision upheld a governing board's decision to expel a student for an altercation on a campus the student was not attending (*Fremont Union High School District v. Santa Clara County Board of Education*). In *Fremont*, Matthew was attending an alternative program when he went to a comprehensive high school campus within the district. Matthew was not taking any classes at the high school. On the high school campus, he used a stun gun on another student. Expulsion proceedings led to the governing board voting to expel Matthew for possessing a dangerous object without permission while on a district campus and causing, attempting to cause, or threatening to cause physical injury to another person. Matthew appealed the expulsion order to the county board of education. The county board reversed the order to expel because Matthew was not attending his own school or engaged in his own school activity when he used the stun gun. The school district petitioned a court to reverse the county board and prevailed. The court held that as long as the prohibited act is related to school activity or attendance within the district, discipline is permissible.

However, the off-campus behavior must have some legitimate relation to the school's interests and must not involve constitutionally protected activity. Education

Code Section 44807 extends the discipline authority of school personnel to student conduct on the way to and from school. Thus, should a fight break out at an off-campus bus stop, the school would have authority to discipline the guilty students. But suppose students at the bus stop were to distribute a newspaper of their own making that is highly critical of the school principal. Because expression is involved, school officials would have a harder time justifying disciplinary action. As we noted in Chapter 6, for expression to be ground for discipline, school officials must be prepared to show that it creates material disruption or substantial interference with the rights of others. In this scenario, if an investigation established that the distribution of the newspaper interfered with students boarding or exiting the bus, discipline might then be warranted.

Or consider a situation where student athletes engage in drinking at a private residence following a football game. In this situation, the disciplinary arm of the school may not reach far enough to suspend or expel the students for violating the school's rule against drinking. As the U.S. Court of Appeals for the Fifth Circuit noted some years ago, "the width of a street might very well determine the breadth of the school board's authority" (*Shanley v. Northeast Independent School District,* 1972, p. 974). Students engaged in wrongdoing off campus are within the jurisdiction of the police and, of course, their parents. In our drinking scenario, the school could conceivably remove the athletes who consumed alcohol from the team if they had signed training rules committing them not to consume alcohol on or off campus during the season. Unlike compulsory schooling, participation in extracurricular activities is considered a privilege, not a right, and can be conditioned in this way. Of course, an investigation will be necessary to identify those students who had in fact been drinking.

Involuntary Transfer

Education Code Section 48432.5 permits the involuntary transfer of a student to a continuation school. The governing board of each high school must adopt rules and regulations for the involuntary transfer of students. If a transfer is initiated, the student and the student's parents must be given written notice of their right to request a meeting with a designee of the district superintendent prior to the transfer. At the meeting, the student and the parents are to be informed of the specific facts and reasons for the transfer. The meeting must also permit the student and the parents an opportunity to inspect all documents relied on, question any evidence and witnesses presented, and present evidence on the student's behalf. A student may bring a representative and/or witnesses to the meeting with the superintendent's designee.

An involuntary transfer must be based on a finding that the student committed an act in Education Code Section 48900 or has been habitually truant or irregular in attendance at school. Involuntary transfer can be imposed only when other means of correction fail to bring about school improvement. However, a student may be involuntarily transferred the first time the student commits an act in Education Code Section 48900 (see cell A3 in Table 9.1) if the principal determines that the student's presence causes a danger to persons or property or threatens to interrupt the educational process.

A decision to involuntarily transfer a student to a continuation school must be in writing, state the facts and reasons for the decision, and be sent to the student and the student's parents. The written notice must also indicate whether the decision to involuntarily transfer the student is subject to periodic review and the procedures for review. None of the individuals involved in making a final decision to involuntarily transfer a student may be staff at the school where the student is currently enrolled. The involuntary transfer must not extend beyond the end of the semester following the semester during which the acts leading directly to the involuntary transfer occurred. A governing board with an adopted procedure for yearly review of an involuntary transfer may extend the time period for review of the transfer.

THE EXPULSION PROCESS

Education Code Section 48900 details the acts qualifying a student for suspension and/or expulsion. Education Code Section 48915 notes the particular circumstances when a student committing an act in Section 48900 may or must be recommended for expulsion. Section 48915 also notes whether a governing board may or must order expulsion for a particular act. Education Code section 48918 governs the expulsion hearing. We can conceptualize the expulsion process in four components.

The first component requires a determination by a principal or superintendent that a student has committed an act warranting expulsion. As previously noted, the administrator may or may not have discretion in recommending expulsion. The second component of the process is the expulsion hearing. The hearing may result in no recommendation for expulsion, which terminates the entire process, or a recommendation for expulsion made to the governing board. The third component of the expulsion process occurs when the governing board considers the recommendation from the hearing. The governing board must review the evidence from the hearing and determine whether to adopt the recommendation for expulsion through a vote. Depending on the findings and the offense, the governing board may or may not be able to exercise discretion in voting for expulsion. The final component of this process is the enforcement of the expulsion order. The governing board, in its discretion, may suspend enforcement of the expulsion order.

Recommendation for Expulsion

The expulsion process starts when a principal or superintendent determines that a student has committed one of the acts in Education Code Section 48900 warranting expulsion and thereafter recommends expulsion. As noted previously, a recommendation for expulsion may be discretionary or mandatory depending on the particular circumstances. Because expulsion from school implicates the student's property right to attend school, a formal expulsion hearing is held. Note the distinction between the relatively formalized components of an expulsion hearing, which are detailed next, and the informal notice and meeting that accompany a suspension.

The Expulsion Hearing

Education Code Section 48918 details the rules governing expulsion procedures and hearings. Special rules applicable to an expulsion hearing for committing or attempting to commit sexual assault or battery are set forth in Section 48918.5. An expulsion hearing must be held within thirty days after the principal or superintendent determines that the student has committed an expellable offense. A student may request a postponement of an expulsion hearing in writing. The first request for a postponement must be granted for a period not to exceed thirty days. The school district's governing board may, but does not have to, grant additional postponement requests. If a postponement is granted, the reason for the postponement must be included as part of the record when the expulsion hearing is conducted.

Is a student entitled to any educational instruction after the recommendation for expulsion but before the expulsion hearing? No, unless the student is eligible for special education and related services under IDEA. Chapter 8 addresses special education in detail. We comment at the end of this chapter on the educational programming a special education student must receive while awaiting an expulsion hearing. General education students do not have a similar entitlement. Under Education Code Section 48913, a teacher of any class from which a student is suspended *may* require the student to complete assignments and tests missed during the suspension. The Education Code contains no other reference to the educational instruction to be provided to a general education student pending the student's expulsion hearing. A school district's governing board, however, may adopt a policy requiring a student awaiting an expulsion hearing to receive homework.

Written notice of an expulsion hearing must be sent to the student at least ten calendar days prior to the start of the hearing. The notice must include

- The date and place of the hearing.
- A statement of the specific facts and charges upon which the proposed expulsion is based.
- A copy of the disciplinary rules of the district that relate to the alleged violation.
- A notice of the parent's obligation to inform the next school the student may attend of the basis of the expulsion for an act in cell A3 of Table 9.1.
- A notice of the student or parent's opportunity to appear in person or be represented by an attorney or nonattorney adviser, to inspect and obtain copies of all documents to be used at the hearing, to question all other evidence presented, and to present oral and documentary evidence on the student's behalf, including witnesses.

The school district or student may request subpoenas from the governing board to compel the attendance of percipient (individuals with firsthand knowledge) witnesses. A request for a subpoena may be made before the hearing starts or after its commencement. The governing board is not required to issue a subpoena. Does this mean a governing board can always refuse to issue subpoenas for expulsion hearings? No, according to a 2003 California court of appeal decision (*Woodbury v. Brown-Dempsey*). In *Woodbury*, six students were alleged to be involved in a number of inappropriate (to put it mildly) acts occurring in the football squad's locker room. Curious readers can review the decision, which details the graphic allegations (including the use of a wooden dildo) and circus-like atmosphere of the expulsion hearing. Prior to the start of the expulsion hearing, the students requested the governing board to issue subpoenas for numerous witnesses, including some current district employees. The governing board denied the request, noting that it had never issued subpoenas in the past. Current district employees, however, were voluntarily made available for the expulsion hearing.

The students were expelled by the governing board and went to court to challenge the expulsion. The students argued, and the trial court agreed, that the Education Code imposes a mandatory duty on the governing board to issue subpoenas on request and that a failure to issue the subpoenas was a denial of due process. The school district appealed. The appellate court held that while the governing board is not required to issue a subpoena in response to every request, the governing board cannot act arbitrarily by refusing to exercise discretion in considering a request for subpoenas. Despite the board's procedural error, the appellate court found no miscarriage of justice and denied the expelled students' demand that subpoenas be issued for certain witnesses. The lesson of *Woodbury* is that although a governing board does not have to issue a subpoena, consideration should at least be given to the request for one.

A school district, through the superintendent or superintendent's designee, may object to the issuance of a subpoena. The governing board can meet in closed or open session, if requested by the student, to consider an objection to the issuance of a subpoena. The governing board's decision regarding an objection to the issuance of a subpoena is final.

Expulsion hearings are closed to the public unless the student makes a written request for an open hearing five days before the start of the hearing. The school district's governing board, a hearing officer, or an impartial hearing panel of three or more certificated persons may conduct the hearing. The hearing officer may be from the county office of education or the Office of Administrative Hearings, which provides hearing officers for a variety of administrative hearings throughout the state. If an impartial administrative panel conducts the expulsion hearing, no individual on the panel may be a member of the district's governing board or employed on the staff of the school in which the student is enrolled.

Is a student denied a fair hearing if all members of the administrative panel are teachers employed by the school district? No, according to a 1982 California Supreme Court decision (*John A. v. San Bernardino City Unified School District*). John was expelled from school for his involvement in a fight after a football game. The county board of education adopted the governing board's expulsion order, and John sought court intervention to overturn the expulsion. Among other arguments, John urged the court to reverse his expulsion because teachers have a "built-in bias in disciplinary matters against students" (p. 308). To the court, potential bias in and of itself was not sufficient to reverse the expulsion. If fairness requires a total absence of preconception in the mind of the judge, the court wrote, "'no one has ever had a fair trial and no one ever will' because all have attitudes which affect them in judging situations" (p. 309). Because none of the administrative panel members was on the staff of the school where John was enrolled (as required by the Education Code) when the fight occurred, John's argument was rejected and his expulsion upheld.

Unlike criminal and civil proceedings, expulsion hearings are not subject to the technical rules of evidence. Evidence is considered relevant and admissible in an expulsion hearing if it is the kind of evidence upon which reasonable persons are accustomed to rely in the conduct of serious affairs. Testimony by a student witness in an expulsion hearing is privileged, like testimony in court (Educ. Code § 48918.6). This means student witnesses can testify without fear of subsequent legal action for defamation of character. Section 48918.6 was enacted in response to an incident where a student was sued for defamation after reporting another student's comment that he wanted to kill people. Although the lawsuit was dismissed, the reporting student and her family incurred approximately $40,000 in legal expenses.

An expulsion hearing resembles an informal trial, with each side presenting opening statements, documentary evidence, questioning witnesses, making legal arguments if appropriate, and concluding with a closing statement. A record of the hearing must be made that is clear enough to permit a reasonably accurate and complete written transcription. In criminal law, evidence obtained in violation of the Fourth Amendment of the Constitution of the United States is inadmissible under the exclusionary rule. The Fourth Amendment prohibits unreasonable searches (e.g., a search without reasonable cause). The question of whether the exclusionary rules applies to expulsion hearings arose in a 1984 California court of appeal decision (*Gordon J. v. Santa Ana Unified School District*). Gordon was approached by the vice principal of his high school and asked to turn out his pockets. The vice principal's suspicions were based on what the court characterized as "stale information, previous misbehavior, and the student's unusually heavy use of a telephone" (p. 532). Marijuana was found in Gordon's pocket. Gordon was expelled for a year and challenged the expulsion in court. Gordon argued that because he was searched in violation of the Fourth Amendment, the evidence obtained during the search should not have been used against him in a disciplinary proceeding. While the court agreed that the vice principal did not have sufficient cause for a lawful search of Gordon's pockets, the court declined to extend the exclusionary rule to high school disciplinary proceedings. A student may therefore be disciplined on the basis of evidence obtained in violation of the Fourth Amendment, though this area of the law remains murky and school officials are advised to have reasonable cause to conduct a search. The law regarding student searches is discussed in Chapter 10.

If an allegation of committing or attempting to commit sexual assault or battery is the basis for the expulsion hearing, special rules may be used for questioning of the complaining witness. The complaining witness must be given five days notice prior to being called to testify and is allowed to have up to two adult support persons present. Evidence of specific instances of the complaining witness's prior sexual conduct is presumed inadmissible, absent a determination that extraordinary circumstances exist requiring the evidence to be heard. Prior to determining if such evidence may be heard, the complaining witness must be given notice and an opportunity to present opposition to the introduction of the evidence. Under no circumstances is reputation or opinion evidence regarding the sexual behavior of the complaining witness admissible.

Regardless of the act at issue in the expulsion hearing, there is another unique circumstance in which a witness may not have to testify in the usual manner. A hearing officer, administrative panel, or governing board may determine that the disclosure of either the identity of a witness or the testimony of that witness would subject the witness to an unreasonable risk of psychological or physical harm. In this scenario, the testimony of the witness is introduced through a sworn declaration examined solely by the hearing officer, administrative panel, or governing board. A copy of the declaration is given to the student with the name and identity of the witness redacted. The use of a declaration under these circumstances is also appropriate even if a subpoena is issued for the witness to testify at the expulsion hearing.

The individual or group of individuals charged with determining if expulsion is warranted at the conclusion of the hearing may meet in closed session for deliberation. However, if any other individual is admitted to the closed session aside from the hearing officer, administrative panel, or governing board (as the case may be), the student, the student's parent, and legal counsel may also attend the closed-session deliberations.

If an expulsion hearing is conducted before a hearing officer or administrative panel, a recommendation regarding whether to expel must be made to the governing board within three days after the hearing's conclusion. If expulsion is not recommended, the expulsion proceedings are terminated and the student is immediately returned to a classroom instructional program, a rehabilitation program, or any combination of these programs. The superintendent or superintendent's designee determines the student's placement after consultation with school district personnel, including the student's teachers and the student's parent(s). A decision not to recommend expulsion is final.

Final Determination by the Governing Board

If a hearing officer or administrative panel recommends expulsion, findings of fact in support of the recommendation must be prepared and submitted to the governing board. If the governing board itself conducts the expulsion hearing, a decision regarding whether to expel must be made within ten school days. For a hearing held by a hearing officer or administrative panel, a decision to expel by the governing board must be made within forty school days after the date of the student's removal. In either situation, the student may make a written request to delay the decision.

Failure to observe the applicable ten- or forty-day time period does not invalidate a governing board's decision to expel a student (*Board of Education v. Sacramento County Board of Education,* 2001). In *Sacramento County Board of Education,* the governing board expelled a student for possession of a pipe bomb. Due to a summer break occurring after the expulsion hearing but before the governing board's vote to expel, there was disagreement as to whether the forty-day time period was met. Adopting the student's position, the county board of education to which the expulsion order had been appealed reversed the expulsion order after determining that the governing board took longer than forty days to issue an expulsion order. The governing board petitioned a court to reverse the county board of education. The court agreed with the governing board, holding that a failure to adhere to the forty-day time period does not invalidate an order to expel.

The findings of fact and recommendation submitted to the governing board can be based only on evidence from the expulsion hearing. The governing board can accept a recommendation for expulsion in one of two ways. First, the governing board can accept the recommendation based on a review of the findings of fact and recommendation submitted by the hearing officer or administrative panel. Education Code Section 48918 (f) requires a decision by a governing board to expel a student to be "based upon substantial evidence relevant to the charges adduced at the expulsion hearing or hearings." Although hearsay evidence is admissible in an expulsion hearing, an expulsion cannot be based solely on hearsay evidence. Alternatively, the governing board can order a supplementary hearing. If the supplementary hearing results in a recommendation for expulsion, the governing board can adopt the recommendation.

As in the initial decision to recommend expulsion, a governing board may or may not be able to exercise discretion in ordering expulsion. As noted in cell D1 of Table 9.1, a governing board must order expulsion for a student who commits an act described in cell A1. All other offenses in column A permit the governing board to exercise discretion in determining whether to order expulsion as noted in cells D2 and D3. To order expulsion for all acts aside from those in cell A1, a governing board must determine that the student committed both the act and either of the following, as noted in cells C2 and C3:

- Other means of correction are not feasible or have repeatedly failed to bring about proper conduct.
- Due to the nature of the act, the presence of the student causes a continuing danger to the physical safety of the student or others.

This is the same analysis that occurs during the expulsion hearing to determine if a recommendation for expulsion to the governing board can be made for an act aside from those included in cell A1.

A written notice of the governing board's decision to expel must be sent to the student's parent and be accompanied by:

- Notice of the right to appeal the expulsion to the county board of education
- Notice of the educational alternative placement to be provided to the pupil during the time of expulsion
- Notice of the obligation of the parent or student to inform the student's next school of the basis for the expulsion acts listed in cell A3

The expulsion order is then placed in the student's record and sent to any California public elementary, middle, or high school in which the student subsequently enrolls. After adopting a recommendation for expulsion, a governing board may suspend enforcement of the expulsion. Suspension of an order to expel is detailed later in this section.

A governing board must maintain a record of each expulsion, including the cause for each expulsion. The Education Code refers to this record as a "nonprivileged, disclosable public record" (Educ. Code § 48918 (k)). A federal law, entitled the Family Educational Rights and Privacy Act (FERPA), however, classifies this type of record as personally identifiable information that cannot generally be disclosed unless a specific provision of FERPA permits disclosure (e.g., court order, subpoena, written consent for disclosure, etc.). A school district's receipt of federal funding is conditioned on compliance with FERPA. In response to a request for an expulsion record, should a school district release the record and risk a loss of federal funding, or not release the record and violate Section 48918 (k)?

A California court addressed this query in a 2002 decision (*Rim of the World Unified School District v. Superior Court*). In *Rim of the World Unified School District*, the school district received a request for expulsion records and did not release the records. The school district reasoned that the terms of FERPA, as a federal law, controlled over Education Code Section 48918 (k), which is a state law. The court agreed with the school district because section 48918 (k) presents an "obvious obstacle to accomplishing Congress' purpose and objectives in enacting FERPA" (p. 1399). The court also declared that Education Code Section 48918 (j) requiring the governing board to announce an expulsion order in open session violated FERPA. Violating Sections 48918 (j) and (k) to adhere to FERPA is the appropriate choice for a school district faced with our initial question.

A determination by a governing board to expel a student does not necessarily mean the student will be expelled. A governing board may suspend enforcement of an order to expel. Education Code Section 48917 governs suspension of an order to expel. A suspension of an order to expel is a probationary reprieve for the student. During suspension of the expulsion order, the student is on probationary status and on a rehabilitation plan. The suspension cannot exceed one year and may require the student to enroll in a different school, class, or program that is "deemed appropriate for rehabilitation" of the student. The suspension order can include a rehabilitation program mandating parent involvement. Refusal or failure of a parent to abide by this requirement, however, cannot be considered by a governing board to determine whether the student satisfactorily completed the rehabilitation program. May enforcement of an expulsion order based on one of the acts mandating expulsion (e.g., possession of a firearm, brandishing a knife, etc.) be suspended? Yes, according to a 1997 California attorney general opinion (80 Ops. Atty. Gen. 85). It is therefore possible for a student to avoid the implementation of an expulsion order for even the most serious acts.

A student may have his or her probationary status revoked for committing any of the acts in Education Section 48900 or violating any of the district's rules and regulations governing student conduct. Revoking the suspension of an expulsion order may result in the student being expelled pursuant to the terms of the original expulsion order. A student who successfully completes the student's rehabilitation assignment must be reinstated to a school of the district (assuming the student was placed elsewhere as part of his or her rehabilitation program) and may have all records of the expulsion proceeding expunged from his or her record. A governing board's decision to suspend an order to expel does not affect the time period and requirements for filing an appeal of the expulsion order.

Post-Expulsion Educational Programming

A student expelled for one of the acts listed in cell A1 of Table 9.1 must be placed in a program that is appropriately prepared to accommodate students who exhibit discipline problems (Educ. Code § 48915 (d)). The program cannot be at a comprehensive elementary, middle, junior, or senior high school, nor at the school site the student attended when he or she committed the offense warranting expulsion. If a student is being expelled for any other act (cells A2 and A3 of Table 9.1), the student generally must also be referred to a program of study that meets this requirement. In the case of a student expelled for an act in cells A2 or A3 of Table 9.1, however, a county superintendent of schools may certify that an alternative program of study is not available away from a comprehensive campus. Thus the student may be permitted to attend a comprehensive campus for the duration of his or her expulsion. The governing board may also require a student who is expelled for a drug or alcohol offense to enroll, with the permission of the student's parent(s), in a county-supported drug rehabilitation program prior to readmission (Educ. Code § 48916.5). And, as with suspension, a school district may require a student to perform community service on school grounds during nonschool hours in lieu of expulsion or a portion thereof (Educ. Code § 48900.6).

A plan of rehabilitation must accompany a student's expulsion order (Educ. Code § 48916 (b)). Section 48916 (b) suggests, but does not require, the following elements for a plan of rehabilitation: "periodic review as well as assessment at the time of review for admission," and "recommendations for improved academic performance, tutoring, special education assessments, job training, counseling, employment, community service, and other rehabilitative programs." The governing board must also provide a description of the readmission process to a student for whom expulsion is ordered.

Readmission Following Expulsion

Education Code Section 48916 governs readmission of a student after expulsion. For a student expelled for an act in cell A1 of Table 9.1, the governing board must set a date one year from the expulsion on which to review readmission of the student to a district school. On a case-by-case basis, an earlier date for review may be set. For all other acts resulting in an expulsion, the governing board must set a date for reviewing readmission not later than the last day of the semester following the semester in which the expulsion occurred. A student expelled during summer session or the intersession period of a year-long program must have the student's review for readmission set by the governing board no later than the last day of the semester following the summer session or intersession period in which the expulsion occurred.

A school district's governing board must adopt rules and regulations establishing a procedure for the filing and review of requests for readmission. A governing board must readmit a student who completes the readmission process unless the governing board determines that the student did not meet the conditions of the student's rehabilitation plan or continues to pose a danger to campus safety or to other students or employees of the school district. If readmission is denied, the governing board must determine if the student is to remain in the current alternative educational program or attend another program, which may include a placement serving expelled students such as a county community school. A denial of readmission must be accompanied by written notice to the student and the student's parent describing the reasons for the denial and a determination of the educational program for the student. The student must enroll in the educational program chosen by the governing board unless the parent(s) elect to enroll the student in another school district.

Appeal of an Expulsion Order

After a governing board orders an expulsion, a student has thirty days to file an appeal with the county board of education. Education Code Sections 48919 to 48924 govern the appeal of an expulsion order. A student on probationary status under a suspended expulsion order may not challenge revocation of the student's probationary status and the subsequent implementation of the expulsion order if the student did not appeal the expulsion order. The appeal must be heard within twenty school days. The appeal is heard by the county board of education, or in a class one or class two county, by a hearing officer or impartial administrative panel. An appeal heard by a county board of education results in a final decision by the county board of education. An appeal heard by a hearing officer or impartial administrative panel, however, results in a recommendation to the county board of education regarding the appeal. Like the governing board's role in the expulsion process, the county board of education has the final say on an expulsion appeal.

The time period for calculating the time to file an appeal starts on the day the governing board votes to expel the student. A request for an appeal by a student must be accompanied by a simultaneously written request to the school district for a copy of the written transcripts and supporting documents from the expulsion hearing. The school district must provide the student with the requested documents within ten school days. The student then files these documents with the county board of education. The student must pay for the cost of the transcript unless the student's parent certifies that he or she cannot reasonably afford the cost of the transcript because of limited income or exceptional necessary expenses. If the student pays for the cost of the transcript and the expulsion is reversed on appeal, the school district must reimburse the student for the cost of the transcript.

A county board of education must adopt rules and regulations for expulsion appeals. Regardless of whether the county board of education or a hearing officer or administrative panel hears an expulsion appeal, the rules and regulations must detail and explain:

- Requirements for filing a notice of appeal
- Setting of a hearing date
- Furnishing of notice to the student and the governing board regarding the appeal

- Furnishing of a copy of the expulsion hearing record to the county board of education
- Procedures for the conduct of the hearing
- Preservation of the record of the appeal

Hearing officers and administrative hearing panel members may not be members of the governing board of the school district or employees of the school district from which the appeal is filed. A hearing officer or member of the administrative panel that oversaw the expulsion hearing cannot hear the appeal. Three school days after the hearing officer or administrative panel hears the appeal, a recommended decision, including any findings or conclusions required for that decision, must be sent to the county board of education.

The county board of education's review of the governing board's decision to expel is limited to four questions:

- Whether the governing board acted without or in excess of its jurisdiction
- Whether there was a fair hearing before the governing board
- Whether there was a prejudicial abuse of discretion in the hearing
- Whether there was relevant and material evidence that, in the exercise of reasonable diligence, could not have been produced or that was improperly excluded at the hearing before the governing board

A proceeding without or in excess of jurisdiction "includes, but is not limited to, a situation where an expulsion hearing is not commenced within the requisite time period, where an expulsion order is not based on an act in Education Code Section 48900, or a situation involving acts not related to a school activity or attendance" (Educ. Code § 48922 (b)). An abuse of discretion is established if "school officials have not met the procedural requirements for an expulsion, the decision to expel is not supported by the findings required by [Education Code] Section 48915," or the "findings are not supported by the evidence" (Educ. Code § 48922 (c)). However, a determination of an abuse of discretion does not result in an automatic reversal of the expulsion order. The county board of education must also determine that the abuse of discretion was prejudicial, meaning that it unfairly tainted the expulsion decision.

The county board of education has four options after its review of the underlying hearing and decision by the governing board: remand to the governing board for reconsideration or adoption of required findings, order a new hearing, affirm the expulsion, or reverse the expulsion. The county board of education may remand the matter to the governing board for reconsideration, or order a new hearing if the county board of education finds that "relevant and material evidence exists which, in the exercise of reasonable diligence, could not have been produced or which was improperly excluded at the hearing" (Educ. Code § 48923 (a)). If reconsideration is ordered, the student may be readmitted to school pending the reconsideration. A new hearing must conform to the requirements of Education Code Section 48918 discussed earlier. If the county board of education determines that the decision of the governing board is not supported by the findings required by Section 48915, but evidence supporting the findings exists in the record of the proceedings, the county board of education must remand the matter to the governing board for adoption of the required findings. A remand for adoption of the required findings does not result in an additional hearing for the student; however, the final action of the governing board to expel upon adoption of the required findings must be taken consistent with Education Code Sections 48918 (j) and (k) as judicially interpreted. Subdivisions (j) and (k) contain the notice requirements discussed on page 360 and the governing board's obligation to maintain a record of each expulsion.

Otherwise, the county board of education must enter an order either affirming or reversing the decision of the governing board. If the county board reverses the governing board's decision to expel the student, the county board of education may direct the governing board to expunge the records of the school district of any references to the expulsion action. A reversal of the expulsion also requires that the expulsion is deemed not to have occurred. A county board of education can remand or reverse a governing board's decision to expel only for the circumstances noted earlier in this section. In 1997, the California attorney general opined that a decision by the county board of education to reverse a governing board's decision for any other reason is an abuse of discretion (80 Ops. Atty. Gen 91). Does the governing board have any recourse if the county board of education reverses the governing board? Yes; the 1997 attorney general opinion also concludes that the governing board may seek judicial review of the county board of education's decision.

DISCIPLINE AND SPECIAL EDUCATION

Additional care and attention must be given to the discipline of students who are, or are suspected of being, eligible for special education services under the Individuals with Disabilities Education Act (IDEA). IDEA, a comprehensive statutory scheme governing the rights of children with disabilities and the duties of school districts in educating these children, is discussed in detail in Chapter 8. Because special education law contains numerous unique terms, phrases, and concepts, readers should consult, or perhaps read in its entirety, Chapter 8 prior to reading this section.

For purposes of completing the discussion of student discipline, it is important to note the additional rights IDEA affords students who are, or are suspected of being, eligible for special education services. The key inquiry to determine if these additional rights apply in a given situation is whether or not the discipline will result in a "change in placement." If no change in placement results from the discipline, the student can be disciplined in the same manner as a general education student. However, if the discipline will result in a change in placement, special procedures detailed more fully in upcoming subsections must be followed.

Different Types of Disciplinary Removals

The best way to understand when a change in placement occurs is to view disciplinary removals in four different categories. These categories are a short-term removal of ten days or less (category one); a series of short-term removals of more than ten cumulative days that do not constitute a change in placement (category two); a series of short-term removals of more than ten cumulative days that do constitute a change in placement (category three); and long-term removals of more than ten consecutive school days (category four). Categories one and two are not considered a change in placement. Categories three and four are considered a change in placement.

When is a special education student removed for purposes of the four noted categories? A special education student is "removed" when the student cannot continue to progress in the general curriculum, receive the services in the student's individualized education program (IEP), and/or participate with nondisabled children to the extent the student would in the student's current placement. Given this broad definition, a removal can include an in-school suspension (e.g., spend the last two periods of the day in a detention room without instruction) and a bus suspension. In the latter circumstance, an inability to get to school clearly prevents a student from receiving the services in the student's IEP. A school district is required to provide an alternative form of transportation to a student at no cost to the parent if the student is excluded from bus transportation and transportation is specified in the student's IEP (Educ. Code § 48915.5 (c)).

Short-Term Removals

Categories one and two are short-term removals because they do not constitute a change in placement. Special education students in categories one and two may be disciplined in the same manner as general education students. A student in category one has no right to educational services during the student's disciplinary removal. However, school districts do have to provide educational services to students in category two on the eleventh day of the student's disciplinary removal. The educational services made available must constitute a free appropriate public education (FAPE).

For example, if Amy (our hypothetical special education student in Chapter 8) is suspended from school for five days, she is a category one student to whom no special education services are owed. The difficult question is whether Amy is entitled to special education services after being suspended for five days in one month, an additional five days a few months later, and after a few more months, an additional three days. In this latter scenario, Amy may be subject to a change in placement (thereby moving her from category two to three) on the eleventh day of removal.

Long-Term Removals

Long-term removals can result from a series of short-term removals that constitute a change in placement (category three), or a single removal of more than ten consecutive days (category four). A special education student in a long-term removal is entitled to receive educational services that constitute a FAPE. A series of short-term removals may, in the aggregate, constitute a pattern of removals that is considered a change in placement. A pattern may result because of factors such as the length of each removal, the total amount of time the student is removed, and the proximity of the removals to each other. A school district can also consider whether the child's behavior in the most recent removal was similar to behavior demonstrated in prior removals (34 C.F.R. § 300.536 (a)). If the behaviors are not substantially similar, the school district could consider this to be a factor mitigating against a determination that a change in placement occurred. Determining when such a pattern of removals exists is no easy task. In the example posed with Amy, some school districts might provide services on the eleventh day to err on the side of caution.

If a dispute arises regarding a long-term removal, a parent may request a due process hearing. Stay put generally requires the school district to maintain the student in the student's last agreed upon and implemented placement until completion of the hearing or the parties agree otherwise. A significant change brought about by IDEA 2004, however, provides that a student's stay-put placement during a due process hearing concerning discipline is the disciplinary placement chosen by the school district.

If a removal constitutes a change in placement, there are three steps that a school district must undertake before further disciplining a special education student. First, the school district must immediately notify the student's parents of the disciplinary action and provide a copy of IDEA's procedural safeguards to the parents. Second, the school district must conduct a manifestation determination (i.e., determine whether the student's behavior was a manifestation of the student's disability) and convene an IEP meeting. The manifestation determination must be conducted within ten school days of the decision to change the placement of the student. Third, the IEP team must discuss behavior interventions or the necessity of a functional behavioral assessment (FBA).

Steps two and three may result in a single meeting (referred to as a manifestation determination meeting) that should be held immediately, but no later than ten school days after the date the school district decides to impose a removal that results in a change in placement. The meeting's purpose is twofold: to prevent disciplining a student for behavior that is a result of the student's disability and to determine if any changes need to be made to the student's IEP to address behavioral concerns.

A manifestation determination does not try to determine why a student committed a particular act. Rather, the inquiry focuses on the relationship between the student's behavior and the student's disability. The basic premise is that a student should not be disciplined if the student's behavior is a result of the student's disability.

IDEA 2004 provides that a special education student's conduct is a manifestation of the student's disability if:

- The conduct in question was caused by, or had a direct and substantial relationship to, the child's disability; or
- The conduct in question was the direct result of the local educational agency's failure to implement the IEP.

Thus, IDEA 2004 heightens the connection that must exist between the student's conduct and disability, or the conduct and the school district's failure to implement an IEP before the conduct is determined to be a manifestation of the student's disability.

If the members of the manifestation determination meeting determine that the behavior in question was a manifestation of the student's disability, no disciplinary action can result. Alternatively, if the determination of the meeting is that the student's behavior was not a manifestation of the disability, disciplinary rules applicable to general education students apply. In this latter scenario, all disciplinary and special education records must be sent to the final person (e.g., the principal for an expulsion) or entity (the governing board for an expulsion) charged with making a decision regarding discipline for the student.

If the student already has a behavior intervention plan (BIP), the members of the manifestation determination meeting must review the plan to determine if revision is necessary. We refer to this as an IDEA BIP to avoid confusion with the behavior intervention plan (BIP) contained in Title Five, California Code of Regulations. Chapter 8 details the purpose and function of a BIP. The IDEA BIP is akin to a behavior plan or behavior support plan and does not require the level of detail of a BIP. To further confuse matters, a BIP can serve as an IDEA BIP. If a student does not have an existing IDEA BIP when the behavior giving rise to the change in placement occurs, a school district must undertake a functional behavioral assessment (FBA), which is a federal law requirement.

IDEA does not define FBA. An FBA can consist of a file review or a formal assessment and is undertaken to determine why a student is engaging in inappropriate behavior. An FBA should not be confused with a functional analysis assessment (FAA). As we discuss in Chapter 8, an FAA is a particular type of behavior assessment that is required when the instructional/behavioral approaches in a student's IEP are ineffective. In discussing an FBA or IDEA BIP, however, the members of the manifestation determination meeting may conclude that an FAA is warranted because of the student's behavior. IDEA requires an FBA no later than ten school days after imposing the change in placement if the student does not have an existing IDEA BIP. Failure to timely complete an FBA may result in a reversal of the school district's disciplinary action by an OAH hearing officer.

Interim Alternative Educational Settings and a *Honig* Injunction

Federal law permits school districts to order a special education student to an interim alternative educational setting (IAES) for up to forty-five school days if the student carries a weapon to school or to a school function, knowingly possesses or uses illegal drugs, sells or solicits the sale of a controlled substance, or has inflicted serious bodily injury on another while at school or at a school function. A special education student committing one of these acts can be ordered to an IAES regardless of whether the act was a manifestation of the student's disability.

Aside from weapons offenses, drug offenses, or infliction of serious bodily injury, a hearing officer may order a student into an IAES for up to forty-five school days if certain criteria are met. To obtain such an order, a school district must show that maintaining the current placement of the student is substantially likely to result in injury to the child or others.

A school district may believe that a special education student presents a substantial risk of injury (to the student or others), yet not be able to meet the criteria for implementing an IAES or obtaining an administrative order to change the student's placement. A court order, referred to as a *Honig* injunction (after a 1988 U.S. Supreme Court case), can be sought by a school in order to change a student's placement. A school district must demonstrate that maintaining the student in his or her current placement is substantially likely to result in injury to the student or to others (*Honig v. Doe*). If it agrees with the school district, the court will issue an injunction permitting the school district to change the student's placement.

Students Not Yet Identified as Special Education Students

The foregoing disciplinary procedures also can apply to general education students who are not yet identified as special education students. If a school district is "deemed to have knowledge" that a general education student is a child with a disability under IDEA, the procedures applicable to disciplining special education students subject to a category three or four removal apply to the student. This inquiry also is referred to in terms of whether the school district has a "basis of knowledge." IDEA's implementing regulations identify the following circumstances in which a school district is deemed to have knowledge that a student is a child with a disability:

- The parent of the child has expressed concern in writing to personnel of the appropriate educational agency that the child is in need of special education and related services.

- The parent of the child has requested an evaluation of the child.

- The teacher of the child, or other personnel of the school district, expressed specific concerns about a pattern of behavior demonstrated by the child directly to the director of special education of the agency or to other supervisory personnel.

A school district is not deemed to have knowledge that a student is a child with a disability if the child's parent has not permitted an evaluation by the school district to determine special education eligibility, the child's parent has refused special education services, or the child has been evaluated and determined not to be eligible for special education services under IDEA.

The Office of Administrative Hearings (OAH), which adjudicates special education disputes in California, can conduct an expedited due process hearing to determine if a school district had a basis of knowledge that prevents the school district from disciplining the student as a general education student. A determination that a basis of knowledge exists will result in an order returning the student to his or her prior placement unless the parties agree otherwise.

SUMMARY

Student discipline rules are necessary for the maintenance of order in public schools. The acts for which suspension or expulsion is permissible are in Education Code Section 48900. Section 48900 and following sections were enacted in response to the U.S. Supreme Court's decision in *Goss v. Lopez. Goss* notes the type of due process required by the Fourteenth Amendment to the U.S. Constitution prior to discipline resulting in a removal from school. Suspensions of ten days or less require an informal conference and an opportunity for the student to present the student's interpretation of the events at issue. Removals from school in excess of ten school days require the more formalized procedures of an expulsion hearing.

Table 9.1 details those acts for which a student may or must be suspended and/or expelled. While Section 48900 details all of the grounds for which suspension and/or expulsion are permissible, Section 48915 notes the particular circumstances for which immediate suspension and/or a mandatory recommendation for expulsion are required. The "Big Five" are described in cell A1 and mandate immediate suspension and recommendation for expulsion. A secondary category of acts, detailed in cell A2, mandates expulsion unless inappropriate under the circumstances. All remaining acts listed in cell A3 vest discretion in school administrators on whether to recommend expulsion. Suspension for a first-time offense is not appropriate unless the student violates Education Code Section 48900 (a)–(e), the student's presence causes a danger to persons or property or threatens to disrupt the instructional process, or the student commits one of the Big Five. Nontraditional disciplinary options are also available to school administrators. These include supervised classroom suspensions, requesting parents to attend school with their child, an involuntary transfer, and community service.

All acts aside from those in cell A1 of the table require an additional finding of one of the following before the governing board can order expulsion: other means of correction are not feasible or have repeatedly failed to bring about proper conduct; or due to the nature of the act, the presence of the student causes a continuing danger to the physical safety of the student or others. The governing board reviews the findings of the individual or panel conducting the expulsion hearing and must order an expulsion of a student who commits one of the Big Five. The governing board may exercise discretion in ordering expulsion for all other acts. The governing board may also suspend an order to expel. A student may pursue an appeal of an expulsion order with the county board of education.

The Individuals with Disabilities Education Act (IDEA) contains its own requirements for the discipline of a special education student resulting in a change of placement. A change of placement may occur through a series of separate removals that are more than ten school days in the aggregate or through a single removal for longer than ten school days. For a change in placement, a school district must notify the parents and provide a copy of the IDEA's procedural safeguards, conduct a manifestation determination (which determines whether the student's behavior was a manifestation of the student's disability), and convene an individualized education program (IEP) team meeting to discuss behavior interventions. Certain offenses (drugs, weapons, and inflicting serious bodily injury) permit a school district to place a special education student in an interim alternative educational setting (IAES). A school district can also petition a court or the Office of Administrative Hearings (OAH) to change a special education student's placement.

10 | PUBLIC ACCESS, PRIVACY, AND STUDENT SEARCH AND SEIZURE

The law requires that the public's business must be conducted in public. Yet, while the public has access to governing board meetings and to the records that are generated through the business of operating schools, some matters are shielded from view. Both federal and state laws provide a cloak of privacy for students and parents. What employees do on their own time is largely beyond the purview of the school. And while school officials must maintain a safe environment for learning, students have a constitutional right to be free from unreasonable searches and seizures. Balancing the needs of the public against the privacy interests of students, parents, and employees is no easy task, but one that courts have had to address. In this chapter, we sort through the law to explain what aspects of school operation are governed by public access laws, what matters remain private, and what kinds of searches and seizures can be conducted without violating student rights.

PUBLIC ACCESS

While federal and state law offers a cloak of privacy for families and students, state law brings the affairs of government out into the open. The reason is that in a democracy, members of the public have a right to know what the governmental entities they elect and support are up to. So-called sunshine legislation is evident in open access to governmental meetings and records. We discuss both in turn.

The Brown Open Meetings Act

Added in 1953, the Ralph M. Brown Act begins by noting that "public commissions, boards and councils and other public agencies in this state exist to aid in the conduct of the people's business. It is the intent of the law that their actions be taken openly and that their deliberations be conducted openly" (Govt. Code § 54950). To this end, California courts have interpreted the law broadly and the exceptions to open meetings narrowly. The Brown Act applies to the governing boards of traditional public schools and charter schools. It also applies to the board of a nonprofit benefit corporation that is created by an elected body to exercise delegated power or that receives funds from the elected body and includes a member of that body as a voting member on its governing board. Thus, nonprofit benefit corporations formed to operate charter schools must comply with the act.

The Education Code stipulates that governing board meetings are to be conducted in accord with the terms of the Brown Act (Educ. Code § 35145 and following sections). This is true for both monthly or quarterly board meetings as well as those held at other times. In conformity with the Brown Act, the Education Code specifically provides that agendas must be posted, minutes taken and made available to the public, and members of the public able to place matters on the board agenda. In addition, every agenda for regular meetings must provide members of the public an opportunity to address the board on agenda items of interest to them. This does not preclude a board's hearing testimony on matters not on the agenda, provided that no action is taken on the matter being addressed.

Several court decisions have indicated that the open portion of a governing board meeting constitutes a limited open forum; as a result, the authority of governing boards to control what persons say is curtailed. A case in point involves two parents in the Vista Unified School District who challenged a governing board bylaw permitting the board president to terminate a presenter's comments if the presenter persists, after being warned, to engage in improper conduct or remarks (*Leventhal v. Vista Unified School District*, 1997). At a board meeting, the parents attempted to address the qualifications and performance of the school superintendent, including his social relationship with a board member. At one point the board member responded, triggering an animated exchange. The board president cut the parents off, noting that personnel criticisms could not be made in a public board meeting. Later, the parents filed a lawsuit in federal court, contending the restriction violated their First Amendment right of free speech.

The federal judge noted that under both the Brown Act and the Education Code, open board meetings are limited open forums, meaning that they are open to public comment on matters within the subject matter of the jurisdiction of the governing board. As such, the district's interests in controlling public commentary "cannot outweigh the public's fundamental right to engage in robust public discourse on school issues" (p. 957). The school board argued that a provision of the

Brown Act permitting closed sessions for personnel matters specifically lists hearing complaints or charges against an employee unless the employee requests a public session. Thus, the school board president acted appropriately in limiting criticism. But the court did not agree. The Brown Act favors open meetings, and the personnel exception under Government Code Section 54957 cannot preclude a person from raising personnel issues in public session. The board can then deliberate about them in closed session. In effect, the privacy rights of district employees cannot trump the First Amendment rights of members of the public. Further, the court noted, permitting a board member to criticize members of the public who address the board but then prohibiting the latter from responding is a form of viewpoint discrimination. We discussed a similar decision to this effect in Chapter 6 (*Baca v. Moreno Valley Unified School District*, 1996). Since there was no disruption of the public meeting, the board president was in error when he terminated the parents' right to speak. The court left open the possibility of channeling calls for actual disciplinary action against an employee to closed session under the personnel exception of the Brown Act.

Key provisions. While the Brown Act and its interpretive law are quite extensive, a few of the more salient features are summarized here. First, public meetings are to be open and public; though as described later, the board may go into executive session for specific purposes after announcing in open session the intention to do so. Meetings must be held within the boundaries of the district or the charter school's serving area except in certain situations (e.g., to interview a potential employee from another district). Meetings must be held in facilities that accommodate persons without reference to race, religion, color, national origin, ancestry, sex, and disability and that do not require a payment or purchase from attendees. An agenda describing each item of business or discussion for both open and executive sessions must be posted in an accessible location at least seventy-two hours before a regular meeting. If requested, the agenda must be made available in appropriate alternative formats for persons with disabilities and include information about accommodations for them at the meeting. While agenda items need not be described in detail, they should be understandable to the average citizen.

Special meetings of the governing board may be called at any time by the board president or by a majority of the board (Govt. Code § 54956). This requires a twenty-four-hour written notice both to board members and the media describing the time and place of the meeting and the business to be transacted or discussed. The notice also must be posted in a place accessible to the public at least twenty-four hours prior to the special meeting. No other business may be conducted at a special meeting beyond that described in the notice. The notice of adjournment of both regular and special meetings is to be conspicuously posted on or near the door where the meeting was held within twenty-four hours of adjournment. Emergency meetings are permitted when some crippling activity or disaster strikes. In this event, the media who have so requested are to be notified by telephone one hour prior to the emergency meeting in lieu of the twenty-four-hour notice and posting requirement for special meetings. If telephone service is not available, the media are to be notified of the purpose and actions taken at the meeting as soon as possible. Emergency meetings may be held in executive session if agreed to by two-thirds of those members present or, if less than two-thirds are in attendance, by unanimous vote. After the meeting, the minutes must be posted for at least ten days in an accessible place.

The governing board may use video teleconferencing to receive public comment or testimony and to deliberate. However, board members may not use technological devices or otherwise communicate among themselves to reach a collective concurrence (Govt. Code § 54952.2). The California attorney general has advised that this provision precludes the use of e-mail for this purpose (84 Ops. Atty. Gen. 30, 2001). If video teleconferencing is used, the agenda must be posted at all teleconference locations and a quorum of the governing board must participate from within the boundaries of the district.

A member of the public does not have to sign a register or provide other information as a condition of attendance. If an attendance sheet is circulated during the meeting, there must be an indication that signing it is voluntary. Audio- and video-taping of open sessions are permitted unless disruptive. An official audio- or videotape of the session is a public record available for inspection without charge, though it may be destroyed after thirty days. Broadcasting of open meetings is permissible unless it would prove disruptive. There is no requirement that minutes or recordings must be made during closed sessions.

Government Code Section 54957.9 provides that if a meeting is willfully interrupted and order cannot be restored by removing disruptive persons, the members of the governing board may order the room cleared and continue in session. The media must be allowed to attend, except for those who are involved in the disturbance. The governing board may establish a procedure for readmitting persons not responsible for the disruption. Though the First Amendment protects robust interaction among members of the public and board members during an open session, its protection is not unlimited. A case in point involves the arrest of an attendee after he dumped bags of garbage on the floor of a multipurpose room in an elementary school where the governing board meeting was being held. The incident occurred during the portion of the meeting reserved for public comments.

The speaker had sought to demonstrate how derelict the school was in preventing high school students in the district from littering neighborhoods surrounding the campus. He did take the precaution of spreading a tarp on the floor and donning gloves before opening the bags and pouring their contents on the tarp. Some of the contents spilled out onto the floor. The principal of the elementary school was present and warned the speaker that the room would be used as the school's cafeteria the next day. The meeting was adjourned and the police called. Meanwhile, the speaker continued talking to the audience and dumping trash. The police advised that they were without authority to make an arrest, whereupon the superintendent made a citizen's arrest of the speaker for willfully disturbing a public meeting. The speaker filed a lawsuit against the district, its board members, and its superintendent for, among other things, violating his First Amendment rights.

The appellate court affirmed dismissal of the lawsuit. It noted that the speaker was arrested for violating California Penal Code Section 403, which provides in part that anyone who willfully disturbs or breaks up any lawful assembly or meeting is guilty of a misdemeanor. The California Supreme Court interpreted this statute narrowly in 1970 to pertain to disruptive actions, not to the content of the speech. Here, the appellate court agreed with the jury that the speaker had crossed the line when he began dumping the garbage. His actions were not a legitimate part of the meeting but rather had become a significant impairment of it (*McMahon v. Albany Unified School District*, 2002).

Education Code Section 35147 provides that meetings of school site councils and advisory committees must be open to the public and members of the public given a chance to address agenda items. Notice of the meetings must be posted at the school or other appropriate place accessible to the public at least seventy-two hours before the meeting. The notice is to specify date, time, and location and to include an agenda. Action cannot be taken on matters not on the school site agenda unless those present unanimously vote to take immediate action on a matter that came to their attention after the agenda was posted. Questions or brief statements made at meetings by members of the council, committee, or public that do not significantly affect students or employees or that can be resolved informally need not be included on the agenda. If a person complains about a violation of these procedures, the matter is to be reconsidered at the next meeting following an opportunity for public comment. Finally, any materials provided to a school site council must be made available under the terms of the California Public Records Act to a member of the public upon request.

Defining open meetings. The term "open meetings" as used in the Brown Act applies both to gatherings at which action is taken and to meetings where deliberation takes place. Thus, an informal luncheon where school board members talk among themselves about school matters is governed by the act. However, advisory committees composed solely of board members and consisting of less than a quorum are not legislative bodies subject to the terms of the act unless they are standing committees (Govt. Code § 54952 (b)). For example, meetings of an ad hoc advisory committee comprised solely of less than a quorum of board members to advise the full board of qualifications of candidates for appointment to a vacant board position are not open to the public (*Henderson v. Los Angeles City Board of Education*, 1978).

A 1993 California appellate court decision sheds some light on the scope of the open meetings portion of the Brown Act. The case involved a school board faced with complaints from some parents about a recently adopted reading series known as "Impressions." In accord with board policy, two committees were appointed, one to review the merits of the complaints and a second to hear testimony from the first committee and then make a recommendation to the board about retaining the series. During this time, district staff members sent board members information about the work of the committees, including the views of the director of instruction about the issue. A quorum of board members met with members of the school's curriculum council to view a videotape relating to censorship and to be brought up to date on parent complaints. The curriculum council was overseeing the work of the two committees. The school board eventually voted in open session to retain the series after hearing all sides to the issue. Parents upset about the way the matter was handled filed suit. Among their arguments were that the two committees should have held their deliberations in public session and that the board violated the Brown Act by viewing the videotape with the curriculum council.

The court ruled that the two committees were subject to the Brown Act. Government Code Section 54952 provides that the term "legislative body" includes a "commission, committee, board, or other body of a local agency, whether permanent or temporary, decisionmaking or advisory, created by charter, ordinance, resolution, or formal action of a legislative body." The fact that the superintendent and his staff actually set up the committees and appointed their members was irrelevant, because they were acting under a formal board policy dealing with complaints about instructional materials. The court also agreed with the parents that because a quorum of the board viewed the videotape with the curriculum council, the viewing constituted a "meeting" under the Brown Act. In addition to viewing the tape, the board engaged in discussion with members of the council. The court noted that the Brown Act is not limited to gatherings where a quorum of board members takes some form of formal action. Deliberative gatherings are included as well. However, the sending of information by district staff to members of the governing board did not involve communication among board members or any collective action and so did not violate the act. Whether the board's violations of the Brown Act tainted its decision reached in open session to continue the "Impressions" reading series was a matter to be determined by the trial court (*Frazer v. Dixon Unified School District*, 1993).

Exceptions to open meetings. The Brown Act lists a number of exceptions to holding government meetings in open session. Among them are real property transactions discussed with the governing board's negotiators, provided the property being discussed and the persons with whom the negotiators will deal have been announced in open session (Govt. Code § 54956.8). Another exception is conferring with legal counsel in closed session on existing or anticipated litigation (Govt. Code § 54956.9). The attorney general has advised that this exception encompasses discussing and taking action on proposed settlement of lawsuits (75 Ops. Atty. Gen. 14, 1992). The attorney general also has advised that a school board member may not publicly disclose information that was received and properly discussed in closed session concerning pending litigation unless authorized by law to do so (80 Ops. Atty. Gen. 231, 1997).

The personnel exception specifies that closed sessions are permissible for considering the "appointment, employment, evaluation of performance, discipline, or dismissal of a public employee or to hear complaints about or charges brought against the employee by another person or employee unless the employee requests a public session" (Govt. Code § 54957). The purpose of the personnel exception is to protect employees from public embarrassment and to permit free and candid discussions of personnel matters by members of the governing board. But its scope is limited. A principal in the Los Angeles Unified School District was unsuccessful in contending that the superintendent and area superintendent had breached the personnel exception when they commented critically to newspaper reporters about the principal's handling of disturbances at his high school. The comments were later reported in the *Los Angeles Times*. The appellate court affirmed the trial court's dismissal of the lawsuit. Both courts found the personnel exception inapplicable, because the newspaper comments were not the equivalent of a personnel evaluation. The appellate court added that the principal's argument "turns the Brown Act on its head, because the general purpose of the Brown Act is to *increase* public awareness of issues bearing on the democratic process" (emphasis in original). Citing the *Leventhal* decision discussed earlier, the judges noted that the personnel exception must be read narrowly (*Morrow v. Los Angeles Unified School District*, 2007).

The degree to which the personnel exception limits what board members can discuss in closed session was addressed in a 2001 California court of appeal ruling.

The case involved a school governing board's indication on several meeting agendas that closed meetings would be conducted to evaluate the superintendent's performance. Plaintiffs contended that the board violated the Brown Act by discussing only the form to be used for evaluation and not the superintendent's performance, then later taking action to find the evaluation sufficiently positive to renew the superintendent's contract. The appellate court rejected the contention. Evaluation of performance as used in Section 54957, the judges observed, may be confined to a particular aspect of job performance and may include discussion of the means of evaluation. Similarly, providing the superintendent with positive feedback about the evaluation during closed session is part of the evaluation process (*Duval v. Board of Trustees*).

When the governing board decides to hold a closed session on a specific complaint or charge against an employee, the employee is entitled to written notice within twenty-four hours of the right to have the matter held in open session. There must be a specific complaint or charge to trigger the closed meeting option. Under the Education Code, a governing board has an absolute right not to reelect probationary teachers to employment for any reason without a hearing. Does a negative evaluation of a probationary teacher constitute a specific complaint or charge sufficient to give the teacher the right to a twenty-four-hour notice to request an open meeting? No, according to a 1999 California court of appeal ruling. The twenty-four-hour requirement pertains only to specific complaints and not to employee appointment, employment, evaluation of performance, discipline, or dismissal. The evaluations of the teachers in this case did not fall into the specific complaint category. Rather, they were evaluations of performance (*Fischer v. Los Angeles Unified School District*, 1999).

By contrast, a high school football coach who also was a tenured instructor was successful in bringing such a claim against the Vista Unified School District's governing board when it voted in closed session to remove him from his coaching assignment with no loss in pay. The California Interscholastic Federation (CIF), which supervises interscholastic athletic competition in the state in consultation with the California Department of Education, ruled that the coach had used undue influence in the enrollment of an Australian student to play football. CIF placed the school's athletic program on probation, suspended its membership in the federation, and ordered the school district to review the matter and take whatever actions it deemed appropriate with regard to the coach. The school board scheduled a special closed meeting to address these matters. One of the items on the agenda was "public employee discipline/dismissal/release." The coach alleged that the board violated the Brown Act when it did not inform him within twenty-four hours of specific complaints against him in the form of presentations at the meeting by the school superintendent and an associate superintendent who also served as CIF board chair. The appellate court agreed. When the school officials presented the CIF undue influence finding against the coach to the governing board, it evolved into a specific complaint or charge against him by another person or employee. This triggered the twenty-four-hour notice, which would have given him a chance to clear his name and avoid disciplinary action. Thus, the board violated the act (*Bell v. Vista Unified School District*, 2000). It is apparent from this decision and several others along the same lines that when deliberation strays from personnel evaluation to discuss specific complaints and possible disciplinary action, the twenty-four-hour notice requirement comes into play.

Another important exception to public meetings is that of conducting closed sessions for conferring with labor negotiators regarding salaries, salary schedules, and fringe benefits. However, prior to going into executive session, the governing board must disclose the identities of its representatives in open session (Govt. Code § 54957.6). The attorney general has advised that a county board of education may not meet in closed session under this section to consider salaries or compensation paid in the form of fringe benefits to certificated or classified employees of the county superintendent because, while the county board has an interest in the ultimate results of negotiation, the superintendent, and not the board, is the employer (85 Ops. Atty. Gen. 77, 2002).

Following the closed session, the board must reconvene in public session to disclose the actions taken in closed session and the votes of each member present (Govt. Code § 54957.1). The governing board may designate an employee to take minutes at the closed session. The minutes, which could be in the form of an audio recording, are confidential and available only to governing board members or a court if litigation ensues. Absent approval of the governing board, no person can disclose to an unauthorized person confidential information that has been presented in a closed session dealing with selected matters such as real estate, pending litigation, personnel matters, and salaries (Govt. Code § 54963). An exception is if the person questions the propriety or legality of the action taken.

Enforcement. The statute provides that every governing board member who attends a meeting where action is taken in violation of the Brown Act and intentionally deprives the public of information to which they are entitled is guilty of a misdemeanor (Govt. Code § 54959). The Brown Act also provides for civil actions against the governmental entity. If a member of the public or the media believes a violation has occurred or may occur, the person first must contact the entity, its representative, its superior agency if there is one, or the district attorney to resolve the matter. If this is not successful, the next step is to seek an injunction to prevent or stop a violation (Govt. Code § 54960). The act also provides for having the entity's action declared null and void (Govt. Code § 54960.1). In this instance, the person or district attorney must first request that the board take corrective measures by giving it written notice within ninety days of the date the questioned action was taken. The board has a period of time following receipt of the notice to do so. If nothing is done, an injunction may be sought declaring the action null and void.

The Public Records Act

Modeled on the federal Freedom of Information Act, the California Public Records Act (PRA) provides that any public record in the possession of a governmental body must be disclosed upon request unless specifically exempt (Govt. Code § 6253). The first section of this statute conveys its intent: "In enacting this chapter, the Legislature, mindful of the right of individuals to privacy, finds and declares that access to information concerning the conduct of the people's business is a fundamental and necessary right of every person in this state" (Govt. Code § 6250). The term "person" is broadly defined in the statute to include any natural person, corporation, partnership, limited liability company, firm, or association. In 2007, a California court of appeal ruled that the term encompasses a public agency and its attorney seeking disclosure of public records held by another public agency. The case involved an effort by the City of Long Beach and its attorney to seek records from the Los Angeles Unified School District relating to a school construction project that they were concerned could impact Long Beach (*Los Angeles Unified School District v. Superior Court*). Disclosable public records are open to inspection at all times during regular office hours. Upon request for copies of records, agencies have ten days—fourteen days in unusual circumstances—to determine if the information sought is disclosable and, if so, the estimated date and time when the records will be made available. Agencies may charge a fee for making copies, but the fee must be limited to the direct cost of duplication or to an amount permitted by another statute, if applicable (*North County Parents Organization v. Department of Education*, 1994). Any information that is exempted from disclosure must be deleted. Exact copies are required unless it is impracticable to do so.

Public record means "any writing containing information relating to the conduct of the public's business prepared, owned, used, or retained by any state or local agency regardless of physical form or characteristics" (Govt. Code § 6252 (e)). The term "writing" encompasses just about every form of communication, including faxes and e-mail. If records are maintained in an electronic format, they must be made available in that same format. PRA permits persons to seek a court order to enforce their rights under the statute. Those who prevail are entitled to court costs and attorneys' fees, but if the claims are deemed frivolous, requestors must pay the agency's costs and attorneys' fees (Govt. Code § 6259). The legislature's concern about protecting privacy is evident in the numerous exemptions from disclosure. The burden is placed on the agency to establish that a requested record falls into one of the exceptions when denying access. Exempted records that pertain most directly to public schools include routine preliminary drafts and memoranda not retained by the school and of little interest to the public, records pertaining to pending litigation, personnel records (but not employment contracts) that if released would constitute a clearly unwarranted invasion of personal privacy, test questions and examination data, and computer software developed by the school district (but not the public information stored on computers).

However, these exemptions are not ironclad. For example, in 2006 a California appellate court ruled that the personnel record exception does not prevent the disclosure of an investigatory file pertaining to allegations of student verbal and sexual harassment by a school superintendent. The case involved the superintendent of the Dunsmuir Joint Union High School District who resigned pursuant to a resignation agreement negotiated by his attorney and the district's attorney. Among other things, the agreement provided that the board would not release any documents in the superintendent's personnel file without the latter's approval. The investigatory report containing written summaries of numerous interviews was placed in a sealed envelope in the file. Concerned about a possible "sweetheart deal," the publisher of a newspaper sought release of the investigatory report. Overruling the trial court, the California court of appeal held that the report had to be released, because, while the superintendent as a public official has a right of privacy in his personnel file, that right is not absolute. The public also has an interest in knowing how the school board responds to allegations of misconduct by the district's chief administrator. Here, that interest far outweighed the privacy concerns of the board and superintendent. Accordingly, the investigatory report and supporting documents had to be released, but with the names of any students, parents, staff members, and faculty members redacted (*BRV, Inc. v. Superior Court,* 2006).

The home addresses and telephone numbers of school and county district employees are exempt from disclosure to anyone other than a family member or agent, an officer or employee of another education entity, an employee organization, and health benefit plan employees (Govt. Code § 6254.3). The statute permits the employee to request that such information not be released to employee organizations, and the school district must delete the employee's home address and telephone number from all its mailing lists except those necessary to contact the employee.

One recent addition to the list of exempted records involves documents that assess a local agency's vulnerability to a terrorist attack or similar criminal act and that are intended for closed-session deliberation.

In 1999 the legislature added several sections to PRA describing information collected pursuant to various state and federal statutes that may be exempt from disclosure (Govt. Code § 6254 and following sections). The purpose of this extensive list is to assist public agencies and members of the public in deciding what must be released and what must not be. The legislature intends that any statutory changes that exempt information in a public record from disclosure will be added to the list in the future. Among the items listed relating to education are information showing proof of majority support submitted by an employee organization to the Public Employment Relations Board, student records protected by provisions of the Education Code, disclosure of witness testimony presented in closed session during a student expulsion hearing under Education Code Section 48918, student personal information conveyed to school counselors under Education Code Section 49602, teacher credentialing information submitted to the California Commission on Teacher Credentialing under Education Code Section 44341, and certified school personnel examination results under Education Code Section 44289.

The statute also has a catchall provision that permits a public agency to refuse to disclose records that, on the facts of a particular case, would not serve the public interest (Govt. Code § 6255). The burden is upon the agency to establish the justification in writing. This provision has been relied on to justify refusal to release the identities of confidential law enforcement informants and the governor's daily appointment schedule. Poway Unified School District sought to rely on this section in arguing that it did not have to release a claim form against it to the media. A claim form is the first step in a lawsuit under the California Tort Claims Act. In this case, the claim form contained information about an incident in which a high school student was sodomized with a broomstick as part of an initiation ritual. The form was submitted by one of the perpetrators who sought to sue the district. The victim's identity previously had been revealed in juvenile court proceedings attended by the media, and the victim had participated in a press conference to announce the settlement of his lawsuit against the district. [In a related case, the court overruled the victim's objections to having the amount of the settlement released to the press because the public has a right to know how public funds are spent (*Copley Press, Inc. v. Superior Court,* 1998)]. The perpetrators also had consented to release of their confidential juvenile court records and files because they wanted to publicize a pattern of hazing at the high school.

The school district sought to have the claim form exempted from disclosure to a local newspaper, though the newspaper had a policy of protecting the identity of juvenile offenders and the victims of sex crimes. The trial court ordered the claim form to be released, with information about the students involved deleted. The school district appealed. The appellate court upheld the lower-court decision that claim forms do not fall within the exception for nondisclosure of records pertaining to pending litigation. Nor did protecting the privacy of those involved justify refusing to release the claim form under the "catchall" provision of Section 6255. Because the students' privacy interests already had been diminished by their own actions and because the district could still delete identifying information, the claim form had to be released. The appellate court also rejected the school district's contention that the claim form constitutes a protected educational record under the Family Educational Rights and Privacy Act, a federal law discussed in some detail later in the chapter, as defying "logic and common sense" (*Poway Unified School District v. Superior Court*, 1998, p. 776).

According to a 2004 decision from another California court of appeal, the standard that judges are to use in deciding when a complaint against an employee must be disclosed under Section 6255 is whether the documents reveal sufficient indicia to support a reasonable conclusion that the complaint was well founded (*Bakersfield City School District v. Superior Court*). Neither a finding of truth nor the imposition of employee discipline is a prerequisite to release. The case involved a newspaper's request to view a school employee's disciplinary records. The trial judge denied disclosure of some of the records, but did order the release of seven pages dealing with an incident of alleged sexual conduct and threats of violence. The names, addresses, and telephone numbers of all persons except the employee were to be deleted prior to release. The appellate court upheld this ruling.

PERSONAL PRIVACY

Personal privacy, as a matter of federal constitutional law, has its roots in a series of U.S. Supreme Court rulings beginning in 1965. That year, the Court struck down a state ban on the use of contraceptives by married couples as intruding on the right of privacy (*Griswold v. Connecticut*). The Court later extended the decision to encompass unmarried persons (*Eisenstadt v. Baird*, 1972). In 1973 the Court ruled that the right of privacy encompasses a woman's right to secure an abortion (*Roe v. Wade*). Thirty years later, the U.S. Supreme Court relied on the *Griswold* decision to invalidate a Texas law criminalizing same-sex intimate relations among consenting adults (*Lawrence v. Texas*, 2003).

Because privacy is not a specifically enumerated right in the U.S. Constitution, the Supreme Court justices inferred it from other provisions of the U.S. Constitution, most notably the word "liberty" in the due process clause of the Fourteenth Amendment ("nor shall any state deprive a person of life, liberty, or property without due process of law"). In addition to privacy, the justices similarly have protected marriage, procreation, and parental rights. These interpretations remain a matter of some contention among literalists, who argue that judges should stick to the written words. In California, inference is unnecessary because the state constitution specifically mentions privacy. Article I, Section 1 states: "All people are by nature free and independent and have inalienable rights. Among these are enjoying and defending life and liberty, acquiring, possessing, and protecting property, and pursuing and obtaining safety, happiness, and privacy." Privacy was added to the former version of this section in 1972 and retained when the section was readopted in 1974.

Minors also have privacy rights. The U.S. Supreme Court struck down a restriction on the sale or distribution of contraceptives to minors under the age of sixteen in 1977 (*Carey v. Population Services, International*). In writing for the Court a year earlier that the right to an abortion extends to minors, Justice Harry Blackmun observed that "Constitutional rights do not mature and come into being magically only when one attains the state's defined age of majority. Minors, as well as adults, are protected by the Constitution and possess constitutional rights" (*Planned Parenthood of Central Missouri v. Danforth*, 1976, p. 74). In 1997 the California Supreme Court relied on the right of privacy in the state constitution to hold that a minor cannot be required to secure permission from her parent or guardian before seeking an abortion, even if there is resort to a court if the parent or guardian refuses (*American Academy of Pediatrics v. Lungren*). In this section, we review exactly what rights of privacy employees and students have in the context of public schooling.

Employee and Student Lifestyle

Years ago, it was not unusual for schoolteachers to be dismissed because the school board disapproved of their behavior out of school. A teacher could jeopardize his or her employment by obtaining a divorce or by not going to church. More recently, a few governing boards in parts of the country have sought to terminate the contracts of teachers for cohabitation outside of marriage. For the most part, these efforts have been unsuccessful. Basically, what a school employee does outside of school is beyond the control of school authorities unless the behavior is so notorious as to jeopardize the employee's effectiveness on the job and there is evidence to support the contention.

An important ruling on teacher personal behavior came from the California Supreme Court in 1969. In *Morrison v. State Board of Education*, a case discussed in more detail in Chapter 5, the court was confronted with a schoolteacher's challenge to the termination of his credential by the California State Board of Education for unfitness to teach. The teacher resigned when confronted with evidence of a private, consensual homosexual relationship. The court ruled that, in the absence of any evidence that his behavior had rendered him unfit to teach, the state board's action was unwarranted. The California high court revisited the matter nearly ten years later, when the board of education of the Long Beach Unified School District sought to terminate a veteran elementary teacher who had been arrested for allegedly engaging in homosexual solicitation in a public restroom. Though no charges were ever filed against the teacher, the school board maintained that his behavior had rendered him unfit to teach. In rejecting the school board's arguments, the justices noted that the teacher's behavior was not known by his students, that he had testified he would not engage in such behavior again, and that he had not improperly influenced his students (*Board of Education of Long Beach Unified School District v. Jack M.*, 1977).

A teacher's claim to privacy must yield in the face of a compelling state interest. This is clear from a 1981 court of appeal decision involving a teacher in the Los Angeles Unified School District who refused to secure a chest X-ray contrary to the requirement of Education Code Section 49406. The California court of appeal noted that chest X-rays for teachers and even students are constitutional as a health measure for the protection of society in general (*Garrett v. Los Angeles City Unified School District*, 1981). Note that under Subsection (g) of the statute, a religious objection may provide an exemption from the requirement.

Several state statutes support the right of privacy and lifestyle behavior. The California Fair Employment and Housing Act prevents discrimination on a number of grounds, including marital status and sexual orientation. Education Code Section 49091.24 gives teachers the right to refuse to participate in surveys that address personal values, sexual orientation, political views, religious beliefs, and family life. One section of the Code provides that no tape recorders are permitted in classrooms without the permission of both the teacher and the principal (Educ. Code § 51512), though another provision of the Code permits teachers to tape themselves in the interest of improving their teaching (Educ. Code § 44034). Interestingly, a California court of appeal ruled in 1999 that an audiotape that students had secretly made in a classroom and turned over to the school board for use in a disciplinary action against the teacher did not violate this provision (*Evens v. Los Angeles Unified School District*). The judges rejected the teacher's claim that the taping intruded on the teacher's privacy, noting that classroom teaching by its nature is sufficiently open that a teacher must always expect public dissemination of what transpires there. Nor did the school board's use of the purloined tape violate the California Invasion of Privacy Act (Govt. Code § 630 and following sections). Except for limited law enforcement purposes, that statute restricts the use of eavesdropping via electronic devices and techniques without consent of all parties.

Students also have lifestyle rights. In 2007 the legislature reworded and broadened state antidiscrimination law by enacting a bill entitled the California Student Civil Liberties Act. Section 200 of the Education Code was amended to read, "It is the policy of the State of California to afford all persons in public schools, regardless of their disability, gender, nationality, race or ethnicity, religion, sexual orientation, or any other characteristic that is contained in the definition of hate crimes set forth in Section 422.55 of the Penal Code, equal rights and opportunities in the educational institutions of the state." The statute applies to private schools as well, except those controlled by religious organizations whose tenets are in conflict with its terms. Other provisions of the Education Code were amended to be consistent with the broadened antidiscrimination law. The legislature also enacted a law called the Safe Place to Learn Act that requires the California Department of Education to assure that schools have adopted antidiscrimination and harassment policies and disseminated them broadly. Antidiscrimination policies are to be posted in staff lounges and student government meeting rooms (Educ. Code § 234 and following sections).

Courts have relied on both constitutional and statutory provisions to protect student lifestyle rights. A federal district court in California ruled in 2003 that removing an eighth-grade student from her physical education class and making her sit in the principal's office because she told her teacher and fellow students that she is a lesbian constituted a violation of the equal protection clause of the Fourteenth Amendment to the U.S. Constitution. Accordingly, school officials were not entitled to immunity from her lawsuit (*Massey v. Banning Unified School District*). In 2007 another federal district court recognized that students have a constitutional right to express their sexuality at school. However, the right can be abused. In this case, a female student was suspended for openly and repeatedly engaging in French kissing with another female student, making out, and groping. The judge upheld the suspension. Nor was there a violation of the student's equal protection rights, because heterosexual students engaging in the same behavior would have been treated similarly. The court also recognized that students have a right under both the federal and California constitutions to informational privacy about their sexual identity. Here, however, the principal's disclosure to the mother that the student had been kissing another girl did not violate that right, because the principal was merely following through with his statutory responsibility to give the mother a factual explanation for the basis of the suspension (*Nguon v. Wolf*).

Student Records and Surveys

Student records. The Family Educational Rights and Privacy Act (FERPA) is a federal law that applies to any educational institution receiving federal funding (its provisions can be found in 20 U.S.C. § 1232 g). Basically, the law gives parents access to, and the right to challenge, the content of their children's school records. It also restricts the release of personally identifiable information contained in student records without permission of the parents or eligible student. FERPA rights transfer to a student when the student reaches eighteen or attends a postsecondary educational institution (hence the term "eligible student"). However, parents continue to have access if the student is financially dependent on the parents for federal income tax purposes. The term "parent" includes a natural parent, guardian, or any person acting as a parent in the absence of a parent or guardian. Even if the parent does not have custody of the child, the parent has access to student records unless contrary to a court order.

Each school year, the school must notify parents and students over eighteen of their right to inspect the student's education records, seek an amendment to those portions believed to be inaccurate or misleading or a violation of the Act, consent to disclosure of personally identifiable information, and file a complaint with the Family Policy Compliance Office in the U.S. Department of Education. FERPA regulations require effective notice to persons with disabilities and to non-English speakers. While fees can be charged to make copies of records on an ability-to-pay basis, educational agencies may not charge a service fee to retrieve the requested document.

An education record consists of records maintained by the school, or by a party acting for the school, regardless of where they are kept. The records can be in writing; in print; or in the form of a video- or audiotape, film, microfilm, or microfiche. Notes about particular students kept in the sole possession of school personnel for their own use and not revealed to anyone other than a temporary substitute are not within the definition and thus do not have to be disclosed. Also falling within this category are records maintained by a law enforcement unit of the school. While parents have a right of access to information about their children, they do not have access to information about other children. For example, a parent who asks to see a surveillance videotape of his student acting up on the school bus would not be entitled to view the tape if it includes the images of other students. But the parent would be entitled to see an official evaluation form on the child's misbehavior completed by the bus monitor and used as the basis for disciplinary action.

The U.S. Supreme Court ruled in 2002 that a teacher's having students grade each other's papers in class and call out the results does not violate FERPA (*Owasso Independent School District v. Falvo*). This is so because the term "education record" refers to records maintained by the school; and until grades are entered into a teacher grade book, they are not within the definition. Also not within the definition are records of the school's law enforcement entity and records about former students. Information in these records can be revealed without violating FERPA.

Personally identifiable information cannot be disclosed in any form without prior written consent from the parent or eligible student. This information encompasses the student's name, family member names, addresses, social security number, personal characteristics that would identify the student, and similar traceable information. While parents and eligible students can waive their FERPA rights, as in the case of confidential recommendations for college or employment, the waiver must be a knowing one, that is, voluntary and with full knowledge of what is being waived. The school must maintain a record of every person who requests or obtains access to a particular student's record, except for the student's parents and school officials.

Directory information falls into a different category with regard to disclosure. Directory information consists of information in an education record that would not be considered a significant invasion of privacy if revealed. It includes such general information as a student's name, date and place of birth, photograph, weight and height, and so on. By local policy, school districts can define what they mean by directory information. This information can be routinely included in school directories, athletic rosters, and the like without seeking permission from the parent or eligible student, provided that the school gives parents annual notice and an opportunity to request that such information not be released without prior written consent.

FERPA and its implementing regulations provide a long list of exceptions to nondisclosure. Chief among them is disclosure of student records to others within the school or school district who have a legitimate educational interest in the information. For example, it would not violate the act if a supervisor included the names of students in a memorandum to a teacher following a classroom observation, because the teacher needs to know which students are not being well served. Among the other more notable exceptions are disclosure to another educational institution the student wishes to attend, to accrediting bodies, to organizations that are conducting research on testing and instructional programs, and to law enforcement personnel. In this connection, the California attorney general has advised that a school district may permit the district attorney to view a school bus videotape of an assault of one student on another for law enforcement purposes without parental consent, court order, or subpoena (84 Ops. Atty. Gen. 146, 2001). FERPA also permits release of student records to appropriate persons in an emergency situation when necessary to protect the health or safety of the student or other persons. Thus, it would not violate the act to release to police officers the records of a student who threatens to blow up the school. However, a California court of appeal has ruled that the portion of Education Code Section 48918 requiring that formal action to expel a student be taken during the open session of a governing board meeting violates FERPA and is null and void (*Rim of the World Unified School District v. Superior Court*, 2002). The same is true of making the student's expulsion record available to anyone for the asking.

The Individuals with Disabilities Education Act (IDEA) provides additional protection for these students. Parents have a right to receive copies of the child's eligibility report and related documentation, as well as the individualized education program (IEP), at no cost. There are specific time lines for providing parents with this information. Parents also have the right to have their representatives inspect and review the education records on their behalf. The details of this law are discussed in Chapter 8.

What happens if a schoolteacher or official violates FERPA? In the past, violations of the act not only could trigger lawsuits filed against the institution and its personnel under 42 U.S.C. Section 1983 but also could potentially result in the loss of federal funds. However, a few months after deciding that student peer grading does not violate FERPA (the *Owasso* decision), the U.S. Supreme Court ruled that the sole remedy for FERPA violations involves administrative sanctions imposed by the U.S. Department of Education (*Gonzaga University v. Doe*, 2002). In rare instances, these sanctions could include loss of federal funding. Additionally, it should be noted that an employee who violates the act could be subject to discipline.

California law tracks the provisions of FERPA and goes beyond them to some extent (Educ. Code § 49060 and following sections). Under state law, if parents are divorced or legally separated, only the parent having legal custody of the child may challenge the contents of the child's record, offer a written response to a record, or consent to release of records to others unless there is a written agreement to the contrary. The annual notice to parents about the district's policy on student records includes a long list of components. Among them are types of records the school keeps and their location, the person responsible for the maintenance of each record type, the location of the log of those requesting or receiving student records, the costs for reproducing records, the school's policies for reviewing and expunging records, and what constitutes directory information (Educ. Code § 49063). Another section provides that while a school can charge for copying, it may not charge for up to two transcripts of former students or up to two verifications of various former student records (Educ. Code § 49065). It also may not charge for retrieving records.

As we saw in Chapter 1, parents in California have an absolute right of access at both public and private schools to student records during school hours and within five days of making a request (Educ. Code § 49069). Any editing or withholding of records is prohibited. In conformity with FERPA, the Education Code describes the due process procedures to be followed when parents challenge the content of their child's education records (Educ. Code § 49070). Basically, within thirty days of filing a request to challenge the contents of a student's record, the parent is entitled to meet with the superintendent or designee and the school employee who recorded the information. If the superintendent denies the request, the parent can appeal to the governing board, whose decision is final. The parents can file an objection to the decision, which becomes part of the student's school record.

Among other provisions of note, Education Code Section 49602 provides that personal information conveyed by a student over the age of twelve to a school counselor is confidential and cannot become part of the student's record without the student's permission. Nor can it be revealed, even to the student's parents, except in narrow circumstances as described in Chapter Twelve regarding legal liability of school counselors. Education Code Section 45345 prohibits an instructional aide from giving out personal information about a student to anyone other than a teacher or administrator in the school. Section 49068 requires the transfer of student records to a new school upon request. These records may not be withheld because of any charges or fees owed by the student or parent. Section 49072 permits parents to file a written statement or response in their child's record about any disciplinary action taken against the child. Section 49073.5 states that the legislature's intent is to minimize the release of student telephone numbers in the absence of parental consent because of harassment concerns. This would appear to have bearing on the school's use of directory information. Section 49076 includes a student who is sixteen or older and has completed tenth grade as one of those who have access to records under the legitimate educational interest exception to nondisclosure without parental consent. That same section permits school districts to participate in interagency computerized data systems that contain student information, provided the systems are secure so that unauthorized personnel cannot gain access and privileged or confidential information is not disclosed.

Finally, Section 49079 requires school districts to inform a student's teachers based on information contained in school records or obtained from law enforcement that within the past three years the student has engaged in, or is reasonably suspected of having engaged in, a suspendable or expellable offense other than the use or possession of tobacco. Failure to do so is a misdemeanor, punishable by confinement in county jail of up to six months and a $1,000 fine. The teacher is prohibited from disseminating this information to anyone else.

Student surveys. Shortly after it was enacted, FERPA was amended to give parents and guardians the right to inspect instructional material and request exemptions from material they found objectionable for their children (20 U.S.C. § 1232 h). At first, there was some confusion about the extent of these provisions. It was not until the amendment's sponsor, Republican Senator Orrin Hatch of Utah, explained that the amendment to FERPA applied only to instructional material used in teaching programs sponsored by the federal government that the matter was clarified. Now known as the Protection of Pupil Rights Amendment (PPRA), the act applies to hard copy or electronic/digital instructional material used in applicable programs other than tests.

The term "applicable program" means a program administered or funded by the U.S. Department of Education and its secretary. PPRA does not apply to school curriculum and instructional material. For programs to which it does apply, the act restricts the use of surveys to gather information on such topics as political affiliations, sex behavior of family members, critical appraisals of family members, religious practices, and income without prior consent of the parent or eligible student. The act requires districts to develop policies in consultation with parents to implement it.

California law tracks PPRA. Education Code Section 49091.12, part of a chapter entitled the Education Empowerment Act of 1998, provides that a student may not be compelled to affirm or disavow any worldview, religious doctrine, or political opinion. Nor may students be given a behavioral, mental, or emotional evaluation without written parental consent. The statute also provides that neither the student's family nor the student can be asked to participate in an assessment of home life, any form of parental testing, a nonacademic home-based counseling program, a parent training program, or a family education service plan. Education Code Section 51513 states that no test, questionnaire, survey, or examination with questions about student or family personal beliefs or practices in sex, family life, morality, and religion can be administered in public school unless the parent or guardian has given written consent.

STUDENT SEARCH AND SEIZURE

Since the late 1970s, California public school students have been protected from unreasonable searches and seizures by the state constitution and then later by the federal constitution as well. In recent years, drug trafficking and violence at school have increased the vigilance of school officials over student behavior. Whenever possible, school officials seek to take preventive action to keep the school safe. Inevitably, doing so raises questions of how far they can go without violating student search-and-seizure rights. The judicial decisions discussed in this section provide good insight into what school officials can and cannot do.

Student Searches

We begin with a discussion of the standards laid down by the U.S. and California supreme courts for conducting legally valid student searches. We then examine how lower courts have applied the standards in specific situations to gain a better understanding of how school officials can go about conducting a legally valid student search.

Standards. The U.S. Supreme Court first faced the question of student searches in a New Jersey case involving a student who denied that she had been smoking in the girls' restroom contrary to school rules (*New Jersey v. T.L.O.*, 1985). A teacher discovered the girl, T.L.O., and a companion apparently doing so and herded the two girls to the office. There, the other girl confessed; but T.L.O. did not. The principal, bearing the no-nonsense name of Theodore Choplick, demanded to see T.L.O.'s purse. When Choplick looked inside, he found a pack of cigarettes. He also spotted a package of cigarette rolling papers, raising his suspicions about possible drug involvement. He searched further and found a small amount of marijuana, a number of empty plastic bags, a substantial amount of money, a list of names of students who owed T.L.O. money, and a letter implicating the student in drug dealing. His suspicions confirmed, he turned the student over to the police. T.L.O. was suspended from school and later declared delinquent in juvenile court and placed on probation. She sought to overturn her conviction by arguing that the purse search violated her right under the unreasonable search provision of the Fourth Amendment to the U.S. Constitution. That provision, which applies to the states and their political subdivisions through the Fourteenth Amendment, reads:

> The right of the people to be secure in their persons, houses, papers, and effects, against unreasonable searches and seizures, shall not be violated, and no Warrants

shall issue, but upon probable cause, supported by Oath or affirmation, and particularly describing the place to be searched, and the persons or things to be seized.

The U.S. Supreme Court first observed that the Fourth Amendment applies to searches of public school students. That question answered, the next question for the justices was whether the standards for a lawful search require school officials to establish probable cause and obtain a warrant from a judge in conformity with the wording of the Fourth Amendment. In other decisions, the high court has permitted exceptions to the probable cause/warrant requirements when exigent circumstances exist. These exceptions include a search incident to lawful arrest, a search conducted by police pursuant to a stop and frisk for weapons, and a consensual search. The State of New Jersey argued that the need to maintain a safe educational environment is so compelling that any search of student personal property brought into the school is justified. Writing for the majority, Justice Byron White noted that the Court had ruled to this effect with regard to prisoners but observed, "We are not yet ready to hold that the schools and the prisons need be equated for purposes of the Fourth Amendment" (p. 742).

The Supreme Court set forth two standards for a search of a public school student to conform to the Fourth Amendment. First, there must be *reasonable cause* to believe that a student has violated a school rule or a law. Second, the search that is conducted must not be *excessively intrusive* in light of the age and gender of the student and the nature of the infraction. Applying the standards to the search that Choplick conducted of T.L.O.'s purse, the Court observed that the principal had reasonable cause to suspect the student had been smoking, based on the teacher's report. Thus, the initial search of her purse met the reasonableness standard. When Choplick was conducting this search, he spotted the cigarette rolling papers. The Court previously had ruled that evidence "in plain view" during a search can be used against a person even though the evidence was not suspected of being there. Since the rolling papers were in plain view during the initial cigarette search, they justified the second, more intrusive search resulting in discovery of the drug paraphernalia. The search of T.L.O.'s purse was therefore lawful. The Court upheld her delinquency conviction.

A few months after this decision, the California Supreme Court reached a different decision in a case involving the search of a student's calculator case (*In re William G.*, 1985). In the *T.L.O.* decision, the U.S. Supreme Court had observed in footnote that a state constitution might confer greater rights on students, but the New Jersey courts had not relied on its state constitution in that case. In *In re William G.*, the

California high court did so. It pointed out that a student's right to be free from unreasonable searches emanates both from the Fourth Amendment and from Article 1, Section 13 of the California Constitution, which is nearly a word-for-word repeat of its federal counterpart. Five years earlier, the court had ruled that this section applies to juveniles outside of school and protects them from a warrantless search even if their parents consent (*In re Scott K.*, 1979). In addition, the justices noted the relevance of Article 1, Section 1 of the state constitution for protecting privacy. "Homage to personhood is the foundation for individual rights protected by our state and national Constitutions," the California high court observed. "The privacy of a student, the very young or the teenager must be respected" (pp. 125–126). The justices applied these provisions to the case at hand.

The facts of the *William G.* case are relatively simple. At Chatsworth High School in Los Angeles, assistant principal Reno Lorenz confronted William G., a sixteen-year-old student, and two male companions walking through the campus. Wondering why the students were not in class, Lorenz walked toward them. As he did so, he noticed William G. was carrying a small black bag, later identified as a vinyl calculator case, that had an odd-looking bulge. The students' attention was focused on the bag. The assistant principal's suspicions aroused, he asked William G. why he was not in class. The student responded that his classes were over for the day. As he spoke, the student placed the case to his side and then behind his back. Lorenz asked what William G. had in his hand and received the reply, "Nothing." The student added, "You can't search me; you need a warrant for this." Lorenz took William G. to the office. There Lorenz forcefully took the case and unzipped it. Inside he found marijuana and drug paraphernalia. The police were contacted and the student placed under arrest. The juvenile court refused to accept William G.'s argument that the evidence was illegally obtained, and the student appealed.

Viewed from the perspective of the federal and state constitutions, the California Supreme Court concluded, the search violated the student's rights. The search was not based on articulated facts but rather on a hunch. Lorenz had no reason to believe that William G. was involved in drug dealing. And there was no evidence of exigent circumstances requiring an immediate nonconsensual search. This point is important because in a situation where school officials have reason to believe a student has a concealed weapon, they may well have no alternative to conducting a nonconsensual search. The search of William G. being illegal, the evidence obtained from it could not be used in the juvenile court. The student's conviction of delinquency was overturned.

The California Supreme Court sidestepped the issue of the standards to be applied when school security officers or law enforcement officials are involved in the search. The U.S. Supreme Court had done the same in *T.L.O.* The California high court also did not discuss whether evidence seized in an illegal search could nevertheless be used against the student in a school disciplinary proceeding as contrasted with a criminal prosecution, noting in a footnote that the matter had not been raised in the case. However, the year before, a California court of appeal ruled that the exclusionary rule did not apply in student disciplinary proceedings and that marijuana seized in what turned out to be an unjustified search could be used to suspend the student from school (*Gordon J. v. Santa Ana Unified School District*, 1984). How strong a precedent this case presents today is questionable, given that it was decided before both the *T.L.O.* and *In re William G.* decisions. Clearly, aside from emergency situations, it is always wise for administrators to have articulated facts justifying a student search and then to make sure the search is not excessively intrusive on student privacy.

The lesson learned from the *In re William G.* decision is that the California constitution is more protective of the student right to be free from searches and seizures than is the federal constitution, even when the searches are of school property assigned to students. In 2005, a state court recognized the continuing validity of *In re William G.* in a case involving the search of a student's purse. Lisa G, a San Diego High School student, and several other students were disruptive in class. The teacher told the students to sit down and focus on their work. Lisa requested permission to go to the bathroom. The teacher refused, unaware of information from the school nurse that the student should be permitted to use the bathroom upon request because of a medical condition. Becoming more agitated and insistent, Lisa walked to the classroom door. The teacher attempted to block her from leaving, but Lisa pushed the teacher aside and left the classroom. The student could not reenter the classroom because the door was locked. At the end of class, the teacher decided to write a discipline referral for Lisa. However, the teacher did not know Lisa's name. When the student left the classroom, the teacher had taken Lisa's purse for safekeeping. The teacher decided to open the purse in hopes of finding identification information. She found a knife and called security. Lisa was arrested and subsequently declared a ward of the state and placed on probation. Lisa sought to suppress the evidence used against her as a violation of her Fourth Amendment right to be free from unreasonable searches. The California court of appeal found the search little different from the one in *In re William G.* As in that case, there was no justification for the search. The fact that the student had been disruptive in class was irrelevant. In a key passage, the judges pointed out that "mere disruptive behavior does not authorize a school official to rummage through his or her students' personal belongings" (p. 166). Thus, the search was unreasonable, and the evidence resulting from it had to be suppressed. Without the evidence, there was no evidence to support Lisa's conviction of possession of a knife on school grounds (*In re Lisa G.*). Whether it would have made any difference if the student had just been disciplined internally is not clear. The best advice is always to have reasonable cause—meaning clearly articulated facts—before conducting student searches.

So far we have been discussing the standards of an individualized search of a student. General searches are more problematic because they run counter to the purpose of the Fourth Amendment. That amendment was included in the Bill of Rights because the American Founders wanted to eliminate the capricious searches the colonists had experienced at the hands of the British. Still, general searches have been permitted where the expectations of personal privacy are limited and the needs of government substantial. A good illustration is the metal detector searches conducted at airports. The U.S. Supreme Court confronted the general search issue in 1995 in a case involving random, unannounced drug testing of public school athletes (*Vernonia School District v. Acton*). The school district in that case had experienced a serious drug and alcohol problem among its students. The district asserted that the leaders of the drug culture in the school were student athletes and instituted a general drug-testing program to combat it. The program required a written consent form from parents. One student, Wayne Acton, and his parents refused to sign the consent form, arguing that it violated their Fourth Amendment rights. The Ninth Circuit agreed. The Supreme Court reversed that decision. The *Vernonia* decision is important because it sets the standards for a lawful student drug test under the federal constitution.

The Court first observed that students who voluntarily participate in interscholastic sports have a diminished expectation of privacy. "School sports are not for the bashful," wrote Justice Antonin Scalia for the majority. At the same time, the school's interest in curtailing illicit drug use among students and protecting student athletes from injury is significant. The drug-testing policy minimally intruded on student privacy. Female students produce samples in an enclosed bathroom stall within earshot of a school official of the same gender. Male students do so at a urinal with a school official standing at some distance behind them. The samples are sent to a laboratory with a nearly 100 percent accuracy rate. The laboratory does not know the identity of the students and sends the results to the superintendent. Only school administrators have access to the testing results, which are not kept for more than one year. Significantly, the consequences of a positive test are limited. A student who tests positive must undergo a second test. If the result again is positive, the student is given an option of participating in a six-week assistance program or being suspended from athletics for the remainder of the season and the next season. A second offense results in a similar penalty, while a third offense results in suspension for the remainder of the season and the next two athletic seasons. Students are neither expelled nor turned over to the police.

The Court was not of one mind on the question. Justice Ruth Bader Ginsburg concurred in the judgment but limited her concurrence to the facts of the case. Three justices dissented. Writing for them, Justice O'Connor pointed to the core principle of individualized suspicion inherent in the Fourth Amendment and asserted that testing students who gave signs of drug use would have addressed the problem while at the same time safeguarding student Fourth Amendment rights. A few years later, these four justices opposed the majority's extension of the *Acton* ruling to a similar general drug testing encompassing students participating in all extracurricular activities. The case involved Lindsay Earls, a high school student in an Oklahoma school district who was a member of several nonathletic extracurricular activities including the show choir, the marching band, and the National Honor Society. While the district's drug-testing policy covered all extracurricular activities, in practice it applied only to competitive extracurricular activities such as band, choir, pom-pom, cheerleading, Future Farmers of America, Future Homemakers of America, and athletics. For the same reasons advanced in the *Acton* decision, the majority upheld the policy. Writing for the four dissenters, Justice Ginsburg expressed skepticism about the safety concerns advanced by the school with this colorful statement:

> Notwithstanding nightmarish images of out-of-control flatware, livestock run amok, and colliding tubas disturbing the peace and quiet of Tecumseh, the great majority of students the school district seeks to test in truth are engaged in activities that are not safety sensitive to an unusual degree. (*Board of Education v. Earls*, 2002, p. 2577)

In sum, the standards for legally permissible individualized searches of public school students and school property assigned to students arising from these decisions require articulated facts of alleged wrongdoing and a search that is not excessively intrusive on student privacy. A general search is permissible in the context of student drug testing of student athletes and those participating in extracurricular activities in general. We now examine how these standards have been applied to a variety of searches conducted in California public schools.

Individual searches. In its *In re William G.* ruling, the California Supreme Court did not distinguish between searches of school property assigned to students and searches of student possessions. In an important passage, the justices wrote, "Neither indiscriminate searches of lockers nor more discreet individual searches of a locker, a purse or a person, here a student, can take place absent the existence of reasonable suspicion. Respect for privacy is the rule—a search is the exception" (p. 126). A California appellate court followed this directive in 1995 in upholding a locker search triggered by a call from a parent on a Wednesday to the school's vice principal, informing him that the previous Friday night her son had seen another student with a pistol at the high school football game. Fearing for her son's safety, the parent asked for confidentiality. Based on the tip, the vice principal and security guard searched the student's locker the next day but found nothing except books. A short time later they saw the student place his backpack in the locker. They waited a few minutes and then searched the locker a second time. This time they found a loaded handgun in the student's backpack.

The student sought to overturn his conviction as a delinquent minor by arguing that the initial locker search was unjustified because the tip came from an anonymous source and was too remote in time. The second locker search, he contended, was completely without cause. The appellate court disagreed. The tip was not anonymous, and even if it had been, that would be but one factor to weigh regarding reasonable cause. The court also rejected the argument that the information about the weapon was stale because it was based on an incident occurring five days earlier outside of school. With regard to the second search, the judges observed that school officials reasonably could conclude that a student who brings a gun to school will keep it in a locker, in a backpack or purse, or on his or her person. The judges advised:

> School officials should investigate reports that particular students are carrying firearms on to campuses by the minimal intrusion of checking the contents of a student's locker. Such a minimal intrusion is justified particularly when school officials observe the student putting a backpack, a likely place for carrying a gun, into a locker. (*In re Joseph G.*, p. 906)

Thus, the second search of the locker and the backpack, which was in plain view, was justified. Whether a school could condition student use of its lockers and desks by having students consent to periodic unannounced inspections remains unclear.

In 2003 a federal district court in California provided additional guidance for conducting individualized searches on public school campuses. The case involved a nonstudent who argued that his conviction for possessing a sawed-off shotgun on a public school campus should be overturned because school security personnel could not rely on the relatively lax *T.L.O.* standards to conduct the search. The court rejected the contention, noting that the purpose of the *T.L.O.* ruling was to provide a safe school environment and "must surely encompass the conduct of non-students who pose a threat to that environment" (*United States v. Aguilera*, p. 1209). The court also observed that reliance on an anonymous tip to conduct a search satisfies the reasonable cause standard of *T.L.O.* as long as the tip is reliable. In this case the anonymous tip came from the mother of a student, who had observed the youth with a gun tucked into his shorts walk past her car and toward the campus and who then used her cell phone to alert the office staff. In the view of the court, the tip exhibited "sufficient indicia of reliability" to provide reasonable suspicion.

Searching lockers and asking students to empty their pockets or purses is quite different from conducting searches of students themselves. While personally intrusive searches have been upheld in a few states, they are not permissible in California. Education Code Section 49050 prohibits searches involving the removing or rearranging of the clothing of a student to permit visual inspection of "the underclothing, breast, buttocks, or genitalia of the pupil." Body-cavity searches are likewise outlawed. Given the reluctance of many judges to condone excessively intrusive searches of students and the thrust of this California Education Code section, personally intrusive searches should be left to parents and to law enforcement except in the most exigent circumstances, when maintaining student safety is paramount.

So far, there is little case law regarding searches and seizures of student electronic devices such as cell phones, iPods, and BlackBerries at school. One informative ruling comes from a federal district court in Pennsylvania holding that a student's right to freedom from unreasonable seizures is not violated when his cell phone is confiscated after the student uses the device contrary to a school rule. However, the court refused to dismiss the student's Fourth Amendment unreasonable search claim against school officials for searching his phone for alleged drug activity by checking text messages and voice mail. Nor was there justification for school officials to call other students whose numbers were listed on the cell phone to determine if these students might be involved in drug matters (*Klump v. Nazareth Area School District*, 2006).

As we all know from watching television crime shows, the police are required to read persons under arrest their *Miranda* rights, based on the famous 1966 U.S. Supreme Court *Miranda v. Arizona* decision: "You have a right to remain silent. Anything you say can be used against you in a court of law. You are entitled to an attorney. If you cannot afford one, an attorney will be appointed to represent you." Are these rights required before searching a student? In a 1988 decision, a California appellate court ruled in the negative, following a long line of similar rulings by courts in other parts of the country. The case involved an Oakland middle school student, Corey L., who consented to being searched after the school principal had learned from three students that someone on the school grounds had drugs. One of the three identified Corey L. as possessing cocaine. The principal found two baggies containing what turned out to be cocaine. The student said he had gotten it from someone else and denied that he intended to sell it on campus. A month earlier, the principal had suspected Corey L. to be involved in drug dealing because the student had a large amount of cash without credible explanation. The police were summoned, and Corey L. was arrested. The student sought to suppress the evidence against him by arguing that the principal should have read him his *Miranda* rights. The principal had not done so.

The court rejected the contention, noting that *Miranda* comes into play after a person is taken into police custody and does not apply to student questioning by school officials. The court observed that "Questioning of a student by a principal, whose duties include the obligations to maintain order, protect the health and safety of pupils and maintain conditions conducive to learning, cannot be equated with custodial interrogation by law enforcement officers" (*In re Corey L.*, p. 361).

Group searches. Suppose a school administrator suspects that some members of a group of students have contraband but is unsure exactly which ones. Can the administrator subject them all to a search? This was the question before a California court of appeal in a case involving the detention and subsequent search of a group of students in connection with a confrontation between rival gangs at Grant High School in the Los Angeles Unified School District. The dean of students heard yelling of slogans and noticed one group of students running toward another group. He separated the two groups and ordered them to the office. An unidentified boy in one of the groups said, "Don't pick on us; one of those guys has a gun," gesturing to a third group of five or six students who had been egging the others on from the sidelines. The dean directed an officer from the district's police department who had been standing nearby to check the third group of students for a weapon. The officer ordered the third group to sit on the curb while he began searching each student. One of the students refused to comply with the officer's order to remain sitting. When the student attempted to leave, the officer wrestled the student to the ground. As he did so, the officer noticed a black handle sticking out from the student's belt. A machete knife and scabbard were removed from inside the student's trouser leg. The student sought to overturn an order declaring him a ward of the juvenile court by arguing in part that the evidence was the product of an illegal search.

The court of appeal rejected the student's contention. Here, the district police officer had received information from the dean that someone in the group reportedly was in possession of a weapon. Given the need to provide students with a safe school environment, "a cursory search of appellant and others in his group for dangerous weapons was not only reasonable, it was constitutionally compelled" (p. 344). The fact that the search was focused on five or six students rather than a particular student was immaterial. The officer had acted appropriately in deterring the student from attempting to leave and conducting the search (*In re Alexander B.*, 1990).

There are two noteworthy comments to make about this case. First, the court did not decide the standards to be followed had the police officer conducted the search on his own volition or had ordered the dean of students to do so. The general assumption is that when the police initiate a search, the standards are higher. However, if the police officer is assigned to the school, then the police officer may conduct searches under the relaxed *T.L.O.* standards just like a school administrator or security officer paid by the school (*In re William V.* 2003). Second, in a later decision discussed in the next section, the California Supreme Court distinguished searches from seizures, noting that brief detentions of students do not require reasonable cause. Thus, it would not have been necessary for the district police officer to show reasonable cause to detain either the group of students or the student who attempted to leave. To this extent, the California high court disapproved the *In re Alexander B.* decision.

The U.S. Court of Appeals of the Ninth Circuit also has upheld group searches. In 1997 the court was confronted with a case involving the search of a group of students reported to be smoking on a cul-de-sac near Orange Glen High School in Escondido. Apparently, the school had a rule against smoking both on and in the vicinity of the school. The vice principal and a security guard herded the group to school, where they were searched individually over a two-hour period. The search of one of the students produced three knives, including a double-edged dagger with a four-inch blade. Even though the juvenile court judge suppressed the evidence and dismissed the charges, the student sued the vice principal for conducting an illegal search. Noting that the U.S. Supreme Court had left open the possibility of exceptions to individualized suspicion in *New Jersey v. T.L.O.* and later approved a general drug-testing program in *Vernonia School District v. Acton*, the Ninth Circuit ruled against the student's argument that it was unreasonable for the principal to conduct a general search without asking first which students had been smoking. Even if some students had confessed, there was no way of knowing whether those who did not were lying. The student's argument that the two-hour delay in completing the search violated her liberty right to be in class was rejected out of hand (*Smith v. McGlothlin*, 1997).

Two of the three judges in a concurring opinion directed some scathing comments to the student, her parents, and her attorneys. They characterized the student's complaint as "a triumph of petulance over common sense" and found it ironic that a student who lacked the common sense not to bring knives to school thought she was the one who had been wronged. Before bringing the lawsuit, the parents should have considered their own culpability, the judges observed, and the student's lawyer should have pondered whether it was right to impose the burden of a lawsuit on the school principal. As for the student, she "might have thanked her lucky stars when she got off easily because her juvenile court judge misread the law and suppressed the evidence" (p. 788).

Employing drug-detecting sniffer dogs to search for drugs in school is not uncommon. In a 1999 decision, the Ninth Circuit set a limit on the use of such dogs. The case involved a sniffer dog search at Quincy High School in the Plumas Unified School District. School officials ordered students out of their classroom, and as the students exited, they passed a drug-sniffing dog. The students waited while the dog entered the room to sniff their desks and belongings. The students again walked past the dog as they returned to their room. No drugs were found. One of the students, B. C., filed suit. After reviewing the law in other jurisdictions, the Ninth Circuit ruled that the use of sniffer dogs to sniff students is a search under the Fourth Amendment. Further, it is offensive and intrudes on personal privacy. Agreeing that school officials have an important, even compelling, interest in deterring drug use, the judges noted that relying on a sniffer dog to conduct a random, suspicionless search of students as they left and reentered the classroom was unreasonable in the absence of any evidence that there was a drug crisis or even a drug problem at the high school. Thus, the search of B. C. was unconstitutional (*B. C. v. Plumas Unified School District*).

Note that the appeals court did not rule out the use of sniffer dogs to conduct a general search of students if there were documented evidence of a major drug problem at school. In the absence of such a showing, sniffer dogs can be used only to search a particular student based on individualized suspicion. One of the three judges disagreed that the sniffing of students was all that intrusive. The dog was at a distance of three or four feet from students and did not touch them. The judge also questioned how the school district could achieve its compelling interest in deterring a major drug problem without taking preventive action through the use of general sniffer dog searches. All three judges differentiated sniffer dog searches of objects from searches of persons. Thus, it appears that sniffer dogs can be used to sniff lockers, desks, and cars without violating student rights.

To keep campuses and school events weapon-free, schools often employ magnetometers, through which persons pass, and handheld metal detectors to conduct general searches. The California attorney general has advised that these searches are similar to administrative searches conducted at airports and at courthouses and only minimally intrude on student privacy (75 Ops. Atty. Gen. 155, 1992). Further, the attorney general found their use consistent with provisions of the Education Code permitting school employees to remove injurious objects from students (Educ. Code § 49330 and following sections). An "injurious object" means something that is capable of inflicting substantial bodily harm. School personnel must notify parents and have the option of notifying law enforcement. School officials can turn the object over to the parents or to the student at the end of the day if the object can be lawfully possessed off school grounds. The attorney general also advised that the use of metal detectors is consistent with provisions of the Education Code requiring the school site council or school safety planning committee to develop a comprehensive school safety plan (Educ. Code § 32280 and following sections). In short, the compelling interest to secure safety outweighs the minimal intrusions on personal privacy.

A California court of appeal also has upheld the use of metal detectors to protect students and staff from weapons at school (*In re Latasha W.*, 1998). The metal detectors were used randomly in conformity with the high school's written policy. If a detector was triggered, the student was asked to open his or her jacket or pockets to reveal the source. When Latasha W. opened her jacket, a knife with a blade longer than two-and-one-half inches came into view. The student sought to overturn her conviction in juvenile court, arguing that the knife was the product of an illegal search. She was unsuccessful. While noting an absence of cases dealing with such searches in California, the appellate court reviewed decisions elsewhere and found that metal-detector searches have been upheld in the absence of individualized suspicion. Given the substantial interest of the school in keeping guns and knives off campus coupled with the minimally intrusive nature of the search, the court found that the random, general use of metal detectors did not violate student rights. The judges noted no other effective way for the school to achieve a weapon-free environment. Later the same court (different judges) cited *Latasha W.* in holding that not only are completely random weapons searches of students entering school groups permissible, a nonstudent has a lesser right of privacy than a student who is properly on school grounds. The case involved a pat-down search of a student from another high school who was taken to the security office and searched by a police officer assigned to the school. During the search the officer discovered a knife. The nonstudent contended that because the pat-down search violated his rights, his being placed on probation for violating a Penal Code provision against possessing a locking blade knife on school property should be tossed out. The court of appeal rejected the student's motion (*People v. Jose Y.*, 2006).

In sum, the case law relevant to California tells us that group searches of public school students are permitted when there is reasonable suspicion that someone in the group possesses contraband. The search must not be excessively intrusive in light of the circumstances. When students refuse to comply with the request for a search or when a particularly invasive search is necessary, the best policy is to contact law enforcement and let them handle the search. Any contraband they find usually will be admissible for a juvenile or criminal prosecution and also can be used in the school's administrative discipline procedures. General administrative searches using magnetometers and metal detectors are permitted when there is a need to conduct them. The use of sniffer dogs to detect drugs on school property also is permitted as long as the dogs are not used to sniff students. How much justification would be necessary to allow dogs to sniff students in a general manner is not known. In part, the answer will depend on the degree to which the dogs intrude on the students' zone of personal privacy.

Student Seizures

Both the federal and California constitutions prevent unreasonable seizures as well as searches. What is an unreasonable seizure? The leading ruling on the issue comes from the California Supreme Court in a case involving a fourteen-year-old male student, Randy G., who was spotted by a campus security officer in an area on campus where students were not permitted to congregate. When the student saw the security aide, he fixed his pocket nervously, leaving some of the lining sticking out. The aide thought the student acted very paranoid. Together with another security official, the aide went to the classroom where Randy G. had gone and asked him to step outside to the hallway. The aide asked the youth if he had something on him. He said he did not. Asked if he would consent to a patdown search, Randy G. replied in the affirmative. The search produced an illegal knife. The student argued in juvenile court that use of the knife against him should be excluded because the ten-minute detention in the hallway amounted to a seizure without reasonable cause.

The justices first observed that minors are compelled to be in school, and while they are there, school officials have a responsibility to keep them safe. During the school day, students are ordered to be in various places at various times. Stopping a student to ask a question does not intrude on the student's liberty any more than these requirements do. Because a seizure is less intrusive than a search, the same reasonable suspicion standard does not apply. "Detentions of minor students on school grounds do not offend the Constitution," the justices unanimously concluded, "so long as they are not arbitrary, capricious, or for the purposes of harassment" (*In re Randy G.*, 2001, p. 525). In the *B. C. v. Plumas Unified School District* case discussed in the previous section, the Ninth Circuit similarly rejected the student's argument that by requiring him to stand with others in a nearby snack bar area while the drug-detecting dog sniffed the room, school officials had violated his Fourth Amendment right to be free from unreasonable seizures. Such a brief detention, the court noted, does not fall within the terms of the Fourth Amendment.

In making its ruling in the *In re Randy G.* case, the California Supreme Court did not differentiate between school administrators and school security personnel. The title "security officer" itself is not constitutionally significant, the justices noted, so long as the latter are not acting as law enforcement officers. The court did not comment on what the appropriate standard would be for seizures of students conducted by school personnel on campus or at school-sponsored events in conjunction with or at the behest of law enforcement agencies.

A federal district court in California later followed the same line of thinking evidenced by the California Supreme Court in its *In Randy G.* ruling in a case involving a three-hour office detention of a student after numerous students reported that she had possessed and used drugs during the day. An earlier search of her backpack, pockets, and shoes had revealed no drugs. The federal judge accepted the school's assertions that the detention served to prevent disruption, discipline the student, and prevent possible drug distribution and use. Much like the two concurring Ninth Circuit judges in the *Smith v. McGlothlin* case discussed earlier in this chapter, the federal judge expressed some impatience with the lawsuit, noting that "It is ironic and unfortunate that [school officials] were dragged into federal court and required to defend themselves against a civil rights lawsuit for simply doing their duty." The case was dismissed (*Bravo ex rel. Ramirez v. Hsu*, 2005).

Not all detentions, however, will automatically pass judicial inspection. In 2003 the Ninth Circuit was confronted with an odd case involving a vice principal's taping a second-grade student's head to a tree as a disciplinary measure. The student had been sent to the school official for fighting. The vice principal told the child to stand against the wall for punishment. If the child did not stand still, the vice principal said he would take the student outside and tape his head to a tree. The official carried through with his threat. The child was released when a fifth grader came upon the scene and told the vice principal what he was doing was wrong. The child through his parents later filed suit against the Hawaiian Department of Education (all schools in Hawaii constitute one district operated by the department) and the vice principal. The Ninth Circuit ruled that the taping constituted an unreasonable seizure under the Fourth Amendment, noting that "Taping [the student's] head to a tree for five minutes was so intrusive that a fifth grader observed it was inappropriate" (*Doe v.*

Hawaii Department of Education, 2003, p. 910). The case was sent back to the trial court to determine the extent to which the vice principal could be held liable.

SUMMARY

The Brown Act mandates public access to meetings of the governing board and many of its committees when deliberation or action takes place. Members of the public have the right to comment at these meetings as well. The act permits closed meetings, but only in specific situations. The Education Code tracks the Brown Act and goes beyond it to some extent by requiring that school site councils and advisory committees must be open to the public. Likewise, the Public Records Act tilts in the direction of disclosing government documents that are not specifically exempted from disclosure. Among the exceptions are personnel records that would constitute a clearly unwarranted invasion of personal privacy if released.

While the law generally requires that the public's business must be conducted in public, neither school employees nor students and their families lose their right to personal privacy. The Education Code protects the privacy rights of teachers in several specific situations, and other statutes protect teacher lifestyle choices. The support for student and family privacy rights is well anchored in both federal and state law, especially in the context of school records and the use of surveys and questionnaires.

While concerns about student drug use and violence on campus have increased, students have a right to be free from unreasonable searches and seizures under constitutional law. Aside from general drug-testing programs administered to students participating in extracurricular activities and metal-detector searches for concealed weapons, school officials must search students only if they have reasonable cause to do so and the searches they conduct are not excessively intrusive. Though individualized suspicion is preferred, group searches are permissible when there are grounds to believe that someone in the group is in possession of contraband. Personally intrusive searches intended to permit visual inspection of underclothing and private body parts are outlawed by the Education Code. While students have asserted that being detained for questioning by school officials is a seizure and requires reasonable cause, both state and federal courts have rejected the contention.

It is evident from the privacy and search-and-seizure cases discussed in this chapter that this area of the law requires careful balancing of student rights with school interests. Given continuing concern about school safety, judges will continue to be called upon to redress the balance. School authorities are best advised to monitor legal developments carefully.

11 | RACE AND GENDER DISCRIMINATION

California's public school population of 6.3 million students is racially diverse. In 2007, 48 percent was Latino, 29 percent white, 9 percent Asian/Pacific Islander, and 8 percent black. Seventy percent of the population is now composed of students of color, with Latinos being the most rapidly growing segment. The fact that the population is racially diverse does not mean that each school reflects the state's student demographics. In fact, quite the opposite is true. In the state's large metropolitan areas, urban districts that serve mostly low-income students of color are surrounded by suburban school districts that are much more heterogeneous by race and class or, in some cases, are mostly white and high income. San Diego Unified School District, for example, had a 26 percent white enrollment in 2007 compared with 60 or more percent white in surrounding districts such as Coronado, Alpine, Santee, Del Mar, Solana Beach, Rancho Santa Fe, and Carlsbad. Race and class isolation in public schools remains among the most problematic and contentious public policy issues. The law in California for dealing with it is complex and confusing, reflecting crosscurrents in the thinking of judges, legislators, and voters.

We begin this chapter with a review of federal desegregation law; then we concentrate on California law. Included is a discussion of the consequences of racial isolation and why educators seek to integrate schools by both race and class. We then look at gender discrimination and the current state of the law regarding single-sex programs and schools. Finally, because racial and gender harassment are forms of discrimination, we include a section discussing both federal and California law targeted at their elimination.

RACIAL DISCRIMINATION

May 17, 2004, was the fiftieth anniversary of the U.S. Supreme Court's *Brown v. Board of Education of Topeka, Kansas* decision declaring state-maintained racial segregation in public schools unconstitutional. The nation's observance of the watershed decision was in some ways less a celebration than a commemoration. How the decision is viewed depends in large measure upon whether one considers *Brown* a case about race or a case about education. If seen as a case about race, *Brown* is applauded because it outlawed state-sanctioned apartheid. But if viewed as a decision about education, *Brown* is observed with some disappointment because the public schooling system remains highly segregated. For a time, federal and state judges in California were vigorous in advancing the cause of racial integration in public schools. In recent years, however, a retreat has been evident.

Racial Discrimination under Federal Law

The movement to eradicate racial segregation in schools has been one of the most monumental developments in school law in the twentieth century. The vigorous efforts of the federal judiciary, followed by those of the federal government, have effectively eradicated the once-common legally segregated schooling system. As often happens, the achievement of this goal led to the discovery of more fundamental questions, ones that have stirred much controversy in the educational arena in the years since the civil rights movement. If the cessation of forced racial segregation does not result in racially integrated student bodies, should public school administrators be forced to use racial or ethnic heritage information to diversify them? Are racially homogenous schools a detriment to their students? These are important questions, and, at least for now, we will merely raise them as issues that merit consideration and that illustrate the contemporaneity of race and schooling.

In 1954, the U.S. Supreme Court first recognized the right of students to be free from government-imposed racial segregation in *Brown v. Board of Education of Topeka, Kansas*. Until the Court's seminal opinion in *Brown*, states had been free to maintain separate public facilities for people of different races, provided those facilities were substantially equal in physical quality. In reality, however, facilities accessible to whites were far superior in quality than those assigned to blacks. The same was true for public schools. Minority children who lived in towns with segregated schools often attended class in inadequate buildings with few educational resources and poorly trained teachers. When the African American elementary school students of Topeka, Kansas—together with students in similarly segregated districts—asked the Supreme Court for help in gaining access to the white schools, the Court could have simply abolished the inferior schools because they did not comport with the prevailing "separate but equal" doctrine. But the Court was not satisfied with such a narrow holding.

Instead, a unanimous Court held that the separation of children by race, even into buildings of equal quality, deprives minority children of equal educational opportunities. According to the Court, the act of separating nonwhite students "solely because of their race generates a feeling of inferiority as to their status in the community that may affect their hearts and minds in a way unlikely ever to be undone" (p. 494). Therefore, separate facilities are "inherently unequal," and as a result they violate the equal protection clause of the Fourteenth Amendment, which prevents any state from denying "to any person within its jurisdiction the equal protection of the laws."

In the two decades following *Brown*, the Court sanctioned increasingly intrusive federal court involvement in local educational administration for the purpose of eradicating racially segregated schools. For example, the Court held that once a judge finds that a school purposefully engaged in discriminatory acts, the judge may gerrymander attendance zones and compel busing programs to integrate the schools (*Swann v. Charlotte-Mecklenburg Board of Education*, 1971). In 1964, the federal government joined the Supreme Court in condemning governmental racism with the passage of the monumental Civil Rights Act. Two key provisions of the act are Title VI, which prohibits discrimination on the basis of race, color, or national origin by recipients of federal funds, and Title VII, which prohibits discrimination by public and private employers on the basis of race, color, national origin, religion, and sex. Title VI is most significant today in the remedies it provides for the harassment of protected classes. It will be discussed in more detail later in this chapter. Title VII plays an important role in employment law and is discussed in Chapter 5.

Despite the initial zealousness after *Brown*, the scope of the developing federal law was curtailed in the early 1970s. Though the language of *Brown* was expansive enough to encompass de facto segregation (segregation due to societal factors) as well as de jure segregation (government-imposed segregation), the Court had never explicitly stated in the ruling whether de facto segregation alone was sufficient to prove a violation of the Constitution. It was not until 1973 that the Court clarified that *Brown* applied only to situations of government-sanctioned segregation. In *Keyes v. School District No. 1*, the Court held that a plaintiff trying to prove a violation of the equal protection clause by unlawful racial segregation has to show "not only that segregated schooling exists but also that it was brought about or maintained by intentional state action" (p. 198). Shortly thereafter, the Court expanded its emphasis on intent, holding that desegregation plans may not involve schools outside the desegregating district unless those schools also had engaged in de jure segregation (*Milliken v. Bradley*, 1974). As a result of these decisions, de facto segregated school districts are beyond the reach of the equal protection clause. In his outspoken dissent in *Milliken*, Justice Thurgood Marshall wrote, "In the short run, it may seem to be the easier course to allow our great metropolitan areas to be divided up each into two cities—one white, the other black—but it is a course, I predict, our people will ultimately regret" (pp. 814–815). Marshall had argued *Brown* before the U.S. Supreme Court.

The Court also has backed away from its early support for judicial intervention in the local administration of de jure segregated schools. The remedy for such purposeful segregation—court oversight and involvement in school board decisions—had always engendered considerable controversy because of the judicial intrusion into local affairs. Since the Court's decision in *Brown*, some school districts have been operating under continual judicial supervision because of decades-old findings of de jure segregation. The districts will return to self-control only when the supervising court determines they have become "unitary," a status indicating that the district has successfully eradicated all traces of the prior segregation. In the 1970s, a declaration of unitary status was hard to obtain, particularly because the standard was so ill defined. Several Supreme Court decisions, however, have eliminated much of this uncertainty.

In 1976, the Court held in *Pasadena City Board of Education v. Spangler* that a desegregation court order should not be modified to account for de facto demographic changes occurring after the creation of the order. In that case, several students had brought suit against the school district in Pasadena, alleging that it unconstitutionally segregated students on the basis of race. The federal district court agreed with the plaintiff students and issued an order requiring the school district to develop a student assignment plan that would prevent any school from having a majority of its students be of a minority racial status. The school district complied with the order, and the plan successfully achieved its goals during the first year of implementation. In succeeding years, however, the minority student population at several schools exceeded 50 percent due to changing residential patterns in Pasadena. The Supreme Court found that the "normal pattern of human migration" was not a product of purposeful actions by the school administrators and therefore was not a violation of the Fourteenth Amendment equal protection clause, even though the changing demographics exacerbated racial isolation in the schools (p. 436).

In 1991 the Court held that once all "vestiges of past discrimination [have] been eliminated to the extent practicable," a court should terminate its supervision of a school district (*Board of Education of Oklahoma City Public Schools v. Dowell*, p. 250). The Court rejected the contention by the plaintiffs in that case that the judiciary should renew its involvement in the affairs of a school district that had previously been subject to a desegregation court order when the district's schools resegregated. The Court emphasized that judicial supervision is only a temporary remedy, with the ultimate goal being to return a desegregated school district to autonomous control. Courts facing the decision of whether to declare a district unitary should examine whether the district complied in good faith with previous court orders and whether all remnants of the district's former discriminatory acts have been erased as much as possible. To make this determination, courts must look "not only at student assignments, but . . . 'every facet of school operations—faculty, staff, transportation, extracurricular activities and facilities'" (p. 250). One year after the Court decided *Dowell*, it unanimously held that a court may declare certain aspects of a district's operation unitary before the entire district has reached that stage (*Freeman v. Pitts*, 1992). In short, a supervising court has the authority to reduce its role in school district affairs as the district makes progress toward unitary status.

One notable exception in this trend away from racial integration was the Court's decision in 2003 upholding the use of race as one factor in a public law school's admissions policy. The five-to-four ruling in *Grutter v. Bollinger* surprised many, because there had been a general assumption that the Court would take the opportunity to end affirmative action. Yet, the Court basically affirmed a controversial 1978 decision permitting the use of race as one factor in student admissions to the University of California at Davis Medical School (*Regents of the University of California v. Bakke*). The majority pointed out in the *Grutter* decision that the University of Michigan Law School has a multifaceted admissions policy designed to assure a diversified student body. Racial diversity was part of this policy. The policy sought a "critical mass" of heretofore underrepresented groups—blacks, Latinos, and Native Americans enrolling at the school. The school was not attempting to remedy its own past racial discrimination or societal discrimination in general. Rather, the policy was intended to enrich legal education by assuring a variety of viewpoints among students. The critical mass was important to prevent minority students feeling either isolated or pressured to be spokespersons for their race. Assuring student body diversity, the Court ruled, constitutes a compelling state purpose sufficient to withstand a challenge under the Fourteenth Amendment equal protection clause. If this is true of higher education, would it not be equally compelling for elementary and secondary education?

In 2007 the Court confronted this question. It ruled five-to-four that admitting or rejecting public school students based solely on their race is unconstitutional. *Parents Involved in Community Schools v. Seattle School District No. 1* involved two school districts, one in Seattle and one in metropolitan Louisville (Jefferson County), Kentucky. Seattle, which had never engaged in racial segregation, adopted a school choice plan for its ten high schools and used race as a tie-breaker to further diversity if more students sought to attend a school than there were places. The Jefferson County system continued to use race in assigning students to school to achieve racial balance after a desegregation court order had ended. In striking down the use of race in both districts, four of the five justices in the majority agreed that any use of race in public school assignment is unconstitutional. In the words of Chief Justice John Roberts, who wrote for himself and three other justices on this point, "For schools that never segregated on the basis of race, such as Seattle, or that have removed the vestiges of past segregation, such as Jefferson County, the way 'to achieve a system of determining admission to the public schools on a nonracial basis' is to stop assigning students on a racial basis" (p. 2768). Writing for the four dissenters in the case, Justice Stephen Breyer minced no words in criticizing the majority for turning their backs on *Brown v. Board of Education*: "This is a decision that the Court and the Nation will come to regret," he wrote (p. 2837).

Justice Anthony Kennedy, who agreed with the four justices that the use of race by Louisville and Seattle violated the equal protection clause, did not endorse total exclusion of race in student assignment and refused to sign on to this aspect of the majority opinion. In his view, public schools have a compelling interest in avoiding racial isolation and addressing the problem of resegregation. He noted that "In the administration of public schools by the state and local authorities, it is permissible to consider the racial makeup of schools and to adopt general policies to encourage a diverse student body, one aspect of which is its racial composition" (p. 2792). To this end, he noted that race could be considered in choosing sites for new schools, drawing attendance zones, allocating resources for special programs, and targeted recruiting of both students and teachers. Given that four justices disapproved of any use of race in student assignment and four justices took the opposite position, Justice Kennedy's opinion carries great weight. Just what it all means in terms of using race in a more nuanced way to further integration awaits future litigation.

Racial isolation in education is increasing for a variety of reasons including demographic changes, housing patterns, the termination of desegregation court orders, and less interest in racial integration. The Civil Rights Project/*Proyecto Derechos Civiles* at UCLA published a study in 2007 on the extent of racial isolation in public schools in the United States. Among the findings in *Historic Reversals, Accelerating Resegregation, and the Need for New Integration Strategies* is one showing that in 1968 when school desegregation got under way, 77 percent of black students attended a school that was predominately nonwhite. In 1988, that figure dropped to 63 percent, but by 2005 had climbed to 73 percent. In 2005–2006 the average black and Latino student attended a school that was less than one-third white, while the average white student attended a school that was 77 percent white. There is also a significant link between race and socioeconomic status. In 2005–2006, the study shows that 84 percent of students received free or reduced-price lunches at schools with less than 10 percent white students. By contrast, only 18 percent of students received free or reduced-price lunches at schools with less than 10 percent black and Latino students.

The overlap between race and poverty is important because income is related to student achievement. The higher a family income level, the higher the student achievement. For example, according to statistics released by the College Board a few years ago, students from families earning less than $10,000 a year average 859 on the combined verbal and math Scholastic Aptitude Tests (SAT), while students from families earning more than $100,000 a year average 1123.

Attendance and test score patterns in California mirror those at the national level. In 2005–2006, 40 percent of California's black students attended schools that were between 90 and 100 percent nonwhite, and 50 percent of Latino students attended such schools. But because the California schooling system is now over 70 percent nonwhite, only 4 percent of white students attended schools that were 90 to 100 percent white. Isolation by class is as big a concern in California as isolation by race and ethnicity. California also is plagued by a nagging racial student achievement gap. In 2007, for example, 40 percent of white fourth graders were at or above proficiency in reading on the National Assessment of Educational Progress (NAEP), a standardized achievement test administered by the U.S. Department of Education to a cross section of students in all states. But only 14 percent of black students and 11 percent of Latino students reached this level. While scores of all racial groups have increased over the years, the already large gap in the percentage of white students scoring proficient or above as compared with both Latino and black students had not narrowed since 1992. A similar pattern was evident on the fourth-grade math test, with the large gap between California white students and both black and Latino students scoring proficient or higher expanding by twenty percentage points over the same time period. A similar student performance gap is evident on the California Standards Tests.

Statistics like these carry immense implications for educators struggling to meet the No Child Left Behind Act mandate that all students must reach proficiency or higher levels on state standardized achievement tests by 2014. Recall from Chapter 2 that the rigor of state tests must correlate with NAEP. These statistics also stimulate efforts to increase the proportion of resources spent on schools populated by low-income minority students and to foster integration across racial and socioeconomic lines in these schools in the interest of providing an achievement-oriented peer group in all schools.

Racial Discrimination under California Law

Historical perspective. Though long considered among the most educationally progressive states, California does not have an unblemished record regarding racial segregation in public schooling. In 1860, the legislature passed a law providing public schooling for white children but excluding "Negroes, Mongolians, and Indians." The law did permit district governing boards to establish separate schools for educating these minority children. A few years later, the legislature deleted "Mongolians" from the provision for separate schooling, thus denying Chinese American students, most of whom lived in San Francisco, any form of public education.

In 1874 in the case of *Ward v. Flood*, the California Supreme Court confronted a challenge to the separate education of Negroes. The father of Mary Ward, an eleven-year-old black child, filed suit after a San Francisco school principal refused to admit her to the neighborhood school. The principal of the school, Noah Flood, maintained that he was following state law and that the black school to which Mary was assigned provided her with an equal education. The father contended that the exclusion of his daughter constituted a badge of servitude contrary to the Thirteenth Amendment and violated the Fourteenth Amendment equal protection clause. The California high court rejected the first contention out of hand, noting no relationship between exclusion from a school and forced slavery. As to the equal protection argument, the justices cited with approval an 1849 Supreme Judicial Court of Massachusetts ruling that racially segregated schooling was no different from educating students separately by age, gender, and special needs. When the U.S. Supreme Court handed down its notorious 1896 *Plessy v. Ferguson* ruling that "separate but equal" public facilities (including schools) does not violate the federal constitution, it cited a number of state court decisions in support of this position, including *Ward v. Flood*.

Though an historical anachronism from a racial perspective, *Ward v. Flood* did declare public education to be a vested right under state law that had to be provided equally to all children. This prompted the legislature to remove the white-children-only provision from the school law in 1880 and delete the provisions for separate schools for other races. When the San Francisco school district tried a few years later to exclude a Chinese American student from its public schools, the California Supreme Court cited the statutory change to require her admission (*Tape v. Hurley*, 1885). In 1890 the California high court declared that a black student could not be directed to attend a black school in the Visalia school district, because state law no longer permitted racial segregation in public schools (*Wysinger v. Crookshank*). However, in both these decisions, the court recognized that the legislature could change the status quo and opt for racially separate schools should it choose to do so.

In fact, after the *Tape* ruling, the California Legislature did amend the statute to permit school districts to establish separate schools for Indian children and those of "Mongolian or Chinese descent." If separate schools were not established, then a school district was required to admit the students into its regular schools. These provisions were not removed until 1947. Redress in federal court was unavailing, particularly after the U.S. Supreme Court permitted Mississippi to classify Chinese students as "colored" so that they had to attend black schools (*Gong Lum v. Rice*, 1927). Interestingly, the California Legislature did not permit separate schools for Japanese Americans until 1921, but by then most of these students were already attending white schools and continued to do so. The combination of increasing numbers of Chinese students in San Francisco and the costs of maintaining separate schools eventually forced the governing board to end segregated schooling in the city.

While California never sanctioned separate schooling for Latino students, local officials routinely segregated them based on language deficiencies. The first decision involving the so-called Americanization schools occurred in 1931. The all-white Lemon Grove school board decided to educate children of Mexican descent in a separate school. In ruling against the school board, the state superior court judge noted that segregation "denies the Mexican children the presence of the American children, which is so necessary to learn the English language" (Leonel Sanchez, "Before Brown," *San Diego Union-Tribune*, May 18, 2004). As noted in Chapter 2, the state in recent years has wrestled with some of the same concerns over bilingual education. However, the Lemon Grove decision did not become a legal precedent in the state, because the district never appealed the trial judge's decision.

It was not until 1947 that segregation of Mexican American students based on claims of language deficiency ended. The case involved students of Mexican descent in several Los Angeles area school districts who contended in federal court that such segregation violated the equal protection of the laws under both the California and U.S. constitutions. In affirming the federal trial court's decision against the district, the U.S. Court of Appeals for the Ninth Circuit first noted that the legislature had not authorized the segregation of Mexican students. In fact, a state law at the time allowed admission of Mexican children to California schools. Thus, the judges held that the California Supreme Court's ruling in *Ward v. Flood* and the U.S. Supreme Court's later ruling in *Plessy v. Ferguson* did not apply, thus sidestepping the question of state-sanctioned racial segregation in public schools. Among those urging the appeals court to confront the matter head on were Thurgood Marshall and Robert Carter of the National Association for the Advancement of Colored People (NAACP), who filed an amicus brief in the case and a few years later would successfully argue *Brown v. Board of Education of Topeka, Kansas* before the U.S. Supreme Court. Because the state did not authorize segregation of Mexican students, the Ninth Circuit ruled that the actions of local school officials in doing so were unconstitutional (*Westminster School District of Orange County v. Mendez*). Following this decision, the California Legislature eliminated all references to racially separate public schools in the attendance law. However, as will become clear in the following sections, concern about racial segregation in California public schools has never abated.

Remedying racial isolation regardless of cause. In 1963, the California Supreme Court addressed the segregation of the Pasadena schools in an opinion that would mark a major shift in California school law away from the trend of the developing federal law. In July of 1961, one of the junior high schools in Pasadena withdrew from its district, leaving its students in need of a new school. Many of the students and their families, who were predominately white, did not want to be included in the attendance zone for the nearest junior high school, which had a student body of predominately minority children. In response to all the political pressure, the school district gerrymandered the school zones to allow the white students to attend a more distant, primarily white school. A thirteen-year-old black student objected to the maintenance of the new zoning system because it led to the denial of his application to transfer out of his primarily minority school.

The California Supreme Court found that the redrawing of attendance zones to maintain the demographic status quo qualifies as de jure segregation. While relying primarily on the *Brown* decision, the court also cited State Board of Education regulations to the effect that "The right to an equal opportunity for education and the harmful consequences of segregation require that school boards take steps, insofar as reasonably feasible, to alleviate racial imbalance in schools regardless of its cause" (*Jackson v. Pasadena City School District*, 1963, p. 610).

Though the *Jackson* decision clearly established an affirmative obligation of school officials to integrate schools, the impact of the decision on the daily lives of administrators was highly uncertain due to a technical aspect of the ruling that rendered it merely advisory rather than binding law. Because of this ambiguity, the California political community had to contend with the divisive issues left unresolved by *Jackson*.

Developing a coherent plan to address racial imbalances in student populations proved to be a difficult task. The controversy surrounding policies of forced integration through means such as busing or rezoning divided much of the population of California. The state legislature sought to respond to the will of the voters, but the temporary nature of any political majority made efforts at lawmaking short lived. In 1970, the legislature declared that schools could not require "any student to be transported for any purpose or for any reason without written permission of the parent or guardian" (Cal. Educ. Code § 1009.5). The apparent purpose of this statute was to eliminate the forced busing of students to achieve racial integration in schools. The California Supreme Court found such a purpose to be unconstitutional and construed the statute as simply preventing students from being forced to use school-provided transportation without parental consent (*San Francisco Unified School District v. Johnson*, 1971). In 1971, the same year the California Supreme Court decided *Johnson*, the state legislature made an abrupt about-face and enacted the Bagley Act, which effectively codified the *Jackson* doctrine by placing the responsibility on school officials to operate racially integrated schools and gave the California Department of Education enforcement power.

However, the Bagley Act was short lived. One year following its enactment, the people of California approved by referendum Proposition 21 (now Educ. Code § 35351), which repealed the Bagley Act. Proposition 21 also tried to effectuate the real purpose of Section 1009.5 by denying school officials the power to assign students to schools on the basis of their racial or ethnic identity. Once again, however, the California Supreme Court foiled the legislature's efforts. In *Santa Barbara School District v. Superior Court*, the court held that the repealing of the Bagley Act was constitutional. But the court found the portion of the proposition preventing school authorities from using racial classifications for student assignments unconstitutional as applied to districts experiencing either de jure or de facto segregation (1975). The court clarified that the fatal flaw in Proposition 21 and its predecessor, Section 1009.5, was their failure to exempt the use of racial classifications by schools remedying past segregation. Without this exemption, the laws interfered with a school board's ability to remedy a violation of federal law. Education Code Section 35351, which remains on the books, thus appears to have limited applicability in the racial context. In 2007, the statute was expanded to prohibit assigning students to schools on the basis of disability, gender, nationality, race or ethnicity, religion, sexual orientation, or any other characteristic that is contained in the definition of hate crimes in Penal Code Section 422.55.

In 1976, the California Supreme Court stepped back into the fray with a decision that established the limits as well as the reach of *Jackson*'s affirmative obligation to integrate schools. The decision concerned a class of minority students in the Los Angeles Unified School District who had filed a lawsuit in 1963 against the school district to force the integration of its schools. It was undisputed that the district's schools were segregated—in 1968 a significant number of student bodies within the district's schools were either 90 percent minority or 90 percent white. After several years of unsuccessful settlement negotiations, a trial, and appeals, the case came before the California Supreme Court.

The court affirmed the *Jackson* ruling by this time explicitly noting that Article I, Section 7 (a) of the California Constitution mandating equal protection of the laws requires all public school districts to undertake "reasonably feasible steps to alleviate school segregation, regardless of its cause" (*Crawford v. Board of Education of the City of Los Angeles*, 1976, p. 726). By ignoring its responsibility to integrate its schools as required by *Jackson*, the Los Angeles district had violated the state constitution. But the court's opinion stressed that the obligation does not impose on school districts a duty to ensure their schools reflect the ethnic makeup of the district as a whole. The court found "nothing inherently invalid in the fact that percentages of various racial or ethnic groups may vary, even significantly, in different schools throughout a school district, or even that a particular minority group may be completely unrepresented in a particular school" (p. 740). Rather, school authorities are charged under the California Constitution with taking "reasonable and feasible steps" to address racially segregated schools, which are "schools in which the minority student enrollment is so disproportionate as realistically to isolate minority students from other students and thus deprive minority students of an integrated educational experience" (p. 739).

The *Crawford* court added that whether a school is unconstitutionally segregated will depend on a fact-intensive inquiry sensitive to the circumstances of each case, with acknowledgment of the limited resources available to a school district to adopt corrective measures. Factors that should be considered include the racial makeup of the student body, faculty, and staff, as well as community attitudes toward the schools. Additionally, the court emphasized that the primary responsibility for compliance with the constitutional mandate and the determination of corrective measures should rest with school administrators. California courts should not intervene in the desegregation process, regardless of the efficiency of the district's plans. Only upon a finding that a district has failed to take any reasonable steps to ameliorate segregation may a trial court step in and order the district to follow certain guidelines or adopt certain procedures. Once a trial court has intervened, however, the *Crawford* court emphasized that the judge may use his or her full equitable powers to formulate a desegregation plan.

Limits on busing. Three years after *Crawford* invoked the equitable power of the intervening courts, those powers were drastically reduced by California voters. Proposition 1, which passed in 1979 and became part of Section 7 (a) of Article I of the California Constitution, successfully did what Proposition 21 had failed to achieve seven years earlier. It removes from state courts the ability to require schools to implement busing and student reassignment plans unless such remedies are necessary to comply with federal law. In effect, the constitutional amendment prevents courts that are addressing situations of de facto segregation from requiring the use of what is often considered one of the most effective tools to desegregate schools. With this law, the voters clearly indicated their discontent with the broad and potentially intrusive power of the state judiciary that *Jackson* and *Crawford* had authorized.

In 1982, the California Supreme Court confronted a case requiring it to clarify how Article I, Section 7 (a) interacts with the *Jackson* doctrine. A group of parents and taxpayers had filed suit against the Oxnard Union High School District, claiming that the district's procedure for complying with *Jackson* was inadequate. For proof, they cited that the district had declared a school not segregated whose student body was 86 percent white and 14 percent students of color. In considering the case, the California Supreme Court rejected the contention that the "antibusing" aspect of Article I, Section 7 (a) lessens the extent of the *Jackson* obligation. While the constitutional amendment reduces the power of judicial intervention in desegregation cases, it does not prevent school administrators from *voluntarily* implementing desegregation measures to comply with *Jackson* and *Crawford*. Specifically, the court stated that "the amendment neither releases school districts from their state constitutional obligation to take reasonably feasible steps to alleviate segregation regardless of its cause, nor divests California courts of authority to order desegregation measures other than pupil school assignment or pupil transportation" (*McKinney v. Oxnard Union High School District*, p. 556).

The court then applied the *Jackson* and *Crawford* criteria to the situation at Oxnard Unified. Noting the emphasis in *Crawford* on deferring to localized decision-making, the court upheld the district's conclusion regarding the segregated status of its schools, stating that "the admittedly substantial disparity between minority and white racial percentages at Camarillo High School was not 'so disproportionate as to realistically to isolate minority students from other students in the district'"(p. 553).

Three months after the *McKinney* decision was handed down, the U.S. Supreme Court upheld the constitutionality of the Proposition 1 amendment to Article I, Section 7(a). The Court clarified that "having gone beyond the requirements of the Federal Constitution, the State was free to return in part to the standard prevailing generally throughout the United States" (*Crawford v. Board of Education of the City of Los Angeles*, 1982, p. 542). In other words, a state is not legally obligated, having placed the bar of state constitutionality higher than the bar of federal constitutionality, to forever maintain such a position. As applied to California, state desegregation law generally does require "more" than federal desegregation law because of the *Jackson* and *Crawford* holdings. But with respect to busing and pupil reassignment, state and federal law are congruent.

Limits on affirmative action and racial balancing. In 1996, California voters again altered the tenuous balance of state desegregation law, this time with even more restrictive results. Proposition 209, which passed by a vote of 54 percent, added Section 31 to Article I of the California Constitution prohibiting any governmental entity, including public schools, from discriminating or granting preferences on the basis of race. In 1997, the Ninth Circuit affirmed the initiative's constitutionality (*Coalition for Economic Equity v. Wilson*). As a result of Section 31, school administrators may not adopt any racially discriminatory or preferential measures unless they are ordered to do so by a court enforcing the federal prohibition of de jure segregation. There is a small but significant exception to this rule. The amendment grandfathered in existing court orders and consent decrees requiring schools to desegregate, so school districts under continuing court supervision are unaffected by the new law. For districts without ongoing court orders, the effect of the amendment is more uncertain.

At least nominally, all school districts in California must comply with the *Jackson* and *Crawford* requirement that schools retain some measure of diversity. Section 31, however, appears to undercut the thrust of these rulings by preventing school officials from employing policies that have the effect of discriminating against white students or preferring minority students. At the time of this writing, the apparent conflict between Section 31 and the California Supreme Court rulings, and racial balancing measures more generally, is still unresolved. The courts and the legislature have not yet clarified what methods of maintaining or obtaining racial balance in a school amount to racial preferences forbidden by Section 31.

For example, does it constitute a racial preference to operate a transfer policy that allows only transfers that would improve the racial balance at the sending and receiving schools? Currently, there are two California statutes governing the effect of transfers on the racial balance of schools. Education Code Section 35160.5 (b)(2)(A) conditions the receipt of state funds on a school district's establishment of an intradistrict enrollment policy that allows parents to choose the school their children attend, provided the policy allows district officials the authority to comply with a court order or district policy on maintaining racial or ethnic balance. Education Code Section 48204 (b)(2), in contrast, concerns interdistrict transfer policies. That statute permits a district's governing board to reject a student's application to transfer to a school within the district if the transfer would negatively impact a court-ordered or voluntary desegregation plan. The statute added in 2004 that implements the interdistrict transfer option contains the same provision (Educ. Code § 48301 (b)).

In 2002, a California appellate court examined the effect of Section 31 on the intradistrict transfer statute, Education Code Section 35160.5 (b)(2)(A). In that case, a taxpayer in Huntington Beach objected to the racial and ethnic balancing component of the local district's transfer policy. Under the policy, transfers in and out of the "ethnically isolated" Huntington Beach High School could occur on a one-for-one basis only, meaning that a white student residing in the attendance area could transfer out only if another white student transferred in; and a minority student residing outside the attendance area could transfer in only if another minority student transferred out. The taxpayer viewed this as a form of racial discrimination. The California appellate court agreed, finding that the transfer policy "creates different transfer criteria for students solely on the basis of their race" (*Crawford v. Huntington Beach Union High School District*, p. 102). The court then concluded that the racial and ethnic balancing component of Education Code Section 35160.5, which would allow for a policy like the one at Huntington Beach Unified, amounts to a granting of racial preferences in violation of Section 31 of the California Constitution. The court pointed out that the California Constitution has changed since the California Supreme Court decided the *Jackson* and *Crawford* cases and that Section 31 now controlled.

This ruling has not been accepted by the federal courts. In 1999, a teacher at Van Nuys High School in Los Angeles sought to transfer to a similar position at another school in the district, but the faculty transfer policy of the Los Angeles Unified School District would not permit him, as a white teacher, to move to a school with more than a specified percentage of white faculty members. The teacher sued in federal court, claiming the policy was a violation of Section 31 of the California Constitution. The federal district court held that the transfer policy at Los Angeles Unified did not give preferential treatment to or discriminate against a racial group. The policy required only that school faculties remain within a specified number of percentage points above or below the district-wide percentage of minority faculty members. The district court reasoned that the policy did not prefer one race of teachers over another. Furthermore, the district court noted that Los Angeles Unified is exempted from the operation of Section 31 because it is still operating under a court order mandating it to comply with *Jackson* and desegregate its schools to the extent feasible. The teacher appealed to the U.S. Court of Appeals for the Ninth Circuit.

The Ninth Circuit found the question presented a closer one than the trial court had believed it to be. The transfer policy could not definitively be declared neutral, because while it erects both a minimum and a maximum applicable to each racial group, such that the policy's macroscopic effect—keeping whites and nonwhites in balance—touches both groups with equal force, "its microscopic effect—denying a transfer to a teacher who would upset that balance—operates to exclude an individual from a position based on his race" (*Friery v. Los Angeles Unified School District*, 2002, p. 1123). The Ninth Circuit did not find the *Huntington Beach* decision controlling, because the student transfer policy in that case limited the transfers of white students out of a particular high school and of nonwhites into the school but did not apply to the transfer of nonwhites out and the transfer of white students in. By operating only in one direction, the Huntington Beach policy did not apply to each racial category equally. Because no California court decisions elucidate whether the type of teacher transfer policy employed by the Los Angeles district constitutes preferential treatment, the Ninth Circuit submitted the question to the California Supreme Court and held up further proceedings in the case.

The Ninth Circuit also expressed reluctance to follow the California court of appeal's conclusion in *Huntington Beach* that *Jackson* and *Crawford v. Board of Education* have been diminished by the enactment of Section 31. "[T]he safer course," the judges observed, "is to seek an authoritative resolution of this question from the California Supreme Court" (p. 1124). The judges added that the Ninth Circuit is bound by the decisions of the California intermediate courts on matters of state law "only to the extent that the California Supreme Court would likely reach the same conclusions" (p. 1124). In a similar vein, the judges were uncertain whether the Los Angeles district was still sufficiently under court order to fall within the exception to Section 31 and asked for clarification on this matter as well. Subsequently, the California Supreme Court refused to take up the request from the Ninth Circuit. The Ninth Circuit eventually sent the entire matter back to the trial court in 2006 to determine whether Friery even had standing to file the lawsuit.

Several years prior to the Supreme Court's *Grutter* decision upholding the limited use of race in a public law school's admissions policy, the Ninth Circuit was confronted with a similar admissions policy used at the Corinne A. Seeds University Elementary School, operated as a research laboratory by the University of California at Los Angeles Graduate School of Education. To assure a student body appropriate for conducting research on issues relevant to children in urban settings, the school's admissions committee considered various factors in deciding whom to enroll, including race, ethnicity, gender, and family income. In a two-to-one decision, the appeals court upheld the policy. The majority concluded that the research mission of the laboratory school provided the requisite compelling governmental interest to justify the consideration of race and ethnicity in admissions decision making (*Hunter ex rel. Brandt v. Regents of the University of California*, 1999). The majority clearly was influenced by the testimony of expert witnesses about the importance of using race as a factor in admissions decisionmaking to fulfill the school's research mission.

The parents who initiated the lawsuit in federal court after their daughter was denied admission to the laboratory school also filed a lawsuit in state court, arguing that the racial preference policy violated the Section 31 embodiment of Proposition 209 in the California Constitution. A few years after the Ninth Circuit issued its decision in *Hunter*, a California court of appeal affirmed a trial court's decision that the parents' state law action should be dismissed. In an unpublished opinion—which has no value as legal precedent—the court noted that as a tuition-supported, selective-admissions-based laboratory school operated by UCLA, the school did not meet the definition of public school contained in Section 31 (*Hunter v. Regents of the University of California*, 2001). Thus, Section 31 does not invalidate the laboratory school's admissions process.

The fact that the laboratory school is the only one of its type in the state limits the reach of these judicial decisions. This is significant for California charter schools, which are considered public schools, not laboratory schools, and are therefore prohibited by Section 31 from granting racial preferences. Despite this restriction, charter schools are required by the Education Code to address in their charter petition "the means by which the school will achieve a racial and ethnic balance among its pupils that is reflective of the general population residing within the territorial jurisdiction of the school district to which the charter petition is submitted" (Educ. Code § 47605 (b)(5)(G)). In their efforts to comply with this statute, charter schools may not implement race-conscious admissions policies and then attempt to avoid accountability under Section 31 by pointing to the U.S. Supreme Court's *Grutter* decision. *Grutter* does not apply to public schools. Even if it did, the decision does not convey an entitlement to a race-conscious admissions policy.

While the U.S. Supreme Court struck down most general uses of race in student assignment it its 2007 *Parents Involved in Community Schools v. Seattle District No. 1* as discussed earlier, the impact of this ruling on California appears minimal, given that Proposition 209 already prohibits governmental entities including public schools from discriminating or granting preferences based on race, color, ethnicity, gender, and national origin. As noted in the next section, school districts and charter schools have used proxies for race with varying degrees of success to satisfy the obligation under the *Crawford v. Board of Education of the City of Los Angeles* decision and provisions of the Education Code to eliminate racial isolation regardless of cause. Whether the nuanced use of race itself as Justice Kennedy suggests in *Parents Involved* will pass judicial muster in California and elsewhere awaits future litigation. One thing is certain: School districts seeking to reduce racial isolation must design their plans carefully to avoid conflict and litigation.

In sum, it is clear from this review that the state courts, the state legislature, and the voters have played equally significant roles in shaping desegregation law in California since the early 1960s. We have provided a capsule summary of the major developments in Table 11.1. The apparent divide between popular political sentiment and judicial interpretation of the state constitution through the 1960s and 1970s produced a legal landscape that has become complex and in many ways contradictory. Though *Crawford* offered guidance to school officials in defining the extent of their obligation under state law regarding de facto segregation, Propositions 21, 1, and 209 have chipped away at the strength of the *Jackson* and *Crawford* opinions. While the affirmative obligation on school officials to remedy racial segregation in public schooling regardless of cause still exists, the only way noncomplying school officials can be forced to do so is through a suit brought by a student-plaintiff alleging violation of *Crawford*. However, even this avenue may be closing. The California Supreme Court last cited the *Crawford* decision in 1992. Though the affirmative obligation to address de facto segregation is still controlling law, it is unclear at this time where the California Supreme Court stands on the matter.

Finding other means of fostering diversity. Let us return to the question of how a charter school operator can comply with the Education Code requirement that it have a student body that reflects the racial and ethnic mix of the general community of the school district within which it is located. As we have noted, under federal law, a school can implement policies designed to achieve a measure of racial integration

TABLE 11.1
Major Developments in California Desegregation Law

Year	Development	Content	Significance
1963	*Jackson v. Pasadena City School District*	California Supreme Court supports efforts to alleviate racial imbalance in public schools regardless of cause.	Unclear to what extent school officials must take action to alleviate racial imbalance.
1972	Proposition 21 amends the Education Code	Denies school officials the power to assign students to schools on the basis of race or ethnicity.	Limited ability of school officials to comply with *Jackson*.
1975	*Santa Barbara School District v. Superior Court*	California Supreme Court holds the portion of Proposition 21 preventing use of student assignment based on race unconstitutional.	Restores the use of racial classifications for student assignment.
1976	*Crawford v. Board of Education of the City of Los Angeles*	California Supreme Court affirms *Jackson* that equal protection clause of California Constitution requires school districts to undertake reasonably feasible steps to alleviate racial segregation regardless of cause.	Court suggests but does not dictate the means by which integration is to be accomplished. Places primary responsibility on school administrators and directs judges to become involved only as a last resort.
1979	Proposition 1 amends Section 7(a) of Article I of the California Constitution	Limits state courts from requiring busing or student assignment to bring about integration unless necessary to comply with federal law.	Limits use of two significant tools for integrating school districts.
1982	*McKinney v. Oxnard Union High School District*	California Supreme Court rules that Proposition 1 does not curtail voluntary use of busing and student assignment by school districts.	Clarifies that school districts can continue to use busing and student assignment if they choose to do so. However, federal courts disapprove their use unless necessary to comply with a court order.
1996	Proposition 209 adds Section 31 to Article I of the California Constitution	Prevents government entities from discriminating or granting preferences on the basis of race.	Ends affirmative action measures unless required to comply with a court order.

only if the court first finds that the school officials had engaged in some explicit or implicit discriminatory behavior. Section 31 of Article I of the California Constitution explicitly prohibits the use of race for affirmative action purposes in the absence of a court order. Thus, for the moment, both federal law and Section 31 prohibit school officials from voluntarily using racial classifications for benign purposes such as assuring a diversified student body. It is thus not possible for a charter school to set aside a certain percentage of its student enrollment for students of various races. Are there other ways that charter schools and public schools in general can achieve a racially diversified student body? Perhaps. But the task is not easy. An illustration is afforded by the experience of the San Francisco Unified School District. In 1983, the district entered into a consent decree with the NAACP providing that no school shall have fewer than four racial/ethnic groups represented in its student body and that no racial/ethnic group shall constitute more than 45 percent of the student enrollment at any traditional school and no more than 40 percent at any alternative school. The district committed itself to monitor the enrollment at each school to assure that the racial percentages were observed.

In 1994, Chinese students filed suit against the use of the racial balancing system as discriminatory. The district first contended that it was not employing a racial balancing system, but both the federal trial court and the Ninth Circuit found to the contrary. All parents were required to indicate their race on a preregistration form that stated that black and Latino students were given priority over other students in granting optional enrollment requests. The president of the governing board maintained that the district had not yet eliminated vestiges of past segregatory acts against black and Latino students and was striving to do so. Because this might be true, the Ninth Circuit refused to overturn the trial judge's decision that a trial would be necessary to see if the district could prove its case (*Ho by Ho v. San Francisco Unified School District*, 1998).

Before the trial was held, the district, the Ho plaintiffs, and the San Francisco NAACP agreed to a settlement that in effect ended use of race and ethnicity in student assignment. The parties agreed to seek other ways to achieve racial integration in the district, and in 2001 a new settlement was reached that included a student assignment provision known as the diversity index. The index encompassed family socioeconomic status, mother's educational background, language status, academic performance, and home language. It did not include assigning students to schools by geographic zones or the use of race as one factor in student assignment. Despite the diversity index, the district became increasingly segregated. Frustrated with the lack of progress by the parties in fixing the diversity index, the federal judge refused to extend the consent decree beyond its termination date of December 31, 2005, despite the urging of the parties that he do so. As it turned out, the high point of integration occurred in 1997–98 when only one school in the district enrolled more than fifty percent of a single racial group. By 2005, over one in three schools had resegregated. The court pointed out that the overwhelming majority of schools that had been successful in closing the achievement gap among racial groups had been the ones maintaining ethnically and racially diverse student bodies. The resegregated schools had declining Academic Performance Index (API) scores and growing achievement gaps. The court noted that the diversity index allowed, if not caused, the resegregation and that extending the consent decree not only would prevent the parties from modifying it but would add the court's imprimatur to a failed plan. It was time, the judge added, to turn control of the district over to school officials "subject to the rough and tumble of local politics and government" (*San Francisco NAACP v. San Francisco Unified School District*, 2005, p. 1072).

Contrary to the San Francisco experience, other California school districts (e.g., Berkeley) and charter schools (e.g., High Tech High in San Diego) have been successful in using what the law calls "non-suspect classifications" like family income, parent education, geography, targeted recruiting, and admission by lottery to assure that their student bodies reflect at least to some extent the racial and ethnic mix of the communities within which they operate. In this way, the benefits of diversity are preserved without engaging in impermissible racial discrimination, though any kind of assignment system, including the altering of neighborhood attendance zones, is likely to generate controversy.

GENDER DISCRIMINATION

Beliefs in the inferiority of women are at least as old as the written history of Western civilization. Under English common law, women could not own property or enter into contracts. The American founders simply assumed that voting rights would not include women. Women did not gain the right to vote until the Nineteenth Amendment was ratified in 1920, and they only recently have gained entry into the top echelons of corporate and nonprofit organizations and the government.

There are two major differences between discrimination against racial minorities and discrimination against women. First, because there are more women than men, women have had the political power in recent years that racial minorities have lacked. Second, physiological differences between men and women sometimes warrant different treatment under the law. Both may have played a role in the failure to amend the U.S. Constitution to provide gender equality under the law through ratification of the Equal Rights Amendment (ERA). That amendment read, "Equality of rights under the law shall not be denied or abridged by the United States or any State on account of sex" and would have authorized Congress to enact enforcement legislation. ERA never received sufficient state ratification to be added to the U.S. Constitution by the time the period for ratification had ended in 1982. Thirty-five states had ratified it, including California, but three more were necessary.

With the failure of ERA, attention shifted back to judicial and statute law to advance the cause of women's rights. We begin by addressing constitutional dimensions in this section.

Constitutional Dimensions

For much of its history, the U.S. Supreme Court paid little attention to gender discrimination. When it did consider gender, it took a paternal posture. Consider Justice Joseph P. Bradley's concurring opinion in an 1873 ruling upholding an Illinois law that prevented women from being lawyers:

> Man is, or should be, woman's protector and defender. The natural and proper timidity and delicacy which belongs to the female sex evidently unfits it for many of the occupations of civil life. . . . The paramount destiny and mission of woman are to fulfill the noble and benign offices of wife and mother. This is the law of the Creator. (*Bradwell v. State*, p. 141)

It was only in the early 1970s that the Court began to question the constitutionality of gender-based classifications. The equal protection clause of the Fourteenth Amendment, which the Court had interpreted to forbid racial classifications in the school desegregation cases discussed earlier, was the logical starting point for the Court's analysis. In its first case recognizing gender discrimination as grounds for invalidating a statute, the Court held that the government may not treat similarly situated men and women differently merely because of archaic stereotypes, even if doing so would promote administrative convenience in some cases (*Reed v. Reed*, 1971). Holding otherwise would permit the continuation of "romantic paternalism" that, as the Court noted in a similar case, "put[s] women, not on a pedestal, but in a cage" (*Frontiero v. Richardson*, p. 684).

Despite their determination that gender qualifies for constitutional protection, the justices did not initially agree on whether gender classifications merit the same level of protection as racial classifications. Several justices considered gender to be innately different from race because of the physical differences separating men and women, thus necessitating that there be some situations in which state actors can constitutionally take account of gender-based differences. In a series of several decisions, the Court established that governmental gender classifications merit close review, though they are not as disfavored as racial classifications. Under no circumstances may gender be used to perpetuate stereotypes or foster the legal, social, or economic inferiority of women. Gender preferences, however, that seek to compensate women for past inequities may receive slightly less stringent review by courts. Regardless of the purpose, all such classifications must serve important governmental objectives by means that are substantially related to the achievement of those objectives.

Two important decisions illustrating the scope of protection afforded gender arise in the context of higher education. In 1982, the Supreme Court considered the gender-based admissions policy at an all-female Mississippi school for nursing. A male applicant who was refused admission because of his gender sued the school, claiming that its policy violated the Fourteenth Amendment's equal protection clause. The Supreme Court agreed. Writing for the Court, Justice Sandra Day O'Connor stated that "the party seeking to uphold a statute that classifies individuals on the basis of their gender must carry the burden of showing an 'exceedingly persuasive justification' for the classification" (*Mississippi University for Women v. Hogan*, p. 724). In this case, the state had failed to show that its stated purpose for the restrictive admissions policy, compensating women for generations of educational discrimination, was the real justification for the policy. The Court also found that the policy did not actually help women overcome their stereotyped roles, because women already had considerably more opportunities than men in the nursing profession.

In 1996, the Court refined the standard it had set out in *Mississippi University for Women*. At issue was the Virginia Military Institute's (VMI) refusal to admit women to its rigorous educational program designed to produce "citizen-soldiers" (*United States v. Virginia*, p. 549). Virginia argued that the presence of women would require accommodations so extreme as to destroy the unique adversative educational program. The state's alternative school for women, a gentler and less prestigious program than what was offered at VMI, fell far short of comparability. The lack of a comparable alternative, together with the historical exclusion of women from opportunities in higher education, led the Court to find that Virginia had failed to show that it had an "exceedingly persuasive justification" for its gender-based admissions policy at VMI. The Court also emphasized that Virginia's stated purpose for providing the two single-sex programs was merely formulated after the challenge began and was not the actual motivation that had prompted the state to set up the two-school system.

In 1974, the Court of Appeals for the Ninth Circuit struck down an admissions policy at the prestigious Lowell High School in the San Francisco Unified School District seeking to achieve gender diversity by setting higher admissions requirements for female applicants than for male applicants. The school district instituted the policy to ensure the numerical equality of male and female students in entering classes. The court rejected the school's contention that gender diversity is necessary for a quality education, because the school had failed to provide any proof to support its claim. The school, therefore, could not meet the required showing under the equal protection clause of the Fourteenth Amendment that the gender-specific admissions policy substantially furthered the school's purpose of enhancing the education provided (*Berkelman v. San Francisco Unified School District*).

School athletic programs receive considerable attention for their impact on students of different genders and are subject to the same constitutional constraints as the academic programs discussed earlier. Title IX, which governs many of the details of these programs, will be discussed in depth in the following section of this chapter. In 1982, a class of male high school students in Arizona sued the Arizona Interscholastic Association (AIA), seeking access to their high schools' all-female interscholastic volleyball teams. AIA has a policy preventing male students from playing on all-female teams, though female students are allowed to play on all-male teams for noncontact sports. The Ninth Circuit held that AIA is subject to the strictures of the Fourteenth Amendment because its activities are closely intertwined with the state. The court then noted that while male students in Arizona may have less access to interscholastic all-female volleyball teams, they do not have less access to interscholastic sports teams overall. AIA supported its policy of forbidding male students from participating in all-female volleyball teams by citing the history of discrimination against female students in athletic activities. Because male students could potentially overwhelm the all-female team and reduce the opportunities for the female team members to play, the court upheld the policy (*Clark v. Arizona Interscholastic Association*, 1982).

Later, AIA authorized interscholastic competition among male-only volleyball teams, but the school where Clark's brother, the lead plaintiff in the earlier AIA case, played had none. The brother then sought to participate on the female team. As before, the Ninth Circuit found past discrimination against women justified the female-only restriction (*Clark v. Arizona Interscholastic Association*, 1989). In light of this case law, school districts must carefully consider the constitutionality of policies involving gender-based classifications. Such policies must, at the least, seek to further important—potentially even exceedingly persuasive—governmental objectives by means substantially related to those objectives. Further, those objectives cannot be formulated after the fact. Rather, they must be real expressions of the district's purposes in establishing the policies.

The California Constitution has both an equal protection clause and a provision that has been construed as the equivalent of the unsuccessful Equal Rights Amendment. The equal protection clause is found in Article I, Section 7 (a). As discussed in Chapter 3, it was used in the school finance case, *Serrano v. Priest* (1976), to strike down the California foundation program that permitted substantial interdistrict disparities in per-pupil expenditures. The gender-equality provision is Article I, Section 8, which states that "a person may not be disqualified from entering or pursuing a business, profession, vocation, or employment because of sex, race, creed, color, or national or ethnic origin." State judicial decisions have concluded that government classifications in these areas are suspect and must represent the narrowest and least restrictive means by which the statute's objectives can be achieved. And, as discussed in the race section of this chapter, Proposition 209, now codified as Article I, Section 31 of the California Constitution, outlaws discrimination and preferential treatment on the basis of gender as well as race, color, ethnicity, and national origin in public education, public employment, and public contracting. Thus while school districts must provide equal educational opportunities to both males and females under Article I, Section 8, they cannot engage in affirmative action efforts that prefer one gender over another under Section 31.

The door remains open for single-sex schooling under federal and state constitutional law, though proponents of such schemes will have to be prepared to withstand searching judicial inquiry into their motives and into the comparability of the programs offered. Consider in this context California's Single Gender Academies Pilot Program, enacted in 1996 (Educ. Code §§ 58520–58524). Its purpose is to increase the diversity of the state's public educational offerings by making single-gender academies available to those pupils of each gender who because of their unique educational needs will benefit from single-gender education. The statute requires that if a particular program or curriculum is available to one gender, a similar opportunity shall be available to those pupils of the other gender, though tailored to the differing needs and learning styles of each. Only a handful of schools were started before funding cutbacks curtailed further development. The availability of evidence supporting the justification for a school's gender-based policies appears to be essential.

Title IX and Its Regulations

Title IX of the 1972 Education Amendments provides in part that "No person in the United States shall on the basis of sex, be excluded from participation in, be denied the benefits of, or be subjected to discrimination under any education program or activity receiving federal financial assistance" (20 U.S.C. § 1681). The U.S. Department of Education's Office for Civil Rights (OCR) is charged with implementing and enforcing the law. Education Code Section 270 requires that the thrust of its regulations be posted on the California Department of Education's website. OCR can impose sanctions on funding recipients, including the loss of federal money. In addition to OCR enforcement, victims of discrimination may file lawsuits under Title IX and its implementing regulations against school districts and private schools receiving federal funds, seeking both injunctive relief and, if discrimination is intentional, compensatory damages. In 2005 the U.S. Supreme Court ruled that third parties who suffer retaliation can file lawsuits as well (*Jackson v. Birmingham Board of Education*). The case involved a high school basketball coach who complained about unequal treatment of the girls' basketball team. He sued the school district, alleging retaliation against him in the form of negative evaluations and removal from coaching. The removal cost him supplemental pay. The case was returned to the trial court to determine if the coach could prove his claims.

Title IX applies primarily to students in public schools and in private schools receiving federal funds. Gender discrimination in employment discrimination and harassment falls under Title VII of the 1964 Civil Rights Act, as discussed in Chapter 5 on Employment. An organization qualifies as receiving federal funds if any part of it receives "scholarships, loans, grants, wages or other funds" that are "payment to or on behalf of students admitted to that entity, or extended directly to such students for payment to that entity." It does not matter whether the district receives the money for educational purposes directly from the government or indirectly through its students. Title IX excludes from its coverage the admissions policies of single-sex public high schools that have been single-sex since their establishment as well as parochial schools that espouse religious principles contrary to the intent of the statute.

Title IX is most often cited in its application to school athletic programs. Schools subject to Title IX must ensure that their athletic programs offer equal opportunities for athletic participation to students of both genders. Though this requirement does not necessitate equal funding, a failure to provide necessary financial support for one gender's athletic programs is considered as a factor in determining whether a school has violated its Title IX obligations. Additional factors include the variety of sports and competition opportunities offered and whether they accommodate each gender's level of interest; the provision of equipment; game times and practice times; funding for travel expenses; coaching and academic tutoring opportunities; compensation for coaches and academic tutors; the quality of locker rooms; and the facilities provided for practice, housing, dining, and medical attention.

Title IX does not prevent schools from operating single-sex sports teams if members are selected on the basis of competitive skill or if the team plays a contact sport. Contact sports include boxing, wrestling, rugby, ice hockey, football, basketball, and other sports involving bodily contact. For noncontact sports, schools may offer teams to one gender and not to the other; but they must allow students of the excluded gender to try out for such teams if opportunities in that particular sport have previously been limited for students of that gender. Scholarships must be made available to students of each gender on an equal basis in proportion to the number of students of each sex participating in interscholastic or intercollegiate athletics.

While schools subject to Title IX generally may not offer different courses on the basis of gender, they may separate students of different genders for physical education classes or for activities involving contact sports. The regulations also allow for schools to utilize standards that have the effect of separating students of different genders for vocal chorus classes. Such standards having disparate impacts may not be utilized when measuring skill or progress in a physical education class, however. Students may also be separated by gender for sex education classes. The U.S. Department of Education currently is modifying Title IX regulations to accommodate the growing interest in single-gender schooling.

Additionally, schools subject to Title IX may not discriminate on the basis of pregnancy, childbirth, termination of pregnancy, or marital status unless the student volunteers to attend a comparable educational program separate from other students.

RACIAL AND GENDER HARASSMENT

Harassment on the basis of race and gender is a form of discrimination and is outlawed under both federal and California law. We begin by examining federal statutes that govern harassment of this type and then discuss California's Unruh Civil Rights Act.

Racial Harassment under Title VI

Ending racial segregation nationally and in California under the terms of the equal protection clauses of both the federal and state constitutions is only part of the story. In this section, we examine how Title VI of the 1964 Civil Rights Act has become an important means of combating racial harassment in public schooling. In Chapter 5 we discussed how Title VII of the same act has targeted discrimination on the basis of race, color, religion, sex, and national origin in public and private employment.

Title VI of the 1964 Civil Rights Act provides that "No person in the United States shall, on the ground of race, color, or national origin, be excluded from participation in, be denied the benefits of, or be subjected to discrimination under any program or activity receiving federal financial assistance" (42 U.S.C. § 2000 d). As with Title IX, OCR in the U.S. Department of Education has developed a set of administrative rules for implementing Title VI and has the power to levy sanctions against entities for violations, including curtailing federal funding. Since virtually all public and many private schools receive some form of federal funding, the consequences of violating the act are real.

In addition to OCR enforcement, victims of discrimination may file lawsuits under Title VI and its implementing regulations against school districts and private schools receiving federal funds, seeking both injunctive relief and compensatory damages. Lawsuits may be filed against public school personnel as individuals under 42 U.S.C. Section 1983, a matter discussed in Chapter 12. To be successful in either case, plaintiffs must show an intent to discriminate. The U.S. Supreme Court has ruled that merely establishing that some action has a racially discriminatory impact is insufficient to trigger a violation under both the equal protection clause and Title VI (*Washington v. Davis*, 1976) and under Title VI's implementing regulations (*Alexander v. Sandoval*, 2001). This does not mean that activities having an unintentional discriminatory effect are always immune to judicial challenge under Title VI. Some federal agencies, including the Department of Education, have enacted implementing regulations that prohibit recipients of federal assistance from engaging in activities that have a disparate impact on different racial groups (34 C.F.R. § 100.3 (b)(2)). Though individuals may not sue on the basis of these regulations, the federal agencies that have established them may impose sanctions (*Alexander v. Sandoval*).

In a 1998 decision, the Ninth Circuit laid out the conditions for establishing a viable racial harassment claim under Title VI. The case involved African American parents who objected to having their children read *The Adventures of Huckleberry Finn,* by Mark Twain, and the short story *A Rose for Emily,* by William Faulkner, in public school ninth-grade English class. The parents filed suit, asserting that the requirement was discriminatory and created a racially hostile environment at school. The trial court dismissed their complaint, and the parents appealed. As discussed in Chapter 6 ("Rights of Expression"), the court concluded that use of the books in class did not constitute a violation of Title VI but rather served the interests of the school in exposing students to classic literary works and the interests of the students in reading them. But the judges were sufficiently concerned about the alleged racial harassment that they permitted this part of the lawsuit to go forward. The complaint alleged that after reading the books, white students repeatedly called the African American students "nigger," and racist graffiti was scrawled about the school. Though the Ninth Circuit could find no reported decision applying Title VI to student-to-student racial harassment, it did so in this case. Drawing upon U.S. Department of Education guidelines, it laid out three conditions for peer racial harassment to violate Title VI.

First, it must be established that a racially hostile environment exists. This requires a showing that the harassment is sufficiently severe that it interferes with the ability of targeted students to obtain an equal benefit from schooling. Second, it must be established that the district knew or should have known about the racially hostile environment. Third, as in sexual harassment cases, it must be shown that the district was deliberately indifferent to the need to take action to stop the harassment. Here, the complaint met all three tests, and the matter was sent back for trial (*Monteiro v. Tempe Union High School District*, 1998).

A 2002 racial discrimination claim filed in state court by two black students at Tamalpais High School against the Novato Unified School District over racial harassment occurring at a basketball game was not successful, because the school district had taken action in response to the harassment. Before the game at San Marin High School, a number of San Marin students arrived in costumes, some racist in character. At least one student wore a black Afro wig, and others had blackface. During the warm-up period, some of the students chanted "nigger." School officials intervened to stop the racist comments, but the racial slur again was hurled at a Tamalpais player during the game. Following the game, officials in the Novato district conducted an investigation and followed that up with letters of apology to the Tamalpais students. The two students bringing the lawsuit asserted that school officials knew of a long-standing racially hostile environment at San Marin High School and had failed to redress the situation effectively. They cited racial slurs directed to the only black teacher at the school, a slave day when some students wore chains and torn clothing with brown shoe polish on their faces, and display of the confederate flag in the school yearbook. The two students argued that the response of district personnel to the basketball incident was inadequate and constituted deliberate indifference under Title VI.

In an unpublished decision, the California court of appeal carefully examined the efforts that San Marin High School and school district officials took following the basketball game. They noted a number of actions in addition to the letters of apology. These included a nine-point plan to address racial issues, a diversity advisory committee, a policy on expected student behavior, and an equity plan designed to stop discrimination before it starts by teaching civility and acceptance. As a result of these and other actions, the court found that the district was not deliberately indifferent. Similarly, claims filed against several school administrators in their individual capacities under 42 U.S.C. Section 1983, a federal civil rights law discussed in Chapter 12, were dismissed because the administrators had not been deliberately indifferent (*Malcolm W. v. Novato Unified School District*, 2002).

In addition to missed educational opportunities and negative publicity, these cases demonstrate that failing to take steps to root out racial harassment can result in liability for both the district under Title VI and individual school personnel under Section 1983.

Sexual Harassment and Abuse under Title IX

Earlier in this chapter we examined gender discrimination and equity issues in public schools from the perspective of both federal and state law. Here, we look at how Congress and the courts have addressed sexual harassment and abuse under Title IX of the 1972 Education Amendments and its implementing of federal regulations.

To provide an effective remedy for victims of sexual harassment and abuse, the U.S. Supreme Court ruled in 1992 that victims can file their own lawsuits against school districts (*Franklin v. Gwinnett County Public Schools*). The case involved a female student who alleged that she was harassed and pressured into sexual intercourse by one of her male teachers. She sought monetary damages. The Court recognized that monetary damages can compensate a victim in a way that administrative sanctions imposed on the school district cannot, but the justices did not specify the conditions under which a district could be liable for employee-on-student sexual harassment. The answer was forthcoming six years later in the case of *Gebser v. Lago Vista Independent School District* (1998).

Gebser was a fourteen-year-old high school student who was in a sexual relationship with her fifty-two-year-old social studies teacher over a six-month period. None of the encounters occurred at school. The parents of two other students had complained to the high school principal that the teacher had made inappropriate sexual remarks in class. But the district found no evidence to support the complaint and, in any case, the complaint did not relate to Gebser and did not suggest the teacher had engaged in sexual relations with a student. After the pair was discovered in a wooded area, the teacher lost his job and his teaching certificate. He also served jail time on a charge of attempted sexual assault. Gebser sued the school district under Title IX, asserting that the teacher had used his position at school to sexually assault her and that the district should be accountable for the acts of its employees.

The Supreme Court established two standards for determining school district liability under Title IX. First, the matter has to be reported to a school official who has authority to institute corrective measures; and second, the official has to be deliberately indifferent. Here, the district was not liable. As soon as the matter became known, the teacher was dismissed. Gebser argued that she did not know what to do about the continued harassment because the district had failed to provide her with a copy of Title IX procedures. The Court did not find liability on this basis but did note that the U.S. Department of Education could impose sanctions on the district for failing to comply with its Title IX administrative regulations. Further, the Court noted that nothing precludes the student from seeking remedies under state law and suing school personnel individually for damages under 42 U.S.C. Section 1983.

In 1999, the Supreme Court confronted a case involving prolonged sexual harassment of a female student by one of her fifth-grade male classmates. The mother of the student alleged that the male student attempted to touch her daughter's breasts and genital area, made vulgar statements such as "I want to get in bed with you" and "I want to feel your boobs," rubbed his body against her, and placed a doorstop in his pants. The complaint claimed that school officials took no effective action. Only after three months of reported harassment was the daughter permitted to change her classroom seat so she wouldn't be next to the male student. The complaint further alleged that the girl's high grades had dropped, she wrote a suicide note, and she told her mother she did not know how long she could keep the student off of her. The incidents ended when the male student pleaded guilty to sexual battery. The Supreme Court ruled in *Davis v. Monroe County Board of Education* that peer sexual harassment is covered by Title IX and that the district can be liable if the harassment is reported to an official who has authority to take corrective action (presumably this could be the teacher as well as the campus administrator), the official is deliberately indifferent to doing so, and the harassment is so severe that it constitutes deprivation of equal access to educational opportunities or benefits.

Same-sex student peer harassment falls within the parameters of Title IX, just as it does with 42 U.S.C. Section 1983. A case in point involves an eighth-grade student in the Antioch Unified School District who was beaten severely on the way home by a fellow male student who taunted him about being homosexual, due in part to the fact that the victim's mother was a transgendered female. According to the allegation, the boy and his mother repeatedly reported harassing behavior of students to school district officials, but no action was taken. The boy asserted that the district knew that his attacker was violence prone. He also asserted that the attack left him so emotionally impaired and fearful of his safety as to deny him access to equal educational opportunities. The federal district court ruled that same-sex harassment is actionable under Title IX and refused to dismiss the case against the school district (*Ray v. Antioch Unified School District*, 2000).

California law both mirrors Title IX and goes beyond it. Education Code Section 200 and following sections prohibit public and private educational institutions from discriminating against persons on the basis of gender as well as disability, nationality, race or ethnicity, sexual orientation, or any other characteristic that falls within the definition of hate crimes under Section 422.55 of the Penal Code. Private schools are exempt from this requirement if compliance would violate their religious tenets. Section 210.7 defines "gender" to include a person's gender identity and gender-related appearance whether or not related to a person's biological sex. In other words, transgender persons are accorded equal rights in the state's schools. For example, while it may be possible in some states to prevent a male dressed as a female from attending the school prom, this could not occur in California. In 2008 a California court of appeal ruled that money damages for violating these sections of the Education Code are available (*Donovan v. Poway Unified School District*). The case involved sustained harassment against two gay students by their peers in the Poway district that resulted in their cutting classes and eventually enrolling in a home-study program. Holding that the standards for seeking damages under Section 220 are the same as under Title IX, the appellate court ruled that there were adequate grounds for the jury to conclude that the district had actual notice of the harassment and was deliberately indifferent to taking action to stop it, thus denying the two students access to equal educational opportunities. Significantly, the two students kept detailed logs chronicling the numerous anti-gay peer harassment incidents they encountered at school and their reports to school administrators. The $300,000 damage award under Section 220 was upheld.

California school districts may not utilize state funds for sports programs that do not provide male and female students with equal opportunities and equal use of facilities (Educ. Code § 221.7). Districts may not operate programs that exclude students from participation in equivalent athletic programs on the basis of their gender (Educ. Code § 230). Districts may meet this obligation in a number of ways: (1) by providing opportunities for the participation of male and female students in proportion to their respective enrollments; (2) by establishing a program that is responsive to underrepresentation of a particular gender in athletic participation, provided there has been a history of such underrepresentation; or (3) by fully accommodating the interests and abilities of the underrepresented students, provided there has been a history of such underrepresentation and the district does not have a program in place to encourage participation.

California Unruh Civil Rights Act

In a dramatic effort to eradicate societal discrimination, the California legislature enacted the Unruh Civil Rights Act in 1959. Its key provision now states:

> All persons within the jurisdiction of this state are free and equal, and no matter what their sex, race, color, religion, ancestry, national origin, disability, medical condition, marital status, or sexual orientation are entitled to the full and equal accommodations, advantages, facilities, privileges, or services in all business establishments of every kind whatsoever. (Civil Code § 51)

The phrase "business establishments" appears to encompass public and private schools, though courts are divided. For a claim to be viable, it must be established that the discrimination was arbitrary or intentional. Practices that have an unintentional disparate impact on a class of persons are not actionable. Penalties include both compensatory damages and injunctive relief, and can encompass both entities and individual employees. Punitive damages also are available.

In the schooling context, litigation under the Unruh Act has been limited, in part because the act deals only with equal access to establishments and in part to the availability of other remedies for discrimination. One important decision is *Nicole M. v. Martinez Unified School District*. After her daughter was allegedly sexually harassed and assaulted in school, the student's mother filed a lawsuit in federal court, advancing a number of federal and state claims. The student contended that the actions taken by the principal were so inadequate as to constitute a violation of her civil rights. She cited suspension of her attacker for one day and the placement of one of the worst perpetrators in a class to which she had been reassigned. Following the mandate of the California Supreme Court to apply the Unruh Act "in the broadest sense reasonably possible," the federal judge concluded that, if true, the lack of effective action may have deprived the student of the advantages and privileges of a public education. The school district argued that the Unruh Act had not been applied to claims of sexual harassment, but the judge could see no reason why it should not be (*Nicole M. v. Martinez Unified School District*, 1997). The judge also permitted the lawsuit to go forward against the school district under Title IX and against the school principal individually under 42 U.S.C. Section 1983. For reasons discussed in the next chapter, the federal judge rejected the portion of the lawsuit contending that the school district and principal were liable under the California Tort Claims Act. The case was set for trial to determine if the allegations were true and whether they amounted to intentional discrimination.

This potential barrage of litigation should encourage school districts to take preventive action. Districts should inform both personnel and students about Title IX, Education Code Section 200, and the Unruh Act and emphasize their commitment to enforcing the law in sexual harassment training programs. Education Code Section 231.5 requires educational institutions to have a written policy on sexual harassment as part of its general operating procedures. The policy is to be provided to new employees and students and is to be prominently displayed at the school site and administration building. It is to include information on where to obtain information about reporting charges of sexual harassment and seeking remedies. School personnel should avoid compromising situations with students. Consider, for example, the possible negative implications of teacher hugs and stroking of younger students and sexual banter exchanged with older students. Teachers should act aggressively to halt and report student-on-student sexual harassment. Supervisors should treat complaints of sexual harassment and abuse seriously by conducting thorough investigations in association with the district's Title IX coordinator and taking appropriate action.

A year after the *Nicole M.* ruling, another case arose in the context of racial harassment. An African American high school student sued the Santa Barbara Unified High School District and various school officials after she was subjected to repeated racial harassment. Among other things, the student alleged that several students placed a drawing on her desk of an African American person hanging from a tree by rope. The name "Sharoon" was written next to the body. The student, whose first name was Cheron, claimed the word combined her name and the word "coon." The student contended that her teacher did nothing except to excuse her from class and that school administrators did little to protect her. The student also contended that a racially hostile environment existed at the high school, noting that the NAACP had petitioned the district two years before to do something about it. The federal judge dismissed the student's claims under the Tort Claims Act. But he refused to do so under the Unruh Civil Rights Act, noting that, as in *Nicole M.*, the student had advanced sufficient allegations of a racially hostile environment to warrant a trial (*Davison v. Santa Barbara High School District*, 1998).

A violation of the Americans with Disabilities Act (ADA), which accords persons with disabilities meaningful access to programs and facilities of public and private schools as well as most businesses in the country, also is a violation of the Unruh Act. Thus, victims of disability discrimination can seek relief under either or both federal and state law. This is particularly significant in the case of private schools because damage remedies are available in this instance under the Unruh Act but not under the ADA.

SUMMARY

In 1954, the U.S. Supreme Court declared in *Brown v. Board of Education of Topeka, Kansas* that government-sanctioned racial segregation in public schools was unconstitutional. It soon became apparent that this goal could not be achieved simply by ending de jure segregation because of the legacy of harm suffered by generations of schoolchildren. To compensate them and to assure equality of opportunity, the U.S. Supreme Court directed that steps be taken to integrate previously segregated schools. But the question arose whether this requirement applied to all racially segregated schools, not just those in the South. In 1974, the U.S. Supreme Court said no. Only where it could be proven that schools had practiced racial segregation could such a remedy be imposed. The result was a system of racially integrated schools in the South but not necessarily elsewhere. In the decades thereafter, the enthusiasm of federal judges to pursue racial integration waned. Many districts resegregated as judicial oversight came to an end.

The California experience has been somewhat different. The California Supreme Court did not draw the line between forced segregation and segregation by circumstance. Rather, beginning in the 1970s, school districts had to take effective action to address racial isolation regardless of cause. Public opposition resulted in constitutional amendments limiting the use of busing, pupil assignment, and affirmative action to achieve this goal. These limitations, coupled with the retreat of federal courts from vigorously pursuing the cause of integration, have prompted school officials to resort to creative ways of reducing racial isolation. These include the development of thematic choice schools in racially isolated areas and assigning students to schools based on socioeconomic and geographic factors. In the case of charter schools, which have a statutory responsibility to achieve a racial and ethnic mix reflective of the general population of the district within which they are located, focused recruitment in underrepresented areas is an oft-employed effort. Despite efforts to overcome it, racial and economic isolation in California's public schools remains extensive.

Because of physiological differences between the sexes, the quest for gender equality has not ended the practice of separate but equal in facets of public schooling. However, school officials must advance an exceedingly persuasive justification under both the federal and California constitutions to warrant separate treatment. Title IX of the 1972 Education Amendments and its implementing regulations describe what is and is not permitted in treating students differently based on gender. This federal law applies to both public and private schools that receive federal funding. It has been especially important in advancing the cause of gender equity in extracurricular and athletic activities.

Racial and gender harassment is strictly forbidden under both federal and California law. Given the rigor with which Title VI and VII of the 1964 Civil Rights Act, Title IX, Section 220 of the Education Code, and California's Unruh Civil Rights Act are enforced, school authorities must take immediate action to stop harassment of employees and students on these grounds to avoid both district and employee liability.

LEGAL LIABILITY

The threat of lawsuits and legal liability are serious concerns for educators. In this chapter, we examine the extent to which school districts, board members, and employees can be held legally accountable in California state and federal courts. We do not discuss all legal claims, but focus on those involving personal injury and civil rights because these are the most prevalent in public schools. The matter is quite complex. To make the discussion more understandable, we provide numerous illustrations drawn from judicial decisions. We begin by discussing liability under California law, then turn to examine liability for federal wrongs. The clear message from this review is that the best way to avoid legal liability is to know and follow the law.

LIABILITY UNDER CALIFORNIA LAW

Before we examine California law specifically, we need to point out that the No Child Left Behind Act enacted by Congress in 2001 contains an important section entitled the Paul D. Coverdell Teacher Protection Act. This federal law is intended to shield school employees and individual members of a governing board from liability in state court for maintaining order and ensuring safety at school. It applies to states like California that receive federal assistance and that have not elected to be exempt from the act.

Specifically, the law extends immunity protection when school employees or individual board members take action in conformity with federal, state, and local laws to control, discipline, expel, or suspend a student or maintain order or control in the classroom or school. However, the immunity is carefully conditioned.

There is no immunity if school personnel are not acting within the scope of their employment or if they engage in willful or criminal misconduct, gross negligence, reckless misconduct, or flagrant indifference to the rights of the individual. Nor is there any immunity for crimes of violence, sexual offenses, violations of civil rights, or acts or omissions occurring while alcohol or drug impaired. Nothing precludes a school or other governmental entity from filing a civil suit against a teacher or other school official. The act also does not apply to cases involving harm caused by the use of a motor vehicle, nor to those involving the imposition of corporal punishment.

Presumably, the Coverdell Act is a response to the flurry of lawsuits against school officials that arose after the student shootings at Columbine and other high schools. However, as we will see in the ensuing discussion, its application in California is limited because state law already broadly protects school employees and governing board members.

California Tort Claims Act

The standards relating to liability of California governmental entities and their employees for damages under state law are set forth in the California Tort Claims Act (Govt. Code § 810 and following sections). School districts and charter schools are considered governmental entities. However, it remains unclear whether a charter school is sufficiently independent from the school district granting the charter to constitute a separate legal entity subject to being sued in its own right. The California attorney general has opined that such independence is lacking (81 Ops. Atty. Gen. 140, 1998). If charter schools are operated as nonprofit benefit corporations, Education Code Section 47604 provides that the authorizing entity—school district, county board of education, or state board of education—will not be liable "for the debts or obligations of the charter school, or for claims arising from the performance of acts, errors, or omissions by the charter school" if the authorizing entity has complied with all of its oversight responsibilities as delineated in the charter school law. Of course, this provision does not preclude the inclusion of the authorizing entity in a lawsuit. Whether or not the entity has performed all of its oversight responsibilities will be question of fact. County boards of education and county superintendents are considered governmental entities because the Education Code assigns governing duties to both (*Ross v. Campbell Union School District*, 1977).

While the Tort Claims Act encompasses a range of actions for damages beyond those commonly known as torts, we are primarily concerned with the latter. A tort is a civil wrong for which a court will award money damages. There are all kinds of torts. Included among them are libel, slander, maintaining a nuisance, and negligence. Negligence is the most common tort in the context of personal injury. It means that a person who has a legal duty toward another and fails to carry out the duty can be held liable for damages to the injured person if the failure was the most direct cause of the injury (what is termed "proximate cause" in the law).

Because the Tort Claims Act specifies the situations when California governmental entities, officials, and employees can be held liable, its key provisions relating to personal injuries are summarized in Table 12.1 in the context of public school employees and school districts. These same provisions may apply to charter schools and their employees. Other provisions of the act will be referenced in the ensuing discussion. The act has a claims presentation requirement that necessitates submitting a written claim to the school district before legal action can be initiated for damages. The claims requirement, however, does not apply to charter schools operated by nonprofit benefit corporations, because they do not meet the definition of a public agency (*Knapp v. Palisades Charter High School*, 2007). Many provisions of the Tort Claims Act are quite detailed, and only the general thrust of their contents is conveyed here. Readers will find it useful to consult the table periodically while reading this chapter.

A few key points emerge from reviewing the Tort Claims Act. First, as specified in Sections 820 and 820.2, school employees are shielded from personal injury lawsuits when they are using discretion in carrying out their responsibilities. Because most acts of school employees are discretionary in the sense of their choosing among a variety of courses of action, the law provides a strong shield against employee liability. However, remember that we are discussing state, not federal, law. Immunity under state law does not extend to claims involving federal law. Second, if the employee is immune, the district bears no liability unless otherwise provided by state law under Section 815.2. If the employee is not immune, then the district bears the liability. The assumption of liability by the employer is called vicarious liability or respondeat superior, meaning that the district is held accountable for the acts of its employees. The purpose of the respondeat superior doctrine is to spread the risk for losses caused by employees through insurance and to provide greater assurance of compensation for victims. In effect, vicarious liability becomes a cost of doing business. Third, as policymakers, school board members enjoy broad immunity for their acts under Section 820.9.

In the following sections, we examine how these and other provisions of the Tort Claims Act have played out in California courts in the context of public schooling.

Injury to students on campus. Under the terms of the California Tort Claims Act, the district is vicariously liable for the acts of its employees when they are acting in the scope of their employment and not undertaking a duty imposed by the

TABLE 12.1

Key Provisions of the California Tort Claims Act

Sections 820 and 820.2	A school employee is liable for an injury proximately caused by the employee's act or failure to act as would a private person, *except* when the employee is exercising discretion, whether or not such discretion is abused, unless otherwise provided by statute.
Section 820.8	A school employee is not liable for an injury caused by the act or failure to act of another person, unless otherwise provided by statute.
Section 822	A school employee is not liable for money stolen from his official custody, unless the loss was attributable to the employee's negligent or wrongful act or failure to act.
Section 825	Upon timely request, a school district must pay defense costs and any judgment against the employee arising out of an act or omission of the employee acting within the scope of employment. The employee must reasonably cooperate in the defense of the claim. A school district is not liable for punitive damages intended to punish the transgressor for acting recklessly or with malice or deceit. However, the district may choose to pay punitive damages assessed against an employee of the district when the latter is deemed liable.
Section 815.2	A school district is liable for injury proximately caused by an act or failure to act of an employee of the district if the employee was acting within the scope of his/her employment. However, if the employee is immune, the district bears no liability unless otherwise provided by state law.
Section 815.4	A school district is liable for injury caused by an independent contractor, except if the district would not have been liable for the injury had it been caused by the act or failure to act of a district employee.
Section 815.6	If a school district is under a mandatory duty imposed by law designed to protect against the risk of a particular kind of injury, the district is liable for an injury caused by its failure to carry out the duty, unless it can establish that it acted with reasonable diligence.
Section 820.9	School board members are not held liable for injuries caused by the act or failure to act of the school district.
Section 835	Unless otherwise provided by statute, a school district is liable for injury caused by a dangerous condition of its property if the dangerous condition resulted either from the negligence of its employees or from the district's failure to correct a known dangerous condition.
Section 831.7	Neither a school district nor its employees are liable to any person who participates in a hazardous recreational activity, including any person who assists the participant, or to any spectator who knew or reasonably should have known that the hazardous recreational activity created a substantial risk of injury to himself or herself and was voluntarily in the place of risk, or having the ability to do so failed to leave, for any damage or injury to property or persons arising out of that hazardous recreational activity. "Hazardous recreational activity" means a recreational activity conducted on property of a school district which creates a substantial (as distinguished from a minor, trivial, or insignificant) risk of injury to a participant or a spectator.

Education Code. Thus, for example, when the California Education Code charges employees with the duty to supervise students and they fail to do so, the district can be liable because there is no discretion not to supervise students. A case in point is a 1993 California appellate court decision involving a ten-year-old student who was struck in the eye by a dirt clod during unsupervised recess when the student and others were throwing dirt clods at each other. The court ruled that the district was liable because school employees had failed to carry out the requirement of Education Code Section 44807 that students are to be supervised while on the school playground (*Lucas v. Fresno Unified School District*). This section of the Education Code imposes a duty to discipline students for misconduct occurring while going to and from school, on the playgrounds, and during recess. When the duty is breached, the Tort Claims Act provides the means for those injured to seek redress from the school district.

Similarly, a school district may be held liable when school employees fail to use reasonable care in protecting students from injury by nonstudents on school grounds. A high school student wrestler in the Stockton Unified School District sued his school district, school principal, and wrestling coach when he was assaulted by a nonstudent in an unsupervised school restroom where he was changing his clothes before wrestling practice. The California court of appeal noted that the defendants owed him a duty of reasonable care under Education Code Section 44807 and that he did not have to establish that prior acts of violence had occurred in the restroom to warrant some degree of supervision. The fact that it was unsupervised was enough to establish a claim. The case was sent back to the trial court for a determination of liability, a matter to be determined by the facts and the provisions of the Tort Claims Act (*Leger v. Stockton Unified School District*, 1988).

The *Leger* case is interesting because the court drew from practices in private schools to define the extent of liability under the Tort Claims Act. The statute specifies that a public employee is liable for his acts or omissions "to the same extent as a private party." Therefore, both the employee and the public entity are entitled to any defenses that a private employee or employer might assert. Noting that private schools have a duty under the law to supervise if school officials reasonably could anticipate that it is necessary, the court concluded that, had the public school employees been in the private sector, they would have been liable if the facts alleged by the student turned out to be true.

There is a consensus among judges that the duty to supervise is not so high as to require schools to be absolute insurers of the physical safety of students. This would require schools to be operated as lockdown prisons. However, such a duty does exist when students constitute a threat of foreseeable harm to other students. In a 2003 ruling, a California court of appeal was confronted with a lawsuit seeking damages from the school district for an assault committed during the school day on one high school student by another student in a restroom. The perpetrator, Damascus, had a record of disciplinary problems in elementary and middle school. He had been expelled from the middle school for fighting. After he was admitted to high school, his disciplinary infractions lessened. There were no incidents of threatening or violent behavior toward others, though the day before the assault, Damascus had gotten into an argument with a female student and was accused of setting fire to a bulletin board poster. He was told that failure to undergo anger management would result in a three-day suspension. The next day, Damascus and another student heard a rumor that the victim, Thompson, was carrying marijuana. The pair lured Thompson into the restroom and asked him to empty his pockets. The youth refused and ran out of the restroom. The fight broke out a few feet outside.

The appellate court found that the principal did not owe a duty to Thompson to immediately suspend Damascus from school following the argument the previous afternoon with the female student and the poster-burning allegation. These incidents were not related to Thompson. Indeed, the court noted that Damascus apparently did not know Thompson. Nor was there any evidence that the restroom or the area immediately outside it were known areas of danger. In fact, a school monitor had just passed the restroom before the incident occurred and immediately returned to the area when the fight broke out. Thus, there was insufficient causation to link the prior incidents involving Damascus to the assault on Thompson. The school principal had exercised reasonable care in supervising students. Dismissal of the lawsuit was upheld (*Thompson v. Sacramento City Unified School District*).

Liability in a failure-to-supervise case is especially likely when special education students are involved because of their special needs. This is the teaching of a 2003 California appellate court decision involving the sexual assault of a fifteen-year-old male mentally retarded student by another male special education student with a history of disciplinary problems (*M. W. v. Panama Buena Vista Union School District*). The act occurred in a boy's bathroom at approximately 7:15 a.m. The gates of the junior high school were unlocked at 7 a.m., but direct supervision did not begin until 7:45 a.m. Parents were not informed of the lack of supervision during the early morning hours. Indeed, the victim's mother believed that her son was being supervised. School officials knew the victim to be vulnerable to teasing during this period because he frequently retreated to the office to escape it. Given the circumstances, the court of appeal in a two-to-one ruling found it foreseeable that the special education student was at risk for a physical or sexual assault. It affirmed a jury award against the district in the amount of $2.4 million under the California Tort Claims Act.

A few months later, a different California appellate court drew from the *M. W.* ruling to advise that the expectation level for securing student safety is higher today than in the past because of the increasingly foreseeable risks to students at school. The case involved a high school student who arrived at school early, then moved to the sidewalk outside the school where he was shot by another student. The school was operated as a closed campus during the school day. However, prior to the beginning of school the campus was open and the school gates unsupervised. In an unpublished but informative decision, the court noted that "it is well established that a school's duty to supervise students begins before students sit down at their desks when the school bell rings" (*Durant v. Los Angeles Unified School District*, 2003). The court overturned the lower court's dismissal of the case. The lesson of the *M. W.* and *Durant* rulings is that, to reduce the risk of liability, a school either should preclude students from coming on campus before the opening of school or be prepared to provide supervision if students are allowed on campus prior to this time. The same holds true at the end of the day.

Education Code Section 49079 imposes a mandatory duty on school districts to inform teachers about students who have engaged in, or are reasonably suspected of having engaged in, suspendable or expellable acts. Section 815.6 of the California Tort Claims Act provides that a governmental entity may incur liability for breach of a mandatory duty imposed by statute if the failure to carry out the duty was the proximate cause of an injury and the entity did not exercise due diligence. Does this include warning teachers about a student's potential for future violence, and if there is no warning, is the school district liable? The Vacaville Unified School District sought to overturn a jury award against it on this basis after a ninth-grade male student attacked the co-captain of the volleyball team, breaking her jaw and inflicting severe and permanent injuries. The victim claimed that the district was negligent in failing to warn the physical education teacher of the student's propensity to violence. There was no question that school administrators had not warned the teacher, though they knew that the ninth grader had a history of fighting.

The appellate court found the question "very close." While the ninth grader had not inflicted injury on other students and had not been expelled prior to the incident, the court concluded that the evidence supported the jury finding that school administrators had breached their duty under the statute to notify the teacher of the student's record of fighting. However, in a lucky break for the district, the failure to warn the teacher was judged not to be the proximate cause of the injury. The teacher already knew that the student could be a problem and had been keeping her eye on him. Because any additional information from the district may not have made a difference, the appellate court found insufficient evidence to support the jury finding of causation. The judgment against the district was overturned (*Skinner v. Vacaville Unified School District*, 1995). Even though the district escaped liability in this instance, the lesson is clear. School officials must always inform teachers of students with discipline problems stemming from suspendable or expellable acts.

Can a school district be liable under Section 815.6 of the Tort Claims Act when school officials fail to assure that students never will be subjected to corporal punishment? This was a question facing another California appellate court in a case involving parents who contended that their special education child had been subjected to beatings by his teacher in addition to physical, psychological, and verbal abuse. In their lawsuit, the parents claimed that the school district had breached its mandatory duty under Education Code Sections 49000–49001, which prohibit the use of corporal punishment in public schools. The parents construed these provisions to mean that the district had a mandatory duty to see that corporal punishment never was used. The appellate court decided against the parents, pointing out that the corporal punishment statutes "do *not* create any mandatory, affirmative duty on the part of public schools and school districts to take action or carry out measures to ensure that students are never subjected to corporal punishment by teachers" (*Clausing v. San Francisco Unified School District*, 1990, pp. 80–81, emphasis in original). Acceptance of the parents' position, the court noted, would transform the prohibition on corporal punishment into a requirement that schools take affirmative action to protect students from ever being disciplined in this way. This would subject schools to civil liability and damages at great cost. That the legislature did not intend this to be the case, the judges noted, is apparent from reading another provision of the Tort Claims Act providing that public entities are not liable for injuries caused "by failing to enforce any law" (Govt. Code § 818.2). The parents also argued that the California Constitution gave them grounds to sue the school district. They cited Article I, Section 28 requiring that all public school students "have the inalienable right to attend campuses which are safe, secure, and peaceful," as well as Article I, Section 1 protecting the right of privacy. The appellate court again decided against the parents. Section 28 does not provide a damage remedy. As for Article I, Section 1, the court held that it supports a cause of action seeking only an injunction against alleged privacy violations, not one seeking money damages.

The outcome in the *Clausing* case does not mean that educators can use corporal punishment or violate a student's right to a safe school environment or to privacy without consequences. For example, a teacher who uses corporal punishment in violation of the statute and district policy may be liable to the student injured, because the teacher would be acting outside the scope of employment. The district may be liable if it condones the use of corporal punishment. While Education Code Section 44807 does give educators the same degree of physical control over a student that a parent has as a matter of law, it provides no immunity from criminal prosecution or criminal penalties if the physical force exceeds that reasonably necessary to maintain order, protect property, safeguard students, or maintain conditions conducive to learning. Further, school administrators who fail to halt inappropriate use of physical force or corporal punishment as well as teachers who use it as a discipline technique are in danger of disciplinary action from their employers for failure to follow state law. The thrust of the *Clausing* decision is that the district does not have a mandatory duty under the provisions of the Education Code to prevent such actions from ever happening. In fact, in some situations, physical force may be necessary to protect a student from harm and shield the district and its personnel from liability. Education Code Section 49001 does permit a reasonable amount of force necessary to prevent physical injury to persons or damage to property, for self-defense, and to divest a pupil of weapons and dangerous objects. If school officials do not use force in such situations and a student is injured as a result, there could be liability against both the school district and its personnel.

A 2002 unreported California appellate court ruling involving the death of a fifteen-year-old student who was play-fighting on school grounds with friends during a tutorial period sheds light on the importance of school disciplinary rules. One of the friends had hurt his hand earlier and wanted to show Sean, the victim, that his hand had healed. The friend punched Sean in the chest. Sean collapsed and died of a very rare phenomenon whereby a blow to the chest delivered at the precise moment in the cycle of the heartbeat causes an arrhythmia, leading to cessation of heart function. Sean's parents sued the school district under the Tort Claims Act, claiming that it had failed to have a rule specifically against play-fighting and had not exercised reasonable care to protect their son from harm. The school district countered that it had a behavioral code and had taken steps to control the behavior of the group Sean was associating with, including stopping play-fighting when it got out of control. School personnel had passed by when Sean and others were play-fighting but did not make them stop. The court ruled that, while school employees do have a mandatory duty under Education Code Section 44807 to enforce rules and regulations necessary for the protection of children on school grounds, the school district does not have a mandatory duty to create or enforce a rule directed toward conduct that is not unsafe. Play-fighting, the court noted, is not inherently unsafe. Thus, the school administration had the discretion to permit it. School employees who passed by during the play-fighting also bore no liability because they were simply following district practice in not halting the play-fighting that led to Sean's death. However, the court observed that had it been evident that play-fighting was likely to create real injury, the district would have been liable for not carrying out its mandatory duty to have and enforce rules protecting students (*Schug v. Sonoma Valley Unified School District*). The lesson from this decision is to make sure that the student code of conduct contains rules against behavior that may lead to injury and that the rules are enforced.

Liability when school employees act outside the scope of their employment. Under Sections 820 and 820.2 of the California Tort Claims Act, employees are shielded from liability when they are acting within the scope of their employment and are using appropriate discretion in carrying out their responsibilities. And if employees are immune, so too are districts under Section 815.2 of the act, unless otherwise provided by state law. Discretion means choosing among a range of alternatives and making a decision. Employees are entitled to immunity even if the decision actually made was not effective. School administrators, for example, who responded to a student's sexual harassment and assault claim by allegedly suspending the perpetrator for one day and taking other actions that were not effective, were exercising discretion and hence immune from liability under the Tort Claims Act (*Nicole M. v. Martinez Unified School District*, 1997). However, lawsuits often involve numerous causes of action. As we noted in Chapter 11, administrators in the *Nicole M.* case were not immune from liability under California's Unruh Civil Rights Act. Further, the judge in that case cited case law in California indicating that the exercise of discretion means making a decision about what is just and proper under the circumstances. Thus, as a matter of taking preventive action, school employees should exercise care in making discretionary decisions.

If employees are not acting in the scope of their employment, the district bears no liability unless state law specifies otherwise. The California Supreme Court ruled in 1989, for example, that a district is not vicariously liable under the Tort Claims Act for a teacher's allegedly sexually assaulting a fourteen-year-old student at the teacher's home. The student was participating in a district-sanctioned work-experience program supervised by his teacher at the time of the assault. The court found the relationship between the teacher's act and his employment too attenuated for the district to be liable. Were it otherwise, the supreme court noted, the risk of a lawsuit would force school districts to foreclose all informal interaction between teachers and their students (*John R. v. Oakland Unified School District*).

A California appellate court relied on the *John R.* decision to rule that a school district could not be liable under the Tort Claims Act for an alleged sexual molestation upon a five-year-old student by her teacher, because such an act is not encompassed within the teacher's scope of employment (*Kimberly M. v. Los Angeles Unified School District*, 1989). Similarly, a janitor who sexually assaulted a student in the janitor's office was not acting within the scope of his employment. The alleged assault was judged not incident to his employment and could not be reasonably foreseen by the district under the facts of the case (*Alma W. v. Oakland Unified School District*, 1981).

In circumstances like these, when employees acting outside the scope of their employment injure students, the employees themselves will be the target of the lawsuit and possible criminal penalties and cannot rely on the district to defend them or pay any judgment against them. Nor can they depend on a professional insurance policy to shoulder a judgment against them. Parents of a third grader who was sexually abused by her teacher tried to secure a judgment against the Horace Mann Insurance Company, which issued the man an educator's employment liability policy. The court of appeal agreed with the insurance company that sexual abuse was not encompassed within the policy. Wrote the judges: "We cannot fathom a more personal activity less related to the goal of education than [the teacher's] acts" (*Horace Mann Insurance Company v. Analisa N.*, 1989, p. 64).

It is important to note that these state court rulings cannot shield the school district from lawsuits in federal court based on Title IX, as discussed in Chapter 11. It also is important to note that more recent decisions indicate that if district officials are negligent in hiring or supervising employees who injure students, the district may be liable. This is most apt to occur in the context of sexual abuse. A junior high school student who alleged that she had been sexually harassed and assaulted by her teacher argued that the school district's hiring procedures were deficient. A proper background check would have revealed that the teacher had been terminated from another school for sexual misconduct. The California court agreed with the student that the district does have a duty to protect her from sexual assault by her teacher. While the *John R.* ruling precludes holding the district liable for the conduct of teachers who commit such acts, the court noted that nothing shields the district from lawsuits premised on the district's own negligence in hiring and supervising teachers. If it could be established that the district employees knew or should have known of the teacher's prior misconduct and that he posed a reasonably foreseeable risk of harm, the district could be held liable under the Tort Claims Act for failing in its duty to take all reasonable steps to protect the student from harm (*Virginia G. v. ABC Unified School District*, 1993).

The California Supreme Court weighed in on the issue in a 1997 ruling involving a student who allegedly was sexually assaulted by an administrator. The student sued her school district, along with a number of other school districts that had previously employed the administrator. She argued that the previous employers were negligent because they had written glowing recommendations of the administrator's performance, yet knew he had a history of sexual misconduct with students. In a detailed analysis, the court ruled that the writer of a letter of recommendation owes a duty to third parties not to misrepresent the facts in describing the qualifications and character of a former employee if making the misrepresentations would present a foreseeable risk of physical injury to third persons. Absent a fore-seeable risk of physical injury, no duty of care exists. The court found that the rec-ommendations in this case contained misleading half-truths indicating the admin-istrator to be fit to interact with female students, even though prior experience with the administrator indicated otherwise. The student's complaint thus constituted an exception to the general rule excluding liability for nondisclosure (*Randi W. v. Muroc Joint Unified School District*).

Based on these rulings, it is important to be honest in recommendations. An ad-ministrative regulation issued by the California Commission on Teacher Creden-tialing specifies that a certificated person is not to sign a letter or memorandum to be used as a positive letter of reference that intentionally omits significant facts re-lating to the fitness of the employee for future employment or includes those that the writer does not know to be true. The rule does not pertain to statements that reflect personal opinions (Admin. Code, Title 5, § 80332). Truth is always a de-fense—a point underscored by California Civil Code Section 47 (c), which pro-vides a privilege against defamation suits for recommendations made without mal-ice. A superintendent was successful in defeating a libel action against him on this basis by a teacher who discovered the superintendent's candid comments about her qualifications for future employment in a letter the superintendent had written. The court of appeal ruled that the qualified privilege applies in such a situation un-less there is substantial evidence of hatred or ill will, or without a reasonable belief that the comments are true, or of improper intent (*Manguso v. Oceanside Unified School District*, 1984). Some attorneys advise that in the absence of a waiver, the best way to avoid the threat of litigation is to stick to established facts.

Occasionally, school administrators will file lawsuits seeking damages for defamation of character. The chances of success are slim. A recent case involving a former charter school superintendent who sued the Anti-Defamation League (ADL) and its officers for libel over the contents of a letter posted on its website provides a good illustration. The letter had been sent to the State Superintendent of Public Instruction (SPI) calling for an immediate suspension of Gateway Acad-emy's funding and urging an investigation of religious instruction and of the school's link to the Islamic terrorist organization Al-Fuqra. At the time, the SPI was investigating newspaper reports that Gateway was having students study Islam and charging tuition at certain of its multiple school sites contrary to state law. Later, the Fresno Unified School District, the chartering authority, terminated the char-ter for fiscal mismanagement. After the termination, the ADL posted on its web-site the letter it had sent to the SPI. The charter school superintendent contended that the contents were maliciously false and defamatory in stating that the charter

LEGAL LIABILITY | 457

school director was a member of the virulently anti-Semitic Islamic extremist group and in linking the official and the charter school to a terrorist organization. The appellate court agreed with the trial court that the letter sent to the SPI was privileged under the "anti-SLAPP" (Strategic Lawsuit Against Public Participation) law (Civil Proc. § 425.16). That law was enacted to give courts more authority to reject lawsuits over speech on public matters. The court also agreed that the charter school superintendent, like her counterparts in the public schools, was a "public official." This means that to prevail against ADL on the website-posting issue, the charter school superintendent would have to show that the statements in the letter were made with knowledge of their falsity or with reckless disregard for their truth. This so-called "actual malice" test comes from *New York Times v. Sullivan,* a famous 1964 U.S. Supreme Court decision intended to protect freedom of the press (it has been applied to California public school teachers as well). Whether or not the charter school superintendent could show actual malice behind the letter posting was addressed in a section of the opinion that was not published (*Ghafur v. Bernstein,* 2005).

Injury to student athletes and cheerleaders. Education Code Section 44807 places responsibility on teachers to supervise students on the way to and from school, on the playground, and at recess. California courts have recognized that the primary assumption of risk that student participants must shoulder when they engage in many extracurricular and athletic events lessens employee liability in these instances and, through them, the liability of the district. For example, a high school student was not successful when he sued both his wrestling coach and the school district after the student broke his arm during an exhibition with the coach on the use of the control hold. The student tried to brace himself by jamming his arm into the wrestling mat. The appellate court concluded that the type of injury the student suffered is an inherent risk of wrestling. The court did not accept the student's contention that Section 44807 precludes application of the primary assumption of risk doctrine to extracurricular sports. If otherwise, instructors would fear requiring their students to stretch beyond their present level of performance (*Lilley v. Elk Grove Unified School District,* 1998).

The same assumption of risk applies to cheerleaders. A cheerleader who was injured when she attempted an acrobatic activity known as "the cradle" claimed inadequate supervision in her lawsuit against the district. The cradle requires two cheerleaders to form a base and then launch a third cheerleader into the air. After the flyer touches her toes, she is caught by the base cheerleaders. Denning, the injured student, had been part of the base and was hurt when the elevated cheerleader fell on her. Denning had attended a cheerleading camp, had been given safety instruction, and had received instruction in how to do a gymnastic stunt. She maintained that the coach failed to protect her from harm, especially because she has having trouble learning how to do the stunt and was afraid that she might get hurt. She argued that because students had not mastered the stunt, the coach's duty of care was greater in this instance. The district countered that students who participate in athletic activities must assume the risk of being injured and that no greater duty of care was required here. The appellate court agreed. A coach is not an insurer of the student's safety and cannot be liable unless the coach were to increase the risk of harm over and above that inherent in the sport. Here, there was no evidence that the coach had increased the risk of harm. The appellate court concluded that ruling to the contrary would fundamentally alter the nature of high school cheerleading, perhaps ending it altogether (*Aaris v. Las Virgenes Unified School District*, 1998).

A 2003 ruling from the California Supreme Court expanded on the discussion about assumption of risk in sports activities. The case involved a fourteen-year-old competitive swimmer, Olivia Kahn, who broke her neck when she dived into a shallow pool just prior to a swim meet at Mount Pleasant High School in the East Side Union High School District. The student had a strong fear of diving. In response, her coach had assigned her to the first leg of the relay in previous swim meets where she could start from inside the pool. But on the day of the accident, he told Olivia that she would not be swimming the first leg of the relay. The student alleged that she pleaded with the coach to change the rotation. But he did not do so. Before the relay race began and apparently without her coach's knowledge, the student practiced shallow dives with two fellow swimmers. The accident occurred on the third dive. Through her mother, Olivia sued the coach and the school district. In upholding the trial court's dismissal of the case, the court of appeal in a two-to-one decision noted that there is a primary assumption of risk when students voluntarily participate in sporting events. The risk is inherent if its elimination would alter the fundamental nature of the activity. Diving, the court concluded, is an integral part of competitive swimming. Either eliminating it or requiring deeper pools would fundamentally alter the sport. Therefore, a student must assume the risk of diving in shallow pools if the student wishes to participate in competitive swimming.

The California Supreme Court disagreed and sent the case back to the trial court for further proceedings against the coach (*Kahn v. East Side Union High School District*). The student did not appeal the trial court's decision to dismiss the case against the school district. The high court pointed out that in 1992 it had ruled that the standard of liability of a sports participant for an injury to a co-participant is if the participant "intentionally injures another player or engages in conduct that is so reckless as to be totally outside the range of the ordinary activity involved in the sport" (*Knight v. Jewett*, p. 17). In a lengthy review of a number of lower-court rulings on the matter, the justices concluded that the same standard should be applied to coaches. The supreme court noted that Olivia presented evidence that the coach failed to provide training to Olivia in shallow-water diving, had lulled her into a false sense of security by telling her she would not have to dive at competitions, and had breached that promise. The coach disputed these assertions. To resolve whether the coach had acted recklessly, a trial would have to be conducted. The importance of the ruling is the California Supreme Court's articulation of the standard for determining when a coach can be liable for accidents resulting in student injury. It is clear that while there is a primary assumption of risk when students participate in competitive athletics and that nothing precludes a coach from encouraging students to go beyond their current level of competence, a coach has a duty of care reasonably to prepare students to engage in the activity so that the risk of harm is not heightened.

But it is important to note that when a student injury is *not* attributable to participating in the athletic activity, the standard of care exercised by the school and its personnel is the same as for students generally. Thus a California appellate court refused to dismiss a case filed by a middle school student's parents when the student was struck in the mouth by a golf club swung by another student during a physical education class. The court noted that in California, a prudent standard of care has been imposed for injuries occurring during PE classes or physical exercise free periods, which are part of the curriculum. Being hit in the head by a golf club is not an inherent risk in the game of golf. Rather, it relates to such matters as the size of the class (in this case, 54 students), staffing, and similar matters. The case was remanded to the trial court to determine whether the parents could establish that the class was disorganized and poorly supervised (*Hemady v. Long Beach Unified School District*, 2006).

As discussed in more detail later in the chapter with regard to injury to nonstudents, Section 831.7 of the Tort Claims Act provides immunity for districts and employees when persons engage in hazardous recreational activities on school property. Does this provision apply to student athletes who are injured? In the first California case confronting this question, the court of appeal in a two-to-one decision responded in the negative. The facts of the case are particularly wrenching. A high school gymnast, Omar, was working out one evening during the off-season at the school gymnasium while it was open for community use. His coach was assisting him. He was practicing a maneuver on the high bar called a "front catch" in which the gymnast swings forward and, at the top of the arc, lets go of the bar, performs a somersault, and catches the bar on the way down. Omar missed catching the bar and fell, landing on his neck. He was rendered a quadriplegic and died shortly thereafter.

The school district and Omar's coach argued that they were immune from liability because the student was engaged during nonschool hours in a hazardous recreational activity, not a school-directed extracurricular activity. The appellate court disagreed. The judges began by noting that school-sponsored extracurricular athletic activities that are under the supervision of school personnel are not hazardous recreational activities. If they were so considered, schools would be immune for negligent supervision for a whole range of contact sports. The majority noted that school districts have a duty to supervise students at school-sponsored athletic activities, even if the events occur after school hours and during the off-season. Here, the coach ran a structured practice for members of the gymnastics team during the community recreational program. At the time of the accident, Omar was practicing on school equipment under the supervision of the coach, who had suggested he learn the catch maneuver. There was no question, the majority concluded, that Omar was engaged in a school-sponsored and supervised activity at the time of the injury. The case was sent back to the trial court for a determination of the amount of damages the district owed Omar's family. The dissenting judge agreed that school-sponsored extracurricular activities are not hazardous recreational activities, but he preferred to have the jury decide whether the activity in question was in fact school sponsored (*Acosta v. Los Angeles Unified School District*, 1995).

In a case decided the same year as *Acosta*, a fourteen-year-old student sought recovery from the school district after he suffered a double fracture of his right arm during a soccer match conducted during school hours as part of the school's physical education program. The school district sought immunity under the hazardous recreational activity provision of the Tort Claims Act, contending that the student had voluntarily placed himself at risk and knew or reasonably should have known that such an injury might occur in a bodily contact sport like soccer. The student argued that he was engaging in a compulsory class when the accident occurred and had no choice but to participate. The court of appeal agreed with the student, noting that a body contact sport incorporated into a physical education class during the school day is not a recreational activity, however hazardous it might be. Under Education Code Section 44807's duty to supervise students, it was up to a jury to determine if there was negligence in supervision and what damages, if any, were due the injured student (*Iverson v. Muroc Unified School District*, 1995).

Is there liability when students don't learn? Educators often wonder if they and the school district can be held liable if a student does not learn. Outside the context of special education, the answer to date is generally no. Under special education law, a school district can be taken to an administrative hearing and perhaps beyond into federal court if a student does not receive some educational benefit. For regular education students, the first and most famous case involving "educational malpractice" is *Peter W. v. San Francisco Unified School District*, decided in 1976. The student in that case argued that the district had failed in its duty to provide him an adequate instruction in basic academic skills. As a result, when he graduated from high school, he could be employed only as a manual laborer. The appellate court was not supportive, noting the complexity of the teaching-learning process: "Unlike the activity of the highway or the marketplace, classroom methodology affords no readily acceptable standards of care, or cause, or injury" (p. 860). Due to the absence of criteria to isolate the contribution of the school to a student's learning from the myriad other factors that affect it, the court dismissed the lawsuit.

In 2006 the California Supreme Court cited the *Peter W.* ruling in upholding a lower court's decision throwing out the portion of a lawsuit filed by parents who contended that the distance learning charter schools operated by One2One Learning Foundation failed to teach their children. However, the high court noted that nothing in *Peter W.* precludes a claim that a school operator failed to provide equipment and supplies, failed to employ appropriately credentialed teachers, violated rules governing independent study, or charged improper fees. Claims like these do not involve a court in determining educational quality or results. The parents in this case had filed their claim against the charter school operator under the California False Claims Act (Govt. Code § 12650 and following sections). That law provides civil penalties against anyone who knowingly presents a false claim to a government entity for payment or approval. Basically, the False Claims Act (FCA) is intended to protect the treasury from those who seek to defraud the government. Here the parents claimed that the charter schools, their operator, and the authorizing school districts bilked the state out of some $20 million in average daily attendance (ADA) money. The high court agreed with the lower court that charter schools operated as nonprofit benefit corporations are "persons" under the FCA and can be held liable for defrauding the state or school district for three times the amount of damages, costs of the lawsuit to recover the money, and civil damages up to $10,000. However, the court concluded that the legislature did not intend to permit such lawsuits against school districts. Thus the authorizing districts could not be sued. The high court also ruled that the parents could sue the charter schools and their operators under the California Unfair Competition Act to seek restoration of lost money or property (Bus & Prof. Code § 17200 and following sections). Thus the lawsuit was allowed to go forward under both laws (*Wells v. One2One Learning Foundation*).

Injury to students off campus. In addition to requiring teachers to hold students strictly accountable for their conduct on the playground and at recess, Education Code Section 44807 extends the responsibility to students going to and from school. This is known as "portal to portal" responsibility. But it does not mean that teachers must supervise students on their way to and from school, for clearly this would be an impossibility when students are not riding school buses. Rather, it is intended to give teachers the authority to discipline students who misbehave on the way to and from school (e.g., the grudge fight that occurs on the way home).

Education Code Section 44808 provides that no school district, city or county board of education, county superintendent of schools, or their officers or employees shall be responsible or liable for student conduct and safety off school property *unless* they have undertaken to provide transportation to students to and from school premises, have undertaken a school-sponsored activity off school premises, have otherwise specifically assumed such responsibility or liability, or have failed to exercise reasonable care under the circumstances. The "or have failed to exercise reasonable care under the circumstances" generally has been construed as pertaining to one of the previously listed undertakings. Only a few courts have viewed it as an independent source of liability. When a school district assumes responsibility for students when they are off campus, the statute provides that the district, board, or employee is liable or responsible for the conduct or safety of the student only when the student is or should be under the immediate and direct supervision of an employee.

A number of cases have focused on the application of Section 44808. One of the earliest dealt with a student who decided to play hooky from summer school and left without anyone's knowledge. He was struck by a motorcycle at an intersection and seriously injured. Was the district liable? The district claimed that it was not, because the accident happened off campus and it had not assumed responsibility for students when they were off campus. In this case, the California Supreme Court recognized that while school districts are not insurers of their students' safety, they do have a legal duty to exercise reasonable care in supervising students. The court avoided the problem of deciding how much supervision a district must bear for off-campus behavior. Here, the problem was whether the district had exercised reasonable care in preventing students from leaving school in the first place. The court sent the case back to the trial court to determine whether the district had exercised the degree of care that a reasonable person would have exercised in the same circumstances. The district tried to argue that its duty to supervise a voluntary summer school should be less than during the regular school year, but the court rejected the assertion. The judges observed:

> Since at least the days of Huck Finn and Tom Sawyer, adults have been well aware that children are often tempted to wander off from school, and a jury might well conclude that defendants could have reasonably foreseen that this temptation might be especially strong during the summer session when a student's friends might not be in school. (*Hoyem v. Manhattan Beach City School District*, 1978, p. 8)

More recent cases have limited district liability under this section. In one, a teacher who was driving home from school encountered some of his students along the way. His curiosity aroused, he stopped to talk with them. One of the students climbed on the rear bumper of the teacher's van and was injured when the teacher drove off. The court found that the teacher had not assumed responsibility for the off-campus conduct of the students and thus the district was not liable (*Torsiello v. Oakland Unified School District*, 1987). In another case, school officials strongly encouraged a student to attend a nonprofit summer camp in the Sequoia National Forest for low-income, at-risk students. The school district provided applications and general information about the camp. The school superintendent was a camp board member. The youth's mother repeatedly asked about camp safety and was assured by school personnel that the camp was safe. But the facts indicated otherwise. The youth drowned when swimming during a backpacking outing at the camp. There were no life jackets or other emergency equipment, and camp counselors were not trained in life-saving techniques. The mother sued the school district. The school district was judged not liable under Section 44808 because the camp program was not a school-sponsored activity. While the district may have encouraged his participation, the youth was not required to attend the camp and received no credit for doing so. The school district did not provide transportation or assume responsibility for the youth's safety at the camp. No one at the camp was employed or supervised by the district, and the district did not formulate the camp's program (*Ramirez v. Long Beach Unified School District*, 2002). In 2006, an appellate court upheld the dismissal of the portion of a lawsuit against the Lake Tahoe Unified School District filed by parents of a student who was killed after being struck by a drunk driver when she was crossing a street to reach a designated bus stop. While the court observed that the superintendent has the authority to designate bus stops and that their location could amount to a dangerous condition of public property as described below, Section 44808 limits the district's liability. The student was not on school property when the accident occurred and not under the direct supervision of the school (*Bassett v. Lakeside Inn, Inc.*).

Section 44808.5 exempts districts and employees from liability when high school students are allowed to leave school grounds during the lunch period with parental permission. Another exemption encompasses voluntary field trips and excursions. In addition to describing the conditions under which field trips can be conducted, Education Code Section 35330 specifies that "all persons making the field trip or excursion shall be deemed to have waived all claims against the district, a charter school, or the State of California for injury, accident, illness, or death occurring during or by reason of the field trip or excursion." This provision encompasses lawsuits against school employees acting within the scope of their duties of employment as well (*Casterson v. Superior Court*, 2002). Some districts have parents sign a statement to make them aware of this statute. If the field trip is out of state, all adults, including parents and guardians of participating students, are required to sign a statement waiving such claims. A school district successfully asserted its immunity under this section against a lawsuit filed by parents of a first grader who was injured on the way home from a voluntary field trip. The student was riding in a car driven by a parent volunteer when the accident happened. The parents claimed that because the trip constituted a school-sponsored activity off campus and the district had arranged for transportation, the district had assumed responsibility under Education Code Section 44808. Their claim was rejected (*Wolfe v. Dublin Unified School District*, 1997). The judges in this case cited an earlier ruling to the effect that when students participate in non-required field trips or excursions, the voluntary nature of the event absolves the district of liability. Other courts have questioned limiting the protection against liability just to voluntary field trips. It may well be that both voluntary and required field trips are included. While district and employee liability is thus restricted when students leave school grounds for lunch and field trips, Education Code Section 48900 (r) gives districts the authority to discipline students at these and other times such as going to and from and during school-sponsored activities.

Injury to nonstudents. It is the last day of school, and student exuberance is high at the high school. When the final bell sounds, students flock to their cars. The high school has two parking lots. One is a main lot under adult supervision, and the second is an overflow lot that is not. A car driven by a sixteen-year-old student (who has never been a discipline problem at the school) peels out of the overflow parking lot. The car jumps the curb and strikes a pedestrian who is walking along the sidewalk. The injured pedestrian sues the school district, claiming the district breached its duty to protect him. Is the district liable?

The injured pedestrian, Hoff, first argued that under common law—meaning the precedents established by the judiciary over time—a special relationship exists between the school district and the student, Lozano, who was driving the car. This special relationship imposes a duty upon school district personnel to protect Hoff from the acts of Lozano. Because school personnel failed to supervise Lozano as he exited the parking lot, Hoff argued, the district is liable under the Tort Claims Act for its employees' negligence. The California Supreme Court recognized that state law long has imposed a duty on school personnel to supervise the conduct of students at all times on school grounds and to enforce rules and regulations necessary for their protection. The standard of care imposed upon school personnel in carrying out this duty is one of ordinary prudence. But the duty runs to protect students, not to nonstudents like Hoff who are injured off campus.

Hoff sought to strengthen his argument by pointing out that the law recognizes a special relationship between parent and child, such that the parent has a duty to protect innocent third parties from foreseeable danger inflicted by the child. Because school officials stand in loco parentis with regard to their students, Hoff contended, they have the same duty. The concept of in loco parentis means, literally, "in place of the parent." Traditionally, the law has recognized that the in loco parentis doctrine gives educators considerable authority to control students at school. The concept has been eroded somewhat as students have gained such rights as freedom of speech and due process. This is particularly true at the secondary school level. Nevertheless, the in loco parentis doctrine remains viable, and Hoff argued here that school employees had breached it by not supervising the overflow parking lot. But the justices did not agree. Parents have a duty to protect third parties from the acts of their children only when there is foreseeable danger. Because Lozano had not been a discipline problem at school and school officials had no reason to question his driving ability, there was no in loco parentis responsibility placed on school personnel to protect Hoff from Lozano.

Hoff next contended that the California Education Code requires the district and its employees to supervise students on and off school grounds, and when they are negligent in doing so, the district is liable under the Tort Claims Act for injuries sustained by innocent third parties. Hoff maintained that teenage automobile driving on school grounds is the most dangerous activity that students can engage in and thus is within the ambit of Education Code Section 44807, requiring teachers to supervise students on campus and going to and from school. Since teachers did not supervise Lozano, the district is vicariously liable. The California Supreme Court did not support Hoff's contention, noting that Section 44807 requires teachers to enforce those rules and regulations necessary for the protection of students.

It is not intended to protect nonstudents who are not on school property against the risk of injury. Further, Hoff could not rely on this provision to sue the school district directly under the Tort Claims Act for failure to carry out a mandatory duty, because Section 44807 places the duty on teachers and not districts.

Hoff additionally argued that the district had assumed responsibility for supervising the main parking lot and thus under Education Code Section 44808 was responsible for student driving into and out of school parking lots. As noted earlier, that provision imposes liability on the district and employees if they have assumed responsibility for student conduct and safety off campus. But the California high court did not agree that supervising the main parking lot signified a district decision to assume responsibility for a student's off-campus conduct. The accident had not happened in the parking lot. In any event, the district had not assumed any responsibility for students driving in the overflow parking lot. Thus, all of Hoff's arguments were rejected (*Hoff v. Vacaville Unified School District*, 1998). His only recourse was to attempt to hold Lozano and his parents responsible.

The *Hoff* decision constitutes an important precedent in California on district liability for injuries sustained by nonstudents. A California court of appeal later relied on *Hoff* to reject a lawsuit against the coach of the Chico High School Ski and Snowboard Team over a snowboarding accident. The accident occurred when an eighteen-year-old member of the team was snowboarding at a high rate of speed down a run at Mammoth Mountain Ski Area. The student allegedly was racing his friends, looking back several times to see where they were, and was unable to swerve before slamming into an adult skier who had just completed the run, causing severe injuries to her. In addition to suing the student, the adult skier sued the coach and the Chico school district, among others. Citing *Hoff*, the appellate court noted that the coach had no reason to think the student required close and direct supervision, never having been reckless before. Thus the coach owed no duty to protect innocent third parties from injury. Because the coach was immune under the Tort Claim Act, so was the school district. However, the court ruled that there was a question whether the student had acted recklessly and sent the case back for trial on that issue (*Lackner v. North*, 2006). These decisions are instructive with regard to liability to third parties resulting from the acts of students. First, school authorities have a well-recognized responsibility to supervise and protect students, and if they believe that students are dangerous, the duty extends to protecting third parties. For example, if school officials have reason to believe that a student is alcohol or sleep impaired after attending an all-night prom, they would have a duty under common law as set forth in the *Hoff* decision to prevent the student from driving. Similarly, if the coach in the *Lackner* case had reason to believe that the student would maneuver the snowboard recklessly on the ski slope, the coach would have had a duty to prevent him from doing so. Failure in either case to protect innocent third parties could be viewed as negligence and, if the proximate cause of the injury, could result in liability. Second, if school officials assume responsibility under Education Code Section 44808 for supervising students when they are off campus and then do not exercise reasonable care, they may be liable for injuries sustained by third parties.

Under the Tort Claims Act, school districts and their employees enjoy considerable immunity from liability for injuries sustained by nonstudents who participate in hazardous recreational activities on school premises (Govt. Code § 831.7). This provision is intended to offer protection from lawsuits when members of the public use public facilities after hours, on weekends, or during vacations. The statute defines a hazardous recreational activity as creating a substantial risk of injury to participants or spectators. The statute includes a long list of activities that fall within this definition, including trampolining and sports that involve bodily contact. The statute does not provide immunity from liability if the entity or employee knows about a dangerous condition that cannot be assumed to be inherent in the activity and provides no warning, if a specific fee is charged to engage in the activity, if the structure or equipment is not in good repair, if the public entity or employee recklessly or with gross negligence promotes participation in the activity, or if gross negligence by the entity or employee is the proximate cause of the injury.

Despite the exceptions, the provision does give considerable immunity to both school districts and employees. For example, the Oakland Unified School District was entitled to immunity when Yarber, a member of the public, was injured in an after-hours adult basketball game at a junior high school gymnasium. Yarber and others had rented the gym and had played there before. He was injured when the impact of another player propelled him against an unpadded concrete wall. He sued the district. The district claimed immunity from liability under the hazardous recreational activity provision. The appellate court agreed with the district, noting that playing basketball in a full-court game is a body contact sport and that being struck by another player and running into obstacles near the court are inherently part of the game. Yarber should have been aware of the unpadded wall, especially since he had played basketball in that gym before. The district was under no obligation to warn him of the hazard (*Yarber v. Oakland Unified School District*, 1992).

Dangerous condition of school property. Section 835 of the Tort Claims Act provides that a school district can be liable when a dangerous condition of its property causes injury. The condition must be caused either by the negligence of employees (e.g., failure to install protective guards on shop equipment) or by a known condition that the district did nothing to correct. A case in the latter category involved two elementary students in the Conejo Valley Unified School District who were injured when a car driven by a parent jumped the curb in a parking lot designated as the student pickup area. The parking lot originally had been used as a bus loading zone. It was quite small and badly congested, in part because the school had ended staggered dismissal times. The driver of the car had just spoken with another driver, asking her for room to park. When she returned to her car and began to maneuver it into the space, the car rapidly lurched forward over the curb, striking the students. The parents of the injured students settled their claims against all defendants except the school district, which sought dismissal of the case.

The jury found that the district knew that the pickup area was dangerous but had not taken corrective action. The district was found liable, and it appealed. The California court of appeal affirmed the judgment. The court noted that principals at the school had complained over the years to district officials about hazardous congestion in the parking lot. Two experts had testified that, though no accidents had occurred in the past, the lot was an "accident waiting to happen." Thus, it could be foreseen that the impact of a driver's negligence would be exacerbated because of the congested space. The court wrote, "When a public entity has actual or constructive notice [i.e., should have known] of a dangerous condition, it has a duty to take reasonable steps to protect the public from the danger even if such dangers are not necessarily created by the entity." Since a special relationship existed between the district and its students requiring a heightened duty to make the school safe, the district was negligent in not erecting barriers or taking other corrective measures (*Constantinescu v. Conejo Valley Unified School District*, 1993, p. 739).

The condition of property must have something to do with the injury for there to be liability under this section of the Tort Claims Act. If the property is merely the site of the injury, no liability will incur. A student who props his bike against the school's chain-link fence so he can climb upon it to pick oranges from a tree on the other side and is injured when the bike slips cannot recover damages from the school district, because the fence did not constitute a dangerous condition of public property (*Biscotti v. Yuba City Unified School District*, 2007). "The lesson learned," the court observed, "is that tort law does not protect [the student] from the consequence of his careless decision."

Conversely, if the condition of property increases the risk of injury, the district may incur liability. This is true even when the injury occurs on adjacent property not controlled by the school. Government Code Section 830 provides as much. An appellate court ruled in 2003 that if an open schoolyard gate encourages students to cross the street at an unguarded crosswalk with a history of "near misses" rather than walk to an intersection with a traffic light some distance away, the school can be liable for injuries sustained when a student is struck by a car in an adjacent crosswalk (*Joyce v. Simi Valley Unified School District*). The principal had ordered the fence opening to facilitate student entry to the junior high school. It would make no difference if the gate itself was not physically defective, or if the driver of the car was negligent. The appeals court upheld a damage award of $2.8 million against the district.

Some years earlier, another court held that an opening in a school fence through which two boys gained access to the school playground after hours did not subject the school district to liability. Once on the playground, one of the boys was killed when he fell while playing a version of crack-the-whip while on his skateboard. The district was judged not liable because the opening in the fence merely allowed access to the area. The only thing that was dangerous was the activity of the boys (*Bartell v. Palos Verdes Peninsula School District*, 1978). This seems to be a narrow distinction, and different juries and judges may reach different outcomes. In any event, the best way to avoid litigation is to prevent injuries. This could have been accomplished in these cases simply by closing the gate and fixing the hole in the fence.

Waivers of liability. How useful are waivers of liability? Unless they are explicitly worded, not very. This is the teaching of a 1990 ruling involving the San Diego Unified School District. A high school student was injured during a campus hypnotism show sponsored by the Parent, Teacher, and Student Association (PTSA) at a fund-raiser. The student's father had signed a release form permitting his daughter to participate and waiving all liability against the PTSA, its members, the high school, and the school district. Both the student and her father signed another form indemnifying the hypnotist and any third parties from liability in connection with the show. The student had seen the show the previous year and wanted to participate. During the show, she was injured when she slid from her chair to the floor several times. The court of appeal first ruled that waivers of liability are not contrary to public policy. Without them, many school-sponsored activities and events could not be held at all. While a minor can disaffirm a previously signed contract, such is not the case when the contract is signed on the student's behalf by her parent. In this case, there was a binding agreement. However, the wording was vague. There was no language regarding bodily injury or negligence. Nor was there any language indicating that the child could not recover for bodily injury. Given the ambiguity in the agreement, the district could not rely on it to have the case dismissed. The matter was returned for trial (*Hohe v. San Diego Unified School District*).

For a waiver to be valid, the person signing it must be aware of what is being given up. This poses a challenge to drafters. As the court noted in the *Hohe* case:

A valid release must be simple enough for a layman to understand and additionally give notice of its impact. A draftsman of such a release faces two difficult choices. His Scylla is the sin of oversimplification and his Charybdis a whirlpool of convoluted language which purports to give notice of everything but as a practical matter buries its message in minutiae. (p. 650)

What was missing from the *Hohe* waiver was an explicit indication that both the parent and the daughter were giving up the right to sue, even if the sponsors and actors were negligent and the student physically injured as a result.

Counselors and the duty to warn. In 1976 the California Supreme Court issued an important decision that has implications for counselors and psychologists. In *Tarasoff v. Regents of the University of California*, the court had to consider the extent to which confidentiality protects the doctor-patient relationship. The case involved a lover's quarrel between two students at the University of California at Berkeley. The situation confronted health officials at the institution with a difficult choice. They could maintain confidentiality with the male student, who said he intended to kill his girlfriend, or they could break the confidentiality and warn the intended victim. They chose not to warn the girlfriend. Two months later, the boyfriend murdered Tatiana Tarasoff. The girl's parents sued the doctors and the university. The university and the health officials asserted they owed no duty of reasonable care to Tarasoff and were thus immune from liability under the Tort Claims Act. A majority of the justices disagreed, ruling that when a therapist knows or should know that his patient presents a serious danger of harm to another person, the therapist has a duty to use reasonable care to protect the intended victim from harm. The cloak of confidentiality between doctor and patient cannot insulate the therapist from liability. As the court noted, "The protective privilege ends where the public peril begins" (p. 27).

Education Code Section 49600 specifies the functions of certificated school counselors. Included among them are student personal and social counseling. In these instances, students often reveal sensitive information. Are counselors protected by a shield of confidentiality, or can they be liable for not disclosing information that may pose a threat to others? Education Code Section 49602 delineates what must be kept confidential and what must be revealed. The statute provides that personal information disclosed by a student who is twelve years old or older is confidential and that the counselor is not to be subjected to any civil or criminal liability for nondisclosure. The same is true of confidential information disclosed to the counselor by a parent or guardian of a student who is twelve years old or older. Information is not to become part of the student's record without written consent of the person who disclosed it and may not be revealed to anyone.

The statute then goes on to list exceptions to nondisclosure. They include reporting of child abuse or neglect, communication between the counselor and psychotherapists or other health providers for student referral purposes, and disclosure to persons specified in a written waiver signed by the student and kept in the student's file. Two exceptions to confidentiality specifically track the *Tarasoff* ruling. The first permits reporting information to the principal or parents of the student when the counselor has reasonable cause to believe that disclosure is necessary to avert a clear and present danger to the student or other persons in the school community. The second permits disclosure to the principal, the student's parents, or other persons outside the school when the student indicates that a crime involving personal injury or significant property loss has been or will be committed. However, the statute prohibits disclosure of information to the parents of the student when the counselor has cause to believe that the disclosure would result in a clear and present danger to the health, safety, or welfare of the student. The statute also requires school counselors to disclose confidential information to law enforcement agencies pursuant to a court order when necessary to aid in the investigation of a crime, or for purposes of testifying in an administrative or judicial proceeding.

It is important to note that the federal Family Educational Rights and Privacy Act provides that disclosure of personally identifiable information about students and their families for health or safety emergency reasons does not violate the act. In addition, California Civil Code Section 48.8 provides immunity from defamation liability for reporting information to a public or private school official that a person has threatened to use a firearm or other deadly weapon on school property. Liability occurs only if there is clear and convincing evidence that the report was made with knowledge of its falsity or with reckless disregard for the truth or falsity.

A word about insurance. Education Code Section 35208 requires school districts to secure liability insurance for themselves, their board members, and their employees for personal injury, property damage, and death. In lieu of securing insurance, districts can provide protection from their own funds. One way or another, employees are indemnified when they are acting within the scope of their duties of employment. Additionally, Section 32220 and following sections require school districts to assure that members of athletic teams have specified amounts of insurance protection for medical and hospital expenses resulting from accidental bodily injuries, including those experienced while being transported to and from athletic events under the auspices of the district or a student body organization. The term "athletic team" includes members of team members, school bands, cheerleaders, team managers, and others involved in athletic activities, but it does not include student rooting sections or spectators unless the district so chooses. The expense of the insurance is to be paid by the district; funds of the student body; or by parents, guardians, or other persons. However, if parents, guardians, or persons having change of an athletic team are not able to pay the costs, then districts assume this responsibility. Section 32221.5 requires a written notice regarding insurance sent to members of school athletic teams to include a statement regarding no-cost or low-cost local, state, or federally sponsored health insurance programs. If 15 percent or more of the covered groups speak a primary language other than English, the notice must be translated in accord with Education Code Section 48985.

An area of particular concern to administrators and teachers is transporting students in private automobiles to and from school events. If an accident occurs due to the negligence of the school employee, is the district or the employee liable? The first question is whether the school employee is acting within his or her scope of employment when the accident occurred. If not, then the school employee's insurance company will have to pay; or, if the insurance coverage is inadequate, the employee personally will be responsible. For example, a teacher would have a difficult time arguing that he was acting within the scope of his duties of employment when driving students to school as part of a neighborhood carpool or transporting students to their homes from a movie theater on a Saturday night.

But suppose a teacher is transporting students in his car to a school event in compliance with an administrative directive to do so. As the result of negligent driving, the teacher's car strikes a pedestrian, causing serious injury. Can the teacher seek indemnification from the school district when the pedestrian files suit? The California Insurance Code requires that California drivers must carry liability insurance. Thus, the teacher is protected by his own insurance, subject to policy limits. The teacher also is protected by the school district's insurance because every school district must provide insurance for its employees. Section 11580.9 of the Insurance Code specifies that when two or more policies provide coverage for the same vehicle, the owner's policy is the primary insurer and the other policy or policies are secondary. Thus, in our hypothetical, the teacher's insurance will bear the initial burden and, if the settlement or judgment is more than the policy limit, the school district's insurance will provide the remainder. Nothing precludes the school district from satisfying its obligations under the Tort Claims Act in this way. Districts routinely advise employees to make sure that they have adequate liability insurance coverage for their vehicles and to advise their insurance companies that the vehicle might be used while on the job.

Recall that the Tort Claims Act also requires the school district to defend the employee in any legal action as well, as long as the employee is acting within the scope of employment. Where liability involves motor vehicles, the Insurance Code provides that defense costs are shared between the primary and secondary insurers. If the employee is not acting within the scope of employment, then the district has no responsibility either to defend the employee or pay any judgment. Sometimes there may be a dispute about this, and the district's legal representative may decline to represent the employee. In this event, the employee will have to shoulder his own legal costs through a personal or professional insurance policy or through personal funds. As a matter of preventive action, it is always wise to check on the extent of insurance coverage under both personal and district policies before accidents happen and to make any necessary adjustments.

Fair Employment and Housing Act

As we discussed in Chapter 5, the California Fair Employment and Housing Act (FEHA) prohibits a broad range of discrimination and harassment in public and private employment. FEHA is the state counterpart to Title VII of the federal 1964 Civil Rights Act and can be found in California Government Code Section 12900 and following sections. FEHA is more comprehensive than its federal counterpart, and its remedies are broader. FEHA applies to public and private employers, labor organizations, employment agencies, apprenticeship training programs, or any training program leading to employment. In addition to discrimination, FEHA prohibits harassment on the basis of race, religious creed, color, national origin, ancestry, physical disability, mental disability, medical condition, marital status, sex, age over forty, or sexual orientation. Claims involving disability discrimination are easier to pursue under FEHA than under the federal Americans with Disabilities Act because FEHA requires only that the disability "limits," rather than "substantially limits," a major life activity. California Government Code Section 11135, which applies to programs and activities operated or funded by the state or any state agency, now includes sex and sexual orientation, and these terms are to have the same meaning as set forth in FEHA. A provision has been added as well to Section 11135 that expands coverage to include a perception of having one or more of the named characteristics or associating with one who does. While this law is worded in terms of the state, school districts and charter schools are within its sweep, because both receive funding from the state.

Harassment on any of the grounds specified in FEHA is unlawful if the employer or the employer's agents or supervisors know, or should know, of the conduct and fail to take immediate and appropriate corrective action. An employee need not suffer loss of tangible job benefits in order to establish harassment. After exhausting the administrative remedies specified in the statute, victims can sue both employers and individual employees for money damages.

The California Supreme Court discussed the relationship between FEHA and the Tort Claims Act in a 1995 decision involving a superintendent whose contract was not extended by a three-to-two vote. Based on newspaper reports, he alleged that one of three board members voted as he did because the superintendent was not Hispanic or Latino. The superintendent also alleged that the other two voted for termination of his contract because he was sixty-six years old. If the allegations were true, it is hard to imagine a clearer case of impermissibly motivated personnel decisionmaking.

The California high court first noted that the common law, in the form of judicial precedent, long has provided government officials broad immunity from lawsuits so that they have maximum discretion to make policy decisions without fear of liability. Votes by members of the school board whether to renew the contract of a superintendent fall into this category. The court then turned to the question of whether FEHA overrides the grant of immunity in Section 820.2 of the Tort Claims Act. That section conveys immunity to employees for discretionary acts "except as otherwise provided by statute." Board members are entitled to the same immunity. Because FEHA is a statute that prohibits the very kinds of reasons allegedly used by the three school board members, the superintendent argued that he could sue each of the board members individually. The justices did not agree. For this to be the case, the legislature would have had to include language in FEHA specifying that its provisions revoke the immunity provided in Section 820.2 for discretionary acts. Because there is no such indication in FEHA, the immunity provision of the Tort Claims Act protects the three board members in their individual capacities from the lawsuit. However, the court observed that while the board members are immune, the school district itself likely could be sued because FEHA specifically states that both private and public *employers* can be held accountable for violating its terms. However, the justices did not decide the question of district liability, because the issue was not before them (*Caldwell v. Montoya*, 1995).

Caldwell, the superintendent, subsequently did pursue litigation against the school district under FEHA. The jury concluded that the board members were motivated by legitimate job-related reasons for not renewing his contract. Caldwell appealed once again, but the appellate court sustained the jury verdict (*Caldwell v. Paramount Unified School District*, 1995). Aside from clarification of how FEHA affects the liability of school board members, the extensive litigation evident in the *Caldwell* case is a good illustration of why employers should avoid any reliance upon, or even mention of, impermissible reasons for negative employment decisions. The focus should always be on job-related deficiencies.

LIABILITY UNDER FEDERAL LAW

Earlier in this book, we briefly examined the extent of liability under various federal statutes. Chapter 1 contains a chart describing the major federal laws impacting public schools and the consequences for violating them (see Table 1.1). We discussed federal statutes pertaining to employment discrimination in Chapter 5, federal disability law in Chapter 8, and racial and sexual harassment in Chapter 11. Here we discuss liability of schools and school employees under a well-known civil rights law, 42 United States Code (U.S.C.) Section 1983.

Liability of Schools under 42 U.S.C. Section 1983

Personal injury and property damage cases are routinely the province of state courts. Aside from actions regarding disputes between citizens from different states involving at least $75,000 in controversy, the jurisdiction of federal courts is limited to federal wrongs. These fall primarily into the categories of violations of the U.S. Constitution and federal statutes. As we noted in Chapter 1 and elsewhere, many federal statutes have provisions describing how violations are to be addressed and what remedies are available. However, such is not the case for provisions of the federal constitution. To bring federal wrongs committed by states and their political subdivisions within the jurisdiction of the federal courts, Congress enacted a key civil rights act after the Civil War. This statute, 42 U.S.C. Section 1983, provides that

> Every person who, under color of any statute, ordinance, regulation, custom, or usage, of any State or Territory . . . subjects, or causes to be subjected, any citizen of the United States or other person within the jurisdiction thereof to the deprivation of any rights, privileges, or immunities secured by the Constitution and laws, shall be liable to the party injured in an action at law, suit in equity, or other proper proceeding for redress [in federal court]. . .

Section 1983, as it is commonly called, enables those who believe they are the victims of federal wrongs committed by persons employed by the government to bypass state courts and bring their claims directly to federal court. It is the primary basis for lawsuits involving alleged violation of federal constitutional rights such as freedom of speech and right to due process.

In an early decision, the U.S. Supreme Court interpreted the term "person" as used in the first part of Section 1983 to encompass municipalities. Thus, in most states the meaning of a "person" encompasses a public school district, as well as the individuals it employs, such as administrators, teachers, custodians, and the like, who are functioning in their official capacities. Likewise, charter schools as newly created mini-school districts are considered "persons" and thus subject to suit, as are their employees. At the same time, states themselves are immune from liability under the Eleventh Amendment to the U.S. Constitution. That amendment prevents states from being sued in federal court by citizens from other states or their own citizens without state permission, unless Congress has abrogated the immunity. Congress has not done so in Section 1983.

Unlike school districts in other states, California school districts are not considered municipalities under Section 1983 and cannot be sued under this statute. The U.S. Court of Appeals for the Ninth Circuit ruled in 1992 that California school districts are an arm of the state and thus immune under the Eleventh Amendment from federal claims (*Belanger v. Madera Unified School District*). The *Belanger* case involved a school principal who was reassigned to classroom teaching. She filed a Section 1983 lawsuit against the district, claiming she was denied equal protection of the laws because of her gender and was the victim of retaliation for testifying against the district in another gender discrimination lawsuit. Because the state controls school district funding as a result of the *Serrano v. Priest* equalization litigation and Proposition 13, as discussed in some detail in Chapter 3, the court noted that any judgment against the school district would have to be paid out of what essentially is a state fund. Second, while public schooling is generally considered a municipal function, this is not true in California. The court cited provisions of the California Constitution and the Education Code giving the state great control over the operations of school districts. The court also noted a California Supreme Court decision recognizing public schools as "a matter of statewide rather than local or municipal concern."

For all these reasons, the judges concluded that California school districts are not political subdivisions but rather agents of the state performing central governmental functions. Because Congress did not abrogate state Eleventh Amendment immunity in enacting Section 1983, the lawsuit was dismissed due to lack of federal jurisdiction. Whether California charter schools, which are less subject to state control, might be similarly immune remains unclear.

In 1999 the Ninth Circuit revisited the question, this time in a case involving a suit in federal court against the Oakland school district based on allegations of a denial of rights protected by the California Fair Employment and Housing Act

(FEHA). Once again, the Ninth Circuit refused to let the lawsuit continue because the Eleventh Amendment barred the claim (*Freeman v. Oakland Unified School District*). There was no indication that either California or Congress had abrogated the state's immunity from a FEHA lawsuit filed in federal court. However, the Ninth Circuit did note that the plaintiff could refile his claim in state court. This assumes, of course, that the period of time during which such a lawsuit can be filed had not ended while the federal action was under way.

While the Eleventh Amendment bars lawsuits for damages against California school districts under Section 1983, it does not preclude courts from issuing court orders defining rights and legal relationships (known as declaratory judgments) or requiring or halting actions (known as injunctions). For example, in the case discussed in Chapter Seven involving a teacher who was restricted from using supplemental materials with religious content, the federal judge did not bar the teacher's lawsuit against school officials acting in their official capacities (which, as discussed in the next section, is the same as suing the school district itself) because the teacher was not seeking damages but rather a declaratory judgment. Attorneys' fees associated with such lawsuits also are not barred by the Eleventh Amendment (*Williams v. Vidmar*, 2005). And it is important to note that Congress can abrogate state Eleventh Amendment immunity under the Fourteenth Amendment, which prohibits states from denying persons of life, liberty, or property without due process of law and of equal protection of the laws. Congress has done so in statutes such as Section 504 of the 1973 Rehabilitation Act, the Age Discrimination Act, Title VI of the 1964 Civil Rights Act against racial discrimination, and Title IX of the 1972 Education Amendments against gender discrimination.

Liability of School Employees under 42 U.S.C. Section 1983

If a school district with its deep pockets cannot be sued in federal court for federal wrongs under Section 1983, what about individual employees? When a lawsuit is filed against the employee in the employee's official capacity, that amounts to suing the district directly. Employees act in their official capacity when they are carrying out school district policies and administrative procedures. And since school districts are immune under the Eleventh Amendment, so too are employees in this instance.

However, public employees can be sued in their individual, as contrasted with their official, capacity under Section 1983. And in this instance, immunity is less certain. Employees are sued in their individual capacities when they stray beyond district policy and administrative procedures. Consider this situation. A school administrator routinely uses force to maintain discipline. In one instance, he slaps a student across the mouth and grabs him by the neck after the student said what the administrator thought was "Heil Hitler." The student, who is hospitalized, reports the incident to the police. The administrator pleads guilty to assault and battery and is placed on probation. Later, the administrator punches a student who was making noise during a special program held at the half-time of a basketball game; he throws another student into the lockers when he spots the student wearing a hat. The three students file a Section 1983 lawsuit against the school administrator, seeking damages.

The first question in a case like this is to identify what federal right is at stake. If there is no recognized federal right, the matter is at an end, and the case will go nowhere under Section 1983. In some instances, stating the right is easy. As we have seen, students have rights to freedom of speech, religious exercise, and due process, among others. In other instances, identifying the right may be more difficult. Is there a constitutional right to be free from being manhandled? In the case from which these facts were taken, the Ninth Circuit recognized that there is a Fourteenth Amendment liberty right to be free from injury inflicted by a school official. This right is clearly established, originating with the 1977 U.S. Supreme Court decision involving the use of corporal punishment (*Ingraham v. Wright*). The Court ruled in that case that "where school authorities, acting under color of state law, deliberately decide to punish a child for misconduct by restraining the child and inflicting appreciable physical pain, we hold that Fourteenth Amendment liberty interests are implicated" (p. 674). Citing that ruling, the Ninth Circuit recognized that the students' right to be free from physical attacks is well recognized.

Once a federal right is found, the next question is whether school employees acting in their individual capacity are entitled to qualified immunity. The U.S. Supreme Court has ruled that a public official is entitled to immunity unless the official knew or should have known that his actions would violate a clearly recognized federal right (*Harlow v. Fitzgerald*, 1982). Applying this test, the Ninth Circuit concluded that the administrator knew or should have known that his excessive use of force violated the students' clearly recognized constitutional right to be free from harm. Therefore, he was not entitled to qualified immunity (*P.B. v. Koch*, 1996). A few years later, the Ninth Circuit ruled that a vice principal's taping an elementary student's head to a tree for five minutes because the student would not stop horsing around constituted a violation of the student's well-recognized Fourth Amendment right to be free from unreasonable seizures. This being the case, the school official was not entitled to qualified immunity under Section 1983 (*Doe v. Hawaii Department of Education*, 2003). In 2007 the Ninth Circuit relied on its analysis in *P.B. v. Koch* to hold that a special education teacher who slaps a four-year old disabled child repeatedly and slams the child into a chair violates the child's constitutional right to be free from excessive force. Because a special education teacher should know that such actions contravene the heightened protections for these children, the teacher is not entitled to qualified immunity from a Section 1983 lawsuit. Nor are school officials who permitted such acts to occur (*Preschooler II v. Clark County School Board of Trustees*).

However, parents cannot use Section 1983 to sue for money damages when allegations are made that IDEA provisions have been violated. The Ninth Circuit ruled as much in a 2007 case involving a parent who sought to link Section 1983 with IDEA so she could receive compensation for lost income and the emotional distress of advocating for IDEA benefits for her son (*Blanchard v. Morton School District*). The appellate judges held that Section 1983 cannot be used in combination with IDEA, because IDEA is a sufficiently comprehensive statute and provides its own remedies (e.g., compensatory education, reimbursement for private school expenses). Note, however, that if a Section 1983 claim is anchored in other law, as is the case with the *Preschooler II* case above, then monetary damages may be sought.

As we noted in Chapter 11, students have a recognized right to be free from both racial and sexual harassment under Title VI of the 1964 Civil Rights Act and Title IX of the 1972 Education Amendments, respectively. Lawsuits under these statutes are filed against school entities. Section 1983 opens up lawsuits against school employees, including those working in charter schools. A 2003 ruling from the Ninth Circuit conveys good insight into the application of Section 1983 in this context. The case involved same-sex student-on-student sexual harassment. Students who either were or were perceived to be lesbian, gay, or bisexual sued school officials in the Morgan Hill Unified School District for responding ineffectively to repeated harassment over a number of years. They alleged that teachers and administrators failed to stop name-calling and antigay remarks and that administrators responded to physical abuse with inadequate disciplinary action. The judges ruled that the Fourteenth Amendment's equal protection clause has been construed in the Ninth Circuit as early as 1990 to protect persons from harassment based on their sexual orientation.

Accordingly, school district antiharassment policies had to be enforced against peer harassment of homosexual and bisexual students in the same manner as against peer harassment of heterosexual students. The court found that not only had the named school officials taken ineffective action to stop the harassment, they also lacked an effective training program on how to deal with sexual orientation discrimination. The court ruled that there was sufficient evidence for a jury to conclude that the school officials intentionally discriminated against the students in violation of the equal protection clause, and therefore the officials were not entitled to qualified immunity (*Flores v. Morgan Hill Unified School District*, 2003).

A federal district court judge ruled similarly in another 2003 case involving an eighth-grade student in the Banning Unified School District who was barred from gym class and forced to sit in the office after she had told other students that she was a lesbian. There was no evidence that the student had made inappropriate remarks or engaged in inappropriate conduct with other students. The court ruled that the individual defendants, including the school principal and physical education teacher, were not entitled to qualified immunity, because they should have known that discrimination based on sexual orientation violates the equal protection clause of the Fourteenth Amendment. The judge also observed that the district employees were not entitled to immunity under the Tort Claims Act, because there is no discretion to engage in discriminatory acts. The defendants' motion to dismiss the case was denied (*Massey v. Banning Unified School District*).

It is important to note that if no recognized federal right is at stake, then liability under Section 1983 is unlikely. A case in point involves a teacher who sued the district and the school superintendent in his official and individual capacities over a letter of reprimand the teacher received from the superintendent. The superintendent sent the letter after the teacher spoke in class about a contentious school board meeting over the rights of gay and lesbian teachers. The teacher had helped establish the faculty Gay-Straight Alliance at the high school and had earlier discussed such issues as diversity and the rights of gay students in his English class. The teacher claimed that the letter violated his rights of free speech. Basing its judgment on Eleventh Amendment immunity, the federal district court dismissed the claims against the school district and the superintendent in his official capacity. This left the claim that the school superintendent, acting in his individual capacity, had violated the teacher's right. The federal district court ruled that the superintendent was entitled to qualified immunity because there is no clearly recognized right for a teacher to depart from classroom instruction to discuss a controversial matter of public interest without risk of reprimand (*Debro v. San Leandro Unified School District*, 2001).

Can a supervisor be liable for a subordinate's violation of federal rights in a Section 1983 lawsuit? The answer is yes, if the supervisor knew or should have known about the acts and failed to stop them. This is the teaching of a 1998 Ninth Circuit ruling involving a sixth grader whose student teacher allegedly fondled, kissed, straddled, and otherwise inappropriately touched her and other girls in the class. Boys in the class also were alleged to have engaged in harassment. The parents sought to have the student teacher removed from the class, but they maintained the principal declined to do so. The parents claimed the classroom teacher did not stop the harassment, but did retaliate against the student by lowering her grade and depriving her of awards she had won. The teacher, principal, and director of elementary education sought dismissal of the claims against them. The Ninth Circuit first observed that a public school student has a clearly recognized right under federal law to be free from sexual abuse and harassment. Accordingly, "a supervisor may be found liable under Section 1983 if the supervisor is 'aware of a specific risk of harm to the plaintiff.'" Here, the teacher, principal, and director of elementary education were all in a supervisory capacity over the student teacher. They all had a duty to take action to protect students from the student teacher's sexual harassment and discrimination. Thus, they were not entitled to qualified immunity (*Oona R. S. By Kate S. v. McCaffrey*).

The lesson of these cases is quite clear. Because school personnel can be held liable in their individual capacities when federal rights are violated, it is wise to learn what these rights are and to act expeditiously to protect them.

SUMMARY

The California Tort Claims Act conveys broad immunity to school districts and their employees. As a general rule, neither the district nor the employee is liable when the employee is using appropriate discretion in carrying out the employee's duties. However, if the employee is not exercising appropriate discretion while acting within the scope of employment when an injury occurs, the district bears the liability. This is particularly true where the law imposes a duty on school employees to assure student safety. For this reason, districts carry insurance. An exception is when the employee is not acting within the scope of employment. In these instances, the employee alone will face liability. Clearly, the implication for employees is to carry out their responsibilities conscientiously. The implication for school districts is to make sure that school employees know what their job requirements are and that they follow school district policies and regulations in carrying them out. This is particularly true when there is a mandatory duty under the law, because the district bears liability if the duty is not performed. The best example of a clearly established mandatory duty is the duty to supervise and protect students. However, that duty is mitigated somewhat in the context of athletic events because courts have ruled that students themselves must assume the risk of participating.

The school district's duty under the Tort Claims Act to protect innocent third parties from the actions of students arises only when the district has assumed the responsibility or when district officials have reason to believe that students could pose a harm to others. In either event, it must be established that the district's action constituted the proximate cause of the nonstudent's injury for there to be liability. Concern about injury to nonstudents is most apt to arise when counselors receive sensitive information from students and when students are attending school-sponsored activities off campus. The California Education Code requires disclosure of information from students that could harm others. Care must be taken in arranging school-sponsored activities so that student safety is assured and innocent third parties are protected.

A school district also bears liability under the Tort Claims Act for injuries caused by a dangerous condition of its property that it knew about but did not fix or that resulted from the negligence of its employees. Consequently, school personnel should make certain that school grounds and equipment are safe. At the same time, the Tort Claims Act provides considerable protection to school districts and their employees from liability for injuries sustained by nonstudents participating in hazardous recreational activities on school premises. Often, districts and district personnel try to ward off the threat of liability through the use of waivers. However, unless very carefully worded, waivers are not foolproof. While districts routinely provide insurance for school personnel, employees should make sure they have personal coverage as well, because it will be needed in the case of injuries caused by their negligent use of an automobile and when they are determined to have acted outside the scope of employment.

Though judicial rulings have indicated that racial or sexual harassment committed by a school employee may not be actionable under the Tort Claims Act because it is not encompassed within the scope of employment, liability may be imposed on both the school district and the employee under other state laws. In particular, as we have seen in earlier chapters, California's Unruh Civil Rights Act and Fair Employment and Housing Act provide remedies for a wide range of discriminatory actions. Discrimination based on sexual preference is encompassed within the terms of both. Further, the school district may be liable under the Tort Claims Act for its negligence in not having a well-designed hiring process that would screen out employees who pose a danger to students. This also carries implications for the writing of employment recommendations, because nondisclosure of facts when there is a foreseeable danger of harm may result in liability for both the writers and the schools that employ them.

Federal law provides an avenue of redress for wrongs involving federal constitutional and statutory rights. However, school districts are immune from many of these lawsuits, given the interpretation of a major federal civil rights statute by the

U.S. Court of Appeals for the Ninth Circuit. How this applies to charter schools awaits a future ruling. Public school employees, including those in charter schools who are sued as individuals acting on their own, are not entitled to the same immunity if it is established that they knew or should have known that their actions would violate clearly recognized federal rights. Among these are freedom of speech, free exercise of religion, due process, and the right to be free from sexual abuse.

School districts are not immune from liability for racial and sexual harassment. As we noted in Chapter 11, Title VI of the 1964 Civil Rights Act and Title IX of the 1972 Education Amendments provide that the district's federal funding can be curtailed and that the victims of harassment and abuse can sue the district for damages. In addition, 42 U.S.C. Section 1983 permits lawsuits against individuals who committed the acts and even against their supervisors. Given the sanctions under both state and federal law for racial and sexual harassment, it is essential that both school districts and employees make every effort to avoid such situations.

In the end, the key to avoiding liability is to practice effective preventive action. This means knowing and following the law, complying with recognized ethical standards, and using common sense. Because one cannot be assured that a lawsuit or even a valid claim will never arise, it is also important to have adequate insurance protection for defense costs and damage awards.

GLOSSARY OF LEGAL TERMINOLOGY

The words and definitions in this glossary are intended to help the lay reader better understand some of the terminology used in this book, in judicial decisions, in legal memoranda, and in other materials on school law. We have included the legal terms the reader is most likely to encounter. For a more extensive list, consult Bryan A. Garner, ed., *Black's Law Dictionary. Abridged*, 8th ed. (see Appendix C).

actual damages.   The amount awarded to the prevailing plaintiff for out-of-pocket losses such as hospital expenses (compare *compensatory damages* and *punitive damages*).

agency fee.   A service fee that employees must pay to the union once a collective bargaining agent has been recognized as the exclusive representative of the employees in a bargaining unit, if the employees do not wish to become dues-paying members of the union.

amicus curiae.   "Friend of the court"; a person or organization allowed to appear in a lawsuit, usually to file arguments in the form of a brief supporting one side or the other, even though not a party to the dispute.

appellant.   The party appealing a court's decision (compare *plaintiff*).

appellee.   The party opposing an appeal of a court's decision (see *defendant*).

attorneys' fees.   Refers to the practice of according the winning party's costs to the losing party in a civil case. The 1976 Civil Rights Attorneys' Fees Awards Act gives courts this power in civil rights suits.

back pay.   Lost wages that must be paid to employees who have been illegally discharged or laid off.

cause of action.   A legal claim.

certiorari. A writ issued by a court asking the lower court to submit the record in a case, thus indicating the willingness of the higher court to entertain the appeal; "cert." for short.

civil case. Every lawsuit other than a criminal proceeding. Most civil cases involve a lawsuit brought by one person against another and usually concern money damages.

civil liberties. Fundamental individual freedoms that are constitutionally protected. Provisions listed in the Bill of Rights to the U.S. Constitution, such as freedom of speech and religious exercise, are considered civil liberties.

civil rights. Rights that provide access to the legal system and equitable treatment before the law. Civil rights can be provided by a constitution or action of a legislative body. Thus, one is entitled to freedom from discrimination based on race, color, religion, sex, or national origin in public and private employment by provisions of Title VII of the 1964 Civil Rights Act.

class action. A lawsuit brought by one person on behalf of himself or herself and all other persons in the same situation.

code. A collection of laws. The California Education Code is a grouping of state statutes affecting education.

collective bargaining. The negotiating process for reaching an agreement pertaining to wages, hours, and other terms and conditions of employment between management and labor. In California, collective bargaining for public school employees is conducted in accord with the provisions of the Educational Employment Relations Act.

common law. Law that develops by custom and is given expression through court rulings. Many student and teacher rights have developed this way, as has the tort of personal privacy invasion. Many common-law principles have been incorporated into legislative enactments (statutes).

compensatory damages. An amount awarded to the plaintiff to compensate for pain and suffering.

complaint. The first main paper filed in a civil lawsuit. It includes, among other things, a statement of the wrong or harm supposedly done to the plaintiff by the defendant and a request for specific help from the court. The defendant responds to the complaint by filing an "answer."

contract. An agreement that affects the legal relationship between two or more persons. To be a contract, an agreement must involve persons legally capable of making binding agreements, at least one promise, consideration (i.e., something of value promised or given), and a reasonable amount of agreement between the persons as to what the contract means.

criminal case. A case involving crimes against the laws of the state; unlike civil cases, in criminal cases the state is the prosecuting party.

de facto.   "In fact, actual"; a situation that exists in fact, whether or not it is lawful. De facto segregation is that which exists regardless of the law or the actions of civil authorities (compare *de jure*).

defamation.   Impugning a person's character or injuring a person's reputation by false or malicious statements. This includes both *libel* and *slander* (see these terms).

defendant.   The person against whom a legal action is brought. This legal action may be civil or criminal. At the appeal stage, the party against whom an appeal is taken is known as the "appellee." Usually, the appellee is the winner in the lower court.

de jure.   "Of right"; legitimate; lawful, whether or not in actual fact. De jure segregation is that which is sanctioned by law (compare *de facto*).

de minimis.   Trivial, small, unimportant, as in "The matter is sufficiently de minimis that it should not be the subject of a formal lawsuit."

dictum.   See *obiter dictum.*

disclaimer.   The refusal to accept certain types of responsibility. For example, a summer school course listing may disclaim any responsibility for guaranteeing that the courses contained therein will actually be offered because courses, programs, and instructors are likely to change without notice.

due process.   Both the U.S. and California constitutions require that before a governmental entity can deprive a person of life, liberty, or property, due process of law must be provided. *Procedural due process* refers to a set of steps that are designed to elicit truth. They generally consist of notice of wrongdoing, a hearing for the presentation of evidence and of a defense, and a right to appeal to higher authorities. If one's life is at stake, each of these components is quite elaborate. Important liberty and property rights also require formal due process. For example, before a public school employee's contract can be terminated, the governing board must follow a set of formal due process procedures. *Substantive due process* requires that the decision itself must be fair and reasonable. Courts rarely become involved on substantive due process grounds unless a decision is so unreasonable as to constitute a miscarriage of justice even though all the procedural steps have been followed. For the due process clauses of the Fifth and Fourteenth Amendments to the U.S. Constitution to come into play, it first must be established that life, liberty, or property rights are implicated. However, the California Constitution due process clauses found in Article I, Section 7 (a) and Section 15 require only a showing that some statutory benefit or entitlement is at stake. The greater the benefit or entitlement, the more formal the due process requirements are.

eminent domain.   The authority of a governmental entity to claim private property for public use. The government typically has to provide the owner the fair market value of the property. Usually refers to land that the government needs for building roads, erecting schools, and the like.

en banc. The hearing of a case by an appellate court in which the full complement of judges assigned to the court, rather than a small panel, presides.

expunge. Blot out. For example, a court order requesting that a student's record be expunged of any references to disciplinary action during a particular time period means that the references are to be "wiped off the books" (see also *redact*).

fiduciary. A relationship between persons in which one person acts for another in a position of trust. Some courts hold private schools to a fiduciary relationship with students and may intervene if the school has not acted fairly, as, for example, in expelling a student.

forum. A place for communication. In the context of the First Amendment to the U.S. Constitution, a *public forum* means a place where First Amendment rights are almost unlimited in their scope, a *limited public forum* allows government some restriction over speakers and content of expression, and a *closed forum* refers to government property traditionally not open to public communication.

grievance. An employee complaint concerning wages, hours, or conditions of work; that is, literally anything connected with employment. A grievance system consists of steps by which an individual employee or a group of employees seeks a solution to a complaint. First, the grievance is brought to the attention of the employee's immediate superior. If no satisfactory adjustment is made, the employee may continue to appeal to higher levels. While virtually all collective bargaining agreements contain a grievance system, such systems are also increasingly part of organizational life whether or not a union is present since they afford the means to channel and resolve disputes.

hearing. An oral proceeding before a court or quasi-judicial tribunal.

holding. The rule of law set forth in a case to answer the issues presented to the court.

informed consent. A person's agreement to allow something to happen (such as surgery) that is based on a full disclosure of facts needed to make the decision intelligently. Certain types of student searches are best carried out with informed consent of the student being searched or his or her parents.

infra. Later in the article or book. For example, *infra*, p. 235, means to turn to that page, which is further on. Opposite of *supra*.

injunction. A court order requiring someone to do something or to refrain from taking some action.

in loco parentis. "In place of a parent"; acting as a parent with respect to the care, supervision, and discipline of a child. The development of student rights law has somewhat curtailed, especially at the secondary school level, the traditional view that public school officials stand in loco parentis to students.

ipso facto.   "By the fact itself"; by the mere fact that.

jurisdiction.   Right of a court to hear a case; also the geographic area within which a court has the right and power to operate. *Original jurisdiction* means that the court will be the first to hear the case; *appellate jurisdiction* means that the court reviews cases on appeal from lower court rulings.

jurisprudence.   Philosophy of the law; the rationale for one's legal position.

justiciable.   Proper for a court to decide. For example, a justiciable controversy is a real dispute that a court may handle.

law.   Basic rules of order. Constitutional law reflects the basic principles by which government operates. Statutory law consists of laws passed by legislatures and recorded in public documents. Administrative laws are the decisions of administrative agencies, for example, a State Board of Education rule. Judicial law consists of the pronouncements of courts.

libel.   Written defamation; false and malicious written statements communicated to another, such as by publication, that injure a person's reputation.

litigation.   A lawsuit or series of lawsuits.

mandamus.   A court order commanding some official duty to be performed.

mediation.   The involvement of a neutral third party to facilitate agreement between the parties to a dispute.

moot.   For the sake of argument; not a real case involving a real dispute.

negligence.   A tort or civil wrong that involves failure to live up to a standard of care, such as reasonableness, when one has a duty to do so, and as a result, someone or something is harmed. Different degrees of negligence trigger different legal penalties.

obiter dictum.   A digression from the central focus of a discussion to consider unrelated points; often shortened to *dictum*, or in the plural, *dicta*.

parens patriae.   The historical right of all governments to take care of persons under their jurisdiction, particularly minors and incapacitated persons. Thus, states have acted *parens patriae* in establishing public schooling systems for the benefit of all people within their borders.

per curiam.   An unsigned decision and opinion of a court, as distinguished from one signed by a judge.

petitioner.   The one bringing an action; similar to *plaintiff.* Opposite of *respondent.*

plaintiff.   The person who brings a lawsuit against another person. At the appeal stage, the person bringing the appeal is called the "appellant" and is usually the one losing in the lower court action.

plenary.   Complete or full in all respects; total.

police power. The traditional power of governments to establish laws protecting the health, safety, and welfare of its citizens and to enforce them.

precedent. A court decision on a question of law that gives authority or direction on how to decide a similar question of law in a later case with similar facts. Ruling by precedent is usually conveyed through the term *stare decisis.*

prima facie. Clear on the face of it; presumably, a fact that will be considered to be true unless disproved by contrary evidence. For example, a prima facie case is one that will win unless the other side comes forward with evidence to dispute it.

punitive damages. An amount awarded to a person by a court that is over and above the damages actually sustained. Punitive damages are designed to punish the defendant and serve as a deterrent to similar acts in the future. Also termed *exemplary damages* (compare *actual damages* and *compensatory damages*).

quasi-judicial. Refers to the case-deciding function of an administrative agency. Thus, a school board is a quasi-judicial body when it holds a formal hearing on a student expulsion case.

redact. To delete or blot out. For example, in releasing documents to the public, it may be necessary to redact certain information that would violate student privacy rights (see also *expunge*).

remand. To send back; for example, a higher court may send a case back to the lower court, asking that certain action be taken.

res judicata. "A thing decided." Thus, if a court decides the case on its merits, the matter is settled and no new lawsuit can be brought on the same subject by the same parties.

respondent. The party responding to an action; similar to *defendant.* The opposite of *petitioner.*

right to work. Also known as the "open shop," the term is used to apply to laws that ban union-security agreements, such as the union shop, by rendering it illegal to make employment conditional on membership or nonmembership in a labor organization. Unions are particularly opposed to these state laws because they allow "free riders"—those who share in the collective benefit but pay nothing for it. In California, the Educational Employment Relations Act provides that employees must either join a union or pay an agency fee to support the work of the union. Thus California is not a right-to-work state.

sectarian. Of or relating to religion or a religious sect.

secular. Of or relating to worldly concerns; opposite of *sectarian.*

slander. Oral defamation; the speaking of false and malicious words to a third party that injure another person's reputation, business, or property rights.

sovereign immunity. The government's freedom from being sued for money damages without its consent. California school districts do not enjoy sovereign immunity in that they can be sued in state court under the terms of the California Tort Claims Act. However, they do enjoy immunity from most federal claims because they are considered part of the state, and the state enjoys immunity from suit in federal court under the Eleventh Amendment to the U.S. Constitution.

standing. A person's right to bring a lawsuit because he or she is directly affected by the issues raised.

stare decisis. "Let the decision stand"; a legal rule that, when a court has decided a case by applying a legal principle to a set of facts, the court should stick by that principle and apply it to all later cases with clearly similar facts unless there is a good, strong reason not to. This rule helps promote fairness and reliability in judicial decision making and is inherent in the American legal system (see also *precedent*).

state action. Action by the government or an entity closely intertwined with the government. For the Fourteenth Amendment of the U.S. Constitution to apply to a given situation, there must be some involvement by a state or one of its political subdivisions. A public school falls into the latter category. Wholly private action is not covered by the Fourteenth Amendment. Thus, private schools and colleges, like corporate organizations and private clubs, are not subject to its strictures.

statute. A law enacted by a legislative body.

summary judgment. A decision for one side in a lawsuit rendered before the trial begins. Summary judgment occurs when there is no genuine issue of material fact and the court can decide the issue as a matter of law.

supra. Earlier in an article or book. For example, *supra,* p. 11, means to turn to that page, which appeared earlier. Opposite of *infra.*

tort. A civil wrong done by one person to another for which a court may award damages to the person injured. Examples of torts are negligence, battery, and defamation. Lawsuits of this type against California school districts and their employees generally are governed by the terms of the California Tort Claims Act.

trial. A process occurring in a court whereby opposing parties present evidence, subject to cross-examination and rebuttal, pertaining to the matter in dispute.

trial de novo. A completely new trial ordered by a judge or appeals court.

ultra vires. Going beyond the specifically delegated authority to act; for example, a school board that is by law restricted from punishing students for behavior occurring wholly off campus acts *ultra vires* in punishing a student for behavior observed at a private weekend party.

waiver. The means by which a person voluntarily gives up a right or benefit. To be valid, waivers have to be worded very carefully. Thus, in a case where a parent is asked to sign a waiver absolving the school or teacher from liability in the event of an accident to his or her child, waivers must make it clear what the parent is giving up, for example, the right to sue *even if* the school or teacher is negligent. Even if parents sign such a knowing waiver, the child may recover damages in his or her own right. The services of an attorney are best secured in drawing up waivers.

FINDING AND READING STATUTES

AND JUDICIAL DECISIONS

In this book we describe the law and provide references to key legislative enactments, called statutes, and to the court decisions. Some readers may be interested
in consulting the statutes and judicial decisions directly. In this appendix, we describe how to do this efficiently and effectively.

STATUTES

Statutes enacted by Congress and the California Legislature can be found in two
ways. The first is to consult websites that list them, and the second is to consult
printed volumes. The former is preferable because websites are easy to access and
updated frequently. A list of a number of websites for obtaining legal information
is contained in Appendix C.

Both federal and California statutes are grouped into codes. The United States
Code contains all the laws enacted by Congress. In California, there are a number
of codes of relevance to education, including the Penal Code, the Government
Code, and, of course, the Education Code. The first task is to locate the relevant
code. Once this is done, the statute can be found by section number. For example,
an important federal statute that enables persons to bring lawsuits in federal court
alleging federal wrongs is known as 42 U.S.C. Section 1983. The number to the left
of the abbreviation is the volume number, and the number to the right of it is the
section number. The abbreviation stands for "United States Code." Most large
public libraries have one or more sets of volumes containing the United States
Code. It is thus a simple task to find the correct volume number and then locate
the desired section. Volumes entitled "United States Code Annotated" include
brief summaries of judicial decisions involving the section as well, along with other

important information such as the administrative regulations that have been developed by federal agencies to implement the provisions.

Finding all the codes containing the statutes enacted by the California Legislature is easy. Simply access the California Education Department's website at www.cde.ca.gov and click on "Laws and Regulations." Follow the linkages to all twenty-nine California codes, including the Education Code. This website also contains the regulations issued by state agencies and approved by the Office of Administrative Law. Included among them are the regulations issued by the State Board of Education and the California Department of Education.

Hardback volumes containing the California statutes and administrative regulations also can be found in law school libraries and larger public libraries. It is important to consult the pocket part at the back of each volume, along with recently issued paperback supplements, to obtain current law. Volumes containing state statutes include references to administrative law provisions and brief summaries of interpretive judicial law relating to each statute. They also include historical information about the enactment of the statute and later amendments. For ease of reference, many administrators have copies of the paperback *Desktop Code* that is published by Thomson West and updated annually. This volume is useful for accessing statutory provisions quickly, but it does not include references to judicial decisions. Users of the desktop edition must remember to use the most recent edition because statute law is always changing.

JUDICIAL DECISIONS

Judicial decisions can be accessed online, in published volumes, and by CD-ROM. Lawyers and legal commentators subscribe either to Westlaw or LexisNexis, comprehensive online databases for access to legal information. Both databases require training in order to use them effectively. Given user cost and sophistication, these systems are not well suited to the needs of laypersons. However, less-sophisticated online systems for accessing court decisions and other information are available to the general public. We have included several of these in Appendix C. Printed volumes containing both federal and California judicial decisions are available in law libraries and in most public libraries.

Regardless whether they are found on the Web or in a library, judicial decisions are reported in a specific format. We can use as an illustration the seminal decision of the U.S. Supreme Court declaring that government-maintained racial segregation in public schools is unconstitutional. The official citation for the case is *Brown v. Board of Education of Topeka, Kansas*, 347 U.S. 483, 74 S.Ct. 686, 98 L.Ed. 873 (1954). The name to the right of the "v." is known as the plaintiff at the trial court level and as the appellant (or petitioner) in the event of an appeal. Since this case had been appealed to the U.S. Supreme Court, Brown is the appellant. The name to the right of the "v." is the defendant at the trial court level and appellee (or respondent) at the appellate level. Here the appellee is the Board of Education of Topeka. Sometimes the names will reverse order. This occurs if the plaintiff wins at the trial court level, and the defendant initiates an appeal, thus becoming the appellant. In the *Brown* case the names did not change on appeal, because the plaintiffs did not prevail in the lower court. The original defendants remain the appellees. The "v." between the names stands for "versus" and indicates the adversary nature of litigation.

The numbers and letters following the case name identify where the case can be found. As with statutes, the number to the left of the abbreviation refers to printed volumes and the number to the right refers to the first page of the decision. Thus, 347 to the left of the first abbreviation refers to the volume number, and 483 to the right of it refers to the page number. "U.S." is the abbreviation for *United States Reports*, the official volumes issued by the Government Printing Office. So once we locate the *United States Reports* in a library, we will retrieve volume 347 and turn to page 483 to find the first page of the Supreme Court's complete *Brown* decision. The other abbreviations operate similarly and refer to commercially published reporters that contain additional information such as headnotes and summaries useful to attorneys and legal researchers. "S.Ct." is the *Supreme Court Reporter*, and "L.Ed" is the *United States Supreme Court Reports*, Lawyer's Edition.

The published decisions of the U.S. Court of Appeals for the Ninth Circuit are found together with the decisions of the other federal circuits in the *Federal Reporter* series. Recent decisions are reported in the third edition of this series, abbreviated as "F.3d." Published decisions of federal district courts in California are found in the *Federal Supplement* series. Recent decisions are reported in the second edition of this series, abbreviated as "F. Supp.2d." California state appellate court decisions can be found in the editions of the *California Reporter* and the *California Appellate Report*. Earlier decisions can be found in the *Pacific Reporter*. Very recent decisions, along with information about the California court system, also can be found on the California Courts website, www.courtinfo.ca.gov. Many law firms and libraries now have case law on CD-ROM, thus doing away with large collections of printed volumes.

Once a case is located, the reader usually will first find a brief syllabus of the ruling. Following the summary will be a list of headnotes, setting forth key points in the decision and directing the reader to where these points are discussed in the text of the opinion. The headnotes also provide links to other sources dealing with the same legal point. Following the headnotes will be a list of the attorneys who argued the case and the judge or judges who decided it. Next is the opinion of the court, along with the name of the judge who authored it. Federal district court decisions bear the name of the trial judge (the decisions of California trial court judges are not published). Federal and state appellate court decisions bear the name of one of the judges assigned to the case (normally cases at both the federal and state appellate levels are heard by a panel of three judges). Numbers in brackets will be found throughout the opinion. These refer to the headnotes at the start of the opinion. If the opinion has been downloaded from a website, numbers will appear periodically in bold type. These refer to the pages in the printed volumes. If the case is reported in more than one printed volume, asterisks will appear before the numbers to distinguish one volume from another.

The reader may encounter one or more concurring opinions at the end of the court opinion. A concurring opinion indicates that the authoring judge agrees with the outcome of the case, but for different reasons. Any dissenting opinions will follow the concurring opinions. A dissenting opinion indicates that the writer disagrees with the outcome for reasons stated in the dissenting opinion. Depending on the number of judges hearing the case, others may join in supporting concurring or dissenting opinions. And in complex cases, it is not unusual to find judges issuing opinions that concur on some points but dissent on others. Neither the concurring nor the dissenting opinions will affect the actual decision of the court. However, it is often said that today's concurring or dissenting opinion may become tomorrow's majority opinion.

Unlike statute and administrative law, which changes frequently, judicial law is built on the concept of *stare decisis*, meaning that a decision stands unless there is a good reason not to follow it. This adds consistency and reliability to the law over time. Accordingly, in crafting opinions, judges and their law clerks frequently will refer to earlier decisions, often including excerpts to support particular points of law. They also will cite statutes and legal commentary. This extensive referencing sometimes makes opinions hard to read. And it may force the reader to review earlier decisions to understand fully the point of law under discussion.

Depending upon the position of the court in the judiciary hierarchy, the decision may be appealed to a higher court. If affirmed, the lower court's decision becomes judicial precedent on the point or points of law involved. If overruled, the lower-court decision ceases to have value as legal precedent. Sometimes a decision that has not been overruled is viewed as an anomaly by other courts and not followed in later decisions. Or it may be that a statute that the court relied upon in reaching a decision may later be changed by the legislature. Lawyers and legal researchers know this and employ the tools of legal research to track a decision over time to make sure that it is still good law. Fortunately, computerized legal retrieval systems have made this task a lot easier than in the days when only printed volumes were available.

Our advice to educators is not to be afraid of the law; but at the same time, realize that sometimes it requires skill to find and understand it. It is always wise to ask for assistance from legal librarians and others who can offer help when the need arises.

APPENDIX C

REFERENCES

The vast majority of the legal authority in the book can be found on the Internet. There is also print material with the laws, regulations, and judicial decisions noted in the book. In this appendix we summarize these resources and note some additional resources relevant to researching the law.

The law is in constant flux. Cases are appealed and reversed. Statutes are amended and repealed. Courts sometimes invalidate regulations. While the following resources contain generally accurate information, additional legal research and/or consultation of a competent legal professional may be appropriate, depending on the intended use of the information.

LAWS AND REGULATIONS

- United States Code (www.law.cornell.edu/uscode/). Search the entire United States Code by title and section. For example, the citation "20 U.S.C. § 1400" is Title 20, Section 1400 of the United States Code.
- Code of Federal Regulations (www.access.gpo.gov/nara/cfr/cfr-table-search .html). The Code of Federal Regulations contains the implementing regulations for the United States Code. The Code of Federal Regulations is arranged by title, part, and section. For example, the citation "34 C.F.R. § 300.503" is Title 34, part 300, Section 503.
- California Code (www.leginfo.ca.gov). Contains the complete California Code. Search by code and section (e.g., Education Code Section 44942).
- *California Education Code: Desktop Edition.* This softbound desktop edition of the California Education Code is published annually. Order from Thomson West (www.west.thomson.com).

- California Code of Regulations (ccr.oal.ca.gov). Like its federal counterpart in the Code of Federal Regulations, the California Code of Regulations provides additional guidance and detail on the implementation of the California Code. Title Five of the California Code of Regulations is Education.

JUDICIAL DECISIONS

- FindLaw for Legal Professionals (www.findlaw.com). Contains links to state and federal judicial decisions. Decisions available on the Internet, however, may be limited in some instances to those issued in the last eight to ten years.
- Appendix B, "Finding and Reading Statutes and Judicial Decisions," addresses the hardbound collections that contain federal and state judicial decisions.

GOVERNMENT AGENCIES

- United States Department of Education (www.ed.gov). Contains information regarding No Child Left Behind (NCLB), Family Education Rights and Privacy Act (FERPA), charter schools, school choice, and numerous education-related links of interest for students, parents, teachers, and administrators. This site contains a link to the Office for Civil Rights (OCR) and Office of Special Education and Rehabilitative Services (OSERS). OCR's site contains information regarding the laws OCR enforces (e.g., Title IX of the Education Amendments of 1972, Section 504 of the Rehabilitation Act of 1973, and the Americans with Disabilities Act). OSERS's site contains information regarding the Individuals with Disabilities Education Act (IDEA), memoranda with interpretive guidance on IDEA, and links to special education research and statistics.
- United States Equal Employment Opportunity Commission (www.eeoc.gov). Contains comprehensive information regarding federal employment discrimination laws, the filing of a discrimination complaint, and publications to assist employers with compliance.
- United States Department of Labor (www.dol.gov). Contains information regarding employee leave rights under the Family and Medical Leave Act (FMLA).
- California Department of Education (www.cde.ca.gov). Contains information regarding state curriculum, testing, finance, and links to state special education sites like the Office of Administrative Hearings (OAH) special education decisions (click on specialized programs on the upper right, click on special education on the lower left, click on Office of Administrative Hearings).
- Department of Fair Employment and Housing (www.dfeh.ca.gov). Contains information regarding state employment discrimination laws and employee leave rights under the California Family Rights Act (CFRA).

- Public Employment Relations Board (www.perb.ca.gov). Contains information regarding the Educational Employment Relations Act (EERA) and a database of decisions.
- California Attorney General (www.caag.state.ca.us). Includes a searchable database of recent attorney general opinions, including a number of opinions relevant to education.

OTHER RESOURCES

- Cohen, Morris L., and Kent Olson. *Cohen and Olson's Legal Research in a Nutshell*, 9th ed., 2007. Easy-to-use guide to legal research, including how to access and use online legal research. Order from Thomson West (www.west.thomson.com).
- Garner, Bryan A., ed. *Black's Law Dictionary, Abridged*, 8th ed., 2004. Softbound law dictionary that is a useful resource for school personnel who work with attorneys and legal materials. Order from Thomson West (www.west.thomson.com).

LIST OF CASES

The official citations of all of the cases cited in this book are included in this list; page numbers for these cases can be found in the index on page 519. The basic citation system format is discussed in Appendix B. Information about accessing cases is given in Appendix C. We have modified the official legal system of citing cases somewhat in this index for the benefit of lay readers.

Modifications include identification of the districts of the California courts of appeal so that the readers can tell which of the six made the decision. This is apparent in the very first citation in the index. To indicate which decisions come from the California Supreme Court, we have included the simple designation "Cal." along with the date of the decision within the parentheses following the citation. While there are several reporters where the decisions of California courts can be found, we have opted to use the *California Reporter* series (abbreviated "Cal. Rptr.") for ease of reference for all but a few older court decisions. For the same reason, we also have opted to use the official *United States Reports* (abbreviated as "U.S.") for U.S. Supreme Court decisions for all but the most recent decisions. For very recent decisions that may not yet be included in the official reports, we use the *Supreme Court Reporter* (abbreviated as "S.Ct."). The words "*cert. denied*" that occasionally appear after a case citation mean that the U.S. Supreme Court refused to hear the case on appeal. This does not mean that the high court agreed with the lower court's ruling. It merely means that for whatever reason, the Supreme Court refused to take up the case. Except for the U.S. Supreme Court, we do not include the citation history of a case except where important to the continued validity of the decision being cited.

The abbreviation PERC stands for Public Employee Reporter for California, where the decisions of the Public Employment Relations Board (PERB) and its staff on collective bargaining matters can be found. The abbreviation IDELR refers to the *Individuals with Disabilities Education Law Report*, which contains decisions pertaining to children with disabilities.

Aaris v. Las Virgenes Unified School District, 75 Cal. Rptr.2d 801 (Cal. App. 2 Dist. 1998)

Abood v. Detroit Board of Education, 431 U.S. 209 (1977)

Acosta v. Los Angeles Unified School District, 37 Cal. Rptr.2d 171 (Cal. App. 2 Dist. 1995)

Adair v. Stockton Unified School District, 77 Cal. Rptr.3d 62 (Cal. App. 3 Dist. 2008)

Adams v. Oregon, 195 F.3d 1141 (9th Cir. 1999)

Adcock v. San Diego Unified School District, 109 Cal. Rptr. 676 (Cal. 1973)

Adelt v. Richmond School District, 58 Cal. Rptr. 151 (Cal. App. 1 Dist. 1967)

Aguirre v. Los Angeles Unified School District, 461 F.3d 1114 (9th Cir. 2006)

Agostini v. Felton, 521 U.S. 203 (1997)

Alabama and Coushatta Tribes of Texas v. Big Sandy Independent School District, 817 F. Supp. 1319 (E.D. Tex. 1993), *remanded without opinion*, 20 F.3d 469 (5th Cir. 1994)

Alamo Heights Independent School District v. State Board of Education, 790 F.2d 1153 (5th Cir. 1986)

Alexander v. Sandoval, 532 U.S. 275 (2001)

Alex G. ex. el. Stephen G. v. Board of Trustees of Davis Joint Unified School District, 332 F. Supp.2d 1315 (E.D. Cal. 2004)

Allison C. v. Advanced Education Services, 28 Cal. Rptr.3d 605 (Cal. App. 4 Dist. 2005)

Alma W. v. Oakland Unified School District, 176 Cal. Rptr. 287 (Cal. App. 1 Dist. 1981)

Ambach v. Norwick, 441 U.S. 68 (1979)

American Academy of Pediatrics v. Lungren, 66 Cal. Rptr.2d 210 (Cal. 1997)

American Library Association v. United States, 539 U.S. 194 (2003)

Arlington Central School District Board of Education v. Murphy, 126 S.Ct. 2455 (2006)

Association of Mexican-American Educators v. State of California, 231 F.3d 572 (9th Cir. 2000)

Atwater Elementary School District v. California Department of General Services, 59 Cal. Rptr.3d 233 (Cal. 2007)

B. C. v. Plumas Unified School District, 192 F.3d 1260 (9th Cir. 1999)

Baca v. Moreno Valley Unified School District, 936 F. Supp. 719 (C.D. Cal. 1996)

Bacus v. Palo Verde Unified School District, 52 Fed. Appx. 355 (9th Cir. 2002) (unpublished)

Bakersfield City School District v. Superior Court, 13 Cal. Rptr.3d 517 (Cal. App. 5 Dist. 2004)

Bakersfield Elementary Teachers Association v. Bakersfield City School District, 52 Cal. Rptr.2d 486 (Cal. App. 5 Dist. 2006)

Banning Teachers Association v. Public Employment Relations Board, 244 Cal. Rptr. 671 (Cal. 1988)

Bassett v. Lakeside Inc., 44 Cal. Rptr.3d 827 (Cal. App. 3 Dist. 2006)

Bartell v. Palos Verdes Peninsula School District, 147 Cal. Rptr. 898 (Cal. App. 2 Dist. 1978)

Bauchman v. West High School, 132 F.3d 542 (10th Cir. 1997), *cert. denied*, 524 U.S. 953 (1998)

Bekiaris v. Board of Education of City of Modesto, 100 Cal. Rptr. 16 (Cal. 1972)

Belanger v. Madera Unified School District, 963 F.2d 248 (9th Cir. 1992)

Bell v. Vista Unified School District, 98 Cal. Rptr.2d 263 (Cal. App. 4 Dist. 2000)

Bellflower Education Association v. Bellflower Unified School District, 279 Cal. Rptr. 179 (Cal. App. 2 Dist. 1991)

Benjamin G. v. Special Education Hearing Office, 32 Cal. Rptr.3d 366 (Cal. App. 1 Dist. 2005)

Berkelman v. San Francisco Unified School District, 501 F.2d 1264 (9th Cir. 1974)

Bernstein v. Lopez, 321 F.3d 903 (9th Cir. 2003)

Bervcovitch v. Baldwin School, 133 F.3d 141 (1st Cir. 1998)

Bethel School District No. 403 v. Fraser, 478 U.S. 675 (1986)

Beussink v. Woodland R-IV School District, 30 F. Supp.2d 1175 (E.D. Mo. 1998)

Biscotti v. Yuba City Unified School District, 69 Cal. Rptr.3d 825 (Cal. App. 3 Dist. 2007)

Blackwell v. Issaquena County Board of Education, 363 F.2d 749 (5th Cir. 1966)

Blanchard v. Morton School District, 509 F.3d 934 (9th Cir. 2007), *cert. denied*, 128 S.Ct. 1447 (2008)

Board of Curators of the University of Missouri v. Horowitz, 435 U.S. 78 (1978)

Board of Education v. Allen, 392 U.S. 236 (1968)

Board of Education v. Earls, 536 U.S. 822 (2002)

Board of Education of Hendrick Hudson School District v. Rowley, 458 U.S. 176 (1982)

Board of Education of Island Trees v. Pico, 457 U.S. 853 (1982)

Board of Education of Long Beach Unified School District v. Jack M., 139 Cal. Rptr. 700 (Cal. 1977)

Board of Education of Oklahoma City Public Schools v. Dowell, 498 U.S. 237 (1991)

Board of Education of Rogers, Arkansas v. McCluskey, 458 U.S. 966 (1982)

Board of Education of the Round Valley Unified School District v. Round Valley Teachers Association, 52 Cal. Rptr.2d 115 (Cal. 1996)

Casterson v. Superior Court, 123 Cal. Rptr.2d 637 (Cal. App. 6 Dist. 2002)

Cedar Rapids Community School District v. Garrett F., 526 U.S. 66 (1999)

Ceniceros v. Board of Trustees of the San Diego Unified School District, 106 F.3d 878 (9th Cir. 1997)

Chandler v. McMinnville School District, 978 F.2d 524 (9th Cir. 1992)

Chandler v. Siegelman, 230 F.3d 1313 (11th Cir. 2000), *cert. denied*, 533 U.S. 916 (2001)

Charles H. Allen, et al., Petitioners-Appellants, and California School Employees Association and Pleasant Valley Elementary School District, Respondents, 8 PERC P 15051 (1984)

Chicago Teachers Union, Local No. 1 v. Hudson, 475 U.S. 292 (1986)

Circle Schools v. Pappert, 381 F.3d 172 (3rd Cir. 2004)

City of Madison v. Wisconsin Employment Relations Commission, 429 U.S. 167 (1976)

Clark v. Arizona Interscholastic Association, 695 F.2d 1126 (9th Cir. 1982)

Clark v. Arizona Interscholastic Association, 886 F.2d 1191 (9th Cir. 1989)

Clausing v. San Francisco Unified School District, 271 Cal. Rptr. 72 (Cal. App. 1 Dist. 1990)

Coalition for Economic Equity v. Wilson, 122 F.3d 718 (9th Cir. 1997)

Cole v. Oroville Union School District, 228 F.3d 1092 (9th Cir. 2000), *cert. denied sub nom, Niemeyer v. Oroville Union School District*, 532 U.S. 905 (2001)

Colin ex rel. Colin v. Orange Unified School District, 83 F. Supp.2d 1135 (C.D. Cal. 2000)

Collins v. Chandler Unified School District, 644 F.2d 759 (9th Cir.), *cert. denied*, 454 U.S. 863 (1981)

Compton Unified School District v. Compton Education Association, 11 PERC P 18067 (1987)

Connick v. Myers, 461 U.S. 138 (1983)

Constantinescu v. Conejo Valley Unified School District, 20 Cal. Rptr.2d 734 (Cal. App. 2 Dist. 1993)

Copley Press, Inc. v. Superior Court, 74 Cal. Rptr.2d 69 (Cal. App. 4 Dist. 1998)

Corales v. Bennett, 488 F. Supp.2d 975 (C.D. Cal. 2007)

County Sanitation District No. 2 v. Los Angeles County Employees Association, Local 600, 214 Cal. Rptr. 424 (Cal. 1985)

Crawford v. Board of Education of the City of Los Angeles, 130 Cal. Rptr. 724 (Cal. 1976)

Crawford v. Board of Education of the City of Los Angeles, 458 U.S. 527 (1982)

Crawford v. Huntington Beach Union High School District, 121 Cal. Rptr.2d 96 (Cal. App. 4 Dist. 2002)

Honig v. Doe, 484 U.S. 305 (1988)

Hooks v. Clark County School District, 228 F.3d 1036 (9th Cir. 2000), *cert. denied*, 532 U.S. 971 (2001)

Horace Mann Insurance Company v. Analisa N., 263 Cal. Rptr. 61 (Cal. App. 4 Dist. 1989)

Horton v. Whipple, 58 Cal. App. 189 (Cal. App. 3 Dist. 1922)

Hoschler v. Sacramento City Unified School District, 57 Cal. Rptr.3d 115 (Cal. App. 3 Dist. 2007)

Hoyem v. Manhattan Beach City School District, 150 Cal. Rptr. 1 (Cal. 1978)

Hudgens v. National Labor Relations Board, 424 U.S. 507 (1976)

Hunter ex rel. Brandt v. Regents of University of California, 190 F.3d 1061 (9th Cir.), *cert. denied*, 531 U.S. 877 (1999)

Hunter v. Regents of the University of California, 2001 WL 1555240 (Cal. App. 2 Dist. 2001) (unpublished)

In re Alexander B., 270 Cal. Rptr. 342 (Cal. App. 2 Dist. 1990)

In re Corey L., 250 Cal. Rptr. 359 (Cal. App. 1 Dist. 1988)

In re Humberto O., 95 Cal. Rptr.2d 248 (Cal. App. 2 Dist. 2000)

In re Joseph F., 102 Cal. Rptr. 2d 641 (Cal. App. 1 Dist 2000)

In re Joseph G., 38 Cal. Rptr.2d 902 (Cal. App. 4 Dist. 1995)

In re Latasha W., 70 Cal. Rptr.2d 886 (Cal. App. 2 Dist. 1998)

In re Lisa G., 23 Cal. Rptr.3d 163 (Cal. App. 4 Dist. 2004), *as modified* (Jan. 10, 2005)

In re M. S., 42 Cal. Rptr.2d 355 (Cal. 1995)

In re Michael M., 104 Cal. Rptr.2d 10 (Cal. App. 5 Dist. 2001)

In re Rachel L. v. Superior Court, 73 Cal. Rptr.3d 77 (Cal. App. 2 Dist. 2008)

In re Randy G., 110 Cal. Rptr.2d 516 (Cal. 2001)

In re Scott K., 155 Cal. Rptr. 671 (Cal), *cert. denied sub nom. Fare v. Scott K.*, 444 U.S. 973 (1979)

In re William G., 221 Cal. Rptr. 118 (Cal. 1985)

In re William V., 4 Cal. Rptr.3d 695 (Cal. App. 1 Dist. 2003)

Ingraham v. Wright, 430 U.S. 651 (1977)

Irvine Unified School District v. Irvine Teachers Association, CTA/NEA, 11 PERC P 18128 (1987)

Irving Independent School District v. Tatro, 468 U.S. 883 (1984)

Iverson v. Muroc Unified School District, 38 Cal. Rptr.2d 35 (Cal. App. 5 Dist. 1995)

Jackson v. Birmingham Board of Education, 544 U.S. 167 (2005)

Jackson v. Pasadena City School District, 31 Cal. Rptr. 606 (Cal. 1963)

Jacobs v. Clark County School District, 526 F.3d 419 (9th Cir. 2008)

John A. v. San Bernardino City Unified School District, 187 Cal. Rptr. 472 (1982)

Oona R. S. By Kate S. v. McCaffrey, 143 F.3d 473 (9th Cir. 1998), *cert. denied,* 526 U.S. 1154 (1999)

Options for Youth-Victor Valley, Inc. v. Victor Valley Options for Youth Teachers Association, 27 PERC P 104 (2003)

Osborne v. Ohio, 495 U.S. 103 (1990)

Owasso Independent School District v. Falvo, 534 U.S. 426 (2002)

P. B. v. Koch, 96 F.3d 1298 (9th Cir. 1996)

Parents Involved in Community Schools v. Seattle School District No. 1, 127 S.Ct. 2738 (2007)

Parents of Student W. v. Puyallup School District, 31 F.3d 1489 (9th Cir. 1994)

Patten v. Grant Joint Union High School District, 37 Cal. Rptr.3d 113 (Cal. App. 3 Dist. 2005)

Pasadena City Board of Education v. Spangler, 427 U.S. 424 (1976)

Peloza v. Capistrano Unified School District, 37 F.3d 517 (9th Cir. 1994), *cert. denied,* 515 U.S. 1173 (1995)

Pennsylvania Association for Retarded Children v. Commonwealth of Pennsylvania, 343 F. Supp. 279 (E.D. Penn. 1972)

People v. Jose Y., 46 Cal. Rptr.3d 268 (Cal. App. 2 Dist. 2006)

People v. Luera, 103 Cal. Rptr.2d 438 (Cal. App. 2 Dist. 2001)

People v. Ramirez, 158 Cal. Rptr. 316 (Cal. 1979)

Perry Education Association v. Perry Local Educators' Association, 460 U.S. 37 (1983)

Peterson v. Minidoka County School District No. 331, 118 F.3d 1351 (9th Cir.), *amended,* 132 F.3d 1258 (9th Cir. 1997)

Peter W. v. San Francisco Unified School District, 131 Cal. Rptr. 854 (Cal. App. 1 Dist. 1976)

Pickering v. Board of Education, 391 U.S. 563 (1968)

Pierce v. Society of Sisters, 268 U.S. 510 (1925)

Pinellas County School District, 20 IDELR 561 (OCR 1993)

Planned Parenthood of Central Missouri v. Danforth, 428 U.S. 52 (1976)

Plessy v. Ferguson, 163 U.S. 537 (1896), *overruled by Brown v. Board of Education of Topeka, Kansas,* 347 U.S. 483 (1954)

Plyler v. Doe, 457 U.S. 202 (1982)

Poway Federation of Teachers v. Poway Unified School District, 12 PERC P 19102 (1988)

Poway Unified School District v. Superior Court, 73 Cal. Rptr.2d 777 (Cal. App. 4 Dist. 1998)

Preschooler II v. Clark County School Board of Trustees, 479 F.3d 1175 (9th Cir. 2007)

Prince v. Jacoby, 303 F.3d 1074 (9th Cir. 2002), *cert. denied,* 124 S.Ct. 62 (2003)

PruneYard Shopping Center v. Robins, 153 Cal. Rptr. 854 (Cal. 1979), *aff'd*, 447 U.S. 74 (1980)

Public Employment Relations Board v. Modesto City Schools District, 186 Cal. Rptr. 634 (Cal. App. 5 Dist. 1982)

Ramirez v. Long Beach Unified School District, 129 Cal. Rptr.2d 128 (Cal. App. 2 Dist. 2002)

Randi W. v. Muroc Joint Unified School District, 60 Cal. Rptr.2d 263 (Cal. 1997)

Ravenswood Teacher Association v. Ravenswood City School District, 26 PERC P 33118 (2002)

Ray v. Antioch Unified School District, 107 F. Supp.2d 1165 (N.D. Cal. 2000)

Reed v. Reed, 404 U.S. 71 (1971)

Reeves v. Rocklin Unified School District, 135 Cal. Rptr.2d 213 (Cal. App. 3 Dist. 2003)

Regents of the University of California v. Bakke, 438 U.S. 265 (1978)

Regents of the University of Michigan v. Ewing, 474 U.S. 214 (1985)

Reynolds v. United States, 98 U.S. 145 (1878)

Rim of the World Unified School District v. Superior Court, 129 Cal. Rptr.2d 11 (Cal. App. 4 Dist. 2002)

Robb v. Bethel School District #403, 308 F.3d 1047 (9th Cir. 2002)

Robert L. Mueller Charter School, 27 PERC P 46 (2003)

Roe v. Wade, 410 U.S. 113 (1973)

Ross v. Campbell Union School District, 138 Cal. Rptr. 557 (Cal. App. 1 Dist 1977)

Runyon v. McCrary, 427 U.S. 160 (1976)

Ryan v. California Interscholastic Federation—San Diego Section, 114 Cal. Rptr.2d 798 (Cal. App. 4 Dist. 2001)

Sacramento City Unified School District v. Holland, 14 F.3d 1398 (9th Cir. 1994), *cert. denied*, 512 U.S. 1207 (1994)

San Antonio Independent School District v. Rodriguez, 411 U.S. 1 (1973)

San Diego Teachers Association v. Superior Court, 154 Cal. Rptr. 893 (Cal. 1979)

San Dieguito Union High School District v. Commission on Professional Competence, 220 Cal. Rptr. 351 (Cal. App. 4 Dist. 1985)

Sands v. Morongo Unified School District, 281 Cal. Rptr. 34 (Cal. 1991), *cert. denied*, 505 U.S. 1218 (1992)

San Francisco Unified School District v. Johnson, 92 Cal. Rptr. 309 (Cal. 1971)

San Francisco NAACP v. San Francisco Unified School District, 413 F. Supp.2d 1051 (N.C. Cal. 2005)

San Leandro Teachers Association v. Governing Board of the San Leandro Unified School District, 65 Cal. Rptr.3d 288 (Cal. App. 1 Dist. 2007)

San Mateo City School District v. Public Employment Relations Board, 191 Cal. Rptr. 800 (Cal. 1983)

Welsh v. United States, 398 U.S. 333 (1970)

West Virginia State Board of Education v. Barnette, 319 U.S. 624 (1943)

Westminster School District of Orange County v. Mendez, 161 F.2d 774 (9th Cir. 1947)

Wexner v. Anderson Union High School District, 258 Cal. Rptr. 26 (Cal. App. 3 Dist.), *review denied and ordered not published,* 1989 Cal. LEXIS 3129 (Cal. 1989)

Widmar v. Vincent, 454 U.S. 263 (1981)

Williams v. Vidmar, 367 F. Supp.2d 1265 (N.D. Cal. 2005)

Wilson v. State Board of Education, 89 Cal. Rptr.2d 745 (Cal. App. 1 Dist. 1999)

Winn v. Hibbs, 361 F. Supp.2d 1117 (D. Ariz. 2005)

Wisniewski v. Board of Education of Weedsport Central School District, 494 F.3d 34 (2nd Cir. 2007), *cert. denied,* 128 S.Ct. 1741 (2008)

Wisconsin v. Yoder, 406 U.S. 205 (1972)

Wolfe v. Dublin Unified School District, 65 Cal. Rptr.2d 280 (Cal. App. 1 Dist. 1997)

Woodbury v. Brown-Dempsey, 134 Cal. Rptr.2d 124 (Cal. App. 4 Dist. 2003)

Woodland Joint Unified School District v. Commission on Professional Competence, 4 Cal. Rptr.2d 227 (Cal. App. 3 Dist. 1992)

Worth County Schools, 27 IDELR 224 (OCR 1997)

Wysinger v. Crookshank, 82 Cal. 588 (Cal. 1890)

Yarber v. Oakland Unified School District, 6 Cal. Rptr.2d 437 (Cal. App. 1 Dist. 1992)

Zalac v. Governing Board of the Ferndale Unified School District, 120 Cal. Rptr.2d 615 (Cal. App. 1 Dist. 2002)

Zelman v. Simmons-Harris, 536 U.S. 639 (2002)

Zorach v. Clauson, 343 U.S. 306 (1952)

INDEX

complaints, 215. *See also* establishment clause; expression rights
first grade, admission to, 50
Fischer v. Los Angeles Unified School District, 184, 380
Fitzgerald, Harlow v., 478
flag, saluting, 3–4
Fleice v. Chualar Elementary School District, 178
Fletcher, McCarthy v., 62
Flood, Ward v., 416, 418
Florence County School District Four v. Carter, 323
Flores v. Morgan Hill Unified School District, 479–80
Florey v. Sioux Falls School District, 265
Florida: tax credits, 282; voucher program, 42
Florida Union Free School District, Walczak v., 295
Ford, Gerald, 289
Ford v. Long Beach Unified School District, 301
Fortas, Abe, 222, 229, 237
foster children, 49, 50
Foster v. Mahdesian, 158
foundation funding, 96–105, 111–12
four-month positions, 150–51
Fourteenth Amendment: corporal punishment, 478; due process, 4, 25, 39, 169, 333–37, 371, 478, 487; enforcement of, 9; privacy, 386, 394, 411; property rights, 39, 169; and Proposition 13, 107; religion, 247, 248; speaking out on matters of public concern, 209. *See also* equal protection clause
Fourth Amendment: exclusionary rule, 357–59; student searches, 394, 395, 396, 397, 398, 399, 407; student seizures, 407, 478

Franklin v. Gwinnett County Public Schools, 438
Fraser, Bethel School District v., 227–28, 242
Frazer v. Dixon Unified School District, 379
Frederick, Morse v., 227–28
free appropriate public education (FAPE), 285, 289, 293–97, 311, 313, 316–19, 321–29, 367
freedom of the press. *See* expression rights
Freeman v. Oakland Unified School District, 477
Freeman v. Pitts, 413
free speech rights. *See* expression rights
Fremont Unified District Teachers Association, Fremont Unified School District v., 151
Fremont Unified School District v. Fremont Unified District Teachers Association, 151
Fremont Union High School District v. Santa Clara County Board of Education, 351
Fresno Unified School District, 456
Fresno Unified School District, Lucas v., 449
Friery v. Los Angeles Unified School District, 424, 425
Frontiero v. Richardson, 430
functional analysis assessment (FAA), 313–16, 330, 370
functional behavioral assessment (FBA), 313–14, 368, 369

gangs, 56, 59, 233–34, 402
Gann, Paul, 105
Gann Limit. *See* Proposition 4 (1979)
Garcetti v. Ceballos, 214–15
Garcia Marquez, Gabriel, 63
Gardner, John, 63
Garner, Bryan A., 485, 500
Garrett F., Cedar Rapids Community School District v., 312